AP
3A

The Resilience and Vulnerability of Ancient Landscapes: Transforming Maya Archaeology through IHOPE

Arlen F. Chase and Vernon L. Scarborough, Editors

Contributions by

Adrian S.Z. Chase
Arlen F. Chase
Diane Z. Chase
Rafael Cobos
Guillermo de Anda Alaniz
María del Rosario Domínguez Carrasco
Nicholas P. Dunning
Betty Faust (c/o Dr. Carnevali)
Scott L. Fedick
Vilma Fialko
William J. Folan
Roberto García Moll
Joel D. Gunn
Michelle Hegmon
Gyles Iannone
Christien Isendahl
David L. Lentz
Rodrigo Liendo Stuardo
Lisa J. Lucero
Ben A. Nelson
Mario Arturo Ortiz-Pérez
Keith Prufer
Jeremy A. Sabloff
Vernon L. Scarborough
Sergey Sedov
Berenice Solís-Castillo
Elizabeth Solleiro-Rebolledo
Joseph A. Tainter
Fred Valdez, Jr.
Sander E. van der Leeuw
Beniamino Volta
Tony J. Wilkinson

2014
Archeological Papers of the
American Anthropological Association, Number 24

The Resilience and Vulnerability of Ancient Landscapes: Transforming Maya Archaeology through IHOPE

Arlen F. Chase and Vernon L. Scarborough, Editors

COMPARATIVE STUDIES

CONCLUSION

Foreward

This volume represents the concerted efforts of a group of Maya archaeologists to employ a different approach to their archaeological data that is consistent with an effort called IHOPE: Integrated History and Future of People on Earth. IHOPE is a global network of scientists and researchers that seeks to use a wide range of data to examine how changes in the Earth's systems of the past have been correlated with changes in the coupled human-biophysical environment (Costanza et al. 2007). "The specific objectives for IHOPE are to identify slow and rapidly moving features of complex social-ecological systems, on local to continental spatial scales, which induce resilience, stress, or collapse in linked systems of humans and nature. These objectives will be reached by exploring innovative ways of conducting inter and trans-disciplinary science, including theory, case studies, and integrated modeling" (Costanza et al. 2012:1).

The integration of these data, a large portion of which are derived from archaeology, is seen as an important contribution to the accurate and applicable information base for addressing both short- and long-term planning issues facing modern populations.

This is a new direction for archaeology, as it does not simply focus on the immediacy of archaeological site reports or settlement data, but seeks to explicate how these data interplayed with ancient landscapes, environments, and climates over time and across regions. Ultimately, we are interested in how these datasets can be reassessed in light of contemporary problems, so as to allow an evaluation—again—of the constraints and accommodations made by the world today. Because of the focus on coupled human–nature relationships, archaeology is squarely placed within an ecological context that focuses on resilience and complexity theory. Being so positioned, the results of archaeological research have special significance for research carried out in other disciplines and directed toward addressing real-time problems. Rather than just addressing other Maya archaeologists, the chapters in this volume will be useful to a wide variety of scholars—including archaeologists outside the Maya area as well as landscape ecologists, urban planners, and other individuals in a wide variety of disciplines. The volume represents the first attempt by an archaeological group to synthesize an ancient area of the world in terms of the established goals for IHOPE.

Maya archaeology is well positioned to act as a significant component under the greater IHOPE umbrella because of the amount of work that has been and is being undertaken in the Maya area. Scientific excavation and publication of results for the Maya region has been ongoing for more than a century. Over the span of this work, most of the major Maya sites have witnessed some excavation and have been described and temporally positioned. A huge database has been gathered on the ancient Maya by a wide variety of projects and researchers.

However, the large number of people involved in carrying out research on the ancient Maya means that there are different archaeological standards, conventions, terminology, and research methods employed. One of the sub-goals of IHOPE-Maya has been an attempt to use a common vernacular in order to make the archaeological results more accessible for comparison. This has taken a series of meetings to accomplish by the individuals involved within the IHOPE-Maya group, but it will hopefully lead to more discussion within the general field.

IHOPE-Maya held its first meeting in Vancouver, Canada during the 2008 Society for American Archaeology annual meeting. Following this initial gathering, IHOPE-Maya met at the School for Advanced Research in Santa Fe during January 2009 for a short seminar and again at the Amerind Foundation in Dragoon, Arizona for a seminar in August 2009. The next multi-day meeting was at Arizona State University in June 2010. This was followed by a four-day meeting at the University of Central Florida in Orlando in January 2011. In November 2011, the results of all of these labors were presented in an Executive Session at the American Anthropological Association in Montreal, Canada; it was this session that culminated all previous deliberations and forms the core of this volume. Other IHOPE-Maya meetings occurred in June 2012 at the University of Cincinnati and in April 2014 in Austin; future meetings are planned.

The participants in this volume see their efforts as professionally transformative by way of their ability to use their data to provide case studies and information that are helpful to both those outside of Maya archaeology and to other researchers and policy makers grappling with the sustainability issues facing modern populations. We have intentionally tried to do something different in the field in order to make archaeology more relevant to the modern world (e.g., Scarborough et al. 2012).

This volume was envisioned to be a cohesive whole with widespread appeal to scholars outside of Maya archaeology. As designed, the book is sub-divided into four parts. The first part contains chapters that lay the groundwork for the rest of the book. The second part of the book presents detailed case studies that examine the specific areas laid out in Chapter 2 for human–nature coupled relationships. Part 3 of the volume compares the Maya situation with other parts of the world in terms of resilience and complexity theory. The final section of the volume contains a synthetic paper that ties all of the above together in terms of IHOPE. This paper also lays out the importance of using archaeological data for helping to reach decisions about modern ecological and sustainability issues. The presentations in the book are designed to have something to say to current debates about climate, sustainability, and ecological issues. In this way, the volume is seen as a new beginning for Maya archaeology in terms of its relevance for the modern world.

Our work as a subset of IHOPE effectively moves Maya archaeology into a new direction. By involving a dedicated group of researchers in a long-term effort, it is possible to overcome different theoretical preconceptions and to begin to standardize definitions and understand the effects of different archaeological methodology on data production. By incorporating resilience and complexity theory into the discussion, it also means that these archaeological data can transcend disciplinary boundaries. This Maya example of IHOPE is but one of the ongoing efforts being undertaken by groups of archaeologists throughout the world. An earlier successful effort (that continues) has been undertaken by a group of Southwestern archaeologists (e.g., Hegmon et al. 2008). Other IHOPE groups are beginning research in Australia, Africa, Europe, and Polynesia. Because all of these groups will be exploring and researching similar issues, this will eventually provide a broad base of archaeological data for comparative analysis. The work of the Maya group is a pioneering effort.

This volume is only the second book to result from the IHOPE collaborative. The first volume was the tome edited by Robert Costanza and his colleagues (2007) called *Sustainability and Collapse*. That book enjoys widespread use both among researchers and in the classroom; we hope that this volume will be as successful. This is among the first volumes to explicitly note the diversity that was extant in the Maya area and to embrace it for its explanatory potential.

Recognizing the multitude of adaptations that the ancient Maya made to a complex and diverse environment brings into focus the many different groups comprising the ancient Maya, as well as their respective actions and reactions to their environments, landscapes, and one another. Thus, this volume helps to firmly dispel the idea that there was but one solution to the various problems and issues faced by a diverse group of ancient Maya—and, for that matter, to our current worldly problems.

References Cited

Costanza, Robert, Lisa J. Graumlich, and Will L. Steffen, eds.
2007 Sustainability or Collapse? An Integrated History and Future of People on Earth. Cambridge: MIT Press.

Costanza, R., S. van der Leeuw, K. Hibbard, S. Aulenbach, S. Brewer, M. Burek, S. Cornell, C. Crumley, J. Dearing, C. Folke, L. Graumlich, M. Hegmon, S. Heckbert, S. T. Jackson, I. Kubiszewski, V. Scarborough, P. Sinclair, S. Sörlin, and W. Steffen
2012 Developing an Integrated History and Future of People on Earth (IHOPE). Current Opinion in Environmental Sustainability 4:106–114.

Hegmon, Michelle, Matthew A. Peeples, Ann P. Kinzig, Stephanie Kulow, Cathryn M. Meegan, and Margaret C. Nelson
2008 Social Transformation and Its Human Costs in the Prehispanic U.S. Southwest. American Anthropologist 110(3):313–324.

Scarborough, Vernon, Arlen F. Chase, and Diane Z. Chase
2012 Low Density Urbanism, Sustainability, and IHOPE-Maya: Can the Past Provide More Than History? UGEC Viewpoints 8:20–24.

Arlen F. Chase and Vernon Scarborough
Winter Springs, FL and Santa Fe, NM

1

Diversity, Resiliency, and IHOPE-Maya: Using the Past to Inform the Present

Arlen F. Chase
University of Central Florida
and
Vernon Scarborough
University of Cincinnati

ABSTRACT

How can the past inform the present? Archaeologists working though IHOPE-Maya seek to address this question by using archaeological data and ecological reconstructions to explore human–nature couplings. Maya archaeologists are revitalizing and contemporizing the field to focus on issues relevant today: the socio-natural boundary and the coupled human–nature dynamic. The ancient Maya occupied a diverse range of tropical environments that permits a comparative exploration of past permutations in adaptive responses and may also be instructive concerning issues of overexploitation. The variety of places that the Maya occupied afforded diverse opportunities and constraints. By providing access to long-term historical interactions between peoples and their landscapes, archaeology is uniquely qualified to define, examine, and interpret topics like sustainability, resilience, and vulnerability that are as equally significant to the past as they are to the present. Because Maya archaeology is well positioned to analyze ancient variability in political structures and cultural adaptations that can be related to differential societal success and decline, the discipline can contribute to broader, more current, debates concerning climate change, population limits, urban forms, landscape modifications, and stability. The research being undertaken by IHOPE-Maya hopes to serve as a catalyst for transforming the field. [archaeology, resilience, sustainability, vulnerability, Maya]

It would be an understatement to say that the field of archaeology is facing an identity crisis. No longer is it satisfactory to simply study the past for the sake of personal intellectual gratification (e.g., Flannery 1982:278) or to add to a broader academic knowledge base (Willey and Phillips 1958). The tide has shifted. It is not sufficient to have an elegant research design that explicates some arcane academic argument about the past. Rather, researchers are now asking what insight their investigations can offer in terms of solving modern quandaries and dilemmas (Fisher et al. 2009; Scarborough et al. 2012). What lessons can the discipline of archaeology offer contemporary peoples? What relevance do archaeological data have to environmental and social issues facing today's populations? Archaeology is proud of its "time depth," but as a discipline it is only beginning to use that temporal barometer to address modern problems (see Kintigh et al. 2014).

Just as the world has changed and evolved, so too has the field of archaeology. Once largely directed to the collection of artifacts for the world's museums and the ordering of past cultures into unilinear developmental models (Willey and Sabloff 1993), archaeology then became focused on attempting to examine function, process, and change in past societies and civilizations (Sabloff 1994). However, as more and more stakeholders have become engaged in interpreting the past, archaeological interpretation

ARCHEOLOGICAL PAPERS OF THE AMERICAN ANTHROPOLOGICAL ASSOCIATION, Vol. 24, pp. 1–10, ISSN 1551-823X, online ISSN 1551-8248. DOI: 10.1111/apaa.12025.

has become more compartmentalized. The lack of a clear "big picture" approach, combined with a limited focus on explaining the contemporary impact of studies of the past, has marginalized the field. This also means that in times of reduced funding, such as currently exist, archaeology is at risk of being "cut" or, minimally, sidelined.

Maya archaeology is itself symptomatic of the contradictions that face the general field today. While a great wealth of archaeological knowledge exists on the Maya area of subtropical Central America, these data have not generally been applied to broader issues and modern problems. For more than a century, scientific research and excavations have been undertaken on the extraordinary remains of the Maya peoples who call this region "home" (Sharer and Traxler 2006). The ancient Maya adapted to a diverse range of environmental conditions, while simultaneously developing great civilizations and art styles independently of the Old World (Marcus 2007). Spurred on by the Resilience Center at the University of Stockholm and their IHOPE (Integrated History and Future of People on Earth) interests (see Costanza et al. 2007), in the summer of 2008 a group of Maya archaeologists began to focus on the long-term human–nature relationships that exist in the Maya area. The stated goal was to use a multidisciplinary approach to determine what could be gleaned from Maya archaeology that would be of use for modern policy decisions relating to climate change, resilience, sustainability, vulnerability, rigidity, and diversity. Working across diverse regions, research projects, sampling schemes, and time periods has proved both difficult and enlightening. However, after more than a half dozen formal meetings over 5 years, IHOPE-Maya is ready to offer some concrete results related to this concerted effort.

General Considerations

The discipline of archaeology gathers and interprets data relevant to past human societies, specifically how they developed, interacted, and adapted. Most archaeologists use the data that they collect to examine past human development and social change, and many of these data can be brought to bear on modern human–environment interactions associated with climate change and drought. They are also suitable for examining ancient and modern sustainability (Blinman 2008; Marston 2011, 2012; Miller and Marston 2012; Scarborough and Burnside 2010; Tainter 2006; Van der Leeuw 2004). By examining settlement patterns and past demography, the sustainability of ancient agricultural processes can be assessed. Yet, the past is not the only purview of the archaeologist. If properly developed, the archaeological remains themselves may provide a sustainable resource that can be used by modern people and countries to promote tourism and economic development (Sabloff 2008). Archaeological data have also been used to identify cultural continuity between ancient remains and modern people, thus directly engaging modern social issues relating to legal rights about land, human remains, artifacts, and even cultural existence (Boytner et al. 2010; McGuire 2008). But, while modern particularistic issues sometimes have been addressed through archaeology, broader global assessments are rarely aired.

Archaeology is positioned to play a key role in the long-term modeling of agricultural systems, urban systems, tropical adaptations, deforestation, and responses to climate change (Gunn et al. 2002; Lentz and Hockaday 2009; Lucero et al. 2011; van der Leeuw 2009). In some parts of the world, past agricultural systems were far more productive and or integrated into the social fabric than they are today; modeling the sustainability of such systems may yield viable solutions for modern populations. Similarly, many ancient urban areas, particularly those found among the tropical civilizations like the ancient Maya, used a diverse set of strategies to integrate farming and settlement into an interdependent or "single" landscape system. Modern urban planners have only recently discovered the benefits of "greening" (Lehmann 2010) despite its prevalence in ancient contexts (e.g., Fletcher 2009); thus, archaeologists can significantly contribute to this discussion. Finally, climate change was constantly faced by past societies (Ruddiman 2003; van der Leeuw and Redman 2008). The many responses and adaptations to diverse environmental situations found in the long-term archaeological record likely hold clues to both successes and miscalculations that are of use in policy decisions facing modern societies. While the future of archaeology is in the past, the past also holds information vital for the world's future—perhaps yielding solutions in spite of modern denials that problems even exist.

If this is the case, then why has archaeology not already played a larger role in present-day management decisions? The answer to this question resides both in the nature of archaeological data and in the way that archaeologists have traditionally collected and shared it. Because of the variability that is apparent in the archaeological record, each site and region presents different problem sets. Controlling time in the absence of absolute dates is a difficult task. Sometimes the collected sample size does not permit the resolution required to address "big picture" questions. Moreover, different and emergent paradigms within Maya archaeology influence research designs and interpretations of different researchers. Each researcher collects and categorizes archaeological data in slightly different ways, meaning that standardization of archaeological data across sites is often difficult (e.g., van der Leeuw and Redman 2002). The individuals participating in IHOPE-Maya are making a concerted effort to resolve issues of definitions, comparisons, scales, and paradigms that have precluded collaboration in the past. This kind of open communication was not traditionally a hallmark of Maya archaeology. Much of our past meeting time has been devoted to establishing mechanisms for effectively sharing and comparing data.

Changing Perceptions and Models within Maya Archaeology

Within the last 50 years, there have been at least three major changes in archaeological perceptions of the ancient Maya that have ramifications for any attempt to be relevant to the modern world. First, there is recognition that the Maya were not a unitary culture facing a single evolutionary trajectory (e.g., Fash 1994). Second, contrary to arguments originally articulated within a cultural ecological framework, where environment largely determined cultural responses and where the Maya Lowlands were viewed as a redundant and uniform environment (e.g., Sanders and Price 1968), more recent research has conclusively demonstrated the usefulness of newer approaches to human–nature interfaces and that the Maya occupied truly diverse environments in which they employed a wide variety of adaptations (e.g, Dunning and Beach 2010; Dunning et al. 1998; Fedick 1996; Ford and Nigh 2009; Harrison and Turner 1978). Third, archaeological data have demonstrated that ancient Maya societies were far more differentiated and complex than widely embraced, and than epigraphically based sociopolitical models would indicate (e.g., Chase and Chase 1992; Chase et al. 2008; Fox et al. 1996; Scarborough et al. 2003). Any examination of the dynamics behind the coupling of human–nature systems in the Maya area should start with these basic premises.

IHOPE-Maya has adopted several approaches to analyzing the past, with a view to using terminology that can be conversant across disciplines. First, human–nature coupling is considered at different scales of time, from millennia to centuries to decades (Costanza et al. 2007:6–10). This approach recognizes that different questions and concerns may require different scales of temporal analysis, all of which are approachable in the archaeological record. Second, spatiotemporal variability is placed within an environment that is considered to be dynamic, is scaled according to the level of observation, and is viewed in terms of complex behaviors that do not easily resolve into cause–effect explanations or simple overarching syntheses (Dearing 2007; Tainter 2000). Third, much of the terminology that is used is grounded in resilience theory, which focuses on an adaptive cycle concerned with degrees of both stability and transformation (Holling 2001; Holling and Gunderson 2002; Holling et al. 2002). Thus, researchers tend to categorize their case examples using terms that have meaning in ecological studies, such as "resilience," "sustainability," and "rigidity." *Resilience* is "a construct representing positive adaptation despite adversity" (Luthar and Cicchetti 2000:857). *Sustainability* implies the ability to continuously utilize natural resources, such as land, water, or energy, while managing these items for long-term future exploitation (e.g., Tainter 2006). *Rigidity* implies an inability to change in the face of stress, often caused by past decisions or adaptations both cultural and natural (see Hegmon et al. 2008).

Archaeological remains provide direct examples of the complex adaptations of past human societies to a wide variety of ecological circumstances. In many instances ancient populations were larger than the modern populations currently living in the same area; this is clearly seen both in the Maya area (Culbert and Rice 1990) and in the Amazonian basin of South America (Balee and Erickson 2006; Erickson 2008, 2010; Heckenberger et al. 2008; Roosevelt 2000). The lack of substantial numbers of people in these regions today implies both the success and failure of ancient adaptations. These past collapses capture the modern imagination and are often invoked as examples of what our global community is facing (Diamond 2005). The successes and failures of past civilizations and the reasons for these failures or continuities (McAnany and Yoffee 2010; Schwartz and Nichols 2006; Tainter 1988) have a direct bearing on modern problems and issues—and archaeology is in a unique position to address these phenomena.

The Maya provide one of the best examples of complex adaptations to a tropical environment. Their largest, densest, and greatest levels of complexity appear to be located in the harshest environments. Thus, the continuity of archaeological occupation implies that contemporaneous groups of Maya were able to survive periods of drying or drought, rising sea levels and water tables, and differential effects of an already modified environment. However, deforestation occurred early in the Maya area, caused by extensive farming practices and an excessive need for fuel in order to make plaster for architecture (Dunning and Beach 2010:375). Denuding the landscape resulted in severe erosion, which is credited with infilling *bajos* (low areas under water during the rainy season) and, perhaps, even lakes; nevertheless, while part of the landscape was degraded, another part was enriched, meaning that farming practices shifted as an indirect result of deforestation. While wetland farming strategies have been extensively examined in the Maya region (e.g., Scarborough 2009), the dryland farming strategies that supported self-sufficient garden-cities have also been a focus of research (Chase and Chase 1998; Dunning and Beach 1994). Because of the need for intensive agriculture to support large populations, different strategies were employed throughout the Maya area. Large, contemporary, urban cities were supported by: wetland agriculture (e.g., Edzna; see Matheny 1978); terraced agriculture (e.g., Caracol; see Chase et al. 2011); swidden and bajo cultivation (e.g., Tikal; see Dickson 1980); and a combination of strategies that may have included tree-cropping, pot irrigation, and gardens made of imported organic soils (e.g., Chunchucmil; see Dunning and Beach 2010). During the Classic period, there may even have been peripheral marginal areas that functioned as bread-baskets for the interior regions (Dahlin and Chase 2014).

Approaches to the Maya Data

Throughout the Maya area, there are both differences and similarities in environment, human occupational history, and adaptations that were made by the ancient Maya. To approach the human–nature interface, the IHOPE-Maya group subdivided the overall Maya region into a series of zones that were correlated with soils and ecology (Dunning et al. 1998) as well as with the existence of intensive archaeological research within a given zone that could provide needed time depth for human–nature correlations. The subtropical Maya environment ranged from barely elevated coastal areas with mangrove swamps or scrub-forest to karstic uplands covered with jungle forest to cooler mountainous zones containing pine trees. Standing water was rare in much of the Maya area, occurring in the northern Lowlands at Coba, at only a very few points in the central Lowlands (Lakes Civiltuk and Bacalar), and spread inconsistently across the central part of the southern Lowlands (from west to east: Lake Salpeten, Lake Peten-Itza, Lake Yaxha-Sacnab). In the north, the water table resides at some depth and is retrievable primarily through accessing *cenotes* (that is, sinkholes). Seasonally running water, as well as a very few perennial rivers, do bracket the eastern, western, and southern sides of the southern Lowlands and were probably the initial focus for early colonization in this region. These rivers also anchored east-west communication and trade routes through the Yucatan Peninsula in combination with seaborne routes that circumnavigated the entire region. Importantly, during the rainy season, several rivers in the southern Lowlands directly articulated with bajos, forming even more impressive interior routes that could be navigated by canoe (e.g., Fialko 2004).

Vegetation also varied throughout the region, dependent on rainfall, soils, and elevation. There is a vast difference in rainfall totals in the northern Maya Lowlands as compared to the southern area, ranging from 500 millimeters to over 2500 millimeters per year. Airflow patterns also govern the amount of precipitation that a given area might receive. While early and late settlements were concentrated in areas that had permanent or running water, the largest Classic period Maya settlements were located away from such water sources, meaning that the landscape was modified to catch and preserve rainwater. Agricultural soils also varied throughout this region and also over time. With the exception of the Puuc region, the soils in the northern Lowlands were generally thin and poor. In the southern region, however, rich soils infilled some of the bajos as a result of erosion events brought about by the initial deforestation of the landscape by the original settlers. Fertile soils were also found along river margins and were replenished annually because of the rainy season cycle. Soils were also manipulated and moved early in Maya prehistory, as noted by evidence from Chunchucmil in the northern Lowlands (Dunning and Beach 2010) and from terraces in the southern Lowlands (Chase and Chase 1998). Most ancient Maya areas implemented a diverse mix of cultivation practices. Agricultural adaptations included walled gardens in the north, raised field agriculture in the central Maya area, and terraced agriculture in the Vaca Plateau. Ancient social and political systems similarly varied. Thus, different cultural groups in the ancient Maya area exploited a wide variety of resources and emphasized a multitude of adaptations to their environments over both time and space.

The contributions presented within this volume examine the temporal and spatial variability of a number of datasets and questions. An initial overview (Chapter 2) contextualizes the Maya area over time, examining general similarities and differences in archaeologically recorded responses to environmental factors. Chapter 3 specifically examines the Maya as a rainfall-dependent agricultural society, looking at the complexity of their interactions with water (e.g., Iannone in press; Lucero and Fash 2006; Scarborough and Lucero 2010). The introductory sections are followed by a number of case studies. In the northern Lowlands, the archaeology of the Puuc region is examined by way of a Maya adaptation to good soils amidst a lack of water (Chapter 4; see also Dunning 1994; Isendahl 2006). In the western part of the northern Lowlands, where extensive settlements occurred within areas of limited agricultural potential, differential adaptive responses are seen in the archaeological records of Chichén-Itzá (Chapter 5; see also Cobos 2007; Cobos and Fernandez 2011) and the Yalahau region (Chaper 6; see also Fedick and Morrison 2004). The western Maya region (the location of Palenque, Pomona, and Tortugeruo) provided the ancient Maya with rivers, a rich environment, and linear strips of settlement (Chapter 7; see also Liendo 2005)—a very different setting from that seen along the

Belize River in the eastern Lowlands (Garber 2004). Some of the largest-known Maya urban developments, such as those found at Calakmul (Folan et al. 1995) and Caracol (Chase and Chase 2007; Chase et al. 2011), occur in regions that were largely devoid of standing water. Clearly, different settlement adaptations occurred in areas of standing or running water than in areas devoid of such resources. In topographically flatter regions, like the one in which Calakmul is located (Chapter 8), bajos were used as a water source; in more hilly terrain, like the area in which Caracol is situated (Chapter 10), a large number of reservoirs were constructed. The agricultural systems within these centers also differed. Caracol covered its landscape with agricultural terraces (Chase and Chase 1998). In contrast to the more complex adaptations of the larger Maya sites, archaeological survey in the Three Rivers Region of Belize provides examples of a network of small, resilient communities that peaked in terms of settlement at different times (Chapter 9; see also Scarborough et al. 2003). The special circumstances and temporal trajectories of smaller hinterland communities (Chapter 11) provide examples of alternative adaptations that can be explored through comparing and contrasting archaeological data from Minanha (Iannone 2005), Uxbenka (Prufer et al. 2008), and Santa Rita Corozal (Chase and Chase 1988).

With a better understanding of Maya adaptations over time and space, it is possible to examine comparative developmental trajectories and the applicability of these data to modern issues and concerns. Comparing the complexity and sustainability of ancient Rome (Tainter and Crumley 2007) to the Maya trajectory permits the extraction of ideas that are of relevance to our modern society (Chapter 14). The archaeology of the Southwest United States has also received extensive analysis of its human–nature interaction and researchers there have also embraced IHOPE's goals (Hegmon et al. 2008; Redman et al. 2009); comparing and contrasting the archaeological data gained from the U.S. Southwest and northern Mexico with that of the Maya Lowlands provides archaeological examples of resilience, rigidity, and path dependence (Chapter 12; see also Nelson 1995). Of particular interest are general comparisons that may be made between the New World Maya and the Old World Near Eastern societies (e.g., Wilkinson and Rayne 2010) in terms of low-density urban adaptations and settlement dynamics framed to address issues of water usage, sustainability, fragility, and scalar responses to stresses relating to collapse and resilience (Chapter 13). These case studies and comparisons suggest both resilience and rigidity of Maya culture at different places in time and space. Finally, lessons drawn from specific ancient Maya cases and from trajectory comparisons in the archaeological record are informative for modern assessments of sustainability, climate change, and adaptations to various stresses (Chapter 15). The successful use of these data to advise modern policy and to guide related concerns would represent a tidemark for Maya archaeology.

Summary

Once thought to be little more than the erudite study of ancient pottery types, untranslatable hieroglyphs, and dead kings, Maya archaeology is in the midst of recasting and rejuvenating its legacy. Through an alignment with IHOPE, Maya researchers are using their archaeological expertise and their control of variable temporal scales both to remodel the past and to probe for solutions to modern problems. With an infusion of ideas borrowed from ecology, Maya archaeologists are revitalizing and contemporizing the field to focus on issues relevant today: the socio-natural boundary and the coupled human–nature dynamic. The ancient Maya occupied a diverse range of tropical environments that permit a comparative exploration of past permutations in adaptive responses and may also be instructive in evaluating notions of overexploitation. The variety of places that the Maya occupied afforded diverse opportunities and constraints. By providing access to long-term historical interactions between peoples and their landscapes, archaeology is uniquely qualified to define, examine, and interpret topics like sustainability, resilience, and vulnerability that are as significant to the past as they are to the present. These same data showcase how a single society may at different times in its history be alternatively adaptive, flexible, and resilient or rigid and vulnerable. Because Maya archaeology is well positioned to analyze ancient variability in political structures and cultural adaptations at a variety of scales that relate to differential societal success and decline, the discipline can—and should—contribute to broader, more current debates concerning climate change, population limits, urban forms, landscape modifications, and degrees of stability. This volume presents some of the research being undertaken by IHOPE-Maya that is serving as a catalyst for the transformation of Maya archaeology.

Acknowledgments

Sincere thanks are due to Diane Z. Chase, who heavily edited earlier versions of this paper. The authors would also like to thank Sander van der Leeuw for his continued prodding and insistence on the importance of pursuing this line of research.

References Cited

Balee, William L., and Clark L. Erickson

2006 Time and Complexity in Historical Ecology: Studies in the Neotropical Lowlands. New York: Columbia University Press.

Blinman, Eric

2008 2000 Years of Cultural Adaptation to Climate Change in the Southwestern United States. *In* Royal Colloquium: Past Climate Change: Human Survival Strategies. Special issue, Ambio 14: 489–497.

Boytner, Ran, Lynn Swartz Dodd, and Bradley J. Parker

2010 Controlling the Past: Owning the Future: The Political Uses of Archaeology in the Middle East. Tucson: University of Arizona Press.

Chase, Arlen F., and Diane Z. Chase

1998 Scale and Intensity in Classic Period Maya Agriculture: Terracing and Settlement at the 'Garden City' of Caracol, Belize. Culture and Agriculture 20(2):60–77.

2007 Ancient Maya Urban Development: Insights from the Archaeology of Caracol, Belize. Journal of Belizean Studies 29(2):60–71.

Chase, Arlen F., Diane Z. Chase, and Rafael Cobos

2008 Jeroglificos y Arqueologia Maya: Colusion o Colision? Mayab 20:5–21.

Chase, Arlen F., Diane Z. Chase, John F. Weishampel, Jason B. Drake, Ramesh L. Shrestha, K. Clint Slatton, Jaime J. Awe, and William E. Carter

2011 Airborne LiDAR, Archaeology, and the Ancient Maya Landscape at Caracol, Belize. Journal of Archaeological Science 38:387–398.

Chase, Diane Z., and Arlen F. Chase

1988 A Postclassic Perspective: Excavations at the Maya Site of Santa Rita Corozal, Belize. Monograph 4. San Francisco: Pre-Columbian Art Research Institute.

Chase, Diane Z., and Arlen F. Chase, eds.

1992 Mesoamerican Elites. Norman: University of Oklahoma Press.

Cobos, Rafael

2007 Multepal or Centralized Kingship? New Evidence on Governmental Organization at Chichen Itza. *In* Twin Tollans. J. Kowlaski and C. Kristan-Graham, eds. Pp. 315–343. Cambridge: Harvard University Press.

Cobos, Rafael, and Lilia Fernandez Souza, eds.

2011 Vida Cotidiana de los Antiguos Mayas del Norte de la Peninsula de Yucatan. Merida: Universidad Autonoma de Yucatan.

Costanza, Robert, Lisa J. Graumlich, and Will L. Steffen

2007 Sustainability or Collapse: Lessons from Integrating the History of Humans and the Rest of the World. *In* Sustainability or Collapse? An Integrated History and Future of People on Earth. R. Costanza, L. Graumlich, and W. Steffen, eds. Pp. 3–17. Cambridge: MIT Press.

Culbert, T. Patrick, and Don S. Rice, eds.

1990 Prehistoric Population History in the Maya Lowlands. Albuquerque: University of New Mexico Press.

Dahlin, Bruce H., and Arlen F. Chase

2014 A Tale of Three Cities: Effects of the A.D. 536 Event in the Lowland Maya Heartland. *In* The Great Maya Droughts in Cultural Context: Case Studies in Resilience and Vulnerability. G. Iannone, ed. Pp. 127–155. Boulder: University Press of Colorado.

Dearing, John A.

2007 Human-Environment Interactions: Learning from the Past. *In* Sustainability or Collapse? An Integrated History and Future of People on Earth. R. Costanza, L. Graumlich, and W. Steffen, eds. Pp. 19–37. Cambridge: MIT Press.

Diamond, Jared

2005 Collapse: How Societies Choose to Fail or Succeed. New York: Viking Press.

Dickson, D. Bruce

1980 Ancient Agriculture and Population at Tikal, Guatemala: An Application of Linear Programming to the Simulation of an Archaeological Problem. American Antiquity 45(4):697–712.

Dunning, Nicholas P.

1994 Puuc Ecology and Settlement Patterns. *In* Hidden Among the Hills: Maya Archaeology of the Northwest Yucatan Peninsula. H. Prem, ed. Acta

Mesoamericana 7. Pp. 1–43. Mockmuhl: Verlag von Flemming.

Dunning, Nicholas P., and Timothy Beach
1994 Soil Erosion, Slope Management, and Ancient Terracing in the Maya Lowlands. Latin American Antiquity 5:51–69.
2010 Farms and Forests: Spatial and Temporal Perspectives on Ancient Maya Landscapes. *In* Landscapes and Societies. I. Martini and W. Chesworth, eds. Pp. 369–389. New York: Springer.

Dunning, Nicholas P., Timothy Beach, Pat Farrell, and Sheryl Luzzadder-Beach
1998 Prehispanic Agrosystems and Adaptive Regions in the Maya Lowlands. Culture and Agriculture 20:87–101.

Erickson, Clark L.
2008 Amazonia: The Historical Ecology of a Domesticated Landscape. *In* Handbook of South American Archaeology. H. Silverman and W. H. Isabell, eds. Pp. 157–183. New York: Springer.
2010 The Transformation of Environment into Landscape: The Historical Ecology of Monumental Earthwork Construction in the Bolivian Amazon. Diversity 2:618–652.

Fash, William L.
1994 Changing Perspectives on Maya Civilization. Annual Review of Anthropology 23:201–208.

Fedick, Scott L., ed.
1996 The Mananged Mosaic: Ancient Maya Agriculture and Resource Use. Salt Lake City: University of Utah Press.

Fedick, Scott L., and Bethany A. Morrison
2004 Ancient Maya Use and Manipulation of Landscape in the Yalahau Region of the Northern Maya Lowlands. Agriculture and Human Values 21:207–219.

Fialko, Vilma.
2004 Diez anos de investigaciones arqueologicas en la Cuenca del rio Holmul, noreste de Peten. *In* XVIII Simposio de Investigaciones Arqueologicas en Guatemala. J. P. Laporte, B. Arroyo, and H. Mejia, eds. Pp. 253–268. Guatemala: MNAE.

Fisher, Christopher T., J. Brett Hill, and Gary M. Feinman
2009 Introduction: Environmental Studies for Twenty-First Century Conservation. *In* The Archaeology of Environmental Change. C. Fisher, J. Hill, and G. Feinman, eds. Pp. 1–12. Tucson: University of Arizona Press.

Flannery, Kent V.
1982 The Golden Marshalltown: A Parable for the Archeology of the 1980s. American Anthropologist 84(2): 265–278.

Fletcher, Roland
2009 Low-Density, Agrarian-Based Urbanism: A Comparative View. Insights 2:2–19.

Folan, William J., Joyce Marcus, Sophia Pincemin, Maria del Rosario Dominguez-Carrasco, and Larraine Fletcher
1995 Calakmul: New Data from an Ancient Maya Capital in Campeche, Mexico. Latin American Antiquity 6(4):310–334.

Ford, Anabel, and Ronald Nigh
2009 Origins of the Maya Forest Garden: Maya Resource Management. Journal of Ethnobiology 29:213–236.

Fox, John, Scott Cook, Arlen F. Chase, and Diane Z. Chase
1996 Questions of Political and Economic Integration: Segmentary versus Centralized States among the Ancient Maya. Current Anthropology 37(5):795–801.

Garber, James, ed.
2004 The Archaeology of the Belize Valley: Half a Century Later. Gainesville: University Press of Florida.

Gunn, Joel D., Ray T. Matheny, and William J. Folan
2002 Climate Change Studies in the Maya Area: A Diachronic Analysis. Ancient Mesoamerica 13:79–84.

Harrison, Peter D., and Billie L. Turner II, eds.
1978 Pre-Hispanic Maya Agriculture. Albuquerque: University of New Mexico Press.

Heckenberger, Michael J., J. Christian Russell, Carlos Fausto, Joshua R. Toney, Morgan J. Schmidt,

Edithe Pereira, Bruna Franchetto, and Afukaka Kuikuro
2008 Pre-Columbian Urbanism, Anthropogenic Landscapes, and the Future of the Amazon. Science 321:1214–1217.

Hegmon, Michelle, Matthew A. Peeples, Ann P. Kinzig, Stephanie Kulow, Cathryn M. Meegan, and Margaret C. Nelson
2008 Social Transformation and Its Human Costs in the Prehispanic U.S. Southwest. American Anthropologist 110(3):313–324.

Holling, Crawford S.
2001 Understanding the Complexity of Economic, Ecological, and Social Systems. Ecosystems 4(5):394–405.

Holling, Crawford S., and Lance H. Gunderson
2002 Resilience and Adaptive Cycles. *In* Panarchy: Understanding Transformations in Human and Natural Systems. L. Gunderson and C. Holling, eds. Pp. 25–62. Washington, DC: Island Press.

Holling, Crawford S., Lance H. Gunderson, and David Ludwig
2002 In Quest of a Theory of Adaptive Change. *In* Panarchy: Understanding Transformations in Human and Natural Systems. L. Gunderson and C. Holling, eds. Pp. 3–24. Washington, DC: Island Press.

Iannone, Gyles
2005 The Rise and Fall of an Ancient Maya Petty Royal Court. Latin American Antiquity 16(1):26–44.

Iannone, Gyles, ed.
In press The Great Maya Droughts in Cultural Context: Case Studies in Resilience and Vulnerability. Boulder: University Press of Colorado.

Isendahl, Christian
2006 The Puuc Urban Landscape: Settlement Archaeology at Xuch, Campeche. Mexicon 28:111–117.

Kintigh, Keith W., Jeffrey H. Altschul, Mary C. Beaudry, Robert D. Drennan, Ann P. Kinzig, Timothy A. Kohler, W. Fredrick Limp, Herbert D. G. Maschner, William K. Michener, Timothy R. Pauketat, Peter Peregrine, Jeremy A. Sabloff, Tony J. Wilkinson, Henry T. Wright, and Melinda A. Zeder
2014 Grand Challenges for Archaeology. American Antiquity 79(1):5–24.

Lehmann, Steffen
2010 The Principles of Green Urbanism: Transforming the City for Sustainability. London: Rutledge Press.

Lentz, David L., and Brian Hockaday
2009 Tikal Timbers and Temples: Ancient Maya Agroforestry and the End of Time. Journal of Archaeological Science 36:1342–1353.

Liendo Stuardo, Rodrigo
2005 An Archaeological Study of Settlement Distribution in the Palenque Area, Chiapas, Mexico. Anthropological Notebooks 11:31–44.

Lucero, Lisa J., and Barbara W. Fash, eds.
2006 Precolumbian Water Management: Ideology, Ritual, and Power. Tucson: University of Arizona Press.

Lucero, Lisa J., Joel D. Gunn, and Vernon L. Scarborough
2011 Climate Change and Classic Maya Water Management. Water 3:479–494.

Luthar, Suniya S., and Dante Cicchetti
2000 The Construct of Resilience: Implications for Interventions and Social Policies. Development and Psychopathology 12:857–885.

McAnany, Patricia A., and Norman Yoffee, eds,
2010 Questioning Collapse: Human Resilience, Ecological Vulnerability, and the Aftermath of Empire. Cambridge: Cambridge University Press.

McGuire, Randall H.
2008 Archaeology as Political Action. Berkeley: University of California Press.

Marcus, Joyce
2007 Great Art Styles and the Rise of Complex Societies. *In* Gordon R. Willey and American Archaeology. J. Sabloff and W. Fash, eds. Pp. 72–104. Norman: University of Oklahoma Press.

Marston, John M.
2011 Archaeological Markers of Agricultural Risk Management. Journal of Anthropological Archaeology 30:190–205.
2012 Agricultural Strategies and Political Economy in Ancient Anatolia. American Journal of Archaeology 116(3):377–403.

Matheny, Raymond T.
1978 Northern Maya Lowland Water-Control Systems. *In* Pre-Hispanic Maya Agriculture. P. Harrison and B. Turner, eds. Pp. 185–210. Albuquerque: University of New Mexico Press.

Miller, N. F., and John M. Marston
2012 Archaeological Fuel Remains as Indicators of Ancient West Asian Agropastoral and Land-Use Systems. Journal of Arid Environments 86:97–103.

Nelson, Ben A.
1995 Complexity, Hierarchy, and Scale: A Controlled Comparison between Chaco Canyon, New Mexico and La Quemada, Zacatecas. American Antiquity 60(4):597–618.

Prufer, Keith M., Andrews Kindon, and Douglas Kennett
2008 Uxbenka and the Foundation of Sedentary Communities in Southern Belize. Research Reports in Belizean Archaeology 5:241–250.

Ruddiman, William E.
2003 The Anthropogenic Greenhouse Era Began Thousand so Years Ago. Climate Change 61:261–293.

Redman, Charles L., Margaret C. Nelson, and Ann P. Kinzig
2009 The Resilience of Socioecological Landscapes: Lessons from the Hohokom. *In* The Archaeology of Environmental Change. C. Fisher, J. Hill, and G. Feinman, eds. Pp. 15–39. Tucson: University of Arizona Press.

Roosevelt, Anna C.
2000 The Lower Amazon: A Dynamic Human Habitat. *In* Imperfect Balance: Landscape Transformations in the Precolumbian Americas. D. Lentz, ed. Pp. 455–491. New York: Columbia University Press.

Sabloff, Jeremy A.
1994 The New Archaeology and the Ancient Maya. 2nd edition. New York: Scientific American brk Library.
2008 Archaeology Matters. Walnut Creek: Left Coast Press.

Sanders, William T., and Barbara J. Price
1968 Mesoamerica: The Evolution of a Civilization. New York: Random House.

Scarborough, Vernon L.
2009 Beyond Sustainability: Managed Wetlands and Water Harvesting in Ancient Mesoamerica *In* The Archaeology of Environmental Change. C. Fisher, J. Hill, and G. Feinman, eds. Pp. 62–82. Tucson: University of Arizona Press.

Scarborough, Vernon L., and William R. Burnside
2010 Complexity and Sustainability: Perspectives from the Ancient Maya and the Modern Balinese. American Antiquity 75(2):327–363.

Scarborough, Vernon L., Arlen F. Chase, and Diane Z. Chase
2012 Low Density Urbanism, Sustainability, and IHOPE-Maya: Can the Past Provide More than History? UGEC Viewpoints: Connecting Past and Present Lessons in Urbanization and the Environment 8:20–24.

Scarborough, Vernon L., and Lisa J. Lucero
2010 The Non-Hierarchical Development of Complexity in the Semitropics: Water and Cooperation. Water History 2:185–205.

Scarborough, Vernon L., Fred Valdez, and Nicholas Dunning, eds.
2003 Heterarchy, Political Economy, and the Ancient Maya: The Three Rivers Region of the East-Central Yucatan Peninsula. Tucson: University of Arizona Press.

Schwartz, Glenn M., and John J. Nichols, eds.
2006 After Collapse: The Regeneration of Complex Societies. Tucson: University Arizona.

Sharer, Robert J., and Loa P. Traxler
2006 The Ancient Maya. 6th edition. Stanford: Stanford University Press.

Tainter, Joseph A.
1988 The Collapse of Complex Societies. Cambridge: Cambridge University Press.
2000 Problem Solving: Complexity, History, and Sustainability. Population and Environment 22:3–41.
2006 Social Complexity and Sustainability. Ecological Complexity 3:91–103.

Tainter, Joseph A., and Carole L. Crumley
2007 Climate, Complexity, and Problem Solving in the Roman Empire. *In* Sustainability or Collapse. R. Costanza, L. Graumlich, and W. Steffen, eds. Pp. 61–75. Cambridge: MIT Press.

van der Leeuw, Sander E.
2004 Why Model? Cybernetics and Systems: An International Journal 35:117–128.
2009 What is an 'Environmental Crisis' to an Archaeologist? *In* The Archaeology of Environmental Change. C. Fisher, J. Hill, and G. Feinman, eds. Pp. 40–61. Tucson: University of Arizona Press.

van der Leeuw, Sander E., and Charles L. Redman
2002 Placing Archaeology at the Center of Socio-Natural Studies. American Antiquity 67:597–605.
2008 Climate and Society: Lessons from the Past 10000 Years. *In* Royal Colloquium: Past Climate Change: Human Survival Strategies. Special issue, Ambio 14: 489–497.

Wilkinson, James, and Louise Rayne
2010 Hydraulic Landscapes and Imperial Power in the Near East. Water History 2:115–144.

Willey, Gordon R., and Phillip Phillips
1958 Method and Theory in American Archaeology. Chicago: University of Chicago Press.

Willey, Gordon R., and Jeremy A. Sabloff
1993 A History of American Archaeology. 3rd edition. New York: W. H. Freeman.

2

Tropical Landscapes and the Ancient Maya: Diversity in Time and Space

Arlen F. Chase
University of Central Florida
Lisa J. Lucero
University of Illinois, Urbana-Champaign
Vernon L. Scarborough
University of Cincinnati
Diane Z. Chase
University of Central Florida
Rafael Cobos
Universidad Autónoma de Yucatán
Nicholas P. Dunning
University of Cincinnati
Scott L. Fedick
University of California, Riverside
Vilma Fialko
Instituto de Antropologia e Historia
Joel D. Gunn
University of North Carolina-Greensboro
Michelle Hegmon
Arizona State University
Gyles Iannone
Trent University
David L. Lentz
University of Cincinnati
Rodrigo Liendo
University Nacional Autonoma de Mexico

ARCHEOLOGICAL PAPERS OF THE AMERICAN ANTHROPOLOGICAL ASSOCIATION, Vol. 24, pp. 11–29, ISSN 1551-823X, online ISSN 1551-8248. DOI: 10.1111/apaa.12026.

Keith Prufer
New Mexico
Jeremy A. Sabloff
Santa Fe Institute
Joseph A. Tainter
Utah State
Fred Valdez Jr
Texas, Austin
and
Sander E. van der Leeuw
ASU and Santa Fe Institute

ABSTRACT

Archaeologists have begun to understand that many of the challenges facing our technologically sophisticated, resource dependent, urban systems were also destabilizing factors in ancient complex societies. The focus of IHOPE-Maya is to identify how humans living in the tropical Maya Lowlands in present-day Central America responded to and impacted their environments over the past three millennia, and to relate knowledge of those processes to modern and future coupled human–environment systems. To better frame variability in ancient lowland Maya development and decline, the area that they once occupied may be subdivided into a series of geographical regions in which the collected archaeological data can be correlated with environmental differences. Although beginning as small agricultural communities occupying a variety of ecological niches in the humid tropics of Mesoamerica, the ancient Maya became an increasingly complex set of societies involved in intensive and extensive resource exploitation. Their development process was not linear, but also involved periods of rapid growth that were punctuated by contractions. Thus, the long-term development and disintegration of Maya geopolitical institutions presents an excellent vantage from which to study resilience, vulnerability, and the consequences of decision-making in ancient complex societies. [Maya, archaeology, environment, variability, sustainability]

Various individuals and authors—from politicians to philosophers to historians to scientists—have argued that knowledge of the past is an important key to the future and that, conversely, an ignorance of earlier times and events can result in the unnecessary repetition of historically known failures and problems (Burke 1790; Lipe 1984; Oaklander and Smith 1994; Santayana 1905). Archaeologists often focus narrowly on specific sites and issues, eschewing broader applications. In an attempt to remedy this situation, archaeologists have joined with biologists, geographers, meteorologists, and others under the umbrella organization "IHOPE" (Integrated History and Future of People on Earth). This project calls together a broad range of active researchers to explore human–nature relationships. The intent of these efforts is to integrate knowledge of the past with a dynamic global perspective that can be used to meaningfully address current world problems.

One subgroup of the IHOPE team is focused on exploring the adaptations of the ancient Maya of southeastern Mexico and upper Central America. Despite temporal, technological, and environmental differences, many issues that are of interest to archaeologists reconstructing prehistoric Maya lifeways are also of contemporary concern. These issues include, but are not limited to: sustainability and resilience; the role of political and economic factors in collapse and or the disruption and transformation of social stability; maximum or optimal population levels associated with specific environmental adaptations; the impact of climate change; and the nature of past forms of urbanism and landscape modifications. Thus, IHOPE scholars propose not only to develop an integrated history of the ancient Maya, but also to provide rich data from a precocious, non-modern, non-western culture that will add to our understanding of the dynamics of human–environment inter-relationships. The expected end product is the ability to provide multiple "answers" to understanding processes underlying complex, globally relevant issues.

It is important to note at the outset that there is substantial variation in the archaeological past that most researchers currently lump together and call "Maya." The ancient Maya were not a single uniform or unified civilization; as we shall see, variation is both regional and temporal. Not only did languages differ across the Maya region (Sharer and Traxler 2006:25–28), but so too did governmental structures (Roys 1957) as well as cultural and kinship principles (Fox and Justeson 1986); the variable historical and environmental circumstances that were found throughout the Lowlands further compounded the differences (Dunning et al. 1998). This sometimes occurred even when their communities were only a few kilometers apart (Stanton and Garreta 2001). These ancient, and for that matter modern, differences within the Maya Lowlands—and the explicit recognition of the lack of uniformity in and of itself (e.g., Scarborough et al. 2003) —are important to meeting the IHOPE goals because they offer opportunities to test variable effects of the same global-scale phenomena, such as climate change and radical shifts in economic orientations, on differing local situations.

Although greatly changed by historical circumstances, the present-day Maya still comprise distinct language and ethnic groups. Yucatec Maya of the northern Lowlands speak and dress differently than the Chorti Maya in the far southeast of the southern Lowlands and the Tzotzil Maya in the Chiapas region of the southwestern Lowlands; they are still distinct groups of Maya, but more closely related linguistically than the extremely variant Quiche Maya of the Guatemalan Highlands. Some 31 modern languages are classified as "Mayan," and these 31 languages are separated into four major groups that have substantial antiquity (Campbell and Kaufman 1985). Researchers still disagree as to exactly what language was spoken by the "Classic Maya" who produced the carved stone monuments (stelae and altars) during the Classic and Terminal Classic periods (ca. C.E. 250–900; see Figure 2.1 for Maya time periods) and their accompanying hieroglyphic texts (Houston and Lacadena 2000).

Some argue that the Classic Mayan language found in the hieroglyphs was a prestige language that was distinct from the actual languages that were spoken by local populations across the Lowlands (see Houston et al. 1996); this view portrays the Maya as unified in their cultural expression. Linguists, however, posit at least three different contemporary dialects or languages in the hieroglyphic texts of the Classic period (Wichmann 2006).

By C.E. 800, the Maya region was filled with a number of different kinds of polities, some outward-looking and others inward-looking. The polities ranged in size from expansive regional states—some with desires of forming multiethnic, hegemonic empires—to smaller city-states and other more loosely organized "associations" (Chase et al. 2009). While we sometimes refer to this ancient area today as a monolithic "Maya," in reality the groups that comprised these polities not only spoke a variety of different Mayan languages and dialects, but also practiced varied forms of social and political organization, endorsed different religious practices, and evinced a host of other cultural differences. Depending upon proximity and opportunity, many of these diverse groups interacted within a broader Mesoamerican world system that was interconnected and reactive to far-distant shocks and stimuli. Thus, ancient Maya populations followed varied trajectories developmentally and responded differently to climatic and environmental changes, external challenges, and internal stresses.

Some 27 environmental "adaptive regions" have been defined for the Maya Lowlands (Dunning et al. 1998; see also Chapter 1) based on differences in agricultural soils, wet and dry seasons, water supply and quality, and other factors. The southeastern Maya Lowlands are so moist that they support a complex canopy tropical rain forest ranging up to 40 meters in height. Yet, the northwest corner of the peninsula is so dry it approaches desert-like extremes. Although some outliers occur, the northwestern Lowlands appear to have supported less dense human populations than the southeastern Lowlands. Thus, despite the overall diversity, the environmental settings define certain constraints to the structural responses that are possible.

IHOPE researchers have been meeting to assess the differences and similarities in the archaeological, environmental, and climatic records for different parts of the Maya Lowlands. We are attempting to develop a meta-language that permits the integration of disparate groups of data collected over more than one hundred years from dozens of intensively excavated sites. Through the use of the same analytical measurements to compare and communicate archaeological and environmental information, we hope to ferret out an understanding of diverse past processes of adaptation to a varied landscape, thereby gaining insights into how the ancient Maya successfully lived as farmers in the lowlands of present-day Mexico, Guatemala, Belize, and Honduras for millennia. The Maya adapted and survived in the Lowlands for 3000 years; nevertheless, their success was punctuated by periodic disruptions, the most dramatic being the disintegration of their Classic period civilization around C.E. 900 (Demarest et al. 2004). Their history, therefore, holds clues for the successful adaptations of modern societies to rapidly changing conditions.

Examining Maya Landscapes

To provide an integrated Maya history, scholars working in the Maya Lowlands have joined together to compare and contrast diverse data sets from key areas. Ten "zones"

Beginning	End	Period Name	MAJOR EVENTS	Symbol
CE 1958	2000	Post-IGY	International Geophysical Year Earth System observations	IGY
1920	1958	Instrumental observation	Carnegie Institution of Washington research	Inst
1550	1920	Historic	Maya integrated into modern nation states	Hist
1250	1550	Late Postclassic	northern Lowlands heavily occupied	Lpo
1000	1250	Early Postclassic	florescence of eastern Yucatec coastal sites	Epo
900	1000	Terminal Classic 2	florescence of Chichén Itzá in northern Lowlands	T2
800	900	Terminal Classic 1	political collapse in the southern Lowlands	T1
700	800	Late Classic 2	regional polities dominate the Lowlands	L2
550	700	Late Classic 1	florescence of regional centers in southern Lowlands	L1
450	550	Early Classic 3	transition to stratified regional polities	E3
350	450	Early Classic 2	vaulted buildings and Teotihuacan-like elite pottery	E2
250	350	Early Classic 1	widespread appearance of polychrome ceramics	E1
1 BCE/CE	250	Late Preclassic b	changes potentially reflective of a mini-collapse	Plb
-300	1	Late Preclassic a	large vertical monumental constructions	Pla
-800	-300	Middle Preclassic	large horizontal monumental constructions	Pm
-2000	-800	Early Preclassic	first recognizable Maya peoples	Pe
-3500 BCE	-1500	Archaic	Paleo-Indian lithic points	Ar

Figure 2.1. Maya cultural periods.

were designated as the basic building blocks for a comparative database. These archaeological regions are distributed across the Maya Lowlands and represent long-term established research areas from which extensive collected data already exist. While they are not exhaustive of the variability in environments or of the different ethnic groups that were once manifest across this region, they are representative of the diversity in the ancient Maya Lowlands (Figure 2.2).

These zones provide the basis for compiling standardized comparative data sets that address long-term change and transformation within the quarter-million square kilometers identified as the Maya Lowlands. The ancient population for this region is estimated as having been between three and thirteen million people by C.E. 700 (Turner 1990:302); the most recent estimate places at least 4,665,000 people in the Maya area (Storey 2012:910). The archaeological data provide information about how these societies coped with, cared for, and or destroyed both their environment and themselves. It is only in modern times that the Maya are within reach of their ancient population numbers (Leventhal et al. 2012:51). Thus, a comparative examination of these zones provides important clues concerning stability, resilience, and sustainability that have relevance for modern societies.

For each of these ten zones, a controlled dataset can be formulated that focuses on both the biophysical environment and the past cultural landscape. The biophysical setting is characterized in terms of the general availability of water (climate [including seasonality and precipitation patterns], water-table, surface water, natural sinkholes, and or *aguadas* [naturally occurring low areas where water pools]), the richness of resources (biomass availability), and the potential of the terrain for agriculture (soils and topography [including slope and elevation]). A characterization of the ancient environment can also be reconstructed directly from the archaeological record—ranging from ancient flora (including pollen) and faunal remains to highly visible cultural modifications of the landscape related to water retention

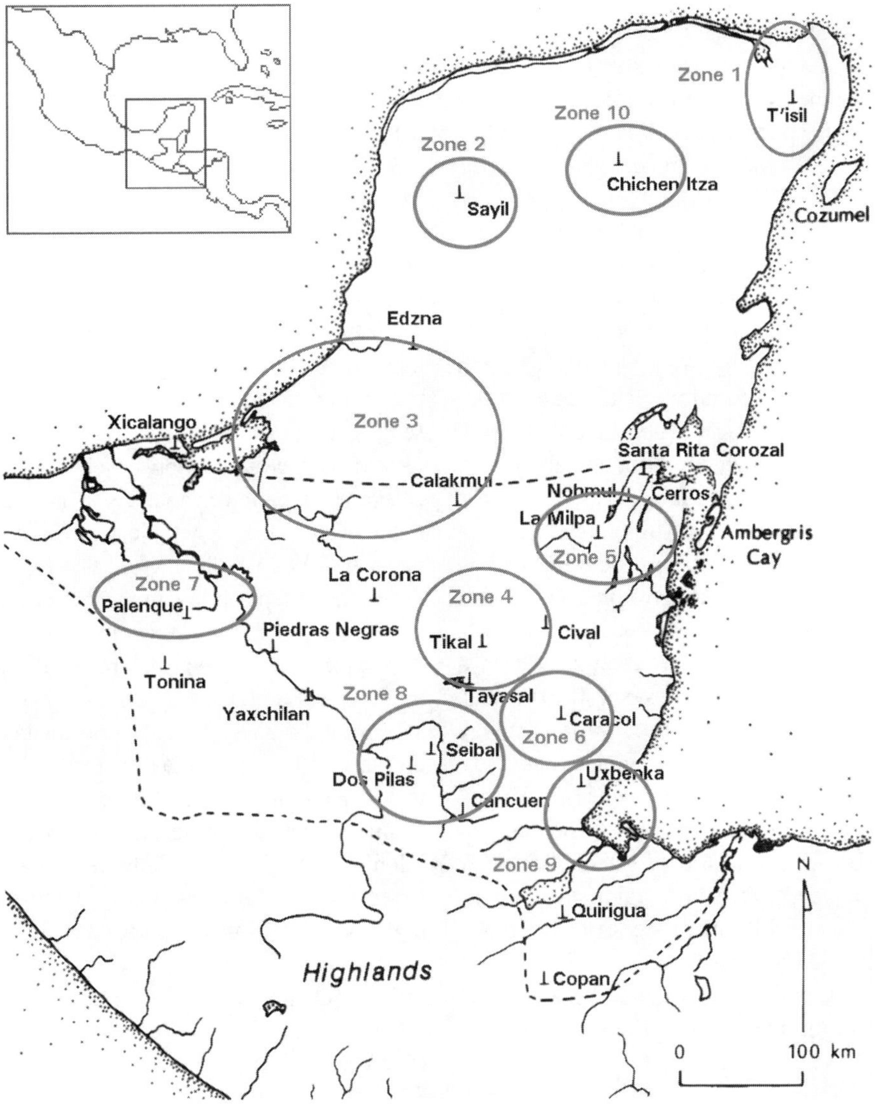

Figure 2.2. Location of lowland Maya zones: (1) T'isil and Yalahau; (2) Sayil and the Puuc; (3) Calakmul and Campeche; (4) Tikal and east-central Petén; (5) La Milpa and northern Belize; (6) Caracol and the Vaca Plateau; (7) Palenque and Sierra de Chiapas foothills; 8) Seibal and the Rio Pasion (9) Uxbenka and the Toledo foothills; (10) Chichén Itzá and Yucatan.

(constructed bedrock chambers [called "chultuns" by Maya researchers], wells, and reservoirs), hydraulic management (canals and dams), and enhanced agricultural production (terraces and raised or drained fields).

The ancient cultural landscape is sometimes more difficult to interpret than the past biophysical environment. In the Maya area, however, settlement density (structures per square kilometer) is quantifiable because of the proclivity of the ancient Maya to build their architectural constructions atop raised stone foundations, meaning that they can be mapped and recorded largely without excavation These same constructions can be subdivided into public spaces (ballcourts, palaces, range buildings, or temples) versus non-public spaces (solitary constructions, residential plaza groups). In some cases, architectural remains of infrastructure (roadways, public plazas, dry storage facilities) can also be identified. An architectural footprint for the landscape can be established for each site that distinguishes between built and non-architectural space. Such metrics permit a different comparative view of settlement density that is not solely based on structure count. Architectural mass and energetics add yet another dimension to this quantification.

Archaeological excavation permits a reconstruction of shifting site layout and development over time by providing needed temporal control for dating the architectural remains. Usually, temporal depth is added to the architectural stratigraphy through the use of contextually controlled ceramic analysis combined with radiocarbon dating and or with the ancient Maya calendar (e.g., A. Chase 1994). While Maya dates in tombs can sometimes be dated to a specific year, ceramics generally provide a chronological precision on the order of 50 to 200 years and radiocarbon dates provide a similar range of accuracy. While ceramic style and form are used in the Maya area to anchor archaeological time and track sequenced developments, pottery and other artifacts (e.g., obsidian, grinding stone, chert, jade, and marine shell) are also utilized to infer broader interactions within the Mesoamerican world system beyond the level of the polity. Skeletal remains provide information about diet, health, migration, social divisions, and adaptive success. Analyses of floral and faunal remains from archaeological sites provide not only the substance for radiocarbon dating, but also evidence for agricultural practices, forest management approaches, and other subsistence activities. Finally, besides sometimes refining the time scale, Maya hieroglyphs provide direct data about past social structures.

While the rich databases available to Maya archaeology are often taken for granted in broader regional syntheses, it is possible to examine different expressions of this civilization by looking at assorted archaeological and ecological zones. While the dry season usually occurs from May through December in most of the Maya region, topography, temperature, elevation, rainfall totals, access to water, and patterns in vegetation diverge across the geographic space occupied by the Maya; their ancient cultural patterns are similarly varied. Thus, diverse environmental zones tend to be associated with different developmental trajectories and spatial signatures.

T'isil and Yalahau (Zone 1)

The Yalahau region of northern Quintana Roo, Mexico, is a distinctive physiographic zone characterized by a system of inland freshwater wetlands. These north-south trending wetlands follow the underlying Holbox fracture zone and represent the exposure of the water table. Archaeological research has found that nearly all of the wetlands contain evidence of ancient engineering features that most likely functioned to control movement of soil and water and to facilitate the cultivation of crops or the management of wetland resources (Fedick and Mathews 2005; Fedick and Morrison 2004; Fedick et al. 2000; Glover 2012). The generally flat terrain surrounding the wetlands averages only about six meters above sea level; the water table is further exposed by numerous natural sinkholes (cenotes). Water can also be easily accessed through the excavation of wells. The freshwater aquifer of the region is perhaps the thickest in the northern Yucatan Peninsula and serves today as the sole source of water for the Cancun-Tulum development area, the fastest growing urban area in Mexico. The location of the Yalahau region in the northeast corner of the Yucatan Peninsula places it in a rainfall anomaly that receives an average of 2000 millimeters of annual rain, often in the context of hurricanes that pass through with great frequency. The region does experience a distinct dry season, usually between March and May, when rain rarely falls. Vegetation in the wetlands includes a range of aquatic plants (e.g., sedges and cattails) and swamp forest; uplands are characterized by medium-canopy deciduous tropical forest. The earliest occupation in the region is represented by a very scant occurrence of Middle Preclassic ceramics that date between 700 and 400 B.C.E. The region appears to have experienced rapid population growth during the Late Preclassic into the Early Classic, from 100 B.C.E. to about C.E. 350 or 450. The region has relatively little in the way of monumental architecture, although many larger sites (such as Kantunilkin and Naranjal) do include platforms reaching up to 50 meters on a side coupled with pyramids of 5 to 14 meters in height. The well-documented site of T'isil attained a settlement density of 731 structures per square kilometer (Fedick and Mathews 2005:39), unusually high for an ancient Maya community. After achieving a relatively high level of regional population, there seems to have been a dramatic depopulation, leaving only traces of occupation throughout the Late Classic into the Postclassic, with the exception of a Terminal Classic or Early Postclassic presence centered on the northern coastal site of Vista Alegre. Beginning in the Late Postclassic, around C.E. 1250, there was an influx of people into the region that focused on reoccupying previously abandoned sites. While not achieving the population levels of the Late Preclassic, the Postclassic occupation appears to have continued to the time of initial Spanish contact, after which the population declined rapidly. The region is still sparsely occupied today.

Sayil and the Puuc (Zone 2)

The Terminal Classic city of Sayil is located in the Puuc region of western Yucatan state (Sabloff and Tourtellot 1991, 1994). The Puuc region is the only significantly hilly area in the northern Lowlands and is the home of such major archaeological sites as Uxmal, Kabah, Labna, Kiuic, and Oxkintok (Pollock 1980). While the basal area is approximately 25 meters above sea level, the relatively low hills

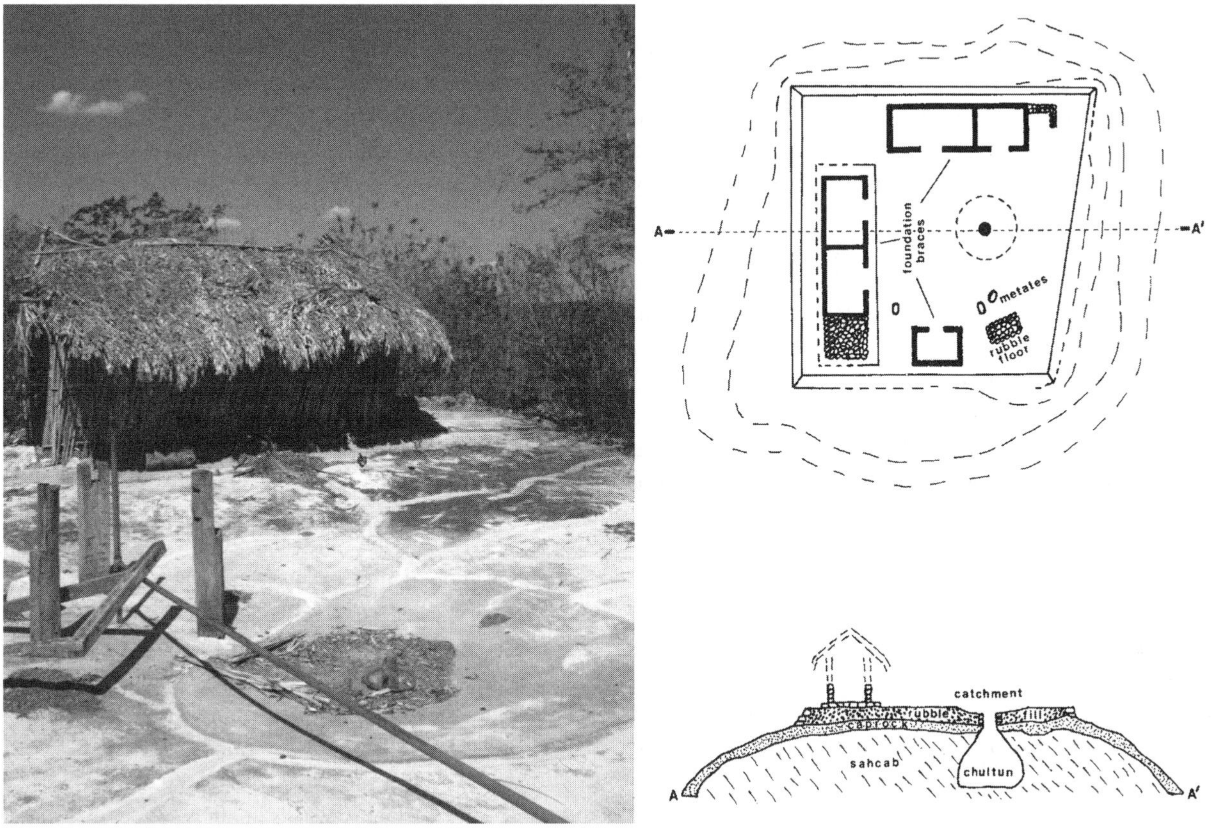

Figure 2.3. Water storage chultun from the Puuc region (Zone 2) of the northern Lowlands, showing the use of a paved plaza area for water collection.

rise an additional 40 to 100 meters in height. The region also has a deep water table and lacks readily available water with no rivers, lakes, or cenotes. Thus, the inhabitants of Sayil, in particular, and the region, in general, constructed numerous bedrock water cisterns (*chultuns*) to capture rainwater during the rainy season in order to provide potable water during the spring dry season (Figure 2.3). The extreme effort needed to secure water in the Puuc region may have fortuitously adapted its inhabitants to withstand the onset of coming drier conditions (Carmean et al. 2004). There is evidence at Sayil that open spaces around houses in the urban core were used for gardens and that zones beyond the first row of hills around the Sayil Valley were used for the cultivation of maize and other crops (Smyth and Dore 1992).

Surprisingly, there is only limited evidence for terracing and other intensive agricultural features in the Puuc region. The principal florescence of Puuc region cultural development was from the middle of the 8th century to the early 10th century C.E., although there is some variation from site to site. In recent years, new evidence has emerged for important earlier development going back as far as the Preclassic period. During the Terminal Classic florescence, the Puuc region reached its maximum Precolumbian population with both city and village size increasing and with population expansion into areas between previously occupied sites (Dunning and Kowalski 1994). Sizable cities like Kabah, Sayil, and Labna were located within 5 to 7 kilometers of each other. This also was the time that the heights in monumental architecture and art—for which the region is most notably famous—reached their apogee (Pollock 1980). Postclassic period occupation is found scattered throughout the zone and there is a sizeable modern population in this part of Mexico.

Calakmul and Campeche (Zone 3)

Located on the western slopes of the Yucatan Peninsula between 0 and 400 meters above sea level, the Campeche Zone consists of a series of north-south trending hill systems and valleys that step upward from the coast to the central spine of the peninsula. The topography is karstic and there are no standing lakes in the interior valleys. However, the coastal plain in the middle reaches of the Candelaria and Champoton Rivers are broad swamps. The

Edzna Valley is the most northerly clay basin (Matheny 1983). Running water is present toward the coast in the Candelaria and Champoton River basins. Rainfall ranges between 1300 millimeters of rain per year in the south to 700 millimeters in the north. Monthly average temperatures in the modern city of Campeche vary from 17°C in January to 33°C in late May or early June. Approximately 25 meters-high forest covers most of the region, excepting those areas where modern agriculture has been developed, such as the Edzna Valley. In antiquity, a major component of the population concentrated in the interior Calakmul Basin with the ancient city of Calakmul being one of the larger capitals among the many Maya polities of the Classic period (Folan 1992; Carrasco 1996). Earliest settlement in the region dates to approximately 600 B.C.E. By C.E. 700, over 50,000 Maya occupied the urban center of Calakmul (Folan et al. 1995; calculated as 55% occupation of over 6000 structures mapped). Calakmul is thought to have been composed originally of many small barrios located around natural water holes (called "aguadas" in the Maya area) in the gullies that cross the city and run into swamps (called "bajos" in the Maya area) to the north and west. A focal plaza was eventually constructed near El Laberinto Bajo at the southern edge of the city. This plaza is surrounded by many formal structures, including the imposing Structure II, which at 55 meters in elevation is one of the largest human-made structures in the Maya Lowlands (Folan 1992). The scale of the administrative structure of the city is reflected in the size of these buildings. Most agriculture is thought to have taken place on slumped sediments around the edge of the bajos and in upland *milpas*—rain-dependent tropical gardens adapted to rough, rocky terrain. Hot burns during the milpa cycle restored vital trace elements to the soils, probably explaining much of the 1500-year longevity of the city. At the very beginning of the 9th century, environmental instability appears to have precipitated abandonment of Calakmul, followed by a reoccupation of the center by a smaller population from the north. By the end of the 9th century the city was abandoned except for pilgrimage visitors who left *ocarinas* and *incensarios* on the steps of the city's architectural complexes (see Braswell et al. 2004).

Tikal and East-Central Peten (Zone 4)

This limestone region is characterized by a chain of interior land-locked lakes as well as rivers that run east-west, ultimately emptying into the Caribbean Sea to the east. Ancient settlement is located on the shores of Lakes Yaxha and Petén-Itzá (Figure 2.4a) and along the banks of the Rivers Holmul and Ixcanrio. The hydrology of the zone is also characterized by the presence of a system of stationary *bajos*, or seasonal wetlands, that fill with water in the rainy season, making seasonal canoe transport possible over great distances. The vegetation of the upland areas in this zone is largely tropical deciduous forest dominated by broadleaf trees with a canopy height as high as 40 meters. The climate in the area is generally hot with a maximum temperature of 39°C and an average temperature of 30°C. The humidity in the region averages 78% and often reaches 100%. The average annual precipitation is 1800 millimeters, distributed over approximately 180 days of the year. The highest point in the east-central Peten is 300 meters above sea level.

More than 300 Maya sites occur within the zone, including the major centers of Tikal, Yaxha, Nakum, Naranjo, Xultun, Holmul, Rio Azul, and Uaxactun. Tikal is probably the best documented site archaeologically, having been excavated for almost 50 years (Coe 1990; Coe and Haviland 1982; Laporte and Fialko 1995; Sabloff 2003). Like other major centers in the zone, Tikal exhibits large-scale architecture in the form of temples and palaces (Figure 2.5) and has a rich history contained within its hieroglyphic texts that document ancient political inter-relationships with other areas (Martin and Grube 2000). Intermediate-level sites within this zone also exhibit urban development and impressive architecture (see Puleston 1983). Smaller centers occur at the peripheries of the major and intermediate centers and represent aggregated residential settlement where specialized activities were practiced (Fry 2003). Many major and intermediate centers of this zone present archaeological evidence for continuous occupation from the Preclassic through Late Classic periods; however, many smaller centers only appear to have been occupied during the Late Classic period.

La Milpa and Northern Belize (Zone 5)

Extending from the Three Rivers Region of northwest Belize, down the escarpment(s) and across a broad plain to Lamanai, this zone continues east to the Belize coast. The region ranges from sea level to approximately 240 meters above sea level. The area is underlain by a limestone shelf that displays significant topographic variation along its western border, as demonstrated by a series of karst terraces. The Rio Azul becomes the Blue Creek and, when joined by the Rio Bravo, is then the Rio Hondo. The New River flows from the Hill Bank area and passes Lamanai on its course to Chetumal Bay. Numerous smaller drainages feed the larger flowing streams and water holes of the zone. Both on the western escarpments and in the lower zones close to the coast are many bajos, aguadas, and swamps that are often fed by the many smaller drainages. The forest canopy ranges

Figure 2.4. Water was crucial for the survival of the ancient Maya in the tropics and it came in many forms: (a.) Lake Péten-Itza in northern Guatemala (Zone 4); (b.) a constructed reservoir at Caracol (Zone 6); (c.) natural waterfalls near Palenque (Zone 7); (d.) the Cenote Sagrado, a limestone sinkhole, at Chichén Itzá (Zone 10).

to a height of 25 meters in a large portion of the western part of the zone and in segmented patches across the lower plain. Rainfall is typical of the Maya Lowlands with a rainy season from June through January and a dry season from February through May. The amount of rain across the zone is approximately 1500 millimeters per year with some slightly wetter areas in the west. Human activity in the region began in Paleo-Indian times and continued through the Archaic, as evidenced by lithic artifacts in both the western and coastal areas (Lohse 2010). Archaic occupation occurs near Colha, where some evidence of deforestation and cultigens appear by 3400 B.C.E. Maya occupation is continuous from about 800 B.C.E. through the Postclassic (C.E. 900–1532) and into the Historic period (Shafer and Hester 1991). Throughout the region there is evidence of significant Maya occupation, as represented by numerous hamlets, villages, and cities, including: Lamanai, La Milpa, Dos Hombres, Chan Chich, Rio Azul, and Kinal (Scarborough et al. 2003). Agricultural methods are documented by the physical remains of channelized fields and terraces that are found across the zone (Lauzader-Beach et al. 2012). Water management features are also a significant component of Maya activity in the

Figure 2.5. View of the ruins of Tikal (Zone 4) showing remains of vaulted buildings within the covering tropical forest.

region. Most sites appear to have been rapidly abandoned between C.E. 800 and 900, as was the case in most other regions, but the circumstances of the abandonment remain obscure. One significant exception to any collapse scenario is Lamanai, which continues directly into the Postclassic and also into the Historic era without interruption (Pendergast 1986). As at Lamanai, archaeological data also show that Santa Rita Corozal extended into the Historic period (Chase and Chase 1988).

Caracol and the Vaca Plateau (Zone 6)

Located between 450 and 600 meters above sea level, the Vaca Plateau is a level plain located amidst the karst topography of west-central Belize. Even though the Macal River borders the area to the west and the Chiquibul River borders the area to the east, no running water can be found in the uplands. This part of Belize receives between 2000 and 2400 millimeters of rain per year with temperatures varying from 6˚C to 39˚C, sometimes within the same 24 hour period. Today, subtropic moist rainforest canopy averages approximately 25 meters in height and covers the entire region. In antiquity, the entire Vaca Plateau and the karst topography south of it was densely occupied by the ancient Maya. Earliest settlement in the region dates to approximately 600 B.C.E. By C.E. 650, approximately 100,000 Maya had integrated a 200 square kilometer area into the single urban center of Caracol (Chase and Chase 2007; Chase et al. 2011). Caracol is characterized by thousands of residential groups set among constructed agricultural terraces with an embedded road system that dendritically linked public architecture throughout the region. To store water in this region, the ancient inhabitants constructed hundreds of reservoirs (Figure 2.4b), most loosely attached to mundane residential groups. Extensive systems of terraces covered most of the hills and valleys within Caracol and these constructed features served to manage the landscape hydrology and retain water for crops (Figure 2.6; see also Chase and Chase 1998). These agricultural fields were developed and used over approximately 600 years. At the very beginning of the tenth century C.E., however, the entire region appears to have been abandoned. Today, the Belizean part of the zone is unoccupied while the adjacent parts of Guatemala are being rapidly settled.

Palenque and Sierra de Chiapas Foothills (Zone 7)

The upper Usumacinta River area encompasses three environmentally diverse geological systems that run from approximately 25 to 150 meters above sea level. From north to south these are the Pleistocene fluvial terraces, the Intermediate Plains, and the Tertiary formations of the Sierra de Chiapas. The Intermediate Plains are generally not suited for agriculture because of shallow soils and poor drainage.

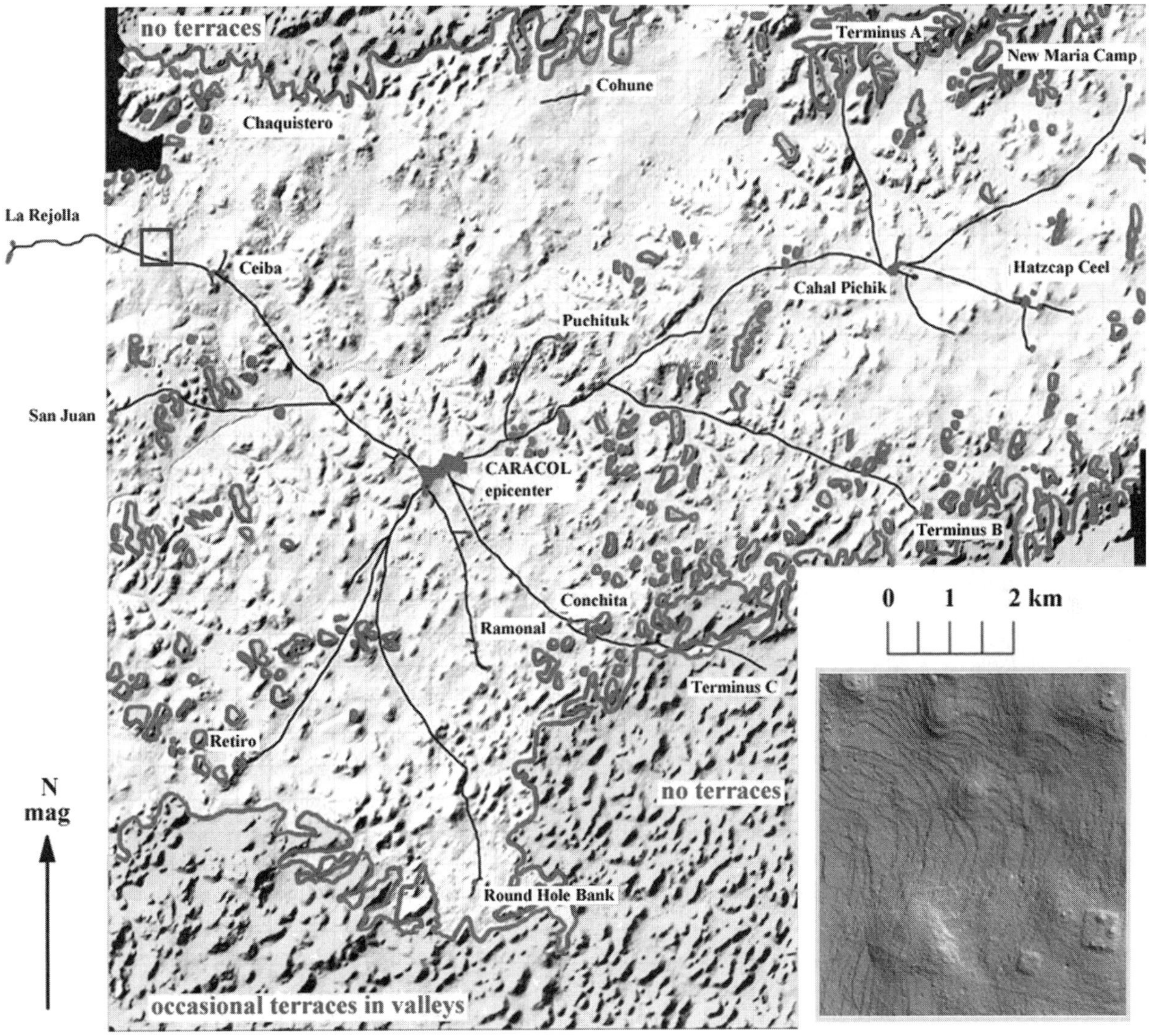

Figure 2.6. LiDAR Digital Elevation Model of Caracol, Belize (Zone 6) showing location of causeways, major architectural groups, and agricultural terracing (after Chase et al. 2011). Most of the site is terraced (see inset LiDAR image and its location on DEM) and represents an anthropogenic landscape. Settlement is continuous throughout this area and represents a Maya low-density urban adaptation that was successful for approximately 500 years.

In contrast, the comparatively high settlement densities for the ancient Maya found in the Tertiary foothills demonstrate the importance of this zone during Precolumbian times; the vast majority of ancient sites are located along the first escarpments of the Sierra de Chiapas. Several factors account for the presence of population concentrations: transportation along the base and through the valleys of the Chiapas foothills; rich non-agricultural resources; and a varied ecosystem. Site variability in terms of settlement characteristics or density might be due to differences in subsistence adaptations to the contrasting landscapes present within the Usumacinta drainage; however, other aspects of settlement variation (location of civic ceremonial centers, settlement layout) might be the result of historical and social circumstances tied to the development of social inequalities and hierarchical organizations associated with the rise of political complexity in the region. Some of these historical processes indicate that important changes occurred in the region with the rise of particular places—Palenque (Figure 2.7), Pomoná, Chinikihá, El Arenal, and Reforma-Moral—as centers of paramount political power.

The Middle Preclassic (800–300 B.C.E.) seems to have been a moment of noticeable population growth in the Middle Usumacinta area. The sites at Tierra Blanca, Tiradero, and Povicuc—located on rich Usumacinta River alluvial soils and adjacent bluffs—functioned as central points for

Figure 2.7. Palenque is located in the foothills of the Sierra de Chiapas overlooking the vast Tabasco Plain (Zone 7).

a series of smaller mounds located on either margin of the river. The dispersed settlement pattern along rivers during the Late Preclassic (300 B.C.E.–C.E. 250) and Early Classic periods (C.E. 250–550) has been explained as the logical result of an early agricultural population seeking the most favorable lands along river levees (Liendo 2008). Populations were low during the Early Classic, a fact that suggests little competition for resources; and, it appears that there was a population decline along the middle Usumacinta during this era. However, the end of the Early Classic marks a change in the trends described for earlier periods with population nucleation taking place along the Tertiary foothills of the Sierra de Chiapas, as represented by the development of new settlements at Chinikihá, Chancalá, Yoxihá, and Palenque. Research in Palenque and, more recently, in the Chinikiha region indicates that the Late Classic period (especially during the 8th and the first half of the 9th centuries) was a time of great development and innovation for this zone (Liendo 2005).

Seibal and the Rio Pasion (Zone 8)

Sandwiched between upland regions to the east, west, and south, the area comprising the south-central portion of the Maya Lowlands is characterized by a limestone and shale landscape that rises approximately 100 to 150 meters above sea level. The numerous streams and lagoons in this zone provided permanent water sources; these perennial water courses also facilitated transport and communication. Rainfall in this zone is slightly less than that found to the east and west in areas of higher elevation. As in other zones, the upland soils are agriculturally productive. While alluvial soils are plentiful within this zone and would have been productive had they been well drained, the many kilometers of natural river levees and floodplains are actually low-lying, marshy, and seasonally inundated. Thus, these swamplands are too waterlogged or leached to have been agriculturally productive without human management, for which there is currently no evidence. A series of Maya sites are known from the Pasion region, including Altar de Sacrificios (Willey 1973) and Seibal (Willey 1982; Tourtellot 1988). Settlement of the Rio Pasion zone occurred in the early part of the Preclassic period (ca. 900 B.C.E.) and continued through the 10th century C.E. Recent information from Dos Pilas, Aguateca, Cancuen, and smaller Guatemalan sites east of Yaxchilan, Mexico indicate a complex and contentious political history for this zone during the Late Classic period (Demarest 2013; Golden et al. 2011). Later Postclassic occupation is rare in this zone, which is only sparsely occupied today.

Uxbenka and the Toledo Foothills (Zone 9)

Ranging from sea level to almost 700 meters in elevation, the southern Belize zone stretches from the coastal plain to the eastern flank of the Maya Mountains, the largest relief feature in the Maya Lowlands. The majority of archaeological communities in the region—Uxbenka, Lubaantun, Pusilha, and Nimli Punit—are found in the Toledo Uplands and the Bladen, Columbia, and Deep River valleys in the eastern slope of the Maya Mountains. The Toledo Uplands are characterized by extremely fertile soils derived partly from weathered mud, sand, and silt-stone. The region is circumscribed geographically and difficult to access: to the north it is bounded by inhospitable pine-barrens; to the west, by the formidable Maya Mountains; to the south, by the swampy Temash and Sarstoon River basins; and to the east, by the Caribbean Sea. Annual precipitation can exceed 5000 millimeters. Today, much of the region is populated by Mopan and Q'eqchi' subsistence farmers, though the mountainous areas remain unoccupied since the 10th century C.E. The earliest human presence dates to the late Paleoindian period, with the first sedentary communities likely emerging between 1500 and 800 B.C.E. Despite highly productive soils and abundant rainfall, polities of the Classic period are diminutive compared to neighboring regions (Leventhal 1990). A range of biotic and mineral resources not found elsewhere in the Maya Lowlands may have fueled regional economic growth in the Late Classic, when no fewer than 12 monument-bearing polities dotted the landscape (Braswell and Prufer 2009). By the 10th century the region was in decline and there is little evidence of reoccupation before the 15th century.

Chichén Itzá and Yucatan (Zone 10)

The karstic plain of the northern-central portion of the Yucatán Peninsula has an average elevation of 25 meters above sea level that corresponds with the Eocene-derived Pisté Formation in which Chichén Itzá is located. Natural features of the Pisté Formation include cenotes, dry depressions, and fertile soils. At Chichén Itzá, the principal architectural groups of the settlement are located close to these natural features and next to limestone quarries. Their construction was due in large part to the easy access to potable water, areas with excellent soils for agricultural practices, and quarries to procure construction materials. Two great cenotes, Sagrado (Figure 2.4d) and Xtoloc, are located in the center of Chichén Itzá; around these water sources are many massive constructions with vaulted buildings and elaborate architecture. The Great Terrace (Figure 2.8), the Monjas Complex, the Initial Series Group, and the Groups of the Three and Four Lintels are distributed among various dry depressions of great size, which are located either to the east or west of these architectural groups.

The spatial distribution of the physiographic elements that dominate Chichén Itzá's landscape played a key role in determining the construction and internal arrangement of this ancient city (Ruppert 1952). The area in which the site developed was sparsely settled by 300 B.C.E. During subsequent phases of occupation, the settlement developed at Chichén Itzá by combining green areas with monumental architecture made of masonry and vaults, domestic and residential structures, monumental art, and internal causeways. Between C.E. 800 and 1000, Chichén Itzá was a dominant center in Mesoamerica (Cobos 2004). In the later Postclassic period the site served as a destination for religious pilgrimage. Sizeable other ancient centers, such as Yaxuna, exist a short distance from Chichén Itzá and modern communities overlay many other ancient Maya sites in the general vicinity.

Discussion and Summary

Even a cursory review of the selected zones demonstrates the diversity and variability in and among Maya Lowland environments and adaptations. There were marked differences with regard to water availability, with each area investing in slightly different approaches and innovations (Lucero 2006). For example, during an acute drought in the early 9th century, the Maya of the Puuc Hills (Zone 2) appear to have increased their population levels by constructing sizable household water collection systems using chultuns. Evidence from neighboring western Yucatan (Zone 3), however, indicates that this same drought coincided with a loss of population (Gunn and Folan 2000). In contrast, northeastern Yucatan (Zone 1) was more influenced by fluctuations in its water table due to changes in sea level (Fedick and Morrison 2004).

Similarities are evident across all zones. For the most part ancient Maya settlement is characterized by low-density urbanism. This appears to be an important organizational principle for an area with high ecological diversity and low individual species density (Scarborough and Burnside 2010). Such low-density agrarian urbanism (Fletcher 2009) provided a successful adaptation to hot and humid environments with a mosaic pattern of fertile soils, an inconsistent water supply, and the likelihood of rapid disease vector growth. At large centers like Caracol (Zone 6), the anthropogenic landscape contains dispersed residential units situated amidst terraces and reservoirs, all linked by an extensive causeway system (Chase and Chase 1996, 2007). The Maya also created garden space within and between rural communities (Fialko 2004; Scarborough et al. 2003).

Figure 2.8. The western side of the Castillo at Chichén Itzá (Zone 10), a construction dating to the Terminal Classic period, showing 2009 excavations into the Great Terrace.

During the Late Classic, the pollen record indicates that major tree species were depleted. This has been interpreted to mean that native tropical vegetation sustained growing populations and was sacrificed to construct built environments (Lentz and Hockaday 2009; Ford and Nigh 2009). That both hardwoods and softwood species were declining in unison in the Late Classic could suggest a stressed overall interior environment. Notwithstanding the decline in the interior forests, however, there is widespread evidence that the ancient Maya were skilled at the practice of arboriculture (Lentz 1999) and, at least to some degree, replaced "natural" forests with orchards of domesticated trees with high economic value. By standardizing the data sets within each of the ten zones and facilitating communication among the researchers working in these areas, a significantly improved understanding of ancient Maya societies is assured. Identification of types and degrees of resilience, stability, rigidity (integration, hierarchy, conformity), and pan-regional interaction within the ancient Maya context is overdue. Such considerations will not only elucidate temporal and spatial variation within the Maya Lowlands, but also permit the ancient Maya to be more directly compared to the developmental trajectories of other civilizations.

In spite of over a hundred years of rich and well-reported archaeological data and complementary natural scientific research in the Maya area, until recently, we have thought of the Maya as a monolithic culture and have not focused on the social and landscape differences within this region, which surely had an impact on past adaptations and management strategies. By considering the constituent units of the ancient Maya, both the cultural and environmental variability become evident; comparing and contrasting these microcosms also serves to highlight aspects that may have been responsible for different developmental trajectories.

At several points in their long history, the Maya reached a precarious imbalance with their environments that proved unsustainable; when exactly this occurred differs throughout the Maya area. For some Maya groups, this imbalance was reached in the Late Preclassic period. For others, it occurred at the end of the 9th century C.E. The causes of any "collapse" varied spatially and temporally throughout the Maya region and likely included political mismanagement, warfare, and shifting economic opportunities—as well as environmental issues (Kennett et al. 2012; Turner and Sabloff 2012). However, by the end of the Late Classic period, food production had been repeatedly intensified in many parts of the Maya region to support ever larger populations. Refuse was carefully managed and recycled into building projects. Arable lands were manufactured from residual soils. Supplies and resources were imported from distant places and administratively marketed to populations. Governance systems employed a variety of techniques to control and manage populations. The situation was not unlike that of today in which population pressure places great demands upon the underlying ecology to support the infrastructure of society. To some extent, the globalization models that are used to describe variability within today's world are just as pertinent for the past Maya world.

The environments and the social systems in the ancient Maya Lowlands constituted a highly complex and nuanced set of relationships and interdependencies that operated at many scales. The ancient Maya landscapes resulted from a series of past decisions that placed many of their societies on trajectories that eventually became unsustainable. By examining the ecological and climatic variability that exists in this region in relation to the various cultural responses that are evident in the archaeological record, it becomes possible to use these long-term temporal data to inform modern policy debates. To understand the kinds and degrees of change in this ancient society, commonly held blanket statements about the effects of climate change, human-induced degradation, human-induced ecological enhancement, causation, and fundamental dating concerns—as well as geographical and temporal scaling—must be reassessed. By employing both quantitative and qualitative measures of variable dependency and interdependency based on our working methodology, we hope to contribute to broader worldwide comparative goals. The enterprise is timely and should serve as a model for subsequent research both for the immediacy of the tropical Maya Lowlands and for other research and planning efforts elsewhere in the world.

References Cited

Braswell, Geoffrey E., Joel D. Gunn, Maria del Rosario Dominguez Carrasco, William J. Folan, Larraine A. Fletcher, Abel Morales Lopez, and Michael D. Glascock

2004 Defining the Terminal Classic at Calakmul, Campeche. *In* The Terminal Classic in the Maya Lowlands: Collapse, Transition, and Transformation. A. A. Demarest, P. M. Rice, and D. S. Rice, eds. Pp. 162–194. Boulder: University Press of Colorado.

Braswell, Geoffrey E., and Keith M. Prufer

2009 Political Organization and Interaction in Southern Belize. Research Reports in Belizean Archaeology 6:43–55.

Burke, Edmund

1790 Reflections on the Revolution in France. London: J. Dodsley.

Campbell, Lyle, and Terrence Kaufman

1985 Mayan Linguistics: Where are We Now? Annual Review of Anthropology 14:187–198.

Carmean, Kelli, Nicholas Dunning, and Jeff Karl Kowalski

2004 High Times in the Hill Country: A Perspective from the Terminal Classic Puuc Region. *In* The Terminal Classic in the Maya Lowlands: Collapse, Transition, and Transformation. A. A. Demarest, P. M. Rice, and D. S. Rice, eds. Pp. 424–449. Boulder: University Press of Colorado.

Carrasco V., Ramon

1996 Calakmul, Campeche. Arqueologia Mexicana 3(18):46–51

Chase, Arlen F., and Diane Z. Chase

1996 A Mighty Maya Nation: How Caracol Built an Empire by Cultivating its 'Middle Class.' Archaeology 49(5):66–72.

1998 Scale and Intensity in Classic Period Maya Agriculture: Terracing and Settlement at the 'Garden City' of Caracol, Belize. Culture and Agriculture 20(2):60–77.

2007 Ancient Maya Urban Development: Insights from the Archaeology of Caracol, Belize. Journal of Belizean Studies 29(2):60–71.

Chase, Arlen F., Diane Z. Chase, and Michael E. Smith

2009 States and Empires in Ancient Mesoamerica. Ancient Mesoamerica 20(2):175–182.

Chase, Arlen F., Diane Z. Chase, John F. Weishampel, Jason B. Drake, Ramesh L. Shrestha, K. Clint Slatton, Jaime J. Awe, and William E. Carter

2011 Airborne LiDAR, Archaeology, and the Ancient Maya Landscape at Caracol, Belize. Journal of Archaeological Science 38:387–398.

Chase, Diane Z., and Arlen F. Chase

1988 A Postclassic Perspective: Excavations at the Maya Site of Santa Rita Corozal, Belize. Monograph 4. San Francisco: Pre-Columbian Art Research Institute.

Cobos P., Rafael
2004 Chichen Itza: Settlement and Hegemony during the Terminal Classic Period. *In* The Terminal Classic in the Maya Lowlands: Collapse, Transition, and Transformation. A. A. Demarest, P. M. Rice, and D. S. Rice, eds. Pp. 162–194. Boulder: University Press of Colorado.

Coe, William R.
1990 Excavations in the Great Plaza, North Terrace, and North Acropolis of Tikal. 6 vols. Tikal Report, 14. Philadelphia: The University Museum.

Coe, William R., and William A. Haviland
1982 Introduction to the Archaeology of Tikal, Guatemala. Tikal Report, 12. Philadelphia: The University Museum.

Costanza, Robert, Lisa J. Graumlich, and Will L. Steffen, eds.
2007 Sustainability or Collapse? An Integrated History and Future of People on Earth. Cambridge: MIT Press.

Demarest, Arthur A.
2013 Ideological Pathways to Economic Exchange: Religion, Economy, and Legitimization at the Classic Maya Royal Capital of Cancuen. Latin American Antiquity 24(4):371–402.

Demarest, Arthur A., Prudence M. Rice, and Don S. Rice, eds.
2004 The Terminal Classic in the Maya Lowlands: Collapse, Transition, and Transformation. Boulder: University Press of Colorado.

Dunning, Nicholas P., and Jeff K. Kowalski
1994 Lord of the Hills: Classic Maya Settlement Patterns and Political Iconography in the Puuc Region, Mexico. Ancient Mesoamerica 5(1):63–95.

Dunning, Nicholas P., Timothy Beach, Pat Farrell, and Sheryl Luzzadder-Beach
1998 Prehispanic Agrosystems and Adaptive Regions in the Maya Lowlands. Culture and Agriculture 20:87–101.

Fedick, Scott L., and Jennifer P. Mathews
2005 The Yalahau Regional Human Ecology Project: Introduction and Summary of Recent Research. *In* Quintana Roo Archaeology. J. M. Shaw and J. P. Mathews, eds. Pp. 33–50. Tucson: University of Arizona Press.

Fedick, Scott L., and Bethany A. Morrison
2004 Ancient Maya Use and Manipulation of Landscape in the Yalahau Region of the Northern Maya Lowlands. Agriculture and Human Values 21:207–219.

Fedick, Scott L., Bethany A. Morrison, Bente Juhl Andersen, Sylviane Boucher, Jorge Ceja Acosta, and Jennifer P. Mathews
2000 Wetland Manipulation in the Yalahau Region of the Northern Lowlands. Journal of Field Archaeology 27(2):131–152.

Fialko, Vilma
2004 Diez anos de investigaciones arqueologicas en la Cuenca del rio Holmul, noreste de Peten. *In* XVIII Simposio de Investigaciones Arqueologicas en Guatemala. J. P. Laporte and B. Arroyo, eds. Pp. 253–268. Guatemala: MNAE.

Fletcher, Roland
2009 Low-Density, Agrarian Based Urbanism: A Comparative View. Insights 2(4):1–19.

Folan, William J.
1992 Calakmul, Campeche: A Centralized Urban Administrative Center in the Northern Peten. World Archaeology 24(2):158–168.

Folan, William J., Joyce Marcus, Sophia Pincemin, Maria del Rosario Dominguez-Carrasco, and Larraine Fletcher
1995 Calakmul: New Data from an Ancient Maya Capital in Campeche, Mexico. Latin American Antiquity 6(4):310–334.

Ford, Anabel, and Ronald Nigh
2009 Origins of the Maya Forest Garden: Maya Resource Management. Journal of Ethnobiology 29: 213–236.

Fox, John A., and John S. Justeson
1986 Classic Maya Dynastic Alliance and Succession. *In* Supplement to the Handbook of Middle American Indians, v 4: Ethnohistory. V. Bricker, general ed. R. Spores, volume ed. Pp. 7–34. Austin: University of Texas Press.

Fry, Robert E.
2003 The Peripheries of Tikal. *In* Tikal: Dynasties, Foreigners, and Affairs of State: Advancing Maya Archaeology. J. A. Sabloff, ed. Pp. 143–170. Santa Fe: School of American Research Press.

Glover, Jeffrey B.
2012 The Yalahau Region: A Study of Ancient Maya Socio-Political Organization. Ancient Mesoamerica 23:271–295.

Golden, Charles, Andrew K. Scherer, Arturo R. Munoz, and Zachary X. Hruby
2011 Polities, Boundaries, and Trade in the Classic Period Usumacinta River Basin. Mexicon 34(1):11–19.

Gunn, Joel D., and William J. Folan
2000 Three Rivers: Subregional Variations in Earth System Impacts in the Southwestern Maya Lowlands (Candelaria, Usumacinta, and Champoton Watershed). *In* The Way the Wind Blows: Climate, History, and Human Action. R. MacIntosh, J. Tainter, and S. McIntosh, eds. Pp. 263–270. New York: Columbia University Press.

Houston, Stephen D., and Alfonso Lacadena G.
2004 Maya Epigraphy at the Millennium: Personal Notes. *In* Continuity and Change in Maya Archaeology: Perspectives at the Millennium. C. Golden and G. Borgstede, eds. Pp. 115–124. New York: Routledge.

Houston, Stephen D., John Robertson, and David Stuart
1996 The Language of the Classic Maya Inscriptions. Current Anthropology 41:321–356.

Kennett, Douglas J., Sebastian F. M. Breitenbach, Valorie V. Aquino, Yemane Asmerom, Jaime Awe, James U. L. Baldini, Patrick Bartlein, Brendan J. Culleton, Claire Ebert, Christopher Jazwa, Martha J. Macri, Norbert Marwan, Victor Polyak, Keith M. Prufer, Harriet E. Ridley, Harald Sodemann, Bruce Winterhalder, and Gerald H. Haug
2012 Development and Disintegration of Maya Political Systems in Response to Climate Change. Science 338:788–791.

Laporte, Juan Pedro, and Vilma Fialko
1995 Un Reencuentro con Mundo Perdido, Tikal, Guatemala. Ancient Mesoamerica 6:41–94.

Lauzader-Beach, Sheryl, Timothy P. Beach, and Nicholas P. Dunning
2012 Wetland Fields as Mirrors of Drought and the Maya Abandonment. Proceedings of the National Academy of Science 109(10):3646–3651.

Lentz, David L.
1999 Plant Resources of the Ancient Maya. *In* Reconstructing Ancient Maya Diets. C. White, ed. Pp. 3–18. Salt Lake City: University of Utah Press.

Lentz, David L., and Brian Hockaday
2009 Tikal Timbers and Temples: Ancient Maya Agroforestry and the End of Time. Journal of Archaeological Science 36:1342–1353.

Leventhal, Richard M.
1990 Southern Belize: An Ancient Maya Region. *In* Vision and Revision in Maya Studies. F. S. Clancy and P. D. Harrison, eds. Pp. 125–141. Albuquerque: University of New Mexico Press.

Leventhal, Richard M., Carlos Chan Espinosa, and Cristina Coc
2012 The Modern Maya and Recent History. Expedition 54(1):46–51.

Liendo Stuardo, Rodrigo
2005 An Archaeological Study of Settlement Distribution in the Palenque Area, Chiapas, México. Anthropological Notebooks 11:31–42.
2008 Fronteras, territorio y estructura de asentamientos en la región de Palenque, Chiapas: Aspectos de Método y Teoría. *In* Memorias de la V Mesa Redonda de Palenque: El Territorio Maya. R. Liendo Stuardo, ed. Pp. 98–107. Mexico: INAH-CONACULTA.

Lipe, William D.
1984 Value and Meaning in Cultural Resources. *In* Approaches to the Archaeological Heritage: A Comparative Study of World Cultural Resource Management Systems. H. Cleere, ed. Pp. 1–11. Cambridge University Press, Cambridge.

Lohse, Jon C.
2010 Archaic Origins of the Lowland Maya. Latin American Antiquity 21(3):312–352.

Lucero, Lisa J.
2006 Water and Ritual: The Rise and Fall of Classic Maya Rulers. Austin: University of Texas Press.

Martin, Simon, and Nikolai Grube
2000 Chronicle of the Maya Kings and Queens. London: Thames and Hudson.

Matheny, Ray T.
1983 Investigations at Edzna, Campeche, Mexico. Paper 46. Provo: New World Archaeological Foundation.

Oaklander, L. Nathan, and Quentin Smith, eds.
1994 The New Theory of Time. New Haven: Yale University Press.

Pendergast, David M.
1986 Stability through Change: Lamanai, Belize, from the Ninth to Seventeenth Century. *In* Late Lowland Maya Civilization: Classic to Postclassic. J. A. Sabloff and E. W. Andrews, eds. Pp. 223–249. Albuquerque: University of New Mexico Press.

Pollock, Harry E. D.
1980 The Puuc: An Archaeological Survey of the Hill Country of Yucatan and Northern Campeche, Mexico. Peabody Museum of Archaeology and Ethnography Memoirs, 19. Cambridge: Harvard University.

Puleston, Dennis E.
1983 The Settlement Survey of Tikal. Tikal Report, 13. Philadelphia: The University Museum.

Roys, Ralph L.
1957 The Political Geography of the Yucatan Maya. Publication 548. Washington, DC: Carnegie Institution of Washington.

Ruppert, Karl
1952 Chichen Itza: Architectural Notes and Plans. Publication 595. Washington, DC: Carnegie Institution of Washington.

Sabloff, Jeremy A., ed.
2003 Tikal: Dynasties, Foreigners, and Affairs of State: Advancing Maya Archaeology. Santa Fe: School of American Research Press.

Sabloff, Jeremy A., and Gair Tourtellot
1991 The Ancient Maya City of Sayil: The Mapping of a Puuc Region Center. Middle American Research Institute Publication 60. New Orleans: Tulane University.
1994 Community Structure at Sayil: A Case Study of Puuc Settlement. *In* Hidden Among the Hills: Maya Archaeology of the Northwest Yucatan Peninsula. H. Prem, ed. Pp. 71–92. Bonn: Verlag von Flemming.

Santayana, George
1905 The Life of Reason: The Phases of Human Progress. New York: Charles Scribner's Sons.

Scarborough, Vernon L., and William R. Burnside
2010 Complexity and Sustainability: Perspectives from the Ancient Maya and the Modern Balinese. American Antiquity 75(2):327–363.

Scarborough, Vernon L., Fred Valdez, and Nicholas Dunning, eds.
2003 Heterarchy, Political Economy, and the Ancient Maya: The Three Rivers Region of the East-Central Yucatan Peninsula. Tucson: University of Arizona Press.

Shafer, Harry J., and Thomas R. Hester
1991 Lithic Craft Specialization and Product Distribution at the Maya Site of Colha, Belize. World Archaeology 23(1):79–97.

Sharer, Robert J., and Loa P. Traxler
2006 The Ancient Maya. 6th edition. Stanford: Stanford University Press.

Smyth, Michael P., and Christopher D. Dore
1992 Large-Site Archaeological Methods at Sayil, Yucatan, Mexico: Investigating Community Organization at a Prehispanic Maya Center. Latin American Antiquity 3(1):3–21.

Stanton, Travis W., and Tomas Gallereta N.
2001 Warfare, Ceramic Economy, and the Itza: A Reconsideration of the Itza Polity in Ancient Yucatan. Ancient Mesoamerica 12:229–245.

Storey, Rebecca
2012 Population Decline During and After Conquest. *In* Oxford Handbook of Mesoamerican Archaeology.

D. L. Nichols and C. A. Pool, eds. Pp. 908–915. Oxford University Press, New York.

Tourtellot, Giar
1988 Peripheral Survey and Excavation Settlement and Community Patterns: Excavations at Seibal, Department of Peten, Guatemala. Memoir 16. Cambridge: Peabody Museum of Archaeology and Ethnology.

Turner II, Billie L.
1990 Population Reconstruction of the Central Maya Lowlands: 1000 B.C. to A.D. 1500. *In* Precolumbian Population History in the Maya Lowlands. T. P. Culbert and D. S. Rice, eds. Pp. 301–324. Albuquerque: University of New Mexico Press.

Turner II, Billie L., and Jeremy A. Sabloff
2012 Classic Period Collapse of the Central Maya Lowlands: Insights about Human-Environment Relationships for Sustainability. Proceedings of the National Academy of Sciences 109:13908–13914.

Wichmann, Soren
2006 Mayan Historical Linguistics and Epigraphy: A New Synthesis. Annual Review of Anthropology 35:279–294.

Willey, Gordon R.
1973 The Altar de Sacrificios Excavation: General Summary and Conclusions. Papers, 64(3). Cambridge: Peabody Museum of Archaeology and Ethnology.
1982 Excavations at Seibal, Department of Peten, Guatemala. Memoirs, 15(1–2). Cambridge: Peabody Museum of Archaeology and Ethnology.

3

Water and Landscape: Ancient Maya Settlement Decisions

Lisa J. Lucero
University of Illinois, Urbana-Champaign
Scott L. Fedick
University of California, Riverside
Nicholas P. Dunning
University of Cincinnati
David L. Lentz
University of Cincinnati
and
Vernon L. Scarborough
University of Cincinnati

ABSTRACT

In this chapter we present the major transitions in Maya history from the Late Preclassic through Terminal Classic periods in the Maya Lowlands, focusing first on major settlement and subsistence systems, followed by major social and environmental costs. We particularly focus on how the Maya built and relied on increasingly complex water and agricultural systems to adapt in the humid tropics where everything in life was rainfall dependent. The seasonality of rainfall required innovative strategies to contain water throughout the long dry season in the face of growing population and socio-political complexity. Drastic changes occurred when several prolonged droughts struck the Maya area, resulting in them exploring new areas and subsistence practices. The chapter concludes with a few thoughts on how understanding ancient Maya water and land use is relevant for today's issues regarding sustainable land and water use. [settlement patterns, water management, seasonal issues, agricultural strategies, climate change]

The ancient Maya lived in a diverse tropical setting with dispersed pockets of soils suitable for agriculture, differential water resources, noticeable seasonality, and an abundance of floral and faunal species. Everything in Maya society was rainfall-dependent, especially agriculture. Timing was crucial, including predicting when the rainy season would start, which is also the onset of intensive agricultural activities. Because of these characteristics, water and agricultural land availability impacted how people lived, built, and moved across the landscape. They also meant that the Maya were more susceptible to major shifts in seasonal or long-term rainfall patterns. To compensate for seasonal vagaries and differential soil distribution, the Maya engineered features that provided access to, control over, and improvement of water and soil resources from small-scale household systems to massive and intricate ones in centers. Reservoirs were particularly critical in the 4–5 month annual dry season, especially in areas without

ARCHEOLOGICAL PAPERS OF THE AMERICAN ANTHROPOLOGICAL ASSOCIATION, Vol. 24, pp. 30–42, ISSN 1551-823X, online ISSN 1551-8248. DOI: 10.1111/apaa.12027.

permanent surface water and, in many instances, low water tables.

In this chapter, we touch upon the transitions in Maya history, and then briefly present the social and environmental costs of the growing reliance on an engineered landscape. We conclude with a few thoughts on how understanding ancient Maya water and land use is relevant for today's issues regarding sustainable land and water use.

Transitions in Maya History

Late Preclassic to Late Classic

In the southern Maya Lowlands, the Maya started migrating into interior areas such as the Petén in Guatemala from riverine or coastal areas in the Early Preclassic period by ca. 1000 B.C.E. (Ford 1986:59, 80–82; Wahl et al. 2006). They moved into areas with fertile agricultural land and little surface water, which presented particular challenges, especially during the long dry season. The dry season in the southern Lowlands, usually from January through May, transforms the landscape into a green desert where it might not rain at all for several months, and where temperatures and humidity noticeably climb (see Graham 1999; Scarborough 1993). Although this season involved few agricultural tasks, the Maya still needed water for daily drinking needs, cooking and food preparation, plaster manufacture and ceramic production, as well as other domestic and production activities (e.g., Marcus 2006). The length and intensity of the rainy and dry seasons also are important variables that impacted agricultural schedules and strategies. The beginning of the rainy season can vary up to five weeks in any given area, and the annual amount of rainfall can vary 30 to 40 percent ranging from 1350 to 3700 millimeters (Gunn et al. 1995; Gunn et al. 2002; Scarborough 1993). Adequate amounts of rain are vital for crops, especially since the major staple of maize is a relatively thirsty plant compared to staples grown elsewhere such as millet and sorghum (Vince 2010).

Tikal and its environs provide an excellent case to illustrate the intricate relationship between water availability, fertile land, and settlement decisions (see Figure 1.2 in chapter 1 for map with major areas and sites mentioned). Relative to other regions, this polity has a noticeable amount of dispersed agricultural soils, but limited water sources (Ford 1986, 1996). It, like other regional capitals such as Calakmul and many other centers without permanent water sources, was surrounded by *bajos*, or seasonally inundated swamps. Forty to 60 percent of the southern Lowlands consists of wetlands, mostly bajos (Dunning et al. 2006), and the Maya exploited them for agriculture, fishing, and hunting (Scarborough 2006). While some bajos were perennial wetlands, many were seasonal (Dunning et al. 2006). In some bajos, the Maya practiced flood–recession agriculture, indicated by the noticeable number of terraces and berms along their margins, as well as terracing, to avert soil loss (Beach et al. 2008; Kunen 2006; Scarborough 2006).

To offset seasonally limited water supplies, the Maya built water retention systems (Scarborough 1993; see Scarborough 2001:354). By the Late Preclassic period (ca. 300 B.C.E.–C.E. 250), these systems included wetland reclamation adaptations (e.g., Cerros, Belize) and "passive" or concave micro-watershed systems where the Maya took advantage of the natural landscape, namely depressions, as found at the major Preclassic center of El Mirador in the Petén (Figure 3.1; Scarborough 1993, 2000). A growing concern would have been increasing sedimentation into these low-lying, gravity-driven water systems due to erosion.

By the Early Classic period (ca. C.E. 250–550), population growth led to a growing reliance on increasingly larger artificial reservoirs, a trend that continued into the Late Classic period (ca. C.E. 550–800) when water systems were further augmented in size and scope. These sophisticated engineered reservoir systems are epitomized by elevated convex micro-watershed systems whereby reservoirs, dams, channels, sluices, filtration systems and switching stations were designed to capture, store and distribute water as seen at, for example, Tikal and Caracol (Figure 3.2; Scarborough 1993, 2003:50–51, 2007; Scarborough and Gallopin 1991; Scarborough et al. 2012). Gravity release of water during the dry season supplied water to urban center inhabitants in lower–lying settlements (Scarborough 2003:110–111). As the dry season wore on and water levels dropped and water quality worsened, the Maya diverted gray water into agricultural fields and holding ponds for other purposes including fishponds, ceramic production, and plaster manufacture. The entire system depended on adequate rainfall and maintaining water quality, especially in the core reservoirs (Lucero 1999; Lucero et al. 2011).

The need for potable water was critical in the tropics where people can lose up to 10 liters per day sweating and thus require more water than their counterparts living in temperate areas of the world (Bacus and Lucero 1999). Maintaining water quality in the humid tropics presents challenges, especially since standing water provides prime conditions for both water-borne diseases and disease carriers such as mosquitoes (Burton et al. 1979; Miksic 1999). To maintain water quality in reservoirs, the Maya applied their understanding and knowledge of wetland biosphere systems by introducing a balance of macrophytic and hydrophytic plants, as well as other organisms such as fish (Lucero

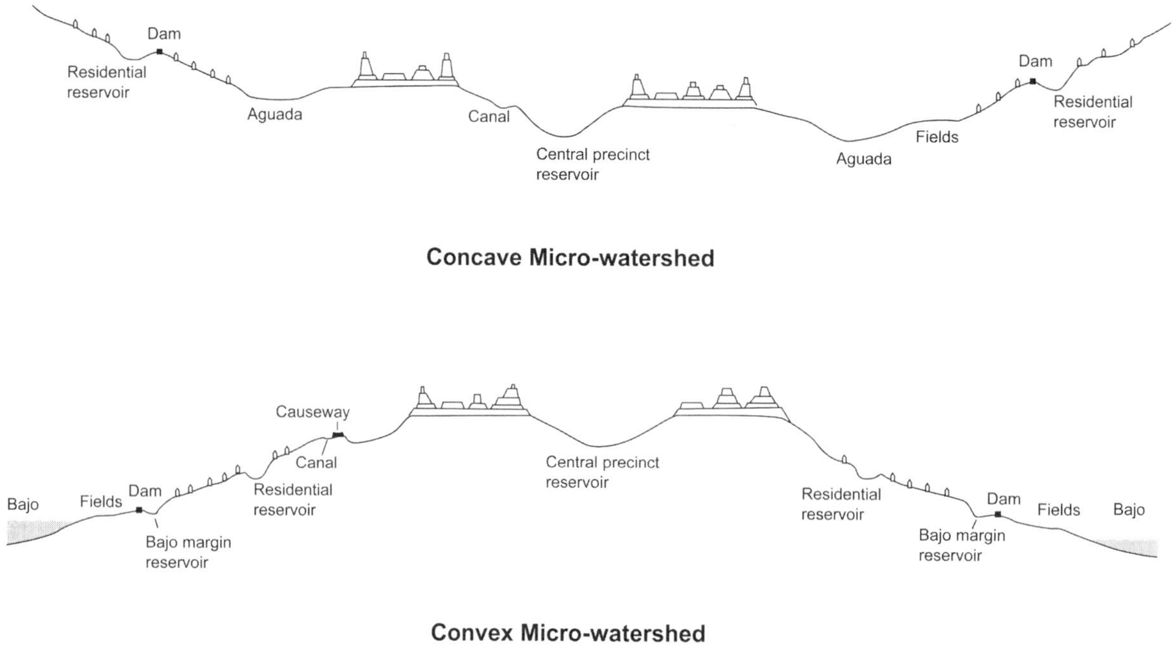

Figure 3.1. Schematic of concave and convex watershed systems (courtesy of V. Scarborough).

Figure 3.2. Tikal and its reservoirs (courtesy of V. Scarborough).

1999). Associated bacteria, along with a certain amount of algae, together purify water since plants absorb phosphorus and nitrogen, elements that accumulate in standing water (Hammer and Kadlec 1980; Nelson et al. 1980). For instance, investigations of both urban and hinterland reservoirs at the Petén sites of San Bartolo and Xultun indicate that the Maya went to great lengths to secure clean water, including investing in plaster linings in some reservoirs and siltation tanks in others fed by surface runoff (Akpinar-Ferrand et al. 2012).

Because a major role of kings was providing clean water to their subjects, it is not surprising that royals highlighted the association between their power and clean water in the iconographic record, especially via water lilies (Finamore and Houston 2010; Lucero 1999; e.g., Rands 1953:figures 3.1–6). Water lilies, *Nymphaea ampla* (Salisb.)

Figure 3.3. Water lilies at Cara Blanca (photo by L. J. Lucero).

DC., on reservoir surfaces actually indicate clean water because they are sensitive aquaflora that require specific conditions to flourish, including relatively shallow depths (1–3 meters) of still, non-acidic water without too much calcium or algae (Figure 3.3; Conrad 1905:116; Lundell 1937:18, 26). Their significance is also highlighted in many inscriptions, where *Nab Winik Makna*, or water lily lords, refers to Maya kings (Ford 1996), while *Ah Nab* refers to Maya nobility as water lily people (Schele and Freidel 1990:94). As we discuss below, significant changes in rainfall patterns had major repercussions for Maya rulers because of the close relationship between water and power in Classic Maya society.

People living in centers located along rivers also built reservoirs for a steady supply of drinking water, as rivers were not always reliable sources of potable water. At the height of the rainy season, the rains churned up sediment (e.g., Davis-Salazar 2003; Fash and Davis-Salazar 2006), while at the height of the dry season, rivers became low, murky, and disease-ridden (e.g., Houston 1998). We should note that in certain situations the Maya built water systems, such as aqueducts and canals, to divert water away from monumental architecture and living areas, as was the case at Palenque. This major center has over 50 streams and springs, not to mention a higher than average annual rainfall exceeding 3600 millimeters (French 2002; French et al. 2006). Evidence also suggests that farmers constructed irrigation canals on the plains below to take advantage of the abundance of water (Barnhart 2001:101; Liendo 2002). In most cases, however, the main goal of water systems was to contain water during the dry season.

In the northern Lowlands, we find a different situation which has to do with its higher water table and thinner soils. For instance, in the Yalahau region of the northeast Yucatán Peninsula, water was readily available in freshwater wetlands, wells that tapped into an abundant freshwater aquifer, and *cenotes*, or steep-sided sinkholes fed by the relatively high water table (Brown 2006). During the Late Preclassic, the Maya extensively modified the wetlands with rock alignments to manage soil and water. The Maya likely tapped the Yalahau wetlands for recession agriculture for domesticated crops, or alternatively for the management of economically important wetland plant and animal species, or as a source for biofertilizer transported to upland gardens (Fedick et al. 2000; Fedick and Morrison 2004). Rising water levels in the Early Classic may have actually contributed to the abandonment of wetlands because there might have been too much water.

Settlement was widespread across the northern Lowlands during the Late Preclassic, with numerous settlements dispersed to take advantage of natural water sources, chiefly cenotes, tracts of higher quality soil, and coastal resources such as salt (Glover and Stanton 2010). While many Preclassic sites were abandoned for unknown reasons by the onset of the Early Classic, including many Puuc centers (Smyth et al. in press), the region as a whole was not completely depopulated. Settlement was sparser in areas such as the Puuc Hills with few natural water sources, but some small and a few large Preclassic centers emerged, including Xcoch and its elaborate system of rain–fed reservoirs (Dunning, Weaver, et al. in press). However, Xcoch exhibits a period of abandonment early in the Early Classic, perhaps related to a period of increased aridity that even its elaborate reservoir system was unable to overcome (Smyth et al. in press).

In summary and in general, the major transition between the Late Preclassic and Late Classic consisted of the Maya successfully having met increasing land and water demands in areas without adequate sources of surface water.

Late Classic to Terminal Classic and Beyond

In the Terminal Classic period (ca. C.E. 800–1000), people no longer could rely on artificial reservoirs in the southern Lowlands because of increasingly frequent multiyear droughts, especially between C.E. 800 and 930 (Medina-Elizalde et al. 2010); ultimately, and through varied trajectories, the Maya largely abandoned major centers. Those Maya who did not leave the southern Lowlands lived in small communities near permanent water sources including the Belize River valley, wetland areas in northern Belize, nearby lakes and rivers in the Petén, and coastal areas in general (e.g., Demarest et al. 2004; Lucero 2006b; Lucero et al. 2004; McAnany et al. 2004; Mock 2004; Willey et al. 1965:292). Living near coasts provided Maya access to marine resources and maritime trade routes as evidenced in the emergence and growth of trade ports (Sabloff 2007). The Maya also practiced wetland agriculture along slow–moving rivers and near shallow lakes.

In the northern Lowlands, surface water was always severely limited due to its relatively small number of *aguadas*, lakes, small springs, and cenotes (Matheny 1982). However, Uxmal, a Late and Terminal Classic center, had at least 13 reservoirs within its sprawling urban area that undoubtedly were an important factor in its explosive growth and the construction of massive monuments in the site core between C.E. 870 and C.E. 910 (Dunning and Beach 2010). While household cisterns were vital to the Maya in the Puuc, urban reservoirs were also employed at some northern sites from an early date (Carmean et al. 2004; Dunning, Weaver, et al. in press; Isendahl 2011).

These apparent limitations in the northern Lowlands did not prevent the Maya from building large centers; nor did they prevent the Maya from migrating from the south into this area. For example, people moved to Chichén Itzá in the Terminal Classic (ca. C.E. 800–1000); it has two major cenotes, one within the site core and the other located at the end of a causeway 400 meters to the north (Sharer and Traxler 2006:562–565). Occupants of Chichén Itzá also benefitted from opportunities in trade and other production activities (Cobos Palma 2004). Maritime trade in subsistence (e.g., salt) and prestige goods became increasingly important (McKillop 1995, 1996). Areas in the Yucatán peninsula, such as the southern areas of Quintana Roo, incorporated the use of irrigation canals to support the growing immigrant populations (Carmean et al. 2004). Interestingly, the Yalahau region of northern Quintana Roo remained virtually vacant through the Late Classic period, despite an abundance of readily available fresh water (Glover 2006).

At Edzná, located along the Río Candelaria in Campeche, the Maya built complex water management systems consisting of extensive canals, reservoirs, and a moat (Forsyth et al. 1983). While built sometime in the Late Preclassic, the Maya used them through the Terminal Classic period. Of the 29 known canals, the most impressive is the Great Canal; it is over 12 kilometers long, up to 50 meters wide, and ca. 1.5 meters deep (pp. 68, 73, table 30). However, Doolittle (2006:6) argues that most of these supposed water systems, other than the Great Canal, are natural geological formations called grikes, or "solution-enlarged structural joints found in karstic landscapes."

In southwest Yucatán, the Maya constructed ridged field systems (ca. 1.5–2 square kilometers in area) and hundreds of canals one to two kilometers in length along the upper Candelaria (Seimens and Puleston 1972). The challenge is dating them since they could have been constructed by 15th–16th century inhabitants of Acalan, or from earlier time periods based on ceramics dating to ca. C.E. 800–1200. Some of the linear features may also have served as fisheries, which also have been found in northern Belize and northern Veracruz (Siemens 1996).

In summary and in general, the major transition between the Late Classic and Terminal Classic periods and beyond consisted of a move away from the interior southern Lowlands out towards coastal and riverine areas and to the northern Lowlands where the Maya could access a different suite of resources and participate in commerce and trade.

Environmental and Social Costs

Late Preclassic to Late Classic

To appreciate the environmental and social costs experienced in the Late Preclassic through Late Classic periods, it is important to reiterate the fact that many people relied on large scale artificial reservoirs in areas with and without permanent water sources (e.g., Ford 1996; Lucero 1999, 2006a, 2006b; Scarborough 1998). The social costs of an increasing reliance on artificial water systems include spending more time and labor constructing and maintaining them coupled with a growing dependency on water systems ostensibly controlled by others. As population densities grew and mobility decreased, the Maya faced increased uncertainty as they became more dependent on engineered landscapes.

Major environmental costs include the impacts from increasing population spread and growth, as well as landscape modification and transformation (e.g., diverting water, trapping soils). Evidence from Tikal (Lentz and Hockaday 2009), Aguateca (Lentz et al. 2014) and the Belize River valley (Lentz et al. 2005) indicate that a growing Late Classic population was associated with an increased demand for forest products in many areas of the Maya Lowlands. Accumulating evidence shows that widespread tropical forest clearance can impact local hydrological cycles, weaken precipitation recycling, and influence rainfall patterns (D'Almeida et al. 2007). In addition to the hydrological impact, reduced forest cover results in greater water run-off and concomitant erosion. In parts of the interior southern Lowlands, soil erosion and sedimentation exacerbated by drying conditions tainted some of the bajos and other water sources (Dunning et al. 2006). All of these factors increased noticeably through the Late Classic when population reached its height, particularly in areas without much surface water (e.g., around Tikal, Caracol, Calakmul).

Some archaeologists suggest that the Maya used sustainable agricultural practices that did not involve monocropping or environmentally destructive practices (Fedick 2003, 2010; Ford 2008; Ford and Nigh 2009). Increasing evidence also suggests that the Maya practiced some degree of sustainable forest management to offset overuse and limit deforestation, for example, through creating "forest gardens" (Ford 2008). Preliminary analysis of botanical samples collected in the tropical forests of central Belize in areas with and without sites suggests that the Maya modified their surroundings by removing some non-beneficial tree and plant species, adding beneficial domesticated ones, and maintaining useful non-domesticated species (Lindsay 2011; see also Ford and Nigh 2009; Lentz et al. 2002; Ross 2011; Ross and Rangel 2011). In conjunction with terraces, raised fields, and other agricultural features, the landscape, if not completely engineered, was significantly modified (e.g., Fedick 2010; Robin 2012). In fact, Gómez-Pompa (1987) hypothesizes that the forest at present actually is a descendant forest reflecting pre-Columbian forest management.

Analysis of pollen from sediment cores collected from cenotes, lakes, and aguadas (rain fed natural sinkholes) provide evidence for both deforestation and forest management (e.g., McNeil et al. 2010; Mueller et al. 2010). For example, analysis of a sediment core from a cenote at Cara Blanca, central Belize dating between C.E. 550 and 1730, has identified pollen from the family Poaceae, which includes grass species such as bamboo (*Merostachys* sp.) and *Paspalum* sp., among others (Lucero and Lindsay 2013). The most common species, however, is *Zea mays*, or maize. The Asteraceae family, also present in the core, includes flowers and other "composite species," both indicative of a cleared landscape. Common tree families, however, are still present; for instance, Moraceae, or flowering trees such as figs, as well as Melastomataceae and pine (*Pinus* sp.). At ca. C.E. 1730, the core still contains abundant Poaceae, but few *Pinus* sp. grains. Aguadas near the sites of San Bartolo and Xultun, Guatemala also produced pollen demonstrating significant land clearance in the Late Classic, but with sizeable amounts of arboreal species still present, including economic species such as Sapotaceae and *Spondias* (Akpinar-Ferrand et al. 2012).

Indications are that the landscape was both cleared and managed throughout the Classic period, though the extent of deforestation and forest management is yet to be completely unraveled. There is little doubt that we are dealing a complex mosaic of local responses to subsistence needs, which makes sense given the diverse and dispersed resources.

Late Classic to Terminal Classic and Beyond

Growing demands for agricultural and drinking water combined with several prolonged droughts (Hodell et al. 2007; Medina-Elizalde et al. 2010) resulted in a population decline over the long-term, especially in interior areas without much surface water. The droughts set in motion events (e.g., crop failure, depletion of reservoirs, decreasing water quality, social upheaval, political factioning, etc.) that ultimately resulted in the Maya abandoning centers and kings in search of areas with more reliable water sources, including rivers and coasts (Lucero 2002). These events culminated not only in rulers being unable to provide adequate food supplies and clean water to their subjects, but also in them being unable to maintain their seats of power. Kings thus eventually disappeared in the southern Lowlands.

A major social cost was that many farmers in the southern Lowlands had to leave their homes to find more suitable areas to support their families. Those who moved north likely had to negotiate with well-established occupants and live in denser communities due to the distribution and limited nature of water sources and thinner soils. Immigrants still were obligated to "pay" for access to some resources in areas into which they moved since other Maya groups had been living there for centuries. Newcomers, however, found diverse economic opportunities, including exploiting salt pans and participating in commerce and maritime trade. They also found a completely different political system—one that emphasized shared leadership rather than individual kings, as suggested in the archaeological record that lacked funerary temples and centralized palaces; and in the iconographic record that de-emphasized kings and instead highlighted the gods, a complete reversal from the Late Classic (Sharer and Traxler 2006:544–569).

The major environmental cost in the southern Lowlands was the repercussions of several prolonged droughts on crops, forests, and water resources. Small groups of farmers continued to live in the areas adjacent to the more dependable aguadas at Tikal (Dunning, Griffin, et al. in press) and likely used the un-maintained center reservoirs as well—after all, archaeologists a millennium later relied on these same reservoirs at both Tikal and Caracol. Some areas were impacted more by overexploitation than others, especially those with limited resources at the outset. For example, the populace at Tikal, which relied almost entirely on rainfall to recharge reservoirs and grow crops, was living close to the carrying capacity of its extractive zone given the available technology and the population it supported during the Late Classic period (Lentz et al. in press). Erosion has been noted in several areas of Tikal, particularly in the bajo margins (Dunning, Griffin, et al. in press). When the droughts of the 9th century became manifest, all of the resiliency had been wrung out of the landscape and the polity was no longer able to support its expanded population.

Copán in Honduras demonstrates a case with a different type of limited resources. The alluvial soils around the site core are concentrated within a 24 square kilometer area, which itself is surrounded by steep hills (Webster 1999). Copán's occupants extracted timber from both pine-oak forests and tropical deciduous forests as paleoethnobotanical studies (Lentz 1991) and sediment core analyses indicate (Fedick 2010; McNeil et al. 2010). These forestry activities likely contributed to bouts of erosion and environmental degradation in susceptible areas (Abrams and Rue 1988).

Severe droughts at the end of the Classic period ultimately resulted in drastic environmental and social costs, especially in parts of the southern Lowlands. In spite of this fact, the Maya adapted by exploring new areas for commerce and trade opportunities.

Discussion and Concluding Remarks

Our concluding remarks highlight some of the main topics discussed in the context of Maya land use and water management, and their implications regarding coping with similar issues today. Needless to say, the story is not as clear-cut as we might hope, especially regarding the quality and quantity of water sources. The Maya have been adapting to this semi-tropical region for millennia quite well, including moving into new areas and identifying sustainable water sources such as springs, lakes, rivers, streams, and aguadas.

Their social, political, and religious life revolved around water. When the dry season became acute in areas without much or any surface water, such as the elevated interior regions of the southern Lowlands (Dunning et al. 2012), they relied on artificial reservoirs found in nearly every major center and maintained water quality by creating their own wetland biospheres (Lucero et al. 2011). No matter the kind and scale of water systems, they were rainfall-dependent. Surviving annual and regional variation in precipitation was a universal challenge since nearly all agricultural production was rainfall-dependent. Yet they adapted and adopted sustainable agricultural practices that have withstood the test of time for millennia.

A vast portion of the northern Lowlands contains aquifers with water tables high and sizable enough to readily access by hand-excavated wells. This was not the case in the southern Lowlands where the water table is generally unreachable with hand-excavation technology. One only has to consider the 1960s University of Pennsylvania and Guatemalan archaeology project at Tikal where archaeologists abandoned mechanical well digging at ca. 180 meters below the surface when they failed to hit water, and instead turned to the ancient Maya reservoirs to meet their water needs (Siemens 1978). Nevertheless, little attempt has been made in the southern Lowlands to look for perched aquifers and their associated springs and shallow water tables. A perched aquifer is situated at a shallower depth than the permanent groundwater table, and is typically created by the presence of an aquitard, or relatively impermeable layer within the bedrock strata. There is also the question about community or household water storage systems, including small natural and artificial depressions, used to supply water year-round in the southern Lowlands (e.g., Weiss-Krejci and Sabbas 2002). However, a major concern with small–scale systems would have been evaporation and decreasing water quality as the dry season wore on. Yet to the north in the Puuc area, the Maya constructed household-scale, potable water cistern systems (Isendahl 2011).

We need to rethink our notions about water scarcity in the Maya Lowlands, and explore why there was such apparent variability in options and resilience when faced with water shortages. Clearly there are complex and multidimensional issues that came into play when adapting and surviving in the humid, seasonal tropics. The fact that the Maya did so quite well has relevance for unraveling long-term solutions to current problems regarding water and landscape use.

One of the most challenging questions when discussing water and landscape use is how to reconcile the noticeable array of systems found in the Maya Lowlands today and in the past. Understanding how these seemingly incongruous features are linked can help us in understanding and addressing today's problems in the face of global climate change. After all, no matter how diverse things have been, there is no doubt that farmers persevered and continue do so at present; there are lessons here that we are getting closer to revealing. In fact, the Intergovernmental Panel on Climate Change (2007) recommends expanding rainfall harvesting, storage, and conservation to offset the impact of global climate change—something the Maya accomplished for at least a millennium (Lucero in press). Some of the strategies we have presented here might be useful today, especially at the community level.

From small to large-scale water systems, the Maya adapted to living in the humid semi-tropics. How they accomplished this feat varied depending on local factors and variable strategies used for long-term success, even when faced with the seasonal vagaries of too much or not enough rainfall (Scarborough and Lucero 2010). A final lesson with which we can leave readers is the knowledge that no matter the type and scale of water features, local social networking, engagement, and interaction were key to keep the system working.

References Cited

Abrams, Eliot M., and David J. Rue
1988 The Causes and Consequences of Deforestation among the Prehistoric Maya. Cultural Ecology 16:377–395.

Akpinar-Ferrand, Ezgi, Nicholas P. Dunning, David L. Lentz, and John G. Jones
2012 The Use of Aguadas as Water Sources in Two Southern Lowland Maya Sites. Ancient Mesoamerica 23:85–101.

Bacus, Elisabeth A., and Lisa J. Lucero
1999 Introduction: Issues in the Archaeology of Tropical Polities. *In* Complex Polities in the Ancient Tropical World. E. A. Bacus and L. J. Lucero, eds. Pp. 1–11. Archeological Papers of the American Anthropological Association, 9. Arlington, VA: American Anthropological Association.

Barnhart, Edwin E.
2001 The Palenque Mapping Project: Settlement and Urbanism at an Ancient Maya City. Ph.D. dissertation, Department of Anthropology, University of Texas.

Beach, Timothy, Sheryl Luzzadder-Beach, and Nicholas Dunning
2008 Human and Natural Impacts on Fluvial and Karst Systems in the Maya Lowlands. Geomorphology 101:301–331.

Brown, Clifford T.
2006 Water Sources of Mayapán, Yucatán, Mexico. *In* Precolumbian Water Management: Ideology, Ritual, and Politics. L. J. Lucero and B. W. Fash, eds. Pp. 171–185. Tucson: University of Arizona Press.

Burton, Thomas M., Darrell L. King, Robert C. Ball, and Thomas G. Baker
1979 Utilization of Natural Ecosystems for Waste Water Renovation. United States Environmental Protection Agency, Region V. Chicago: Great Lakes National Programs Office.

Carmean, Kelli, Nicholas Dunning, and Jeff K. Kowalski
2004 High Times in the Hill country: A Perspective from the Terminal Classic Puuc Region. *In* The Terminal Classic in the Maya Lowlands: Collapse, Transition, and Transformation. A. A. Demarest, P. M. Rice, and D. S. Rice, eds. Pp. 424–449. Boulder: University Press of Colorado.

Cobos Palma, Rafael
2004 Chichén Itzá: Settlement and Hegemony During the Terminal Classic Period. *In* The Terminal Classic in the Maya Lowlands: Collapse, Transition, and Transformation. A. A. Demarest, P. M. Rice, and D. S. Rice, eds. Pp. 517–544. Boulder: University Press of Colorado.

Conrad, Henry S.
1905 The Waterlilies: A Monograph of the Genus

Nymphaea. Publication No. 4. Washington, DC: The Carnegie Institute of Washington.

D'Almeida, Cassiano, Charles J. Vörösmarty, George C. Hurtt, José A. Marengo, S. Lawrence Dingman, and Barry D. Keim
2007 The Effects of Deforestation on the Hydrological Cycle in Amazonia: A Review on Scale and Resolution. International Journal of Climatology 27:633–647.

Demarest, Arthur A., Prudence M. Rice, and Don S. Rice, eds.
2004 The Terminal Classic in the Maya Lowlands: Collapse, Transition, and Transformation. Boulder: University Press of Colorado.

Davis-Salazar, Karla L.
2003 Late Classic Water Management and Community Organization at Copan, Honduras. Latin American Antiquity 14:275–299.

Doolittle, William E.
2006 An Epilogue and Bibliographic Supplement to Canal Irrigation in Prehistoric Mexico: The Sequence of Technological Change. Mono y Conejo 4:3–15.

Dunning, Nicholas P., and Timothy Beach
2010 Farms and Forests: Spatial and Temporal Perspectives on Ancient Maya Landscapes. *In* Landscapes and Societies. I. P. Martini and W. Chesworth, eds. Pp. 369–389. Dordrecht: Springer.

Dunning, Nicholas P., Timothy Beach, and Sheryl Luzzadder-Beach
2006 Environmental Variability Among Bajos in the Southern Maya Lowlands and Its Implications for Ancient Maya Civilization and Archaeology. *In* Precolumbian Water Management: Ideology, Ritual, and Politics. L. J. Lucero and B. W. Fash, eds. Pp. 81–91. Tucson: University of Arizona Press.
2012 Kax and Kol: Collapse and Resilience in Lowland Maya Civilization. Proceedings of the National Academy of Sciences 106(2012):3652–3657.

Dunning, Nicholas P., Robert Griffin, John G. Jones, Richard Terry, Zachary Larsen, and Christopher Carr
In press Life on the Edge: Tikal in a Bajo Landscape. *In* Tikal: Paleoecology of an Ancient Maya City. D. L. Lentz, N. P. Dunning, and V. L. Scarborough, eds. Cambridge: Cambridge University Press.

Dunning, Nicholas, E. Weaver, M. Smyth, and D. Ortegón
In press Xcoch: Home of Ancient Maya Rain Gods and Water Managers. *In* The Archaeology of Yucatan: New Directions and Data. T. Stanton, ed. Oxford: BAR International Series.

Fash, Barbara W., and Karla L. Davis-Salazar
2006 Copan Water Ritual and Management: Imagery and Sacred Place. *In* Precolumbian Water Management: Ideology, Ritual, and Politics. L. J. Lucero and B. W. Fash, eds. Pp. 129–143. Tucson: University of Arizona Press.

Fedick, Scott L.
2003 In Search of the Maya Forest. *In* In Search of the Rain Forest. Candace Slater, ed. Pp. 133–164. Durham: Duke University Press.
2010 The Maya Forest: Destroyed or Cultivated by the Ancient Maya? Proceedings of the National Academy of Sciences 107:953–954.

Fedick, Scott L., and Bethany A. Morrison
2004 Ancient Use and Manipulation of Landscape in the Yalahau Region of the Northern Maya Lowlands. Agriculture and Human Values 21:207–219.

Fedick, Scott L., Bethany A. Morrison, Bente Juhl Andersen, Sylviane Boucher, Jorge Ceja Acosta, and Jennifer P. Mathews
2000 Wetland Manipulation in the Yalahau Region of the Northern Maya Lowlands. Journal of Field Archaeology 27:131–152.

Finamore, Daniel, and Stephen D. Houston, eds.
2010 Fiery Pool: The Maya and the Mythic Sea. New Haven: Peabody Essex Museum and Yale University Press.

Ford, Anabel
1986 Population Growth and Social Complexity: An Examination of Settlement and Environment in the Central Maya Lowlands. Anthropological Papers, 35. Tempe: Arizona State University.
1996 Critical Resource Control and the Rise of the Classic Period Maya. *In* The Managed Mosaic: Ancient Maya Agriculture and Resource Use. S.

L. Fedick, ed. Pp. 297–303. Provo: University of Utah Press.

2008 Dominant Plants of the Maya Forest and Gardens of El Pilar: Implications for Paleoevironmental Reconstructions. Journal of Ethnobiology 28:179–199

Ford, Anabel, and Ronald Nigh
2009 Origins of the Maya Forest Garden: Maya Resource Management. Journal of Ethnobiology 29:213–236.

Forsyth, Donald W., Deanne L. Gurr, F. Richard Hauck, and Ray T. Matheny
1983 Investigations at Edzná, Campeche, Mexico, Volume 1, Part 1: The Hydraulic System. Papers of the New World Archaeological Foundation, 46. Provo: Brigham Young University.

French, Kirk D.
2002 Creating Space through Water Management at the Classic Maya Site of Palenque, Chiapas, Mexico. M.A. thesis, Department of Anthropology, University of Cincinnati.

French, Kirk, David S. Stuart, and Alfonso Morales
2006 Archaeological and Epigraphic Evidence for Water Management and Ritual at Palenque. *In* Precolumbian Water Management: Ideology, Ritual, and Politics. L. J. Lucero and B. W. Fash, eds. Pp. 144–152. Tucson: University of Arizona Press.

Gómez-Pompa, Arturo
1987 On Maya Silviculture. Mexican Studies/ Estudios Mexicanos 3(1):1–17

Glover, Jeffrey B.
2006 The Yalahau Regionial Settlement Pattern Survey: A Study of Ancient Maya Social Organization in Northern Quintana Roo, Mexico. Ph.D. dissertation, Department of Anthropology, University of California, Riverside.

Glover, Jeffrey B., and Travis W. Stanton
2010 Assessing the Role of Preclassic Traditions in the Formation of Early Classic Yucatec Cultures. Journal of Field Archaeology 35:58–77.

Graham, Elizabeth
1999 Stone Cities, Green Cities. *In* Complex Polities in the Ancient Tropical World, E. A. Bacus and L. J. Lucero, eds. Pp. 185–194. Archeological Papers of the American Anthropological Association, 9. Arlington, VA: American Anthropological Association.

Gunn, Joel, William J. Folan, and Hubert R. Robichaux
1995 A Landscape Analysis of the Candelaria Watershed in Mexico: Insights into Paleoclimates affecting Upland Horticulture in the Southern Yucatan Peninsula Semi-Karst. Geoarchaeology 10:3–42.

Gunn, Joel D., Ray T. Matheny, and William J. Folan
2002 Climate-Change Studies in the Maya Area. Ancient Mesoamerica 13:79–84.

Hammer, David E., and Robert H. Kadlec
1980 Wetland Utilization for Management of Community Water: Concepts and Operation in Michigan. Industrial Development Division, Institute of Science and Technology. Ann Arbor: University of Michigan.

Hodell, David A., Mark Brenner, and Jason H. Curtis
2007 Climate and Cultural History of the Northeastern Yucatan Peninsula, Quintana Roo, Mexico. Climatic Change 83:215–240.

Houston, Stephen D.
1998 On the River of Ruins: Explorations at Piedras Negras, Guatemala, 1997. Mexicon 20:16–22.
2007 Summary for Policymakers of the Synthesis Report of the IPCC Fourth Assessment Report. Accessed http://www.ipcc.ch/index.htm, accessed November 15, 2013.

Isendahl, Christian
2011 The Weight of Water: A New Look at Pre-Hispanic Puuc Maya Water Reservoirs. Ancient Mesoamerica 22:185–197.

Kunen, Julie L.
2006 Water Management, Ritual, and Community in Tropical Complex Societies. *In* Precolumbian Water Management: Ideology, Ritual, and Politics. L. J. Lucero and B. W. Fash, eds. Pp. 100–115. Tucson: University of Arizona Press.

Lentz, David L.
1991 Maya Diets of the Rich and Poor: Paleoethnobotanical Evidence from Copan. Latin American Antiquity 2:269–287.

Lentz, David L., B. Lane, and K. Thompson
2014 Food, Farming and Forest Management at Aguateca. *In* Life and Politics at the Royal Court of Aguateca: Artifacts, Analytical Data, and Synthesis. T. Inomata and D. Triadan, eds. Pp. 203–217. Monographs of the Aguateca Archaeological Project First Phase, 3. Provo: University of Utah Press.

Lentz, D. L., L. Haddad, S. Cherpelis, H. J. Mary Joo, and M. Potter.
2002 Long-Term Influences of Ancient Maya Agroforestry Practices on Tropical Forest Biodiversity in Northwestern Belize. *In* Ethnobiology and Biocultural Diversity. J. R. Stepp, F. S. Wyndham, R. Zarger, eds. Pp. 431–442. Athens: University of Georgia Press.

Lentz, David L., and Brian Hockaday
2009 Tikal Timbers and Temples: Ancient Maya Agroforestry and the End of Time. Journal of Archaeological Science 36:1342–1353.

Lentz, David L., Kevin Magee, Eric Weaver, John Jones, Kenneth Tankersley, Angela Hood, Gerald Islebe, Carmen Ramos, and Nicholas P. Dunning
In press Agroforestry and Agricultural Practices of the Ancient Maya at Tikal. *In* Tikal: Paleoecology of an Ancient Maya City. D. L. Lentz, N. P. Dunning, and V. L. Scarborough, eds. Cambridge: Cambridge University Press.

Lentz, David L., Jason Yaeger, Cynthia Robin, and Wendy Ashmore
2005 Pine, Prestige and Politics of the Late Classic Maya at Xunantunich, Belize. Antiquity 79:573–585.

Liendo Stuardo, Rodrigo
2002 The Organization of Agricultural Production at a Maya Center: Settlement Patterns in the Palenque Region, Chiapas, Mexico. Pittsburgh: Instituto Nacional de Antropología e Historia, Mexico City and University of Pittsburgh.

Lindsay, Colleen
2011 Assessing Ancient Maya Forest Management in Peripheral Yalbac. *In* Results of the 2010 Valley of Peace Archaeology Project: Cara Blanca and Yalbac. L. J. Lucero, ed. Pp. 137–150. Report submitted to the Institute of Archaeology, National Institute of Culture and History, Belize.

Lucero, Lisa J.
1999 Water Control and Maya Politics in the Southern Maya Lowlands. *In* Complex Polities in the Ancient Tropical World, E. A. Bacus and L. J. Lucero, eds. Pp. 34–49. Archeological Papers of the American Anthropological Association, 9. Arlington, VA: American Anthropological Association.
2002 The Collapse of the Classic Maya: A Case for the Role of Water Control. American Anthropologist 104:814–826.
2006a Agricultural Intensification, Water, and Political Power in the Southern Maya Lowlands. *In* Agricultural Strategies. J. Marcus and C. Stanish, eds. Pp. 281–305. Los Angeles: The Cotsen Institute of Archaeology, UCLA.
2006b Water and Ritual: The Rise and Fall of Classic Maya Rulers. Austin: University of Texas Press.

In press Water Management in Lowland Mesoamerica. *In* Water and Humanity: Historical Overview. V. Scarborough, ed. Paris: UNESCO.

Lucero, Lisa J., and Colleen Lindsay
2013 Into the Depths of Cara Blanca: Exploring the Maya Underworld. Research Reports in Belizean Archaeology 10:165–175.

Lucero, Lisa J., Scott L. Fedick, Andrew Kinkella, and Sean M. Graebner
2004 Ancient Maya Settlement in the Valley of Peace area, Belize. *In* Archaeology of the Upper Belize River Valley: Half a Century of Maya Research. J. F. Garber, ed. Pp. 86–102. University Press of Florida.

Lucero, Lisa J., Joel D. Gunn, and Vernon L. Scarborough.
2011 Climate Change and Classic Maya Water Management. Theme Issue, "Managing Water Resources and Development in a Changing Climate," Water 3(2):479–494.

Lundell, Cyrus
1937 The Vegetation of Petén. Publication No. 478.

Washington, DC: The Carnegie Institute of Washington.

Marcus, Joyce
2006 The Roles of Ritual and Technology in Mesoamerican Water Management. *In* Agricultural Strategies. J. Marcus and C. Stanish, eds. Pp. 221–254. Los Angeles: The Cotsen Institute of Archaeology, UCLA.

Matheny, Ray T.
1982 Ancient Lowland and Highland Maya Water and Soil Conservation Strategies. *In* Maya Subsistence: Studies in Memory of Dennis E. Puleston. K. V. Flannery, ed. Pp. 157–178. New York: Academic Press.

McAnany, Patricia A., Eleanor Harrison, Polly A. Peterson, Steven Morandi, Satoru Murata, Ben S. Thomas, Sandra L. López Varela, Daniel Finamore, and David G. Buck
2004 The Deep History of the Sibun River Valley. Research Reports in Belizean Archaeology 1: 295–310.

McKillop, Heather
1995 Underwater Archaeology, Salt Production, and Coastal Maya Trade at Stingray Lagoon, Belize. Latin American Antiquity 6:214–228.
1996 Ancient Maya Trading Ports and the Integration of Long-Distance and Regional Economies. Ancient Mesoamerica 7:49–62.

McNeil, Cameron L., David A. Burney, and Lida Pigott Burney
2010 Evidence Disputing Deforestation as the Cause for the Collapse of the Ancient Maya Polity of Copan, Honduras. Proceedings of the National Academy of Sciences 107:1017–1022.

Medina-Elizalde, Martín, Stephen J.Burns, David W. Lea, Yemane Asmerom, Lucien von Gunten, Victor Polyak, Mathias Vuille, and Ambarish Karmalkar
2010 High Resolution Stalagmite Climate Record from the Yucatán Peninsula Spanning the Maya Terminal Classic Period. Earth and Planetary Science Letters 298:255–262.

Miksic, John N.
1999 Water, Urbanization, and Disease in Ancient Indonesia. *In* Complex Polities in the Ancient Tropical World, E. A. Bacus and L. J. Lucero, eds. Pp. 167–184. Archeological Papers of the American Anthropological Association, 9. Arlington, VA: American Anthropological Association.

Mock, Shirley B.
2004 Maya Traders on the North-Central Belize Coast. Research Reports in Belizean Archaeology 1:359–370.

Mueller, Andreas D., Gerald A. Islebe, Michael B. Hillesheim, Dustin A. Grzesik, Flavio S. Anselmetti, Daniel Ariztegui, Mark Brenner, Jason H. Curtis, David A. Hodell, and Kathryn A. Venz
2010 Climate Drying and Associated Forest Decline in the Lowlands of Northern Guatemala during the Late Holocene. Quaternary Research 71:133–141.

Nelson, Stephen G., Barry D. Smith, and Bruce R. Best
1980 Nitrogen Uptake by Tropical Freshwater Macrophytes. Water Resources Research Center. Technical Report, 10. University of Guam, Mangialo.

Rands, Robert L.
1953 The Water Lily in Maya Art: A Complex of Alleged Asiatic Origin. Bureau of American Ethnology Bulletin 151, Anthropological Papers, 34. Pp. 75–153. Washington, DC: Smithsonian Institution.

Robin, Cynthia, editor
2012 Chan: An Ancient Maya Farming Community. Gainesville: University Press of Florida.

Ross, Nanci J.
2011 Modern Tree Species Composition Reflects Ancient Maya "Forest Gardens" in Northwest Belize. Ecological Applications 21(1):75–84.

Ross, Nanci J., and Thiago F. Rangel
2011 Ancient Maya Agroforestry Echoing Through Spatial Relationships in the NW Belize. Biotropica 43(2):141–148.

Sabloff, Jeremy A.
2007 It Depends on How You Look at Things: New Perspectives on the Postclassic Period in the Northern Maya Lowlands. Proceedings of the American Philosophical Society 151:11–25.

Scarborough, Vernon L.
1993 Water Management in the Southern Maya

Lowlands: An Accretive Model for the Engineered Landscape. Research in Economic Anthropology 7:17–69.
1998 Ecology and Ritual: Water Management and the Maya. Latin American Antiquity 9:135–159.
2000 Resilience, Resource Use, and Socioeconomic Organization: A Mesoamerican Pathway. *In* Natural Disaster and the Archaeology of Human Response. G. Bawden and R. Reycraft, eds. Pp. 195–212. Albuquerque: Maxwell Museum of Anthropology and the University of New Mexico Press.
2001 Hydrology. *In* Archaeology of Ancient Mexico and Central America: An Encyclopedia. S. T. Evans, and D. L. Webster, eds. Pp. 352–356. New York: Garland Publishing.
2003 The Flow of Power: Ancient Water Systems and Landscapes. Santa Fe: School of American Research Press.
2006 An Overview of Mesoamerican Water Systems. *In* Precolumbian Water Management: Ideology, Ritual, and Politics. L. J. Lucero and B. W. Fash, eds. Pp. 223–235. Tucson: University of Arizona Press.
2007 Colonizing a Landscape: Water and Wetlands in Ancient Mesoamerica. *In* The political economy of ancient Mesoamerica: Transformations during the Formative and Classic Periods. V. L. Scarborough and J. E. Clark, eds. Pp 163–174. Albuquerque: University of New Mexico Press.

Scarborough, Vernon L., and Gary C. Gallopin
1991 A Water Storage Adaptation in the Maya Lowlands. Science 251:658–662.

Scarborough, Vernon L., and Lisa J. Lucero
2010 The Non-Hierarchical Development of Complexity in the Semitropics: Water and Cooperation. Theme Issue, "Ancient Near East and Americas," Water History 2(2):185–205.

Scarborough, Vernon L., Nicholas P. Dunning, Kenneth B. Tankersley, Christopher Carr, Eric Weaver, Liwy Grazioso, Brian Lane, John G. Jones, Palma Buttles, Fred Valdez, and David L. Lentz
2012 Water and Sustainable Land Use at the Ancient Tropical City of Tikal, Guatemala. Proceedings of the National Academy of Sciences 109:12408–12413.

Schele, Linda, and David Freidel
1990 A Forest of Kings: The Untold Story of the Ancient Maya. New York: William Morrow and Company.

Siemens, Alfred H.
1978 Karst and the Pre-Hispanic Maya in the Southern Lowlands. *In* Pre-Hispanic Maya Agriculture. P. D. Harrison and B. L. Turner, eds. Pp. 117–143. Albuquerque: University of New Mexico Press.
1996 Benign Flooding on Tropical Lowland Floodplains. *In* The Managed Mosaic: Ancient Maya Agriculture and Resource Use. S. L. Fedick, ed. Pp. 132–144. Provo: University of Utah Press.

Siemens, Alfred H., and Dennis E. Puleston
1972 Ridged Fields and Associated Features in Southern Campeche: New Perspectives on the Lowland Maya. American Antiquity 37:228–239.

Sharer, Robert J., and Loa P. Traxler
2006 The Ancient Maya. 6th edition. Stanford: Stanford University Press.

Smyth, M. P., D. Ortegón, N. Dunning, and E. Weaver
In press Settlement Dynamics, Climate Change, and Human Response at Xcoch in the Puuc Region of Yucatan, Mexico. *In* The Archaeology of Yucatan: New Directions and Data. T. Stanton, ed. Oxford: BAR International Series.

Vince, Gaia
2010 From One Farmer, Hope—and Reason for Worry. Science 327:800.

Wahl D., R. Byrne, T. Schreiner, and R. Hansen
2006 Holocene Vegetation Change in the Northern Peten and Its Implications for Maya Prehistory. Quaternary Research 65:80–389.

Webster, David L.
1999 The Archaeology of Copán, Honduras. Journal of Archaeological Research 7:1–53.

Weiss-Krejci, Estella and Thomas Sabbas
2002 The Potential Role of Small Depressions as Water Storage Features in the Central Maya Lowlands. Latin American Antiquity 13:343–357.

Willey, Gordon R., William R. Bullard, John B. Glass, and James C. Gifford
1965 Prehistoric Maya Settlements in the Belize Valley. Peabody Museum of Archaeology and Ethnology Papers, 54. Cambridge: Harvard University.

4

Growth and Decline in Classic Maya Puuc Political Economies

Christian Isendahl
University of Gothenburg
Nicholas P. Dunning
University of Cincinnati
and
Jeremy A. Sabloff
Santa Fe Institute

ABSTRACT

The Classic period Puuc region presents Maya archaeologists with significant challenges. One challenge to interpretation lies in the fact that, despite a form of agro-urban settlement that proved highly resilient in the Maya Lowlands overall, Puuc cities flourished relatively briefly, beginning on a grand scale in the sixth century C.E. and with a halt in major building construction and depopulation in the tenth century C.E. This chapter focuses on analyzing how the Puuc economy depended on sustained economic growth and ultimately suffered its consequences for long-term agro-ecological sustainability. We suggest that an important clue to understanding urban collapse in the Puuc is found by looking at transitions in the net energy gain of the agricultural economy over the long-term. The boom-and-crash character of Puuc economic history follows a series of opportunities, challenges, and problem-solving with varying efficacy for long- and short-term sustainability and resilience. These factors include the highly fertile soils as the main resource; water scarcity as a limiting factor; effective water management as a key solution; and costly social complexity a driving force of agro-economic growth. The diminishing returns on energy invested were consequences of a dependency on economic growth as the supply of the primary resource decreased. The elite segments of polities were unable to adjust to decreasing returns, which led to economic decline and, eventually, organizational collapse. The boom-and-crash character of Puuc settlement suggests a political economy that had locked into dependency on constant growth and failed to adapt to diminishing returns. [Puuc Maya, political economy, agro-ecological sustainability, growth, decline]

Introduction

The broad intellectual intent of this volume is to provide insights into the long- and short-term dynamics of social-ecological interactions "useful" to humanity at large, both today and in the future. These studies are useful in the sense that archaeological work can offer socio-ecological system examples, suggest how people in the past managed resources and dealt with climate variability and related crises, as well as provide background for the economic decision-making that has compromised or set the stage for subsequent generations to manage the resources available to them. Investigating the resilience capacity of past socio-ecological systems expands our understanding of sustainability and gives other scholars, planners, and political decision-makers a broader range of options to consider

ARCHEOLOGICAL PAPERS OF THE AMERICAN ANTHROPOLOGICAL ASSOCIATION, Vol. 24, pp. 43–55, ISSN 1551-823X, online ISSN 1551-8248. DOI: 10.1111/apaa.12028.

when evaluating sustainability in the contemporary world. Archaeology is now ready for the world—but is the world ready for us?

To Pierre Bourdieu, at least, archaeology must have seemed quite irrelevant to society at large when he argued that "archaeologists ... are never asked what use they are, what their work is for, who they work for or who needs it" (Bourdieu 1993:27). This view of archaeology as self-absorbed and marginal to current social concerns is largely our challenge when addressing today's social and environmental issues—and in attempting to meaningfully disseminate our research results. Perhaps the embodied conceptualization of the past in Andean cognition (Bengtsson 1998) can provide a source of inspiration for countering the notion of the past as irrelevant and instead encourage the idea that archaeology indeed matters in the present (Sabloff 2008). These ideas are lucidly expressed in the Quechua words *ñawpa*, which signifies that the past is "in front of us" and can be seen and known; and *qhepa*, a term for the future that places it "behind us" where we cannot see it. Such embodiment of time in Andean cognition reverberates within the historical ecological argument that the present is contingent on the past (e.g., Balée 2006; Crumley 1994). Although much has happened over the last couple of decades—especially with regard to the research questions that archaeology poses and to the public's view of archaeology's relevance—the greatest challenge to the discipline remains the need to overcome jargon and better communicate beyond our disciplinary and academic boundaries (see Dawdy 2009; Little 2002, 2007; Little and Shackel 2007; Sabloff 1998, 2008, 2009, 2011, among many others). An important first step is to connect archaeological findings to current issues and to establish a general position that historical ecological cases are not simply idiosyncratic or limited to a specific point in time, but rather that the nature of socio-ecological relations today differ to those of the distant past in degree rather than in kind. A second step is to offer historical narratives—case stories of socio-ecological interactions that are thoroughly based in empirical research—that are meaningful to a broader audience by introducing something profound about the human condition on key issues, such as adjusting to climate change, managing diversity, or building food and water security.

This chapter focuses on analyzing how the economy of the Classic period Puuc region of the northwestern Maya Lowlands (Figure 4.1) depended on sustained economic growth and ultimately suffered its consequences for long-term agro-ecological sustainability. Our work offers a brief historical narrative of a complex series of events and conditions detailing a set of opportunities and challenges dealt with by the ancient Maya, as well as the long- and short-term environmental, economic, and social outcomes of their decisions. The Puuc region is particularly interesting since it presents Maya archaeologists with significant intellectual challenges. One is the contradiction of great regional agricultural potential combined with an archaeological record that indicates large-scale urbanization was comparatively late to develop. Although a few earlier centers are now known (Rivera Dorado 1996; Smyth 1998; Smyth et al. in press), large-scale urbanization did not occur until the end of the Late Classic (ca. C.E. 550–800). Once underway, however, regional population multiplied fast and established numerous urban settlements, making the early Terminal Classic (ca. C.E. 800–900) Puuc one of the most densely populated regions of the Maya Lowlands. Sayil, Uxmal, and Xkipché are some of the best known centers and, where mapping data are available, these cities display a low-density settlement pattern of nodal civic-ceremonial cores with dispersed urban sprawl that cluster into neighborhoods around subsidiary civic-ceremonial areas, similar to elsewhere in the lowlands (e.g., Isendahl 2002; Prem 2003; Sabloff and Tourtellot 1991). To a large extent, this low-density settlement pattern of Maya cities is conditioned by a heavy emphasis on urban agriculture analogous to many early cities in lower latitudes globally; for example, in the ancient Khmer civilization of Southeast Asia (Fletcher 2009, 2012) and among the Aztecs of Highland Mexico (Isendahl and Smith 2013). The most basic component of these settlements—the household farmstead (Dunning 2004)—collectively formed agro-urban landscapes (Isendahl 2012) that provided social and ecological frameworks for significant production of food resources, ranging from subsistence to surplus. We also argue that this settlement system located a host of ecosystem services within cities, provided urban resilience capacity to stress, and was an energy-efficient strategy to produce food in societies that lacked wheeled transport and beasts of burden (Barthel and Isendahl 2013; Isendahl and Smith 2013).

Another challenge to interpretation lies in the fact that, despite a form of settlement that proved highly resilient in the Maya Lowlands overall, Classic Puuc Maya cities flourished relatively briefly, with a halt in major building construction and depopulation beginning in the tenth century C.E. We suggest that an important clue to understanding urban collapse in the Puuc is found by looking at transitions in the net energy gain of the agricultural economy over the long-term (Allen et al. 2003; Tainter et al. 2003). In the narrative of the Puuc that we propose, the boom-and-bust—or perhaps boom-and-crash—economic history of the Puuc follows a series of opportunities, challenges, and problem-solving with varying efficacy for long- and short-term sustainability and resilience. The following step-by-step factors were critical to the Puuc narrative: (1) highly

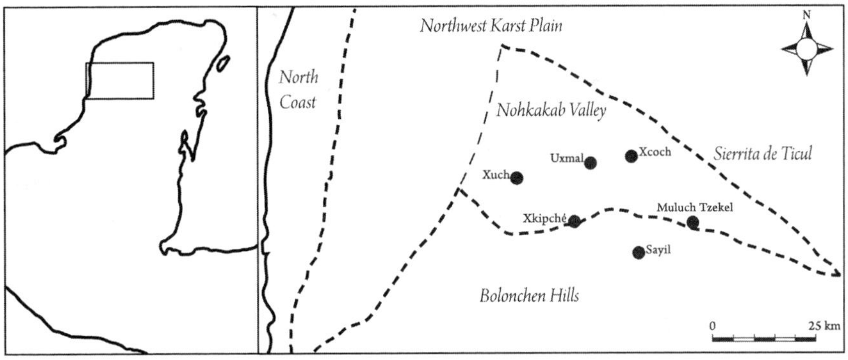

Figure 4.1. Map of the Puuc region on the northwest Yucatán Peninsula, with Classic period Puuc cities mentioned in the text and physiographic districts as described by Dunning and Beach (2010) and Isendahl (2011). Map by Christian Isendahl.

fertile soils were the key resource; (2) water scarcity was a limiting factor; (3) effective water management was a key solution; (4) costly social complexity and ceremonialism was a driving force of agro-economic colonization, growth, and maximization; (5) diminishing returns on energy invested were consequences of a dependency on economic growth as the supply of the primary resource, highly productive unused farmland, decreased; (6) the elite segments of polities were unable to adjust to a phase of decreasing returns on investments; (7) which led to economic decline and, eventually, organizational collapse. The boom-and-crash character of Puuc settlement suggests a political economy that had locked into dependency on constant growth and failed to adapt to diminishing returns.

Although our sample size is inadequate for general conclusions about urban sustainability and vulnerability, we suggest that there are leads to be drawn from analyzing how the Classic Puuc Maya socio-ecological system functioned over time. Our work identifies decisive points in the narrative where the system locked into a path, dependent on rigid economic growth that proved unsustainable and eroded system resilience capacity over time. We believe that these are not simply idiosyncratic insights, but assessments applicable to a better understanding of the resilience of complex, contemporary socio-ecological systems.

Energy Regimes and Transitions in Energy Gain

Joseph Tainter and colleagues have adopted and developed a method of socioeconomic analysis from ecological theory and applied it to the analysis of changes in the long-term sustainability of the Roman imperial economy (e.g., Allen et al. 2003; Tainter 1988; Tainter et al. 2003). This approach examines patterns of large-scale social change based on transitions in net energy gain over time and the consequences of such transitions for the sustainability and resilience capacity of social-ecological systems. The orientation offers an overall theoretical framework that can be applied in basic form for a narrative history of Puuc political economies. The critical concept in this scheme is energy gain, or energy returned on energy invested (Hall et al. 1992), and how transitions between phases of high-gain energy returns and low-gain energy returns are dealt with in an economy. In any early complex agricultural society, the basis of economic and political power is the ability to accumulate capital or resources that can ultimately be interpreted as forms of energy, according to Odum's (1996) use of the term. For the purposes of our analysis, we think of political economies as the social processes in which energy was accumulated among certain social segments in a society at the expense of other groups. While the details of Maya political economies are matters of debate (e.g., Masson and Freidel 2002; McAnany 2013; McAnany and Wells 2008), the economic foundation of elite culture was ultimately based on different ways of controlling past solar energy transformed into agricultural produce and human labor. In a competitive agricultural economy, taking control over a readily available and previously under-exploited resource such as areas of highly fertile soils yielded a high return and financed the establishment of central institutions. In Tainter's model, such high-gain phases are usually relatively short in duration because the key resource is at first abundant and concentrated, but then tends to rapidly diminish owing to subsequent inefficient management. A transition from high-gain to low-gain energy returns occurs as the demand for the resource increases (based, for instance, on the effects of an increasing population, costly organizational complexity, or conspicuous consumption); or, it is maintained at a relatively high level at the same time as the primary resource becomes more scarce and requires higher investment costs to maintain production levels, thus forcing the ratio of energy returns to energy invested to drop. In such low-gain phases, the key resource is usually scarce, dispersed, produces relatively little surplus per capita, and requires efficient management to be sustained. This broad explanatory framework of transitions in energy-gain ratios can be effectively applied to the broad trends of the social and economic history of the Classic period Puuc region.

The Puuc Maya Boom-and-Crash Economy

1. *Highly Fertile Soils were the Key Resource*

The Puuc covers some 3000 square kilometers and comprises a diverse soilscape. Some of the soils that predominate, including large tracts of Nitisols (in the FAO system of soil classification; Alfisols in USDA taxonomy; Buol et al. 2011), are ranked among the best for cultivation on the Yucatán Peninsula (Dunning 1992), as well as in the tropics at large (Driessen et al. 2001), and may have formed a "bread basket" for neighboring areas with poorer soil resources, particularly the northern coastal Karst Plain (Dunning 1992). Indeed, there is some ethnohistoric evidence to indicate that the Classic Puuc Maya thought of the region as *Nohkakab*, "the place of good earth" (Dunning 2008).

2. *Water Scarcity Constituted a Limiting Factor*

Paradoxically, however, while providing good farming soils, the Puuc is highly vulnerable to drought and access to sufficient amounts of freshwater is the main limiting biogeophysical factor for living and farming in the region (e.g., Isendahl 2011). Like much of the Maya Lowlands, the climate is seasonally dry with very low precipitation outside the rainy season that takes place during May to October. Furthermore, during the rainy season, two common anomalies in the rainfall pattern potentially cause distress to local farmers. One is the mid-summer dry spell, which in some extreme years starts in June and may last for about two months. Since farmers in the region plant maize, beans, squash, and many other crops as soon as the rainy season starts, a severe and prolonged dry spell may jeopardize the planting. Moreover, the fractured structure of the limestone bedrock drains surface water to the deep aquifer and there are very few permanent bodies of water, rivers, or streams in many lowland sub-regions (cf. Fedick, this volume). Setting the Puuc apart from many other parts of the northern peninsula, there are no karst water-bearing landforms such as sinkholes (*cenotes*), few deep, water-bearing caves, and the water table is too deep-lying to provide an accessible resource, thus making rain-fed agriculture and the capture and storage of drinking water that was necessary for surviving the dry season even more vulnerable to erratic rainfall (Dunning et al. 2012). Another potential obstacle is the hurricane season during August to October. Hurricanes and tropical storms strike the Yucatán Peninsula on an average of one per year, and the heavy rains and strong winds hurricanes bring may devastate harvests on a very broad scale—and certainly did so occasionally in the prehispanic past (Dunning and Houston 2011). To live and farm in the Puuc involves considerable effort to deal with water scarcity and the Classic-period Puuc Maya managed seasonal water scarcity by using a number of different techniques to collect and store rainwater.

3. *Effective Water Management was an Important Solution*

To cope with water scarcity and take advantage of the valuable soil resources of the land, Puuc residents developed two main hydro-technological inventions: large, open still-water reservoirs (*aguadas*) and small, underground water cisterns (*chultuns*). Aguadas and chultuns captured and stored rainwater for multiple purposes, including household consumption, garden and field pot irrigation, and ritual and ceremonial activities. Small underground water cisterns were constructed in close proximity to household-based residences, commonly in the center of residential patio groups. These formed the main source of freshwater for domestic use in each household, possibly including pot irrigation of kitchen gardens, and were managed by the farmstead dwellers themselves (McAnany 1995; Zapata Peraza 1989). Large, open, still-water reservoirs with the potential to store much greater volumes of freshwater are quite widespread in the Puuc (Figure 4.2; Dunning 2008) and were managed at a higher level in the social-administrative organization. At both the neighborhood and the city or polity leadership level, the organizing principles depended on how groups were situated on the landscape, on the degree of labor investment in fashioning reservoirs from natural depressions in the topography, and on water storage capacities (Dunning 2008; Isendahl 2011; see also Davis-Salazar 2003; Scarborough 1998). Modified from karst depressions, the construction of reservoirs in large tracts of fertile land (indicating their use in pot irrigation) often involved considerable labor investment at most Puuc cities; these features emphasized control of key large-scale land and potential water resources as an important economic and political basis for Puuc polities (Dunning 2008; Isendahl 2011; Dunning et al. in press). These two systems of water collection and storage may have been integrated; water in reservoirs may have been used to replenish household cisterns (Dunning et al. in press), similar to how water from the large *cenote* sinkhole features may have been used at Chichen Itza (Cobos, this volume).

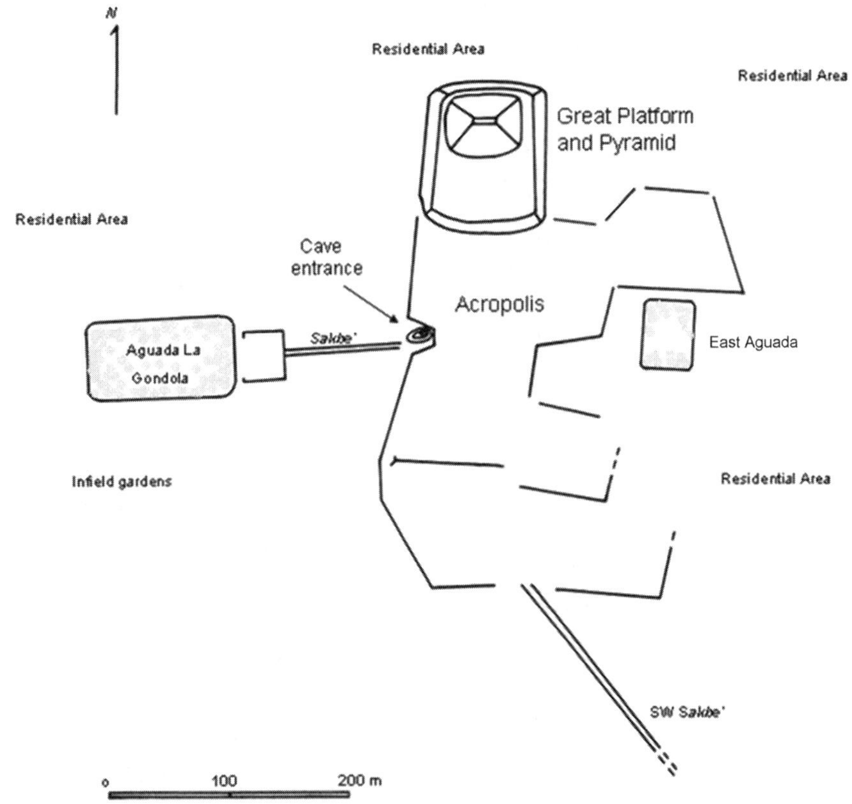

Figure 4.2. The central civic-ceremonial complex at Xcoch showing the location of two large, open, still-water reservoirs (Aguada La Gondola and East Aguada). Map by Nicholas Dunning (adapted from Smyth et al. in press).

Most major Puuc cities are located near large tracts of fertile soil and near geostructural fracturing that increased the frequency of karst depressions, a basic requirement for the construction of large water reservoirs (Dunning 2008; Isendahl 2011). However, it should be noted that not all Puuc cities had large reservoirs, and it remains to be investigated how water was managed at these cities and what consequences the absence of large, open water reservoirs had on their political and subsistence economy.

4. *Costly Social Complexity and Ceremonialism Formed a Driving Force of Agro-Economic Colonization, Growth, and Maximization*

Initial conditions of the Puuc in the sixth century C.E. presented a reserve of under-exploited terrain which, under favorable climatic conditions and efficient water management, formed a great opportunity for highly productive farming in a high-gain phase of energy accumulation. In a competitive agricultural economy, taking control of a readily available and previously un- or under-exploited fertile soil resource yielded a high return on investment and would have financed the rapid establishment of central institutions and their associated urban services and functions in the Puuc. Evidence of conspicuous consumption in the form of Maya monumental architecture and costly ceremonialism suggests that the high-gain phase was accompanied by political integration and economic maximization rather than resilient resource exploitation strategies (see Adams 1978; Alexander 2005). In Tainter's model, high-gain phases are usually relatively short in duration because, while the key resource is initially abundant, it is typically inefficiently managed and rapidly depleted—something that seems partially to be the case in the Puuc region (Andrews 2004; Dunning 1992).

The settlement pattern of the Puuc area was not determined by resource availability alone. Instead, each agro-urban landscape also integrated lower and higher level social institutions. Ethnohistoric documentation of a sixteenth century C.E., four-tiered sociopolitical structure of polity, city, neighborhood, and household (Okoshi Harada 1992; Quezada 1993; Roys 1957) fits very well with Classic period archaeological settlement data (McAnany 1995; Prem and Dunning 2004; Williams-Beck 1998) and offers

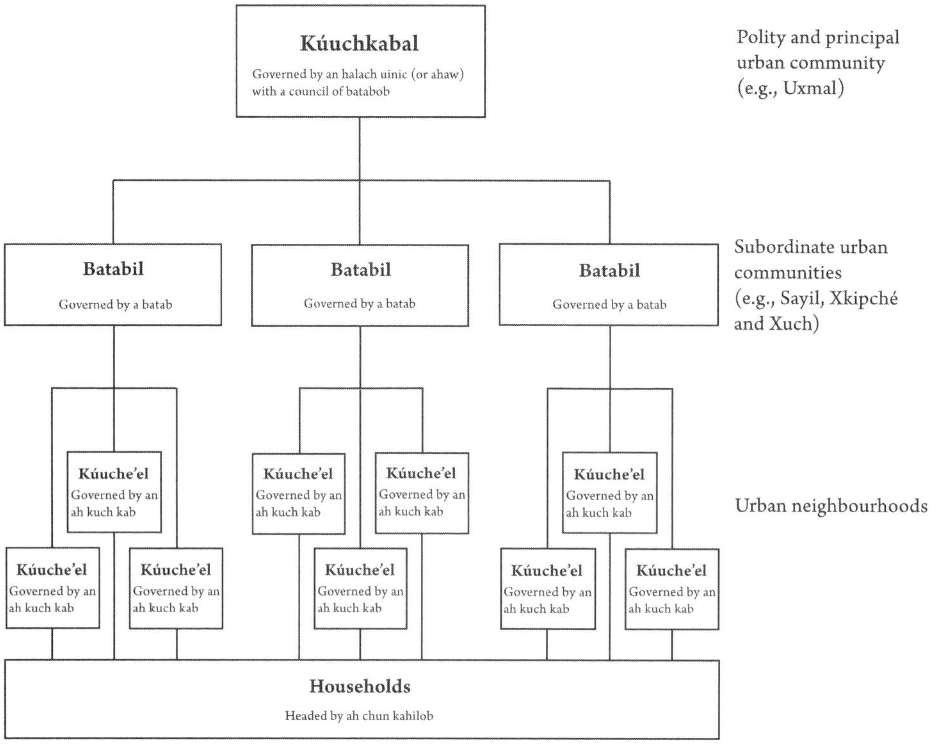

Figure 4.3. Political-settlement hierarchy for Puuc Maya cities. Figure by Christian Isendahl (based on Isendahl 2010:figure 5).

insight as to how resources, in particular farmland and water, were managed and distributed. At the highest level in the hierarchy is the overarching polity (the *kúuchkabal*), a principal settlement governed by a hereditary lord (the *halach uinic* or *ahaw*) and a council of other lords drawn from subordinate cities (Figure 4.3). Uxmal, the largest of the Terminal Classic cities (at least in terms of its presently-known central civic-ceremonial core complex, as urban sprawl at Uxmal has not been adequately investigated), was probably the Puuc capital, or kúuchkabal, in the latter part of the Terminal Classic and possibly before that (Carmean et al. 2004; Ringle and Bey 2001; but cf. Carmean and Sabloff 1996). At the next social-administrative level is a series of subordinate urban communities (*batabilob* [*-ob* is the plural suffix in Yukatek Maya]), each ruled by a *batab* who paid tribute to the ruler of the polity (the *halach uinic*). The batab was the chief executive, judicial, and military officer of each city and ruled over the local city council.

The kúuchkabal was a modular construction of smaller territorial units largely maintained through lineage affiliations of batabob (Quezada 1993). The relatively loose character of such "atomistic polities" indicates that the polity structure likely changed continuously as alliances between and within lineages were renegotiated (Okoshi Harada 1992). Each batabil was divided into several lineage-based neighborhoods (*kúuchte'elob*). Each neighborhood had its own administration, its own subordinate population, and its own lineage head (*ah kuch kab*). The neighborhood and its leadership assumed a central role in the management of natural resources (Isendahl and Smith 2013; McAnany 1995). The lineage head supervised agrarian and commodity production within the *kúuchte'el*, organized agrarian labor, and distributed land and resource rights to household heads (*ah chun kahilob*); he also coordinated and controlled the flow of tribute to the batab. Thus, the urban farming that took place between residential patio groups within neighborhoods and between urban neighborhood clusters in Puuc cities was governed by social interaction and negotiation between different levels in a complex social-administrative organization.

Even if these sociopolitical structures were hierarchically organized in the classic pyramidal sense, recent work on elements of heterarchy in prehispanic social organization suggests that many aspects of the sociopolitical domain of household and communities were socially contested and negotiated—and not simply governed by top-down control (e.g., Scarborough et al. 2003, see also Crumley 1995). The kúuchkabal Puuc polity-model suggests four different kinds of interconnected institutions involved in natural resource management. From the lowest to highest sphere of influence these are the household farmstead, the neighborhood, the urban community, and the polity; with their own respective forms of leadership and administration, each had its own driving goals and motives and degree of resource connectivity.

As the managing institution most directly connected to the primary food and water resources (Ashmore and Wilk 1988; Wilk 1990), the decisions made by the household farmstead had potential repercussions throughout the system. These were the farmers that tended their gardens, worked the soil and planted, weeded, watered, nurtured, and harvested the plants. We assume here, perhaps simplistically, that the primary goal of the household was to provide dependable sustenance, income security, and other basic human needs for the closest kin. Although we must be careful of anachronistic attribution of current concerns and motivations to people in the past (Smith 2010), each level was likely concerned primarily with its own well-being. However, as we move up the system from lower-to higher-level institutions—from the household to the political leadership of the polity—the immediate connectivity to the primary resource decreases. Higher-level institutions depend on an ability to command the rights to surpluses from lower-level managing institutions—i.e., ultimately farmers' labor and produce. In the Puuc, we argue that such rights were regulated through lineage-based systems of labor and tribute obligations. In Puuc neighborhoods and subsidiary towns and villages, the costs associated with maintaining the kúuchte'el administration (including the construction and maintenance of elite residential buildings and ceremonial buildings, as well as the underwriting large-scale integrative ceremonial events at each kúuchte'el)—as well as the surplus produce and labor obligations the ah kuch kab channeled to the batab and the leadership of the agro-urban community—ultimately burdened the primary producers at the household level. Complex organization is a costly endeavor that needs to be financed in one way or the other (D'Altroy and Earle 1985; Tainter et al. 2003); in agrarian-based prehispanic economies, the products of the farming population were the ultimate source of matter and energy financing complexity. Hence, a lower degree of resource connectivity in higher-level institutions is coupled with elevated political power that is dependent on a costly support system sustained by an expansive farming-sector.

5. *Diminishing Returns on Energy Invested were the Consequences of Long-Term Growth Dependency as the Supply of the Primary Resource—Highly Productive Unused or Under-Used Farmland—Decreased*

Initial conditions of the Puuc region in the sixth century C.E. presented a reserve of un- or under-exploited terrain that, under favorable climatic conditions and efficient water management, formed a great opportunity for highly productive farming in a high-gain phase of energy accumulation. Evidence of conspicuous consumption in the "Monstrous Visual Symbols" (Fletcher 1977; Rathje 2002) of Maya elite residential, civic, and ceremonial monumental architecture suggests that the high-gain energy extraction phase was accompanied by political integration and economic maximization rather than resilient resource exploitation strategies (see Adams 1978; Alexander 2005). For instance, in the Uxmal kúuchkabal at the end of the ninth century C.E., monumental constructions like the House of the Governor and the Nunnery Quadrangle required a huge labor investment to construct (Kowalski and Dunning 1999).

6. *The Elite Segments of Polities were Unable to Adjust to a Low-Gain Energy Phase Transition*

By the end of the tenth century C.E., if not before, cities throughout the Puuc area were depopulated (Braswell et al. 2011; Carmean et al. 2004). Depopulation seems to have extended into the countryside, though this phenomenon has been less studied. Simms et al. (2012) document the rapid abandonment of farmsteads around Kiuic in the Terminal Classic. Peaking energy gain seems to have occurred in the Puuc sometime during the early Terminal Classic, followed by a transition from high-gain to low-gain energy returns as a result of increasing regional population, diminishing available farmland per capita, intensified cropping, and decreasing surplus production, while costly demands to maintain central institutions persisted. Tainter's model suggests that in such low-gain phases the key resource is usually scarce, dispersed, produces little surplus per capita, and requires efficient management that often increases costs. In this view, regional settlement abandonments in the latter half of the Terminal Classic indicate that Puuc kúuchkabalob and batabilob were not resilient to transitions in energy gain. These institutions were unable to make the organizational decisions necessary to manage a transition from a high- to a low-gain mode. Decreasing revenues combined with an inability to finance higher-level institutions prompted an organizational crisis. The boom-and-crash character of Puuc settlement suggests a political economy that had locked into a dependency on sustained growth and failed to adapt to diminishing returns. Indeed, perhaps counter to more economically "sensible" measures, the leadership of Uxmal initiated large-scale monumental building programs in the city that might have been ideologically motivated but that its economy hardly could afford at this point in time—and the city seems to have crashed soon thereafter (see Culbert 1973 and Hosler et al. 1977 for broader discussions of this point for cities throughout the Maya Lowlands). Here we see a growing conflict between the decentralizing tendencies within Maya agriculture and the statist goals of the Uxmal city and polity leadership—a drama that has repeated itself historically in other contexts (Nair 1979). While the cultural logic of the ancient Maya may have supported the idea of greater investment in deified rulers, it became increasingly inconsistent with the subsistence needs of the society as a whole (McAnany and Gallareta Negrón 2010). This scenario seems to illustrate well the point of resilience theory in that the connectivity to the primary resource decreases as we move up the system from lower- to higher-level institutions—from the household to the political leadership of the city and polity.

7. *Failing to Adapt to Diminishing Returns Led to Economic Decline and Eventually Polity Collapse*

Once the Puuc agricultural system had been pressed into delivering maximum crop yields, the region's soil resources could only sustain such high levels of productivity for a limited time—no more than 75 years before crashing (Andrews 2004). This non-sustainable system likely deteriorated even more catastrophically under the influence of drought induced stresses (Medina Elizade et al. 2010). The Puuc region was doubly vulnerable to drought because both agricultural production and basic water-based sustenance were dependent on the collection and storage of water in adequate quantity and quality. Like other parts of the elevated interior region of the Yucatan Peninsula, urbanization in the Puuc area required a significant "up front" investment in large-scale water management infrastructure such as reservoirs. Once depopulation occurred, revenues significantly dropped and urban hydraulic systems deteriorated; reoccupation would have required a sizable investment to refurbish these systems (Dunning et al. 2012). These resettlement costs may help explain the relative slowness of interior regions like the Puuc to be reoccupied and form large urban settlements after the economic and organizational crises of the Terminal Classic period.

Implications

Archaeological and historical ecological research that offers a synthetic historical narrative of growth dependency and decline in Classic Puuc Maya political economies provides potentially useful information on the challenges and opportunities for building resilience capacity in social-ecological systems over the long-term. We suggest that these insights are relevant for understanding contemporary sustainability concerns in at least three interrelated domains.

1. *A Systemic Dependence on Maximizing Economic Production Limits Options*

The Late and Terminal Classic proliferation of cities and polities in the Puuc represents a period of expanding exploitation of regional agricultural lands or niche filling. As all prime lands were eventually brought into cultivation and political dominion, production intensified to levels that were not sustainable in the long term. Ultimately, outside of technological innovation, which did not occur, the best possible step for continued growth was the capture of neighboring land and labor through military conquest, most notably visible in the rise of the Uxmal kúuchkabal. However, this effort failed under a maximizing management regime in a heavily populated region. The Puuc case highlights that maintaining a diversity of options for spreading risk and planning for diminishing returns are essential strategies for long-term resilience.

2. *Large-Scale Investments in Infrastructure are Long-Term, High-Risk Ventures*

For those Puuc communities that chose to invest in reservoirs, this decision had major economic implications with start-up costs. At places such as Xuch and Muluch Tzekel, berms constructed to enhance the water storage capacity of reservoirs represent among the largest labor investments made in these settlements (Dunning 2008; Isendahl 2011). Maintenance in the form of dredging, re-flooring, and berm heightening represented further investments, such as seen in the huge city center reservoir of Aguada La Gondola at Xcoch and the hinterland Xcoch South Aguada 1 (see Figure 4.2; Dunning et al. in press). While these investments undoubtedly helped reduce water-related risks for a time, long-term risk may have actually increased. The security provided by the reservoirs likely facilitated urban population concentrations, ultimately putting these people at risk as the traditional pattern of a more resilient dispersed settlement was disrupted.

3. *Maintaining a Dynamic Capacity of Social Institutions to Fragmentize and Re-Coalesce Provides Adaptive Capacity to Temporal Oscillations in Economic Returns*

For millennia, the resilient capacity of Maya communities on the Yucatan Peninsula has been at its best when options for population mobility were retained, allowing dispersal in times of environmental stress such as drought. Resilience has been worst when populations have been forcibly concentrated, such as during the Colonial-era *reducciones* (forced settlement in Spanish towns) that likely contributed to several regional famines (Farriss 1984). In the Terminal Classic Puuc, the concentration of population at Uxmal during a period of intensifying drought likely hastened subsequent regional depopulation. The Puuc Maya cities followed a growth trajectory that was path dependent on maximized management regimes to maintain urban functions and services; this growth proved unsustainable over the long term when key resources were depleted and revenues decreased. However, in the agro-urban landscape, the household-based farmstead garden retained some degree of agro-economic autonomy, upheld farming practices, and preserved and developed agro-ecological pools of knowledge of how to produce food. Thus, these lower-level social institutions maintained resilience capacity over the long-term and provided a potential to reorganize into less complex forms of organization in times of urban crises.

The high risk associated with locking into economic growth for the long-term maintenance of societal functions and ecosystem services, suggested by the historical ecological case of the Puuc, reverberates profoundly in relation to the growth mantra of contemporary globalized economies as well as in mainstream political discourse. Archaeologists are increasingly proficient at inferring the factors that contributed to the resilience of past societies and that introduced vulnerabilities. We argue that these insights can be useful for understanding pathways to sustainable trajectories in the contemporary world.

Acknowledgments

We are most grateful to our colleagues within the IHOPE network for sharing with us an intellectually stimulating and creative milieu. In particular, we thank Arlen and Diane Chase for organizing the IHOPE-Maya workshop in Orlando, January 2011, in which the ideas expressed in this paper took shape, and Arlen Chase and Vernon Scarborough for organizing the session at the AAA annual meetings in Montreal in November 2011 where a skeletal version of this paper was presented. We also thank the volume editors, the book series editor, and anonymous reviewers for their sharp comments that have helped us to make the argument pursued in this chapter stronger.

References Cited

Adams, Robert M.
1978 Strategies of Maximization, Stability, and Resilience in Mesopotamian Society, Settlement, and Agriculture. Proceedings of the American Philosophical Society 122:329–335.

Alexander, Rani T.
2005 Isla Cilvituk and the Difficulties of Spanish Colonization in Southwestern Campeche. *In* The Postclassic to Spanish-era Transition in Mesoamerica: Archaeological Perspectives. Susan Kepecs and Rani T. Alexander, eds. Pp. 161–181. Albuquerque: University of New Mexico Press.

Allen, T. F. H., Joseph A. Tainter, and T. W. Hoekstra
2003 Supply-Side Sustainability. New York: Columbia University Press.

Andrews, Bradford W.
2004 Sayil Revisited: Inferring Terminal Classic Population Size and Dynamics in the West-Central Yucatan Peninsula. Human Ecology 32:593–613.

Ashmore, Wendy A., and Richard R. Wilk
1988 Household and Community in the Mesoamerican Past. *In* Household and Community in the Mesoamerican Past. Wendy A. Ashmore and Richard R. Wilk, eds. Pp. 1–27. Albuquerque: University of New Mexico Press.

Balée, William
2006 The Research Program of Historical Ecology. Annual Review of Anthropology 35:75–98.

Barthel, Stephan, and Christian Isendahl
2013 Urban Gardens, Agriculture, and Water Management: Sources of Resilience for Long-Term Food Security in Cities. Ecological Economics 86:224–234.

Bengtsson, Lisbet
1998 The Concept of Time/Space in Quechua: Some Considerations. *In* Past and Present in Andean Prehistory and Early History. Sven Ahlgren, Adriana Muñoz, Susanna Sjödin, and Per Stenborg, eds. Pp. 119–127. Ethnological Studies, 42. Gothenburg: Ethnographic Museum.

Bourdieu, Pierre
1993 Sociology in Question. London: Sage.

Braswell, Geoffrey E., Iken Paap, and Michael D. Glascock
2011 The Obsidian and Ceramics of the Puuc Region: Chronology, Lithic Procurement, and Production at

Xkipche, Yucatan, Mexico. Ancient Mesoamerica 22:135–154.

Buol, Stanley W., Randal J. Southard, Robert C. Graham, and Paul A. McDaniel
2011 Soil Genesis and Classification. 6th edition. Oxford: Wiley-Blackwell.

Carmean, Kelli, Nicholas P. Dunning, and Jeff K. Kowalski
2004 High Times in the Hill Country: A Perspective from the Terminal Classic Puuc Region. *In* The Terminal Classic in the Maya Lowlands: Collapse, Transition, and Transformation. Arthur A. Demarest, Prudence M. Rice, and Don S. Rice, eds. Pp. 424–449. Boulder: University Press of Colorado.

Carmean, Kelli, and Jeremy A. Sabloff
1996 Political Decentralization in the Puuc Region, Yucatan, Mexico. Journal of Anthropological Research 52:317–330.

Crumley, Carole L., ed.
1994 Historical Ecology: Cultural Knowledge and Changing Landscapes. Santa Fe: School of American Research Press.

Crumley, Carole L.
1995 Heterarchy and the Analysis of Complex Societies. *In* Heterarchy and the Analysis of Complex Societies. Robert M. Ehrenreich, Carole L. Crumley, and Janet E. Levy, eds. Pp. 1–5. Arlington, VA: American Anthropological Association.

Culbert, T. Patrick, ed.
1973 The Classic Maya Collapse. Albuquerque: University of New Mexico Press.

D'Altroy, Terence N., and Timothy K. Earle
1985 Staple Finance, Wealth Finance, and Storage in the Inka Political Economy. Current Anthropology 26:187–206.

Davis-Salazar, Karla L.
2003 Late Classic Maya Water Management and Community Organization at Copan, Honduras. Latin American Antiquity 14:275–299.

Dawdy, Shannon Lee
2009 Millennial Archaeology: Locating the Discipline in the Age of Insecurity. Archaeological Dialogues 16(2):131–141.

Driessen, Paul, Jozef Deckers, Otto Spaargaren, and Freddy Nachtergaele, eds.
2001 Lecture Notes on the Major Soils of the World (World Soil Resources Reports, 94). Rome: FAO.

Dunning, Nicholas P.
1992 Lords of the Hills: Ancient Maya Settlement in the Puuc Region, Yucatán, Mexico. Monographs in World Archaeology, 15. Madison: Prehistory Press.
2004 Down on the Farm: Classic Maya Houselots as Farmsteads. *In* Ancient Maya Commoners. Jon Lohse and Fred Valdez, eds. Pp. 96–116. Austin: University of Texas Press.
2008 Hill Country Chronicles: Puuc Landscapes as Texts. Paper presented at the 6th Annual Mesa Redonda de Palenque, Palenque, Mexico, November 2008.

Dunning, Nicholas P., and Timothy Beach
2010 Farms and Forests: Spatial and Temporal Perspectives on Ancient Maya Landscapes. *In* Landscapes and Societies I. Peter Martini and Ward Chesworth, eds. Pp. 369–389. Berlin: Springer.

Dunning, Nicholas P., Timothy Beach, and Sheryl Luzzadder-Beach.
2012 Kax and Kol: Collapse and Resilience in Lowland Maya Civilization. Proceedings of the National Academy of Sciences 106:3652–3657.

Dunning, Nicholas P., and Stephen Houston
2011 Chan Ik': Hurricanes as a Destabilizing Force in the Pre-Hispanic Maya Lowlands. *In* Ecology, Power, and Religion in Maya Landscapes. Christian Isendahl and Bodil Liljefors Persson, eds. Pp. 57–67. Markt Schwaben: Verlag Anton Saurwein.

Dunning, Nicholas P., Eric Weaver, Michael Smyth, and Davíd Ortegón
In press Xcoch: Home of Ancient Maya Rain Gods and Water Managers. *In* The Archaeology of Yucatan: New Directions and Data. Travis Stanton, ed. Oxford: BAR International Series.

Farriss, Nancy M.
1984 Maya Society Under Colonial Rule: The Collective Enterprise of Survival. Princeton: Princeton University Press.

Fletcher, Roland
1977 Settlement Studies (Micro and Semi-Micro). *In* Spatial Archaeology. David L. Clarke, ed. Pp. 47–162. New York: Academic Press.
2009 Low-Density, Agrarian-Based Urbanism: A Comparative View. *In* Institute of Advanced Studies Insights 2(4). Susan J. Smith, ed. Pp. 2–19. Durham: Durham University.
2012 Low-Density, Agrarian-Based Urbanism: Scale, Power, and Ecology. *In* The Comparative Archaeology of Complex Societies. Michael E. Smith, ed. Pp. 285–320. Cambridge: Cambridge University Press.

Hall, Charles A. S., Cutler J. Cleveland, and Robert Kaufmann
1992 Energy and Resource Quality: The Ecology of the Economic Process. Niwot, CO: University Press of Colorado.

Hosler, Dorethy, Jeremy A. Sabloff, and Dale Runge
1977 Simulation Model Development: A Case Study of the Maya Collapse. *In* Social Process in Maya Prehistory. Norman Hammond, ed. Pp. 553–590. New York: Academic Press.

Isendahl, Christian
2002 Common Knowledge: Lowland Maya Urban Farming at Xuch. Studies in Global Archaeology 1. Uppsala: Uppsala University.
2010 Greening the Ancient City: The Agro-Urban Landscapes of the Pre-Hispanic Maya. *In* The Urban Mind: Cultural and Environmental Dynamics. Paul J. J. Sinclair, Gullög Nordquist, Frands Herschend, and Christian Isendahl, eds. Pp. 527–552. Uppsala: Uppsala University.
2011 The Weight of Water: A New Look at Prehispanic Puuc Maya Water Reservoirs. Ancient Mesoamerica 22(1):185–197.
2012 Agro-Urban Landscapes: The Example of Maya Lowland Cities. Antiquity 86(334):1112–1125.

Isendahl, Christian, and Michael E. Smith
2013 Sustainable Agrarian Urbanism: The Low-Density Cities of the Mayas and Aztecs. Cities 31:132–143

Kowalski, Jeff K., and Nicholas P. Dunning
1999 The Architecture of Uxmal: The Symbolics of Statemaking at a Puuc Maya Regional Capital. *In* Mesoamerican Architecture as a Cultural Symbol. Jeff K. Kowalski, ed. Pp. 274–297. London: Oxford University Press.

Little, Barbara J., ed.
2002 Public Benefits of Archaeology. Gainesville: University Press of Florida.

Little, Barbara J.
2007 Historical Archaeology: Why the Past Matters. Walnut Creek, CA: Left Coast Press.

Little, Barbara J., and Paul A. Shackel, eds.
2007 Archaeology as a Tool of Civic Engagement. Lanham, MD: AltaMira Press.

Masson, Marylin A., and David A. Freidel, eds.
2002 Ancient Maya Political Economies. Walnut Creek, CA: Altamira Press.

McAnany, Patricia A.
1995 Living with the Ancestors: Kinship and Kingship in Ancient Maya Society. Austin: University of Texas Press.
2013 Artisans, Ikats, and, and Statecraft: Provisioning Classic Maya Royal Courts. *In* Merchants, Markets, and Exchange in the Pre-Columbian World. Kenneth Hirth and Joanne Pillsbury, eds. Pp. 229–253. Washington, DC: Dumbarton Oaks Research Library and Collection.

McAnany, Patricia A., and Tomas Gallareta Negrón
2010 Bellicose Rulers and Climatological Peril? Retrofitting Twenty-First-Century Woes on Eigth-Century Maya Society. *In* Questioning Collapse: Human Resilience, Ecological Vulnerability, and the Aftermath of Empire. Patricia A. McAnany and Norman Yoffee, eds. Pp. 142–175. New York: Cambridge University Press.

McAnany, Patricia A., and E. Christian Wells, eds.
2008 Dimensions of Ritual Economy. Research in Economic Anthropology, 27. Bingley, UK: JAI Press.

Medina Elizade, Martín, Stephen J. Burns, David W. Lea, Yemane Asmerom, Lucien von Gunten, Victor Polyak, Mathias Vuille, and Ambarish Karmalkar
2010 High Resolution Stalagmite Climate Record from

the Yucatán Peninsula Spanning the Maya Terminal Classic Period. Earth and Planetary Science Letters 298:255–262.

Nair, Kusum
1979 In Defense of the Irrational Peasant. Chicago: University of Chicago Press.

Odum, Howard T.
1996 Environmental Accounting: EMERGY and Environmental Decision Making. New York: Wiley.

Okoshi Harada, Tsubasa
1992 Los Canules: Análisis Etno-Histórico del Codice de Calkiní. Ph.D. dissertation. Instituto de Investigaciones Antropológicas. Mexico City: Universidad Nacional Autónoma de México.

Prem, Hanns J.
2003 Xkipché I: El Asentamiento. Mexico City: Instituto Nacional de Antropología e Historia.

Prem, Hanns J., and Nicholas P. Dunning
2004 Investigations at Hunto Chac, Yucatan. Mexicon 26:26–36.

Quezada, Sergio
1993 Pueblos y Casiques Yucatecos: 1550–1580. Mexico City: El Colegio de México

Rathje, William L.
2002 The Nouveau Elite Potlatch: One Scenario for the Monumental Rise of Early Civilizations. *In* Ancient Maya Political Economies. Marylin A. Masson and David A. Freidel. Eds. Pp. 31–40. Walnut Creek, CA: Altamira Press.

Ringle, William M., and George Bey III
2001 Post-Classic and Terminal Classic Courts in the Northern Maya Lowlands. *In* Royal Courts of the Maya, Vol 2: Data and Case Studies. Takeshi Inomata and Stephen D. Houston, eds. Pp. 266–307. Boulder: Westview Press.

Rivera Dorado, Manuel
1996 Los Mayas de Oxkintok. Madrid: Ministerio de Educación y Cultura.

Roys, Ralph L.
1957 The Political Geography of the Yucatán Maya. Carnegie Institution of Washington Publ. 613. Washington, DC: Carnegie Institution.

Sabloff, Jeremy A.
1998 Communication and the Future of Archaeology. American Anthropologist 100:869–875.
2008 Archaeology Matters: Action Archaeology in the Modern World. Walnut Creek, CA: Left Coast Press.
2009 How Can Archaeologists Usefully Contribute to Public Policy Considerations? Archaeological Dialogues 16(2):169–171.
2011 Where Have You Gone, Margaret Mead?: Anthropology and Public Intellectuals. American Anthropologist 113:408–416.

Sabloff, Jeremy A., and Gair Tourtellot
1991 The Ancient Maya City of Sayil: The Mapping of a Puuc Region Center. Middle American Research Institute Publication 60. New Orleans: Tulane University.

Scarborough, Vernon L.
1998 The Ecology of Ritual: Water Management and the Maya. Latin American Antiquity 9:135–159.

Scarborough, Vernon L., Fred Valdez Jr., and Nicholas P. Dunning, eds.
2003 Heterarchy, Political Economy, and the Ancient Maya: The Three Rivers Region of the East-Central Yucatán Peninsula. Tucson: University of Arizona Press.

Simms, Stephanie R., Evan Parker, George Bey III, and Tomas Gallareta Negrón
2012 Evidence from Escalera al Cielo: Abandonment of a Terminal Classic Puuc Maya Hill Complex in Yucatan, Mexico. Journal of Field Archaeology 37:270–288.

Smith, Michael E.
2010 Sprawl, Squatters, and Sustainable Cities: Can Archaeological Data Shed Light on Modern Urban Issues? Cambridge Archaeological Journal 20:229–253.

Smyth, Michael P.
1998 Before the Florescence: Chronological Reconstructions at Chac II, Yucatan, Mexico. Ancient Mesoamerica 9:137–150.

Smyth, Michael P., Davíd Ortegón, Nicholas Dunning, and Eric Weaver
In press Settlement Dynamics, Climate Change, and Human Response at Xcoch in the Puuc Region of Yucatan, Mexico. *In* The Archaeology of Yucatan: New Directions and Data. Travis Stanton, ed. Oxford: BAR International Series.

Tainter, Joseph A.
1988 The Collapse of Complex Societies. Cambridge: Cambridge University Press.

Tainter, Joseph A., T. F. H. Allen, Amanda Little, and Thomas W. Hoekstra
2003 Resource Transitions and Energy Gain: Contexts of Organization. Conservation Ecology 7. http://www.ecologyandsociety.org/vol7/iss3/art4/, accessed October 18, 2010.

Wilk, Richard R.
1990 Household Ecology: Decision Making and Resource Flows. *In* The Ecosystem Approach in Anthropology: From Concept to Practice. Emilio F. Moran, ed. Pp. 323–356. Ann Arbor: University of Michigan.

Williams-Beck, Lorraine A.
1998 El Dominio de los Batabob: El Área Puuc Occidental Campechana. Campeche: Universidad Autónoma de Campeche.

Zapata Peraza, René L.
1989 Los Chultunes: Sistemas de Captación y Almacenamiento de Agua Pluvial. Mexico City: Instituto Nacional de Antropología e Historia.

5

Ancient Climate and Archaeology: Uxmal, Chichén Itzá, and Their Collapse at the End of the Terminal Classic Period

Rafael Cobos
Universidad Autonóma de Yucatán
Guillermo de Anda Alanís
Universidad Nacional Autónoma de México-NGS
and
Roberto García Moll
Instituto Nacional de Antropología e Historia

ABSTRACT

Archaeological data and evidence of climatic change are used to suggest that the collapse of Uxmal and Chichén Itzá in the Northern Maya Lowlands was the result of long and recurrent drought episodes in the eleventh century. Although environmental evidence indicates that drought episodes might have begun in the ninth century, they gradually increased in frequency through the eleventh century and generated devastating effects on the late Terminal Classic period civilization. Evidence of recurrent drought episodes in the Northern lowlands is reported from the Holtún Cenote at Chichén Itzá. This *cenote* (sinkhole) shows two moments of the climatic change that affected Northern Yucatán. First, it corroborates the existence of extreme dry environmental conditions during the Terminal Classic period dated between the ninth and eleventh centuries. Second, after C.E. 1100, the water level rose inside the Holtún Cenote when environmental conditions turned wetter at the beginning of the Postclassic period. [northern Yucatán, climatic change, drought episodes, wetter environment, Maya collapse.]

The interpretation of archaeological data collected over the last five decades in the northern Maya Lowlands confirms the collapse of Classic period civilization in this area at the end of the eleventh century (Figure 5.1; Andrews et al. 2003; Cobos 2004; García Moll and Cobos 2009). The end of the Classic Maya cultural tradition and civilization in the northern Lowlands was an event that neither occurred at the same time throughout this region nor involved all the major prehispanic communities that occupied this area. For instance, Yaxuná, Ek' Balam, and Cobá collapsed sometime during the ninth century, contemporaneous with Southern Classic Maya settlements (Aimers 2007; Cobos 2004; Demarest, Rice, and Rice 2004). In contrast, the tenth and eleventh centuries are associated with the apogee of Chichén Itzá, although after C.E. 1100, Chichén Itzá became a pilgrimage center. The Postclassic visitors to this ancient city performed rituals and ceremonies at the Sacred Cenote (sinkhole), cultural practices that continued until the arrival of the Spaniards in the sixteenth century (Cobos 2004, 2007, 2010; Coggins 1992; García Moll and Cobos 2009).

In Western Yucatan, which is part of the northern Maya Lowlands in the Yucatan Peninsula, the collapse of Uxmal has been dated to C.E. 950 (Kowalski 1987:48–51). This

ARCHEOLOGICAL PAPERS OF THE AMERICAN ANTHROPOLOGICAL ASSOCIATION, Vol. 24, pp. 56–71, ISSN 1551-823X, online ISSN 1551-8248. DOI: 10.1111/apaa.12029.

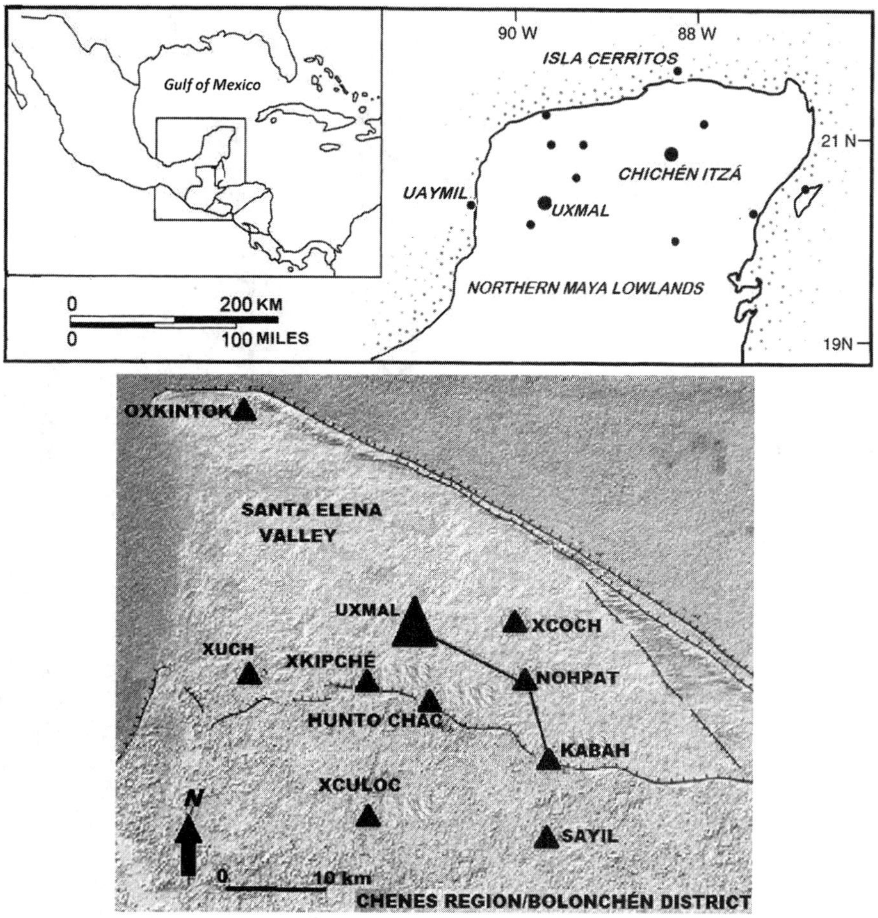

Figure 5.1. Location of Uxmal (Western Yucatán), Puuc region sites, and Chichén Itzá mentioned in the text.

date also continues to be used to date the end of Classic period civilization and complexity in the Puuc region (Braswell et al. 2011; Carmean et al. 2004; Dunning and Beach 2010; Dunning and Kowalski 1994; Kowalski 1994, 2003, 2006; Reindel 1998; Walters and Kowalski 2000). However, in contrast to this earlier date, a review of the architectural, ceramic, and epigraphic evidence reported from the Puuc region suggests that the collapse of Uxmal occurred sometime in the eleventh century.

What caused the collapse of Chichén Itzá and Uxmal in the eleventh century? Several theories have been posited to explain the collapse of Maya civilization generally, including endemic warfare (i.e., political competition, conquest of new territories, elite rivalry), ecological changes (erosion, soil exhaustion), demographic changes (migrations, overpopulation), and climatic change (long and recurrent periods of drought; see Culbert 1995; Curtis et al. 1996; Dahlin 2002; Demarest, O'Mansky, et al. 2004; Gallareta 2000; Gill 2000; Hodell et al. 1995; McAnany and Gallareta 2010; Shaw 2003; Webster 2012; Yager and Hodell 2008). However, considering regional variability in the Maya area as well as social and cultural factors, researchers agree that is not possible to name a single theory and use it to explain the collapse for such a vast area.

In some regions, such as in the Western Petén in Guatemala, endemic warfare might have brought to an end political entities and settlements in the eighth century, well before the period of long and recurrent droughts that occurred in the ninth century (Demarest, O'Mansky, et al. 2004). In the Copán Valley in Honduras, violence associated with erosion and soil exhaustion resulted in the end of Classic civilization at the site of Copán in the ninth century (Abrams et al. 1996; Andrews and Fash 1992; Paine and Freter 1996), although the valley itself continued to be occupied until the eleventh century –but with a reduced number of residents (Fash et al. 2004; Manahan 2004; Webster et al. 1992).

In the Yucatan Peninsula, a different picture is gained. The overwhelming climatic evidence dating to the last 2000 years (Curtis et al. 1996; Hodell et al. 1995; Hodell, Brenner, and Curtis 2005, Hodell, Brenner, Curtis et al. 2005; Leyden et al. 1998; Medina et al. 2010; Metcalfe et al. 2009; Torrescano and Islebe 2006), along with the interpretation of archaeological data from Uxmal and Chichén Itzá, suggest that long and recurrent periods of drought played a determinant role in the collapse of these two Northern Maya settlements at the end of the Terminal Classic period.

Ancient Climatic Conditions in the Yucatan Peninsula

Data recovered from sediment cores at Punta Laguna, San José Chulchacá, and Chichancanab lagoons, as well as stalagmite oxygen isotope records from cave Tzabnah in Yucatán, suggest three broader periods of climatic variability in the Yucatán Peninsula (Curtis et al. 1996; de Menocal 2001; Hodell, Brenner, and Curtis 2005; Hodell, Brenner, Curtis, et al. 2005; Medina et al. 2010). Period I dates between 1300 B.C.E. and C.E. 215 and is characterized as having had wet climatic conditions based on low values of oxygen isotopes.

Period II dates between C.E. 215 and 1050/1100. Results from the analyses of sediment cores and stalagmite show a continued increase in oxygen isotopes values, indicating progressively drier climatic conditions (Curtis et al. 1996; Medina et al. 2010). Climate data have been used to suggest a mega-drought for the northern Maya Lowlands that lasted between 50 and 130 years (Curtis et al. 1996; Gill 2000; Hodell et al. 1995). Medina and his colleagues (2010:256–257), however, did not find a 130 years mega-drought in their speleothem data; instead, they suggest four episodes of drought each lasting between 10 and 20 years. These episodes of drought occurred between C.E. 800 and 950, during the "Medieval Climatic Anomaly" that affected the world. Medina and his colleagues (2010:257) acknowledge that, during the century and a half that those episodes of drought took place, rain precipitation were reduced between 36% and 52% in comparison to rain precipitation values reported in modern times for the Yucatán Peninsula. If rain precipitation were reduced between 36% and 52% during the ninth and tenth centuries, the northern Maya Lowlands would have experienced the most severe droughts documented in the last 1500 years in that region.

Period III began after C.E. 1100 and continued to the 19th century. It is characterized by a reduction in oxygen isotopes values, which suggests wetter climatic conditions. Period III is known worldwide as the "Little Ice Age" (Curtis et al. 1996; Hodell, Brenner, Curtis, et al. 2005; Medina et al. 2010).

Figure 5.2. Inside the Holtún Cenote (photograph by James Balog, NGS).

The severe climatic conditions that produced long and recurrent droughts between C.E. 800–950 (or possibly C.E. 800/900–1100), along with the 36%–52% decrease in rainfall during Period II, might have drastically affected the large number of residents of Uxmal and Chichén Itzá, all of whom depended on yearly rainwater to irrigate their agricultural fields. There are no rivers in the northern Maya Lowlands; therefore, prehispanic Maya agriculture depended on plentiful rainfall to wet their agricultural fields in order to harvest enough food to feed the dwellers of Uxmal and Chichén Itzá. Moreover, the permanent residents at Uxmal depended on rain precipitation year after year to obtain abundant water to fill the ponds or *aguadas* that surround Uxmal, as well as their cisterns (*chultunes*) built to store water for daily drinking.

The permanent residents at Chichén Itzá also built chultunes to collect water from the rain and dug wells at the bottom of sinkholes to reach the water table. The inhabitants of Chichén Itzá procured water all year long from the Xtoloc and Sacred cenotes or sinkholes, as well as from caves (i.e. Balankanché). However, Chichén Itzá's agriculturalists depended on rain precipitation on a yearly basis to produce enough crops to feed a population of at least 30,000 permanent dwellers. Although the physiography of Chichén Itzá is very different from the physiography of the Santa Elena Valley where Uxmal is located, these two complex political units depended on abundant and excellent agricultural production year after year to sustain large populations. This production was possible, but it depended on a wet environment and not a dry one.

In this chapter, we use the abundant information on climatic change that affected the northern Maya Lowlands to interpret the archaeological data from Uxmal and the Puuc region as well as archaeological and water level changes data collected from the Holtún Cenote at Chichén Itzá. The combination of data on climatic change with archaeological evidence suggests that both Uxmal and Chichén Itzá were abandoned in the eleventh century. The permanent inhabitants of these two political units that dominated Western and central Yucatán, respectively, faced long and recurrent episodes of drought during the eleventh century. The climatic conditions deteriorated to such a degree that it was impossible to inhabit Chichén Itzá or Uxmal by the end of that century. If rainfall decreased up to a 52%, this would have had a severe effect on drinking water and agricultural production, especially at Uxmal. Therefore, the most important capital of Western Yucatán was completely abandoned whereas Chichén Itzá, with its limited number of permanent water sources, was still used for pilgrimages. These limited visitors to Chichén Itzá were probably aware that there was enough water to drink but not to revitalize a settlement that once formed a large pre-industrial city.

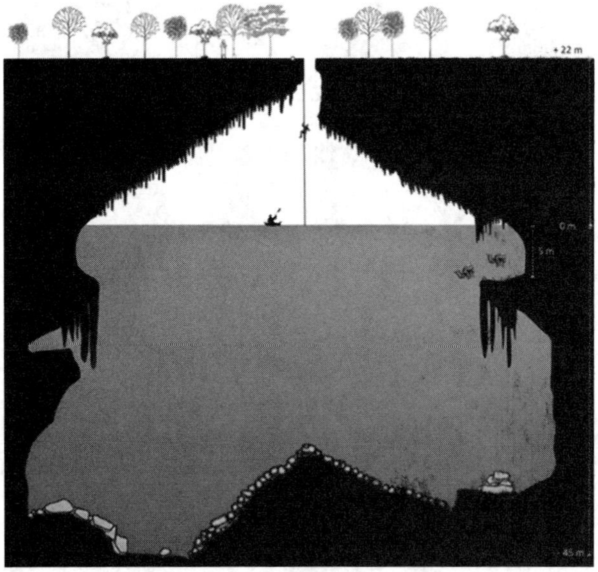

Figure 5.3. Limestone shelf and underwater archaeological context of the Holtún (drawing by Guillermo de Anda).

Uxmal

Traditional interpretation of the abundant archaeological information currently available on Uxmal and neighboring sites suggests that at the end of the ninth century and beginning of the tenth century, this political entity was conducting military campaigns against small settlements located in the Santa Elena Valley and the Chenes region (see Figure 5.1). In these military campaigns, Uxmal and Chichén Itzá were allies; however, the alliance did not survive the tenth century (Dunning and Kowalski 1994:90; Kowalski 2006). Events dating to the ninth and tenth centuries in Uxmal and the Puuc region also suggest that the alliance between Uxmal and Chichén Itzá did not last too long due to the fact that the former settlement ended its supremacy as a regional state in the beginning of the tenth century. Therefore, Uxmal's supremacy only lasted between 20 and 40 years (Carmean et al. 2004:444; Walters and Kowalski 2000:214–215). Following the traditional interpretation, it is suggested that in the first half of the tenth century (around C.E. 950), all monumental construction came to an end at Uxmal, with only a remnant population occupying the buildings and sacred edifices located at the site center. These few residual dwellers were devoted to performing sporadic acts of religious veneration during the drought that affected Uxmal in C.E. 950 (Braswell et al. 2011:141; Carmean et al. 2004:432, 445; Dunning and Beach 2010:384; Dunning and Kowalski 1994:67; Kowalski 1987:51; Kowalski 1994:93; Kowalski et al. 1996).

According to the traditional interpretation, the military campaigns against Uxmal's neighboring communities were orchestrated by Lord *Chac*, the last ruler of Uxmal. Lord *Chac* ordered the construction of several architectural compounds such as the Nunnery Quadrangle, the House of the Governor, and the ballcourt located just to the South of the Nunnery Quadrangle (Dunning and Beach 2010:384; Dunning and Kowalski 1994:63, 86–89). The dates C.E. 895 and C.E. 907 are associated with Uxmal's hegemony, the alliance between Uxmal and Chichén Itzá, all the construction activity that took place at Uxmal, the military campaigns and territorial expansion of this site, and Lord *Chac*'s rule (Dunning and Kowalski 1994; Kowalski 2006). In fact,

Figure 5.4. Ceramics inside the Holtún Cenote: (a) Cumpich incised jar; (b) Chen Mul molded jar (photographs by Guillermo de Anda).

the explanation of the social and political development of Uxmal at the end of the ninth century and beginning of the tenth century are based on Kowalski's (1987:48–51) interpretation of the architectural, ceramic, epigraphic, and sculptural evidence suggested a quarter of century ago.

A critical review of the same line of evidence, however, along with data collected over the past two and a half decades at Uxmal and neighboring sites, permits a new explanation of this time period. Contrary to the traditional interpretation, we suggest that Uxmal consolidated its political power in the tenth century and became the political unit that dominated Western Yucatán in the tenth and eleventh centuries. Our explanation and dating frame differs by some 150 or 200 years from the traditional Uxmal and Puuc interpretation.

Between C.E. 900 and 1100, Uxmal was an administrative city and the seat of a state. To understand the interaction between Uxmal and its neighbors during the tenth and eleventh centuries, we take into account several lines of archaeological evidence, including: volume of constructed edifices; the architecture of different structures and vaulted buildings to identify hierarchical differences between Uxmal and smaller sites; the causeway that connects Uxmal with Kabah; the Cehpech Puuc ceramic component associated with Sotuta-Chichén Itzá ceramics (that additionally suggests contemporaneity among Uxmal, Kabah, Xkipché, and Chichén Itzá); and Uxmal's procurement patterns of obsidian that suggests its active participation in an administrative market economy along with Chichén Itzá during the tenth and eleventh centuries.

When we consider volume of construction, spatial distribution of built structures and compounds, and the elaborate architecture of vaulted buildings, it is evident that a clear hierarchical difference existed between Uxmal and contemporaneous regional settlements such as Kabah, Nohpat, Hunto Chac, Xkipché, Xcoch, Xuch. Uxmal is a first rank settlement whereas Kabah and Nohpat are classified as second rank settlements. Third rank sites include Hunto Chac, Xkipché, Xcoch, and Xuch (Andrews 1986; Dunning 1992; Dunning and Kowalski 1994; Garza and Kurjack 1980; Isendahl 2002; Prem 2003; Prem and Dunning 2004; Reindel 2003; Zubrow et al. 2010). The hierarchical difference between Uxmal and other Puuc sites suggests that the administrative city might have regulated the agricultural production as well as the manufacture or production of other goods or merchandise. Through its political and economic influence, Uxmal probably controlled the labor force of the second and third rank settlements in the tenth century, when rain precipitation was still abundant in the Santa Elena Valley.

Uxmal and Kabah are connected by a causeway whereas third rank sites in the Santa Elena Valley are not linked to Uxmal by those man-made features. The existence of a causeway linking Uxmal with Kabah is a clear reminder that causeways are the material evidence of social, political, and economic interactions that existed in the past (Kurjack 1979; Kurjack and Garza 1981). The Uxmal-Kabah causeway also suggests that an unequal relationship existed between these two contemporaneous prehispanic communities. According to Kurjack and Garza (1981), Uxmal is a first rank settlement whereas Kabah is a second rank site considering construction volume and spatial extension of both prehispanic communities. The causeway that connects Uxmal with Kabah is 19 kilometers long and was probably constructed in the tenth century, at a time when both sites were in their apogee.

At Uxmal, the causeway begins in the southeastern portion of the site and runs through an architectural compound known as Chetulix (Carrasco 1993). A long-rectangular building with columns was constructed near the Northwestern corner of the main platform at the site (Carrasco 1993:207, figure 5.4). This long rectangular building with columns is morphologically similar to Structure 13M4, which is part of an architectural compound built after the construction of the House of the Governor (Barrera Rubio 1991:46–53; Barrera Rubio and Huchím Herrera 1989:271; Barrera Rubio and Huchím Herrera 1990:22). If the Chetulix long-rectangular building (along with associated structures) is contemporaneous with Structure 13M4, this would suggest that construction activity continued at Uxmal during the tenth century, not only in the site-center but also in the periphery.

About one kilometer south of the House of the Governor and the Nunnery Quadrangle, in Quadrants 17L and 18L, an architectural compound housed Altar 10. Three individuals—*Chac-Nal Ajaw*, *Wak Eb Chac E-Wits-Ahau*, and Lord *Chac*—are named in Altar 10. Lord *Chac* has been identified as Kabah's Ruler II, who governed this site in the tenth century (Carrasco and Pérez de Heredia 1996).

At Kabah, in the Plaza Mirador, a jamb associated with Structure 2A3 depicts Ruler II of this site. Ruler II wears a large and elaborate headdress made of feathers, loincloth, gaiters, and sandals with ankle-guards. An earplug and a tubular noseplug that goes through his septum are some of the ornaments that he also wears. A stylistic comparison between the jamb of Structure 2A3 and Stela 14 of Uxmal show great similarities between the individuals depicted on these carved monuments. Similar iconography and dress appear on both monuments (see Carrasco and Pérez de Heredia [1996:figure 5.3], and compare with Graham [1992:108]). Perhaps, the individual depicted on the jamb of Structure 2A3 is Lord *Chac* who conquered Kabah, ordered the construction of the causeway that links this site with Uxmal, introduced the *Chac* rain-god masks to Kabah, and also utilized Chichén Itzá's Sotuta ceramics at Kabah in the middle of the tenth century (Carrasco and Pérez de Heredia 1996). All of this probably started in the first half of the tenth century and lasted until the onset of the eleventh century; this inference for Kabah is supported by the presence of new architectural arrangements, sculptural designs, and ceramics; three calibrated radiocarbon dates also corroborate Kabah's role during that time (Carrasco and Pérez de Heredia 1996:299–301).

The traditional interpretation of Uxmal acknowledges only one ruler using the name Lord *Chac*. This political leader was the last ruler of Uxmal and orchestrated the architectural construction of the site (Carmean et al. 2004; Dunning and Kowalaski 1994; Kowalaski 1987, 1994, 2006; Walters and Kowalski 2000). However, we favor the proposal made by Bricker and Bricker (1996) who suggested that there were at least two, and perhaps up to five, rulers referred to as Lord *Chac* in the hieroglyphic writing of Uxmal.

One of the Lord *Chac* mentioned in the hieroglyphic texts of Uxmal is depicted on Stela 14 standing on the back of a two-headed jaguar. Apparently, the long count date 10.4.0.0.0 (C.E. 909) carved on Stela 14 commemorates his accession to the throne. García Barrios (2009:16; see also García Barrios 2008:476–481) identifies this Lord *Chac* as "smoky sky" and noted his role as a warrior. According to García Barrios (2008, 2009), individuals depicted as *Chac* (or *Chaahk* as García Barrios refers to them) specifically acquired a belligerent role when represented in the Late and Terminal Classic iconography of the northern Maya Lowlands.

If Lord *Chac* "smoky sky" became the paramount ruler at Uxmal in the year C.E. 909, this supports Andrew's (1986), Barrera Rubio and Huchím's (1989, 1990), Gendrop's (1983) as well as Bricker and Bricker's (2000) proposal to date the construction of the Palace of the Governor after C.E. 900. This palace is associated with Lord *Chac*, although Kowalski (1987, 1994, 2003, 2006) suggests to date the construction of such a palace during the second half of the ninth century. Moreover, the construction of the northern, eastern, and western buildings of the Nunnery Quadrangle could also date to the tenth century as Andrews (1986:72–73) suggested based upon his architectural analysis. A one-sigma range recalibrated C-14 date from a lintel associated with the north building at the Nunnery Quadrangle suggests the year C.E. 982 as the date of the lintel (Andrews and Andrews 1980:table 4; Ringle et al. 1991:table 5.1). Ceramic evidence, consisting of Sotuta materials (Tohil Plumbate, Silho Fine Orange) associated with Cehpech Puuc ceramics, found inside the rooms of the Nunnery Quadrangle, as well as in its central patio and the Birds Quadrangle [Cuadrángulo de Los Pájaros], further indicate that these architectural compounds were built and occupied by local dwellers during the tenth century (Huchím and Toscano 1999; Kowalski 2006:320–321; Ruz 1952). The local inhabitants used both Sotuta and Cehpech ceramics as a result of the sociopolitical changes that took place at Uxmal after C.E. 900. Kowalski (2006:320–321), however, argues that "intruders" arrived at Uxmal, utilized Sotuta pottery, dismantled earlier buildings, and built C-shaped structures at the site.

Therefore, it is quite possible that Lord *Chac* "smoky sky" and other rulers—also named Lord *Chac*—whom succeeded him after the middle of the tenth century, spatially arranged Uxmal's internal morphology. The massive construction of elaborate architectural compounds as well as the numerous domestic units with their associated chultunes

Table 5.1. Chronology of sociocultural events associated with climatic periods.

Cultural period	Dates	Climatic periods	Socio-cultural events
Postclassic	C.E. 1100–1550	Period III Wet climatic conditions	Rise of Mayapán and Tulúm in the northern Maya Lowlands
Terminal Classic	C.E. 800–1100	Period II Drier climatic	Collapse of Chichén Itzá and Uxmal
Late Classic	C.E. 600–800	conditions	Apogee and collapse of lowland Maya cities
Early Classic	C.E. 200/300–600		Rise of Maya civilization
Preclassic	1500 B.C.E.–C.E. 200/300	Period I Wet climatic conditions	

took place during the time when rain precipitation was still abundant and there was no water shortage. In fact, Uxmal's extraordinary and efficient hydraulic infrastructure to manage abundant water is a salient testimony of the drought episodes that occurred in the Santa Elena Valley and the Puuc region during the tenth (as Dunning and Beach [2010]) suggest) and eleventh centuries. Then, after Uxmal had already reached its apogee as a political unit, had functioned as the capital of a state, had expanded and controlled the Santa Elena Valley and small settlements, and had participated in an administrative market economy, the site faced severe episodes of recurrent and long droughts that made it impossible to continue living in this part of the Yucatán Peninsula.

After Lord *Chac* "smoky sky" became the ruler of Uxmal and conquered Kabah, he initiated a new political phase in Western Yucatán. In this new phase, Uxmal and Chichén Itzá established strong political and commercial ties along with cooperation programs (such as regional military collaboration). Proskouriakoff (1950:164; see also Kowalski 2003:239; Kowalski 2006:306–308) indicated that one of the figures standing to the left of Lord *Chac* "smoky sky" on Stela 14 carries an atlatl, shield, and necklace with two large beads similar to the weapons and ornaments worn by warriors depicted in Chichén Itzá's iconography. Therefore, we posit that from the first half of the tenth century until the middle of the eleventh century, Uxmal benefited from its alliance with Chichén Itzá and that this alliance was used to consolidate Uxmal's supremacy in Western Yucatán. Furthermore, Uxmal also took advantage of Uaymil, one of Chichén Itzá's seaports located on the Northern coast of Campeche and 90 kilometers directly West of Uxmal, to acquire luxury goods and merchandise that were being exchanged in the sphere of an administrative market economy in which Chichén Itzá was a key player (Cobos 2010, 2012; Cobos et al. 2005). Chichén Itzá's Sotuta ceramics might have arrived at Uxmal via Uaymil, and these connections would explain the presence of Tohil Plumbate, Silho Fine Orange, Chichen Slate, and Chichen Unslipped ceramics associated with Cehpech Puuc ceramics in different archaeological contexts in Uxmal (Ball 1979; Barrera and Huchím 1990; Cobos 2004; García Ayala 2004; Huchím and García 2000; Huchím and Toscano 1999; Konieczna and Mayer 1976; Kurjack et al. 1991; Robles 2006; Ruz 1952; Sáenz 1975, 1976).

Uxmal, Xkipché, and Kabah were occupied during the tenth and eleventh centuries. Evidence of this occupation is supported by the presence Cehpech Puuc ceramics reported at these three settlements, which coexisted with Chichen Unslipped, Chichen Slate, Silho Fine Orange, and Tohil Plumbate found at Uxmal and Xkipché, as well as Chichen Unslipped, Chichen Slate, and Silho Fine Orange reported from Kabah.

The influence of the alliance between Uxmal and Chichén Itzá also reached sites such as Kabah and Xkipché where local Cehpech Puuc ceramics are associated with Chichén Itzá's Sotuta ceramics. For instance, Cehpech Puuc Slate large jars with high, out-curving necks reported from Uxmal, Kabah, and Xkipché (Xkipché phases V and VI) show motifs and decoration very similar to the Chichen Slate jars. Moreover, Puuc Unslipped jars with long, out-curving necks and horizontal interior neck striation "replaced earlier Puuc Unslipped jars without striation and with short necks" (Vallo 2003:329). The changes that occurred in some Puuc Unslipped ceramics types suggest contemporaneity and full collaboration between Uxmal, its subordinate sites, and Chichén Itzá.

In a recent publication, Braswell et al. (2011) constructed a chronology for Xkipché using exclusively obsidian data. Braswell and colleagues (2011:140) chronology dates the end of Xkipché and Uxmal to the first half of the tenth century, but, they commented on a problem in dating by pointing out that Vallo's (2003) ceramic sequence for Xkipché (and particularly the Terminal Classic Xkipché VI phase [C.E. ca. 1000–1100]) "is at least 100 years too late" (Braswell et al. 2011:141). Although Braswell and colleagues (2011) name Cehpech and Sotuta ceramic forms as being associated with Xkipché VI phase, they comment that a modal analysis of ceramics associated with this phase lacks "the uncommon yet temporally diagnostic Sotuta types" (140–141). Braswell and colleagues (2011) seem to have missed distinctive features that reveal Sotuta types influence on Uxmal and Puuc Terminal Classic ceramics. For instance, Cehpech diagnostic types such as Puuc Slate large jars with high, out-curving necks show motifs and decoration very similar to the Chichen Slate jars, as do Puuc Unslipped jars with long, out-curving necks decorated with horizontal striation in the interior of the necks. Finally, the presence of Tohil Plumbate and obsidian (see below) during Xkipché V phase strongly suggests that Xkipché elite members participated of the administrative market economy through Uxmal. Tohil Plumbate is a common diagnostic Sotuta type that was controlled by Chichén Itzá and exchanged in Northern Maya communities whose apogee occurred in the tenth and eleventh centuries (Cobos 2004; García Moll and Cobos 2009). Tohil Plumbate was not exchanged in settlements that were either abandoned or uninhabited. In fact, at Uxmal, Tohil Plumbate has been found in a variety of structures, including the Grand Pyramid (13L3), the Round Structure (12L52), elite compounds (Structure 11N23 in the northern sector of the Birds Quadrangle [Cuadrángulo de Los Pájaros] as well as the central patio of the Nunnery Quadrangle), the northern sector of the House of the Governor's foundation, and in domestic units located in Quadrants 10O, 10P, and 11O (Barrera and Huchím 1990; García Ayala 2004; Konieczna and Mayer 1976; Kowalski 2006; Ruz 1952; Sáenz 1976).

Obsidian is another line of evidence that strongly supports the cooperation that existed between Uxmal and Chichén Itzá in the tenth and eleventh centuries. Uxmal acquired obsidian from the same ten volcanic sources utilized by Chichén Itzá (Braswell and Glascock 2007; Braswell et al. 2011). The arrival of obsidian at Uxmal from all of those sources suggests its participation in the same exchange system in which Chichén Itzá was engaged. Moreover, as the primary regional state in Western Yucatán, Uxmal seems to have regulated obsidian distribution among Puuc communities under its political and economic control. This would explain the presence at Xkipché and Kabah, both sites under direct control of Uxmal, of obsidian imported from the same sources utilized at Uxmal (Braswell and Glascock 2007; Braswell et al. 2011; Pérez de Heredia 2001:appendix II-A).

In summary, it appears that in the first half of the tenth century, just when Uxmal initiated its regional political and economic control over neighboring settlements, climatic conditions began to gradually deteriorate. However, we suggest that it was not until the eleventh century when recurrent and long drought episodes occurred more frequently and rain precipitation was not enough to produce the high agricultural production used to support the state and feed the large population residing at Uxmal. It was at this time that water from rain was not enough to fill in the aguadas and chultunes of this prehispanic community. The remarkable and extraordinary hydraulic infrastructure developed by Uxmal's ancient inhabitants to manage water became ineffective before the severe climatic change that affected the northern Maya Lowlands. Without water to drink and wet the agricultural fields, Uxmal was eventually abandoned in the middle to second half of the eleventh century.

Chichén Itzá

The permanent residents of Chichén Itzá obtained water from cenotes, caves, and wells dug at the bottom of sinkholes to reach the water table. Water for human drinking was, therefore, permanent and available all year long; however, for irrigation purposes, Chichén Itzá prehispanic farmers relied upon rainfall during the tenth and eleventh centuries. Both of these centuries are associated with the apogee of Chichén Itzá as a major political unit that dominated central and Northern Yucatán (Cobos 2003, 2004, 2010; García Moll and Cobos 2009).

Medina and colleagues (2010:257) have suggested the existence of four drought episodes dating between C.E. 800 and 950 and that these episodes were recurrent and lasted for a decade or more at time (see also Curtis et al. 1996; deMenocal 2001; Hodell, Brenner, and Curtis 2005); rainfall was reduced between 36% and 52% in comparison to rainfall values reported presently. However, archaeological evidence strongly supports the functioning of Chichén Itzá as a city and its participation within an administrative market economy throughout Mesoamerica and beyond during the last drought episode. Again, and according to our reasoning in Uxmal's case, we suggest that the people who settled Chichén Itzá made this city function when the climatic conditions gradually began to worsen. Toward the second half of the eleventh century, as a result of the long and constantly recurrent droughts, rainfall was insufficient to allow the agricultural fields produce enough food to feed the residents of Chichén Itzá. At this time, the city collapsed.

A dry environment existed during the tenth and eleventh centuries in central Yucatán where Chichén Itzá is located. The archaeological evidence found at the Holtún Cenote in Chichén Itzá demonstrates that a dry environment was replaced by a wetter environment indicating improved climatic conditions between C.E. 1100 and 1200. According to our interpretations, the surface of a limestone shelf located inside the Holtún Cenote was above the water level during the Terminal Classic period (or at the end of Period II; Table 5.1). The inhabitants of Chichén Itzá used that dry surface inside the Holtún Cenote to perform rituals and probably considered it as a "sacred place" according to their ideological perspective. They intentionally placed cultural objects and offerings on the summit of the dry limestone shelf. After the beginning of the Postclassic period (or during the beginning of Period III ca. C.E. 1100), the limestone shelf was covered by water and the archaeological evidence suggests that this event occurred rapidly.

The Holtún Cenote is located in the southern edge of Quadrant 21Y in the Northwestern section of Chichén Itzá. This cenote is surrounded by Structures 21Y27–21Y30 to its North and by the end of Causeway 40 to its South. Analysis of the ceramic materials found inside the Holtún Cenote indicates that they mostly belong to the late Sotuta ceramic complex (C.E. 900–1100), which is associated with the apogee of Chichén Itzá. Other pottery recovered from the cenote is associated with the Terminal Classic-Postclassic transition and the Postclassic. The presence of all of these ceramic materials and the association of the Holtún Cenote with Causeway 40 indicates its use both by residents of Structures 21Y27–21Y30 and by people using the causeway (Figures 5.2 and 5.3).

Water level inside the Holtún Cenote is presently 21 meters below ground surface. From this water level, the bottom of the cenote is found 50 meters deep. Access to the interior of the Holtún Cenote is through a rectangular opening measuring 3.00 meters long by 2.70 meters wide. Whoever utilized the Holtún Cenote for ceremonies and rituals probably used ropes to slide down from the ground surface to reach the water. Once in the water, some sort of floating device might have been employed to transport people and objects closer to the Western wall of the Holtún Cenote where a considerable number of archaeological objects were placed upon a limestone shelf.

The Holtún Cenote limestone shelf is currently underwater. One meter of water covers that natural feature near the Southwestern area of the cenote, but five to six meters of water rise above the shelf to the Northeast. The limestone shelf measures 16 meters long by six meters wide and follows the natural contour of the cenote's wall. A detailed analysis of the archaeological contexts inside the cenote suggests that the cultural objects found inside got there by two ways. First, objects were carefully and orderly placed along the 16 meters of dry limestone shelf. Second, objects were thrown from the ground entrance into the cenote waters; these objects rest deep within the bottom of the cenote.

Some of the objects found on the Holtún Cenote limestone shelf include: human skulls, pelvis, and femurs; the skull of a dog associated with a human tibia; bifacial knives made of chert; sculptures of porta-estandarte and atlantean figures; jade beads, stingrays, spindle whorls, and charcoal. Ceramic analysis of the pottery found on the limestone shelf reveals late Sotuta (C.E. 900–1100) materials and a variety of jars of the following ceramic types: Dzibiac Red, Timak Composite, Dzitas Slate, Sisal Unslipped, Silho Fine Orange, and Muna Slate.

The careful array and spatial distribution of the objects along the limestone shelf indicates that these cultural materials were placed there when that surface was dry and the water level was below this feature. Based upon current evidence, we cannot determine if this cultural material was placed during a relatively short period of time or throughout several decades. What we are sure of is that these materials were placed on a dry limestone shelf during the Terminal Classic period at a time when Chichén Itzá was a functioning city and the most important political unit of central Yucatán (Cobos 2004, 2010; García Moll and Cobos 2009).

Artifacts that were tossed into the cenote from the ground surface comprise a second group of cultural objects that were introduced into the Holtún Cenote. After the objects were thrown away into the cenote, they sank to a debris mound covered by water, falling down until they came to rest at different depths. Apparently, the water reduced the impact and spread of the objects tossed from ground level. It is worth mentioning that the limestone shelf and the debris mound are separated by more than ten meters, so the cultural artifacts found on the limestone shelf could not have reached their present context if they had been thrown into the cenote from above.

An analysis of the pottery vessels associated with the debris mound shows the presence of Peto Cream jars dating to the late Terminal Classic and Early Postclassic periods; Chen Mul molded and Mama Red jars belonging to the Postclassic period are also present (Figure 5.4).

Peto Cream, Chen Mul molded, and Mama Red ceramics have also been reported from the Sacred Cenote. Thus, after C.E. 1100, Chichén Itzá inhabitants were using both bodies of water to perform ritual practices and ceremonies that involved tossing objects into the water from the ground surface.

The archaeological evidence reported from Chichén Itzá corroborates the proposal that after C.E. 1100, climatic conditions improved in the Yucatán Peninsula (Curtis et al. 1996; Hodell, Brenner, Curtis et al. 2005; Medina et al. 2010). The decrease of oxygen isotopes values indicates wet environmental conditions, an event known worldwide as the "Little Ice Age." The rise of the water level recorded in the Holtún Cenote suggests that plentiful rain returned to the Yucatán Peninsula after two and a half centuries of long and recurrent droughts that affected the northern Maya Lowlands during the Terminal Classic period. The archaeological evidence from Chichén Itzá suggests that severe droughts occurred in Yucatán during the eleventh century—and not only in the middle of the tenth century. We acknowledge that the droughts might have started sometime in the ninth century and that it was a gradual drying process that reached its peak after C.E. 1000.

When the top of the Holtún Cenote limestone shelf was used for ritual practices and ceremonies, it would have had to occur after a period of severe drought in central Yucatán. During the Terminal Classic period, the climatic change that affected the Yucatán Peninsula had already begun and Chichén Itzá farmers would have realized during the tenth century that drought episodes continued to increased and last longer. For a society whose members depended on the agricultural production to feed themselves, the lack of abundant rainfall to irrigate their agricultural fields would have had a dramatic impact leading to the collapse of the city of Chichén Itzá at the end of the eleventh century. In other words, the severe drought ended the agricultural surplus that helped to support a hierarchical society. Without the benefit of the rainfall, the surplus-dependent socioeconomic hierarchy collapsed in the eleventh century, as well as the rest of the society.

Conclusion

Archaeological data and evidence of climatic change have been used to posit the collapse of Uxmal and Chichén Itzá as a result of long and recurrent drought episodes in the eleventh century. Although environmental evidence indicates that drought episodes might have begun in the ninth century, they gradually increased in frequency through the eleventh century and generated devastating effects on the late Terminal Classic permanent dwellers of Uxmal and Chichén Itzá. With the worsening of climatic conditions in the northern Maya Lowlands in the eleventh century, rainwater could neither fill the aguadas and chultunes at Uxmal and Chichén Itzá, nor irrigate the agricultural fields of these two prehispanic communities. The drastic drop off in rainfall seriously affected the functioning of Uxmal and Chichén Itzá, whose large populations depended on abundant rainwater to produce enough food to feed not only the non-farmers, but also farmers as well.

The year C.E. 950 has been suggested by Medina and colleagues (2010) as dating one of the long and recurrent drought episodes. However, our interpretation of the archaeological evidence suggests that population lasted for a century or century and a half beyond C.E. 950 at both Uxmal and Chichén Itzá. We agree with Medina and colleagues (2010) in acknowledging severe drought episodes in the ninth and tenth century, but the interpretation of the archaeological record suggests that these episodes were part of a gradual process that reached its peak in the eleventh century. We acknowledge that environmental conditions had worsened during the tenth and part of the eleventh centuries, and rain precipitation was not copious in Northern Yucatán. Settlements such as Uxmal and Chichén Itzá reached their political, social, economic, and cultural apogees at the same time when environmental conditions deteriorated. Furthermore, ascribing the collapse of Uxmal and Chichén Itzá to climatic change in the eleventh century complements Dunning and Beach's (2010) explanation of the effects of environmental change during the Terminal Classic period in the northern Lowlands.

Archaeological evidence reported from the Holtún Cenote at Chichén Itzá shows two moments of the climatic change that affected Northern Yucatán. First, it corroborates the existence of extreme dry environmental conditions during the Terminal Classic period, or toward the end of Period II, as is demonstrated by the placement of cultural materials on a dry natural limestone shelf within the cenote. Second, the water level rose inside the Holtún Cenote when environmental conditions turned wetter at the beginning of the Postclassic period, or Period III (after C.E. 1100). Apparently, the rise of the water level occurred rapidly and the natural limestone shelf and the debris mound inside the cenote were completely submerged under water. The association of Postclassic ceramic vessels with the debris mound suggests that they were dropped into the cenote from the ground surface.

Finally, environmental change has affected and continues to affect the earth; this is an unstoppable process and is part of our planet's natural evolution. Apparently, Classic period Maya civilization experienced environmental change, but could neither explain how and why it occurred nor face it in a successful manner. Contemporary twenty first century society, however, with its broad and vast scientific knowledge acquired through several centuries, can look back in time and manage explanations as to how and why environmental changed happened. The archaeological and environmental reconstructions of the ancient Yucatán Peninsula are useful today in helping us understand how large populations inhabiting outsized settlements depend on excellent climatic conditions and water to develop. A change or changes in climatic conditions might result in a negative effect in rain precipitation, leading to the reduction or full desiccation of water sources.

Currently, large populations live in full-size cities and due to changes in climatic conditions, water has once again become a key resource for the survival of those settlements. A lesson that we can learn from the prehispanic Maya is that it is not enough to know how to manage abundant water, but also how to manage this vital resource when it becomes insufficient or scarce. Twenty-first century technology, along with the enormous knowledge acquired over the centuries by humankind, should help us manage water at a time when it is in short supply due to extreme climatic conditions. If this occurs, our knowledge of the past might help us in the present to face climatic change in a successful manner before—long before—our own civilization collapses.

Acknowledgments

Research at the Holtún Cenote is part of the "Chichén Itzá: estudio de la comunidad Clásico Tardío" project sponsored by the Instituto Nacional de Antropología e Historia (INAH) and the Universidad Autónoma de Yucatán (UADY). We thank Alfonso de María y Campos, director of INAH, M.V.Z Alfredo Dájer Abimerhi, Rector of UADY, and Dra. Genny Negroe Sierra, Directora de la Facultad de Ciencias Antropológicas, for their support.

References Cited

Abrams, Elliot M., Ann Corinne Freter, David Rue, and J. Wingard
1996 The Role of Deforestation in the Collapse of the Late Classic Copán Maya site. *In* Tropical Deforestation: The Human Dimension. L. Sponsel, T. Headland, and R. Bailey, eds. Pp. 56–75. New York: Columbia University Press.

Aimers, James J.
2007 What Maya Collapse? Terminal Classic Variation in the Maya Lowlands. Journal of Archaeological Research 15:329–377.

Andrews, Anthony P., E. Wyllys Andrews V, and Fernando Robles C.
2003 The Northern Maya Collapse and Its Aftermath. Ancient Mesoamerica 14:151–156.

Andrews, George F.
1986 Los Estilos Arquitectónicos del Puuc, Una Nueva Apreciación. Colección Científica 150, Serie Arqueología. México, D.F.: Instituto Nacional de Antropología e Historia.

Andrews, E. Wyllys, IV, and E. Wyllys Andrews, V
1980 Excavations at Dzibilchaltun, Yucatán, México. Middle American Research Institute Publication, 48. New Orleans: Tulane University.

Andrews, E. Wyllys, V, and Barbara W. Fash
1992 Continuity and Change in a Royal Maya Residential Complex at Copan. Ancient Mesoamerica 3:63–88.

Ball, Joseph W.
1979 Ceramics, Culture History, and the Puuc Tradition: Some Alternative Possibilities. *In* The Puuc: New Perspectives. L. Mills, ed. Pp. 18–35. Scholarly Studies in the Liberal Arts, 1. Pella, IA: Central College.

Barrera Rubio, Alfredo
1991 La gran plataforma del Palacio del Gobernador de Uxmal. *In* Cuadernos de Arquitectura Mesoamericana 12:41–56.0 México, D.F.: Facultad de Arquitectura, Universidad Nacional Autónoma de México.

Barrera Rubio, Alfredo, and José Huchím Herrera
1989 Exploraciones recientes en Uxmal (1986–1987). Memorias del II Coloquio Internacional de Mayistas Volume I. Pp. 265–286. México, D.F.: Instituto de Investigaciones Filológicas, Centro de Estudios Mayas, Universidad Nacional Autónoma de México.
1990 Restauración Arquitectónica en Uxmal, 1986–1987. University of Pittsburgh Latin American Archaeology Reports Number 1. Pittsburgh: Department of Anthropology, University of Pittsburgh.

Braswell, Geoffrey E., and Michael D. Glascock
2007 El Intercambio de la Obsidiana y el Desarrollo de las Economías de Tipo Mercado en la Región Maya. *In* XX Simposio de Investigaciones Arqueológicas en Guatemala 2006. Juan Pedro Laporte, Bárbara Arroyo y Héctor Mejía, eds. Pp. 15–28. Guatemala: Museo Nacional de Arqueología y Etnología.

Braswell, Geoffrey E., Iken Paap, and Michael D. Glascock
2011 The Obsidian and Ceramics of the Puuc Region: Chronology, Lithic Procurement, and Production at Xkipche, Yucatan, Mexico. Ancient Mesoamerica 22:135–154.

Bricker, Harvey M., and Victoria R. Bricker

1996 Astronomical References in the Throne Inscription of the Palace of the Governor at Uxmal. Cambridge Archaeological Journal 6:191–229.

2000 La Inscripción del Trono del Palacio del Gobernador en Uxmal. *In* Arquitectura e Ideología de los Antiguos Mayas: Memoria de la Segunda Mesa Redonda de Palenque. Silvia Trejo, ed. Pp. 213–230. México, D.F.: Consejo Nacional para la Cultura y las Artes e Instituto Nacional de Antropología e Historia.

Carmean, Kelli, Nicholas Dunning, and Jeff Karl Kowalski

2004 High Times in the Hill Country: A Perspective from the Terminal Classic Puuc Region. *In* The Terminal Classic in the Maya Lowlands: Collapse, Transition, and Transformation. Arthur A. Demarest, Prudence M. Rice, and Don S. Rice, eds. Pp. 424–449. Boulder: University Press of Colorado.

Carrasco Vargas, Ramón

1993 Formación Sociopolítica en el Puuc: El Sacbe Uxmal-Nohpat-Kabah. *In* Perspectivas Antropológicas en el Mundo Maya. María Josefa Iglesias Ponce de León and Francesc Ligorred Perramón, eds. Pp. 199–211. Publicaciones de la Sociedad Española de Estudios Mayas, 2. Spain: Catalunya.

Carrasco Vargas, Ramón, and Eduardo Pérez de Heredia

1996 Los Últimos Gobernantes de Kabah. *In* Eighth Palenque Round Table, 1993. Martha J. Macri and Jane McHargue, eds. Pp. 297–307. San Francisco: The Pre-Columbian Art Research Institute.

Cobos, Rafael

2003 Antiguas Formas de Comunidad y Complejidad Social en Chichén Itzá, Yucatán. *In* El Urbanismo en Mesoamérica, Volume 1. William T. Sanders, Alba Guadalupe Mastache, and Robert H. Cobean, eds. Pp. 451–472. México, D.F.: Instituto Nacional de Antropología e Historia.

2004 Chichén Itzá: Settlement and Hegemony during the Terminal Classic Period. *In* The Terminal Classic in the Maya Lowlands: Collapse, Transition, and Transformation. Arthur A. Demarest, Prudence M. Rice, and Don S. Rice, eds. Pp. 517–544. Boulder: University Press of Colorado.

2007 Multepal or Centralized kingship? New Evidence of Governmental Organization at Chichén Itzá. *In* Twin Tollans: Chichén Itzá, Tula, and the Toltecs. Jeff Karl Kowalsky and Cynthia Kristan-Graham, eds. Pp. 315–343. Washington, DC: Dumbarton Oaks.

2010 Más allá del Centro de Yucatán: Reconstruyendo el Dominio Territorial de Chichén Itzá en las Tierras Bajas Mayas del Norte. *In* VI Coloquio Pedro Bosch Gimpera. Edith Ortiz Díaz, ed. Pp. 333–348. México, D.F.: Instituto de Investigaciones Antropológicas, Universidad Nacional Autónoma de México.

2012 La Arqueología de Uaymil, una Comunidad Costera del Norte de Campeche. *In* Arqueología de la Costa de Campeche: La Época Prehispánica. R. Cobos, ed. Pp. 319–329. Mérida: Ediciones de la Universidad Autónoma de Yucatán.

Cobos, Rafael, Lilia Fernández Souza, and Nancy Peniche May

2005 Las Columnatas de Uaymil: su Función durante el Clásico Terminal. Los Investigadores de la Cultura Maya 13(1):245–253. Campeche: Universidad Autónoma de Campeche.

Coggins, Clemency C.

1992 Artifacts from the Cenote of Sacrifice Chichen Itza, Yucatan. Memoirs of the Peabody Museum of Archaeology and Ethnology, 10(3). Cambridge: Harvard University.

Culbert, T. Patrick

1995 Población, Subsistencia y el Colapso de los Mayas del Clásico. *In* VIII Simposio de Investigaciones Arqueológicas en Guatemala, 1994. Juan Pedro Laporte and Héctor Escobedo, eds. Pp. 666–672. Guatemala: Museo Nacional de Arqueología y Etnología.

Curtis, John H., David A. Hodell, and Mark Brenner

1996 Climate Variability on the Yucatan Peninsula (Mexico) during the Past 3500 Years, and Implications for Maya Cultural Evolution. Quaternary Research 46:37–47.

Dahlin, Bruce H.

2002 Climate Change and the End of the Classic Period in Yucatán. Ancient Mesoamerica 13:327–340.

Demarest, Arthur A., Prudence M. Rice, and Don S. Rice, eds.
2004 The Terminal Classic in the Maya Lowlands: Collapse, Transition, and Transformation. Boulder: University Press of Colorado.

Demarest, Arthur A., Matt O'Mansky, Nicholas Dunning, and Timothy Beach
2004 ¿Catastrofismo, Procesos Ecológicos o Crisis Política? Hacia una Mejor Metodología para la Interpretación del "Colapso" de la Civilización Maya Clásica. *In* XVII Simposio de Investigaciones Arqueológicas en Guatemala, 2003. J. P. Laporte, B. Arroyo, H. Escobedo, and H. Mejía, eds. Pp. 478–501. Guatemala: Museo Nacional de Arqueología y Etnología.

DeMenocal, Peter B.
2001 Cultural Responses to Climate Change during the Late Holocene. Science 292:667–673.

Dunning, Nicholas P.
1992 Lords of the Hills: Ancient Maya Settlement in the Puuc Region, Yucatán, México. Monographs in World Archaeology, 15. Madison: Prehistory Press.

Dunning, Nicholas P., and Timothy Beach
2010 Farms and Forests: Spatial and Temporal Perspectives on Ancient Maya Landscapes. *In* Landscapes and Societies. I. P. Martini and W. Chesworth, eds. Pp. 369–389. New York: Springer Science and Business Media B. V.

Dunning, Nicholas P., and Jeff Kowalski
1994 Lords of the Hills: Classic Maya Settlement Patterns and Political Iconography in the Puuc Region. Ancient Mesoamerica 5:63–95.

Fash, William L., E. Wyllys Andrews V, and T. Kam Manahan
2004 Political Decentralization, Dynastic Collapse, and the Early Postclassic in the Urban Center of Copán, Honduras. *In* The Terminal Classic in the Maya Lowlands: Collapse, Transition, and Transformation. Arthur A. Demarest, Prudence M. Rice, and Don S. Rice, eds. Pp. 260–287. Boulder: University Press of Colorado.

Gallareta Negrón, Tomás
2000 Sequía y Colapso de las Ciudades Mayas del Puuc. INAJ 11:13–21. México: CONACULTA/INAH.

García Ayala, César A.
2004 Unidades Habitacionales en la Región del Puuc: Análisis de los Conjuntos Ich y Koot de Uxmal, Yucatán. Tesis de Licenciatura, Facultad de Ciencias Antropológicas. Mérida: Universidad Autónoma de Yucatán.

García Barrios, Ana
2008 Chaahk, el Dios de la Lluvia, en el Período Clásico Maya: Aspectos Religiosos y Políticos. Memoria para optar al grado de Doctor. Facultad de Geografía e Historia. Madrid: Universidad Complutense.
2009 El Aspecto Bélico de Chaahk, el Dios de la Lluvia, en el Período Clásico Maya. Revista Española de Antropología Americana 39:7–29.

García Moll, Roberto, and Rafael Cobos
2009 Chichén Itzá, Patrimonio de la Humanidad. México, D.F.: Grupo Azabache.

Garza Tarazona, Silvia, and Edward B. Kurjack
1980 Atlas Arqueológico del Estado de Yucatán, vols. 1–2. México, D.F.: Instituto Nacional de Antropología e Historia.

Gendrop, Paul
1983 Los Estilos Río Bec, Chenes y Puuc en la Arquitectura Maya. México, D.F.: Universidad Nacional Autónoma de México.

Gill, Richardson B.
2000 The Great Maya Droughts: Water, Life, and Death. Albuquerque: University of New Mexico Press.

Graham, Ian
1992 Corpus of Maya Hieroglyphic Inscriptions, vol. 4 part 2: Uxmal. Peabody Museum of Archaeology and Ethnology, Harvard University. Cambridge.

Hodell, David A., Mark Brenner, and John H. Curtis
2005 Terminal Classic Drought in the Northern Maya Lowlands Inferred from Multiple Sediment Cores in Lake Chichancanab (Mexico). Quaternary Science Review 24:1413–1427.

Hodell, David A., Mark Brenner, John H. Curtis, Roger Medina-Gonzalez, Enrique I. Chan Chan, Alma Albornoz-Pat, and Thomas P. Guilderson
2005 Climate Change on the Yucatan Peninsula during the Little Ice Age. Quaternary Research 63:109–121.

Hodell, David A., Jason H. Curtis, and Mark Brenner
1995 Possible Role of Climate in the Collapse of Classic Maya Civilization. Nature 375:391–394.

Huchím Herrera, José, and César García Ayala
2000 La Arquitectura que Denota una Ocupación Tardía en Uxmal, Yucatán. Los Investigadores de la Cultura Maya 8(1):138–154. Campeche: Universidad Autónoma de Campeche.

Huchím Herrera, José, and Lourdes Toscano Hernández
1999 El Cuadrángulo de los Pájaros de Uxmal. Arqueología Mexicana 37:18–23.

Isendahl, Christian
2002 Common Knowledge: Lowland Maya Urban Farming at Xuch. Studies in Global Archaeology, 1. Department of Archaeology and Ancient History. Uppsala: Uppsala University.

Konieczna, Bárbara, and Pablo Mayer Guala
1976 Uxmal, Yucatán, Informe de la Temporada 1973–1974. *In* Investigaciones Arqueológicas en el Sureste. B. Konieczna and P. Mayer, eds. Pp. 1–18. Cuadernos de los Centros No. 27 (Dirección de Centros Regionales, Centro Regional del Sureste). México, D.F.: Instituto Nacional de Antropología e Historia.

Kowalski, Jeff K.
1987 The House of the Governor: A Maya Palace. Norman: University of Oklahoma Press.
1994 The Puuc as Seen from Uxmal. *In* Hidden among the Hills: The Archaeology of Northwestern Yucatán. Hanns J. Prem, ed. Pp. 93–120. Acta Mesoamericana, 7. Möckmül: Verlag von Flemming.
2003 Collaboration and Conflict: An Interpretation of the Relationship between Uxmal and Chichén Itzá during the Terminal Classic/Early Postclassic Periods. *In* Escondido en la Selva. Hanns J. Prem, ed. Pp. 235–272. Colección Obra Diversa. México, D.F.: Instituto Nacional de Antropología e Historia.
2006 ¿Destrucción? Una Interpretación de Uxmal, Chichén Itzá y el Abandono de las Ciudades del Puuc. *In* Los Mayas de Ayer y Hoy: Memorias del Primer Congreso Internacional de Cultura Maya, vol. 1. A. Barrera Rubio and R. Gubler, eds. Pp. 305–339. Yucatán-Cultur, CONACULTA-Instituto Nacional de Antropología e Historia. Mérida: Universidad Autónoma de Yucatán.

Kowalski, Jeff K., Alfredo Barrera R., Heber Ojeda M., and José Huchím H.
1996 Archaeological Excavations of a Round Temple at Uxmal: Summary Discussion and Implications for Northern Maya Culture History. *In* Palenque Round Table, 1993. Martha J. Macri and Jan McHargue, eds. Pp. 281–296. San Francisco: Pre-Columbian Art Research Institute.

Kurjack, Edward B.
1979 Sacbeob: Parentesco y Desarrollo del Estado Maya. XV Mesa Redonda. Vol. 1. Pp. 117–239. México, D.F.: Sociedad Mexicana de Antropología.

Kurjack, Edward B., and Silvia Garza T.
1981 Pre-Columbian Community Form and Distribution in the Northern Maya Area. *In* Lowland Maya Settlement Patterns. Wendy Ashmore, ed. Pp. 287–309. Albuquerque: University of New Mexico Press.

Kurjack, Edward B., Rubén Maldonado C., and Merle Green Robertson
1991 Ballcourts of the Northern Maya Lowlands. *In* The Mesoamerican Ballgame. Vernon L. Scarborough and David R. Wilcox, eds. Pp. 145–159. Tucson: University of Arizona Press.

Leyden, Barbara W., Mark Brenner, and Bruce H. Dahlin
1998 Cultural and Climatic History of Cobá, a Lowland Maya City in Quintana Roo, Mexico. Quaternary Research 49:111–122.

Manahan, T. Kam
2004 The Way Things Fall Apart: Social Organization and the Classic Maya Collapse at Copan. Ancient Mesoamerica 15:107–125.

McAnany, Patricia A., and Tomás Gallareta Negrón
2010 Bellicose Rulers and Climatological Peril? *In* Questioning Collapse. Human Resilience,

Ecological Vulnerability, and the Aftermath of Empire. P.A. McAnany and Norman Yoffee, eds. Pp. 142–175. New York: Cambridge University Press.

Medina Elizalde, Martín, Stephen J. Burnsa, David W. Lea, Yemane Asmerom, Lucien von Gunten, Victor Polyak, Mathias Vuille, and Ambarish Karmalkar
2010 High Resolution Stalagmite Climate Record from the Yucatán Peninsula Spanning the Maya Terminal Classic Period. Earth and Planetary Science Letters 298:255–262.

Metcalfe, Sarah, Ann Breen, Malcolm Murray, Peter Furley, Anthony Fallick, and Angus McKenzie
2009 Environmental Change in Northern Belize since the Latest Pleistocene. Journal of Quaternary Science 26:627–641.

Paine, Richard R., and Ann Corinne Freter
1996 Environmental Degradation and the Classic Maya Collapse at Copan, Honduras (A.D. 600–1250). Ancient Mesoamerica 7:37–47.

Pérez de Heredia Puente, Eduardo J.
2001 El Edificio de Manos Rojas de Kabah, Yucatán: Datos para la Cronología. Tesis de Licenciatura, Facultad de Ciencias Antropológicas. Mérida: Universidad Autónoma de Yucatán.

Prem, Hanns J.
2003 Aspectos de los patrones de asentamiento en la región Puuc central. *In* Escondido en la Selva. Hanns J. Prem, ed. Pp. 273–308. Colección Obra Diversa. México, D.F.: Instituto Nacional de Antropología e Historia.

Prem, Hanns J., and Nicholas P. Dunning
2004 Investigations at Hunto Chac, Yucatán. Mexicon 26:26–36.

Proskouriakoff, Tatiana
1950 A Study of Classic Maya Sculpture. Publication 593. Washington, DC: Carnegie Institution of Washington.

Reindel, Markus
1998 El Abandono de las Ciudades Puuc en el Norte de Yucatán. *In* 50 Años de Estudios Americanistas en la Universidad de Bonn. Sabine Dedenbach-Salazar Sáenz, Carmen Arellano Hoffman, Eva Köning, andy Heiko Prümers, eds. Pp. 239–257. Bonner Amerikanistische Studien 30. Bonn: Verlag Anton Saurwein.
2003 El Apogeo de la Arquitectura Puuc. Evolución de una Cultura Regional del Clásico Tardío en el Norte del Área Maya. *In* Escondido en la Selva. Hanns J. Prem, ed. Pp. 79–96. Colección Obra Diversa. México, D.F.: Instituto Nacional de Antropología e Historia.

Ringle, William, George Bey, and Carlos Peraza
1991 An Itza Empire in Northern Yucatán: A Neighboring View. Paper presented at the 47th International Congress of Americanists, New Orleans, Louisiana. May.

Robles Castellanos, Fernando
2006 Las Esferas Cerámicas Cehpech y Sotuta del Apogeo del Clásico Tardío en el Norte de la Península de Yucatán. *In* La Producción Alfarera en el México Antiguo, vol. 3: La Alfarería del Clásico Tardío (700–1200 d.C.). Beatriz Leonor Merino Carrión and Ángel García Cook, eds. Pp. 281–344. México, D.F.: Instituto Nacional de Antropología e Historia.

Ruz Lhuiller, Alberto
1952 Uxmal: Temporada de Trabajos 1951–1952. Manuscript. México, D.F.: Archivo Técnico de Monumentos Prehispánicos del Instituto Nacional de Antropología e Historia.

Sáenz, César A.
1975 Exploraciones y Reconstrucciones en la Gran Pirámide de Uxmal, Yucatán. Boletín del INAH 12:39–44. México, D.F.: INAH.
1976 Cerámica de Uxmal, Yucatán. Anales del INAH, 5(53):171–186. México, D.F.: INAH-SEP.

Shaw, Justine M.
2003 Climate Change and Deforestation. Ancient Mesoamerica 14:157–167.

Torrescano, Nuria, and Gerald A. Islebe
2006 Tropical Forest and Mangrove History from Southeastern Mexico: A 5000 Yr Pollen Record and Implications for Sea Level Rise. Vegetation History and Archaeobotany 15:191–195.

Vallo, Michael
2003 Xkipché Ceramics: On Current Data, Methods, Results and Problems. *In* Escondido en la Selva.

Hanns J. Prem, ed. Pp. 309–338. Colección Obra Diversa. México, D.F.: Instituto Nacional de Antropología e Historia.

Walters, Rachel E., and Jeff Karl Kowalski
2000 Los Murales de Mulchic: La Guerra y la Formación de un Estado Regional Puuc. *In* La Guerra entre los Antiguos Mayas: Memoria de la Primera Mesa Redonda de Palenque. Silvia Trejo, ed. Pp. 205–223. México, D.F.: Consejo Nacional para la Cultura y las Artes e Instituto Nacional de Antropología e Historia.

Webster, David
2012 The Classic Maya Collapse. *In* The Oxford Handbook of Mesoamerican Archaeology. Deborah L. Nichols and Christopher A. Pool, ed. Pp. 324–334. Oxford: Oxford University Press.

Webster, David, William T. Sanders, and Peter van Rossum
1992 A Simulation of Copan Population History and Its Implications. Ancient Mesoamerica 3:185–197.

Yager, Jason, and David A. Hodell
2008 The Collapse of Maya Civilization: Assessing the Interaction of Culture, Climate, and Environment. *In* El Niño, Catastrophism, and Culture Change in Ancient America. Daniel H. Sandweiss and Jeffrey Quilter, eds. Pp. 187–242. Washington, DC: Dumbarton Oaks.

Zubrow, Ezra B. W., Michael P. Smyth, David Ortegón Z., Nicholas P. Dunning, and Eric W. Weaver
2010 Paleoclimatic Reconstruction and Archaeological Investigations at Xcoch and the Puuc Region of Yucatan, Mexico: Exploratory Research into Arctic Climate Change and Maya Culture Processes. 2009–2010 Preliminary Report for the Early-Concept Grants for Exploratory Research, Artic Social Sciences Program. Washington, DC: National Science Foundation.

6

A Reassessment of Water and Soil Resources in the Flatlands of the Northern Maya Lowlands

Scott L. Fedick
University of California, Riverside

ABSTRACT

Often characterized as a low, flat, limestone shelf with thin soils and restricted water resources, the northern lowlands are now proving to have supported high population levels and complex social development from the earliest Preclassic times through the Postclassic, though striking differences in developmental trajectories exist. The karstic plain of the north-central portion of the Yucatán Peninsula is characterized by the presence of dry depressions or *rejolladas* with wells, cenotes, and caves with water. The spatial distribution of these hydrological features played a key role in the occupation of the region since the Late Preclassic period, while the archaeological data suggest population growth during the eighth and ninth centuries C.E., reaching its peak in the tenth and eleventh centuries. Various agricultural technologies provided adaptations to the resource base, while the general settlement history may be linked to the dynamics of water-table fluctuations and resulting suitability of the wetlands for subsistence production. [Maya, archaeology, Yucatan Peninsula, rejolladas, hydrology]

To fully understand issues of resilience and vulnerability of ancient landscapes one must have an accurate perception of their attributes. This contribution will begin a reassessment of subsistence resources in the northern flatlands of the Yucatan Peninsula that could alter our perceptions of resilience and vulnerability of this landscape under changing trajectories of cultural development and climate change.

All agricultural systems are dependent primarily on two fundamental elements: soil and water. The northern flatlands of the Yucatan Peninsula are generally characterized as severely lacking in both of these resources. The physical environment of the Maya Lowlands as a whole has long been misunderstood through the eyes of the non-Maya visitor, conqueror, farmer, scientist—and archaeologist (Fedick 2003). Perhaps the most misunderstood area within the Maya Lowlands are the flatlands that make up the far northern Yucatan Peninsula, defined herein as the contiguous area of the northern peninsula that falls below 40 meters elevation, and is constrained on the south primarily by the foothills of the Sierrita del Ticul, or Puuc hills (Figure 6.1).

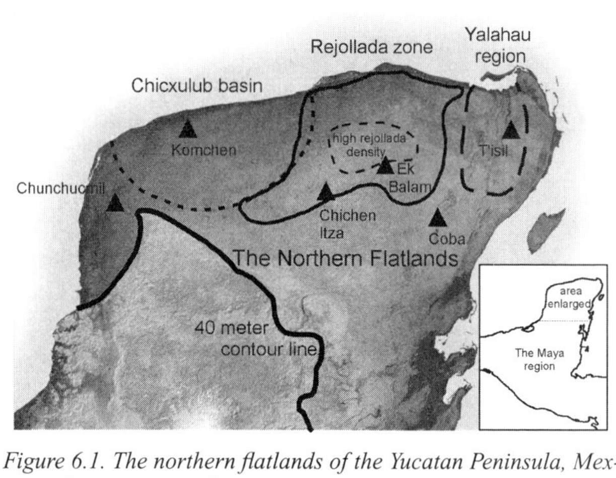

Figure 6.1. The northern flatlands of the Yucatan Peninsula, Mexico with partitions and sites mentioned in text. Background shaded relief image courtesy of SRTM Team/NASA/JPL/NIMA, image acquired February 2000.

These misperceptions of the northern flatlands have their roots in Spanish and Mexican domination of the region that included a long history of failed experiments

ARCHEOLOGICAL PAPERS OF THE AMERICAN ANTHROPOLOGICAL ASSOCIATION, Vol. 24, pp. 72–83, ISSN 1551-823X, online ISSN 1551-8248. DOI: 10.1111/apaa.12030.

in commercial-scale agricultural production. Diego De Landa, bishop of Yucatan in the 16th century, provided an oft-quoted description of the landscape of the northern flatlands: "Yucatan is the country with the least earth that I have seen, since all of it is one living rock and has wonderfully little earth" (Tozzer 1941:186). The Spaniards of Colonial times found little of the land to be arable, meaning literally that it could not be plowed due to the shallowness of the soil over limestone bedrock. The region was considered of little value for "proper" agriculture, as practiced in Spain at the time (Alonso de Herrera 2006[1513]).

In the 16th century, indigo (*Indigofera suffruticosa*) plantations flourished for a short time, until the industry was banned by the government in 1581 because of dire health consequences among the Maya, who were forced to run the mills and wade in the vats of dye (Patch 2003:564). The Spanish also found limited success in the northern flatlands with non-indigenous crops such as rice, which proved to be an important commercial crop during the 18th century, at least in limited areas of Campeche and Yucatan where soils suitable for rice cultivation were found (Patch 2003:566). After experimentation with establishing sugarcane plantations as early as 1530, the crop came to be widely cultivated in the northern peninsula from the final decades of the Colonial period, up until the time that harsh treatment of Maya workers in the cane fields proved one of the major factors leading to Maya rebellion and the outbreak of the Caste War in 1847 (Patch 2003:566–568). The final burst of commercial crop production in the northern peninsula was the henequen (*Agave fourcroydes*) boom of the late 19th to early 20th centuries (Peniche Rivero 2003). An ancient native domesticate (Colunga-GarcíaMarín 2003), henequen produced much wealth for non-Maya plantation owners, while leading to deforestation in much of the northern peninsula. The henequen industry fell into decline with the Mexican Revolution and the decreasing demand for rope to rig sailing ships. Nearly all henequen plantations were abandoned by 1950. The 20th century also saw the final blow to the commercial agricultural potential of the northern Yucatan Peninsula as agricultural scientists from the United States declared the region to be nearly useless for modern agriculture, as perceived by the United States Department of Agriculture (and relayed to archaeologists working in the region; e.g., Morley 1946:141–150, 448).

The other perceived limiting factor to agriculture, and to human subsistence in general in the northern peninsula, is water. Most descriptions of the northern lowlands state that no significant rivers are to be found, and that the only natural sources of freshwater are the *cenotes*, or natural wells, that characterize the region. Rain is generally cited as the only additional source of water. Adding to the apparent hostility to human presence in the northern peninsula is a pattern of annual precipitation that leaves the land without significant rain for several months of the year. As a result, much of the northernmost peninsula has vegetation that is adapted to arid conditions (Gómez-Pompa 1998).

A Reassessment of Water Resources

Given the failure of the European colonizers in agricultural development, how did the ancient Maya manage to live off this land, and support populations much greater than those of historic and modern times?

It would surprise most archaeologists to know that hydrologists have recently determined that the Yucatan Peninsula has the greatest reserve of water in Mexico (Delgado et al. 2010). While it is true that there are no significant rivers on the surface of the northern lowlands, there actually are major rivers located underground. These underground rivers originated as cavern systems that are now below the water table due to rising sea levels. In Quintana Roo, numerous underground river systems have been identified and explored, including the longest underground rivers in the world (Gabriel et al. 2009; Smart et al. 2006).

The cenotes of the northern peninsula are well known. These features originally formed as caves when sea levels, and the inland water table, were much lower. Water levels rose and cave ceilings collapsed, leaving cenotes as openings to the aquifer. In some cases, cenotes provide links between the surface and underground rivers. The number of cenotes in the Yucatan Peninsula is not well defined, though estimates range up to 7,000 in the northwest peninsula alone (Schmitter-Soto et al. 2002). Even after advanced remote sensing technologies are applied, on-the-ground low-tech survey reveals that many cenotes with access to groundwater remain undetected by these modern technologies (e.g., Winemiller 2007). In northern Quintana Roo, dozens of cenotes are shown on 1:50,000 topographic maps, yet surveys in the Yalahau region (see Figure 6.1) indicate that only a small fraction of cenotes are included on the existing maps. The future application of LiDAR (Light Detecting and Ranging) mapping holds the promise of detecting cenote openings with a high degree of resolution (Chase et al. 2012; Weishampel et al. 2011).

The Yalahau region, besides having an abundance of cenotes, is characterized by an extensive freshwater wetland system that covers about 134 square kilometers. The surface water of the Yalahau wetlands is not typical swamp water; it is crystal clear and represents the partially exposed water table of the Holbox-Xel Ha aquifer that is today pumped to supply all of the freshwater needs of the Cancun-to-Tulum

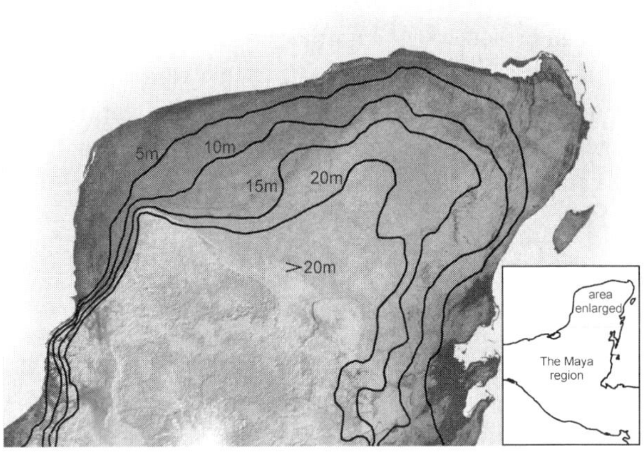

Figure 6.2. Depth to water table with 5 meter contour lines. Background shaded relief image courtesy of SRTM Team/NASA/JPL/NIMA, image acquired February 2000.

resort area (Perry et al. 2003; Tulaczyk et al. 1993). The ancient Maya engineered the Yalahau wetlands for subsistence production (Fedick et al. 2000; Fedick et al. 2010; Leonard 2010).

Additional sources of surface water in the northern flatlands that are often overlooked include about 60 freshwater lakes: 50 in Quintana Roo and 10 in Yucatan (Index Mundi 2012). But the major water reserves of the Yucatan Peninsula, the largest water reserve in Mexico, are the freshwater aquifers (Delgado et al. 2010; Perry et al. 2003).

One of the resource advantages of the northern flatlands is the shallow depth to the freshwater aquifer, and the ease of hand-excavation of wells through the soft limestone bedrock (Winzler and Fedick 1995). Cross-cultural studies suggest that it is easiest to draw water, using containers and rope, from wells that are less than ten meters in depth (Wilken 1987:167; Winemiller 2007). In the case of hand-dug wells in the Maya area, there does seem to be a drop-off in the frequency of wells deeper than 10 meters, with a maximum depth of about 20 meters (Harrison 1993:78). As elevations rise out of the northern flatlands and into the Puuc hills of southwestern Yucatan state, depth to the water table increases beyond 20 meters, and the ancient Maya transitioned from excavating wells to constructing cisterns and reservoirs (Winemiller 2007).

Data has been published by Mexico's National Institute of Geographic Statistics and Informatics on the depth to water table for over 1,100 wells scattered across the Yucatan Peninsula (INEGI 1983–1985). These data have been used to generate an isopleth map of water-table depth, with contours representing five-meter intervals down to the depth of 20 meters, below which hand-excavated wells would be unlikely (Figure 6.2). This analysis demonstrates that water is actually a readily available resource across most of the northern flatlands, accessible through hand-excavated wells.

Besides supplying drinking water, the shallow depth to the water table and the moisture-retaining permeable bedrock above the aquifer, have implications for plant ecology and agricultural systems (see Schwinning 2010). Many perennial species of plants, particularly trees, can develop root systems reaching maximum depths of 30 meters to access the water table (Gillespie et al. 2004:35; Parker 1968). Some species of trees have the demonstrated ability to spread out root systems laterally in the thin soil in order to locate bedrock cracks where roots can be sent down to tap groundwater (Poot and Lambers 2008). Within the northern flatlands, studies have distinguished specialization among tree species, with deciduous varieties dependent on concentrated root systems within shallow surface soil, and evergreen species with roots that reach the groundwater (Hasselquist et al. 2010).

It turns out, however, that the most significant source of water for trees in the northern flatlands is a layer of unconsolidated limestone, known locally as *sascab*, which is particularly characteristic of the northern peninsula. The sascab layer is related to the relatively young Miocene/Pliocene geology of the far northern peninsula (see Hearth and Fedick 2011 for a discussion of geology and implications for chert availability in the northern flatlands). The northern flatlands have a common soil/bedrock profile of soil (0–0.3 meters); a hard calcrete limestone cap, or *laja* layer (0.3–2.5 meters); a sandy, loosely consolidated limestone, or sascab layer (2.5–5.0 meters); and a variable, generally harder *coquina* layer of limestone and mollusk-and-coral wackstone at the bottom (5.0–9 + meters) that intersects with the water table (Estrada-Medina et al. 2012; Lauderdale et al. 1979; Perry et al. 2003; Rebolledo-Vieyra et al. 2000). The upper calcrete laja layer is riddled with cracks, fissures, and cavities that drain surface water, accumulate soil, and allow deep access by tree roots. Cavities and fissures are also common in the sascab and coquina layers, connecting to the aquifer.

A study in the northern flatlands took advantage of freshly exposed quarry walls to examine moisture retention in bedrock and soils, and to distinguish how rooting systems use subsurface water sources (Estrada-Medina et al. 2012). It was found that the greatest water reservoir for tree roots is the sascab layer, followed in descending order of moisture retention by soil-filled cavities, the coquina layer, the laja layer, and finally, the topsoil.

A related study in the same area used analysis of oxygen and nitrogen stable isotopes from tree-stem water, soil, bedrock, and groundwater, to determine the source of water used by seven tree species that are common in the region

(Querejeta et al. 2007). The study distinguished sources of water as deriving from surface soil, bedrock, or the aquifer. The results indicated variation among the species, but overall the trees were not dependent on having roots that penetrated down to the aquifer, but instead derived the majority of water uptake from the upper two to three meters of bedrock (corresponding to the laja and sascab layers), where ample water was stored through the dry season within the soil-filled cracks and cavities, and particularly in the soft, porous limestone sascab.

Field studies are needed to examine the relationship between tree seedling survival and immediate access to bedrock fissures and cavities in the northern flatlands. One study does describe how Maya homegardeners of Yucatan propagate trees such as ramon (*Brosimum alicastrum*) from seed, hand watering them from wells until they are established, with roots growing down through cracks and cavities in the bedrock to reach water reserves (Gillespie et al. 2004). This study also found that hand irrigation of ramon seedlings increases growth rates four-fold (Gillespie et al. 2004). A follow-up study of plantation-grown ramon trees in northern Yucatan demonstrated through carbon stable isotope analysis that the five to nine year old trees relied on water stored in the bedrock to survive (Querejeta et al. 2006). Ramon trees are of particular interest here, as their nutritious seeds have long been suggested as a subsistence alternative (or supplement) to maize for the ancient Maya (Puleston 1982). The Maya are well-aware of the moisture holding limitations of the top soil, and know how to aid the establishment of trees in the unique soil-bedrock environment of the northern flatlands.

A Reassessment of Soil Resources

Turning now to soils, it is necessary to reassess the long held characterization of the northern flatlands as, in De Landa's words, "the country with the least earth that I have seen" (Tozzer 1941:186). This impression of the landscape has been codified in modern soil surveys and maps. The most detailed soil maps that are available for the whole of the Yucatan Peninsula are at a scale of 1:250,000 (INEGI 1984–1985). While these maps do show variability in the edaphic landscape, they are still broadly generalized maps that exclude much of the local and micro-scale detail that may have been of greatest importance to ancient Maya farmers and gardeners. Maps at the scale of 1:250,000 do not delimit variability on the ground of areas less than 252 hectares (Davidson 1980:table 2.1) and thus miss the most valued land resources of the northern flatlands, which range from about 1.5 hectares down to about 80 square centimeters in surface area. On the ground, these range from large karstic depressions, known as *rejolladas*, to the small, yet deep, soil-filled cavities in the bedrock, as described above for their moisture-retaining properties.

Karst sinkholes have been identified by Europeans since Colonial times as resources that were valued by the Maya as micro-environments of deep soil and elevated moisture that could be used for sunken gardens and orchards (Gómez-Pompa et al. 1990). These crater-like features, with gently sloping walls and flat bottoms, are called rejolladas by the Maya. More recent studies have shown that the modern Maya commonly use these natural sunken gardens for cultivation of a wide variety of subsistence crops and other economically useful plants (e.g., Gómez-Pompa et al. 1990; Houck 2006:64; Kepecs and Boucher 1996:77; Triplett et al. 2006). It is only in very recent years that archaeologists have begun to recognize rejolladas as landscape features that could influence patterns of settlement and land-use in the northern flatlands (Cobos 2003:120–121; Houck 2006; Kepecs and Boucher 1996; Munro-Stasiuk and Manahan 2010). While cenotes are common landscape features of the northern flatlands, rejolladas are far more numerous and widespread within that region. As reported in the literature (e.g., Houck 2006; Munro-Stasiuk and Manahan 2010), rejolladas of the northern flatlands range in size from about 15 meters to 140 meters in diameter, or 0.02 to 1.54 hectares in area, and in depth from about two to 15 meters. The soil in rejolladas is reported as averaging between one and three meters in depth, and retaining moisture in the lower profiles, even after several months of no rain (Houck 2006; Kepecs and Boucher 1996; Munro-Stasiuk and Manahan 2010).

Another important aspect of rejolladas is that they provide more ready access to the water table for the excavation of wells. Archaeologists and others have noted ancient and modern wells within rejolladas (see Cobos 2003:120–121). Wells situated in rejolladas not only facilitate access to drinking water, but also allow the possibility for hand (pot) irrigation of sunken gardens, as first suggested by Kepecs and Boucher (1996:79).

In a first approximation of the distribution and number of rejolladas in the northern lowlands, a rapid assessment has been conducted, using Google Earth. The assessment involved following a virtual flight-path every 15 minutes of longitude (87 degrees—91 degrees), moving north from the 19 degree latitude line that is generally used to divide the northern and southern lowlands. The virtual flights were at an average "eye-altitude" of roughly 4,500 meters, providing a flight-path view of about five kilometers width. Although much of the landscape in the southern survey area was obscured by trees, the farther northern area, including nearly all of the northern flatlands, had fairly good visibility due to lower vegetation cover and extensive land clearance.

It proved to be a fairly straight-forward process to define the limits of a rejollada zone in the northern flatlands, as well as a high-density area within that zone (see Figure 6.1). The high density area contained about 1.5 rejolladas per square kilometer, while the rest of the zone has about 1.2 rejolladas per square kilometer. The total area of the rejollada zone covers 11,500 square kilometers and contains an estimated total of 14,430 rejolladas. In rejolladas, the northern flatlands have a fine-scale land resource that has been overlooked by modern soil mapping and land evaluation.

In the Yalahau region, adaptation to even finer scale landscape features is evident in the way that modern Maya gardeners make use of deep, soil-filled bedrock cavities as "containers" for growing crops (Fedick et al. 2008). Clearing off the thin top-soil generally reveals pock-marked limestone bedrock. These fissures and cavities, visible in the bedrock surface, are formed in the hard calcrete laja layer. Non-Maya observers are often shocked to see homegardens, with lush vegetation, including tree crops, seeming to grow out of solid bedrock. A small opening in the bedrock surface often bells-out to contain several cubic meters of rich organic soil; what might be considered a vertical A-horizon.

How wide-spread this micro-scale cavity formation is across the northern flatlands is not currently known, although the previously mentioned study of bedrock dissolution features in Yucatan state found fissures and cavities to be very common (Estrada-Medina et al. 2012). This study also found that the bedrock cavities accounted for over twice the volume of soils as did the topsoil per hectare of land (Estrada-Medina et al. 2011). Ground penetrating radar has been tested in the region for mapping and quantifying bedrock cavities, and shows promise for future research (Estrada-Medina et al. 2010). Given these studies of soil accumulation in bedrock cavities, and the focus of modern traditional gardening on these largely "hidden" soil resources, we see once again how the Maya have successfully adapted cultivation systems to the local resource base.

Implications for Ancient Cultural Trajectories in the Northern Flatlands

Only a few brief comments and questions will be offered here about the various trajectories of culture change that are found in the northern flatlands (and some other areas) over a span of 2,500 years of settlement history preceding European contact.

Evidence for Middle Preclassic Maya occupation in the northern flatlands is growing rapidly. Work at Komchen, in northwest Yucatan state (see Figure 6.1), has documented public architecture and extensive, dense settlement in the Middle Preclassic, perhaps dating to as early as 700 B.C.E. (Andrews 1990; Ringle and Andrews 1988). Survey by the Proyecto Costa Maya in near-coastal areas of the Yucatan state has found dozens of Middle Preclassic settlements that include ball courts (Robles Castellanos and Andrews 2003). An interesting pattern has been identified by Terrance Winemiller (2007), who has characterized the Chicxulub impact crater of the northwest peninsula as a basin that provides shallow access to the water table (see Figure 6.1). Within the Chicxulub basin is a hot-spot for hand-excavated wells, and for a relatively large number of ancient Maya sites (Winemiller 2007), including the majority of the pioneering Middle Preclassic communities documented by the Proyecto Costa Maya (Robles Castellanos and Andrews 2003). The Middle Preclassic ceramics (Early Nabanche tradition) of the northwest flatlands suggest movement of pioneering settlers into the region from the Usumacinta zone and the western lowlands sometime around 650 or 700 B.C.E. (Andrews 1990).

Recent research by the Costa Escondida Project at the north coast of the Yalahau region has found Middle Preclassic ceramics associated with the northeastern-Petén northern-Belize zone (i.e., the Mamom ceramic sphere), dating pioneering occupation in the northeast flatlands, at the mouth of the Yalahau wetland system, to at least as early as that documented for the northwest (Glover et al. 2011).

It is important to note that the reconstructed sea-level curve indicates that, at about 700 B.C.E. when the earliest Maya settlements in northwest Yucatan are thought to originate, sea level would have been about around 1.5 to 2.3 meters lower than today (Toscano and Macintyre 2003:table 4). Given the inland sea-water intrusion of the peninsula, the freshwater aquifer would have also been lower over much of the region. This would have further restricted the area where wells could easily reach the water table, making the Chicxulub basin and the swales of the Yalahau region all the more attractive for pioneer settlement.

There seems to have been major disruptions during the Preclassic to Early Classic transition, leading to demographic and political collapse in the Mirador basin to the south, followed by abandonment of the Yalahau region in the northeast and a shift in the political economy of the northwest, perhaps representing different responses to changing climate and water-table level.

Hodell and his colleagues (2007) have argued that a drought spanning the Late Preclassic to Early Classic transition may have impacted the northern lowlands in a manner similar to what caused disruptions in the Mirador basin to the south. A broad manifestation of climate change may, however, result in dramatically different local consequences in accordance with the initial environmental conditions of the smaller sub-regions.

The Maya of the Mirador basin in north-central Petén, far to the south of the northern flatlands, rose to demographic and political heights from the Middle Preclassic through the Late Preclassic, between about 1000 B.C.E. and C.E. 150. Climate records indicate this to have been a relatively wet, though fluctuating, period (Hodell et al. 2007). It has been suggested that the low-lying *bajos*, around which much of the Mirador settlement focused, may have been shallow lakes at the time, providing water as well as rich soil that was transported for use in gardens and fields (Hansen et al. 2002). The bajos of the interior Petén are associated with localized perched water tables, with the regional aquifer located at a much greater depth than in the northern peninsula. Abandonment of the Mirador basin is suggested to be associated with a drought lasting from about C.E. 100 to 250 (Dahlin 1983; see also Hodell et al. 2007), in conjunction with infilling of the shallow lakes due to human-induced erosion (Dunning et al. 2002).

During the years that El Mirador was in decline, sites in the Yalahau region were flourishing. Given that the water table in the Yalahau region was probably at least a meter lower during the Late Preclassic than today, it is possible that the Yalahau swales were flooded for much shorter intervals, if at all. During most of the Preclassic, the Yalahau uplands would have received relatively high rainfall, and swales may have been farmed throughout much of the year, with engineering improvements (rock alignments) functioning to control rainwater runoff and soil movement within the moisture retaining (but minimally flooded) swales.

In the Yalahau region, the near-abandonment that is documented by about C.E. 400 may be related not so much with a decrease in rainfall that characterizes the Classic period (Hodell et al. 2007), but with a rise in the freshwater aquifer as it was pushed up by rising sea levels and the saltwater intrusion that underlies the region. A rising water table, accompanied by greater fluctuation in rainfall patterns, may have disrupted agricultural production in the Yalahau swales through prolonged, though variable, inundation (Wollwage et al. 2012). The Yalahau abandonment is also coincident with a population rise, and development of the urbanism and political influence of Cobá, situated just south of the Yalahau region in the eastern flatlands (see Figure 6.1; Folan 1983).

As the water table in the northern flatlands steadily rose from the Preclassic into the Classic periods, it may have differentially altered the agricultural potential of the eastern and western flatlands. While prolonged inundation rendered the swales of the northeastern Yalahau area unsuitable for agriculture, it may have increased the availability of subsurface moisture for deep penetrating roots of trees and other perennials in the northwest. The site of Chunchucmil, in the far northwest (see Figure 6.1), developed into a major urban center during Early Classic to Late Classic times (Hutson et al. 2008). It has been a mystery how the population of Chunchucmil could have supported themselves on the thin soils of the area (Beach 1998). Perhaps annual crops, such as corn, would have done poorly and required importation, but cultivation of food-producing trees and other deep rooting perennials within bedrock cavities could have supplied more local produce than has been considered (see discussions in Dahlin et al. 2005; Sweetwood et al. 2009).

During the Terminal/Late Classic, the northern flatlands see the rise of powerful regional centers such as Chichén Itzá and Ek Balám on the southern margin of the rejollada zone (see Figure 6.1). To what extent was the power of these polities linked to control of agricultural production in rejolladas? It is also interesting to note that the central area of Chichén Itzá is situated on a significant topographic rise, adding not only to the dominating view to, and from, the monumental architecture, but also to the dramatic impression of the drop to the water in the sacred cenote, into which offerings, including humans, were tossed. Moving off this rise to the north and west, the elevation descends, and the density of rejolladas rapidly increases, supplying both high quality agricultural resources and ready access to the water table through wells.

Moving into the Postclassic, there is a resurgence of settlement into the interior of the Yalahau region, beginning about C.E. 1250 (Fedick and Mathews 2005; Glover 2006; Wollwage et al. 2012). The still-rising water table, coupled with the peak rain levels of the Postclassic period between about C.E. 1050 and the 15th century, after which drier conditions began to return. The Postclassic occupation at the well-studied site of T'isil in the central-eastern Yalahau region (see Figure 6.1) shows evidence for the importance of fishing during that time, in the form of apparent fishing-net weights made from Postclassic sherds.

These few examples are intended to highlight how resources, previously under-appreciated by archaeologists, may have influenced cultural trajectories in the northern flatlands. They also show how long-term changes in those resources, associated with changes in climate and the water table, also shifted resource endowments and Maya response to those changes.

Summary: Reassessment Reveals the Potential for a Resilient Agricultural System

Contrary to our previous perception of resources in the northern flatlands, a reassessment reveals a landscape with appreciable water and soil resources. Aquifers of the northern peninsula represent the most abundant water reservoir in Mexico, easily accessible through hand-dug wells, and providing ample water for drinking, household needs, and hand (pot) irrigation of gardens and orchards. Soils, while apparently shallow and limited, can be found in deep deposits within thousands of rejolladas. Natural cavities in the bedrock likewise hold deep soil accumulations, rich in moisture and providing access for deeper rooting trees and other food-producing perennial plants to tap another vast reservoir of moisture held in the porous limestone sascab layer between the topsoil and the aquifer. The northern flatlands may not have been such a bad place to live in ancient times, and we have much to learn from the ancient and modern Maya about how best to use under-appreciated resources for sustainable development of the region in the future.

The unique configuration of soil and water resources in the northern flatlands presents a landscape that is pre-adapted to an agricultural system based on the cultivation of deep-rooting perennial crops, and this adaptation should be exploited for future development. Native species adapted to the local environment are best suited for cultivation. The Maya are known to make use of 215 native species of food-producing trees (Fedick and Santiago 2012). These tree species should be evaluated for water source partitioning to identify those best adapted to tapping the moisture retained in the regional sascab layer and aquifers (following Estrada-Medina et al. 2011; Querejeta et al. 2007). Production studies, nutritional analysis and marketing research could then narrow the list of native trees to those with the highest potential for sustainable, marketable orchard cultivation. Existing studies have examined how seemingly depleted and degraded landscapes, such as abandoned henequen plantations in Yucatán state, can be transformed into productive agroforestry systems (Mizrahi et al. 1997). Direct irrigation can be used to greatly increase the survival of native tree seedlings, while after establishment, irrigation could cease (Gillespie et al. 2004). Orchard cultivation and agroforestry based on native species represent a much more sustainable approach than attempts at cultivating non-native species, such as citrus, which often fail, due in part to the need of continuous irrigation (Jiménez-Osornio et al. 2008).

Regional mapping of the water-retaining sascab layer could be conducted to identify areas with the highest potential for supporting orchard crops of native species. Rapid and efficient mapping could be accomplished with airborne ground penetrating radar (GPR), calibrated with boreholes, to identify the reflective signal of interfaces between layers of soil, laja, sascab, and coquina, and to better define at a regional scale the depth of the water table and thickness of aquifers (Annan 2005; Huisman et al. 2003; Lunt et al. 2005). It may also be possible to calibrate airborne GPR to quantify the distribution and volume of soil filled cavities within the geological layers of the vadose zone, following initial field experiments with surface GPR (Estrada-Medina et al. 2010).

In addition to native trees, there are 146 native species of shrubs, lianas, succulents, cactus, and other plants, mostly perennials, that are drought resistant food producers (Fedick and Santiago 2012). In light of future climate change, more consideration should be given to these drought-adapted species. Two examples of drought resistant native plants with high potential for subsistence production and marketing are chaya (*Cnidoscolus chayamansa*/*C. aconitifolius*) and pitaya (*Hylocereus undatus*), both of which are beginning to find high levels of demand for local consumption and export. It is noteworthy that pitaya, a cactus that is native to the northern Maya Lowlands, is under large scale production in Vietnam, Thailand, Malaysia, and Taiwan, being marketed as "dragon fruit" and widely perceived as an exotic product of Asia, with demand far surpassing supplies (ElObeidy 2006; Le Bellec et al. 2006).

Progress is being made in efforts to promote sustainable agriculture in the northern flatlands that incorporate Maya traditional knowledge and the use of native plant species. Promising results are being obtained in several pilot projects initiated by the Department of Management and Conservation of Natural Resources in the Tropics (PROTROPICO), a division of the National Autonomous University of Yucatán (see Jiménez-Osornio 2003; Jiménez-Osornio et al. 2008). These projects have established agroforestry systems, promoted the use of green manuring and cover crops, established community gardens at schools to conserve and promote the use of native food plants, and developed educational programs to promote ecologically appropriate agriculture and application of traditional Maya ecological knowledge. Maya culture has proven to be one of the most resilient on earth, spanning three millennia of climate change, social upheavals, foreign invasion, and misguided attempts at agricultural development. The Maya Lowlands represent a case study in human persistence that can inform us about the past and provide guidance for the future (Allen et al. 2003).

Acknowledgments

I would like to thank all of the IHOPE-Maya participants, and the many guests who have joined us at meetings, for their enthusiasm, knowledge, and companionship. Sander van der Leeuw has been a driving force, mentor, supporter, and inspiration to all of us. Assistance and expertise with GIS analysis of the wells data was provided by Kurt Heidelberg. Mary Baker supplied many helpful comments on a draft of the manuscript.

References Cited

Allen, Michael F., Arturo Gómez-Pompa, Scott L. Fedick, and Juan J. Jiménez-Osornio
2003 The Maya Lowlands: A Case Study for the Future? Conclusions. *In* The Lowland Maya Area: Three Millennia at the Human-Wildland Interface. Arturo Gómez-Pompa, Michael F. Allen, Scott L. Fedick, and Juan J. Jiménez-Osornio, eds. Pp. 623–634. New York: Haworth Press.

Annan, A. Peter
2005 GPR Methods for Hydrogeological Studies. *In* Hydrogeophysics. Y. Rubin and S. S. Hubbard, eds. Pp. 185–213. New York: Springer.

Alonso de Herrera, Gabriel
2006 [1513] Ancient Agriculture: Roots and Application of Sustainable Farming. Juan Estevan Arellano, comp. Layton, UT: Ancient City Press.

Andrews, E. Wyllys, V
1990 The Early Ceramic History of the Lowland Maya. *In* Vision and Revision in Maya Studies. Florence Clancy and Peter Harrison, eds. Pp. 1–20. Albuquerque: University of New Mexico Press.

Beach, Timothy
1998 Soil Constraints on Northwest Yucatán, Mexico: Pedoarchaeology and Maya Subsistence at Chunchucmil. Geoarchaeology: An International Journal 13(8):759–791.

Chase, Arlen F., Diane Z. Chase, Christopher T. Fisher, Stephen J. Leisz, and John F. Weishampel
2012 Geospatial Revolution and Remote Sensing LiDAR in Mesoamerican Archaeology. Proceedings of the National Academy of Sciences 109(32):12961–12921.

Cobos, Rafael
2003 The Settlement Patterns of Chichen Itza, Yucatan, Mexico. Ph.D. dissertation, Department of Anthropology, Tulane University.

Colunga-García Marín, Patricia
2003 The Domestication of Henequen (*Agave fourcroydes* Lem.). *In* The Lowland May Area: Three Millennia at the Human-Wildland Interface. Arturo Gómez-Pompa, Michael F. Allen, Scott L. Fedick, and Juan J. Jiménez-Osornio, eds. Pp. 439–446. New York: Haworth Press.

Dahlin, Bruce H.
1983 Climate and Prehistory on the Yucatan Peninsula. Climatic Change 5(3):245–263.

Dahlin, Bruce H., Timothy Beach, Sheryl Luzzadder-Beach, David Hixson, Scott Hutson, Aline Magnoni, Euginia Mansell, and Daniel E. Mazeau
2005 Reconstructing Agricultural Self-Sufficiency at Chunchucmil, Yucatan, Mexico. Ancient Mesoamerica 16:229–247.

Davidson, D. A.
1980 Soils and Land Use Planning. London: Longman.

Delgado, C., J. Pacheco, A. Cabrera, E. Batllori, R. Orellana, and F. Bautista
2010 Quality of Groundwater for Irrigation in Tropical Kart Environment: The Case of Yucatán, Mexico. Agricultural Water Management 97:1423–1433.

Dunning, Nicholas P., Sheryl Luzzadder-Beach, Timothy Beach, John G. Jones, VernonScarborough, and T. Patrick Culbert
2002 Arising from the *Bajos*: The Evolution of a Neotropical Landscape and the Rise of Maya Civilization. Annals of the Association of American Geographers 92(2):267–283.

ElObeidy, Ahmed A.
2006 Mass Propagation of Pitaya (Dragon Fruit). Fruits 61(5):313–319.

Estrada-Medina, Héctor, Robert C. Graham, Michael B. Allen, Juan José Jiménez-Osornio, and Said Robles-Casolco
2012 The Importance of Limestone Bedrock and Dissolution Karst Features on Tree Root Distribution in Northern Yucatán, México. doi:10.1007/s11104–012–1175-x, accessed September 8, 2012.

Estrada-Medina, Héctor, Robert C. Graham, Michael B. Allen, Wes Tuttle, Louis S. Santiago, and Juan José Jiménez-Osornio
2011 Subsurface Features: Beyond Shallow Soils in Yucatan. Presentation at the 96th Annual Meeting of the Ecological Society of America, August 7–12, Austin, Texas. http://esameetings.allenpress.com/2011/webprogram/Paper27782.html, accessed September 8, 2012.

Estrada-Medina, Héctor, Wes Tuttle, Robert C. Graham, Michael F. Allen, and Juan JoséJiménez-Osornio
2010 Identification of Underground Karst Features using Ground-Penetrating Radar in Northern Yucatán, México. Vadose Zone Journal 9:653–661.

Fedick, Scott L.
2003 In Search of the Maya Forest. *In* In Search of the Rain Forest. Candace Slater, ed. Pp. 133–164. Durham: Duke University Press.

Fedick, Scott L., Maria de Lourdes Flores Delgadillo, Sergey Sedov, Elizabeth SolleiroRebolledo, and Sergio Palacios Mayorga
2008 Adaptation of Maya Homegardens by "Container Gardening" in Limestone Bedrock Cavities. Journal of Ethnobiology 28(2):290–304.

Fedick, Scott L., and Jennifer P. Mathews
2005 The Yalahau Regional Human Ecology Project: An Introduction and Summary of Recent Research. *In* Quintana Roo Archaeology. Justine Shaw and Jennifer P. Mathews, eds. Pp. 33–50. Tucson: University of Arizona Press.

Fedick, Scott L., Bethany A. Morrison, Bente Juhl Anderson, Sylviane Boucher, Jorge Ceja Acosta, and Jennifer P. Mathews
2000 Wetland Manipulation in the Yalahau Region of the Northern Maya Lowlands. Journal of Field Archaeology 27:131–152.

Fedick, Scott L., Daniel Leonard, Jennifer Chmilar, Maria de Lourdes Flores Delgadillo, Alfredo González, Sergio Palacios Mayorga, Sergey Sedov, and Elizabeth Solleiro Rebolledo
2010 Long-term implications for Maya resource use in the pulse-based ecosystem of the Yalahau wetlands, northern Quintana Roo, Mexico. Paper presented at the 70th Annual Meeting of the Society for Applied Anthropology, Merida, Yucatan, Mexico, March 24–27.

Fedick, Scott L., and Louis Santiago
2012 Drought resistance and ancient Maya agriculture. Paper presented at the 77th Annual Meeting of the Society for American Archaeology, Memphis, Tennessee, April 18–22.

Folan, William J.
1983 Summary and Conclusions. *In* Coba: A Classic Maya Metropolis. William J. Folan, Ellen R. Kintz, and Laraine A. Fletcher, Pp. 211–217. New York: Academic Press.

Gabriel, Jeremy J., Eduard G. Reinhardt, Matthew C. Peros, Dawn E. Davidson, Peter J. van Hengstum, and Patricia A. Beddows
2009 Paleoenvironmental Evolution of Cenote Aktun Ha (Carwash) on the Yucatan Peninsula, Mexico and Its Response to Holocene Sea-Level Rise. Journal of Paleolimnology 42(2):199–213.

Gillespie, A. R., D. M. Bocanegra-Ferguson, and J. J. Jimenez-Osornio
2004 The Propagation of Ramón (*Brosimum alicastrum* Sw: Moraceae) in Mayan Homegardens of the Yucatan Peninsula of Mexico. New Forests 27:25–38.

Glover, Jeffrey B.
2006 The Yalahau Regional Settlement Pattern Survey: A Study of Ancient Maya Social Organization in Northern Quintana Roo, Mexico. Ph.D. dissertation, Department of Anthropology, University of California, Riverside.

Glover, Jeffrey B., Dominique Rissolo, Joseph W. Ball, and Fabio E. Amador
2011 Who Were the Middle Preclassic Settlers of Quintana Roo's North Coast? New Evidence from Vista Alegre. Mexicon 33:69–73.

Gómez-Pompa, Arturo
1998 Vegetation of the Maya Region. *In* Maya. Peter Schmidt, Mercedes de la Garza, and Enrique Nalda, eds. Pp. 38–51. New York: Rizzoli.

Gómez-Pompa, Arturo, J. S. Flores, and M. Aliphat Fernandez
1990 The Sacred Cacao Groves of the Maya. Latin American Antiquity 1(3):247–257.

Hansen, Richard D., Steven Bozarth, John Jacob, David Wahl, and Thomas Schreiner
2002 Climatic and Environmental Variability in the Rise of Maya Civilization. Ancient Mesoamerica 13(2):273–295.

Harrison, Peter D.
1993 Aspects of Water Management in the Southern Maya Lowlands. *In* Economic Aspects of Water Management in the Prehispanic New World. Vernon L. Scarborough and Barry L. Issac, eds. Pp. 71–119. Research in Economic Anthropology, Supplement 7. Greenwich, CT: JAI Press.

Hasselquist, Niles J., Michael F. Allen, and Louis S. Santiago
2010 Water Relations of Evergreen and Drought-Deciduous Trees along a Seasonally Dry Tropical Forest Chronosequence. Oecologia 164:881–890.

Hearth, Nicholas F., and Scott L. Fedick
2011 Defining the Chert Paucity Problem in the Northern Maya Lowlands: A First Approximation. *In* The Technology of Maya Civilization: Political Economy and Beyond in Lithic Studies. Zachary X. Hruby, Geoffrey E. Braswell, and Oswaldo Chinchilla Mazariegos, eds. Pp. 69–75. Sheffield: Equinox.

Hodell, D. A., M. Brenner, and J. H. Curtis
2007 Climate and Cultural History of the Northeastern Yucatan Peninsula, Quintana Roo, Mexico. Climatic Change 83:215–240.

Houck, Charles W., Jr.
2006 Cenotes, Wetlands, and Hinterland Settlement. *In* Lifeways in the Northern Maya Lowlands: New Approaches to Archaeology in the Yucatán Peninsula. Jennifer P. Mathews and Bethany A. Morrison, eds. Pp. 56–76. Tucson: University of Arizona Press.

Huisman, J. A., S. S. Hubbard, J. D. Redman, and A. P. Annan
2003 Measuring Soil Water Content with Ground Penetrating Radar. Vadose Zone Journal 2(4):476–491.

Hutson, Scott R., David R. Hixson, Aline Magnoni, Daniel Mazeau, and Bruce Dahlin
2008 Site and Community at Chunchucmil and Ancient Maya Urban Centers. Journal of Field Archaeology 33(1):19–40.

2012 Lakes by Country. www.indexmundi.com/zl/, accessed September 9, 2012.

1983 5 Carta Hidrológica de Aguas Subterraneas. 1:250,000. Mexico, D.F.: Direccion General de Geografia.

1984 5 Carta Edafologica. 1:250,000. Mexico, D.F.: Direccion General de Geografia.

Jiménez-Osornio, Juan J.
2003 The School of Ecological Agriculture: A Viable Liaison Between Campesinos and Researchers in the Yucatán Peninsula. *In* The Lowland Maya Area: Three Millennia at the Human-Wildland Interface. Arturo Gómez-Pompa, Michael F. Allen, Scott L. Fedick, and Juan J. Jiménez-Osornio, eds. Pp. 599–609. New York: Haworth Press.

Jiménez-Osornio, Juan J., Hector Estrada-Medina, William Aguilar-Cordero, Patricia Montañez-Escalante, Rocío Ruenes-Morales, and Rafael Ortíz-Pech
2008 Ecological Land Use Planning for Sustainable Landscapes in Yucatan. *In* Applying Ecological Knowledge to Landuse Decisions. Holm Tiessen and John W. B. Stewart, eds. Pp. 42–48. Sao Paulo, Brazil: Inter-American Institute for Global Change Research.

Kepecs, Susan, and Sylviane Boucher
1996 The Pre-Hispanic Cultivation of Rejolladas and Stone-Lands: New Evidence from Northeast Yucatan. *In* The Managed Mosaic: Ancient Maya Agriculture and Resource Use. Scott L. Fedick, ed. Pp. 69–91. Salt Lake City: University of Utah Press.

Lauderdale, Robert W., William C. Ward, and Alfred E. Weidie
1979 "Carillo Puerto Formation" of Northeastern Quintana Roo, Mexico. The American Association of Petroleum Geologists Bulletin 63:1606.

Le Bellec, Fabrice, Fabrice Vaillant, and Eric Imbert
2006 Pitahaya (*Hylocereus* spp): a New Fruit Crop, a Market with a Future. Fruits 61(4):237–250.

Leonard, Daniel
2010 Resultados Preliminares de la Primera Fase del Reconocimiento de las Sabanas Yalahau. *In* XXIII Simposio de Investigaciones Arqueológicas en

Guatemala, Vol. II. B. Arroyo, A. Linares, and L. Paiz Argón, eds. Pp. 791–803. Guatemala City: Minesterio de Cultura y Deportes.

Lunt, I. A., S. S. Hubbard, and Y. Rubin
2005 Soil Moisture Content Estimation Using Ground-Penetrating Radar Reflection Data. Journal of Hydrology 307:254–269.

Mizrahi, Aliza, José Maria Ramos Prado, and Juan Jiménez-Osornio
1997 Composition, Structure, and Management Potential of Secondary Dry Tropical Vegetation in Two Abandoned Henequen Plantations of Yucatan, Mexico. Forest Ecology and Management 96:273–282.

Morley, Sylvanus G.
1946 The Ancient Maya. Stanford: Stanford University Press.

Munro-Stasiuk, Mandy J., and T. Kam Manahan
2010 Investigating Ancient Maya Agricultural Adaptation through Ground Penetrating Radar (GPR) Analysis of Karst Terrain, Northern Yucatán, Mexico. Acta Carsologica 39(1):123–135.

Parker, J.
1968 Drought-Resistance Mechanisms. *In* Water Deficits and Plant Growth. T. T. Kozlowski, ed. Pp. 195–234. New York: Academic Press.

Patch, Robert W.
2003 The (Almost) Forgotten Plants of Yucatán. *In* The Lowland Maya Area: Three Millennia at the Human-Wildland Interface. Arturo Gómez-Pompa, Michael F. Allen, Scott L. Fedick, and Juan J. Jiménez-Osornio, eds. Pp. 561–569. New York: Haworth Press.

Peniche Rivero, Piedad
2003 From Milpero to Lunero to Henequenero: A Transition to Capitalism in Yucatán, Mexico. *In* The Lowland Maya Area: Three Millennia at the Human-Wildland Interface. Arturo Gómez-Pompa, Michael F. Allen, Scott L. Fedick, and Juan J. Jiménez-Osornio, eds. Pp. 571–584. New York: Haworth Press.

Perry, Eugene, Guadalupe Velazquez-Oliman, and Richard A. Socki
2003 Hydrogeology of the Yucatán Peninsula. *In* The Lowland Maya Area: Three Millennia at the Human-Wildland Interface. Arturo Gómez-Pompa, Michael F. Allen, Scott L. Fedick, and Juan J. Jiménez-Osornio, eds. Pp. 115–138. New York: Haworth Press.

Poot, Pieter, and Hans Lambers
2008 Shallow-Soil Endemics: Adaptive Advantages and Constraints of a Specialized Root-System Morphology. New Phytologist 178(2):371–381.

Puleston, Dennis
1982 The Role of Ramón in Maya Subsistence. *In* Maya Subsistence: Studies in Memory of Dennis E. Puleston. Kent V. Flannery, ed. Pp. 353–366. New York, Academic Press.

Querejeta, José Ignacio, Héctor Estrada-Medina, Michael F. Allen, Juan J. Jiménez-Osornio
2007 Water Source Partitioning among Trees Growing on Shallow Karst Soils in a Seasonally Dry Tropical Climate. Oecologia 152:26–36.

Querejeta, José Ignacio, Héctor Estrada-Medina, Michael F. Allen, Juan J. Jiménez-Osornio, and Rocío Ruenes
2006 Utilization of Bedrock Water by *Brosimum alicastrum* Trees on Shallow Soil Atop Limestone in a Dry Tropical Climate. Plant Soil 287:187–197.

Rebolledo-Vieyra, Mario, Jaime Urrutia-Fucugauchi, Luis E. Marín, Alberto Trijo-García, Virgil L. Sharpton, and Ana María Soler-Archalde
2000 UNAM Scientific Shallow-Drilling Program of the Chicxulub Impact Crater. International Geology Review 42:928–940.

Ringle, William M., and E. Wyllys Andrews V
1988 Formative Residences at Komchen, Yucatan, Mexico. *In* Household and Community in the Mesoamerican Past. Richard R. Wilk and Wendy Ashmore, eds. Pp. 171–197. Albuquerque: University of New Mexico Press.

Robles Castellanos, Fernando, and Anthony P. Andrews, eds.
2003 Proyecto Costa Maya: Reconocimiento Arqueológico en el Noroeste de Yucatán, México.

Reporte Interino, Temporada
2002 Report prepared for Consejo Nacional de Arqueología de México. Mérida, Yucatán: Centro INAH Yucatán—National Geographic Society.

Schmitter-Soto, J. J., F. A. Comín, E. Escobar-Briones, J. Herrera-Silveira, J. Alcocer, E. Suárez-Morales, M. Elías-Gutiérrez, L. E. Marín, and B. Steinich
2002 Hydrogeochemical and Biological Characteristics of Cenotes in the Yucatan Peninsula (SE Mexico). Hydrobiologia 467:215–228.

Schwinning, Susanne
2010 Ecohydrology Bearings—Invited Commentary: The Ecohydrology of Roots in Rocks. Ecohydrology 3:238–245.

Smart, Peter L., Patricia A. Beddows, Jim Coke, Stefan Doerr, Samantha Smith, and Fiona R. Whitaker
2006 Cave Development on the Caribbean Coast of the Yucatan Peninsula, Quintana Roo, Mexico. *In* Perspectives on Karst Geomorphology, Hydrology, and Geochemistry—A Tribute Volume to Derek. C. Ford and William B. White. R. S. Harmon and C. Wicks, eds. Pp. 105–128. Special Paper, 404. Boulder, CO: Geological Society of America.

Sweetwood, Ryan V., Richard E. Terry, Timothy Beach, Bruce H. Dahlin, and David Hixson
2009 The Maya Footprint: Soil Resources of Chunchucmil, Yucatán, Mexico. Soil Science Society of America Journal 73(4):1209–1220.

Toscano, M. A., and I. G. Macintyre
2003 Corrected Western Atlantic Sea-Level Curve for the Last 11,000 Years Based on Calibrated ^{14}C Dates from *Acropora palmata* Framework and Intertidal Mangrove Peat. Coral Reefs 22:257–270.

Tozzer, Alfred M.
1941 Landa's Relación de las Cosas de Yucatan: A Translation. Papers of the Peabody Museum of American Archaeology and Ethnology, Harvard University, 18. Cambridge: Harvard University.

Triplett, K., C. Gutierrez, and T. Ardren
2006 Ethnobotanical Investigations. *In* Report of the 2005 Proyecto Arqueologico Xuenkal Field Season. T. K. Manahan and T. Ardren, eds. Pp. 25–29. Crystal Springs: Foundation for the Advancement of Mesoamerican Studies.

Tulaczyk, S. M., E. C. Perry, C. E. Duller, and M. Villasuso
1993 Influence of the Holbox Fracture Zone on the Karst Geomorphology and Hydrogeology of Northern Quintana Roo, Yucatán Peninsula, México. *In* Applied karst Geology. B. F. Beck, ed. Pp. 181–188. Rotterdam: A. A. Balkema.

Weishampel, John F., Jessica N. Hightower, Arlen F. Chase, Diane Z. Chase, and Ryan A. Patrick
2011 Detection and Morphologic Analysis of Potential Below-Canopy Cave Openings in the Karst Landscape around the Maya Polity of Caracol Using Airborne LiDAR. Journal of Cave and Karst Studies 73(3):187–196.

Wilken, Gene C.
1987 Good Farmers: Traditional Agriculture Resource Management in Mexico and Central America. Berkeley: University of California Press.

Winemiller, Terrance L.
2007 The Chicxlulub Meteor Impact and Ancient Locational Decisions on the Yucatán Peninsula, Mexico: The Application of Remote Sensing, GIS, and GPS in Settlement Pattern Studies. Tampa, Florida: Proceedings of the American Society for Photogrammetry and Remote Sensing 2007 Annual Conference. http://www.asprs.org/a/publications/proceedings/tampa2007/0080.pdf, accessed September 9, 2012.

Winzler, Susan, and Scott L. Fedick
1995 Ancient Maya Wells and Water Resources of the Yalahau Region. *In* The View from Yalahau: 1993 Investigations in Northern Quintana Roo, Mexico. Scott L. Fedick and Karl A. Taube, eds. Pp. 101–113. Latin American Studies Program, Field Report Series, 2. Riverside: University of California.

Wollwage, Lance, Scott Fedick, Sergey Sedov, and Elizabeth Solleiro-Rebolledo
2012 The Deposition and Chronology of Cenote T'isil: A Multiproxy Study of Human/Environment Interaction in the Northern Maya Lowlands of Southeastern Mexico. Geoarchaeology 27:441–456.

7

Population Dynamics and Its Relation to Ancient Landscapes in the Northwestern Maya Lowlands: Evaluating Resilience and Vulnerability

Rodrigo Liendo
University Nacional Autonoma de Mexico
Elizabeth Solleiro-Rebolledo
University Nacional Autonoma de Mexico
Berenice Solis-Castillo
University Nacional Autonoma de Mexico
Sergei Sedov
University Nacional Autonoma de Mexico
and
Arturo Ortiz-Pérez
University Nacional Autonoma de Mexico

ABSTRACT

In this article we present for discussion certain aspects of settlement and paleo-environmental data obtained over the last few years for the northwestern Maya lowlands. Accordingly, our goal is to identify a point of departure for future research by presenting a list of possible "environmental attractors" that might later be used for a better understanding of the seemingly divergent trajectories shown by ancient communities located in different physical settings—particularly in the Sierras region and the Usumacinta plains, Mexico. Our study is based on the paleo-pedological record of the region. Paleosols are good paleo-environmental proxies and, with the climate information, they are indicators of past human activities and land use. In the Maya lowlands, they have been used extensively to register changes in environmental conditions and human impact on the soil cover. Nevertheless, this study represents the first attempt in that same direction in the northwestern Maya lowlands. [settlement patterns, paleoenviromental reconstruction, northwestern Maya lowlands.]

Introduction

The presence of hydrographic elements is a salient feature in the geography of the northwestern Maya lowlands. The role of water in sediment transport and alluvial deposition has conditioned many of the morphogenetic processes at the regional level, while much of natural vegetation and wildlife is aquatic. High levels of precipitation in the lowlands, foothills, and Chiapas mountains create a vast drainage network—coming in and

ARCHEOLOGICAL PAPERS OF THE AMERICAN ANTHROPOLOGICAL ASSOCIATION, Vol. 24, pp. 84–100, ISSN 1551-823X, online ISSN 1551-8248. DOI: 10.1111/apaa.12031.

out of lakes and swamps—that eventually empties into the Gulf of Mexico. This river system drains an area of 63,804 km^2 that includes parts of Tabasco, Chiapas, and Guatemala.

During prehispanic times, this broad region was the seat of many population centers. Through controlled surveys, we know of well over 2,300 archaeological sites (Figure 7.1). Presenting a range of human engineered features, these sites are located mainly in the plains of Tabasco; though a number of sites are surely located in the countless narrow valleys along the Usumacinta River within the Sierras region, an area currently poorly known. Although several archaeological sites recovered from this region correlate with the locations of contemporary population centers, insufficient archaeological data remains a concern in discussing aspects of the socio-political organization of the groups inhabiting the region in pre-Columbian times or their long trajectory of occupation.

Nevertheless, in this chapter we discuss certain aspects of settlement and paleo-environmental data obtained over the last few years for the northwestern Maya lowlands. Our goal is to identify a point of departure for future research by presenting a list of possible "environmental attractors" that might later be used for a better understanding of the seemingly divergent trajectories shown by ancient communities located in different physical settings—particularly in the Sierras region and the Usumacinta plains.

The Northwestern Maya Lowlands: An Archaeological Case Study

This vast region has been subdivided into two main areas: the Lower Usumacinta (from Boca del Cerro to its mouth in the Gulf of Mexico) and the Upper Usumacinta (from Boca del Cerro to the origins of the Usumacinta River in the confluence of the Salinas and Chixoy rivers). In prehispanic times, these geographical zones were the seat of many population centers. Nevertheless, the sociopolitical organization of the groups that inhabited this region in Precolumbian times is still difficult to address, simply because we know too little about their political and territorial organization, the characteristics of their adaptation to the environment, or the sequence of occupation and abandonment of this vast territory.

A yet more disturbing aspect of the history of archaeological research in this region is the overwhelming reliance in recent decades on epigraphic data. Our knowledge based on regional archaeological research is less than that gleaned from the hieroglyphic history. The research emphasis in the northwestern lowlands has focused mainly on a discussion of epigraphic evidence relating to a small number of issues concerning the identification of minor lords, dynastic sequences, relationship subordination of minor lords, royal visits, enthronement ceremonies, and the exchange of women of royal descent (Culbert 1991; Marcus 1976, 1993; Mathews 1991, Schele 1986, 1991; Schele and Freidel 1990; Grube and Martin 1998; Martin and Grube 2000). From these glyphic analyses, it has been argued that Palenque, Piedras Negras, Yaxchilan, and Pomona (among others) emerged as capitals of their respective areas of influence, but we still lack sufficient comparable archaeological information.

General Comments on the Ceramics and Chronology of the Lower and Upper Usumacinta

Ceramic research in the area has established a long sequence of occupation ranging from the Middle Preclassic period (800–300 B.C.E.) to the Terminal Classic period (C.E. 850). Robert Rands (1974, 1977) established the first and most reliable scheme of regional ceramic development based on his excavations at Yoxihá, Chinikiha, Miraflores, Tortuguero, and around Balancán Zapata, Tabasco. Rands' studies—and, more recently, the work of Sandra López at Pomona (2005), Marta Hernandez in the San Pedro River region (1981), and Socorro Jimenez (2009) in the Sierras region—confirm the existence of two ceramic traditions with dissimilar trajectories that coexisted in the Lower and Upper Usumacinta.

Since the early 1950s we have known that the Zapata-Balancán region presents a continuous trend of ceramic element incorporations belonging to the Chicanel ceramic sphere (Berlin 1955; Rands 1967; Ochoa 1978, 1984). Ochoa reported a series of sites in the Balancán Zapata region showing ceramic materials belonging to the Mamom and Chicanel ceramic spheres. These include El Mirador and Tiradero along the Rio San Pedro; and Pomoca, La Concepción, Povictuc, Nueva Esperanza, Río Frío, San José del Rio, and La Soledad Chacavita along the Usumacinta River (see Figure 7.1). The association of the Tabasco plains with ceramic types exhibiting a much wider distribution in the Maya Lowlands is a feature that continues through the long occupation sequence for the region. In contrast, the Sierras region (as Robert Rands used to call it) represents a more local ceramic development, showing marked regional differences. In the former region, the earliest pottery found by Rands (1967:134) and our project (Liendo 2008, 2011) comes from samples collected in caves near Chinikiha, and it is related to the waxy ceramic diagnostics of the Sierra Red group. Early Classic ceramics at Chinikiha and other

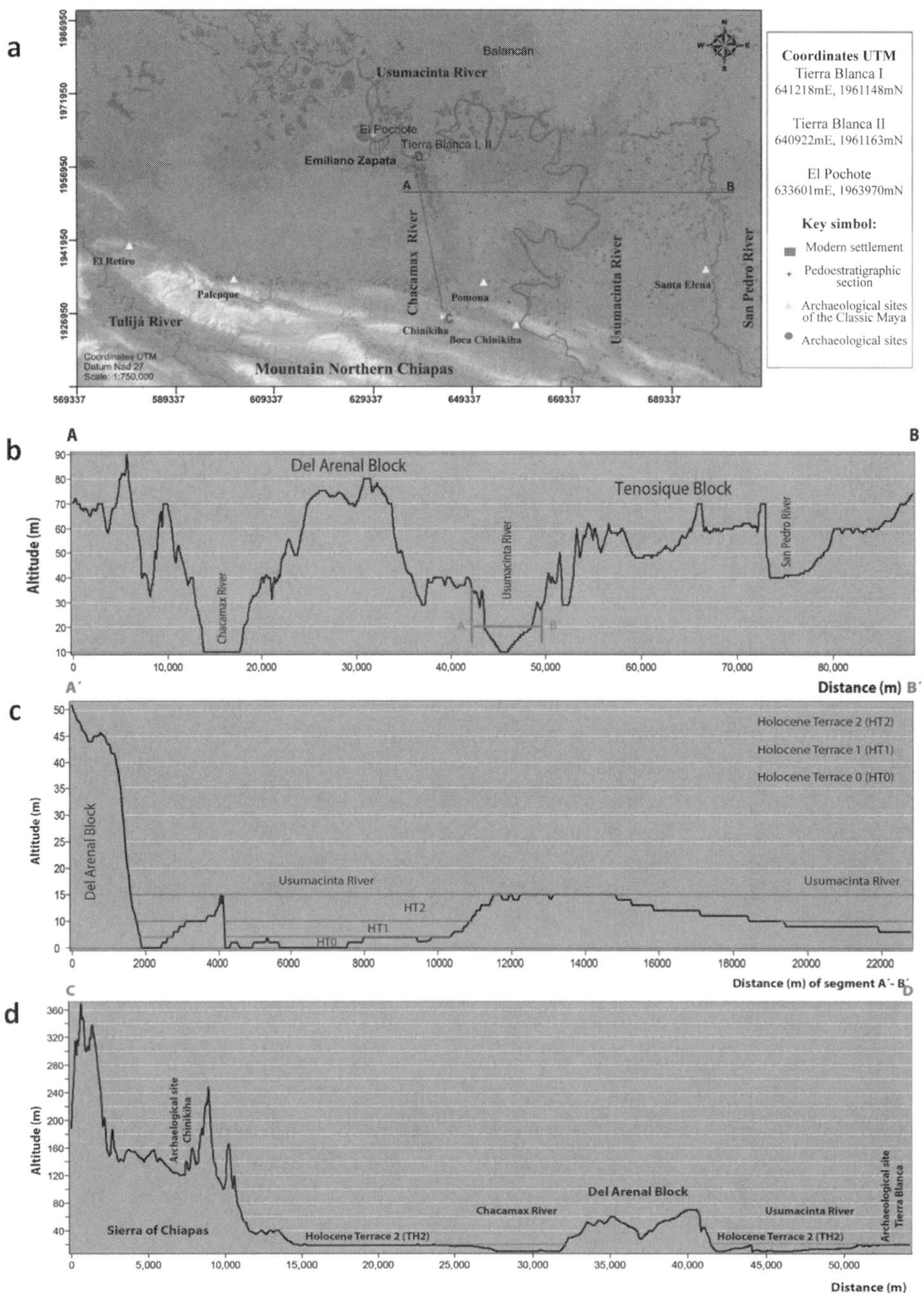

Figure 7.1. Northwestern Maya Lowlands and the Usumacinta River: (a.) study area showing: in circles, the archaeological sites; in triangles, the Classic big urban centers; and the pedological sections. (b.) A—B Cross section with W-E orientation showing the differences in altitude of fluvial terraces according to their age and controlled by tectonic activity; (c.) A´—B´cross section, representing the Holocene terraces in detail and close to the river bank; (d.) C—D cross section, with NW-SE orientation, representing the archeological site of Chinikihá in the Sierra de Chiapas.

settlements of Sierras, however, are more difficult to place. Currently, it is difficult to even establish an Early Classic occupation for the region. It is also unclear to what extent the Sierras Tzakol ceramics (scarce at Chinikiha) might be the result of sporadic ceramic intrusions. This scarcity of Early Classic ceramic material might also be due to inadequate archaeological sampling. Test pit excavations (N = 230) in the Palenque region (Liendo 2002, 2003, 2005) have sampled a large number of settlements (N = 145) without encountering a major occupation for this period. Clearly, the Sierra de Chiapas shows a differing pattern of distribution for the better known Maya ceramic types (Rands 1967:138). Ceramic analysis demonstrates that the Sierras region (including settlements like Palenque, Chinikiha, Pomoná, and Yoxihá) is characterized during Late Classic times (C.E. 560–830) by a markedly regionalized ceramic distribution pattern when compared to other regions in the lowlands (Rands 1967).

Chronology and Population Dynamics in the Lower Usumacinta

The Preclassic Period (600 B.C.E.–C.E. 150)

Based on ceramic materials, we might envision a model of differential use for lowland riverine environments with communities showing an early and continuous development throughout the sequence in contrast to the low hilly landscape (Sierra), which shows a late and short-term explosive development. The rich alluvial banks of the Usumacinta River contain many of the early sites reported for the northwestern lowlands. Several factors may account for the high frequency of prehispanic sites close to the Usumacinta River and its tributaries, the Rio San Pedro and Chacamax. The existence of rich alluvial soils, the lack of evidence for destructive floods on natural banks, and the rich variety of lake resources available to prehispanic inhabitants of the region make the setting especially attractive.

A significant Middle Preclassic occupation has been detected in Trinidad and Tierra Blanca, Tabasco. In the Lower Usumacinta, the Middle Preclassic seems to have been a remarkable period of population growth. Major sites dating to this time—Tierra Blanca, Balancan, and Zapata—are located on the rich alluvial banks of the Usumacinta River. In this vast natural floodplain, Povictuc, La Carmelita, and Tierra Blanca appear to have been large centers straddling the river, as indicated by a series of small mounds located on both banks of the Usumacinta.

This scenario differs radically from the La Sierra region where no contemporary settlements have yet been found. However, our recent surveys have identified some 32 sites with abundant evidence of ceramics belonging to the Late Preclassic Chicanel period along the foothills of the Sierra de Chiapas and along the river Chacamax. If we compare the abundance of early ceramic contexts in Balancán Zapata with these few contexts in the Sierra, we might argue for a marginal demographic development at the regional scale during the Late Preclassic. During the Early and Middle Preclassic periods, it is highly probable that the Sierra region remained sparsely populated and was visited only sporadically by groups of individuals with permanent residency in the northern plains.

The Early Classic Period (C.E. 150–550)

The Sierras Early Classic pottery found in archaeological contexts presents a situation that is difficult to interpret. The Sierras region differs in fundamental ways from better known ceramics from other sectors of the Maya area. During the Early Classic period, settlements appear to be preferentially clustered in low-lying riverine environments along the Lower Usumacinta. With time, populations concentrated in a small number of centers. Following the foothills of the Sierra de Chiapas and intermountain valleys, Chinikiha, Palenque, Santa Isabel, La Cascada, San Juan Chancalaíto, La Reforma, El Retiro, Nututun, Sulusum, and Miraflores (see Figure 7.1) were all settled by the end of the Early Classic period. Along the rivers of the Usumacinta and San Pedro, there are several important sites with evidence of occupation during this period: Pomona, Morales-Reforma, San Claudio, and Santa Elena. The Usumacinta River and the Rio San Pedro seem to have exerted a strong force of attraction to people seeking expedient and appropriate transportation routes. The Early Classic period represents a time of significant population growth along the Usumacinta River and in the Sierra region. It also represents the emergence of important local dynasties at Palenque, Piedras Negras, Yaxchilan, Pomona, Reforma, and certainly Chinikiha—all sites with great influence in later times.

The Late Classic Period (C.E. 550–830)

During the Late Classic period, there was a change in the correlation between the populations living within larger settlements and overall regional population figures. Some researchers (Bishop 1994; Liendo 2002; Rands et al. 1982) argue this evidence is strong enough to suggest that sites like Palenque experienced a marked population increase during the Terminal Classic. Such population spikes may have been the logical result of people searching for new lands, although the evidence is not conclusive in this regard. Whether or not there was a population increase from the Late to Terminal Classic periods requires more detailed demographic studies. The settlement pattern indicates a trend toward the abandonment of nucleated settlements—clear in the case of Palenque, Chinikiha, and Pomoná, but a phenomenon that remains to be demonstrated elsewhere in the northwestern Lowlands—that created a more dispersed pattern than that characteristic of Early Classic times, with settlements occupying spaces near agricultural fields.

The Terminal Classic is characterized by the introduction of a fine paste ceramic tradition, mainly orange ceramic groups related to the Altar, Balancan, and Silho ceramic types. This ceramic phase is underrepresented in the region, with only a few sherds found in la Sierra region at Palenque, Miraflores, and Pomoná. Chinikiha is completely devoid of ceramic material that can be associated with this period. It is evident that the Terminal Classic was a time of substantial decrease in population levels throughout the northwest of the Maya lowlands. Sites located near the Usumacinta River (Balancan, Calatrava, and Trinidad) appear to have survived and prospered into Postclassic times, but, overall, the Terminal Classic represents the end of most sizable communities—Palenque, Piedras Negras, Yaxchilan, Pomona, Morales-Reforma, and Chinikiha—as centers of political importance in the region.

The Paleo-Environment Setting of the Northwestern Maya Lowlands

Paleo-environmental studies in the northwestern Maya lowlands are scarce. Most of the information available for this area has been derived from reconstructions made in Guatemala and Belize. Given the high variability found in modern ecosystems (Ortiz-Pérez et al. 2005), these studies can only be provisionally utilized. There studies include the interpretation of lacustrine records from lake basins in Guatemala and Belize, covering the Late Pleistocene–Early Holocene (Correa-Metrio et al. 2012; Hodell et al. 2005; Hodell et al. 2008; Leyden et al. 1994; Rosenmeier et al. 2002) and, with more detail, the Late Holocene (Gill 2000; Haug et al. 2003; Hodell et al. 1995, 2005). According to these data, climate was highly variable during the last 36,000 years, and neither homogeneous in space nor time.

In general, the environmental conditions for Late Pleistocene–Early Holocene are characterized as humid with a progressive drying trend that began about 4000 years ago (Mueller et al. 2009) and created droughts that affected Maya populations (Gill 2000; Haug et al. 2003; Hodell et al. 1995, 2005). These data document that severe pulses of aridity occurred at the end of both the Late Preclassic and Classic periods, recorded not only in lacustrine sediments (Gunn et al. 1995; Hodell et al. 2001) but also in stalagmites of the Macal Chasm caves in Belize (Webster et al. 2007) and sediments of the Ix Chel cave in Belize (Polk et al. 2007). Dunning and Beach (2010) indicate that intense drought periods affected the Maya Lowlands in the fourth century B.C.E. and in the second, sixth, ninth, and eleventh centuries C.E., as well as in the more recent Little Ice Age. Both paleo-environmental records and archeological evidence show a strong correlation in terms of societal change in the Maya Lowlands associated with these periods.

Regional Setting—The Usumacinta River

The Usumacinta River is located in the southeastern part of Mexico. It runs from the south, starting in Guatemala, to the northeast into the Gulf of Mexico (see Figure 7.1). The river crosses through a mountain range belonging to Sierra de Chiapas that is constituted primarily by Tertiary folded limestones with their folding axis oriented northwest-southeast. The river then continues to the north through the alluvial plain of Tabasco. In the Sierra de Chiapas, the river runs mainly underground because of the karstification processes involving dissolution and infiltration rather than runoff. Consequently, water availability is more limited. Present environmental conditions vary according to the landforms. Near mountain ranges, precipitation is 2000 mm per year; in the alluvial plain, precipitation is slightly lower at 1800 mm per year. The region has an annual mean temperature of 27°C. The distribution of vegetation corresponds with this variability; evergreen tropical rainforest is found in the mountainous area, and grasses and aquatic species occur in the alluvial plain (Bueno and Santiago 2005; Rzedowski 2006).

The main tributaries of the Usumacinta system follow the planes of normal faults: San Pedro in the eastern part, Chakamax in the center, and Tulijá in the western sector.

Faults are also partly responsible for the distribution of the alluvial terraces. The alluvial plain is slightly inclined to the north, formed by clastic materials like sands, silts, and clays. Here the river has a different configuration, characterized by meanders, oxbow lakes, wetlands, lagoons, and swamps. The river was also responsive to tectonic features, providing a morphology of basin and range systems. This morphology is more obvious in the area between the mountain system and the alluvial plain where fluvial terraces from the effluents of the San Pedro, Chakamax, and Tulijá are located at different altitudes. Figure 7.1b shows a schematic section crossing the Usumacinta system from east to west, where the San Pedro River occupies a higher position than the Usumacinta and Chacamax Rivers in the uplift block. These terraces were formed during the Pleistocene, located at altitudes higher than 20 meters; and during the Holocene, at lower altitudes (Figure 7.1c). In the Pleistocene terraces, big urban centers like Palenque, Chinikihá, Pomona, and

Santa Helena developed (Figure 7.1, 1d); on the Holocene terraces, formed by floodplain deposits, middle sized sites are present. At least three levels of Holocene terraces are recognized (HT2, HT1, HT0) (Solís et al. 2013), as shown in Figure 7.1c.

Study Method

This study is based on the paleo-pedological record. Paleosols are good paleo-environmental proxies and, with climate information, they are indicators of past human activities and land use. In the Maya Lowlands, they have been used to register changes in environmental conditions (Cabadas et al. 2010; Dunning et al. 2006; Sedov et al. 2007) and human impact on the soil cover (Beach, 1998; Beach et al. 2008; Beach et al. 2009; Beach et al. 2011; Fedick et al. 2008; Fernández et al. 2005; Johnson, Terry, et al. 2007; Johnson, Wright, and Terry 2007).

We conducted a field survey along the Usumacinta near the town of Emiliano Zapata (see Figure 7.1), studying Holocene pedo-stratigraphy in detail. Four sections were described and sampled: two in the oldest Holocene terrace (HT2), Tierra Blanca I and Tierra Blanca II; and two in the HT1, El Pochote, and Vicente Guerrero (Figure 7.2; Solís et al. 2013).

Five profiles were described and sampled. Here we report the results of two of them, Tierra Blanca and El Pochote, where several pedo-stratigraphic units were recognized. In Tierra Blanca, these soil units are directly associated with the presence of artifacts of different ages. At El Pochote, no artifacts were recovered. Morphological descriptions were done in order to detect the differences in the soil development and sedimentation processes.

In the area of Chinikihá in the mountain system of Sierra de Chiapas (see Figure 7.1), we sampled another profile, taking advantage of the archaeological work undertaken in the core of the settlement. Thus, it is possible to make a comparison between two archaeological sites located in different landform positions: Tierra Blanca in the "open" alluvial plain, where the system is more dynamic; and, Chinikihá in a "protected" position near the Sierra.

Selected properties were evaluated. Colors were determined using Munsell Soil Color Charts (1975). Clay content was separated by gravity after the elimination of aggregating agents: H_2O_2 (15%) was used for soil organic matter (SOM), dithionite-citrate-bicarbonate (DCB) for iron oxides, and HCl (10%) for carbonates. pH was measured in H_2O in a 1:2 soil paste and measured using a potentiometer.

Only A horizons were used to evaluate the stable isotope composition ($\delta^{13}C$), which were obtained by Solís et al. (2013) from samples at Tierra Blanca and El Pochote. Samples from Chinikihá were processed in the Laboratory of Spectrometry of Stable Isotopes of the Institute of Geology at UNAM. A chronological frame for the study area has been constructed by using several AMS (Accelerator Mass Spectrometry) dates from Beta Analytic Laboratory (Solís et al. 2013), pedo-stratigraphy, and the presence of cultural materials.

Paleo-Environmental Results: Geomorphology

Profile Descriptions in the Alluvial Terrace

Tierra Blanca I and II (TBI, TBII)

We studied two sections in Tierra Blanca: the Tierra Blanca I (TBI) profile (1961366 N; 641218 E, 7 meters above sea level) and the Tierra Blanca II (TBII) profile (1961355 N; 641199 E, 7 meters above sea level; see Figure 7.1a). Sections are separated by only 50 meters and occupy the HT2 (Holocene terrace; see Figure 7.1b).

TBI has a more complete sequence that covers a longer time span. The base contains several buried paleosols with strong gleyic features (Gleysols) that were formed in the Late Pleistocene to Middle Holocene. There is no evidence of human occupation. This set of Gleysols is well separated from the upper materials by 1.5 meters of fine laminated sediment. Overlying this sediment we have recognized two paleosols (2, 3) with 2A, 2AB, 2C, 3A, 3AB 3BC horizons (Figure 7.3; Table 7.1) strongly affected by human activities and sedimentary processes. Particularly in 2A and 2AB, there is an artifactual mixture of different cultural periods including Classic ceramics and Postclassic burials containing ceramics. These materials are close to the present-day surface, which has a poorly developed soil only 20 centimeters thick.

In TBII, Gleysols are not present, but the younger paleosols are better developed and are separated from modern soil by one meter of alluvial sediment. The set of paleosol horizons is as follows: 2A, 2AC; 3A, 3C, 4Ck, 5Ass, 5Bss, 5BC, 5C. The latest horizons, belonging to the paleosol 5, are the best developed and contain ceramics from the Preclassic period. This paleosol shows strong dark colored vertic features in the 5Ass horizon, hard angular blocky structure, clayey slickensides, and vertical cracks. The fourth paleosol is a pedo-sediment (4Ck), containing common fragments of soils eroded from the previous surface as well as re-worked pedogenic carbonates and alluvium, indicating a period of landscape instability. Paleosols 2 and 3 are less developed, with similar soil profiles; but in TBII they are well separated by parent material, while in TBI they are welded in

Figure 7.2. Chiniquihá soils: (a.) Landscape view, showing the differences in altitude; (b.) Rendzinas in the slope of the Sierra; (c.) and (d.) Luvisols at the valley bottom.

2A. Abundant artifacts have been found: Postclassic in 2A and 2C, and Classic in 3A, 3C. Modern soil signature of the carbon stable isotope composition is -21.9‰. 2A and 3A have a little bit higher values, -20.2% and -19.4‰, respectively.

El Pochote (POCH)

This section (1964202 N; 633601 E, 7 meters above sea level), located in younger terrace HT1, is constituted by seven paleosols (2, 3, 4, 5, 6, 7, 8; see Figure 7.1b). The modern soil has an AC horizon, preserving characteristics of the parent material (sandy alluvial sediment). The upper first paleosols (2, 3, 4) are poorly developed, showing loose structure and light colors, but the A horizons are slightly darker (see Table 7.1). Paleosol 4 is somewhat better developed and has abundant charcoal fragments. In contrast, underlying paleosols (5, 6 7, 8) have a higher degree of development and are more clayey, with the following horizons: 5Bg, 6Bgk, 6BCg, 7Ass, 7Bg, 8Ass, 8Bg, 8G, all of them with gleyic features (reddish mottling, Fe concretions). A horizons (7Ass and 8Ass) are very dark (see Figure 7.2; see Table 7.1) and have angular blocky structures, very compact and dense. $\delta^{13}C$ in values of the soil organic C are lower in the uppermost paleosols (-22.9% and -21.9‰ for 2A and 4A, respectively). The highest values correspond to paleosols 6 and 7, both having -17.6‰ (see Table 7.1). We did not find artifacts in this section.

All horizons from TBI, TBII, and POCH had pH values ranging from neutral to slightly alkaline (7 to 8), with low to moderate carbonates contents that are low in TBI and TBII (4% to 15%) and high in the Pochote (10% to 26%).

Profile Descriptions inside the Archaeological Site of Chinikihá—Natural vs. Human Affected Soils

Chinikihá is located in the Sierra de Chiapas (1926451.5 N; 643533.5 E, 130 meters above sea level; see Figure 7.1d) and is a large archaeological site. As the Sierra de Chiapas is constituted by folded limestones, it conforms with a karstic system in which soils show a high variability (see Figure 7.2), spanning thick, red, clayey soils or Luvisols to shallow, dark Rendzinas. Luvisols occupy the lowest positions in the valleys (Figure 7.4b, 7.4c), while Rendzinas are found in the hills and on the slopes, contrasting their presence with the limestone outcrops (see Figure 7.2d).

We have described three sections: one corresponds to the Luvisol profile in the bottom valley (see Figure 7.2b, 7.2c); the second is a Rendzina in the limestone ridge

Figure 7.3. Pedological sections, showing the paleosols' stratigraphic location: (a.) Tierra Blanca II; (b.) El Pochote.

(see Figure 7.2d); and the last, inside the archaeological excavation (Operation 114), associated with an interesting midden located behind the Palace at the site of Chinikiha. It is highly plausible that the Chinikihá palace functioned as the residence for the ruling family.

Luvisols were more than one meter thick, with a dominant reddish brown color. The A horizon was shallow (15 centimeters thick) and dense. Underlying the A horizon was a clayey Bt horizon. It presented clay cutans, structured in angular blocks, and was very well developed; however, it was hard and dense, which limited root penetration (see Figure 7.2a). The Rendzina profile was 50 centimeters thick, but this depth was irregular, having an abrupt contact with the limestone (see Figure 7.2b). The Rendzina color was very dark brown with a high root density, and its structure was granular and porous.

In Operation 114 (see Figure 7.4), a Bt horizon was observed that was very clayey (75% of clay), belonged to a Luvisol (Figure 7.4c), and was buried by cultural remains.

The material used for the infillings—like the Bt horizon—were denser and more compact. Both materials, the Bt horizon and the infilling, had similar pH values (7.5 and 7, respectively) and color (see Table 7.1). Overlying the cultural structure, a less developed soil was present (Figure 7.4b). It was 30 centimeters thick, with A and AB horizons that were brownish and had a hard subangular blocky structure (see Figure 7.4).

Age of the Paleosols

The age of the paleosols was determined by several AMS dates from bulk organic matter. Although we do not have dates from all paleosols present in the alluvial terrace, the archaeological artifacts and paleosol morphology help to establish a chronological framework. Accordingly, we propose that 5Ass-TBII, 8Ass-POCH, and 3A in TBI, which were associated with ceramics belonging to a Preclassic culture, were formed during the same era (see Table 7.1). All of these paleosols had well expressed vertic features. Sample 2A-TBI containing ceramics from both the Maya Classic and Postclassic periods correlate with 7Ass-POCH, 3A-TBII, and 2A-TBII. The latter was associated with Postclassic ceramics.

Environmental and Land-Use Interpretation

Contrasting features may be found in the morphology of the alluvial valley paleosols as shown in Figure 7.5, and taking into account the TBII section, which includes all

Figure 7.4. Operation 140 at the archaeological excavation: (a.) remains of a wall; (b.) Soil close to excavation surface; (c.) Buried soil showing similar characteristics of the Luvisol in Figure 7.2.

paleosol units and contains archaeological materials. Vertic features predominate in paleosols 3 in TBI, 5 in TBII, and in 8Ass and 7Ass of El Pochote. Humus accumulation is the main pedogenetic process in the younger paleosols found in the alluvial terrace.

In Chinikihá, however, we observe a different picture: two kind of pedogenesis are noticeable, one related to the plain and bottom valley positions, and another related to the mountainous system. This behavior is common in karstic areas (e.g., Yaalon 1997). Luvisols need a longer time to develop, while Rendzinas suffer from erosion and translocation processes. Consequently, the observed differences might indicate periods of relative landscape stability. In the Sierra de Chiapas, erosional processes take place on the slopes, leading to the accumulation of material in the valley bottom that leads to the formation of thick Luvisols; Rendzinas are consequently thinner.

On the other hand, paleosols in the alluvial terrace are formed in shorter time periods and within a more dynamic environment. In such positions, the influence of alluvial sedimentation is high—limiting the development of the soils, but contributing nutrients to them. These paleosols are less developed and younger than those observed in the mountain region.

In terms of environmental conditions, Luvisols form under humid climatic conditions for periods of several thousands of years; their formation probably covers most of the Holocene. Early Holocene humid conditions have been reported in other parts of the Maya lands as noted earlier (e.g., Hodell et al. 2001, 2007; Islebe et al. 1996; Leyden 2002; Mueller et al. 2009). However, the paleosols of the alluvial terraces demonstrate that this environment was not homogeneous in space and time. First, the Usumacinta River had several pulses of sedimentation and erosion that produced the terrace configuration labeled as HT2, HT1, and HT0 (see Figure 7.1, from oldest to youngest). Second, each pulse of sedimentation generated a new parent material for soil formation. In this way, paleosols in TBI, TBII, and POCH reflect periods of instability (where the river was more active and accumulated sediments) and stability (when the sedimentation stopped and pedogenesis started).

The presence of vertic paleosols, formed during the Preclassic, is evidence of a seasonal climate; a dry season, several months long; and a short rainy season. Such conditions also are necessary for the formation of Vertisols in other parts of the world (Wilding and Puentes 1988). We suggest that a seasonal climate combined with stable conditions permitted the formation of better developed paleosols

Table 7.1. Selected properties of paleosols in Tierra Blanca I and II and Chinikihá.

Horizon	Depth cm	Color dry	Features	Clay (%)	Calendrical Age (2σ)	$\delta^{13}C^{*}$
			Tierra Blanca I (TBI)			
AC	0–20	10YR 4/2	Sandy, weak structured, affected by recent human activities.	24.7		−21.9
2A	20–52	10YR 5/2	Very hard and compact subangular blocky structure. Ceramic and burials (human bones).	32.1		−20.2
2AB	52–80	10YR 6/2	Very hard, subangular blocky structure, abundant artifacts. Abundant charcoal.	33.7		
2C	80–140	2.5Y 6/2	Silty. Colluvial material, with no pedogenic structure.	27.1		
3A	140–155	2.5Y 7/1	Clayey. Fine and very hard subangular blocky structure, slickensides are present in ped surfaces, vertical cracks.	45.6	830–790 B.C.E.	−19.4
3AB	155–170	2.5Y 7/2	Clay. Fine and very hard subangular blocky structure.	45.4		
3BC	170–185	2.5Y 8/2	Silty. Less structured, friable.	35.9		
sediment	185–451	2.5Y 8/2	Silty. Laminated. No signs of pedogenesis.	36.3		
			Tierra Blanca II (TBII)			
AC	0–100		Alluvial sediment poorly affected by pedogenesis.	14.3		
2A	100–130	2.5Y 4/2	Silty. Structure is well developed, with fine subangular blocks. Post-Classic ceramic.	44.2		−22.6
2AC	130–195		More silty and less structured.	31.5		
3A	195–210	2.5Y 5/3	Silty clayey. Brownish gray. subangular blocky structure, compact. Presence of ceramic of Maya Classic.	33.5		−20.3 −25.0
3C	210–270	2.5Y 5/3	More silty and less structured.	20.3		
4Ck	270–290		Silty pedosediment. Reworked soil fragments and carbonate concretions, horizontal alignment.	37.9		
5Ass	290–315	2.5Y 4/1	Clayey. Structure in very hard angular blocks, slikensides, and carbonate concentrations. Ceramic of the Formative period.	57.1	390–350 B.C.E.	−16.5
5Bss	315–340	2.5Y 5/3	Clayey. Slickensides. Concentrations of carbonates in the ped surfaces.	55.3		−18.3 −10.0
5BC	340–365	2.5Y 5/3	More silty. Here, there are also abundant ceramic fragments	44.3		
5C	365–515	2.5Y 5/2	Colluvial sediment. Silty sand. It has incorporated rests of gleyic soils.	30.3		
C	0–38	2.5Y 5/3	Sandy, with low degree of pedogenesis.	19.2		−22.9

(Continued)

Table 7.1. (continued)

Horizon	Depth cm	Color dry	Features	Clay (%)	Calendrical Age (2σ)	$\delta^{13}C^*$
			El Pochote (POCH)			
2AC	38–50	10YR 7/4	Low structured. Sandy.	16.3		
2C	50–71	2.5Y 6/4	Sandy, not structured. Laminated sediment.	20.0		
3A	71–88	2.5Y 5/3	Sandy, with a weak structure.	12.0		
3C	88–120	2.5Y 6/3	Sandy, poorly structured.	9.3		−21.9
4A	120–160	2.5Y 7/3	Sandy. Subangular blocky structure, friable, abundant charcoal fragments.	16.8		
4AC	160–176	2.5Y 7/3	Coarser subangular blocky structure, friable.	30.4		
4C	176–326	2.5Y 6/4	Sandy, laminated sediment.	25.0		
5Bg	326–356	2.5Y 7/3	Sandy. Friable subangular blocks. In the limit with 5Bgk there is a layer of coarser material.	12.8		
6Bgk	356–446	2.5Y 7/3	Silty. Prismatic to columnar structure, very hard and very well developed, with small carbonate hard concretions. Some shells are present.	20.3		
6BCg	446–476	2.5Y 7/3	Clayey. Subangular blocky structure, very hard.	44.8		−17.6
7Ass	476–528	2.5Y 6/2	Clayey. Columnar to prismatic structure, breaks into angular blocks. Slickensides.	47.1	C.E. 640–690	
7Bg	528–616	2.5Y 7/2	Clayey. Subangular blocky structure more friable than 7Ass. dense	52.8		−17.6
8Ass	616–628	2.5Y 6/1	Clayey. Very hard, angular blocky structure, slickensides.	45.9	180–30 B.C.E.	
8Bg	628–672	2.5Y 7/3	Clayey. Subangular blocky structure. Slickensides.	67.9		
8G	672–702	2.5Y 5/3	More sandy, showing redox features.	23.9		
			Chinikihá (Luvisol)			
A	0–15	5 YR 3/3	Subangular blocky structure, dense, low density of roots.	60.0		
Bt	15–80	2.5YR 3/6	Very clayey, subangular blocky structure, very dense and compact. Poor root penetration. Some fragments of limestone are present at different depths. Bright clay cutans on surface of the aggregates.	75.7		
			Chinikihá (Rendzina)			
A	0–20/50	10YR 3/1	Granular structure, very well developed. High density of roots, very aggregated and clayey.	55		−25.6

(Continued)

Table 7.1. (continued)

			Chinikihá (Operation 140)			
A	0–18	7.5YR 4/6	Subangular blocky structure, slightly compacted, but still porous.	51.7		−25.6
AB	18–29	5YR 4/6	Subangular blocky structure, very dense and hard.	65.6		
cultural	29–61	5YR 4/6 (infillings)	Floor made of stones, infilled by reddish, clayey material.	35.7		
Btb	61–80	5YR 4/6	Subangular blocky structure, very well developed, very dense and compact. It has bright clay cutans and shows limestone fragments and ceramic.	75.6		

*According to Solis et al. 2013, except for the samples of Chinikihá

prior to the Classic and Postclassic, when these particular soils were more affected by erosion and sedimentation processes.

Paleosols in the river bank demonstrate better attributes for agriculture and would have been able to sustain a population longer based on high organic content, carbonates and clay, and a neutral pH, as well as a porous structure that permitted good root penetration and aeration. In contrast, in higher terraces and in the Sierra de Chiapas, Luvisols are more clayey, more compact, and contain less organic matter. Rendzinas have better attributes, but they are shallow and discontinuous. Compare values of $\delta^{13}C$, Chinikihá values are very low (-25.6‰); thus, we suggest that the soils were not affected by agriculture. Paleosols in Tierra Blanca and El Pochote show the highest $\delta^{13}C$ value of -16.5‰—evidence for the use of C4 and CAM plants. Maize is a typical C4 plant; thus, the signature that was obtained probably is due to the mixture of maize and C3 plants from humid forest. Whatever the case, it clearly indicates the use of these paleosols in agriculture. Fernández et al. (2005) and Johnson and colleagues (Johnson, Terry, et al. 2007; Johnson, Wright, and Terry 2007) have documented similar variations in the carbon isotope signatures in Guatemalan soils and attribute these variations to changing land use.

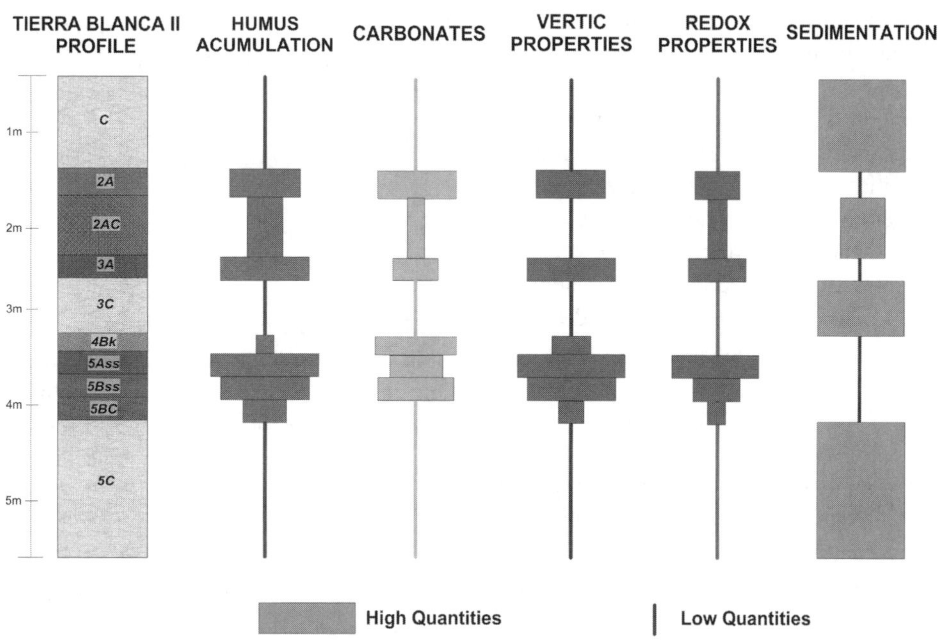

Figure 7.5. Scheme of morphological characteristics of paleosols at Tierra Blanca II, showing contrasting differences between those formed in Post-Classic, Classic, and Formative periods.

Although similar, paleosols in El Pochote and Tierra Blanca show significant differences. In El Pochote, reductomorphic features, related to periods of soil water-saturation, are more frequent. This feature would have developed during seasonal inundations and is probably the reason that no artifacts are found in these soils. However the signature of $\delta^{13}C$ at -17‰ can be attributed to ancient maize agriculture.

Final Remarks: Spatial Differentiation of Occupation Type and Evolution Controlled by Landscape and Soil Cover Structure?

The distribution of archaeological sites of different types and histories shows a clear relation to geomorphic position, geological setting, and soil type. The most ancient (Preclassic) rural settlements have been registered in the lowest river terrace, nearest to the Usumacinta River and in areas that were periodically flooded. In this setting, people inhabited a flat land surface covered by thick cumulic Luvisols that were rich in humus and nutrients and that had a high physical quality. It is important that these original settlements persisted throughout the Classic period and even survived the Terminal Classic collapse, maintaining the same characteristics of minor rural sites.

The higher terraces, more distant from the river and closer to the mountain ridges, were occupied later during the Classic period by larger and more complex settlements. These landforms have a more curved relief and are covered with more developed red soils that have a lower agronomic quality and are poorer in humus and nutrients. Major urban centers are located on the calcareous mountain ridges (see Figure 7.1). These centers, like Palenque, Piedras Negras Yaxchilán, Pomoná, Santa Elena, Reforma Moral, and Chinikihá, flourished during the Classic period. All show high population densities, impressive cultural developments, and a high concentration of political power. These centers suffered a complete abandonment during the collapse that occurred in the Terminal Classic period at the beginning of the 9th century C.E. The mountains are formed of Tertiary limestones subjected to karst processes that in a humid tropical environment demonstrate the highest erosional intensity when occupied by humans. These processes generated a very contrasting relief consisting of profound circular closed or half-closed depressions surrounded by sharp, steep ridges. Underground cavities, caves, and galleries are frequent; some are partly filled with groundwater. The soil mantle is strongly differentiated: the ridges have very thin, stony, discontinuous soils alternating with the limestone outcrops; the depressions contain thick, red, very clayey soils that are compact and hard. Both components of the mountain soil cover are difficult for cultivation and have a much lower agronomic quality than the alluvial soils of the lower terraces.

Obviously for initial colonizing populations focusing on an agronomic viewpoint, the lower terraces present the most attractive landscape in terms of easy access and soil fertility. Nevertheless, floods presented certain risk. That said, however, in the terrace profiles we observed higher soil development and minor alluvial sedimentation features corresponding to occupation during the Classic period. This indicates that the surface was rather stable and that flooding processes were rare and weak.

The Sierras region clearly presented the most hostile environment for agriculture because of relief complexity and poor soil quality. Interestingly, during Preclassic times, this same landscape provided an excellent stage for ritual activities in karstic caves. A better understanding of the factors responsible for drawing population to the Sierras region will need to be detailed through future research. However, we are able to cautiously suggest the following "attractors" as favorable conditions for the development of an urban pattern that concentrated political power:

- High position in the relief allows visual control of the adjacent low territories.
- More defensive settlement positions exist on high relief.
- The stone material for urban and ceremonial constructions is abundant in the more elevated settings.
- The karstic relief presents a specific advantage for urban development. The set of interconnected flat, draining, circular karstic depressions are a perfect base to create small squares—plazas surrounded by habitation areas developed on artificial terraces of surrounding slopes. We can conclude that karstic relief formed part of the urban design in several examples in the Sierras region, especially Chinikiha.
- Subsurface water-filled karstic hollows provided a permanent water supply for urban dwellers.

The comparison of this set of attractors (or new ones) among human communities located in the alluvial flood plains and the Sierras regions are an important avenue for future research in the Usumacinta region. The divergent trajectories and comparative success of settlements located in the plains and Sierras regions can be traced and understood in these terms.

In closing, we note the dynamic role of the karstic environs and the clever landscaping adjustments and alterations made by the Maya of the northwestern Maya lowlands. Our regional case study emphasizes the resilience of these populations in adapting to the oscillations of a changing climate and the behaviors of a human induced erosional cycle. We hope that a careful reevaluation and reassessment of these ancient settings and the people that occupied and utilized them will be allowed before additional urban expansions by our modern world.

Acknowledgments

This research has been funded by PAPIIT, grants No. IN117709 and IN110710 (E. Solleiro-Rebolledo); IN400711 (Rodrigo Liendo); CONACYT-DLR J010/0705/09 and CONACYT 166878 (E. Solleiro-Rebolledo); CONACYT 56573 (Rodrigo Liendo); and the Coordinación de Estudios de Posgrado (UNAM). We very much appreciate the valuable collaboration of Keiko Teranishi, who has recorded the cultural history for Tierra Blanca. We acknowledge the support of Jaime Díaz, Kumiko Alcalá, and René Alcalá for laboratory analyses. Edith Cienfugos and Pedro Morales evaluated the carbon stable isotopic composition.

References Cited

Beach, T.
1998 Soil Constraints on Northwest Yucatán, Mexico: Pedoarchaeology and Maya Subsistence at Chunchucmil. Geoarchaeology 13(8):759–791.

Beach, T., S. Luzzadder-Beach, N. Dunning, and D. E. Cook
2008 Human and Natural Impacts on Fluvial and Karst Depressions of the Maya Lowlands. Geomorphology 101:308–331.

Beach, T., S. Luzzadder-Beach, N. Dunning, J. Jones, J. Lohse, T. Guderjan, S. Bozarth, S. Millspaugh, and T. Bhattacharya
2009 A Review of Human and Natural Changes in Maya Lowland Wetlands over the Holocene. Quaternary Science Reviews 28:1710–1724.

Beach, T., S. Luzzadder-Beach, R. Terry, N. Dunning, S. Houston, and T. Garrison
2011 Carbon Isotopic Ratios of Wetland and Terrace Soil Sequences in the Maya Lowlands of Belize and Guatemala. Catena 85:109–118.

Bishop, Ronald L.
1994 Pre-Columbian Pottery: Reserach in the Maya Region. *In* Archaeometry of Pre-Columbian Sites and Artifacts. David A. Scott and Pieter Meyers, eds. Pp. 15–65. Los Angeles: The Getty Conservation Institute.

Berlin-Neubart, Heinrich
1955 News from the Maya World. Ethnos 20(4):201–209.

Bueno, J., F. Alvarez, and S. Santiago
2005 Biodiversidad del Estado de Tabasco.Instituto de Biología, UNAM, México.

Cabadas, H., E. Solleiro-Rebolledo, S. Sedov, T. Pi, and J. Gama-Castro
2010 Pedosediments of Karstic Sinkholes in the Eolianites of NE Yucatán: A Record of Late Quaternary Soil Development, Geomorphic Processes and Landscape Stability. Geomorphology 122:323–337.

Correa-Metrio, A., M. B. Bush, K. R. Cabrera, S. Sully, M. Brenner, D. A. Hodell, J. Escobar, and T. Guilderson
2012 Rapid Climate Change and No-Analog Vegetation in Lowland Central America during the Last 86,000 Years. Quaternary Science Reviews 38:63–75.

Culbert, T. Patrick
1991 Polities in the Northern Peten, Guatemala. *In* Classic Maya Political History: Hieroglyphic and Archaeological Evidence. T. P. Culbert, ed. Pp. 128–146. Cambridge: Cambridge University Press.

Dunning, N. P., and T. Beach
2010 Farms and Forests: Spatial and Temporal Perspectives on Ancient Maya Landscapes. *In* Landscapes and Societies. I. P. Martini and W. Chesworth, eds. Pp. 369–389. New York: Springer Science Business Media B.V.

Dunning, N. P., T. Beach, and S. Luzzadder-Beach
2006 Environmental Variability among *Bajos* in the Southern Maya Lowlands and Its Implications for Ancient Maya Civilization and Archaeology. *In* Pre-Columbian Water Management. L. Lucero and B. Fash, eds. Pp. 111–133. Tucson: University of Arizona Press.

Fedick, S. L, M. L. Flores-Delgadillo, S. Sedov, E. Solleiro-Rebolledo, and S. Palacios-Mayorga
2008 Adaptation of Maya Homegardens by Container Gardening in Limestone Bedrock Cavities. Journal of Ethnobiology 28(2):305–317.

Fernández, F., K. Johnson, R. Terry, S. Nelson, and D. Webster
2005 Soil Resources of the Ancient Maya at Piedras Negras, Guatemala. Soil Science Society of America Journal 69:2020–2032.

Gill, R. B.
2000 The Great Maya Droughts. Albuquerque: University of New Mexico Press.

Grube, Nikolai, and Simon Martin
1998 Política Clásica Maya dentro de una Tradición Mesoamericana. *In* Modelos de Entidades Políticas Mayas. Silvia Trejo, ed, Pp. 131–146. Mexico: INAH.

Gunn, J. D., W. J. Folan, W. J., and H. R. Robichaux
1995 A Landscape Analysis of the Candelaria Watershed in Mexico: Insights into Paleoclimates Affecting Upland Horticulture in the Southern Yucatan Peninsula Semi-Karst. Geoarchaeology 10:3–42.

Haug, G., D. Gunther, L. Peterson, D. Sigman, K. Hughen, and B. Aeshlimman
2003 Climate and Collapse of Maya Civilization. Science 299(5613):1731–1735.

Hernández, Ayala, Martha Ivón
1981 Cronología y periodificación en la región del río San Pedro Mártir, Tabasco. Ph.D. dissertation, Escuela Nacional de Antropología e Historia. Mexico City, Mexico.

Hodell, D. A., F. S. Anselmetti, and D. Ariztegui
2008 An 85-ka Record of Climate Change in Lowland Central America. Quaternary Science Reviews 27:1152–1165.

Hodell, D. A., M. Brenner, and J. H. Curtis
2005 Terminal Classic Drought in the Northern Maya Lowlands Inferred from Multiple Sediment Cores in Lake Chichancanab (Mexico). Quaternary Science Reviews 24:1413–1427.
2007 Climate and Cultural History of the Northeastern Yucatán Peninsula, Quintana Roo, Mexico. Climatic Change 83:215–240.

Hodell D. A., M. Brenner, J. H. Curtis, and T. Guilderson
2001 Solar Forcing of Drought Frequency in the Maya Lowlands. Science 292:1367–1370.

Hodell, D. A., J. H. Curtis, and M. Brenner
1995 Possible Role of Climate in the Collapse of Classic Maya Civilization. Nature 375: 391–394.

Islebe, G.A., H. Hooghiemstra, M. Brenner, J.H. Curtis, and D. A. Hodell
1996 A Holocene vegetation history from lowland Guatemala. Holocene 6:265–271.

Johnson, K. D., R. E. Terry, M. W. Jackson, and C. Golden
2007 Ancient Soil Resources of the Usumacinta River Region, Guatemala. Journal of Archaeological Science 34:1117–1129.

Johnson, K. D., D. R. Wright, and R. E. Terry
2007 Application of Carbon Isotope Analysis to Ancient Maize Agriculture in the Petexbatún Region of Guatemala. Geoarchaelogy 22:313–336.

Leyden, B. W.
2002 Pollen Evidence for Climatic Variability and Cultural Disturbance in the Maya Lowlands. Ancient Mesoamerica 13:85–101.

Leyden, B. W., M. Brenner, D. A. Hodell, and J. A. Curtis
1994 Orbital and Internal Forcing of Climate on the Yucatan Peninsula for the Past ca. 36 ka. Palaeogeography, Palaeoclimatology, Palaeoecology 109:193–210.

Liendo Stuardo, Rodrigo
2002 The Organization of Agricultural Production at a Maya Center: Settlement Patterns in the Palenque Region, Chiapas, Mexico. Serie Arqueología de México. University of Pittsburgh: Latin American Archaeological Publications/INAH.
2003 Palenque y el problema de la Integración Política. *In* Memoria del VIII Simposio de Investigaciones Arqueológicas en Guatemala. Pp. 65–77. Guatemala: INAH.
2005 An Archaeological Study of Settlement Distribution in the Palenque Area, Chiapas, México. Anthropological Notebooks 11:31–42.

2008 Fronteras, territorio y estructura de asentamientos en la región de Palenque, Chiapas: Aspectos de Método y Teoría. *In* Memorias de la V Mesa Redonda de Palenque: El Territorio Maya. R. Liendo Stuardo, ed. Pp. 98–107. Mexico: INAH-CONACULTA.
2011 B'aakal: Arqueología de la región de Palenque, Chipas, México. BAR International Series 2203. Oxford: Archaeopress.

López, Sandra
2005 Cerámica. *In* Pomoná: un sitio del Clásico Maya en las colinas tabasqueñas. R. García Moll, ed. Pp 75–101. Mexico: Colección Científica INAH.

Marcus, Joyce
1976 Emblem and State in the Classic Maya Lowlands: An Epigraphic Approach to Territorial Organization. Washington, DC: Dumbarton Oaks.
1993 Ancient Maya Political Organization. *In* Lowland Maya Civilization in the Eight Century A.D. J. Sabloff and J. Henderson, eds. Pp. 111–183. Washington, DC: Dumbarton Oaks.

Martin, Simon, and Nikolai Grube
2000 Chronicle of the Maya Kings and Queens: Deciphering the Dynasties of the Ancient Maya. London: Thames and Hudson.

Mathews, Peter
1991 Classic Maya Emblem Glyphs. *In* Classic Maya Political History: Hieroglyphic and Archaeological Evidence. T. P. Culbert, ed. Pp.19–29. Cambridge: Cambridge University Press.

Mueller, A. D., G. Islebe, M. B. Hillesheim, D. A. Grzesikc, F. S. Anselmetti, D. Ariztegui, M. Brenner, J. H. Curtis, D. A. Hodell, and K. A. Venzc
2009 Climatic Drying and Associated Forest Decline in the Lowlands of Northern Guatemala during the Late Holocene. Quaternary Research 71:133–141.

Munsell Color
1975 Munsell Soil Color Charts. Baltimore: Macbeth Division of Koll Morgen Corporation.

Ochoa Salas, Lorenzo
1978 Estudios preliminares sobre los mayas de las Tierras Bajas Noroccidentales. IIF-CEM. Mexico: UNAM.
1984 Introducción. In Investigaciones arqueológicas en el Valle del Río Tulijá Tabasco-Chiapas. Mexico: UNAM.

Ortiz-Pérez, M. A., C. Siebe, and S. Cram
2005 Diferenciación ecogeográfica de Tabasco. *In* Biodiversidad del Estado de Tabasco. J. Bueno, F. Álvarez, and S. Santiago, eds. Pp. 305–322. Instituto de Biología. Mexico: UNAM-CONABIO.

Polk, J. S., P. E. van Beynen, and P. P. Reeder
2007 Late Holocene Environmental Reconstruction Using Cave Sediments from Belize. Quaternary Research 68:53–63.

Rands, Robert L.
1967 Cerámica de la Región de Palenque, México. Estudios de Cultura Maya VI:111–147. Centro de Estudios Mayas. Universidad Nacional Autónoma de México. México.
1974 The Ceramic Sequence at Palenque, Chiapas. *In* Mesoamerican Archaeology: New Approaches. N. Hammond, ed. Pp. 51–75. London: Duckworth.
1977 The rise of Classic Maya Civilizations in the Northwestern Zone: Isolation and Integration. *In* The Origins of Maya Civilization. R. E. W. Adams, ed. Pp. 159–180. Albuquerque: University of New Mexico Press.

Rands, Robert L., R. L. Bishop, and G. Harbottle
1982 A Ceramic Compositional Interpretation of Incense-Burner Trade in the Palenque Area, Mexico. *In* Nuclear and Chemical Dating Techniques. L. A. Currie, ed. Pp. 411–440. Washington: American Chemical Society.

Rosenmeier, M. F., D. A. Hodell, M. Brenner, and J. H. Curtis
2002 A 4000-Year Lacustrine Record of Environmental Change in the Southern Maya Lowlands, Petén, Guatemala. Quaternary Research 57:183–190.

Rzedowski, J.
2006 Vegetación de México. 1st edición digital. Mexico: Comisión Nacional para el Conocimiento y el Uso de la Biodiversidad.

Schele, Linda
1986 Architectural Development and Political History at Palenque. *In* City-States of the Maya: Art and Architecture. E. P. Benson, ed. Pp. 110–138. Denver: Rocky Mountain Institute for Pre-Columbian Studies.
1991 An Epigraphic History of the Western Maya Region. *In* Classic Maya Political History. Hieroglyphic and Archaeological Evidence. T. P. Culbert, ed. Pp.72–101. Cambridge: Cambridge University Press: Cambridge.

Schele, Linda, and David Freidel
1990 A Forest of Kings: the Untold Story of the Ancient Maya. New York: Morrow and Co.

Sedov, S., E. Solleiro-Rebolledo E., S. L. Fedick, J. Gama-Castro, S. Palacios-Mayorga, and E. Vallejo Gómez
2007 Soil Genesis in Relation to Landscape Evolution and Ancient Sustainable Land Use in the Northeastern Yucatan Peninsula, Mexico. Sociedad. Toscana. Sciencias. Naturales., Memorias., Serie A 112:115–126.

Socorro Jiménez, María
2009 Análisis Cerámico. *In* Segundo Informe Parcial. Segunda Temporada Proyecto Arqueológico Chinikihá. R. Liendo Stuardo, ed. http://www.mesoweb.com/resources/informes/Chinikiha2008.html, accessed May 3, 2014.

Solís-Castillo, B., E. Solleiro-Rebolledo, S. Sedov, R. Liendo, S. López-Rivera, and M. A. Ortiz-Pérez
2013 Paleoenvironment and Human Occupation in the Maya Lowlands of the Usumacinta River, Mexico. Geoarchaeology 28:268–288.

Webster, J. W., G. A. Brook, L. B. Railsback, H. Cheng, L. Edwards, C. Alexander, and P. P. Reeder
2007 Stalagmite Evidence from Belize Indicating Significant Droughts at the Time of Preclassic Abandonment, the Maya Hiatus, and the Classic Maya Collapse. Palaeogeography, Palaeoclimatology, Palaeoecology 250:1–17.

Wilding, L. P., and R. Puentes, eds.
1988 Vertisols: Their Distribution, Properties, Classification and Management. Technical Monograph, 18. College Station: Texas A&M.

Yaalon, D. H.
1997 Soils in the Mediterranean Region: What Makes Them Different? Catena 28:157–170.

8

Calakmul: Agent Risk and Sustainability in the Western Maya Lowlands

Joel D. Gunn
University of North Carolina-Greensboro
William J. Folan
Universidad Autonoma de Campeche
Christian Isendahl
University of Gothenburg
María del Rosario Domínguez Carrasco
Universidad Autonoma de Campeche
Betty B. Faust
University of California, San Diego
and
Beniamino Volta[1]
University of California, San Diego

ABSTRACT

Great attention has been focused on the southern trade routes across the Yucatan Peninsula through Tikal but little to the potential for crossing through Calakmul further to the north. This chapter shows that a combination of topography and politics make the Calakmul corridor the more efficient transit route. The political turmoil generated by Teotihuacan's involvement in Lowland trade following C.E. 378 cascaded into centuries of conflict between cities along the Tikal corridor and inhabitants of alternative routes. We trace the evolution of this conflict as influenced by landscape and climate, and decisions of the ambulatory Kaan Dynasty of El Mirador, Dzibanche, Calakmul and finally Calkini. The conflict seems to have played out in the elevated interior of the peninsula, the bone of contention perhaps being control of the Calakmul corridor through the Candelaria River. We suggest there are sufficient parallels between the Calakmul and European Rhône River corridors to draw a productive analogy between two, including that they both fall under the same synoptic climate system. Because the post-Columbian world economic system rose indirectly from the Rhône corridor, the two systems make a good test bed for thinking about the future evolution of the world system. The scale of comparison is rendered feasible by viewing the systems in terms of the scale of information transfer in which

ARCHEOLOGICAL PAPERS OF THE AMERICAN ANTHROPOLOGICAL ASSOCIATION, Vol. 24, pp. 101–123, ISSN 1551-823X, online ISSN 1551-8248. DOI: 10.1111/apaa.12032.

they were embedded. We offer three brief examples of how rise and decline of the Calakmul hegemony suggests ways of thinking about the future of the world economic system: warfare, sustainable design, and climate engineering. [Maya, economic world system, trade routes, climate, agency, landscape]

Introduction: Goals and Assumptions

Ultimately using past civilizations to forecast future conditions of modern states demands the meaningful use of analogy. We suggest that modeling sustainability of communities in the central Maya Lowlands for purposes of analogy minimally requires three groups of variables in mutually causal relationships: landscape, climate, and people. We work out the shape of these three parameters for the Calakmul economic system and its hegemonic community. Our intention is not to provide a definitive analogy between the Calakmul and modern societies, but to suggest significant similarities that might give rise to collaborative efforts in that direction. Although space does not allow extensive exploration of the analogy between the Calakmul and world economic systems, we end by briefly examining key issues in the light of the analogy: warfare, sustainable design, and climate engineering.

Much has been learned in the last 30 years about the underlying variables controlling Maya Lowland society by studying tropical ecology (ecosystem services), archaeology (material culture and social structure), and history (lineages of agents). Our understandings, however, do not yet match our much more comprehensive data picture of modern economies. Nevertheless, simulation can be used to estimate aspects of the unknown variables in the Maya system (Heckbert et al. in press). Alternatively, scenarios designed to experiment with various possibilities can also illuminate ancient systems relative to their modern counterparts. This chapter is largely an example of the latter. It specifically focuses on the relationship between the Kaan or Snake dynasty of Calakmul and a developed understanding of the little-studied trade routes through the older and more northerly polities of Calakmul, El Mirador, Itzamkanak, and Dzibanche (Figures 8.1 and 8.2). With a clearer picture of these histories, we then proceed to compare the Calakmul and western European histories and draw inferences about the future of the world economic system.

Assumption 1

To build a three-variable model of mutually causal influences on the trajectory of Maya polities in southern Campeche and Quintana Roo, we make the following two assumptions. The first is topographic: we assume that by the Late Classic the Maya had structured a highly engineered environment that facilitated and sustained large entrepôts of well over 10,000 persons in precarious environments. Cowgill (2004) supposes a 10,000-person threshold for urban populations to serve as communications nodes of highly complex social systems. For example, Calakmul was located in a marginal environment to oversee an especially good trade route. Being located on the tropical–subtropical boundary, the city was relatively difficult to sustain. It was in the western half of the Yucatan Peninsula where roughly half the precipitation of the eastern half falls. The region is visited annually by dry seasons and periodically by extended droughts (Folan 1981; Folan et al. 1983; Gunn et al. 1994, 1995; Hodell et al. 2001; Torrescano and Islebe 2009; Wahl et al. 2006). This precipitation regime makes hydrological engineering a matter of necessity, especially in the elevated karstic environment of the peninsula's interior or mesoplano (Domínguez Carrasco et al. 2011; Dunning et al. 2006; Dunning et al. 2013; Folan et al. 2011; Gates 1992, 1999; Gunn et al. 2002; Scarborough 1993). Also, the streams that originate in the Mesoplano are seasonally intermittent and need to be controlled to make waterways passable by way of the construction of dams, lakes, and canals. Such engineering projects are observed clearly in the coastal plains around Itzamkanak in the lower Candelaria River (Siemens 2009; Siemens and Puleston 1972; Vargas Pacheco 1999, 2012), Edzna on the Champoton River (Benavides-Castillo 2001; Matheny et al. 1983), and on the eastern coastal plain in the Rio Hondo and Escondido systems (Dunning and Beach 2010; Nalda 2005). In the less investigated interior areas such as those occupied by Calakmul and El Mirador, landscape modifications have been glimpsed on remote imagery but are not as well quantified as they would be, for example, by a LiDAR survey of the area. We assume that travel by water was preferred when possible because of its 40:1 efficiency advantage over the use of overland porter routes.

Alternative overland north–south routes (Baron et al. 2012; Canuto et al. 2012; Domínguez Carrasco 2008) are relatively well understood and are not especially the topic of this chapter. We are curious, however, as to why the Calakmul elites developed an apparently important south-to-north overland route of commerce through the southern Lowlands from Cancuen to Calakmul in the early Late Classic under the Kaan kings (Baron et al. 2012; Canuto et al. 2012). Less expensive marine alternatives appear to have been fully functional by then (Gunn et al. 2010).

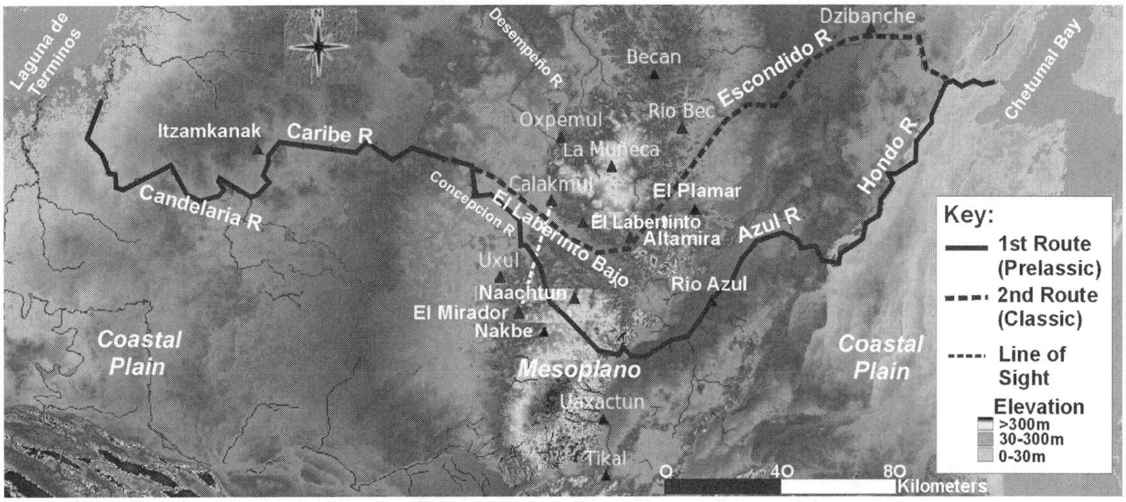

Figure 8.1. Waterways map of the southern Maya Lowlands' northern sector showing a possible Preclassic trade route (dashed), the line of sight from El Mirador to Calakmul, and the Calakmul Classic trade route through the El Laberinto Bajo (solid) overlooked by the city of Calakmul (adapted from Volta and Gunn 2012).

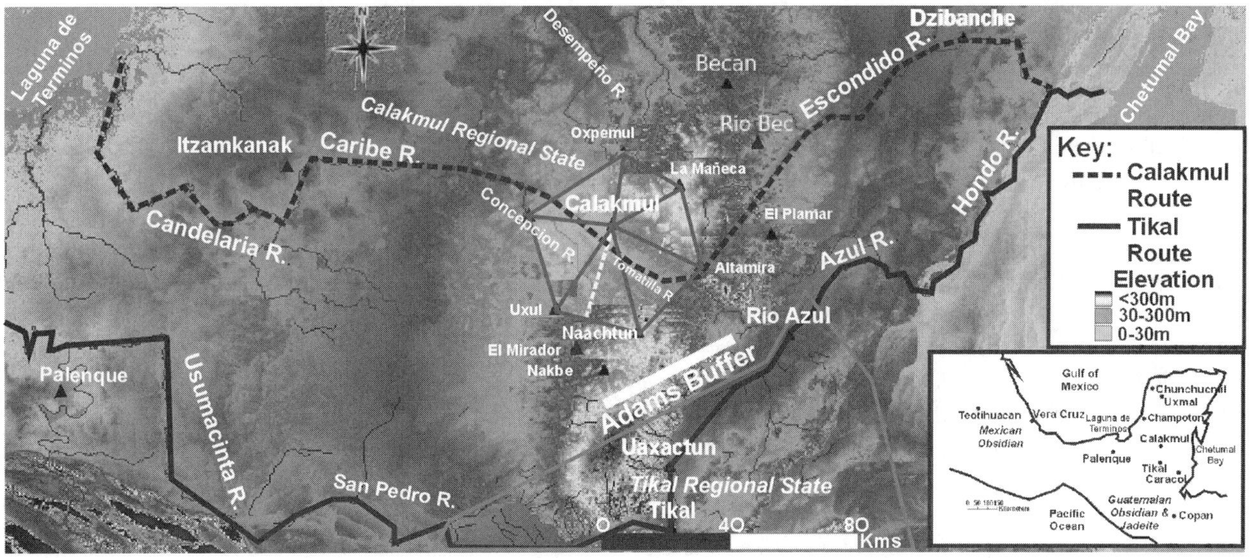

Figure 8.2. Alternative, competing trade routes evolved during the Early Classic (after 378 C.E.) through Tikal (solid) and Calakmul (dashed). The Calakmul regional state is shown as a hexagon (adapted from Folan et al. 2011; Marcus 1976; Volta and Gunn 2012). Inset map shows the relationship between Teotihuacan, the Maya Lowlands, and Copan on the Motagua River in Honduras.

Assumption 2

The second assumption in our model relates to people. A narrative of dynastic succession provides an agent-based context for the evolution of complex society. As with engineering, pieces of the dynastic puzzle are accumulating but remain obscure in their details (H. Robichaux, email, August 10, 2011). However, for purposes of this analysis, we will assume that the narrative developed by Martin (2005) and elaborated by Freidel et al. (2007), Robichaux (2010), Sharer and Traxler (2006:259), Šprajc and Grube (2008), and Folan et al. (2010) are sufficient to provide the basic facts. The story goes that the Snake dynasty was important early on at Late Preclassic El Mirador (Sharer and Traxler 2006:259). In subsequent periods, they moved to Dzibanche, then to Calakmul, and finally to Calkini near the northwest coast. Precise dates are not known but certain central time frames are understood, such as the Golden Ages of El Mirador in the late first millennium B.C.E., Calakmul in the seventh century under Yuknoom the Great (C.E. 636–686), and Tikal in the 8th century C.E.

Van der Leeuw's (2007) concept of agency is helpful in understanding sustainable communities. Agency is the decisions and related activities of individuals, kings, priests and their administrative appointees in the case of the Maya polities. Agency gives energy, provides expectations, institutions, world views, ideas, technological know-how and shared culture by sustained information sharing, and aligns the flow of matter such as trade goods and building materials, and energy, sometimes food surpluses, to produce the outcomes desired by the agents (van der Leeuw 2007:218). Too-small flows of matter and energy cause systems to become incoherent (van der Leeuw 2007:219, 235).

Maya agents implemented their desires through cities. Short of electronic communications, cities are the nodes within which the most information is processed (Cowgill 2004; van der Leeuw 2007:220). The relationships between cities and their hinterlands are measured as information gradients. Information gradients through hierarchies of cities in the Maya Lowlands can be measured by the number of acropoli, usually slightly elevated areas in cities containing administrative structures such as palaces, astronomically oriented temples, triadic structures, plazas, and ball courts. Each acropolis houses a functionally differentiated population of administrators that maintain elements of the social organization such as ritual activities, trade (Nalda 2005), and we might add diplomatic functions. Working up the hierarchy of information flow, small sub-centers had only one acropolis (Villamil and Sherman 2005) that might serve to regulate calendrical cycles such as planting and harvesting. A minimum of four acropoli appear to mark typical, mid-level administrative centers (Villamil and Sherman 2005). In addition to calendrical functions, they might serve to regulate water supply, markets, trade route traffic, and other functions. Super-centers have many more—at least 10 in the case of Golden Age Calakmul (Folan et al. 1995). Added to the previous functions, diplomatic missions and other higher level functional can be suggested. Of course, supporting such supercenters required collecting tribute in food and other necessities to maintain the administrative structure at the highest level of the metropolitan hierarchy. The proxy for inter-metropolitan information flow in this analysis is the IHOPE-Maya database of elite ceramic interactions between polities during 13 Maya Lowlands phases (Gunn et al. 2010). Analysis of the database shows that inter-polity interaction among the interior cities rose to prominence in the Late Preclassic A (300–1 B.C.E) and continued, albeit with fluctuations, until the Terminal Classic 1 (C.E. 800–900).

In a later section of this chapter, we will draw parallels between the Maya metropolises and the somewhat paralleled fortunes of the Dukes of Burgundy. The Dukes of Burgundy and predecessor agents controlled the passage of goods through the Rhône-Sôane-Seine-Rhine corridors between the Mediterranean and North Sea in Post Roman times before circumnavigation of the Iberian Peninsula became possible (Gunn et al. 2004).

Though not mutually influential in any direct sense, the Maya Lowlands and western Europe are influenced by global climate through a common synoptic feature: the Bermuda-Azores Subtropical High. The Bermuda High (for short) spans the Atlantic Ocean between the Yucatan Peninsula and the Peninsula of Europe (see Cunliffe 2008); we will elaborate later. Here we would like to point out that if appropriate compensations are made for the differences in environment, Medieval Europe and the Maya Lowlands were comparable urbanized entities (Adams and Jones 1981). The concept that bridges between tropical Maya and temperate Europe is based on differentiation between moist and arid environments. Scarborough (2007; 2008) identifies two basic orientations, technologically based systems ("technotasking") and labor based ("labortasking"). The place of any given location on this continuum is based on moisture parameters. Tropical systems work better with labortasking systems while temperate systems appear to function better, or at least bear up under, technotasking systems. The reasons may be that the more open urban footprint of tropical urbanization does not allow sufficient information exchange to support a highly technological system. The system can be made dynamic along the continuum by varying the moisture and climate inputs. Since both the Maya and European landscapes have slid back and forth on the moisture continuum (more generally referred to as drought and moist periods) over their histories, both demonstrate locations and times when either format applies (see Crumley 1994; Folan et al. 1983; Gunn and Crumley 1991; Gunn et al. 1995). This sets the stage for very useful analogies between the two areas. In the next section, we will examine some of the climatic dynamics of the Maya Lowlands.

Climate: Variable Atmospheric Environments

It is increasingly apparent that the environmental conditions during which Maya civilization existed were highly variable, both at the global scale and from region-to-region within the peninsula. The most illuminating example is the Terminal Classic, during which the worst drought in 9,000 years is recorded in eastern locales such as Lake Chichancanab near Coba on the east slope of the peninsula (Hodell et al. 1995). At the same time Maya civilization was flourishing as never before in the Puuc Hills to the west. A contributing factor was a system of underground water storage in chultuns (Sabloff 2009; Sabloff and Tourtellot 1991). However, could a climate pattern also have contributed to Puuc Hills' fluorescence?

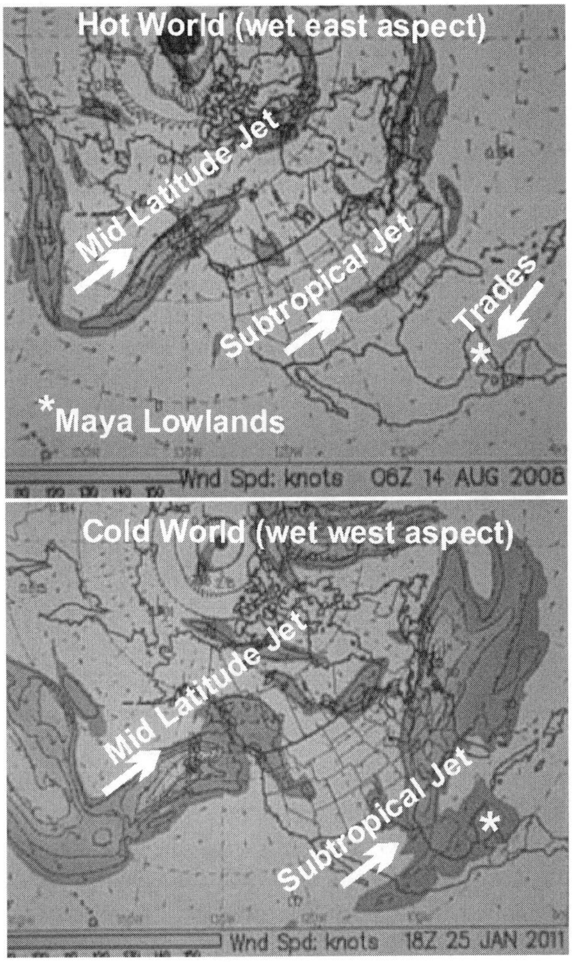

Figure 8.3. Current-day seasonal changes in jet stream storm track flows may approximate changes associated with hotter world conditions such as during the Preclassic, and colder world conditions such as during the Late Classic. During hot world conditions (somewhat equivalent to summer, e.g., June 30, 2012) the Subtropical Jet Stream resided northward over the U.S. Tropical trade winds or easterlies, bringing storm-track precipitation to the Yucatan Peninsula from the east off the Caribbean Sea. During cold world conditions (somewhat equivalent to a cold Northern Hemisphere winter, e.g., January 4, 2010) the Subtropical Jet Stream and associated storm tracts flow eastward over the Yucatan Peninsula from western Mexico. It brings precipitation from the west off the Pacific Ocean and Gulf of Mexico (adapted from California Regional Weather Server web site, http://squall.sfsu.edu/crws/archive/jet_arch.html, accessed December 2, 2013).

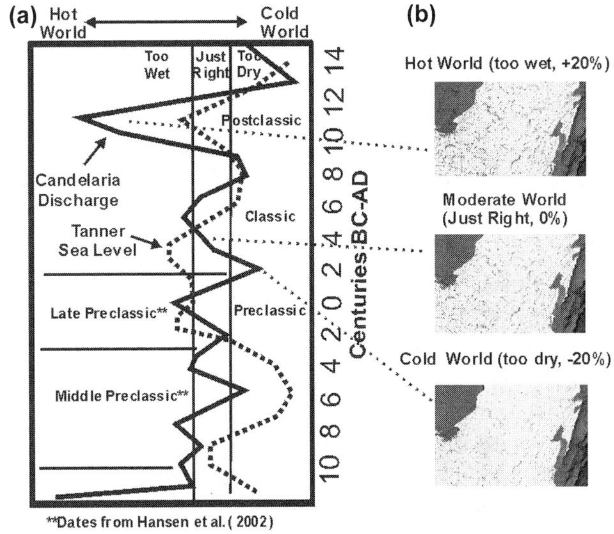

Figure 8.4. At the local level, precipitation is related to global sea level/global temperature. A simulation of precipitation changes shows how increases in precipitation alter the size of waterways. (a) Global-local climate sequence for the Candelaria River system based on regression of instrumental observations of global climate with Candelaria River discharge (1958–1995) in meters cubed per second (m^3s). The solid line is adapted from Gunn et al. (1995). North Atlantic sea level (dotted line) is adapted from Tanner (1993). Note the low sea level and cold global climate in the ninth century C.E. corresponds to the ninth century extended drought. Tanner estimated the range of variation to be about 2–3 meters as reflected in the scale. (b) Simulated stream flows for probable extremes of precipitation changes, Too wet +20%, Just Right 0%, Too dry –20% (adapted from Heckbert et al. [2013]). The number and breadth of waterways increases with precipitation, e.g., see waterways arrows.

A possible climate contribution for the Puuc Hills florescence is that during globally cold periods such the one that coincided with the Terminal Classic (Gunn et al. 1994, 1995) the prevailing winds likely shifted from their current easterly track along the Atlantic Trade Winds (Figure 8.3a) to northwesterlies from the Gulf of Mexico (Figure 8.3b). This shift would have been caused by the natural southward shifting of jet streams and their underlying storm tracts toward the equator as the world cooled, which would have increased rainfall in the Puuc Hills, especially on western slopes.

Utilizing the discharge patterns for the Candelaria River system (Figure 8.4) developed from modern discharge and global temperatures (Gunn et al. 1994, 1995), and adopting Hansen et al.'s (2002) dates for the Preclassic sub-periods so they conform to El Mirador's sequence, suggests that the centuries before C.E. 100 were moister and those after were drier. (Before C.E. 100, dry periods were not as dry and wet periods moister than afterwards.) This conclusion is supported by various botanical analyses (Torrescano and Islebe 2009; Wahl et al. 2006). That this trend is evident in the Candelaria model means that global cooling lies behind these conditions so the actual shifts in moisture would depend on changing seasonal distributions of precipitation and rainshadow effects (see Gunn et al. 1995 for analysis of seasonality). Global cooling would change the major precipitation from summer to fall (see Figure 8.3a) to winter (3b) by changing the storm tracts from easterly to northwesterly, and especially on west-facing slopes such as those in the Puuc Hills or the Campeche-NE Guatemala Mesoplano (i.e., El Mirador), or at Caracol on the west slopes of the Maya Mountains. Rainshadows would have changed correspondingly in opposite direction, changing the western Mesoplano from fall rainshadow to winter rainfall. As in the Puuc Hills, Preclassic water access adaptations in the Mesoplano seem to have turned to chultuns to store water (Reese-Taylor et al. 2012; Šprajc 2008). This tactic served to protect water from long summer dry seasons that would have been manifest under a system without easterlies.

The climate issues will be particularly important relative to the foregoing assumption of substantial landscape modification, as early, moister conditions may have been emulated in terms of travel potentials on water with later landscape modification.

Landscape: The Geomorphic and Topographic Context

Over the last few years, the role of the geomorphic context in the cultural evolution in the southern and western Maya Lowlands has evolved from a simple view of a flat Mesozoic limestone platform upon which the Maya drama played out, to an environmental mosaic of both social and ecological complexity (Fedick 1996). This complexity grew from the realization that soils were highly variable from river system to river system and basin to basin (Dunning 1996; Dunning et al. 1998; Dunning et al. 2006). For example, the bajo sediments in the Mesoplano of southern Campeche (Domínguez Carrasco et al. 2011; Folan et al. 2011) were discovered to be highly saline (Gunn et al. 2002, 2009). The Chicxulub meteorite impact was revealed and found to significantly contribute to the geochemical formation of the landscape, especially with regard to water quality (Perry, Velazquez-Oliman, Wagner, et al. 2010; Perry, Velazquez-Oliman, and Wagner 2011).

Various depressions on the peninsula are the result of gypsum deposit dissolution associated with Chicxulub ejecta (Perry, Velazquez-Oliman, and Wagner 2011), features called "polje" by geomorphologists. Also associated with the Chicxulub ejecta are clay beds that form impermeable surface deposits in the polje basins such as Lake Silvituc and the Edzna Valley. As a result, the subsurface groundwater is rich in sulfur salts, while polje surface pools are generally runoff rainwaters free of contamination. At least one component of these clays is volcanic ash that falls across the peninsula on a generational basis (Tankersley et al. 2011).

Of key importance to this investigation is the El Laberinto Bajo. As a potential traverse of the peninsula, it is the widest pass through the Mesoplano. If the Laberinto is a polje, this may clarify the deep cut of the El Laberinto Bajo across the Mesoplano; it is otherwise inexplicable in terms of surface erosion. N. Dunning (telephone conversation with the author, January 22, 2011), however, thinks the El Laberinto Bajo may be structural rather than a solution feature based on its sharp northern slope. If so, it may be merely a receptor of salts from the ejecta drift. The high salinity of the Laberinto Bajo (Gunn et al. 2002, 2009) probably does explain why Preclassic settlements in the area of Laberinto that antedate the development of convex water systems were associated with extensive use of chultuns as identified at Yaxnohcah (Reese-Taylor et al. 2012) and perhaps other cities with triadic architecture (see below), an interesting topic of future research.

Triadic temples are a highly identifiable, Late Preclassic (300 B.C.E.–C.E. 250) architectural style. They are composed of a dominant structure flanked by two smaller inward-facing structures, all mounted upon a single basal platform (Sharer and Traxler 2006:253). Using triadic temples as a criterion, Šprajc's (2008) survey revealed at least five Late Preclassic cities flanking the El Laberinto Bajo as well as along the headwaters of streams draining down the east slope to the Escondido and Hondo rivers (Šprajc and Grube 2008:table 11.1; Šprajc et al. 2009). There are no additional examples further north into the Mesoplano of Campeche (Figure 8.5).

These settlements, along with the already known triadic sites of neighboring cities in northwestern Guatemala (Hansen 1998; Sharer and Traxler 2006:261) and in Dzibanche near Chetumal Bay (Nalda 2005), suggest triadic centers represent some sort of administrative complex and/or military position relative to trade (see Šprajc and Grube 2008:266 for additional references). Over 40 triadic temples are reported in El Mirador (Dunning et al. 2012:3654), by far the largest number anywhere. There are other examples of cities with triadic temples to the south; do they mark a competing Preclassic route through Uaxactun and Tikal? In the Post-Columbian Historic period (C.E. 1550–1920), triadic temples represented religious, civic and military components of the society (Folan et al. 2001), a feature that appears to set them apart from the social structure of the Usumacinta watershed (Jackson 2013). As one might anticipate, Jackson (2013:19, 90) sees the Maya (Usumacinta) royal courts as being more like the Aztec (highland Mexico, Teotihuacan) courts, which would arise naturally from the inferred relationship between the Usumacinta–Tikal corridor

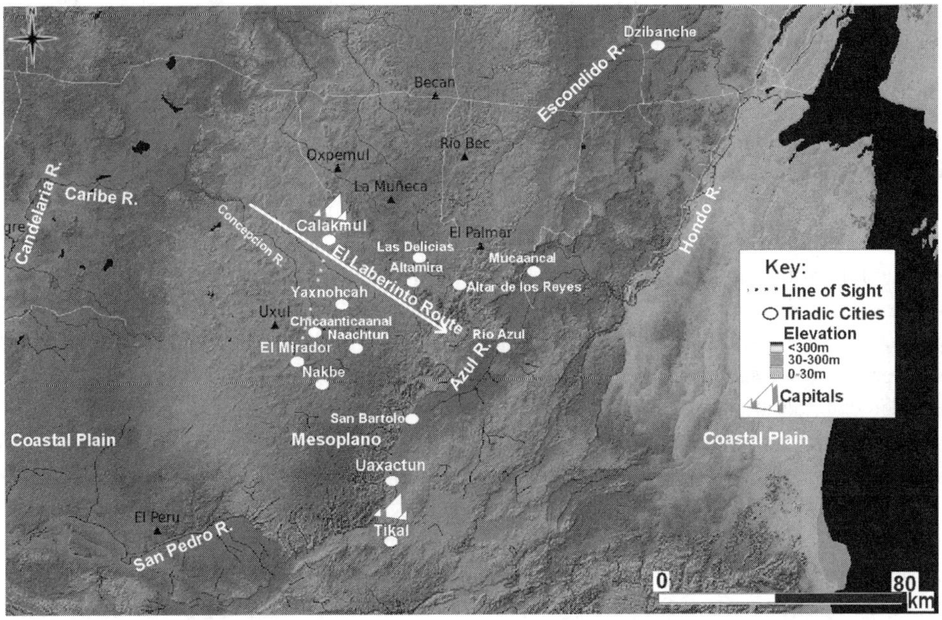

Figure 8.5. Cities with triadic temples overlook key river positions, usually headwaters or portages across the Peninsula through the El Laberinto Bajo. Although examples of triadic structures occasionally occur along the north edge of the peninsula, the north edge of the El Laberinto Bajo seems to mark the furthest they were pushed into the dry lands of the Mesoplano from the south. This suggests their function had something to do with guarding the El Laberinto passage (adapted from Šprajc and Grube 2008).

and Teotihuacan. At least to the north, the triadic courts that arose out of the El Mirador golden age would have continued on the Calakmul corridor.

Another important hydro-geological feature in the search for trade routes is the relative navigability of the rivers of the western peninsula: Usumacinta, Candelaria, and Champoton (see Figure 8.2). Each has very different characteristics. The Usumacinta is a long river, about 1200 kilometers in length, that extends eastward along the foothills of the Sierra Madre de Chiapas, folds back south into the mountains, and drains several internal valleys. It is a typical tropical river with huge differences in discharge between the wet and dry seasons (Aliphat Fernandez 1994; Gunn and Folan 2000; Schele and Freidel 1990). To briefly characterize the river, Canter (2007:14) reports that "the hardest sections of the river were—and still are—Cola del Diablo Canyon with 9 rapids in 9 kilometers; Iguanas Canyon, with 7 rapids and a slot in a 7 kilometer stretch; and finally the two short but powerful Class 3 drops of Raudal de San José pinched between soaring walls." C. Golden (email to the author, March 12, 2012) thinks that in precontact times the river was not navigable most of the year in its middle reaches. Navigation in the wet season was problematic because of torrential discharge. Transportation might have been possible by taking advantage of intermediate discharge periods or by following tow paths. Difficulties with the Usumacinta main stem can be circumvented to some extent by using its Passion tributary (Demarest 2013:377) and overland routes (Volta and Gunn 2012).

The Candelaria–Caribe–Tomatilla, because of vast coastal plain swamps, underground caverns and a broad river bed, is what normally would be thought of as a "river" in the mid latitudes (Gunn and Folan 2000; Gunn et al. 1994, 1995; Siemens 2009; Siemens and Puleston 1972; Vargas Pacheco 2012). A. Siemens (personal communication with the author, November 18, 2011) has experienced the river as navigable most of the year and travel up river can be accomplished by poling. There are shoals below the town of Candelaria at the low edge of the coastal plain and immediately above the delta. Siemens has evidence that the area above the shoals was dammed after ca. 5000 B.C.E., creating a lake that was eventually silted in and used for agricultural fields during the Classic period. The channel was canalized four times. There are probably also shoals at the back edge of the coastal plain where the Candelaria–Caribe enter the Mesoplano and the Laberinto Bajo. To make this navigable, it would also have been dammed and filled with water; possible lake basin features of this sort have been identified on satellite imagery but not ground truthed (C. Brown, email to the author, October 21, 2011).

The Champoton–Desempeño system, further up the coast at Champoton, has no shoals to the edge of the Mesoplano (R. Matheny and A. Lopéz Morales, personal communication, November 18, 2011); it does go underground at the end of the Desempeño and re-emerges at the head of the Champoton from a spring (R. Matheny, personal communication, November 18, 2011). Discharge characteristics of the Champoton are greatly dependent on whether the Edzna Valley was forested or not. Both conditions have been observed in the Post-IGY period (C.E. 1958–1995) because the valley was deforested in 1973 (Gunn and Folan 2000). Most of the year the system is navigable to Edzna, but it would have required engineering to make the Desempeño navigable to Oxpemul–La Muñeca and Calakmul.

As we shall see, the Candelaria system is most tractable in terms of initial navigability, although the Champoton–Desempeño is slightly shorter. There is probably no route through the peninsula that does not require some portaging. Wider passages over intervening uplands are best because they gave engineers room to devise dams, lakes, canals and other means of lengthening the waterborne stages of transport through the El Laberinto Bajo at Calakmul and Bajo de Santa Fe at Tikal, probably the best routes in terms of extensible waterways. Calculation of least cost routes across the peninsula indicate that the Oxpemul–La Muñeca and Calakmul routes are first and second as efficient routes to cross the peninsula, respectively (Volta and Gunn 2012). As discussed above, climatic conditions varied over the ancient history of the Maya and may have given different passages different hydrological characteristics at different times. Drying in the Late Classic, for example, may have made the Candelaria less and the Usumacinta more tractable.

Agency: The Snakes Have Their Way

It has become increasingly clear that human systems are influenced by decision makers (Clark 2000; Jackson 2013), the decline of the "great-man" bias in history notwithstanding. Based on the Martin (2005) reconstruction of Kaan Dynasty history, we see the following train of events falling under their purview.

Snake Dynasty at El Mirador

Although there is epigraphic evidence of the Snake Dynasty in El Mirador in the Early Classic (Guenter 2008), that only indicates they were still there at the dawn of historical writings. How long they were there before is debatable. The Dynasty may have developed with the city in the Middle Preclassic (1000–350 B.C.E.) or Late Preclassic (350 B.C.E.–C.E. 150, Hansen et al.'s 2002 dates for El Mirador periods). A codex-style vase recovered by looters may display a king's list from El Mirador (Sharer and Traxler 2006:259) dating from 396 B.C.E. to the first century C.E. Evidently the presence of the city of El Mirador represents the early stirrings of commerce (Sharer and Traxler 2006:259), perhaps in products that were gathered locally such as cotton and medicinal plants or goods passed through from the Motagua watershed in Honduras and eastern Guatemala to the Gulf Coast. While resident at Calakmul, the Snake dynasty displayed a prodigious appetite for jadeite (Braswell 2010) only available in the Motagua valley (Seitz et al. 2001). The Olmec displayed an evident desire for jadeite in the La Venta period (950–400 B.C.E. according to Milbrath 1979:4; 950–400 B.C.E. according to Sharer and Traxler 2006:165). It therefore seems likely that the trans-peninsular trading of jadeite co-developed in the Middle Preclassic in the Nakbe-El Mirador area (600–400 B.C.E.). It further seems likely that the green stone was a key part of the commercial system for trans-peninsular entrepôts.

A particularly appealing route for the Preclassic system would have been through the 5–10 kilometers wide El Laberinto Bajo (Volta and Gunn 2012; see Figure 8.1). The width is important because it gave engineers room to build dams, lakes, and canals to control floods and retain water to make the passage serviceable through the dry season, the traditional time of commerce (Faust 1988). The El Laberinto Bajo passes midway between the Calakmul and El Mirador line-of-sight. An elevated road (*sacbe*) may have passed between them (Folan et al. 1995; Geovannini Acuña 2008). For such a road to be built, most likely the Snake Dynasty controlled both ends of the road.

The collapse of El Mirador population at the end of the Preclassic and the rise of Calakmul's Golden Age in the Early Classic were broadly coincident. The move of the Snake Dynasty from El Mirador to Calakmul would have been facilitated by evolution in hydrological engineering. In the Preclassic, cities depended on naturally occurring water reservoirs, so-called "concave microwatersheds" (Scarborough 1993; Scarborough and Burnside 2010). Such was the case in El Mirador's locale in the lake district of northwestern Guatemala (Jacob 1995). As noted above, the Late Preclassic would have been moister (Hansen et al. 2002), making such arrangements workable for large communities. Later, by the Calakmul Golden Age, highly engineered convex microwatersheds were developed, allowing the Snakes to move their center of power to Calakmul in the southern Campeche Mesoplano (Domínguez et al. 2011; Folan et al. 2011). There they could have more directly overseen the passage of commerce through the El Laberinto Bajo corridor (the Classic period route in Figure 8.1).

We should mention that well-studied overland trade routes existed down the spine of the Mesoplano as exemplified by ceramic distributions (Baron et al. 2012; Domínguez Carrasco 2008). However, a study of obsidian blade widths at various sites along this route do not support the movement of obsidian cores from the El Chayal source in Guatemala to the southeast to Chunchucmil to the northwest in the western state of Yucatan in the late Early Classic (Hutson et al. 2010:figure 8.5). Regardless, obsidian must have been carried over water by some route. A similar study is required of jade, at least some of which was probably coming overland during the early Late Classic (Baron et al. 2012).

Snake Dynasty at Dzibanche

There is a gap between the time that something broke El Mirador's chain of good fortune late in the Preclassic and the rise of the Calakmul golden age, the latter probably rooted sometime in the fifth or sixth century C.E. An extended drought some time in the third century might have played a role (Dahlin et al. 1980; Gunn et al. 1994, 1995; Wahl et al. 2006). The gap appears to be filled by a Snake Dynasty residence at Dzibanche as evidenced by a set of stairs that celebrate the taking of prisoners in warfare and bearing the Snake Dynasty glyph (Velásquez García 2005). This is also the time that Teotihuacan was actively recruiting allies to control an alternative, competing corridor through the Usumacinta/San Pedro and Hondo/Azul river systems, the Tikal corridor (Freidel et al. 2007; see Figure 8.2). Since the Hondo River parallels the Escondido River and Dzibanche, about 20–30 kilometers apart, it gave the Snake Dynasty access to Chetumal Bay and east coastal trade. A Snake Dynasty presence in this military context is plausible for reason of defense against the Teotihuacan intruders, and perhaps marks the onset of armed confrontation between competing Snake and Tikal factions. Adams (2005) has identified a city-free zone between the two river systems that he judges to be a military buffer zone between the two forces. Two military confrontations between Calakmul and Tikal are reported at Naachtun (Martin and Grube 2008), perhaps marking the elevated Mesoplano as the avenue of conflict.

Several lines of evidence support an important role for Dzibanche in building the Late Preclassic and Early Classic commercial system (Dunning and Beach 2010). Nalda (2005:235) believes the Titul group in Dzibanche to be a market place and residence for traders indicating an active trade link. As would be expected if the Snake kings, builders of El Mirador, were present, the Early Classic on the lower Escondido River was a period of rapid growth (Nalda 2005:239). A triadic complex was built in the Lamay group (Nalda 2005:239), which appears to be the Snake Dynasty's architectural signature of their commercial-military enterprises. Dzibanche is located in an area of rich soils with good water retention, i.e., no karstic seeps (Nalda 2005:237). The general wetness provides the area with low risk agriculture in terms of water abundance but required the additional labor mobilization for raised fields. The size of residential compounds is small enough to imply at least a two-field system of agriculture; they would not have been able to raise enough food in the residential compound alone given the implied size of the associated compound populations. The system suggests the systematic production of agricultural surpluses capable of supporting a bureaucracy to control trade and military. Taken together with additional understanding of commercial warfare tactics adapted from Teotihuacan, the Snake kings were poised for their Golden Age.

Snake Dynasty at Calakmul

Sometime between C.E. 378 and the C.E. 600s a military stalemate seems to have evolved along the Escondido-Hondo front and thus the city-free buffer inferred by Adams (2005; see Figure 8.2, "Adams Buffer"). The buffer allowed the Snakes to return their attention to the central issues of controlling the El Laberinto passage. We might suppose that the Snakes held long time relations with the coastal-maritime city of Itzamkanak on the lower Candelaria, or perhaps were the brokers or descendants of that city. The problem of control now refocused on the Calakmul-Tikal competition for the Candelaria. Two engagements were fought between the factions at Naachtun (Martin and Grube 2008:37), which overlooks the Calakmul-El Mirador line of sight and possible sacbe.

Naachtun can be seen as critical to controlling access to the Candelaria gateway for the following reasons. The first engagement between Calakmul and Tikal over Naachtun was in C.E. 486 (Martin and Grube 2008:39). Tikal was unsuccessful, and there seems to have been no evident effect on the balance of power. Tikal remained a relatively ineffectual entity throughout this period, losing a battle to Yaxchilan in C.E. 508, then succumbing to an alliance between the Snake Dynasty and Caracol in C.E. 562. The Snakes went on to their Calakmul Golden Age that peaked in the seventh century C.E. (Martin and Grube 2008). On the other hand, when Tikal gained the upper hand in the C.E. 695 Naachtun engagement, Calakmul's Golden Age ended abruptly and the city went into decline. In-progress modifications to Temple II were never completed. Final engagements in C.E. 743 at El Peru and C.E. 744 at Naranjo appear to have demolished the Kaan hold on the region south of Tikal (Martin and

Grube 2008:114; Šprajc 2008:75), although they remained interested in the Motagua trade as evidenced by a mention at Quirigua, in the mid-700s C.E. (Martin and Grube 2008:114).

The Snake's move to Calakmul was challenging. Both it and Tikal are located about 40 kilometers from permanent water, apparently to be near commercial passageways. To change Calakmul from a seasonally dry dome or promontory into a world class city (Folan et al. 1995) required up-scaling the water system to support a large, permanent population through the dry season (Domínguez Carrasco and Folan Higgins 1997; Geovannini Acuña 2008). The city has a water catchment descending from the ridge to the northeast. Water had to be collected on the surface and saved from subsurface sediments that are laced with gypsum (Perry, Velazquez-Oliman, and Wagner 2011). Water was canalized into large aguadas east of the main plaza (Figure 8.6; Folan et al. 1990). Platforms with altars are found along the canals (Fletcher and Gann 1994), suggesting that the canals may have been associated with or maintained by a religious order of some sort.

Even an expanded supply of potable water, however, would not have supported an estimated population of 50,000. Agricultural input to the city, for example, would have had to increase by a factor of five since the immediate surrounding landscape will only support about 10,000 persons using both one crop a year (milpa) or two crops where the soils are appropriate (Geovannini Acuña 2008). This was probably accomplished by intensively farming the engineered colluvium along the edge of the El Laberinto Bajo (Geovannini Acuña 2008; Gunn et al. 2002). A canal to transport produce may have been built from Calakmul to the city of El Laberinto 12 kilometers up the bajo; at present, this is only suggested by the canalized arroyo descending from the north edge of the main plaza area that appears to connect to the bajo. Regardless, a more efficient means had to be engineered than that of farmers porting produce to the city, as such efforts appear limited to a range of about 6 kilometers from milpas today (Zetina Gutiérrez and Faust 2011). A transportation canal would have been advantageous because soils below the city of El Laberinto at the upper end of the bajo would be less salinized and therefore agriculturally more productive than those at Calakmul near the lower end of the bajo (Gunn et al. 2002[2]). The arroyo likely served the double purpose of moving produce to the population center at Calakmul and providing a transportation route for trans-peninsular commerce.

Sustaining long-term occupation in Calakmul required special attention to the soils along the upper and lowered edges of the bajo. Ongoing research on the milpa system (Faust et al. 2010; Faust and Gunn n.d.) indicates that limestone bedrock, when subject to the "hot burns" of the milpa system, releases calcium from bedrock fragments. To this are added micronutrients (trace elements) from volcanic ejecta and African dust (Dunning et al. 2013; Tankersley et al. 2011) and bionutrients from night soil and burning vegetation. In this system as it is currently envisioned, the nutrients are released along the 12 kilometers bajo slope, eroded down to the agricultural colluvium, cycled to the cities and villages as produce, recycled out of the urban areas and back down to the aguadas in the colluvium at the beginning of the rainy season, and reintroduced to the fields by irrigation in a continuing, sustainable cycle.

The Calakmul community was sustained for 1500 years, finally becoming a magnificent capital in the seventh century C.E. Taking into consideration the engineered watershed, canals flanked by platforms with altars, high aguadas in the city, low aguadas in the bajo, and other possible modification in the bajo such as the use of water for moving, arranging and desalinized soils, it could be said that the Maya at Calakmul domesticated water rather than animals to do their work.

The Snake Dynasty Moves On

The second engagement at Naachtun between Calakmul and Tikal in C.E. 695 was important, successful for Tikal, and marked the end of the Calakmul Golden Age. An explosion of building in Tikal followed (Martin and Grube 2008:108), and a Calakmul official was soon on display as a prisoner of war in Tikal. Subsequent ramping up of building activity at Tikal resulted in most of what is now seen as the accomplished Tikal, the Northern Acropolis in particular (Martin and Grube 2008:49). This suggests that after 300 years of on-and-off effort, the forces of Tikal had captured access to the Candelaria gateway through Itztamkanak, and thus possessed the wealth to build and control as they might.

Calakmul's fortunes declined over the next two centuries. At some point the Snake Dynasty moved to Calkini on the northwest coast to ply their fortunes there (Folan et al. 2010). The Bat Dynasty, for some centuries resident at Oxpemul, returned to Calakmul and El Mirador. They built small residential structures filled with household and handicraft activities on the zones (faces) of Temple II at Calakmul (Folan et al. 1995) and the Danta complex at El Mirador (Hansen 1994).

During the Terminal Classic (C.E. 800–1000 C.E.), Tikal collapsed and was sacked. The struggles between Calakmul and Tikal no longer obstructed commercial passage, so the old El Mirador corridor was reactivated across

Figure 8.6. Simulated view of Calakmul from the south at its peak of power during the Late Classic. In this north-facing view, the main plaza is to the left of the two aguadas in the center. The Calakmul-El Laberinto Bajo (to the left) waterway can be seen along the top. Up-bajo is to the left (adapted from Winemiller et al. 2011).

the Adam's Buffer (see Figure 8.1). It and other old cities such as Rio Azul, Uaxactun, and El Peru along the original Preclassic trade route revived (Martin and Grube 2008). By moving to the northwestern coastal plain, the Snakes were not only removing themselves from Tikal's military reach, but also taking over directly the brokering of interior and circum-peninsular trade from a vantage that gave them access to the new Postclassic world of dominantly maritime trade.

What if the periodic relocations of the Snake Dynasty are interpreted simply as their efforts to stay on top of the definitive need to maintain sufficient surpluses to support a hierarchy? This suggests that their movements were clocked by the periodic crises noted in Table 8.1. The move from El Mirador to Dzibanche would have been to cope with the 3rd century C.E. crisis. Drier conditions in the elevated interior would have made the agriculturally more reliable moist landscape of the coastal plain appealing. Recentralizing the polity on Calakmul could have come with the 6th century crisis following the world-wide volcanic event of C.E. 536, perhaps a product of an Iloponogo eruption (Dull et al. 2010). Relocation again to a coastal plain at Calkini would have been in response to the 9th century crisis. This of course is a hypothesis to be tested since the dating of the Kaan movements is much more obscure than their settled moments. It is also clear that other economic and political factors figured in each decision. Also, if this hypothesis can be sustained, it suggests a pattern in their decision making. The third and ninth century crises were extended droughts that caused much disruption not only in the Maya Lowlands but worldwide. In both cases of extended drought the Kaans decided to move to the coastal plain. During the 3rd century crisis they abandoned El Mirador, and during the 9th century crisis they abandoned Calakmul. The lower elevations of the coastal plain are less susceptible to extended drought (Dunning et al. 2013). On the other hand, during the C.E. 536 crisis they remained in the elevated interior, apparently able to weather a few years of troubled climate thanks to the convex water systems.

Kaan Dynasty and the World Economic System: A Convenient Analogy

One of the objectives of the IHOPE studies (Scarborough 2007, Chase and Scarborough, this volume), and one of the objectives of this chapter, is to use the past to inform the future. Whatever the use of ancient societies relative to understanding our own possible future, the results will in some sense rely on analogies between the cultural histories of past societies and our current global society. However differentiated globalized society is in cultural origins and current practice, we are one society in the sense that we are all trapped in the same global ecosphere and ecosystem resource base. What has changed is that humans as a species are now huge players in the status of the ecosphere. The truth of this is made all the more evident by a scientific consensus which holds that humans are a major controlling factor in the behavior of the ecosphere (IPCC 2013). Because of a more limited information gradient in antiquity, seemingly small past societies are the information and resource equivalents of modern global society with its internet, jet transport, and United Nations.

Table 8.1. The cultural histories of the southern Maya Lowlands and Burgundy (adapted from Gunn and IHOPE-Maya Members 2010; Gunn et al. 2004; van der Leeuw 2007). The gray lines are periods that are known to have started with global-scale crises: 12th century B.C.E.; 3rd century C.E.; 6th century C.E.; and 9the century C.E. There may have been others

Maya Periods	Start Date	Maya Sub-periods (IHOPE-Maya)	Burgundian Periods (Gunn et al. 2004; van der Leeuw 2007)
	1958	Post-IGY	
	1920	Instrumental Observation	Industrial Revolution (C.E. 1800-2000)
Historic			
	1550	Historic	States of Trading Empires (C.E. 1600-1800)
			Birth of Modern World System (C.E. 1400-1600)
	1250	Late Postclassic	The Renaissance (C.E. 1200-1400)
Postclassic	1000	Early Postclassic	First Stirrings (C.E. 1000-1200)
	900	Terminal Classic 2	
	800	Terminal Classic 1	Carolingian Dynasty (C.E. 687)
Late Classic	700	Late Classic 2	
	550	Late Classic 1	
	450	Early Classic 3	Merovingian Dynasty (C.E. 487)
Early Classic	350	Early Classic 2	Late Roman Empire (C.E. 284)
	250	Early Classic 1	Gallic Empire (C.E. 200)
	C.E. 1	Late Preclassic b	Roman Empire Golden Age
	B.C.E. 300	Late Preclassic a	Roman Republic, Mediterranean Awakening (500 B.C.E.)
Preclassic	800	Middle Preclassic	Greek Dark Age (1200 B.C.E.)
	2000	Early Preclassic	Bronze Age
Archaic	3500	Archaic	Neolithic

Since we are concerned with societies, to begin our analogy we will compare two social entities, the city of Calakmul and its hegemony (both the higher and lower elements of its hierarchy), and global society. Both are diverse and loosely organized confederations. One has run its course (the Calakmul hegemony) and one has not: our own global society that has its roots economic roots in western Europe. In its initial stages, western Europe is surprisingly parallel to the Calakmul hegemony. It has comparable elements of climate, landscape, and willful kings, as we shall discuss in this section.

The analogy required for this exercise is equivalent in some ways to a mathematical proportions problem. In proportions problems, the past (i.e., A = early Maya and B = late Maya) are known, but in global civilization C, our past is known, but D, our future, is unknown.

By solving a proportion's equation, one can obtain, as if by magic, the value of unknown D. This simple but startling procedure has been a fascination in the western intellectual tradition and probably many others since time immemorial. In the 1600s it became Galileo's fascination and he used it in every research context he could think of, including calculating the height of mountains on the moon by measuring the length their shadows through his telescope. In similar manner, we can use it here to obtain alternative scenarios of our own society's future by reference to a past society—let us say the length of the shadow it casts on our own future.

In our current research interest, we would like to take a society, the Classic Maya Calakmul hegemony, for which we know both the beginning and end, and use the experience to understand alternative prospects of our own global society—in the future, the unknown in this case. In the above discussions, we demonstrated that the cultural history of Calakmul society from hunter-gatherer origins to abandonment in favor of maritime trading can be understood in some large part by considering three variables; landscape, climate, and agency. We will now attempt to use this template in an analogy to address the question of the future global society. This should not be considered a definitive analogical analysis, but rather the beginning of a conversation. Basically, the experience of a past society can suggest future scenarios for another society. Given minor manipulations of conditions in the past society especially as regards agency decision based on informed judgments concerning population and climate, one can readily envision alternative outcomes that for one reason or another may provide guidance to researchers and policy makers in our own society. This will be demonstrated in three hypothetical examples.

Global Society

We will view global society as having its origins in Western Europe, and specifically from the point of view of the inhabitants of the Rhône-Saône trading corridor. From the time that the Burgundian Kingdom was established in C.E. 406 until it was absorbed by the French monarchy in C.E. 1477, it was a sometimes-independent state. It earned its independence by sitting astride one of the main trade arteries between the Mediterranean and North Sea (Cunliffe 2008:267, 296, 294, 314–315, 347, 354) at the headwaters of the Rhône-Saône, Loire, Seine, and Rhine rivers transportation corridors. It was frequented since at least the Late Bronze Age (1300–800 B.C.E.), when Mediterranean societies (Greek, Etruscan, and Phoenician) scrambled for the tin supplies of Brittany and Britain. The route was first described in detail by Pytheas of Massalia (Marseille) around 320 B.C.E. He took advantage of frequent cargo ships to explore Loire, Seine, and Rhine passages. Because of the civilization-reset between Antique and Modern times, our analogical concerns begin with the establishment of the Burgundian Kingdom, one of the many German tribes filling the Roman vacuum. This was followed by the complete collapse of the western Roman Empire, the re-Christianization of the area beginning in the sixth century C.E., the re-education of the area in the western tradition beginning during the reign of Charlemagne in the ninth century, and the creation of capitalism beginning at Venice in the tenth century (Braudel 1979). The analogy is therefore rooted in the comparable geographic situations of the rulers of Calakmul and Burgundy sitting astride the best trade routes across the Yucatan Peninsula through the El Laberinto Bajo and the Rhône corridor. Unlike the El Laberinto Bajo route, the Burgundy route remains a busy transportation system today as one can readily experience on the fast train from Paris to Lyon. Its importance as a trading route, however, was diminished with the advent of armed, seagoing sailing ships in the C.E. 1300s, an event that strengthened powerful neighbors to the Rhône corridor, France and Germany. Of course there are many origins to the economic system that became the present day E.U. One could, for example, point out that Spain and Portugal created the worldwide trading sphere that began in the 16th century C.E. However, even then Spain was a recently emerged descendant of the Dukes of Burgundy in the person of Charles V (Davies 2011).

Burgundy is useful as part of western Europe, the root of the current world economic system with comparable economic concerns to the kings of Calakmul as we are able to view them. The eventual shift of centers of power from the central peninsular region to the North Sea following the discovery of the Americas in 1492 corresponds to the shift of power from Calakmul to Calkini on the northwest coast of the Yucatan Peninsula.

Environmentally Linking Yucatan and Europe

The Rhône corridor and the El Laberinto passage have another analogical advantage in that the two systems, though separated by an ocean, are part of the same synoptic climate system. Both are influenced by the Bermuda-Azores Subtropical High (the Bermuda High for short; see Crumley 1993, 1994; Folan et al. 1983: Gunn et al. 1995; Gunn and Crumley 1991). As such, aside from the fact that the Calakmul regional state and the Burgundy state are contemporary, they have common environmental crises, marked in Table 8.1 by gray rows. We take the term "crisis" from classical European history where it is used to describe the third century C.E. collapse of the western Roman Empire. As with the Yucatan Peninsula, Europe was visited by major environmental crises about every 300 years due to sudden negative excursions of global temperatures and consequent movements in the Bermuda High. In even broader perspective, placing both areas in the context of the synoptic scale Bermuda High and thereby the Earth system environment places them on common ground with all other social entities on Earth enabling worldwide comparisons. For example, the third century C.E. crisis in western Europe corresponds to the Preclassic-to-Classic transition in the Maya Lowlands. What were the consequences in China?

Basically the Bermuda High resides in the southern North Atlantic between the Yucatan Peninsula and Europe and circulates in a clockwise rotation forming a cell in the atmosphere that extends from the surface upwards through the lower atmosphere. The location and seasonal movements in the Bermuda High are illustrated in Figure 8.7.

Without going into too much detail, the Bermuda High responds to the Earth system measured as global average temperatures. We will refer to this behavior as the Neilson Effect. Neilson did not invent this understanding but wrote of it eloquently in a 1986 *Science* article (Neilson 1986), and it became the basis of our thinking about how the local climate systems linked to the Earth system (Folan et al. 1983; Gunn et al. 1995). The Neilson Effect has three basic stages that can be observed in microcosm through the seasons. During the northern hemisphere winter, it retreats into the Atlantic just north of the equator and may disappear altogether during globally cold years. In the summer it balloons up over the Atlantic well north of the equator and touches on North America and Europe, influencing the weather in both of those places simultaneously—though frequently with opposite effects, as will be discussed.

Nielson goes on to show that the size of the Bermuda High scales with global temperatures, a concept also

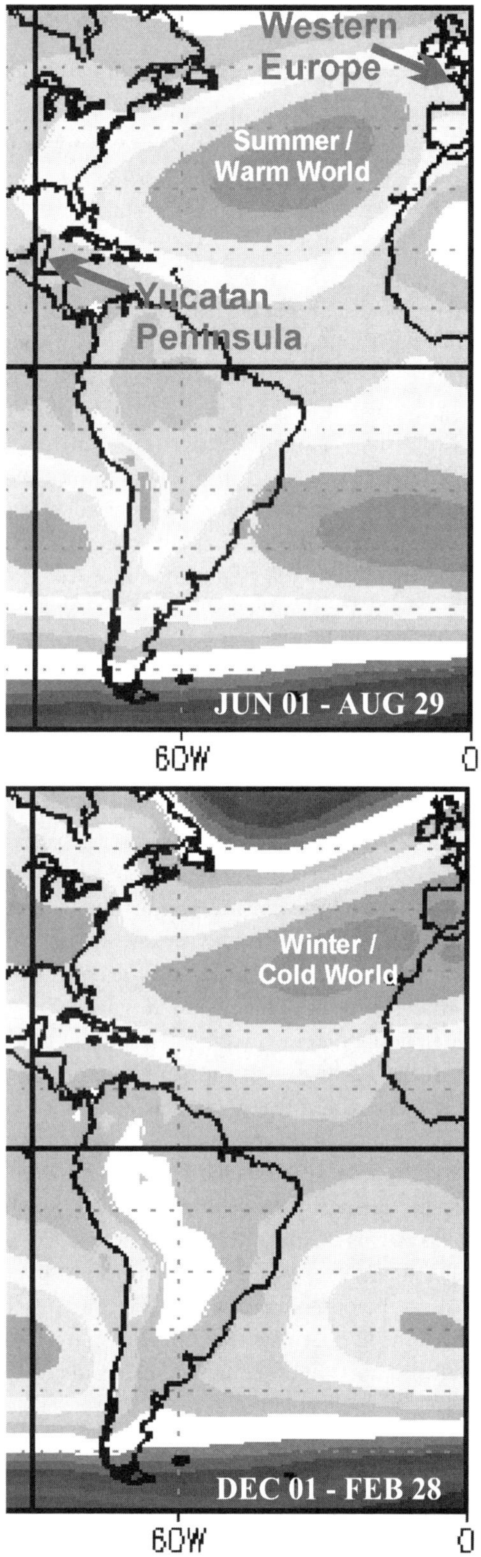

Figure 8.7. The Bermuda High as it currently changes between summer (a) and winter (b). This is based on 2011 averages over three months, but simulates in part the impact of global warming and cooling on the High and how it impacts adjoining lands. If the 1015 millibar line is used to mark the edge of the Bermuda High, in summer (hot) world conditions it moves north of the Yucatan Peninsula allowing more tropical moisture to approach. In winter (cold) world conditions, it encompasses the Yucatan Peninsula blocking tropical Trade Wind moisture. In Western Europe, the effect is the opposite (adapted from California Weather Server web site 2011, http://squall.sfsu.edu/crws/archive/jet_arch.html, accessed December 2, 2013).

investigated by Folan et al. (1983) and Gill (2000). Presumably, under very cold world conditions, it would shrink to nothing year around: this would be the ice ages. Under very hot world conditions, it expands to encircle the globe in one continuous ring, a seasonal condition seldom seen in recent centuries, but probably resembling the much hotter global climate during the time of the Mesozoic dinosaurs. In the Holocene, it shrinks and swells seasonally and, in adjusting to the world temperatures, it changes the climate of landmasses touched by it.

The effects on Yucatan and Europe can be briefly summarized as follows: *Yucatan*: Under cold world conditions, the Bermuda High shrinks southeastward letting dry, continental air into the Yucatan Peninsula from the northwest causing drought (see Figure 8.3B). As the world warms, it expands to center more northward, allowing tropical rains to water the peninsula from the east (Folan et al. 1983; Gunn et al. 1995). *Europe*: Under cold conditions, the Bermuda High shrinks southward, allowing cool, moist air to flow in off the Atlantic in the summer, creating a moist agricultural climate. As the world warms, the Bermuda High balloons up over Europe earlier. Earlier in the summer it blocks moist air and creates a northward-expanded Mediterranean climate zone with dry summers and moist winters (Gunn and Crumley 1991).

Each of these weather patterns has implications for local agriculture. As we have demonstrated, the agricultural system of the Yucatan Peninsula is dependent on about equal parts of the year being dry or wet, so a mid-range "Just Right" global temperature is most productive of food and populations (see Figure 8.4a; Gunn et al. 1994, 1995; Gunn and Folan 2000). In Europe, warmer global conditions are more beneficial because of the highly productive grain- and grape-based Mediterranean agricultural system (Crumley 1994). While other factors can intervene, the ideal conditions in either place generally produce so-called "golden ages" with high agricultural productivity and surpluses that provide for growing populations, social hierarchies, and burgeoning infrastructure.

Since both of the landmasses in our comparison are influenced by the same Bermuda High air mass, we can, to a degree, control for the effects of changing global temperatures on local productivity in the context of related agency and social changes. Thus, an analogy drawn from Yucatan and Europe provides a relatively controlled test bed for analyzing the impacts of climate changes on culturally, distinctly different parts of the world. We might expect that different cultural changes would be occurring in both places as a result of change in global average temperatures and their local synoptic ramifications. They should, however, because of the common climate influence, be occurring on the same climate clock. In fact, as we have discussed elsewhere, serious climate punctuations occur on about a 200–300 year cycle in both areas (Gunn et al. 2004; Gunn et al. 1995). In Table 8.1 these events are labeled as "Crises." These are the most prominent of the crises but others surely exist.

Cultural Histories

The climatic and cultural histories of the Yucatan Peninsula and Europe (also a peninsula of similar size) are some of the best known in the world, thanks to decades of intensive work. For purposes of analysis, we will use cultural histories (Table 8.1) by van der Leeuw (2007) and Gunn et al. (2004) for Europe and the IHOPE-Maya database chronology for the Maya Lowlands (Gunn and IHOPE-Maya Members 2010; Chase and Scarborough, this volume). Van der Leeuw (2007) summarizes the post-Roman Empire period to modern times, the development of the current world system based on the evolution of markets in Europe and their subsequent worldwide expansion. The Gunn et al. (2004) chronology provides details for the first millennium C.E., the time contemporary with the Classic Maya.

The details of Maya chronology are provided in previous sections of this chapter. Links are made between those events with those of Europe for purpose of comparison for the last 3000 years in Table 8.1. Remarks for the Late Classic are as follows:

(1) From the C.E. 536 global climatic event to around C.E. 695 was the Calakmul Golden Age, when the dominant players belonged to the Kaan Dynasty; it lasted C.E. 636–695 (Martin and Grube 2008). This was followed by the Golden Age of the Tikal Dynasty in the eighth century. In Europe, the Calakmul Golden Age corresponds to the Merovingian Dynasty, and the Tikal Golden Age to the Carolingian Dynasty (see Table 8.1). Why there should be nearly simultaneous breaks in dynasties (hegemonies) on both sides of the Atlantic, C.E. 695 and C.E. 687, respectively, is not immediately evident but the previously discussed atmospheric relations suggest a common climate influence of global cooling.

(2) During the 8th–10th centuries: both the Maya Late Classic and the Carolingian Dynasty end about the same time. This is at the lowest point of sea level (see Figure 8.4) and thus the globally coldest period in the first millennium C.E. It is interesting that Charlemagne visited the Pope on Christmas Day of C.E. 800. It has been assumed he was there as a conqueror, but there were reasons for the decision to conquer southward. To give some idea of the character of the time, the Nile froze over in C.E. 829 C.E; the Carolingian trade system on the North Sea collapsed in the face of Vikings fleeing northern areas (Gunn et al. 2004); the Maya Lowland interior cities basically disappeared during this time, and the maritime cities assumed economic control. Some interior cities supported small populations of agriculturists. Trade resumed along the Preclassic route (Martin and Grube 2008) unobstructed by Calakmul–Tikal rivalries.

Analyzing Peninsular Comparisons

Analyzing comparisons between the trajectories of the two cultures requires some mental gymnastics to arrive at useful conclusions. First and foremost, the idea that the Maya "collapsed" is now considered to be an oversimplification (Sabloff 2007). The Maya culture did collapse in the sense that the Classic Maya culture of the southern lowlands, with huge its interior cities, stelae, etc., no longer existed. However, there were significant amounts of reorganization during the ninth century drought and a lot of people undoubtedly lost their lives. On the other hand, there were cities that did not collapse, especially on the coasts; it is clearly a matter that the marine communities, which were more sustainable in the face of extended drought (Dunning et al. 2013), were prepared and able to replace the interior cities as trade entrepôts, and did so. The movements of the Kaan dynasty, as discussed above, suggest that apart from control of then-moribund trade corridors, the elites were better able to maintain surplus production in the coastal plain at levels that supported the lifestyle to which they had become accustomed after about 1200 years of rule.

Obviously parallel shifts to marine dependence occurred in Europe, in a similar time frame. Europeans too extended their ability to travel on the oceans in the post-ninth century C.E. period. However, rather than continuing to rely on rowing goods to distant markets, Europeans built on a long tradition of oceangoing ship construction dating back to the Neolithic (Cunliffe 2008); and when the time came, replaced low energy rowing (galleys existed even on the Atlantic coast in the time of Julius Caesar, around 50 B.C.E.) with sail and then steam. The later would have been the byproduct of the 16th century energy transformation to coal. By way of comparison, in 1504, on his fourth voyage to the Americas, Columbus encountered a Maya oceangoing canoe off the east coast of the Yucatan Peninsula with 21 rowers, passengers, and trade goods.

If the basis of comparison is adjusted, and if the interior cities are taken as the central issue forgetting that the Maya are still here today as they have been for thousands of years, a different perspective can be drawn. Given the interior cities as a subject of analogy, this different question is essentially, How could they have saved their great populations and vast infrastructure from being reduced to forest, chiclero collecting and processing stations, and logger's camps? This approximates the question being asked by those who hold that the Maya simply went away with their interior cities.

There are a number of measures the interior cities could have taken that would have averted their demise. Some were within their capabilities, others were not. We will discuss three possibilities.

(1) The interior cities could have concluded a treaty that foreswore endemic warfare. Warfare has long been thought to be an underlying cause of the externalization of trade relations to the "peripheral" marine communities (Willey 1974; Rathje 1971).
(2) Although the transportation costs of marine trade would have remained far below those of the interior communities, giving them a theoretical edge in transportation competition, the larger populations and accumulated wealth, especially in infrastructure, would have allowed the interior communities to maintain their vested interests and thwart the takeover of the trade system by coastal communities. The coastal cities, however, would always have remained a threat because of their superior ability to maintain agricultural surpluses, even in the face of extended droughts. As we will suggest next, the denizens of Calakmul might have designed a more sustainable economic regime. In that warfare is often a means of capturing additional subsistence resources when one's population overruns local carrying capacity, Maya endemic warfare may have been just a symptom of the need for a more sustainable economy.

The IHOPE-Maya database analysis indicates that during the Late Classic the interior communities were drawing on the forest resources of the coastal communities for food, perhaps because the interior cities were unable to sustain their burgeoning populations by internal means. To maintain a longer historic trajectory of prominence, the interior cities would have had to redesign their use of resources and or controlled population *numbers* to a sustainable budget. Among measures they could have taken was to reduce the opulence to which the kings were accustomed. However,

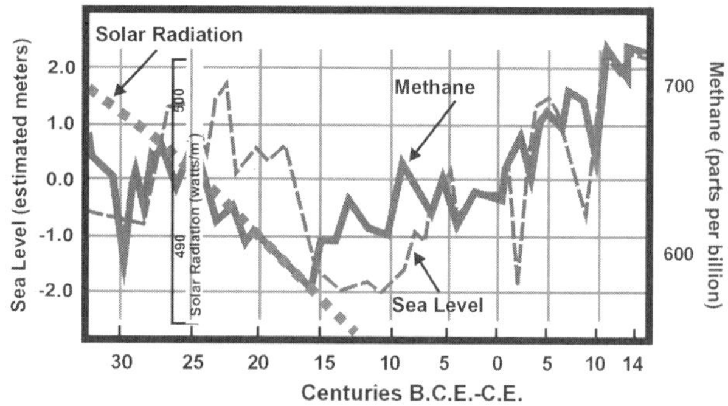

Figure 8.8. Solar radiation (controlled by the rotational wobble of the planet), Holocene methane concentrations in the atmosphere, and north Atlantic sea level as proxies for global temperatures (adapted from Ruddiman 2005; Tanner 1993). Solar radiation is expected to predict the amount of methane in the atmosphere. It does so until 15 centuries B.C.E. (1500 B.C.E.), at which time methane concentrations increase, departing from the predicted decline of solar radiation, apparently due to human intervention (Ruddiman 2005). Sea level and global temperatures follow similar trajectories, though as might be expected with more erratic modes of progress.

there is some consensus that even with convex water systems of the Late Classic, the interior, elevated cities could not withstand the stresses of extended drought.

(3) Investigation of lake core sediments within the Yucatan peninsula indicates that the ninth century drought was the worst in 9,000 years in some locations (Hodell et al. 1995). William Tanner's (1993) reconstruction of Atlantic Basin sea level can be used as a proxy for global temperatures as it measures the amount the global water supply locked up in glaciers. It reflects an approximate 50 year filtering of global temperatures and a slight lag as the oceans warm and cool more slowly than the atmosphere. In Figure 8.8, deep spikes can be seen around the 3rd and 9th centuries. These deep spikes appear to be characteristic of the Late Holocene, and could be associated with the periodic Maya collapses such as occurred in the third and ninth centuries. Comparing the sea level and Candelaria discharge curves indicates that extended droughts occur when low atmospheric temperatures were reinforced by low sea level/water temperatures. Studies by Ruddiman (2005) and several subsequent authors indicate that anthropogenic methane (also plotted in Figure 8.8) generated by wet rice and bovid husbandry has had a significant influence on global temperatures for about 3,000 years. If we suppose that the deep spikes are climate episodes that lack sufficient anthropogenic methane to forestall cooling toward another ice age as declining solar radiation suggests it should, then the interior Maya could have averted the extremes

of the 9th century drought by injecting more methane into the atmosphere. They could also have avoided the hyper-heating of the 12th and 13th centuries by withdrawing methane from the atmosphere. Of course such a suggestion is irrelevant from the perspective of the Classic Maya—but may not be for present-day world society that finds itself trapped between a number of unsustainable conditions, including the threatened onset of another ice age and hyper-heating of the atmosphere by accumulating greenhouse gasses.

While these suggestions drawn from the interior Maya experience are a bit heady, they may on further examination lead to doable corrective actions on the part of modern world communities. Basically Europe and the modern world system, like the Maya interior cities, have been on an unsustainable path since they overran the wood supplies in the 1500s and turned to fossil fuels. All three suggestions drawn from the Maya-Europe comparison could be part of the solution to our current world crisis.

Acknowledgments

The authors like to thank the many members of the IHOPE-Maya community for comments and conversations leading to this article. Also, Scott Hutson, Ivan Sprajc, and Kathy Reese-Taylor provided helpful comments.

Notes

1. Individuals who contributed data to this analysis were David Lentz, Nuria Torrescano Valle, Fred Valdez, Don Forsyth, and Rosario Dominguez Carasco. Other IHOPE members reviewed portions of the manuscript and offered helpful comments and conversations.
2. See cores taken below the city of El Laberinto.

References Cited

Adams, Richard E. W.
2005 Prehistoric Mesoamerica. 3rd edition. Norman: University of Oklahoma Press.

Adams, R. E. W., and Richard C. Jones
1981 Spatial Patterns and Regional Growth among Classic Maya Cities. American Antiquity 46:301–322.

Aliphat Fernandez, Mario M.
1994 Classic Maya Landscape in the Upper Usumacinta River Valley. Ph.D. dissertation, Department of Anthropology, University of Calgary.

Baron, Joanne, Diana Fridberg, and Marcello Canuto
2012 "Entró el Agua" Utilizacion de Especies Acuaticas en Contextos Mortuorios de La Corona, Guatemala. Paper presented at the XXI Encuentro Los Investigadores de la Cultura Maya, Universidad Autónoma de Campeche, Campeche, November 15–18.

Benavides-Castillo, Antonio
2001 La Temporada 2000 del Proyecto Edzna. *In* Los Investigadores de la Cultura Maya, Campeche. Vol. IX. Pp. 28–38. Campeche: Universidad Autonoma de Campeche.

Braswell, Geoffrey E.
2010 The Rise and Fall of Market Exchange: A Dynamic Approach to Ancient Maya Economy. *In* Archaeological Approaches to Market Exchange in Ancient Societies. C. P. Garratty and B. L. Stark, eds. Pp. 127–140. Boulder: University Press of Colorado.

Braudel, Fernand
1979 Civilization and Capitalism 15th–18th Century. Vol. 3: The Perspective of the World. New York: Harper and Row.

Canter, Ronald L.
2007 Rivers among the Ruins: The Usumacinta. The PARI Journal 7(3):1–24.

Canuto, Marcello, Joanne Baron, and Yann Desailly-Chanson
2012 La Corona and Calakul's "Royal Road." Paper presented at the 77th Annual Conference of the Society for American Archaeology, Memphis, Tennessee, April 18–22, 2012.

Clark, John E.
2000 Towards a Better Explanation of Hereditary Inequality: A Critical Assessment of Natural and Historic Human Agents. *In* Agency in Archaeology. M-A. Dobres and J. Robb, eds. Pp. 92–112. London: Routledge.

Cowgill, George L.
2004 Origins and Development of Urbanism:

Archaeological Perspectives. Annual Review of Anthropology 33:525–549.

Crumley, Carole L.
1993 Analyzing Historic Ecotonal Shifts: Ecological Applications 3:377–384.
1994 The Ecology of Conquest: Contrasting Agropastoral and Agricultural Societies' Adaptation to Climatic Change. *In* Historical Ecology: Cultural Knowledge and Changing Landscapes. C. Crumley, ed. Pp184–201. Santa Fe: School of American Research.

Cunliffe, Barry
2008 Europe between the Oceans: 9000 BC–AD 1000. New Haven: Yale University Press.

Dahlin, Bruce H., John F. Foss, and Mary Elizabeth Chambers
1980 Project Acalches: Reconstructing the Natural and Cultural History of a Seasonal Swamp at El Mirador Guatemala; Preliminary Results. *In* El Mirador, Petén Guatemala: an Interim Report. New World Archaeological Foundation. R. Matheny, ed. Pp. 37–57. Provo, UT: Brigham Young University.

Davies, Norman
2011 Vanished Kingdoms: The Rise and Fall of States and Nations. New York: Penguin Books.

Demarest, Arthur A.
2013 Ideological Pathways to Economic Exchange: Religion, Economy, and Legitimation at the Classic Maya Royal Capital of Cancuen. Latin American Antiquity 24:371–402.

Domínguez Carrasco, Maria del Rosario
2008 Análisis químico y sociopolitico de producción cerámica prehispanica en la región de Calakmul, Campeche. Colección Arqueología, 5. Campeche: Universidad Autónoma de Campeche.

Domínguez Carrasco, María del Rosario, and William J. Folan Higgins
1997 El sistema hidráulico de Calakmul. Información 15:51–84.

Domínguez Carrasco, María del Rosario, W. J. Folan, G. Gates, B. Volta, R. González Heredia, J. D. Gunn, A. Morales López, and H. Robichaux
2011 Oxpemul, su altiplanicie Kárstica Ondulada-Calakmul y su Cuenca: El Preclásico. *In* XXV Simposio de Investigaciones Arqueológicas en Guatemala, Ciudad de Guatemala, Guatemala, Vol. XXV. Pp. 887–901. Guatemala City: Museo Nacional de Arqueología y Etnología.

Dull, Robert, J. Southon, S. Kutterolf, A. Freundt, D. Wahl, and P. Sheets
2010 Did the Ilopango TBJ Eruption Cause the AD 536 Event? Abstract. American Geophysical Union 13:2370.

Dunning, Nicholas
1996 A Reexamination of Regional Variability in the Prehistoric Agricultural Landscape. *In* The Managed Mosaic: Ancient Maya Agriculture and Resource Use. S. Fedick, ed. Pp 53–68. Salt Lake City: University of Utah Press.

Dunning, Nicholas P., and Timothy Beach
2010 Farms and Forests: Spatial and Temporal Perspectives on Ancient Maya Landscapes. *In* Landscapes and Societies. I. P. Martini and W. Chesworth, eds. Pp. 369–389. Springer Science+Business Media B. V.

Dunning, Nicholas P., T. Beach, P. Farrell, and S. Luzzadder-Beach
1998 Prehispanic Agrosystems and Adaptive Regions in the Maya Lowlands. Culture and Agriculture 20:87–100.

Dunning, Nicholas P., Timothy Beach, and Sheryl Luzzadder-Beach
2006 Environmental Variability among Bajos in the Southern Maya Lowlands and Its Implications for Ancient Maya Civilization and Archaeology. *In* Precolumbian Water Management: Ideology, Ritual and Power. L. Lucero and B. Fash, eds. Pp. 81–99. Tucson: University of Arizona Press.

Dunning, Nicholas P., Timothy P. Beach, and Sheryl Luzzadder-Beach
2012 Kax and Kol: Collapse and Resilience in Lowland Maya Civilization. Proceedings of the National Academy of Sciences 109(10):3652–3657.

Dunning, Nicholas P., T. Beach, L. Grasiozo Sierra, J. Jones, D. L. Lentz, S. Luzzadder Beach, V. L. Scarborough, and M. P. Smyth
2013 A Tale of Two Collapses: Environmental

Variability and Cultural Disruption in the Maya Lowlands. Diálogo Andino 41:171–183.

Faust, Betty B.
1988 Cosmology and Changing Technologies of the Campeche-Maya. Ph.D. dissertation, Department of Anthropology, Syracuse University.

Faust, Betty B., and Joel D. Gunn
N.d. Gardens, Ceremonies and Cultural Memory in a Maya Village. Unpublished MS, Department of Anthropology, University of North Carolina, Greensboro.

Faust, Betty B., P. Quintana, F. Bautista, and J. D. Gunn
2010 Effect of Agricultural Burning on Chemicals and Mineralogical Soil Properties in Maya Milpas: A Key Ingredient in Maya Lowland Sustainability. Paper presented at the annual conference of the Society for Applied Anthropology, Merida, Mexico, March 24–27, 2010.

Fedick, Scott L., ed.
1996 The Managed Mosaic: Ancient Maya Agriculture and Resource Use. Salt Lake City: University of Utah Press.

Fletcher, Laraine A., and James A. Gann
1994 Analisis Grafico de Patrones de Asentamiento. El Caso Calakmul. *In* Campeche Maya Colonial. W. J. Folan Higgins, ed. Pp. 85–121. Collection Arqueología. Campeche, México: Universidad Autónoma de Campeche.

Folan, William J.
1981 Comments on The Late Postclassic Eastern Frontier of Mesoamerica: Cultural Innovation along the Periphery by J. Fox. Current Anthropology 22:336–337.

Folan, William J., May Hau, R. Couoh Muñoz, and R. González Heredia
1990 Calakmul, Campeche, México: Su Mapa. Campeche: Centro de Investigaciones Históricas y Sociales, Universidad Autónoma de Campeche.

Folan, William J., G. Gates, B. Volta, M. d. R. Domínguez C., R. González H., J. D. Gunn, and A. Morales López
2011 Las ruinas de Calakmul, Campeche, México: sus ciudades tributarias y su altiplanicie kárstica del Petén campechano y el norte de Guatemala. Paper presented at the XXI Encuentro Internacional Los Investigadores de la Cultura Maya, Campeche, Mexico, November 15–18, 2011.

Folan, William J., Joel D. Gunn, and María del Rosario Domínguez Carrasco
2001 Triadic Temples, Central Plazas, and Dynastic Palaces: A Diachronic Analysis of the Royal Court Complex, Calakmul, Campeche, Mexico. *In* Royal Courts of the Ancient Maya, vol. 2: Data and Case Studies. T. Inomata and S. D. Houston, eds. Pp. 223–265. Boulder: Westview.

Folan, William J., J. Gunn, J. D. Eaton, and R. W. Patch
1983 Paleoclimatological Patterning in Southern Mesoamerica. Journal of Field Archaeology 10:453–468.

Folan, William J., J. Marcus, S. Pincemin, M. d. R. Domínguez Carrasco, L. Fletcher, and A. M. López
1995 Calakmul: New Data from an Ancient Maya Capital in Campeche, Mexico. Latin American Antiquity 6:310–334.

Folan, William J., A. Morales L., R. González H., M. d. R. Domínguez C., and A. Anaya H.
2010 El Estado Regional de Calakmul, Campeche, México: Descubrimientos Recientes. *In* La Peninsula de Yucatán: Investigaciones recientes y cronologías alternativas. E. V. P. Antonio Benavides-Castillo, ed. Pp. 59–90. Colección Arqueología. Campeche, Mexico: Universidad Autónoma de Campeche.

Freidel, David A., Hector L. Escobedo, and Stanley P. Guenter
2007 A Crossroads of Conquerors: Waka' and Gordon Willey's "Rehearsal for the Collapse" Hypothesis. *In* Gordon R. Willey and American Archaeology: Contemporary Perspectives. W. Fash, ed. Pp. 187–208. Norman: University of Oklahoma Press.

Gates, Gary
1992 Physiology, Geology, and Hydrology of the Calakmul Biosphere Reserve: Report submitted to the MacArthur Foundation of Chicago through Biocenosis, Mexico S.A. and the Centro de Investigations Históricas y Sociales de la Universidad Autónoma de Campeche.

1999 Fisiografia, Geologia e Hidrologia. *In* Naturaleza y Cultura en Calakmul, Campeche. W. Folan, M. C. Sanchez, and J. M. Ortega, eds. Pp. 31–39. Campeche: CIHS, Universidad Autónoma de Campeche, Mexico.

Geovannini Acuña, Helga
2008 Rain Harvesting in the Rainforest: The Ancient Maya Agricultural Landscape of Calakmul, Campeche, Mexico. BAR International Series, 1879. Oxford: Archaeo Press.

Gill, R. B.
2000 The Great Maya Droughts: Water, Life, and Death. Albuquerque: University of New Mexico Press.

Guenter, Stanley
2008 El Mirador. *In* The Mesoweb Encyclopedia. http://www.mesoweb.com/encyc/index.asp?passcall=rightframeexact&rightframeexact=http%3A//www.mesoweb.com/encyc/view.asp%3Fact%3Dviewfull%26i%3D16%26s%3DTeotihuacan%26ext%3Dn%26sit%3D8%26id%3D19%26expert%3Dy%26sAND%3D%26sANDNOT%3D, accessed May 25, 2014.

Gunn, Joel, and Carole L. Crumley
1991 Global Energy Balance and Regional Hydrology: A Burgundian Case Study. Earth Surface Processes and Landforms 16:579–592.

Gunn, Joel, C. L. Crumley, E. Jones, and B. K. Young
2004 A Landscape Analysis of Western Europe during the Early Middle Ages. *In* The Archaeology of Global Change: The Impact of Humans on Their Environment. C. L. Redman, S. R. James, P. R. Fish, and J. D. Rogers, eds. Pp. 165–185. Washington, DC: Smithsonian Institution Press.

Gunn, Joel D., and William J. Folan
2000 Three Rivers: Subregional Variations in Earth System Impacts in the Southwestern Maya Lowlands (Candelaria, Usumacinta, and Champoton Watersheds). *In* The Way the Wind Blows: Climate, History, and Human Action. R. Mcintosh, J. Tainter, and S. Mcintosh, eds. Pp. 263–270. New York: Columbia University Press.

Gunn, Joel D., W. J. Folan, M. d. R. Domínguez Carrasco, and F. Miller
2002 Bajo Sediments and the Hydraulic System of Calakmul, Campeche, Mexico. Ancient Mesoamerica 13:297–315.
2009 Explicando la Sustentabilidad de Calakmul, Campeche: Eslabones Interiores en el Sistema de Energía del Estado Regional de Calakmul. *In* Encuentro Internacional de Los Investigadores de la Cultura Maya. Pp. 13–40, Vol. XVIII, Toma 1 . Campeche: Universidad Autónoma de Campeche.

Gunn, Joel D., V. Scarborough, A. Chase, J. Sabloff, M. d. R. Domínguez Carrasco, D. Forsyth, F. Valdez, S. Fedick, and R. Liendo
2010 Initial Analysis of Real IHOPE-Maya Data: Did the Maya Manage Woodlands along the Coasts? NCEAS (National Center for Ecological Analysis and Synthesis) IHOPE-Maya Working Group, Santa Barbara, 2010. Unpublished MS, Department of Anthropology, University of North Carolina, Greensboro.

Gunn, Joel, William J. Folan, and Hubert R. Robichaux
1994 Un Análisis Informativo sobre la Descarga del Sistema del Río Candelaria en Campeche, México: Reflexiones acerca de los Paleoclimas que afectaron a los Antiguos Sistemas Mayas en los Sitios de Calakmul y el Mirador. *In* Campeche Maya Colonial. W. J. Folan Higgins, ed. Pp. 174–197. Collección Arqueología. Campeche, México: Universidad Autónoma de Campeche.
1995 A Landscape Analysis of the Candelaria Watershed in Mexico: Insights into Paleoclimates affecting Upland Horticulture in the Southern Yucatan Peninsula Semi-Karst. Geoarchaeology 10:3–42.

Hansen, Richard D.
1994 Investigaciones Arqueológicas en el Norte del Peten de Guatemala: Una Mirada Diacrónica de los Orígenes Mayas. *In* Campeche Maya Colonial: 14.54. W. J. Folan H., ed. Colección Arqueología. Campeche: CIHS, Universidad Autónoma de Campeche.
1998 Continuity and Disjunction: The Pre-Classic Antecedents of Classic Maya Architecture. *In* Function and Meaning in Classic Maya Architecture. S. D. Houston, ed. Pp. 49–122. Washington, DC: Dumbarton Oaks.

Hansen, Richard D., S. Bozarth, J. Jacob, D. Wahl, and T. Schreiner
2002 Climatic and Environmental Variability in the Rise of Maya Civilization: A Preliminary Perspective

from the Northern Peten. Ancient Mesoamerica 13:273–295.

Heckbert, Scott, Christian Isendahl, Joel D. Gunn, Scott Brewer, Vernon L. Scarborough, Arlen F. Chase, Diane Z. Chase, Robert Costanza, Nicholas P. Dunning, Timothy Beach, Sheryl Luzzadder-Beach, David Lentz, and Paul Sinclair

In press Growing the Maya Social-Ecological System from the Bottom Up: Using Complex Systems Models to Test Resilience Theory. *In* Handbook of Historical Ecology and Applied Archaeology. C. Isendahl and D. Stump, eds. Oxford: Oxford University Press.

Hodell, David A., Jason H. Curtis, and Mark Brenner

1995 Possible Role of Climate in the Collapse of Classic Maya Civilization. Nature 375:391–394.

Hodell, David A., J. H. Curtis, M. Brenner, and T. Guilderson

2001 Solar Forcing of Drought Frequency in the Maya Lowlands. Science 292:1367–1370.

Hutson, Scott R., Bruce H. Dahlin, and Danieal Mazeau

2010 Commerce and Cooperation among the Classic Maya: The Chunchucmil Case. *In* Cooperation in Social and Economic Life. R. Marshall, ed. Lanham, MD: Altamira Press.

IPCC (Intergovernmental Panel on Climate Change)

2013 Climate Change 2013: The Physical Science Basis, Working Group I Contribution to the Fifth Assessment Report of the Intergovernmental Panel on Climate Change, Summary for Policymakers. http://www.climatechange2013.org/images/uploads/WGI_AR5_SPM_brochure.pdf, accessed December 18, 2013.

Jackson, Sarah E.

2013 Politics of the Maya Court: Hierarchy and Change in the Late Classic Period. Norman: University of Oklahoma Press.

Jacob, John S.

1995 Archaeological Pedology in the Maya Lowlands. Special Publication, 44. Madison: Soil Science Society of America.

Marcus, Joyce

1976 Territorial Organization of the Lowland Classic Maya. Science 180:911–916.

Martin, Simon

2005 Of Snakes and Bats: Shifting Identities at Calakmul. The PARI Journal 6(2):5–15.

Martin, Simon, and Nikolai Grube

2008 Chronicle of the Maya Kings and Queens: Deciphering the Dynasties of the Ancient Maya. 2nd edition. London: Thames and Hudson.

Matheny, Ray T., D. L. Gurr, D. W. Forsyth, and R. Hauck

1983 Investigations at Edzna, Campeche, Mexico: The Hydraulic System. Papers of the New World Archaeology Foundation, 46. Provo, UT: Brigham Young University.

Milbrath, Susan

1979 A Study of Olmec Sculptural Chronology. Studies in Pre-Columbian Art and Archaeology, 23. Washington, DC: Dumbarton Oaks.

Nalda, Enrique

2005 Kohunlich and Dzibanche. *In* Quintana Roo archaeology. J. M. Shaw and J. P. Mathews, eds. Pp. 228–244. Tucson: The University of Arizona Press.

Neilson, Ronald P.

1986 High-Resolution Climatic Analysis and Southwest Geography. Science 232:27–34.

Perry, Eugene, Guadalupe Velazquez Oliman, and Niklas Wagner

2011 Preliminary Investigation of Groundwater and Surface Water Geochemistry in Campeche and Southern Quintana Roo. *In* Water Resources in Mexico. U. Oswald Spring, ed. Pp. 87–97. Heidelberg: Springer.

Perry, Eugene C., G. Velazquez-Oliman, N. Wagner, A. Paytan, and J. H. Street

2010 Sr Ions and Isotopes in Groundwater Campeche, Mexico: Insight into Development of the Edzna Valley. *In* Water-Rock Interaction. P. Birkle and I. S. Torres-Alvarado, eds. Pp. 349–352. London: Taylor and Francis.

Rathje, William L.

1971 The Origin and Development of Lowland Classic Maya Civilization. American Antiquity 36:275–285.

Reese-Taylor, Kathryn, A. Anaya Hernandez, D. Walker, and A. Flores Esquivel
2012 Resultados y Interpretaciones Preliminaries de la Primera Temporada de investigaciones en Yaxnohcah, Campeche, Mexico. *In* XXI Encuentro Los Investigadores De La Cultura Maya, November 18–22, 2012. Campeche: Universidad Autónoma de Campeche.

Robichaux, Hubert R.
2010 The Ancient Maya Monuments at Oxpemul, Campeche, México: Mesoweb. http://www.mesoweb.com/publications/Robichaux/Oxpemul.html, accessed November 18, 2011.

Ruddiman, William F.
2005 Plows, Plagues, and Petroleum: How Humans Took Control of Climate. Princeton, NJ: Princeton University Press.

Sabloff, Jeremy A.
2007 It Depends on How You Look at Things: New Perspectives on the Postclassic Period in the Northern Maya Lowlands. Proceedings of the American Philosophical Society 151(1):11–25.
2009 The Greater Puuc Region. Paper presented at IHOPE-Maya Workshop: Tropical Sustainability from an Ancient Context, School for Advanced Research, Santa Fe, New Mexico, January 14–17 2009.

Sabloff, Jeremy A., and Gair Tourtellot
1991 The Ancient Maya City of Sayil: The Mapping of a Puuc Region Center. Middle American Research Institute Publication, 60. Tulane University: Middle American Research Institute.

Scarborough, Vernon L.
1993 Water Management in the Southern Maya Lowlands: An Accretive Model for the Engineered Landscape. Research in Economic Anthropology 7:17–69.
2007 The Rise and Fall of the Ancient Maya: A Case Study in Political Ecology. *In* Sustainability or Collapse? An Integrated History and Future of People on Earth (Dahlem Workshop Reports). R. Costanza, L. J. Graumlich, and W. Steffen, eds. Pp. 51–59. Cambridge, MA: The MIT Press.
2008 Rate and Process of Societal Change in Semitropical Settings: The Ancient Maya and the Living Balinese. Quaternary International 184:24–40.

Scarborough, Vernon L., and William R. Burnside
2010 Complexity and Sustainability: Perspectives from the Ancient Maya and the Modern Balinese. American Antiquity 75(2):327–363.

Schele, Linda, and David Freidel
1990 A Forest of Kings: The Untold Story of the Ancient Maya. New York: William Morrow and Company.

Seitz, R., G. E. Harlow, V. B. Sisson, and K. A. Taube
2001 "Olmec Blue" and Formative Jade Sources: New Discoveries in Guatemala. Antiquity 75:687–688.

Sharer, Robert J., and Loa P. Traxler
2006 The Ancient Maya. Stanford: Stanford University Press.

Siemens, Alfred H.
2009 Un Rio en Tierra Maya. Paper presented at Los Investigadores de la Cultura Maya, Campeche, México. November 16, 2009.

Siemens, Alfred H., and Dennis E. Puleston
1972 Ridged Fields and Associated Features in Southern Campeche: New Perspectives on the Lowland Maya. American Antiquity 37(2):228–239.

Šprajc, Ivan
2008 Reconocimiento arqueológico en el sureste del estado de Campeche, México: 1996–2005. Paris Monographs in American Archaeology, 19. Oxford: BAR International Series.

Šprajc, Ivan, and Nikolai Grube
2008 Arqueología del Sureste de Campeche: Una Síntesis. *In* Reconocimiento arqueológico en el sureste del estado de Campeche, México: 1996–2005. I. Sprajc, ed. Pp. 263–275. Paris Monographs in American Archaeology, 19. Oxford: BAR International Series.

Šprajc, Ivan, Carlos Morales-Aguilar, and Richard D. Hansen
2009 Early Maya Astronomy and Urban Planning at El Mirador, Peten, Guatemala. Anthropological Notebooks 15(3):79–101.

Tankersley, Kenneth B., V. L. Scarborough, N. Dunning, W. Huff, B. Maynard, and T. L. Gerke
2011 Evidence for Volcanic Ash Fall in the Maya Lowlands from a Reservoir at Tikal, Guatemala. Journal of Archaeological Science 38:2925–2938.

Tanner, William F.
1993 An 8000-Year Record of Sea-Level Change from Grain-Size Parameters: Data from Beach Ridges in Denmark. The Holocene 3:220–231.

Torrescano, Nuria, and G. A. Islebe
2009 Palynological and Chronological Evidence of Drought in the Yucatan Maya Lowlands during the Late Holocene. Unpublished MS, El Colegio de la Frontera Sur-Unidad Chetumal,Chetumal, Quintana Roo, México.

van der Leeuw, Sander E.
2007 Information Processing and Its Role in the Rise of the European World System. *In* Sustainability or Collapse? An Integrated History and Future of People on Earth. R. Costanza, L. J. Graumlich, and W. Steffen, eds. Pp. 213–241. Cambridge, MA: The MIT Press.

Vargas Pacheco, Ernesto
1999 Itzamkanac y Acalan: Tiempos de Crisis, Anticipando el Futuro, Tesis de Doctorado, INAH, SEP, Mexico, D.F.
2011 El Rio Candelaria, Rio de Encuentros: Ofrendas, Diques, Canales, Campos Levantados. Paper presented at the XXI Encuentro Los Investigadores De La Cultura Maya Conference, Campeche, Universidad Autónoma de Campeche, November 18–22, 2011.

Velásquez García, Erik
2005 The Captives of Dzibanche. The PARI Journal 6(2):1–4.

Villamil, Laura, and Jason Sherman
2005 Investigating Urban Diversity in South-central Quintana Roo. *In* Quintana Roo Archaeology. J. M. Shaw, ed. Pp. 197–213. Tucson: The University of Arizona Press.

Volta, Beniamino, and Joel D. Gunn
2012 Análisis de costo mínimo de posibles rutas de intercambio transpeninsulares en el Petén campechano. Paper presented at the 54th International Congress of Americanists, Vienna, Austria, July 15–20, 2012.

Wahl, David, Roger Byrne, Thomas Schreiner, and Richard Hansen
2006 Holocene Vegetation Change in the Northern Peten and Its Implications for Maya Prehistory. Quaternary Research 65:380–389.

Willey, Gordon R.
1974 The Classic Maya Hiatus: A Rehearsal for the Collapse? In Mesoamerican Archaeology: New Approaches. N. Hammond, ed. Pp. 417–430. London: Duckworth.

Winemiller, Terance L., W. J. Folan, J. May Hau, R. González H., F. Loraine, L. Florey Folan, A. Morales L., and J. D. Gunn
2011 Modelos 3d y Los Sistemas de Informacion Geografica: Descubriendo Nueva Informacion en El Manejo de Los Recursos Hidrologicos Prehistoricos del Sitio de Calakmul, Campeche. Paper presented at the XXI Encuentro Los Investigadores de La Cultura Maya, Campeche, Universidad Autonoma de Campeche, November 18–22, 2011.

Zetina Gutiérrez, María de Guadalupe, and Betty Bernice Faust
2011 De la Agroecología Maya a la Arqueología Demográfica: ¿Cuántas Casas por Familia?

9

The Alternative Economy: Resilience in the Face of Complexity from the Eastern Lowlands

Vernon L. Scarborough
University of Cincinnati
and
Fred Valdez
University of Texas, Austin

ABSTRACT

The ancient eastern Maya Lowlands are characterized by both small, highly resilient communities and the growth of large regional centers. The smaller communities, separated by 2–5 kilometers and dispersed across the landscape, established a circle of interdependency between one another and a spatial separation from the largest centers. Degrees of sustainability were achieved through time by way of a negotiated settlement and land use balance within the relatively fragile biophysical environment. Because tropical ecosystems are identified by low specific species richness in any one patch or microenvironment, humans tend to mimic this spatial dispersion—a high-density "ruralism." When assessed by way of high humidity and precipitation, decomposition and disease were significant deranging factors affecting surplus and storage. Roads and navigable canal systems shorten the time necessary for distribution of organics—principally food; and when coupled with routinized scheduling (calendars), time and distance were reduced. Salting and "natural" root crop preservation techniques are discussed. A dual or alternative economy is proposed in the context social complexity. [periodic market, roads, salt, root crops, sustainability, high-density ruralism]

A recent idiom suggests that seemingly disparate ways of organizing small sets of things or even different worldviews are not necessarily the span between "apples and oranges," but rather—at a more global scale—a reflection of their degrees of similarity or "kinds of roundedness" (see van der Leeuw, this volume). It is in this context that our IHOPE-Maya regional assessments have unfolded to best identify the interconnectivity that was the greater Maya Lowlands. Because of the accelerating accumulation of data acquired over the last fifty years, individual Mayanists have understandably focused their attention and resources on smaller and smaller geographic areas defining their data-rich, but regionally shrinking, research zones. Our interest is not to return to the culture area assessment of those pioneering early scholars invested in Old and New Empires, when data were limited and interpretive license broadly accommodating (Morley 1946; cf. Sharer and Traxler 2006). Rather, pan-Maya interpretation is again our goal, though now drawn from the abundance of carefully collected and reasonably interpreted information. To that end, this chapter introduces another way to assess the economic and political organization of the ancient Maya. Given that IHOPE is a global undertaking committed to employing the past to inform the present and with the goal to pose real-time solutions to today's pressing problems, we close with what we hope is meaningful, relevant, and apparent from an examination of this somewhat remote and still incomplete cultural record within the eastern Maya Lowlands (Figure 9.1).

ARCHEOLOGICAL PAPERS OF THE AMERICAN ANTHROPOLOGICAL ASSOCIATION, Vol. 24, pp. 124–141, ISSN 1551-823X, online ISSN 1551-8248. DOI: 10.1111/apaa.12033.

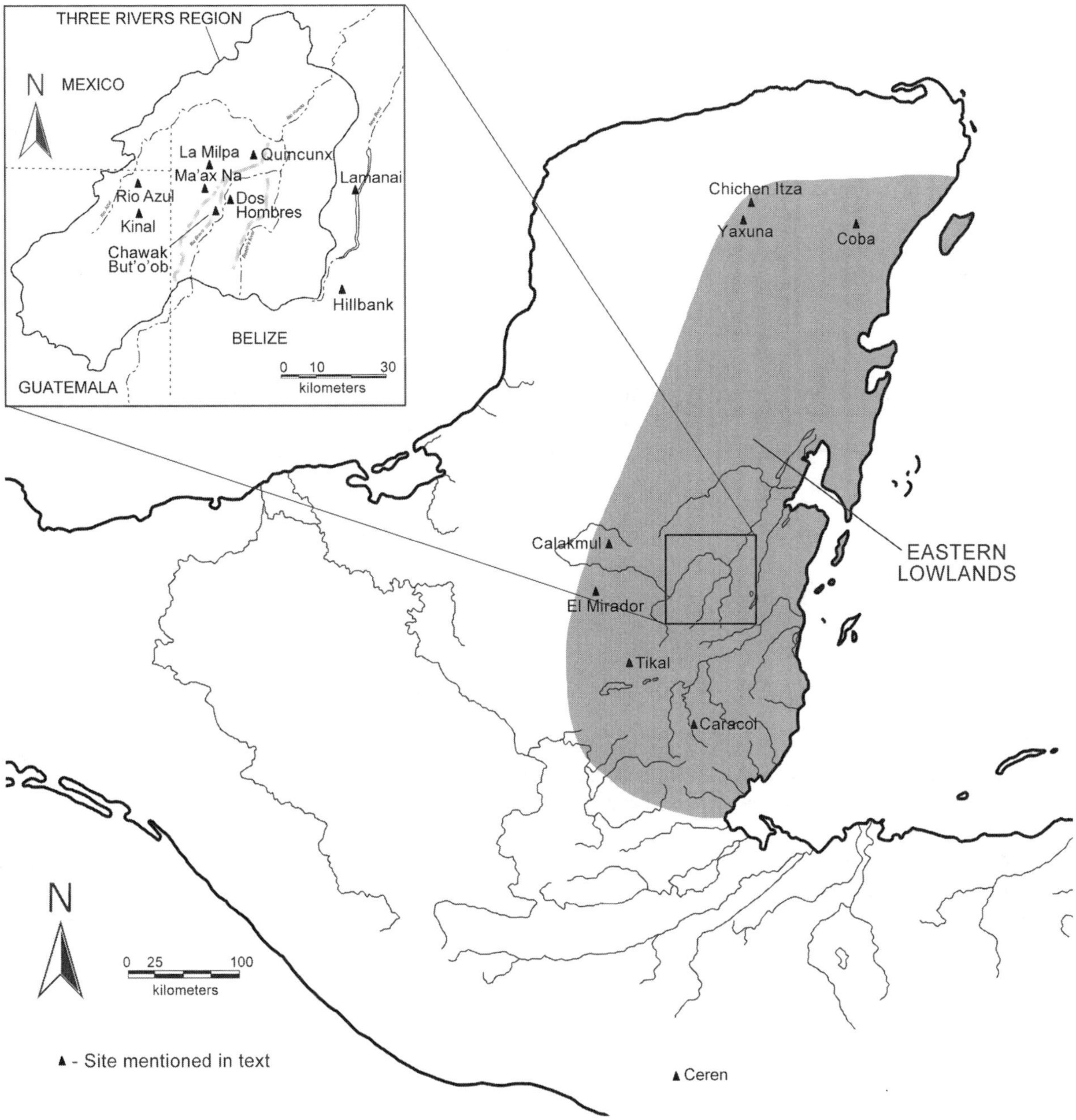

Figure 9.1. Map of Maya area, with sites and areas noted in text.

Our interpretation of ancient Maya economy has changed markedly in the last decade from one of a regional exchange system based on wealth and or staple finance (cf. D'Altroy and Earle 1985 McAnany 2010), associated with processed and refined resources driven by hierarchical access, to an economy based on a highly integrative set of resource-specialized communities contingent upon heterarchical networks (Scarborough and Valdez 2003, 2009). Given the density and diversity of households and communities dispersed throughout the Maya area, the notion that large and powerful Maya centers controlled and administered the regional economy is a less tenable position today (only the historical Aztec are convincingly seen as an administered economy for ancient Mesoamerica—see Isaac 2013; Stark and Garraty 2009; Smith 2009). Clearly, regional low-density cities (cf. Fletcher 2009) significantly influenced political relationships and ideological worldviews guiding the course of Maya (pre)history—with their authority waxing and waning, depending on degrees of geopolitical and ecological stability (Marcus

1993, 1998)—but considerable decision-making about a regional economy's resilience and longevity was rooted at the small community level. A key point of this paper is that subsistence as well as many kinds of surplus wealth were generally in the controlling hands of a hinterland population.

At the most fundamental level, the rural household as the basic unit of socioeconomic identity and the associated "house model" concept set the stage for social complexity (see Gillespie and Joyce 2000; Heitman and Plog 2005; cf. Lohse and Valdez 2004). Payson Sheets (2000) demonstrates the role of redundant behaviors and activities routinely performed in making a daily living as evidenced by the Pompeii-like preservation at Ceren. Although households generate the material remains of daily familial activities, they also invest in a very few production tasks that provide their neighbors with labor intensive activities and tool-use specialized resources. These products might range from textiles to pottery to stone tools that accommodate the community's overall needs and perhaps those of other adjacent groups. The processed resources are not likely to be luxury or status items, but rather mundane products that households provide one another in an interdependency of necessary exchange (see Reina and Hill 1978 for ethnographic examples).

Relatively recently, Gillespie and Joyce (2000) argue that an extended house model for the economy best characterizes the intercommunity exchange network operating widely throughout the Maya Lowlands during the Classic period. At the ecological conservancy of the Programme for Belize (Scarborough et al. 2003)—or the tract of land in northwestern Belize now overseen by the Belizean authorities and the archaeological resources of the Department of Anthropology at the University of Texas at Austin—as well as along the Belize River Valley (Garber 2004), conventional wisdom suggests that small, closely spaced communities were independent and self-reliant, capable only of recreating themselves generationally (Marx 1968 [1853][1853]; Southall 1988). However, many of these communities interacted through a set of socioeconomic interdependencies, knit together in a complicated areal–regional exchange system in which individual communities exploited or harvested specific resources either raw or refined—the latter entailing degrees of craftsmanship (Figure 9.2). Specialized material resources were exchanged as required, but intercommunity special events associated with ballcourts or astronomical alignment architecture were also identified at one site or another; the latter allowing participation in greater intercommunity solidarity and exchange (see again the ethnographic record associated with period marketing). The discovery of an isolated but well-constructed ballcourt at the diminutive community of Chawak But'o'ob (Walling 2011) and an unpretentious astronomical alignment at the small rural site of Quincunx (Zaro and Lohse 2005) indicate the significant role played by these material institutional expressions operating away from the largest cities but linked within a "high density ruralism." Unlike the huge major centers with a concentrated breadth of material, architecture and special event trappings at one location, the regional picture reveals a dispersed version of the activity traits and material culture otherwise identifiable at a center. This highly heterarchical ordering is grounded on a socioecological logic constrained by a tropical biophysical environment of tremendous diversity, but one highly limited by individual species richness (Scarborough 1998; Scarborough and Burnside 2010a). Because of the difficulties in concentrating natural resources, inclusive of the rapid decomposition of stored organics and elevated risk of waterborne disease when living in tight proximity to a neighbor, the Maya developed a dispersed interdependent settlement and land-use adaptation to the engineered landscape.

This is not to say that minor and major centers were anything but hubs for many of the interdigitating regional systems; however, it is unlikely that they functioned as truly centralized economic controllers. Among other functions, centers were loci for political intrigue and religious pilgrimage with their nodal geopolitical positioning significantly affecting and directing the throughput of interregional exchange, but not necessarily its production per se. Centers were important in establishing and maintaining transport infrastructure and scheduling, especially road networks and calendars, but are viewed as heavily dependent on negotiated diplomacy with the producers in the hinterlands. The rural elite, which Bullard (1960) noted five decades ago and has been since reported at numerous small communities throughout the Maya Lowlands, likely coordinated production strategies for a community or a group of communities (Scarborough et al. 2003).

It must be noted that on occasion, a city as engineered and agriculturally intensified as Tikal (Lentz et al. 2014; Scarborough et al. 2012), Calakmul (Gunn et al. this volume), or Caracol (Chase and Chase this volume) emerged. For example, the longevity of Caracol—and its continuous occupation through much of the "great fragmentation" of the Terminal Classic (Chase and Chase 2004; Demarest et al. 2004)—is explained, in part, by its complex and extensive terracing or unique landesque capital adaptation (Chase et al. 2011) accommodated by the specific topography and environments of the Maya Mountains.[1] Although other large centers reveal attempts at such engineered landscapes and a disproportionate access to the means of production—a condition apparent in several other archaic

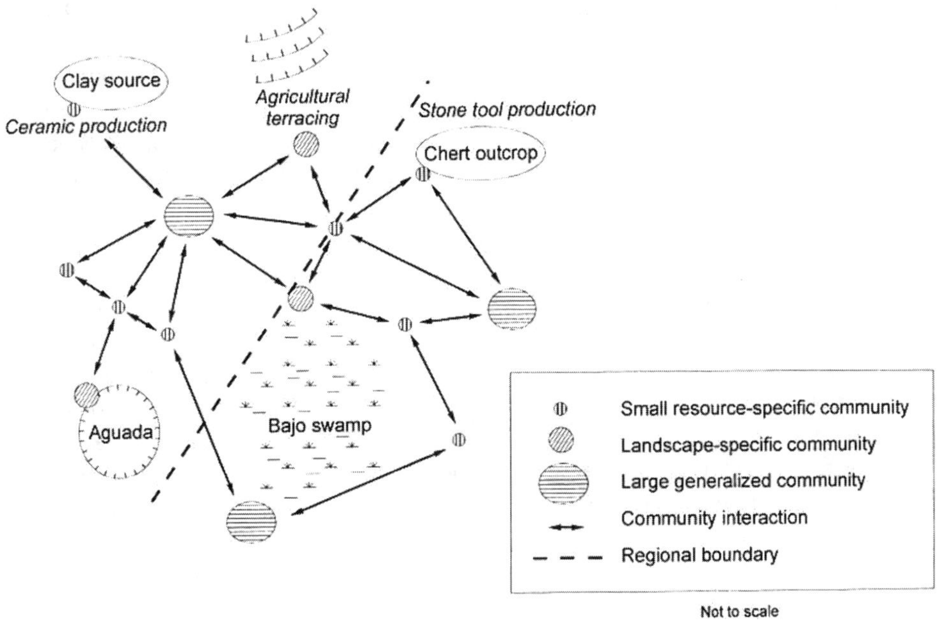

Figure 9.2. Model of community interaction in the Maya Lowlands (after Scarborough and Valdez 2003).

state trajectories elsewhere globally (Marcus and Sabloff 2008)—this transition was less dominate in the Maya case generally.

The dispersed character of both raw materials and the labor necessary to process those resources pulled at society, forcing linkages based on elaborate road systems and highly developed scheduling arrangements. Marketplaces or the grand plazas of most centers accommodated special events at all levels of Maya society, with activity proportional to the size of the site. Long-distant trade items or the occasional highly crafted set of artifacts associated with attached specialists at the largest centers were not the engines driving the economic trains (cf. Costin 1991; contra Inomata 2001). When compared to other archaic states, the Maya example is not a less complex adaptation; it is simply different, one suited to a semitropical setting with clear implications for similar and present-day ecologies (Scarborough and Burnside 2010a). This chapter will introduce the implications of this economic interpretation using data from the eastern Maya Lowlands. We must look to the hinterlands to now understand Maya economic organization.

At the outset, storage and surplus need to be viewed in a different light than frequently understood in other more semiarid or temperate environmental context. By structurally organizing the rapid movement and consumption of (over)ripening organics, surpluses were harvested and exchanged in a highly coordinated and consumptive manner; much of this food apportionment was directed by schedulers within the sizable political centers. More formalized place-bound storage was possible, of course, but it was a highly challenging investment frequently operating and controlled at the domestic level of production.

Periodic Marketing

The periodic market is well documented in the ethnohistoric record of Mesoamerica and specifically in the ethnographic literature of the contemporary Maya (Reina and Hill 1978; cf. Stark and Garraty 2009). Small marketplaces generally operated below the radar of state tributary systems because of their decentralized and diminutive marketplace size (McBryde 1933, 1945). In the Classic period of Maya (pre)history, the scope and scale of the regional economy was considerably more complex than that documented among modern Maya groups, suggesting to some that the period was characterized by an administered economy controlled and manipulated by a few hierarchically powerful cities (see Sharer and Traxler 2006). This commanding and sometime hegemonic power was clearly the pattern associated with archaic states in several other regions of the world, but our assessment of the past economic system of the ancient Maya suggests otherwise and therefore requires explanation.

Periodic markets are found in non-state societies as well as some state-level societies, the former demonstrable by the ancient Hohokam of the U.S. Southwest (Abbot 2010). Here, the ballgame and ballcourts associated with a community drew marketplace participants from an orbit of household and village craftspersons identified by different ceramic wares, which exchanged vessel forms and styles as well as other more perishable goods during the special event. This kind of integrative adaptation functioned well when populations were relatively sparse yet associated with emerging degrees of sociopolitical complexity. Even more environmentally constrained than the ancient Maya, the Hohokam had severe ecological limitations associated with the primacy of water and its deficient availability in spite of highly organized attempts to expand its access through the most sophisticated canalization efforts known anywhere in prehispanic North or Central America (Fish and Fish in press).

For the ancient Maya, the ecological adaptations were somewhat less constraining, though considerable limitations were placed on the concentration of otherwise abundant natural resources and considerations of preservation. Unlike the U.S. Southwest, rainfall was abundant—if somewhat unpredictable—but very seasonal (Me-Bar and Valdez 2003). Given the dispersed set of settlement adaptations made by the Maya and their mimicry of the ecological tempo and rhythms of a tropical forest, they were able to feed and reproduce a huge population. Because of the flexibility in location and the adaptability of local exchange networks, the periodic market in this case adjusted to an evolving engineered landscape by rapidly connecting and reconnecting communities and their subsistence systems (Scarborough and Valdez 2003). Community economic adaptation or "how to make a living" was based on an intricate, though resilient, network of constantly changing and transitory linkages to the environs and to their high-density ruralism juxtaposed with low-density cities. Over generations, the feedback loops were positive in outcome allowing incremental, long-term and sustainable modifications to the environment and society. A structural regularity in this changing set of adaptations resulted by which we recognize the significant longevity of ancient Maya culture from their Preclassic antecedence to their Late Classic florescence. Nevertheless and predictably, cultural identities and population growth had a ceiling especially when degrees of over harvesting of the landscape were coupled with a downturn in the climatic equability of the region (Haug et al. 2003; Hodell and Guilderson 2001; Me-Bar and Valdez 2004, 2005; Medina-Elizalde and Rohling 2012; Scarborough and Burnside 2010a, 2010b; Yaeger and Hodell 2008).

Surplus and Storage

Statecraft has frequently emphasized the role of surplus, a necessary condition to accommodate the year around and predictable demands of non-producers—or those in society holding positions or statuses that separate them from resource extraction or distribution—as well as permitting the acquisition of offsets from otherwise seasonal resource deficits or bad production years (Halstead and O'Shea 2004). However, archaeologically identifying storage and surplus associated with the onset of the earliest experiments in statecraft has not been easy, given sampling and preservation issues. Even in the semiarid setting associated with the first cities of Near East, it has been a challenge (but see Redding 1988); although the standardized "beveled bowls" of subsequent Late Uruk period (3400–3100 B.C.E.) cities suggest parceled grain allocation from formalized granaries to individuals working for the state (Johnson 1973; Redman 1978:254; Yoffee 2005).

Nevertheless, storage and surplus are well reported in the earliest historical states, storage larders identifiable both archaeologically and in ancient texts. The Roman Empire clearly constructed and organized both their broadly distributed grain silos as well as their materiel collections into military magazines (Garnsey 1988; J. Tainter pers. comm. 2010). In the New World, storehouses are found along the elaborate and extensive Inka road system facilitating the movement of the empire's troops and relocated laborers (D'Altroy and Earle 1992; Hyslop 1984; Levine 1992; Stanish 2009; Trombold 1991).

In more tropical regimes, such stores of foodstuffs, goods, and materials are not only less concentrated (for all the reasons noted), but they are environmentally unlikely to store well, given the biophysical decomposition process that accelerates organic matter loss. Elevated humidity and temperatures combine and magnify in ways that are less influential for the storage of food in semiarid or cold settings. By way of example, however, little empirical information is available concerning the storage practices at the great Khmer capital of Angkor, Cambodia nor from Sri Lanka, two tropical settings with archaic statecraft (Evans et al. 2007; Fletcher 2009; Scarborough and Lucero 2011). As a consequence, we have little to compare in suggesting that the storage of organics was any different than that noted among the early states of more arid regions. Or do we?

Fortunately, the study of ancient Maya subsistence has received considerable attention during the last generation resulting in a significant amount of new information. Michael Smyth's (1990) pioneering ethnoarchaeological studies of maize storage among groups in northern Yucatan revealed some of the techniques likely used by the ancient Maya to stem both insect and fungal attack as well as rodent incursions. Nevertheless, a maize storage analogy to present-day populations dependent on truck farming, extensive interstate trade, and the availability of processed foods overstates the similarities to the ancient context. Given the truly grand centers of the Classic period were generally clustered in the Petén, Guatemala and immediately adjacent territories in which precipitation or humidity was markedly higher than further north, ethnographic analogy in this case may not well apply. The preservation of maize for consumption by way of tortilla preparation—a frequently argued technique for accommodating maize flour for extended periods—has been challenged by the more widespread appearance of tamales in the iconographic record (Taube 1989). Although maize was surely a mainstay for most of the populations of the Americas, and the Maya would not be an exception, several other foods would have supplied considerable nourishment and may have been easier to store. And the use of salt as a preservative likely extended the longevity of many tropical foods (see below).

Root Crops and Natural Storage

Several root crops have been noted (Bronson 1966; Hawkes 1989) for the Maya, perhaps the most notable that of manioc. Although exceeding difficult to identify in the pollen record, manioc has recently been identified from root casts in undisturbed subsurface garden contexts; as a substantial food source at Ceren (Sheets et al. 2012),[2] these remains date to the Loma Caldera eruption in C.E. 585–600 (Sheets 1994). Because root vegetables can be left in the ground as part of the living plant for several consecutive years and harvested as needed, they are especially attractive to a tropical society (Cock 1982). The finds at Ceren—a consequence of its unique volcanic ash preservation history—demonstrate that manioc was grown adjacent to maize plots with the soil prepared in mounded ridges to accommodate growth. Consumption was local, at least in part, as midden deposits show the actual sprouting of discarded manioc remains, again identified by their preserved plant casts. Although carbohydrate rich, when coupled with a protein source like fish, manioc provides an important balance to a diet (Langdon 1983).

Sheets and his teams at Ceren have identified several features they interpret as small storehouses with evidence of domesticated plant remains inclusive of maize (Hood 2012). However, the amount of food recovered pales in comparison to the tonnage suggested by the quantities of manioc projected in the ground at Ceren (Sheets et al. 2012). Storage of corn, beans, and squash for the ancient Maya—or those mainstays of greater Mesoamerica—would have been a major storage concern. Even in the context of storehouses, these latter foodstuff likely required rapid (seasonal) harvesting, allocation, and consumption.

Salting and Related Dry Preservation Techniques

What, then, were other ways to store foodstuffs? Fish protein would have been an attractive source in concert with carbohydrate-rich root crops (Piperno and Pearsall 1998). But, again, the problem with storing adequate quantities of fish for subsequent consumption arises, especially if marine and estuarine varieties were the principal sources located away from many of the largest, most prominent urban aggregates of the interior. Although we do not know the intensity of fish harvesting from the internally draining bajos, aguadas, or permanent civales—all low-lying wetland basins of varying water holding capacities—coastal settings were preadapted to such protein storage. Much has been made of the heavy investment in salt works on these elevated marine shelves and the commerce resulting from sea salt production (Andrews 1983; McKillop 2002; Valdez and Mock 1991). Several arguments have addressed the human biological need for salt consumption in the tropics; however, so much salt was generated, as assessed by several authorities (Andrews 1983; McKillop 2002), that it is somewhat difficult to understand the implied consumption rates. If one were still searching for a single causal explanation for the Maya Collapse as was the case two generations ago, we might argue that it was hypertension induced by the amount of salt eaten. But if that is unjustifiable (preposterous), then why so much salt?

Given the elevated temperatures and humidity, how best might the ancient Maya have reduced the accelerated decomposition process associated with some foodstuffs? Perhaps controlled dehydration by way of salting was the intent of salt production. With regard to fish, coastal margins and inlets would geographically "map on" both the fishing and the salt procurement industries providing the kinds of massive salt acquisition investments reported archaeologically. Unfortunately, most of the processed organic product—fish—would be shipped away leaving half of this equation blank to the excavator. And because of the delicacy of fish bone—and for that matter the actual evidence for salt at the consumption end—little material evidence would be expected to preserve. Nevertheless, fish remains are becoming more common in the recovered inventory of ancient Maya communities when flotation techniques are employed (Seymour 2004; Teeter and Chase 2004; Valdez and Mock 1991).

If salt were useful in the storage of fish, then it likely was employed on other animal protein sources and possibly in association with the brining (pickling) of some types of vegetal matter. Evidence remains thin, but little complication is entailed in the processing of salt pork and related perishables for the extended maritime voyages of early Europeans (Fagan 2006). Kepecs (2003) notes from Landa (Tozzer 1941:190) that they did so "on a very large scale, by which they eat and sell fish to all the country. They are accustomed to salt the fish, to roast it and to dry it in the sun." And even if the nutritional salt ingestion habits of the huge populations projected for the ancient Maya are correct, salt-preserved foods would continue to allow its consumption.[3]

In sum, the ability to store perishables in the Maya Lowlands was always a significant challenge, one met by other structural accommodations of the society. The ancient Maya demonstrated the attractiveness of dispersed living arrangements and the coordination of resources without major centralized storage or production systems based on urban places. The structural underpinnings of the periodic market, when complemented by the constraints of organic storage, preadapted the Maya to a different kind of economic organization (Scarborough and Valdez 2003, 2009). In the next sections, we propose that it was scheduling and highly developed road systems that allowed network sophistication like few in the circle of early states. Many of the known *sacbeob* (Maya roads or causeways), constructed as early as those at the Late Preclassic colossus of El Mirador (Dahlin et al. 1980; Graham 1967), extend from sites to *bajos* (expansive, internally draining swamp-like depressions) where land and water portage may have further moved goods over significant distances.[4]

Figure 9.3. A sidewall view of the grand sacbe connecting Coba and Yaxuna (after Sharer and Traxler 2006). The segment emphasizes the scalar effort of road construction at some locations in the Maya Lowands.

Roadways and Navigable Canals

The road systems throughout the Maya area are viewed principally as truncated or short-segment causeways connecting portions of the intrasite architecture within a center. In both large and small sites, causeways are interpreted as avenues for grand spectacle by way of directing highly ritualized processions as well as facilitating the mundane daily foot traffic of community members (Arqueología Mexicana 2006; Folan 1991; Keller 2009; Shaw 2001, 2008). We propose, like the calendar (see below), that there is more embedded in these frequently elaborate and overbuilt conduits than intrasite concerns and affairs. Although difficulties are apparent in identifying significant evidence for inter-site road systems, some old and new evidence suggests the interconnectivity of ancient Maya communities both at the resource-specialized community level as well as between the grand capitals.

Perhaps one of the more perplexing features in the Maya Lowlands is the road—*sacbe*—joining the smaller site of Yaxuna of western Quintana Roo to the much larger city of Coba to the east. Explained as a political effort to control Chichen Itza's expansion by Coba during the Late Classic, it is posited to have acted as a supply chain in defending Coba's western frontier (Sharer and Traxler 2006:554–8; Figure 9.3; see Figure 9.1). We envisage this 100 kilometer-long pavement with segments 4.5 meters wide and elevated 0.5–2.5 meters as more than a defensive strategy, though we are not dismissing its multifunctionality. Although it is the best preserved road in the Maya area, given our understanding of the economy it is unlikely that it is an aberration. The Yaxuna-Coba road system is understood to have a more dendritic lattice, connecting other communities to this "grand trunk." The work of Garza and Kurjack in constructing the *Atlas of Yucatan* (1980) reveals the many causeways linking communities of variable size to one another in a region less vegetated—and therefore with more roadway visibility—in many locations than further south into the heart of Classic Maya statecraft.

The extensiveness of the road systems has recently been documented by the pioneering work with LiDAR imagery at the huge Maya Lowland "city" of Caracol (Chase et al. 2011; Chase and Chase 2001, this volume). Although this imagery has not been fully interpreted, it is clear that Caracol's reach was broad. These paved surfaces account for over 200 kilometers of lineament length and connect numerous small communities (Figure 9.4). Like the

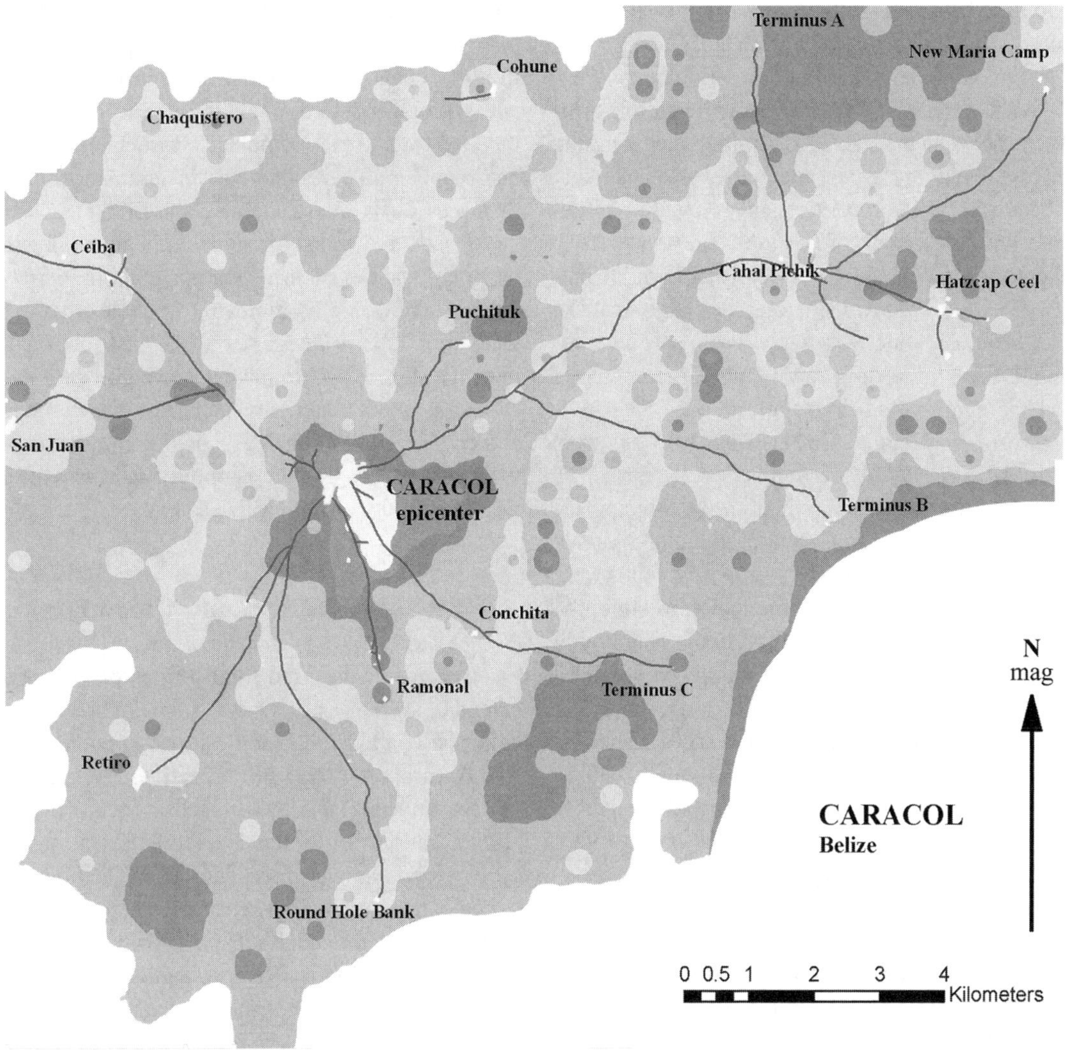

Figure 9.4. Map of Caracol, Belize and its extensive road network (courtesy of Arlen Chase).

Yaxuna-Coba military protectionism argument, a plausible extension of offensive–defensive management might be proposed by way of monitoring or controlling resource-specialized community interactions in Caracol's hegemonic orbit—and the clear sequestering of that interaction back to the center itself. However, this dendritic network may well have interlaced and connected the small rural communities of the region long before the major growth spurts at Caracol's center, as the new aerial imagery (LiDAR) does not preclude the hard work of test excavation and dating control. These widespread roadway linkages throughout the environment and society are likely an indication of a causeway system accretionally developing across the Maya Lowlands perhaps initiated at a very early date; the impressive El Mirador causeways breach several portions of the huge adjacent bajo, and both Cerros and Komchen have well-defined causeways by early in the Late Preclassic period (Scarborough 1991). Caracol may well have appropriated a partial, but preexisting, road network by adding linkages back to the center and strengthening its growing regional controls.

The recent discovery of a low-lying sacbe at Ceren adds to our understanding of the ubiquity of road systems throughout the ancient Maya Lowlands. Sheets (Sheets and Dixon 2011) and his team have identified a linear white plaster surface, under four meters of tephra, leading into–out of the small community. Without the sealed context of immediate burial, it is highly unlikely that a feature of this slight elevation and limited amount of stonework would last in the unforgiving tropical forests that reclaimed much of the southern Maya Lowlands following the great fragmentation of the ninth century. The Ceren sacbeob likely reveals a more widespread use of less substantially constructed roadways elsewhere in the Maya area, roads connecting into the more grand segments like that between Yaxuna and Coba.

Similarly, presumptive sacbeob or their fragmented segments have been observed in the Rio Bravo area of northwestern Belize between the sites of La Milpa, Maax Na, and Dos Hombres, three of the largest site in the area. The likely roads run between the large centers and or smaller settlements across the landscape. Forest cover and poor preservation prevent the identification of a clearly discernible pattern or network. Below the Rio Bravo escarpment, near the Hill Bank Research Station, is a sacbe issuing from a recently mapped site and leading toward the large center of Lamanai on the neighboring drainage, the New River Lagoon (Aylesworth, pers. comm. 2011). This Hill Bank road has not yet been followed to its terminus.

Given the economic underpinnings of the Maya as articulated in previous publications (Scarborough and Valdez 2009; Scarborough et al. 2003), we asserted that roads were a significant investment throughout the region in antiquity. Importantly, we also propose that canoe traffic was highly developed for the rapid movement of goods and services, especially in the huge expanse of bajos that now extend over 40% of the Maya Lowlands (Dunning et al. 2002; Scarborough 2006, 2007). As with roadways, identifying canalization for navigational ends remains difficult, perhaps doubly so because of rapidly infilling sediments associated with a millennium of wetland abandonment and degradation. Nevertheless, a 2 meter-wide, Late Classic canal segment was recently located several kilometers into the sizable Bajo de Azucar; and when coupled with a nearby buried "natural" channel, 10–30 meters in width and of clear navigable dimensions, the ancient role played by the unkempt bajos is suggestive (Garrison and Dunning 2009). Of complementary interest is the large Late Classic community of Kinal positioned on a ridgetop overlooking the Bajo de Azucar, which has a well-defined "causeway" leading into an expansive wetland (Scarborough et al. 1994). Today, stream and river systems are highly fragmented segments and connect only partially during the rainy season. Both Siemens (1998) and Gunn et al. (2002) provide additional support for canalization and the movement of canoe traffic near Calakmul and zones leading to the coast of present-day Campeche state.

The ancient role of canalization for both drained and raised fields as well as navigation is well documented for portions of Amazonia's vastness, the deep-time source for several institutions in the Maya area from the likely origins of cacao use (Piperno and Pearsall 1998) to the rubber ball game (Scarborough and Wilcox 1991; Stern 1949). Clark Erickson (in press) has demonstrated that one can ply a shallow draft canoe 170 kilomters without ever lifting the craft from these waterways. Although few comparisons are made between these two major neotropical wetland settings, in part because of assumed differences in socioeconomic and sociopolitical complexities, recent revelations suggest much greater social complexity associated with significant landscape engineering among ancient Amazonian societies than previously thought (Balee and Erickson 2006).

Roads and transport canals fundamentally shorten exchange distances by directing and routinizing *where* traffic networks flow and by removing obstacles that might otherwise impede movements. However, distributional networks in the context of the tropics require highly scheduled understandings about *when* perishable resource can be harvested and consumed. Although Maya epigraphy remains mute on most topics treating the economy, can any inferences be drawn from the ancient Maya calendar?

Scheduling and Calendars

The mechanics and implications of the ancient Maya calendar system have drawn some of the best minds in anthropological archaeology. From Förstemann (a bit before Anthropology was formalized) to Michael Coe, decoding the concept of Maya time has occupied much scholarly attention. With the broadly consensual acceptance of the Goodman-Martínez-Thompson calendar assessment, our calendar convincingly correlates with theirs (Coe 1992). The origins of time tracking by the Maya is linked to the Sun, Moon, and the planet Venus—and associated with kingly ideals (Helms 1993). For subsequent researchers this understanding of the calendar has provided foundational insights for deciphering Maya hieroglyphic writing; when carved in stone or painted on pots, the care and permanence of the medium served a highly directed set of political and ideological ends (Schele and Freidel 1990). Decipherment in the Near East, however, appears to have had a reverse history, with cuneiform script decoded as a functional recording system put to economic ends from the outset; only later was it used as a tool by the elite to list their kings and related actions. Scheduling of commerce and exchange of any number and variety of goods and service is indicated (Oppenheim 1977; Postgate 1992), suggesting that estate demands for making a living catalyzed the recording of information. Why the variation between the two culture areas by way of writing's origins and the role of the calendar, or are there common forces at work that simply cannot be gleaned just yet?

We are of the opinion that Maya script and, most specifically, the Maya calendar represent an earlier adaptation to the economic underpinnings of the ancient Maya Lowlands—

in addition to subsequent political and ideological associations. If the Maya had opted for a medium of clay—bullae or tablets—for the expedient accounting and trading of goods (Schmandt-Besserat 1977; cf. Graeber 2011:214–5), instead of the stone carved and painted writing that has been preserved, then our understanding of the calendar and its origins would be different. Bark paper simply did not preserve, except for those very few sacred texts that were hidden and sold (Coe 1992). Nevertheless, the Olmec stone tablet that was unearth perhaps a decade ago (Rodríguez Martínez et al. 2006) dating to the early first millennium B.C.E. and now the earliest script reported in the New World may well represent a list of economic things (cf. Goody 1977:chpt 5). If so, our assessment of the origins of writing tied to economic transactions and associated scheduling of both the acquisition or requisition of goods and their movement would be more in line with other parts of the world where the calendar—and writing—developed (Coe 1992; Yoffee 2005:94–96).

Calendars have a sacred quality. They contain and control time "in a bottle" (cf. Goody 1977). Complex societies in tropical settings frequently have several rounds of time. For example, the Balinese identifying several interwoven weeks of variable numbers of days in arriving at a 210 day year; it developed for many occasions and ritualized purposes. This calendar and other semitropical examples are constructed like the gears in a time machine. The interdigitation of smaller cyclical units into larger cycles of time allows the necessary reset associated with natural and artificially induced environmental change (cf. Lansing 1991:67–70). Early calendar systems were linked to seasonality and ultimately the effects of agricultural production, though intercalary adjustments were always made. Although the tantalizing discovery of the Xultun astronomical tables painted on the walls of a small building are interpreted as seeking the "harmony between sky events and sacred rituals.... Each column is self-contained, for reasons still undetermined, to the individual tzolk'in days recorded" (Saturno et al. 2012:716–717). The 260-day calendar or *tzolk'in* likely had more mundane immediacy for the ancient Maya, perhaps similar to the Balinese example. The scheduling of economic activity around planting and harvesting and the subsequent curation of foodstuff for storage and or exchange is the practical dimension of time reckoning. Although remaining speculative, the Maya calendar as discussed here is rooted in the scheduling of goods and labor's movements.

Discussion

In our scenario, then, the Maya had developed a method for coordinating the movement of goods and services based on a network of intricate and well-worn transportation routes. We posit that the principal role of the great centers was in maintaining rapidly received updates on the availability of resources subject to both environmental and social vagaries; the former including droughts, floods, and pests leading to famine, and the latter informed by warfare, human disease, and palace intrigue. These information centers acted as great clocks affecting the timing of goods moved and the relocation of appropriate labor pools. In Flannery's (1968) model of early sedentism and agriculture in Mesoamerica, the ancient Maya were linked to an ancestral set of archaic societal decision-making feedback loops grounded on the notion of scheduling and local knowledge. In an attempt to draw upon the iconographic record, we conjecture that Maya court messengers are identifying the availability of resources in Figure 9.5a, while "accountants" are assessing the timing of their movements in Figure 9.5b.

Given the many deranging forces—from ecological disturbances/disasters to rival centers to impatient consumers—managing this highly complex adaptive system would have drawn on the principles of self-organization (Scarborough and Burnside 2010a). Like the convoluted food webs associated with the fast changing and expedient ecology of a tropical forest, the ancient Maya adapted to its rhythms and tempo by altering the engineered landscape in a manner that best accommodated human societal supply and demand. A ritualized economy by way of the many layers of ideology for which the Maya are well known allowed the necessary routinization of behaviors and tasks, while at the same time permitting the necessary flexibility associated with resource availability and allocation.

Patricia McAnany (2010:91) has recently emphasized the "burden" of maintaining the order of society in her account of a Maya ritualized economy. She points out that the Maya sometimes depicted long-count dates with graphic elements of a stooped burden bearer with his loaded tumpline (Figure 9.5c). As with other symbols and motifs illustrated by the Maya (see Scarborough 1998 and subtle images revealing water's profane and sacred dimensions), the association of physical transport of goods with calendrical time likely captures more than cosmic metaphor. As a window into the scheduling function of coordinated exchange activity and the fleet passage of goods and services, these "Burden Bearers" as time carriers capture the other essence of the calendar; that of a less reified, more mundane aspect to managed time and controlled distance. By reducing distances between harvesting locations, resource collection points and consumers by way of roads and navigable canals, and monitoring schedules and calendars for the distribution of goods, the Maya established a highly networked economy

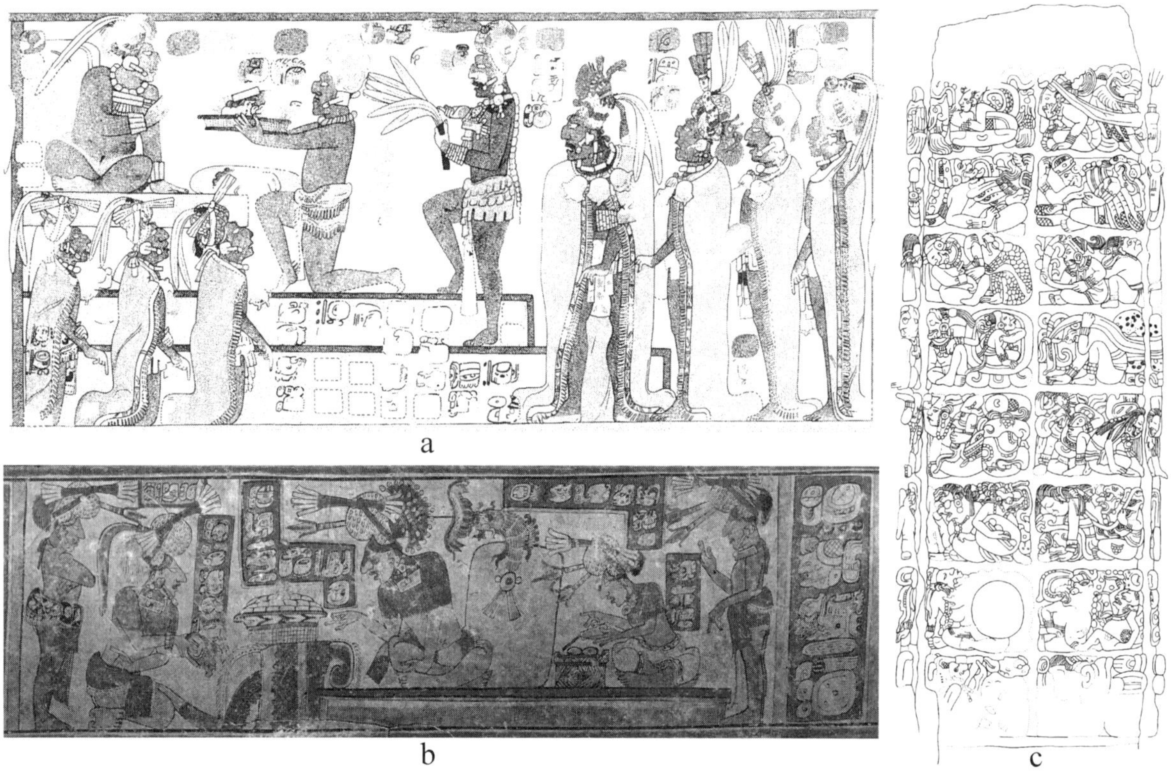

Figure 9.5. (a) Painted throne scene on a cylindrical polychrome vessel from the tomb of Late Classic Tikal ruler, Jasaw Chan K'awil I, showing caped tribute messengers (Courtesy of the University of Pennsylvania Museum, Bur. 116; after Culbert 1993:figure 68A); (b) Fenton vase from Nebaj, Alta Verapaz, Guatemala. The scene shows a scribe, who appears to be keeping a tally, seated to the ruler's left (Copyright, Trustees of the British Museum); (c) Backside of Copan Stela D showing a long-count date of 9.15.5.0.0 10 Ajaw 8 Ch'en or C.E. 736 with full figural substitution for bar-dot numbers. The figure at the upper right literally bears the burden of the bak'tun on a tumpline (drawing by and courtesy of Matthew Looper). Figures noted from selections appearing in McAnany's (2010) book introducing aspects of the ancient Maya economy.

responsive to their tropical setting. In our Western logic, then, distance equals rate multiplied by time:

$$d = rt$$

In this formula, ***d*** is road building; ***r*** is accelerated movement of things; and ***t*** the calendars or schedules shortening journeys and their costs. As Angela Keller recently noted, "for the Maya, however, the conflation of roads and time entails not only a linear path from there to here, but also multiple, interwoven cycles that form the fabric of life.... By walking along the roads, the Maya performed time" (2009:157).

Lessons?

This model of the economy for the ancient Maya differs from many others (McAnany 2010; cf. D'Altroy and Earle 1985). The emphasis on highly flexible road networks and schedules for the distribution of goods and services assumes a production oriented-economy based on a dispersed but populous landscape having adapted to the rhythms and tempos of a tropical rainforest setting. By incrementally modifying the environment, the Maya not only produced a readily accessible set of resources, they transformed their socioeconomic system by way of a complex infrastructure mimicking aspects of a neotropical environment and adhering to its constraints and possibilities. By learning the ecological tolerances over many generations, those social and environmental adjustments made the Maya who they became.

Much has been made of the advantages of urban society and its current advantages for successfully sustaining the future of humanity (Glaeser 2011; Kennedy 2011). However, our assessment is that urban aggregates have frequently developed from models first established by town and country. For the ancient Maya, dispersed rural institutions allowed the occasional coalescence of domesticated landscapes in producing enough resources for the emergence of few great centers or nodes of exchange. These centers for scheduling and coordination of events were many things, but as the hubs for distribution they were a concentrated form of what occurred in the hinterlands always—resource specialized communities knit together in a highly focused manner geographically. Elsewhere, Scarborough (2003; Scarborough and Burnside 2010a; Scarborough and Lucero 2011) has argued that the Maya and several other early experiments in statecraft, especially apparent in tropical environments, emphasized a skilled labor organization different from some other societies and coined "labortasking." Here, trained labor pools adapted flexibly to minor but cumulative environmental and complementary social change without heavy investments in technological breakthroughs.

Clearly the world today is driven by technological advancement and hierarchical power relationships—coined "technotasking" —supporting the view that highly nucleated urban aggregates best accommodate the human densities that generate ideas and synergistic developments. Nevertheless, cities over concentrate resources, energy and wealth, leaving them highly vulnerable to external forces such as warfare, climate change, communicable diseases, extremes in hierarchical divisioning, or social inequality further challenge our infrastructures and social institutions. By delimiting huge population in ever reduced spaces, the city becomes ever more vulnerable and assailable.

However, if something similar to a Maya landscape adaptation were employed with rural communities much less economically subordinated and marginalized by our urban metropolises of today, cities could continue their coordination and regulation of Western institutions. In the context of network resilience, the flexibility and plasticity of hinterland production and exchange less dominated by several megalopolises would accommodate a better distribution of wealth, environmental balance, and overall well-being. The acquisition of goods as well as the coordination of services for a truly regionally integrated economy could be significantly enhanced. With the internet and innovations promoting the interconnectivity and interdependencies among today's resource-specialized communities or cooperatives—small, local community organized, rural operations—it is posited that dying hinterland villages and towns could coordinate in a manner allowing a new economy; one less subject to the imbalances of urban concentrations and a flatter, less pitched hierarchy of cityscape controls. With complex scheduling and rapid exchange, our hinterlands could link into a self-organizing and malleable matrix interfacing with a set of mutually beneficial urban aggregates, each interdependent and helping to distribute economic means more broadly across the landscape.

Notes

1. The influence of natural wealth in the environs is also noted by the longevity of the sizable site of Lamanai, Belize and its permanent supply of freshwater and associated proximity to lagoon resources (Pendergast 1981).

2. Manioc grains have also been identified in northern Belize beginning as early as 3500 B.C.E. (Pohl et al. 1996).

3. A recent example of salting fish for later consumption comes from the archaeological project at Rio Azul, Guatemala—various seasons between1984 and 1991—with the usual field season extending from the end of February to the end of April. At the outset, the project routinely purchased several extra cases of salt packs that were distributed among the workmen. Each weekend during the field season, the workmen would walk a few kilometers south of the research camp and fish in the Rio Azul. The fish caught were brought back to camp, salted and dried in the sun. The salted dried fish were hung from the margins of the *champones* (covered work/storage/sleeping areas), just below the thatch, to allow for additional drying throughout the season. The prepared fish were then gathered the evening before leaving camp for Semana Santa (Holy Week). As reported to us by the workmen, the salted and dried fish served as the base for various foods consumed during Holy Week including mixing of the fish into traditional soups and related meals. The amount of fish processed exceeded personal consumption as it was clearly shared with extended family members or neighbors. The supply of preserved fish for Semana Santa provided an important economic advantage and allowed the workers to focus on "special events" rather than some other costly food purchases.

4. Graham (1967) indicates a road leading across a bajo in proximity to Nakbe, a site with monumental architecture by 600 B.C.E. (Hansen 1991). Also in the Petén, Guatemala, at the Late Classic center of Kinal, a well-constructed "causeway" runs from the sizable "city" center to the huge Bajo de Azucar (Scarborough et al. 1994) demonstrating the clear temporal span of such infrastructure for the ancient Maya.

References Cited

Abbot, David R.

2010 The Rise and Demise of Marketplace Exchange among the Prehistoric Hohokam of Arizona. *In* Archaeological Approaches to Market Exchange in Ancient Societies. C. P. Garraty and B. L. Stark, eds. Pp. 61–84. Boulder: University of Colorado Press.

Andrews, Anthony P.
1983 Maya Salt Production and Trade. Tucson: University of Arizona Press.

Arqueología Mexicana
2006 Rutas y Caminos en el Mexico Prehispanico XIV, Numero 81. Septiembre-Octubre.

Balee, William, and Clark L. Erickson, eds.
2006 Time and Complexity in Historical Ecology. New York: Columbia University Press.

Bronson, Bennet
1966 Roots and the Subsistence of the Ancient Maya. Southwestern Journal of Anthropology 22:251–79.

Bullard, William R.
1960 Maya Settlement Pattern in Northeastern Peten, Guatemala. American Antiquity 25:355–72.

Chase, Arlen F., and Diane Z. Chase
2001 Ancient Maya Causeways and Site Organization at Caracol, Belize. Ancient Mesoamerica 12(2):273–281.
2004 Terminal Classic Status-Linked Ceramics and the Maya Collapse: De Facto Refuse and Caracol, Belize. *In* The Terminal Classic in the Maya Lowlands: Collapse, Transition, and Transformation. A. Demarest, P. M. Rice, and D. S. Rice, eds. Pp. 342–366. Boulder: University of Colorado Press.

Chase, Arlen F., Diane Z. Chase, John F. Weishampel, Jason B. Drake, Ramesh L. Shrestha, K. Clint Slatton, Jaime J. Awe, and William E. Carter
2011 Airborne LiDAR, Archaeology, and the Ancient Maya Landscape at Caracol, Belize. Journal of Archaeological Science 38(2):387–398.

Cock, James
1982 Cassava: A Basic Energy Source in the Tropics. Science 218:755–762.

Coe, Michael D.
1992 Breaking the Maya Code. New York: Thames and Hudson.

Costin, Cathy L.
1991 Craft Specialization: Issues in Defining, Documenting, and Explaining the Organization of Production. *In* Archaeological Method and Theory. Volume 3. M. B. Schiffer, ed. Pp. 1–56. Tucson: University of Arizona Press.

Culbert, T. Patrick
1993 The Ceramics of Tikal. Philadelphia: University Museum of Archaeology and Anthropology.

Dahlin, Bruce H., J. E. Foss, and Mary E. Chambers
1980 Project Acalche: Reconstructing the Natural and Cultural History of a Seasonal Swamp at El Mirador, Guatemala. *In* El Mirador, Petén, Guatemala: An Interim Report. R. T. Matheny, ed. Pp. 43–57. Papers of the New World Archaeological Foundation, 45. Provo: Brigham Young University.

D'Altroy, Terence, and Timothy Earle
1985 Staple Finance, Wealth Finance, and Storage in the Inka Political Economy. Current Anthropology 26:187–206.
1992 Staple Finance, Wealth Finance, and Storage in the Inka Political Economy. *In* Inka Storage Systems. T. Y. Levine, ed, Pp. 31–61. Norman: University of Oklahoma Press.

Demarest, Arthur A., Prudence M. Rice, and Don S. Rice, eds.
2004 The Terminal Classic in the Maya Lowlands: Collapse, Transition, and Transformation. Boulder: University of Colorado Press.

Dunning, Nicholas P., Sheryl Luzzadder-Beach, Timothy Beach, John G. Jones, Vernon Scarborugh, and T. Patrick Culbert
2002 Arising from the Bajos: The Evolution of a Neotropical Landscape and the Rise of Maya Civilization. Annals of the Association of American Geographers 92(2):267–83.

Erickson, Clark L.
In press Pre-Columbian Water Management in Lowland South America. *In* History of Water and Civilization, vol 7: Water and Humanity: A Historical Overview. V. L. Scarborough, ed. Paris: UNESCO.

Evans, Damien, Christophe Pottier, Roland Fletcher, Scott Hensley, Ian Tapley, Anthony Milne, and Michael Barbetti
2007 A Comprehensive Archaeological Map of the World's Largest Preindustrial Settlement

Complex at Angkor, Cambodia. Proceedings of the National Academy of Science USA 104:14277–14282.

Fagan, Brian M.
2006 Fish on Friday. New York: Basic Books.

Fish, Suzannc, and Paul Fish
In press Institutions, Irrigation, and Hohokam Society. *In* Water and Humanity: A Historical Overview. V. L. Scarborough, ed. Paris: UNESCO.

Flannery, Kent V.
1968 Archaeological Systems Theory and Early Mesoamerica. *In* Anthropological Archaeology in the Americas. B. J. Meggers, ed. Pp. 67–87. Washington, DC: Anthropological Society of Washington, Washington, DC.

Fletcher, Roland
2009 Low-density, Agrarian-based Urbanism: A Comparative View. Insights: Institute of Advanced Study, Durham University 2(4):1–19.

Folan, William J.
1991 Sacbes of the Northern Maya. *In* Ancient Road Networks and Settlement Hierarchies in the New World. C. D. Trombold, ed. Pp. 222–229. Cambridge: Cambridge University Press.

Garber, James F., ed.
2004 The Ancient Maya of the Belize Valley: Half a Century of Archaeological Research. Gainesville: University Press of Florida.

Garrison, Thomas, and Nicholas P. Dunning
2009 Settlement, Environment, and Politics in the san Bartolo-Xultun Territory, El Peten, Guatemala. Latin American Antiquity 20:525–552.

Garnsey, Peter
1988 Famine and Food Supply in the Graeco-Roman World: Responses to Risk and Crisis. Cambridge: Cambridge University Press.

Garza Tarazona de González, and Edward B. Kurjack
1980 Atlas Arqueológico del Estado de Yucatán. Mexico City: Instituto Nacional de Anthopología e Historia.

Gillespie, Susan D., and Rosemary A. Joyce, eds.
2000 Beyond Kinship: Social and Material Reproduction in House Societies. Philadelphia: University of Pennsylvania Press.

Glaeser, Edward
2011 Triumph of the City. New York: Penguin Press.

Goody, Jack
1977 The Domestication of the Savage Mind. New York: Cambridge University Press.

Graeber, David
2011 Debt: The First 5,000 Years. Brooklyn: Melville House.

Graham, Ian
1967 Archaeological Explorations in El Petén, Guatemala. Middle American Research Institute Publication, 33. New Orleans: Tulane University.

Gunn, J. D., J. E. Foss, W. J. Folan, M. d. R. Domínguez Carrasco, and B. B. Faust
2002 Bajo Sediments and the Hydraulic System of Calakmul, Campeche, Mexico. Ancient Mesoamerica 13:297–315.

Halstead, Paul, and John O'Shea, eds.
2004 Bad Year Economics: Cultural Responses to Risk and Uncertainty. Cambridge: Cambridge University Press.

Hansen, Richard D.
1991 The Road to Nakbe. Natural History May:8–14.

Haug, Gerald H., Detlef Gunther, Larry C. Perterson, Daniel M. Sigman, Konrad A. Hughen, and Beat Aeschlimann
2003 Climate and the Collapse of Maya Civilization. Science 299:1731–1735.

Hawkes, J. G.
1989 The Domestication of Roots and Tubers in the American Tropics. *In* Foraging and Farming. D. R. Harris and G. C. Hillman, eds. Pp. 481–503. Boston: Unwin Hyman.

Heitman, Carolyn, and Stephen Plog
2005 Kinship and the Dynamics of the House. *In* A Catalyst for Ideas: Anthropological Archaeology and the Legacy of Douglas. W. Schwartz, V. L. Scarborough, ed. Pp. 69–100. Santa Fe: School of American Research Press.

Helms, Mary W.
1993 Craft and Kingly Ideal: Art, Trade and Power. Austin: University of Texas Press.

Hodell, David A., and T. Guilderson
2001 Solar Forcing of Drought Frequency in the Maya Lowlands. Science 292:1367–1370.

Hood, Angela
2012 Testing the Veracity of Paleoethnobotanical Macroremain Data: A Case Study from the Ceren Site, El Salvador. MA thesis, Department of Anthropology, University of Cincinnati, Cincinnati.

Hyslop, John
1984 The Inka Road System. Orlando: Academic Press.

Inomata, Takeshi
2001 The Power and Ideology of Artistic Creation: Elite Craft Specialists in Classic Maya Society. Current Anthropology 42(3):321–349.

Isaac, Barry L.
2013 Discussion. *In* Merchants, Trade and Exchange in the Pre-Columbian World. K. Hirth and J. Pillsbury, eds. Pp. 435–448. Washington, DC: Dumbarton Oaks.

Johnson, Gregory A.
1973 Local Exchange and Early State Development in Southwestern Iran. Anthropological Papers, 51. Ann Arbor: University of Michigan Museum of Anthropology.

Keller, Angela H.
2009 A Road by any other Name: Trails, Paths, and Roads in Maya Language and Thought. *In* Landscapes of Movement: Trails, Paths, and Roads in Anthropological Perspective. J. E. Snead, C. L. Erickson, and J. A. Darling, eds. Pp. 133–157. Philadelphia: University of Pennsylvania Museum of Archaeology and Anthropology.

Kennedy, Christopher
2011 The Evolution of Great World Cities. Toronto: University of Toronto Press.

Kepecs, Susan M.
2003 Chikinchel. *In* The Postclassic Mesoamerican World. M. E. Smith and F. F. Berdan, eds. Pp. 259–68. Salt Lake City: University of Utah Press.

Langdon, Tom
1983 Manioc and Fish: A "Methiononian" Compromise in Amazonia? Nebraska Anthropologist, 156. Lincoln: University of Nebraska Press.

Lansing, J. Stephen
1991 Priests and Programmers. Princeton: Princeton University Press.

Lentz, David L., Nicholas P. Dunning, and Vernon L. Scarborough, eds.
2014 Tikal: Water, Landscapes and Resilience. Cambridge: Cambridge University Press.

Levine, Terry, ed.
1992 Inka Storage Systems. Norman: University of Oklahoma Press.

Lohse, Jon C., and Fred Valdez, Jr., eds.
2004 Ancient Maya Commoners. Austin: University of Texas Press.

Marcus, Joyce
1993 Ancient Maya Political Organization. *In* Lowland Maya Civilization in the Eighth Century A. D. J. A. Sabloff and J. S. Henderson, eds. Pp. 111–83. Washington, DC: Dumbarton Oaks.
1998 The Peaks and Valleys of Ancient States: An Extension of the Dynamic Model. *In* Archaic States. G. M. Feinman and J. Marcus, eds. Pp. 59–94. Santa Fe: School of American Research Press.

Marcus, Joyce, and Jeremy Sabloff, eds.
2008 The Ancient City. Santa Fe: School of Advanced Research Press.

Marx, Karl
1968 [1853] The British Rule of India. *In* Karl Marx on Colonialism and Modernization: His Dispatches and Other Writhing on China, India, Mexico, the Middle East, and North Africa. S. Avineri, ed. Pp. 83–89. Garden City: Doubleday.

McAnany, Patricia A.
2010 Ancestral Maya Economies in Archaeological Perspective. Cambridge: Cambridge University Press.

McBryde, Felix
1933 Solala: A Guatemalan Town and Cakchiquel Market-Center. Middle American Research Series, 5, Pamphlet 3. Pp. 42–152. New Orleans: Tulane University.
1945 Cultural and Historical Geography of Southwest Guatemala. Institute of Social Anthropology Publication 4. Washington, DC: Smithsonian Institution.

McKillop, Heather
2002 Salt: The White Gold of the Ancient Maya. Gainesville: University Press of Florida.

Me-Bar, Y., and F. Valdez, Jr.
2003 Droughts as Random Events in the Maya Lowlands. Archaeological Journal of Science 30:1599–1606.
2004 Recovery Time after a Disaster and the Ancient Maya. Journal of Archaeological Science 31:1311–1324.
2005 On the Vulnerability of the Ancient Maya Society to Natural Threats. Journal of Archaeological Science 32:813–825.

Medina-Elizalde, Martín, and Eelco J. Rohling
2012 Collapse of Classic Maya Civilization Related to Modest Reduction in Precipitation. Science 335:956–959.

Morley, Sylvanus G.
1946 The Ancient Maya. 2nd edition. Stanford: Stanford University Press.

Oppenheim, A. Leo
1977 Ancient Mesopotamia. Chicago: University of Chicago Press.

Pendergast, David M.
1981 Lamanai, Belize: Summary of Excavation Results, 1974–1980. Journal of Field Archaeology 8(1):29–53.

Piperno, Dolores R., and Deborah M. Pearsall
1998 The Origins of Agriculture in the Lowland Neotropics. New York: Academic Press.

Pohl, Mary D., Kevin O. Pope, John G. Jones, John S. Jacob, Dolores R. Piperno, Susan D. deFrance, David L. Lentz, John A. Gifford, Marie E. Danforth, and J. Kathryn Josserand
1996 Early Agriculture in the Maya Lowlands. Latin American Archaeology 7(4):355–372.

Postgate, Nicholas
1992 Early Mesopotamia: Society and Economy at the Dawn of History. London: Routledge.

Redding, Richard W.
1988 A General Explanation of Subsistence Change: From Hunting and Gathering to Food Production. Journal of Anthropological Archaeology 7: 56–97.

Redman, Charles L.
1978 The Rise of Civilization: From Early Farmers to Urban Society in the Ancient Near East. San Francisco: W. H. Freeman and Company.

Reina, Ruben E., and R. M. Hill, II
1978 The Traditional Pottery of Guatemala. Austin: University of Texas Press.

Rodríguez Martínez, Maria Del Carmen, Ponciano Ortíz Ceballos, Michael D. Coe, Richard A. Diehl, Stephen D. Houston, Karl A. Taube, Alfredo Delgado Calderón
2006 Oldest Writing in the New World. Science 313(5793):1610–1614.

Saturno, William A., David Stuart, Anthony F. Aveni, and Franco Rossi
2012 Ancient Maya Astronomical Tables from Xultun, Guatemala. Science 336:714–717.

Scarborough, Vernon L.
1991 The Settlement System in a Late Preclassic Maya Community, Archaeology at Cerros, Belize, Central America. Volume 3. Dallas: Southern Methodist University Press.
1998 Ecology and Ritual: Water Management and the Maya. Latin American Antiquity 9(2): 135–159.
2003 The Flow of Power. Santa Fe: School of Advanced Research Press.
2006 An Overview of Mesoamerican Water Systems. *In* Precolumbian Water Management. L. J. Lucero and B. W. Fash, eds., Pp. 223–235. Tucson: University of Arizona Press.
2007 Colonizing a Landscape. *In* The Political Economy of Ancient Mesoamerica. V. L. Scarborough and J. E. Clark, eds. Pp. 163–174. Albuquerque: University of New Mexico Press.

Scarborough, Vernon L., and William R. Burnside
2010a Complexity and Sustainability: Perspectives

from the Ancient Maya and the Modern Balinese. American Antiquity 75(2): 327–63.

2010b Global Change: Mapping Culture onto Climate. *In* Climate Crisis in Human History. A. B. Mainwaring, R. Giegengack, and C. Vita-Finzi, eds. Pp. 175–187. Philadelphia: American Philosophical Society and Lighting Rod Press.

Scarborough, Vernon L., Robert Connolly, and Steven Ross

1994 The Prehispanic Maya Reservoir System at Kinal, Peten, Guatamala. Ancient Mesoamerica 5(1):97–106.

Scarborough, Vernon L., Nicholas P. Dunning, Kenneth B. Tankersley, Christopher Carr, Eric Weaver, Liwy Grazioso, Brian Lane, John G. Jones, Palma Buttles, Fred Valdez, and David L. Lentz

2012 Water and Sustainable Land Use at the Ancient Tropical City of Tikal, Guatemala. Proceedings of the National Academy of Sciences 109:12408–12413.

Scarborough, Vernon L., and Lisa Lucero

2011 The Non-Hierarchical Development of Complexity in the Semitropics: Water and Cooperation. Water History 2(2):185–205.

Scarborough, Vernon L., and Fred Valdez

2003 The Engineered Environment and Political Economy of the Three Rivers Region. *In* Heterarchy, Political Economy, and the Ancient Maya: The Three Rivers Region of the East Central Yucatan Peninsula. V. L. Scarborough, F. Valdez, Jr, and N. P. Dunning, eds. Pp. 3–13. Tucson: University of Arizona Press.

2009 An Alternative Order: The Dualistic Economies of the Ancient Maya. Latin American Antiquity 20(1):207–27.

Scarborough, Vernon L., Fred Valdez, and Nicholas Dunning, eds.

2003 Heterarchy, Political Economy, and the Ancient Maya: The Three Rivers Region of the East Central Yucatan Peninsula. Tucson: University of Arizona Press.

Scarborough, Vernon L., and David R. Wilcox

1991 The Mesoamerican Ballgame. Tucson: University of Arizona Press.

Schele, Linda, and David Freidel

1990 A Forest of Kings: The Untold Story of the Ancient Maya. William Morrow, New York.

Schmandt-Besserat, D.

1977 An Archaic Recording System and the Origin of Writing. Syro-Mesopotamian Studies 1(2). Malibu: Undena Press.

Seymour, Kevin L.

2004 Empirical Data for Archaeological Fish Weight Analyses. *In* Maya Zooarchaeology. K. F. Emery, ed. Pp. 159–173. Cotsen Institute of Archaeology, Monograph 51. Los Angeles: UCLA

Sharer, Robert J., and Loa P. Traxler

2006 The Ancient Maya. 6th edition. Stanford: Stanford University Press.

Shaw, Justine M.

2001 Maya Sacbeob: Form and Function. Ancient Mesoamerica 12:261–272.

2008 White Roads of the Yucatan. Tucson: University of Arizona Press.

Sheets, Payson

1994 Tropical Time Capsule. Archaeology 47:30–33.

2000 Provisioning the Ceren Household. Ancient Mesoamerica 11:217–30.

Sheets, Payson, and Christine Dixon, eds.

2011 Maya Agriculture South of the Ceren Site, El Salvador, 2011. Unpublished MS, Department of Anthropology, University of Colorado.

Sheets, Payson, David Lentz, Dolores Piperno, John Jones, Christine Dixon, George Maloof, and Angela Hood

2012 Ancient Manioc Agriculture South of the Ceren Village, El Salvador. Latin American Antiquity 23(3):259–281.

Siemens, Alfred H.

1998 A Favored Place: San Juan River Wetlands, Central Veracruz, AD 500 to the Present. Austin: University of Texas Press.

Smith, Michael E.

2009 Regional and Local Market Systems in Aztec-Period Morelos. *In* Archaeological Approaches to Market Exchange in Ancient Societies. C. P.

Garraty and B. L. Stark, eds. Pp.161–182. Boulder: University of Colorado Press.

Smyth, Michael P.
1990 Maize Storage among the Puuc Maya: The Development of an Archaeological Method. Ancient Mesoamerica 1:51–69.

Southall, A.
1988 The Segmentary State in Africa and Asia. Comparative Studies in Society and History 30:52–82.

Stanish, Charles
2009 Labor Taxes, Market Systems, and Urbanization in the Prehispanic Andes: Comparative Perspective. *In* Archaeological Approaches to Market Exchange in Ancient Societies. C. P. Garraty and B. L. Stark, eds. Pp. 185–205. Boulder: University of Colorado Press.

Stark, Barbara L., and Christopher P. Garraty
2009 Detecting Market Exchange in Archaeology: A Methodological Review. *In* Archaeological Approaches to Market Exchange in Ancient Societies. C. P. Garraty and B. L. Stark, eds. Pp. 33–58. Boulder: University of Colorado Press.

Stern, Theodore
1949 The Rubber-Ball Game of the Americas. Monographs of the American Ethnological Society, 17. New York: J. J. Augustin.

Taube, Karl
1989 The Maize Tamale in Classic Maya Diet, Epigraphy, and Art. American Antiquity 54(1):31–51.

Teeter, Wendy G., and Arlen F. Chase
2004 Adding Flesh to Bones: Using Zooarchaeology Research to Answer Big-Picture Questions. Archaeofauna 13:155–172.

Tozzer, Alfred M.
1941 Landa's Relación de las Cosass de Yucatán: A Translation. Papers, 18. Cambridge: Peabody Museum.

Trombold, Charles D., ed.
1991 Ancient Road Networks and Settlement Hierarchies in the New World. New York: Cambridge University Press.

Valdez, Fred, Jr., and Shirley Mock
1991 Additional Considerations for Prehispanic Saltmaking in Belize. American Antiquity 56:520–525.

Walling, Stanley
2011 Overview of Recent Ballcourt Complex Investigations at Chawak But'o'Ob, Belize. *In* Research Reports from the Programme for Belize Archaeological Project, Vol. 5. B. Houk and F. Valdez, eds. Pp. 151–161. Mesoamerican Archaeological Research Laboratory Occasional Papers, 12. Austin: University of Texas.

Yaeger, Jason, and David A. Hodell
2008 The Collapse of Maya Civilization: Assessing the Interaction of Culture, Climate, and the Environment. *In* El Nino, Catastrophism, and Culture Change in Ancient America. D. H. Sandweiss and J. Quilter, eds. Pp. 187–242. Cambridge: Harvard University Press.

Yoffee, Norman
2005 Myths of the Archaic State. Cambridge: Cambridge University Press.

Zaro, Gregory, and Jon C. Lohse
2005 Agricultural Rhythms and Rituals: Ancient Maya Solar Observations in Hinterland Blue Creek, Northwestern Belize. Latin American Antiquity 16(1):81–98.

10

Path Dependency in the Rise and Denouement of a Classic Maya City: The Case of Caracol, Belize

Diane Z. Chase
University of Central Florida
and
Arlen F. Chase
University of Central Florida

ABSTRACT

With an anthropomorphic landscape that completely covered over 130 square kilometers with agricultural terraces in antiquity, Caracol, Belize provides an excellent place to review ancient resilience, rigidity, and path dependency. A population center with over 100,000 people in C.E. 700, Caracol subsisted on change and growth for its initial 1000 years of existence. However, Caracol also developed a relatively unique form of adaptation, one focused on establishing stability through social cohesion during its acme. These adaptations helped Caracol endure the changes wrought by climate change and inter-polity strife until the onset of the 10th century. At this point, elite mechanizations removed the well-established social buffers and Caracol succumbed to external political pressures that combined with environmental forces to create an untenable situation. Path dependency left the ancient Maya of Caracol unable to adapt to the ultimate threat posed by external changes beyond their control. [archaeology, Maya, agricultural terracing, path dependency, resilience]

The ancient Maya site of Caracol is located in the Vaca Plateau of west-central Belize in an area of undulating karst limestone covered by semitropical forest cover. With an elevation of over 500 meters, Caracol was one of the few large sites located within the southern Maya Lowland geographic area that is also situated at an elevation substantially above sea level. Its native soils were relatively thin and less well suited for agriculture than soils in the Belize Valley, and surface water was far less readily available than in areas to the north. Nevertheless, Caracol's population size and the physical extent of the city itself far exceeded that of most of its neighbors at the height of its occupation at approximately C.E. 700. Thus, its development and abandonment are of clear interest in considerations of the Maya human–environment interactions.

The development of Caracol was not without its hurdles. There were constraints to establishing a large population in the Vaca Plateau, particularly with regard to a general lack of surface water and the steeply sloped terrain. The Maya of Caracol achieved relative stability in this environment only through substantial investment of human capital in the construction of site infrastructure that included, but was not limited to, agricultural terracing, reservoir construction, and road systems. It can only be assumed that there were benefits for living in this location that reinforced these heavy investments, such as high rainfall; greater fertility with soil and water management through terracing; proximity to the Maya Mountains with natural resources such as granite, slate, and pine; distance from other large population centers; and a relatively defensible location for the site epicenter. The long-term resilience and stability of Caracol was built upon

ARCHEOLOGICAL PAPERS OF THE AMERICAN ANTHROPOLOGICAL ASSOCIATION, Vol. 24, pp. 142–154, ISSN 1551-823X, online ISSN 1551-8248. DOI: 10.1111/apaa.12034.

cultural adaptations and infrastructure that buffered the population at-large from changing climatic and external forces. These same adaptations reinforced social cohesion at the expense of elite wealth accumulation, encouraging population growth and prosperity. However, the system ultimately failed in the face of internal and external pressures. Without social and economic cohesion and continued investment in landscape management, Caracol could no longer grow or maintain its population; instead, site population declined and the site was abandoned. Thus, Caracol history provides examples of both successful innovation and less successful path dependent adherence to existing practices.

The relationships between environment, climate, society, and change are never clear-cut. However, the variables themselves are linked in ways that sometimes can be explicated through the archaeological record. Modifications made to the built environment at Caracol—particularly the construction of agricultural terracing for agriculture—appears to have set the polity on a trajectory of path dependency (e.g., Berkhout 2002; Kay 2005; Pierson 2000). Once committed to an agricultural strategy that locked the population into continuous landscape modifications and the stabilized placement of residential units, future responses to stress at Caracol became path dependent—largely driven by soil fertility, rainfall, and the spatial constraints of house and field constructions—with variability only in terms of management strategies that could be employed to both placate and integrate the site's population. In such a situation, drought conditions (e.g., Kennett et al. 2012; Luzzadder-Beach et al. 2012; Medina-Elizalde and Rohling 2012) as well as extremely wet or unpredictable conditions would have required a response in the socio-political arena (Turner and Sabloff 2012). The archaeological data from Caracol suggest that periods of drought inspired significant change in elite leaders and leadership strategies at the site. However, rather than causing adversity, elite management of Late Classic period drought conditions appears to have resulted in greater prosperity both in the site core and among its general population—at least in the short term.

Caracol's managerial elite used different strategies for the dispersal of prosperity to the general population at the beginning and at the end of the Late Classic period (C.E. 550–800). We suggest that these distinct strategies—one focused on dispersal of wealth and the other focused on limiting access to key status items—resulted in divergent societal outcomes. Thus, while the subsistence base for the Caracol population made the site extremely path dependent in terms of its possible responses to subsistence and settlement, other managerial elite choices were more open to change, resulting in two very different outcomes to periods of stress. In the earlier period of stress, the managerial elite focused the site on external warfare and then fostered the equitable division of the spoils. In the later period of climatic stress, a new elite also focused on the use of warfare as an integrating strategy for the site, but instead retained the spoils of war and developed greater divisions between the "haves" and the "have-nots." These later decisions further resulted in a lack of attention to the broader site infrastructure, a loss of faith in site leadership, and ultimately in site abandonment.

Path Dependency

The concept of path dependency refers to societal tendencies to continue following a course of action based on tradition and practice or short-term "least cost," even if other alternatives are possible and potentially more desirable in the long-term. Often, there is continued investment in old infrastructure rather than in replacement infrastructure. Once a society makes a specific commitment, it is difficult to change the path or trajectory that is followed, regardless of the outcomes. Path dependency has been defined as occurring under two conditions—contingency and self-reinforcement—and as causing a situational "lock-in in the absence of exogenous shock" (Vergne and Durand 2010:741). It may also be the path of least resistance.

The extensive investment in agricultural terracing evident in the Caracol environment was an innovation that permitted greater agricultural yields and population. However, it also set the city on a developmental trajectory of path dependency. Once it was established that landscape modification led to increased sustainability, further landscape modification followed. The consequences of this practice meant that settlement at the site became rigidified in its placement and spacing; housing units were constructed at a distance rather than in close proximity to each other, adequately spaced to allow sufficient agriculture land. Coincident benefits of this less crowded, low-density urbanism would have been lessened spread of epidemics. Most reservoirs were also placed close to housing in relatively high locations that would provide usable water suitable for drinking. Population increase led to urban sprawl and more landscape modification for terracing, leading to a form of low density urbanism (e.g., Fletcher 2011). But the reliance on agricultural terracing, combined with rigidity in settlement, also led to agricultural involution (Geertz 1963) in which more and more land and labor was required to keep the soils fertile and to maintain sustainable agricultural yields. At the same time, population growth and the need for household spacing required upkeep, enhancement, or new construction of roads and market locations to sustain the system for transporting foods and services throughout the site and to the population. Thus, while the system was stable for a long period of time (Murtha 2009), it became more labor intensive and more stressed over time. It also meant that population growth necessarily led to the horizontal expansion of the site into land that was increasingly further from the site epicenter and was less easily manipulated because of topographic features. Management of the spatial area comprising Caracol would have become more complex over time, with Caracol's causeway system serving to integrate the site horizontally and to move necessary resources from the edges to the center. Thus, both climatic and social issues would have placed stresses on Caracol's managerial elite, but only the severest shock to the system would have ended the population's dependence on their long-enduring agricultural technology.

For Caracol, at least initially, the investment in landscape modification would have led to increasing agricultural yields and immediately produced a positive feedback loop. The ever increasing use of agricultural terracing at Caracol, in conjunction with causeway and market systems for distribution of any surplus, generated higher payoffs for the site's population, producing agricultural yields to support growing subsistence needs and elite infrastructure. Arthur (1994:112–113) has noted that when there are increasing returns for a given practice that unpredictability, inflexibility, and path inefficiency often follow. Initially, it is not clear where the adaptation will lead, but "in applications to technology, a given subsidy to a particular technique will be more likely to shift the ultimate outcome . . . and eventually lock in one solution" (Pierson 2000:253). Small events that occur near the beginning of the process will be reflected in future choices and "in the long-run, the outcome that becomes locked in may generate lower pay-offs than a forgone alternative would have" (Pierson 2000:253). As elaborated by Pierson (2000:254), Arthur (1994:112) pointed to four features of a technology and social context as generating increasing returns: (1) "large set-up or fixed costs" that "create a high pay-off for further investments in a given technology;" (2) "learning effects" in which "knowledge gained in the operation of complex systems also leads to higher returns from continuing use;" (3) "coordination efforts" in which "the benefits an individual receives from a particular activity increase as others adopt the same option" leading to "linked infrastructure;" and (4) "adaptive expectations" in which "projections about future aggregate use patterns lead individuals to adapt their actions in ways that help make those expectations come true." As a widespread technological adaptation, Caracol's agricultural terraces provide a ready example of path dependency that can be studied by examining the archaeological record.

Caracol: Site and Polity

In its final Late Classic period form, the continuous residential settlement of Caracol spread over some 200 square kilometers of the Vaca Plateau, and some 130 square kilometers of the site contained almost continuous agricultural terracing that had been constructed in support of a population of over 100,000 people at C.E. 650 (Figure 10.1; see also Figures 10.3 and 10.5). The Late Classic city was administered by means of solar causeways that articulated outlying administrative nodes and market centers directly with the site epicenter (A. Chase and D. Chase 2001a, 2007; Chase et al. 2011; D. Chase and A. Chase 2014). The epicenter itself was dominated by a massive architectural complex, called "Caana," that served as the hub for the royal family (A. Chase and D. Chase 2001b). Larger public architecture was embedded in the landscape and served as the infrastructure to help integrate and manage the site's population. A number of these monumental architectural concentrations or "nodes" occurred at distances of 5 to 8 kilometers from the epicenter. Formerly independent centers, the public architecture at these sites had been linked to the Caracol epicenter by means of causeways at the beginning of the Late Classic period (C.E. 550). When fully assimilated as a part of metropolitan Caracol, administrative-market plazas were appended to each of these nodes. A second concentration of large architectural plazas occurs at a distance of 3 to 3.5 kilometers from Caana. These, too, served as administrative-market plazas and were purposefully constructed at the onset of the Late Classic period, presumably to support the increasing population levels within the metropolitan area.

We have previously suggested that there was an optimal maximum size for lowland Maya polities; the area that can be effectively controlled is generally located within a 3-day march of the city capital (A. Chase and D. Chase 1998a; D. Chase and A. Chase 2003). In the Maya case this would have been an area roughly 60 kilometers in diameter (Figure 10.2). Thus, most strong Maya polities were capable of directly maintaining an area of approximately 7,000 to 9,000 square kilometers (A. Chase and D. Chase 1996a). We believe that hegemonic control could have extended a tribute area to ca. 30,000 square kilometers. However, larger polity sizes would have become increasingly unstable and likely would have been short-lived. Caracol's political history, as written in the hieroglyphic record and as known through survey and excavation, suggests that it was a strong polity that had extended hegemonic control of the southeastern Southern Maya Lowlands for approximately 50 years at the beginning of the Late Classic period.

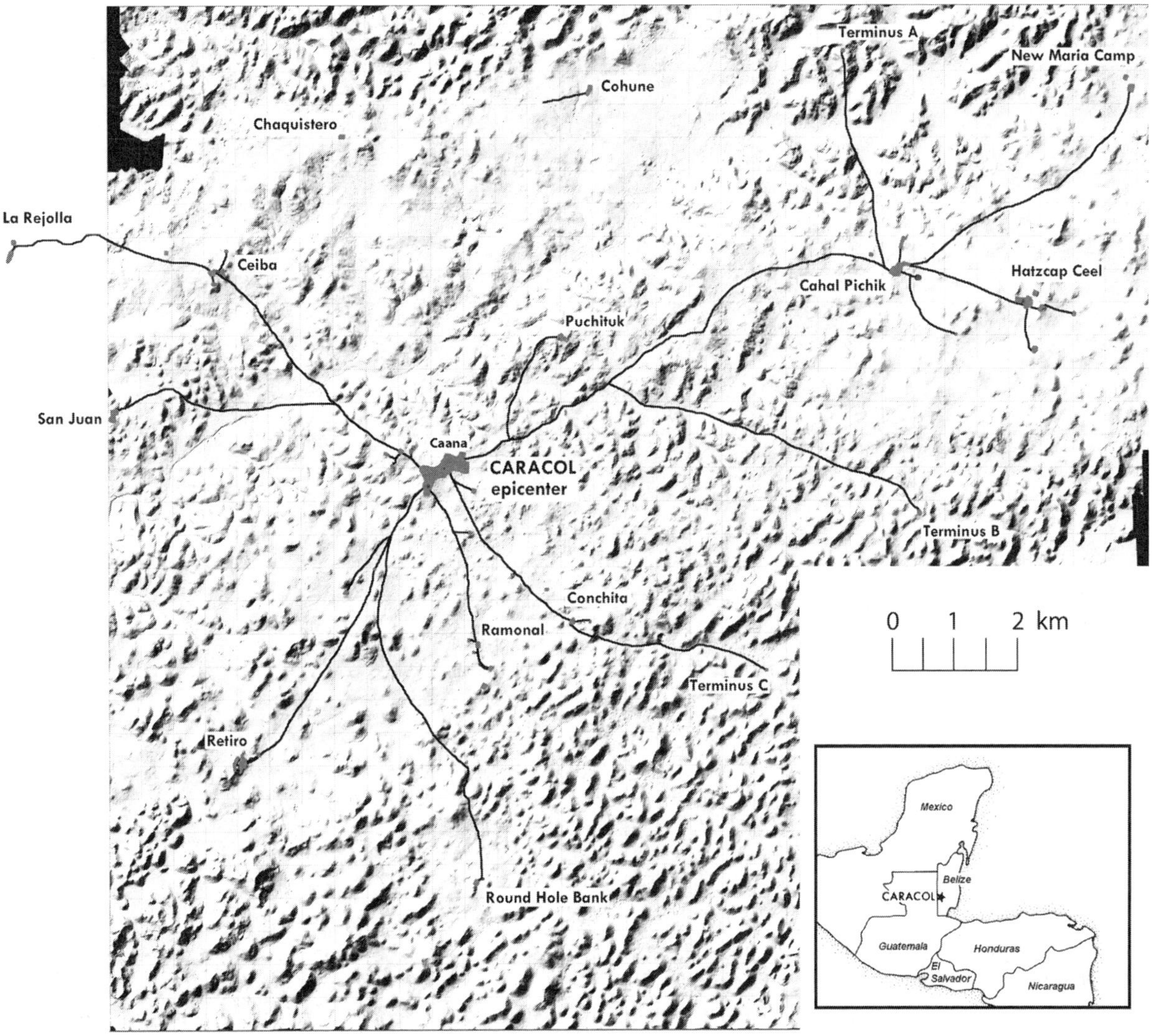

Figure 10.1. Caracol settlement area showing the locations of causeways, market termini plazas, and the epicentral construction of Caana.

Caracol: Site Development and Trajectory

Caracol was first occupied ca. 600 B.C.E. The site continued to be occupied to the onset of the 10th century, when the site epicenter was largely abandoned and burned. Major growth of the Caracol population took place in the first century C.E. Caracol was precocious in some of its developments. Radiocarbon dates indicate that architectural configurations called E Groups (also known as Commemorative Astronomical Complexes; see Laporte and Fialko 1995), as well as elaborate ritual caching and burials, predate their occurrence in what is typically considered the Maya heartland area in the Peten of Guatemala by some 300 years (A. Chase and D. Chase 1995). The last version of the Caracol E Group appears to have been constructed ca. C.E. 41 in celebration of the beginning of the 8th Baktun (A. Chase and D. Chase 2006). Caana reached a height of 38 meters around this same time. The emphasis on this complex suggests that Caracol was already important and had possibly expanded to incorporate the centers of Cahal Pichik and Hatzcap Ceel, both of which contain E Groups, into its borders by the end of the Preclassic era. The causeways linking these two outlying nodes to the Caracol epicenter are presumably among the earliest in the region.

The end of the Preclassic period, in a time sometimes called the "Protoclassic" time frame, ca. C.E. 0–250, was a time of transitions and population movements throughout the Maya Lowlands. Analysis of a speleothem collected from a cave 15 kilometers north of Caracol indicates that there was a drought peak throughout the Maya Lowlands at

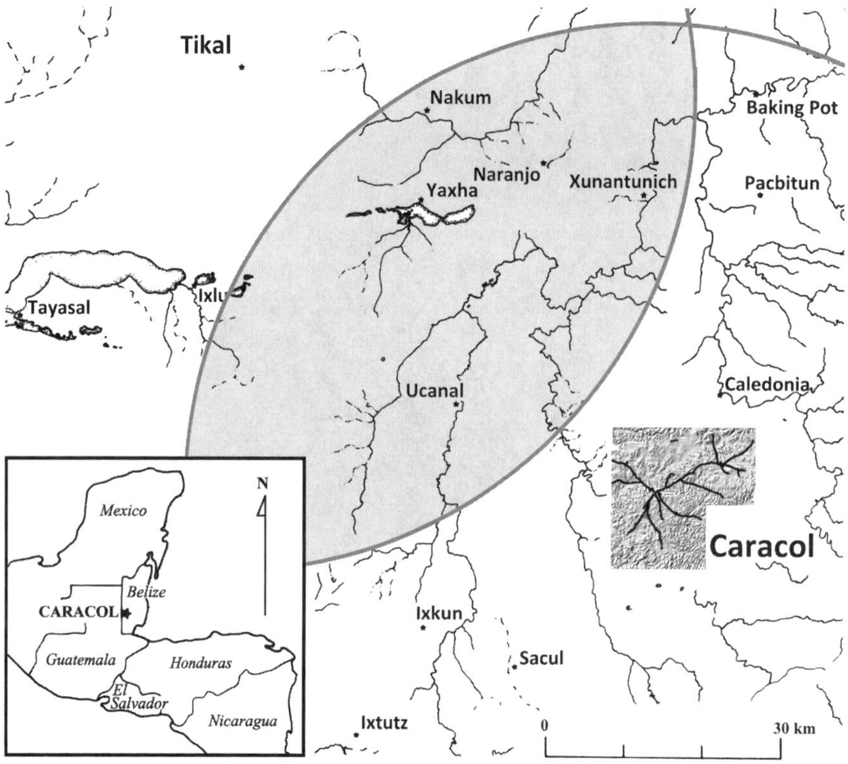

Figure 10.2. Southern Maya Lowlands showing the spatial relationship between Tikal and Caracol and the area of potential territorial overlap, which includes the contested Guatemalan sites of Naranjo and Ucanal. The causeway system of Caracol is indicated within the 2009 LiDAR DEM.

approximately C.E. 141 (Webster et al. 2007). If this drought were severe enough, it might have been responsible for some of the population movement that occurred within the Maya Lowlands during this era. The site of Mirador was essentially abandoned at about this time (Wahl et al. 2007:817) and Caracol may have been the beneficiary of population moving away from areas like the Mirador Basin. At least as early as 100 B.C.E. the occupants of Caracol had begun investments not only in monumental architecture, but also in the construction of agricultural terraces to maintain the soils and moisture necessary for intensive cultivation of inter-household fields (A. Chase and D. Chase 1998b). These agricultural fields were, for the most part, dependent on rainfall and the terraces served not only to redirect and control water flow over the landscape, but also to retain and store water that could be used by plants. The proliferation of constructed reservoirs within the broader settlement region likely also began at this time; there is no natural surface water within this portion of the Vaca Plateau. All of the early architectural concentrations within the Caracol region contain sizeable reservoir constructions that still hold water today, and constructed reservoirs were attached to dispersed residential groups as well (see Crandall 2009 and Chase 2012). While many of the mapped residential reservoirs are associated with Late Classic groups, it can be inferred that much of the earlier buried construction activities were also associated with reservoirs. The landscape manipulation and continuous rebuilding efforts that occurred at Caracol are, to some degree, mirrored in the lack of quarries at Caracol; these features surely existed, but are all now completely obscured beneath agricultural fields and other construction efforts. This early—and massive—labor investment in the built landscape may have helped protect Caracol's populations from fluctuations in rainfall, both through water capture and storage in reservoirs and through managed waterflow and retained moisture in the terraces.

From the end of the Late Preclassic period through the Early Classic period, Caracol was similar to many other lowland Maya sites in that there was stratification and a clear distinction between the elite and other members of Caracol society. Only the elite buried their dead in tombs and used long distance trade items that included imported pottery and jadeite. By the end of the Early Classic period, population levels at Caracol exceeded 30,000 individuals. However, there was sufficient space between household groups or at the edges of settlement to provide basic foodstuffs for the

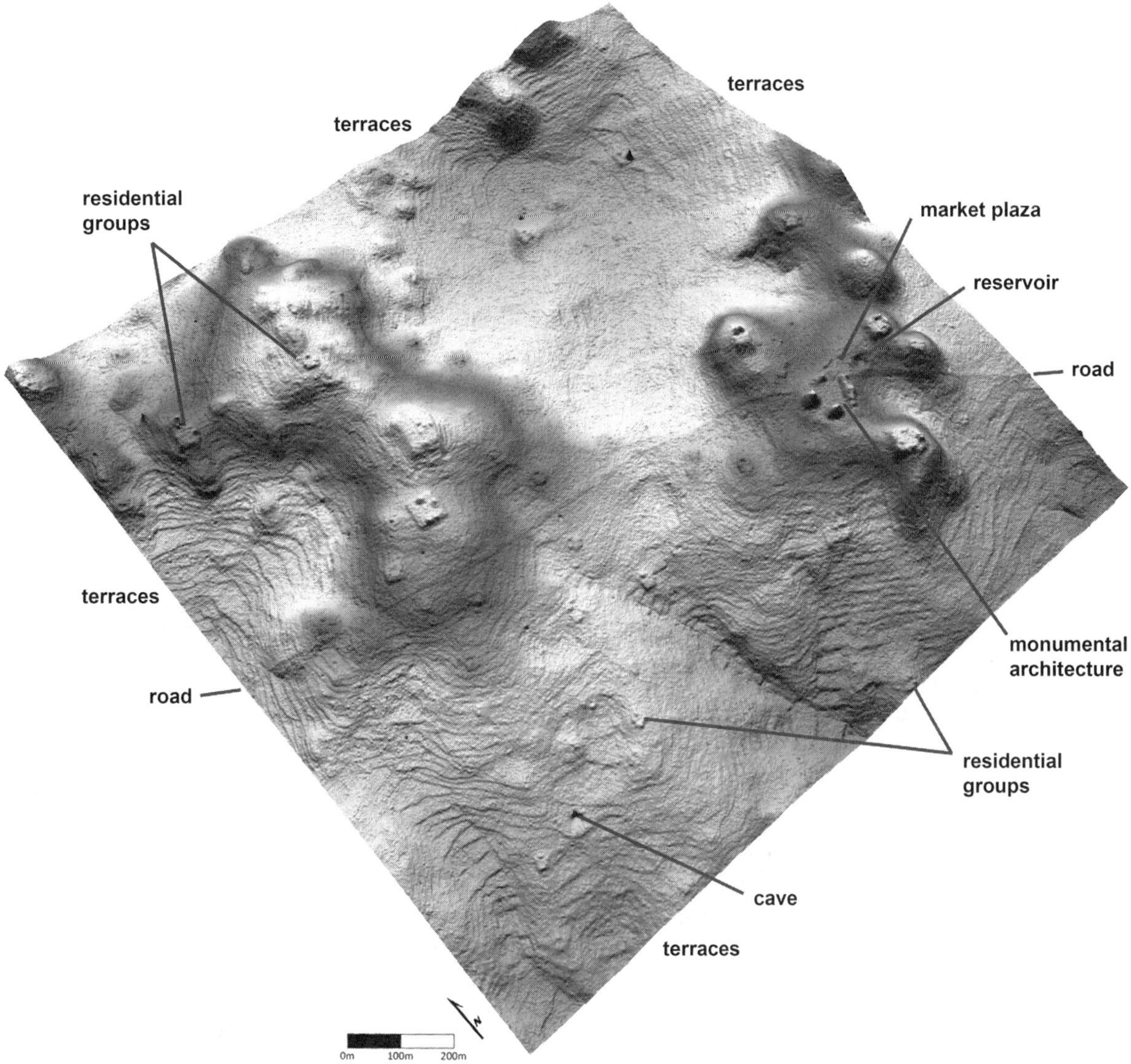

Figure 10.3. Caracol's modified landscape: the area in the vicinity of the Ceiba Terminus showing almost continuous terracing and settlement.

population. Social ties, trade, and migration also existed between Caracol and sites in the Maya heartland in the Peten of Guatemala as well as in the Guatemalan Highlands. Connections are evident in hieroglyphic texts and tradewares (A. Chase and D. Chase 2005). One interment suggests that prior to C.E. 350 there were at least limited ties to the central Mexican site of Teotihuacan (A. Chase and D. Chase 2011).

Caracol began to assert itself into the politics of the Maya lowlands in the 5th century and during the 6th and 7th centuries the balance of power in the eastern portion of the southern Maya Lowlands shifted. The rulers at Caracol established their authority and external control over this region through a series of wars with neighboring polities. The site was important enough to have provided the site of Copan, Honduras, with its founding ruler in C.E. 426/427 (A. Chase and D. Chase 2011; Price et al. 2010). Sometime after this, however, Caracol came under the sway of Tikal, Guatemala (Martin and Grube 2008). Drought conditions are recorded for the southern Lowlands between C.E. 490–580 with a peak at C.E. 517. Caracol appears to have used this climatic stress to strengthen itself politically. The city gained its political independence from Tikal, some 76 kilometers distant, through successful warfare in C.E. 562 and the population materially benefitted from this event (D. Chase and A. Chase 2003). From C.E. 631 through 680—despite periods of continued drought (Kennett et al. 2012)—Caracol maintained Naranjo, Guatemala, 42 kilometers distant, as

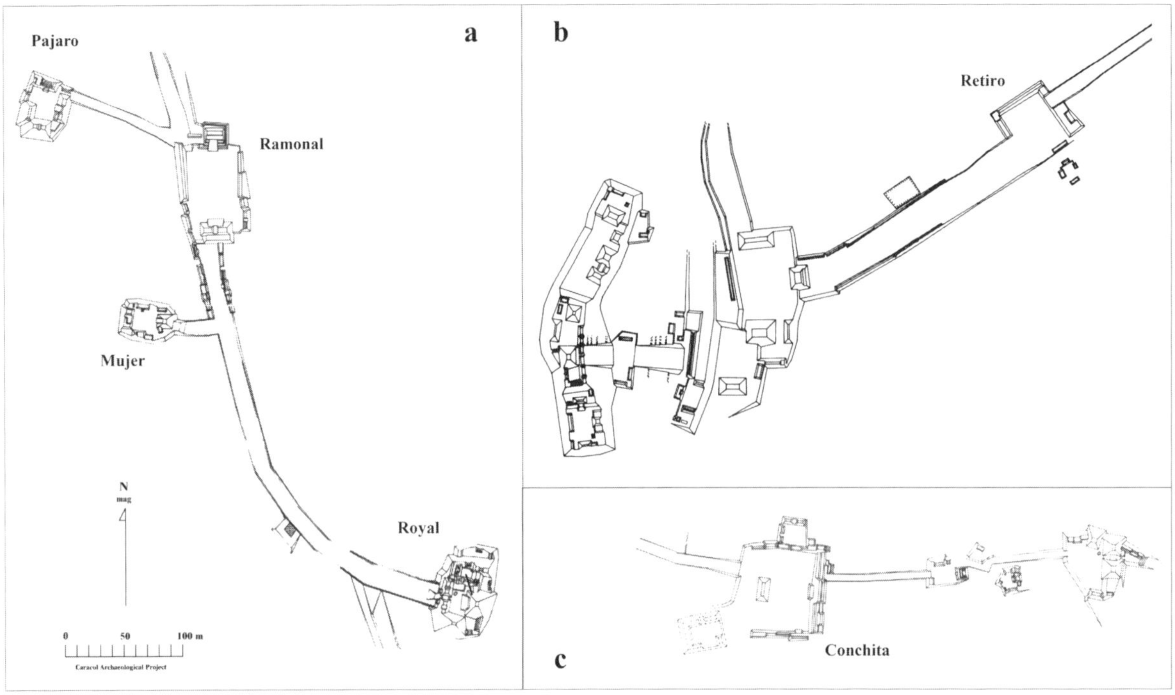

Figure 10.4. Examples of Caracol's market termini (plazas labeled "Ramonal," "Retiro," and "Conchita"); the large termini plazas functioned as markets for the distribution of goods and services to the site's urban population.

a second capitol (see Figure 10.1). As a smaller polity intermediate between Caracol and Tikal, Naranjo provided Caracol with the ability to expand its area of control beyond its own immediate 60 kilometer-radius—at least for a period of time. However, the integration of this larger territory into a broader Caracol polity was not sustainable, given the difficult and time-consuming nature of travel and communication by foot, especially given the hilly terrain and lack of inter-site causeways beyond Caracol-proper.

Immediately following this period of successful warfare, during the early part of the Late Classic period, a different socio-cultural adaption was created by Caracol's elite that did three things: promoted a self-sufficient environment; buffered the population from fluctuating external and internal forces; and served as a magnet for neighboring Maya. Caracol's population grew in numbers and prosperity. There appears to have been a substantial influx of population to Caracol; the site tripled in size to over 100,000 inhabitants by C.E. 700, likely drawn by Caracol's shared prosperity. The human capital that moved into the site was employed in the creation of additional agricultural terracing. Eventually, this terracing covered all areas with fields and completely modified the landscape (Figure 10.3). The system of causeways was extended, easing intra-site mobility and tying the epicentral and core populations together through a system of markets (Figure 10.4; D. Chase and A. Chase 2014). The Caracol urban system was self-supporting and infrastructure grew to meet demand. Spacing between households ensured both health and sufficient agricultural land for kitchen gardens and crops (Figure 10.5). As new population moved into the site, more agricultural terracing was added, and unpopulated areas were filled in with settlement. Water control features were also distributed throughout the landscape (Chase 2012). The result was a landesque-capital landscape (Fisher et al. 2009:10).

Practicing something we have termed "symbolic egalitarianism" (A. Chase and D. Chase 2009), the elite utilized labor to support their own lifestyle, but also re-invested capital in public works and in the inhabitants at-large. A large middle-status level developed in the population (A. Chase and D. Chase 1996b; D. Chase and A. Chase 1992). Caracol's inhabitants had access to basic commodities and luxuries from distant sites, including obsidian, polychrome pottery, jadeite, or spondylus adornments. Common ritual activity, whether the burial of the dead in tombs in eastern mortuary shrines or the interment of caches, was present throughout the urban community (D. Chase and A. Chase 1998, 2010, 2011). Other indicators of what appears to have been an intentionally constructed shared identity included a large percentage of the population with inlaid teeth (22%) and the household use of incense burners (D. Chase and A. Chase 2004). Thus, Caracol was a prime end-destination for

Figure 10.5. Caracol's urban settlement was both dense and fairly evenly distributed over the landscape in response to both health and agricultural needs; this is evident in the square kilometer of terraces and residential groups mapped some 5 kilometers northeast of the Caracol epicenter (after A. Chase and D. Chase 1998:figure 7).

population migration (e.g., Wright 2005), especially as the bulk of the people had access to items not available in other Maya polities. The influx of inhabitants further served te needs of the elite in building fields, roads, and constructions—and, also, through military service. These cultural adaptations, in conjunction with Caracol's built environment, provided resilience for almost two hundred years. However, maintaining Caracol's infrastructure and ensuring the prosperity of the population at-large came at the expense of the elite who, by C.E. 700, no longer monopolized wealth and trade items. Monument erection almost came to a halt in the early part of the 8th century and did not fully resume until C.E. 798. It is likely that a new form of government—one not focused on divine kingship—was instituted at Caracol after the death of K'an II in C.E. 680 (D. Chase and A. Chase 2003).

By the end of the 7th century, the site had pushed the boundaries of its polity size to beyond its "ideal" 60 kilometer radius. In C.E. 680, Naranjo regained its independence from Caracol, at which point it appears that Caracol subsequently focused on internal infrastructure rather than external control. Construction and remodeling of public buildings appears to have continued throughout the 8th century. The summit of Caana was raised over 4 meters and all of its buildings were remodeled sometime in the mid-8th century, but prior to the onset of the Terminal Classic period.

Drought has been noted as occurring in the southern Lowlands between C.E. 754 and 798,with a peak at C.E. 780 (Haug et al. 2003; Hodell et al. 2001; Hodell et al. 2005; Webster et al. 2007; Yaeger and Hodell 2008). Intriguingly, two important events may be correlated with this timespan. First, it is during this era that Late Classic royal tombs at the base of the northern temple of Caana were ritually desecrated and then resealed. Second, Caracol's elite began re-erecting stone monuments in C.E. 798 with a new focus on dynasty and situating the new rulership within a broader Maya worldview (A. Chase and D. Chase 2007). Both of these events imply significant political change at the site. From the epigraphic record, we also know that successful warfare was waged against sites outside of Caracol's sphere, harkening to memories of an earlier era of profitable conflict at the beginning of the Late Classic period. While Terminal Classic monuments were erected from C.E. 798 through 859, rulers appear to have shifted on a regular basis, possibly reflecting a different organizational structure consistent with a non-dynastic *batabil* form of government known from the Postclassic northern Lowlands (Chase et al. 2009).

By C.E. 800, while there remained areas where terracing and housing could be built in the city's core area, these were mostly in less desirable steeply-sloped locations at some distance from the epicenter. At this point, the socio-cultural adaptation appears to have changed. As has been previously noted by van der Leeuw (2009:58), one characteristic of resilient systems is that they make mistakes from which they may not always recover; this seems to be the case at Caracol. One major change was that symbolic egalitarianism was no longer practiced. While elites continued to live in the epicenter palaces and to engage in long-distance trade with other parts of Mesoamerica, trade items were no longer evenly distributed. Two different types of pottery were in use at the site at the same time: one set used by the elite, and another by the rest of the population (A. Chase and D. Chase 2004). Construction efforts appear to have focused on rebuilding the downtown epicenter rather than site-wide infrastructure. Various construction projects were completed or set in progress. During the Terminal Classic period, the Northeast Acropolis was substantially raised and a host of minor building projects were carried out in the epicenter and particularly in the elite residential complex of Caana. Other, clearly unfinished, projects were archaeologically recorded in several locations. For example, just south of the epicenter was a huge agglomeration of Terminal Classic garbage—fill for what would have been a massive platform. Piles of building stones were stockpiled in front of Structure A7 and another stone stockpile was recovered in the Northwest Palace. Thus, a series of large-scale construction efforts were taking place in the site epicenter.

Ultimately, the situation was no longer adaptive. Importantly, however, the situation worsened over a period of nearly 100 years. The lack of infrastructure upkeep, of uneven access to trade items, and of a shared identity no longer provided the incentive for populations to remain invested in the workings of the polity. Without a readily available labor force, projects went unfinished. Other natural and human factors further set what had been a balanced system into disequilibrium. What was once a sustainable adaptation moved out of equilibrium. External forces had an impact on the site and polity. Increased warfare is evident. Stone monuments show both alliances with foreigners and acts of aggression against neighboring peoples. Sites within the 60 kilometer radius of Caracol were no longer directly under its sway, but instead became independent (e.g., Minanha—see Chapter 11 this volume and Iannone 2005). In spite of these pressures, the elite maintained their separation from the rest of society in diet and material remains. We suggest that they ultimately consumed more capital than the system could produce. Climate change, whether to wetter or to drier conditions, would have exacerbated an already fragile human–nature coupling. By the end of 9th century, the "downtown" epicentral area of Caracol was burned (D. Chase and A Chase 2000).

Much of the population abandoned Caracol at the transition from the 9th to the 10th centuries (D. Chase and A Chase 2000). Transformative relocation, described elsewhere in this volume by Nelson and his colleagues, was a factor. However, not all people moved—and, as at other sites, multiple factors likely weakened Caracol's infrastructure (Turner and Sabloff 2012). No substantial Postclassic period settlement exists in the immediate vicinity of Caracol. Rather, there appears to be movement away from the Caracol upland location to lowland coastal or riverine areas. The new settlement locations were both practical—in that they provided transportation and trade access—and symbolic—in that these locations were associated with the watery underworld (D. Chase and A. Chase 1989).

Conclusions

In sum, Caracol provides compelling lessons about the applicability of the past to the present and future. The story of this ancient polity is both uplifting and tragic. Late Classic Caracol is perhaps the best Maya example of positive human–environment interaction; at that time, the population of the city exceeded 100,000. The successful adaptation placed an emphasis on infrastructure and the creation of roads, on agricultural terraces, and on regular settlement distribution as part of a landesque capital landscape (Blaikie and Brookfield 1987:9; Fisher et al. 2009:10) —a landscape anthropogenically modified over the course of centuries to meet Caracol's varied social, economic, political, and ritual needs. The economic system, based on household production and market distribution, utilized labor for city and polity-wide construction investments, and resulted in material well-being for all occupants at the site (even if there were differences between elite and commoners). The city and polity projected shared identity and symbolic egalitarianism, encouraging population movement from other areas. However, the failure of Caracol was also human-induced. Even if climate change was substantial, human actions—decisions to halt public service-oriented infrastructure construction and maintenance in favor of maintaining elite epicentral constructions and lifestyle—in direct contraposition to earlier strategies (as indicated above) set the stage for a downward spiral that needed very little to push things over the edge. The agricultural system placed the site on a trajectory of path dependence on a landscape that was maintained through social practices. While these human adaptations provided a buffer to external circumstances for some two centuries, the Terminal Classic changes that were instituted—changes that took place over the course of a 100 year time-span—left Caracol unstable and exceedingly vulnerable to collapse.

In closing, we would like to take the liberty of quoting from an article written by Costanza, Graumlich, and Steffen (2007:10) and apply it to the Classic Maya. Even though they were writing about the Great Acceleration that occurred at the end of the 20th century, their comments apply equally to the 9th century Maya of Caracol. We quote directly from their text, changing only the dates and tense (marked in italics).

> Towards the end of the *9th* century, there *were* signs that the Great Acceleration could not continue in its present form without increasing the risk of crossing thresholds and triggering abrupt changes. Transitions to new energy systems *were* required. There *was* a growing disparity between wealthy and poor, and, through modern communication, a growing awareness by the poor of this gap, which . . . created a potentially explosive situation. Many of the ecosystem services upon which human well-being *depended were* degrading, with the possible rapid changes when thresholds *were* crossed . . . .

An integrated history of the past can indeed provide us with lessons for the future.

References Cited

Arthur, W. Brian
1994 Increasing Returns and Path Dependence in the Economy. Ann Arbor: University of Michigan Press.

Berkhout, Frans
2002 Technological Regimes, Path Dependency, and the Environment. Global Environmental Change 12:1–4.

Blaikie, Piers, and Harold Brookfield, eds.
1987 Land Degradation and Society. London: Methuen.

Chase, Adrian S. Z.
2012 Beyond Elite Control: Maya Water Management at the Site of Caracol, Belize. Undergraduate Senior thesis, Departments of Anthropology and Computer Science, Harvard University.

Chase, Arlen F., and Diane Z. Chase
1995 External Impetus, Internal Synthesis, and Standardization: E Group Assemblages and the Crystallization of Classic Maya Society in the Southern Lowlands. Acta Mesoamericana 8:87–101.
1996a More than Kin and King: Centralized Political Organization among the Ancient Maya. Current Anthropology 37(5):803–810.
1996b A Mighty Maya Nation: How Caracol Built an Empire by Cultivating its Middle Class. Archaeology 49(5):66–72.
1998a Late Classic Maya Political Structure, Polity Size, and Warfare Arenas. *In* Anatomia de una civilizacion: Aproximaciones Interdisciplinarias a la Cultura Maya. A. Ciudad Ruiz, M. Y. Fernandez Marquinez, J. M. Garcia Campillo, M. J. Iglesias Ponce de Leon, A. Lacadena Garcia-Gallo, and L. T. Sanz Castro, eds. Pp. 11–29. Madrid: Sociedad Espanola de Estudios Mayas.
1998b Scale and Intensity in Classic Period Maya Agriculture: Terracing and Settlement at the 'Garden City' of Caracol, Belize. Culture and Agriculture 20(2):60–77.
2001a Ancient Maya Causeways and Site Organization at Caracol, Belize. Ancient Mesoamerica 12(2):273–281.
2001b The Royal Court of Caracol, Belize: Its Palaces and People. *In* Royal Courts of the Ancient Maya, vol. 2: Data and Case Studies. T. Inomata and S. Houston, eds. Pp. 102–137. Boulder: Westview Press.
2004 Terminal Classic Status-Linked Ceramics and the Maya Collapse: *De Facto* Refuse at Caracol, Belize. *In* The Terminal Classic in the Maya Lowlands: Collapse, Transition, and Transformation. A. Demarest, P. Rice, and D. Rice, eds. Pp. 342–366. Boulder: University Press of Colorado.

2005 The Early Classic Period at Caracol, Belize: Transitions, Complexity, and Methodological Issues in Maya Archaeology. Research Reports in Belizean Archaeology 2:17–38.
2006 Before the Boom: Caracol's Preclassic Era. Research Reports in Belizean Archaeology 3:41–67.
2007 Ancient Maya Urban Development: Insights from the Archaeology of Caracol, Belize. Journal of Belizean Studies 29(2):60–71.
2009 Symbolic Egalitarianism and Homogenized Distributions in the Archaeological Record at Caracol, Belize: Method, Theory, and Complexity. Research Reports in Belizean Archaeology 6:15–24.
2011 Status and Power: Caracol, Teotihuacan, and the Early Classic Maya World. Research Reports in Belizean Archaeology 8:3–18.

Chase, Arlen F., Diane Z. Chase, and Michael E. Smith
2009 States and Empires in Ancient Mesoamerica. Ancient Mesoamerica 20(2):175–182.

Chase, Arlen F., Diane Z. Chase, John F. Weishampel, Jason B. Drake, Ramesh L. Shrestha, K. Clint Slatton, Jaime J. Awe, and William E. Carter
2011 Airborne LiDAR, Archaeology, and the Ancient Maya Landscape at Caracol, Belize. Journal of Archaeological Science 38:387–398.

Chase, Diane Z., and Arlen F. Chase
1989 Routes of Trade and Communication and the Integration of Maya Society: The Vista from Santa Rita Corozal. *In* Coastal Maya Trade. H. McKillop and P. Healy, eds. Pp. 19–32. Occasional Papers in Anthropology, 8. Toronto: Trent University.
1998 The Architectural Context of Caches, Burials, and Other Ritual Activities for the Classic Period Maya (as Reflected at Caracol, Belize). *In* Function and Meaning in Classic Maya Architecture. S. D. Houston, ed. Pp. 299–332. Washington, DC: Dumbarton Oaks.
2000 Inferences about Abandonment: Maya Household Archaeology and Caracol, Belize. Mayab 13:67–77.
2003 Texts and Contexts in Classic Maya Warfare: A Brief Consideration of Epigraphy and Archaeology at Caracol, Belize. *In* Ancient Mesoamerican Warfare. M. K. Brown and T. W. Stanton, eds. Pp. 171–188. Walnut Creek: Alta Mira Press.
2004 Archaeological Perspectives on Classic Maya Social Organization from Caracol, Belize. Ancient Mesoamerica 15:111–119.
2010 Rituales Mezclados: Analizando Comportamientos Públicos y Privados en el Registro Arqueológico de Caracol. *In* El Ritual en el Mundo Maya: de lo Privado a lo Público. A. Ciudad Ruiz, M. J. Iglesias Ponce de Leon, and M. Sorroche, eds. Pp. 107–128. Sociedad Espana de Estudios Mayas Publication 9. Madrid: CEPHIS-UNAM.
2011 Ghosts amid the Ruins: Analyzing Relationships Between the Living and the Dead Among the Ancient Maya at Caracol, Belize. *In* Living with the Dead: Mortuary Ritual in Mesoamerica. J. L. Fitzsimmons and I. Shimada, eds. Pp. 78–101. Tucson: University of Arizona Press.
2014 Ancient Maya Markets and the Economic Integration of Caracol, Belize. Ancient Mesoamerica 25(1):239–250.

Chase, Diane Z., and Arlen F. Chase, eds.
1992 Mesoamerican Elites: An Archaeological Assessment. Norman: University of Oklahoma Press.

Costanza, Robert, Lisa J. Graumlich, and Will L. Steffen
2007 Sustainability or Collapse: Lessons from Integrating the History of Humans and the Rest of the World. *In* Sustainability or Collapse? An Integrated History and Future of People on Earth. R. Costanza, L. Graumlich, and W. Steffen, eds. Pp. 3–17. Cambridge: MIT Press.

Crandall, James M.
2009 Water and the Mountains: Maya Water Management at Caracol, Belize. M.A. thesis, Department of Anthropology, University of Central Florida.

Fisher, Christopher T., J. Brett Hill, and Gary M. Feinman
2009 Introduction: Environmental Studies for Twenty-First Century Conservation. *In* The Archaeology of Environmental Change. C. Fisher, J. Hill, and G. Feinman, eds. Pp. 1–12. Tucson: University of Arizona Press.

Fletcher, Roland
2011 Low-Density, Agrarian-Based Urbanism: Scale, Power, and Ecology. *In* The Comparative Archaeology of Complex Societies. M. Smith, ed. Pp. 285–320. Cambridge: Cambridge University Press.

Geertz, Clifford
1963 Agricultural Involution: The Processes of

Ecological Change in Indonesia. Berkeley: University of California Press.

Haug, Gerald H., Detlef Gunther, Larry C. Peterson, Daniel M. Sigman, Konrad A. Hughen, and Beat Aeschlimann
2003 Climate and the Collapse of Maya Civilization. Science 299:1731–1735.

Hodell, David A., Mark Brenner, and Jason H. Curtis
2005 Terminal Classic Drought in the Northern Maya Lowlands Inferred from Multiple Sediment Cores in Lake Chichancanab (Mexico). Quaternary Science Reviews 24:1413–1427.

Hodell, David A., Mark Brenner, Jason H. Curtis, and Thomas Guilderson
2001 Solar Forcing of Drought Frequency in the Maya Lowlands. Science 292:1367–1370.

Iannone, Gyles
2005 The Rise and Fall of an Ancient Maya Petty Royal Court. Latin American Antiquity 16:26–44.

Kay, Adrian
2005 A Critique of the Use of Path Dependency in Policy Studies. Public Administration 83(3):553–571.

Kennett, Douglas J., S. F. M. Breitenbach, V. V. Aquino, Y. Asmerom, J. Awe, J. U. L. Baldini, P. Bartlein, B. J. Culleton, C. Ebert, C. Jazwa, M. J. Macri, N. Varwan, V. Polyak, K. M. Prufer, H. E. Ridley, H. Sodemann, B. Winterhalder, and G. H. Haug
2012 Development and Disintegration of Maya Political Systems in Response to Climate Change. Science 338:788–791.

Laporte, Juan Pedro, and Vilma Fialko
1995 Un Reencuentro con Mundo Perdido, Tikal, Guatemala. Ancient Mesoamerica 6(1):41–94.

Luzzadder-Beach, Sheryl, Timothy P. Beach, and Nicholas P. Dunning
2012 Wetland Fields as Mirrors of Drought and the Maya Abandonment. Proceedings of the National Academy of Sciences 109(10):3646–3651.

Martin, Simon, and Nikolai Grube
2008 Chronicle of the Maya Kings and Queens: Deciphering the Dynasties of the Ancient Maya. 2nd edition. London: Thames and Hudson.

Medina-Elizalde, Martin, and Eelco J. Rohling
2012 Collapse of Classic Maya Civilization Related to Modest Reduction in Precipitation. Science 335:956–959.

Murtha, Timothy
2009 Land and Labor: Classic Maya Terraced Agriculture. Saarbruken: D. M. Verlag Dr. Muller.

Pierson, Paul
2000 Increasing Returns, Path Dependence, and the Study of Politics. American Political Science Review 94(2):251–267.

Price, T. Douglas, James H. Burton, Robert J. Sharer, Jane E. Buikstra, Lori E. Wright, Loa P. Traxler, and Katherine A. Miller
2010 Kings and Commoners at Copan: Isotopic Evidence for Origins and Movement in the Classic Maya Period. Journal of Anthropological Archaeology 29:15–32.

Turner, B. L., and Jeremy A. Sabloff
2012 Classic Period Collapse of the Central Maya Lowlands: Insights about Human-Environment Relationships for Sustainability. Proceedings of the National Academy of Sciences 109(35):13908–13914.

van der Leeuw, Sander E.
2009 What is an 'Environmental Crisis' to an Archaeologist? *In* The Archaeology of Environmental Change. C. Fisher, J. Hill, and G. Feinman, eds. Pp. 40–61. Tucson: University of Arizona Press.

Vergne, Jean-Phillippe, and Rodolphe Durand
2010 The Missing Link between the Theory and Empirics of Path Dependence: Conceptual Clarification, Testability Issue, and Methodological Implications. Journal of Management Studies 47(4):736–759.

Wahl, David, Roger Byrne, Thomas Schreiner, and Richard Hansen
2007 Palaeolimnological Evidence of Late-Holocene Settlement and Abandonment in the Mirador Basin, Peten, Guatemala. The Holocene 17(6):813–820.

Webster, James W., George A. Brook, L. Bruce Railsback, Hai Cheng, R. Lawrence Edwards, Clark Alexander, and Philip P. Reeder

2007 Stalagmite Evidence from Belize Indicating Significant Droughts at the Time of Preclassic Abandonment, the Maya Hiatus, and the Classic Maya Collapse. Palaeogeography, Palaeoclimatology, Palaeoecology 250: 1–17.

Wright, Lori E.
2005 Identifying Immigrants to Tikal, Guatemala: Defining Local Variability in Strontium Isotope Ratios of Human Tooth Enamel. Journal of Archaeological Science 32:555–566.

Yaeger, Jason, and David A. Hodell
2008 The Collapse of Maya Civilization: Assessing the Interaction of Culture, Climate, and Environment. *In* El Nino, Catastrophism, and Culture Change in Ancient America. J. Quilter and D. H. Sandweiss, eds. Pp. 197–251. Washington, DC: Dumbarton Oaks.

11

Resilience and Vulnerability in the Maya Hinterlands

Gyles Iannone
Trent University
Keith Prufer
University of New Mexico
and
Diane Z. Chase
University of Central Florida

ABSTRACT

Given their grand architecture, intricately carved monuments, and colorful histories, the largest Maya centers have long drawn the attention of archaeologists and non-specialists alike. Early interest in the infamous Maya collapse was, in fact, initially inspired by the discovery of these "lost cities in the jungle." This research focus was further stimulated by advances in deciphering the Maya hieroglyphic script, and the recognition that monument erection—or in other words, the written histories of most of the southern Lowland centers—came to a rather abrupt end in the 9th century C.E. IHOPE scholars are attempting to elucidate the conditions that lead to the decline of these impressive centers. In doing so, the trajectories of smaller communities, and or those located in hinterlands between the more prominent centers, have emerged as interesting counterpoints that provide unique, and no less significant, examples of resilience and vulnerability. The emerging data suggest that these communities had specific strengths and weaknesses, which in turn provided them with a particular set of challenges, as well as a specific range of coping mechanisms they could marshal when dealing with their ever-changing environment circumstances (i.e., climate change, resource availability, landscape modifications), and the highly dynamic geopolitical landscape within which they were embedded. This chapter will discuss some of the key insights derived from our examination of hinterland communities, with particular attention being paid to the broader implications of the contrasting trajectories exhibited by these segments of ancient Maya society. [archaeology, Maya, hinterland, innovation, resilience]

As part of our efforts to explore issues of resilience and vulnerability in the ancient Maya world, IHOPE scholars are not only examining the heartlands of Maya polities, but also their hinterlands. These zones, and their resident communities, are intriguing places to study precisely because of their distinctive characteristics. In this chapter we explore issues relating to resilience and vulnerability in three Maya centers located today in different parts of Belize (Figure 11.1), an area of the eastern Maya Lowlands that can be geographically characterized as encompassing the Caribbean coastal shelf and the Maya Mountains. Not only did these centers emerge in varied ecological, economic, and political settings, their periods of florescence also occurred at different times during the broader Maya developmental trajectory. These case studies provide a glimpse into the dynamic nature of socio-ecological development and denouement in the Maya hinterlands.

ARCHEOLOGICAL PAPERS OF THE AMERICAN ANTHROPOLOGICAL ASSOCIATION, Vol. 24, pp. 155–170, ISSN 1551-823X, online ISSN 1551-8248. DOI: 10.1111/apaa.12035.

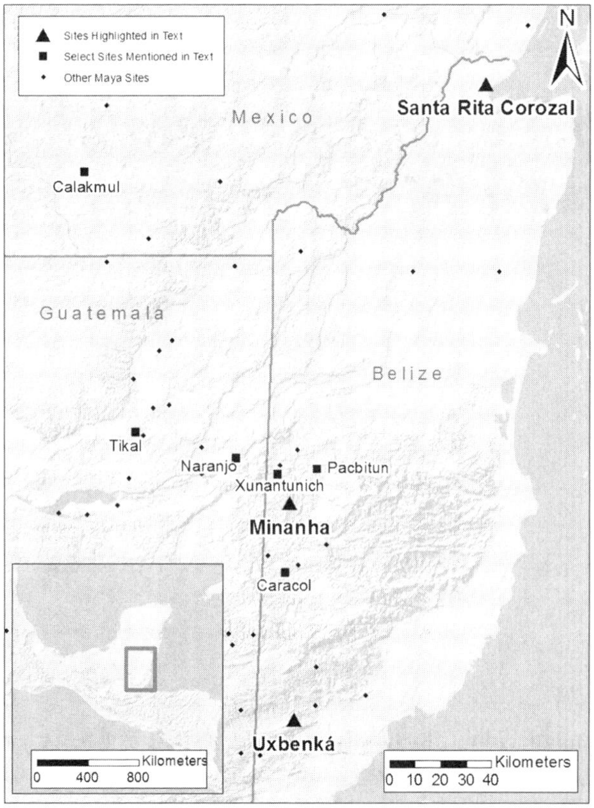

Figure 11.1. Map of the Maya subarea showing the location of the three hinterland case studies.

Resilience and Vulnerability in the Hinterlands

In considering the qualities of hinterlands and how these relate to issues of resilience and vulnerability, it is useful to begin with Igor Kopytoff's (1987, 1999) distinction between internal frontiers, which are zones between two adjacent polities, and external frontiers, which are zones formed as a result of the colonizing expansion of a polity into a sparsely populated and or less politically complex region. When investigating ancient hinterlands, archaeologists study both internal and external frontiers, but often without making a clear distinction between the two. However, the political and economic integration of hinterlands into broader systems, as well as the resilience and vulnerability of hinterland communities, may vary for internal and external frontiers.

Hinterland communities develop in zones that constitute "edges." They may occur not only at the juncture of different political and or cultural units, but also in divergent ecological zones. Thus, the location of a hinterland community may support or minimize its resilience. According to Nancy Turner and her colleagues (2003:456–457), "cultural edges are like ecological edges in that they allow for diversification of resources, in this case cultural resources. . . In both cases they provide increasing social-ecological resilience as they broaden the diversity of biological species and cultural knowledge that can be drawn upon for livelihood."

Others suggest that hinterland communities have an inherent level of resilience because distance from polity capitals affords them a significant level of autonomy (see also Browman 1997:230). The resilience of hinterland communities may also be enhanced because they are located between competing polities and they can, therefore, ally themselves with the polity that is most beneficial to local power structures or institutions, and or the polity that has taken the upper hand in a territorial dispute (Hassig 1992:98).

Hinterlands may also have significant vulnerabilities. For example, considerable debate exists concerning how innovative, and hence resilient, hinterland communities are. Sander van der Leeuw (2007:219) posits that hinterlands are disadvantaged when compared to heartlands because the latter are the centers for innovation; the more peripheral a settlement is, the "more unattainable the innovations are." Others suggest that it is during times of stress that loosely integrated hinterlands become vulnerable, because such "modularity" inhibits the transfer of assistance and innovations precisely when they are most needed (Cumming 2011:138; Walker and Salt 2012:95–96). Similarly, Kopytoff (1999:33) argues that there is often a significant level of "cultural conservatism" in hinterland communities, which stifles innovation on the local scale. According to Kopytoff (1999:33–34), although the inhabitants of hinterland communities tend to see themselves as innovators, with substantial leeway to create any kind of society they wish, in reality they bring a significant level of conformity to their social constructions. This is because they rely on a given "political culture," or "cultural baggage" —including technological traditions and conceptions of power, legitimacy, authority, institution building, and political practice—which manifests itself in the form of "ideal patterns and ideal institutional models, rather than being a matter, as in the metropoles, of active practice."

In contrast to the aforementioned perspectives, others advocate for more significant levels of innovation, and hence resilience, in the hinterlands. For example, Kopytoff's (1999) "cyclical model" for hinterland development underscores the key role played by immigrants from polity capitals, or metropoles, who move into hinterland settings and either set up their own communities or merge with those communities established by earlier settlers, thereby enhancing the innovative capacity of the hinterland communities they now call home. This view does, however, continue to favor the idea that all innovation occurs in the heartlands, which is a stance that has been effectively challenged by those who see hinterlands, themselves, as dynamic places of cultural contact and syncretization, where innovations of all kinds are created, manipulated, and transformed (Lightfoot and Martinez 1995:472). From this perspective, hinterland communities are resilient places precisely because they are centers for innovation, rather than vulnerable peripheries passively awaiting the next innovation to be transferred from the heartland.

Regardless of whether hinterlands are viewed as creators of, or receptors for, innovation—and the previous discussion suggests that the answer lay somewhere in the middle—most scholars agree that the confluence of local and immigrant cultures, the latter often emanating from multiple metropoles, often leads to the emergence of unique hinterland communities, complete with differing social identities (Schortman 1989). The interstitial character of the hinterland, itself, only serves to enhance this uniqueness. As Kopytoff (1987, 1999) has documented using African examples, hinterland communities may eventually develop into capitals of their own polities, re-initiating the process of hinterland formation, as immigrants from the newly established metropole move out and coalesce with new and existing communities in the new hinterland(s). Often, these communities are seen to "emerge as historically changing, multiple, and branching alignments of social groups and segments" (Wells 2006:268). The mixing of local and immigrant cultures within hinterland settings is central to the establishment of distinct hinterland societies and contributes to the different levels of resilience and vulnerability that characterize specific hinterland socioecological systems. While such hinterland dynamics are often the focus of study relative to large ancient empires (see for example Wells 2013 for ancient Rome and Malpass and Alconini 2010 for the Inka), the proximity of hinterland Maya sites to the Maya heartland provides additional depth to this discussion.

We should, in fact, expect considerable variability in the levels of resilience exhibited by specific hinterland communities, over both time and space, especially given that they can interface with neighboring political formations in diverse ways. Where hinterlands are integrated indirectly and local power structures are maintained as long as tax or tribute continue to flow to the heartland, we see loosely integrated geopolitical landscapes defined by continually negotiated alliances and or patron-client relationships (Bedford 2009:42, 48; LeCount and Yaeger 2010:31–39), as well as significant functional redundancy, greater response diversity, limited connectivity, and higher levels of resilience (e.g., Holling 2001; Holling and Gunderson 2002; Gunderson and Holling 2002; Walker and Salt 2006). Alternatively, when hinterlands are under the direct control of a political heartland, usually through the installation of governors emanating from the metropole itself, we see a much more tightly integrated geopolitical landscape consisting of a capital and a series of provinces (Bedford 2009:42, 48; LeCount and Yaeger 2010:31–39), as well as considerable functional specialization, a more limited degree of response diversity, and a high level of interconnectedness—or in other words, "hypercoherence" —leading to diminished resilience over time (Hegmon et al. 2008; Holling and Gunderson 2002; Gunderson and Holling 2002; Walker and Salt 2006:76–77, 164). Of significance here is the fact that a combination of these integrative strategies may be employed at any one time (e.g., see Bedford [2009] for a discussion of the Neo-Assyrian empire, Anderies [2006] for the Hohokom, and van der Leeuw [2005] for the Roman Empire in the Rhone Valley). In summary, as archaeologists we are left to consider whether hinterland communities were: (1) ideally positioned, ecologically, culturally, and politically, so as to promote flexibility and resilience when faced with perturbations; (2) rigid and, thus, vulnerable in the face of negative change because they were tightly connected to heartlands and lacked innovative capacity; and or, (3) highly diverse and inherently dynamic, exhibiting significant variability in terms of their ability to deal with unexpected environmental or cultural shocks. We will now turn to our three case studies to illustrate the complex nature of resilience and vulnerability in the ancient Maya hinterlands.

Uxbenká

Our first case study focuses on Uxbenká, a moderately sized polity spread out across the foothills of the Maya Mountains along the eastern periphery of the Maya Lowlands (Figure 11.2). In this region Uxbenká was the first community with the ability to mobilize labor around significant architectural construction and landscape transformations.

During its evolution, Uxbenká underwent a shift from a small village to a complex polity with social differentiation reflected in distinctions between civic-ceremonial and residential spaces and the installation of carved stelae that record statements attesting to the authority and network interactions of individual elites. Research at Uxbenká focuses on building absolute chronologies for the site core areas and settlement (Culleton et al. 2012; Prufer et al. 2011), on extensive geomorphological analysis assessing productive agricultural strategies (Culleton 2012), understanding economic interactions and the role of trade (Nazaroff et al. 2010), and on placing the development of the polity in the context of its ecological setting and local climate records (Kennett et al. 2012; Walsh et al. in press). These studies are integrated with longitudinal ethnographic work measuring

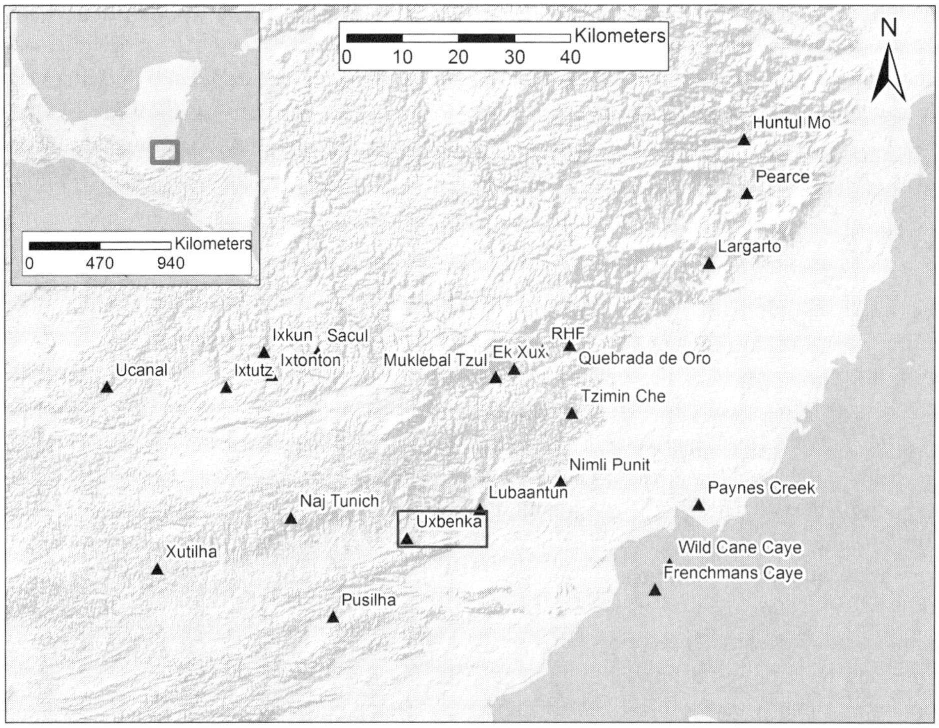

Figure 11.2. Map showing the location of Uxbenka and other centers in, or adjacent to, southern Belize.

agricultural productivity and potential at the Mopan Maya community of Santa Cruz whose residents have recolonized the lands and resources of the ancient polity.

Uxbenká is a peripheral polity (Schortman and Urban 1994) with indicators of economic, political, and ideological links to larger core political centers, but little evidence of having ever fallen under the hegemonic sway of these neighbors (Prufer et al. 2011). The polity began as an agricultural village during the latter part of the Late Preclassic (prior to Cal. 50 B.C.E.–C.E. 50) with small hierarchically undifferentiated households scattered across a series of adjacent hilltops in an otherwise sparsely occupied region. The population that coalesced into a community may have been endogenous. Geomorphological studies at Uxbenka (Culleton 2012) and regional paeloecological records (Walsh et al. in press) indicate land clearing as early as Cal. 1420–1290 B.C.E., with settlers exploiting rich agricultural soils, abundant rainfall, and reliable surface water.

Between Cal. C.E. 60 and 310 Uxbenká underwent significant reorganization, including massive landscape alteration to accommodate public architecture in Groups A, B, and D (Figure 11.3). Entire hilltops and ridges were flattened and expanded by cutting and filling for emergent status-differentiating architectural groups in the core of the Classic Maya center.

A brief period of significantly reduced precipitation from C.E. 400–425 (Kennett et al. 2012) may represent a short hiatus in growth at Uxbenká evidenced by a short cessation of monumental construction (Aquino et al. 2013). During this time there may have been a change in leadership strategies seen in the abandonment of a foundational cave shrine built during the initial development of the polity during the Late Preclassic–Early Classic transition (Moyes and Prufer 2013).

Within several decades of C.E. 400 Uxbenká began to be integrated more fully into the Early Classic Maya traditions. The first carved monuments appear at some point after C.E. 378 but before C.E. 455; some have specific references to Tikal, beginning a three-century tradition of elite texts that describe network interactions and political status. Despite textual references to the Petén heartland, there are no archaeological indicators that suggest Uxbenká was a subordinate of Tikal. The Early Classic was also a period of increasing precipitation (Kennett et al. 2012) and an expansion of settlements away from the site core, including the dispersal of elite households (Thompson and Prufer 2013). Some of these architectural groups have significant investment in landscape alteration, likely reflecting the ability of economic elites to mobilize labor and expand their presence in areas of particularly high quality soils close to

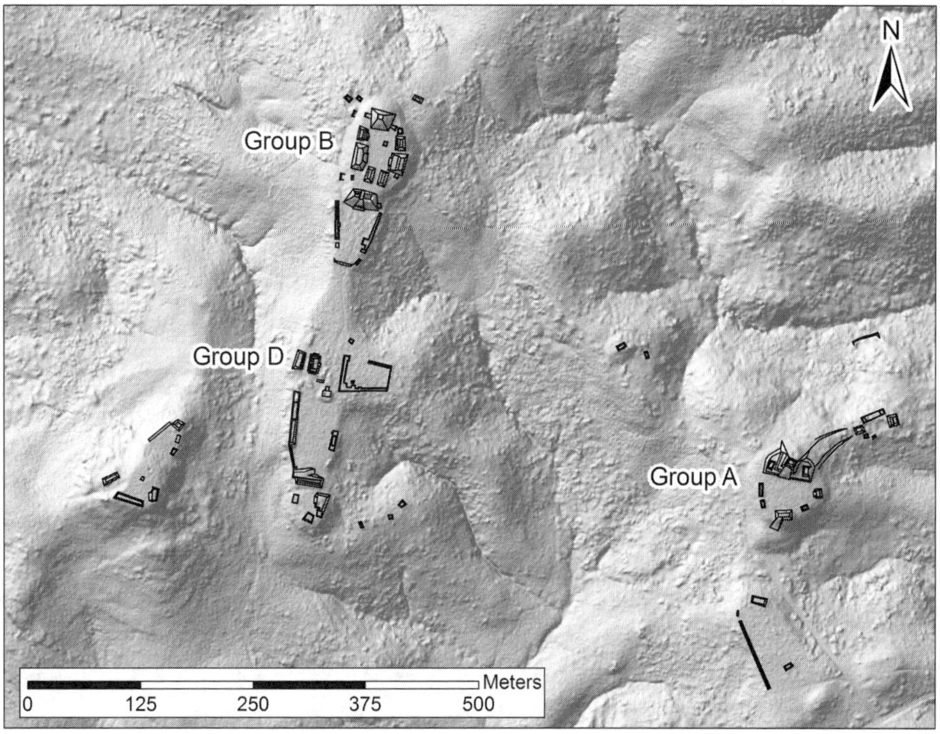

Figure 11.3. LiDAR image of Uxbenka detailing the site core and prominent architectural groups A, B, and D, discussed in the text.

perennial water sources. While this period of rapid growth was likely facilitated by a long period of high rainfall evidenced in a local paleoclimate record (Kennett et al 2012), another factor may have been the unique soils that form in the Rio Blanco Valley. Referred to as the Toledo Beds these sedimentary soils derive from interbedded mudstones, sandstones and limestones that lay close to horizontal. The mudstone strata break down rapidly when exposed to weathering and quickly form new soils (Hartshorn et al. 1984:76–77). Clearing lands for agriculture, including burning, create conditions where soils form rapidly, allowing shortened fallow periods, and allowing more of the landscape to be farmed with minimal intensification (Culleton 2012). These same soils are considered ideal for a range of economically important tree crops, including Cacao (Wright et al. 1959). Combined with some of the highest rainfall rates in Central America (2800–4000 millimeters per year, compared to 1500–2000 millimeters for central Belize and the Peten, Kennett et al. 2012) Uxbenká may have been well suited to maximize agricultural production on less land, and with less investment in terracing or other intensification strategies, thus reducing path dependencies.

The Late Classic also witnessed another reorganization that included the construction of final-phase public buildings in Groups B and D, obscuring earlier architecture and starting after Cal C.E. 650. The final configuration of the site reflects a reorientation of the political center to Group B, a restricted plaza with a northern pyramid and a central ballcourt. In Group A, the Stela Plaza, which housed carved monuments attesting to the dynastic history of the polity and network interactions of leaders, there are no Late Classic constructions, but there is evidence for the re-plastering of surfaces and the continued erection of monuments through the ninth century (Prufer et al. 2011).

Regionally, Uxbenká remained the largest inland polity of any significance until around C.E. 550 when several important polities—including Pusilha, Lubaantun, and Nimli Punit—emerged onto the landscape as regional centers, undoubtedly impacting the geopolitical and economic primacy of Uxbenká on this southeastern periphery (though recent studies indicate that Nim Li Punit may have been founded during the Early Classic; see Fauvelle et al. 2013). Decline appears to have been regional, rapid, and complete with apparent abandonment of political centers and overland trade networks by the end of the ninth century C.E. and only ephemeral evidence of early Postclassic populations, suggesting that the collapse of the political centers was also accompanied by gradual regional depopulation. Paleoecological reconstructions indicate that human use of fire and subsequent erosion in the watershed became less common sometime between C.E. 800–1000 (Walsh et al. in press), likely indicating a reduction of land clearing for agriculture. This occurred at the same time as a decline in rainfall and several protracted droughts well documented across the Maya Lowlands (see Kennett et al. 2012 and references within). It remains unclear whether a reduction of rainfall in this area would alone be sufficient to bring about regional societal collapse, given the overall high precipitation rates in southern Belize. Declines in rainfall in areas of high annual precipitation are unlikely to be as destabilizing as they would be in areas of lower annual precipitation. Stable isotope rainfall reconstructions suggest that multi decadal drought events between C.E. 820–870 were not as severe as the single short event at C.E. 400–425 (Kennett et al. 2012).

In summary, Uxbenká's uniquely rich agricultural soils and location in an area of abundant rainfall likely lent a degree of resilience to both population growth and political stability during its 800 year occupation. Its growth may have also been facilitated by its position along established trade routes linking the Caribbean Sea to the Petén (Nazaroff et al. 2010; Prufer et al. 2011). However, the development of increasingly complex geopolitical regional interaction spheres during the Late Classic, combined with inter-polity competition, population growth, and decisions regarding land-use, may have weakened the polity's ability to withstand the disintegration of political and economic relationships occurring in core areas of the Maya Lowlands (Kennett and Beach, in press).

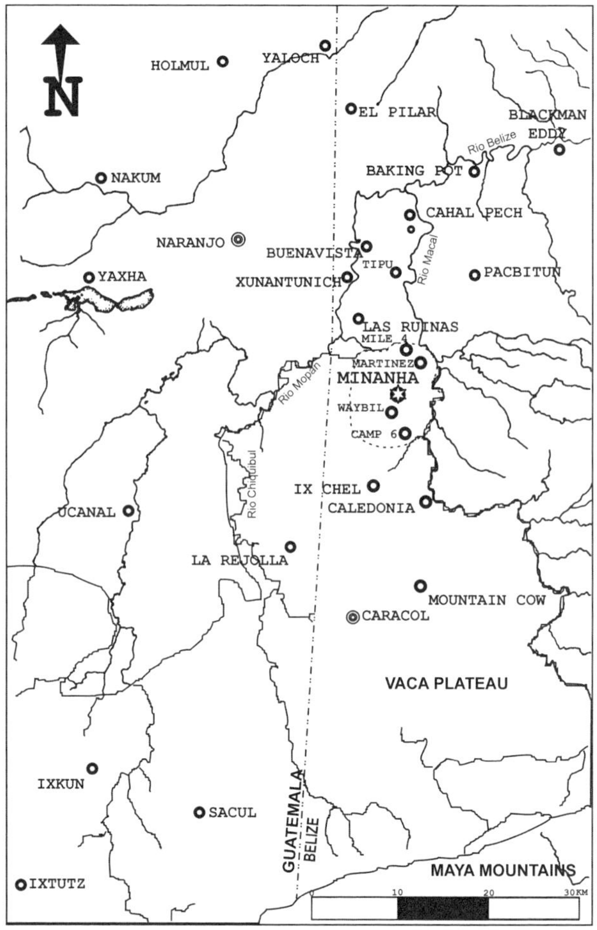

Figure 11.4. Map showing the location of Minanha, its projected polity, and other key centers in, or adjacent to, the Vaca Plateau.

Minanha

The second case study we discuss in this chapter derives from Minanha, located in the north Vaca Plateau of west central Belize (Figure 11.1). Minanha represents an archetypal hinterland community, and is a classic example of an "internal frontier," given its location on both an ecological and cultural "edge"; it lies immediately to the south of the Belize Valley, west of the Mountain Pine Ridge, and equidistant between the heartlands of the powerful, and competing, Naranjo and Caracol polities (Figure 11.4; Iannone 2005, 2010). In terms of resilience modelling, Minanha's location would have enhanced the ability of its inhabitants to respond to perturbations, because they would have had access to diverse natural and cultural resources.

The north Vaca Plateau is characterized by rugged, karstic topography, small valleys, limited surface water, and dispersed pockets of good soil. Although pioneer populations appear to have entered the sub-region earlier, significant occupation of Minanha proper does not appear to have taken place until sometime in the first century B.C.E. (Iannone 2005), during a time thought to be characterized by a modest drought, according to the sequence obtained from a speleothem from the nearby Macal Chasm cave (Moyes et al. 2009; Webster et al. 2007). These early settlements are found scattered across the Minanha micro-region, in or adjacent to small valleys with good soils and perennial water sources, such as springs (Longstaffe and Iannone 2011; Macrae and Iannone 2011; McCane et al. 2010). This seems to fit Van Andel and Runnels' (1995) concept of "saltation," wherein migrant farmers initially populate small alluvial valleys with fertile soils, carry out low-intensity agricultural production for some time, and then move on to exploit similar valleys, leaving vacant intervening areas of limited productively (see also Earle et al. 2011:209).

Over the course of the next six and a half centuries the Minanha community continued to grow in size and extent, albeit slowly, and the earliest courtyard groups tethered themselves more firmly to the landscape through the construction of eastern ancestor shrines and by building terraced agricultural fields, the latter helping to retain soils and soil moisture in the rugged terrain of the Vaca Plateau (Macrae and Iannone 2011). Alongside this program of niche construction, they did, however, maintain a level of biodiversity and productive flexibility because these improved fields only encompassed areas immediately adjacent to their residential courtyards, while the remaining land continued to be "unimproved" (Macrae and Iannone 2011; McCane et al. 2010). Indications are that this small, highly dispersed community was connected to the broader Maya world economically, as is implied by the sharing of ceramic styles and access to raw materials such as shell and jadeite. However, the absence of certain artifacts commonly found at other centers to the north and south (e.g., Pacbitun and Caracol, respectively), such as Charlie Chaplin figures (Lomitola 2012), and Caracol-style face pots (D. Chase and A. Chase 1998), suggests that Minanha continued to be a "deep rural" community that was only loosely incorporated into broader political formations and cultural traditions. On one hand, this would have allowed for some economic and political autonomy, as well as some flexibility to respond to perturbations rapidly, using local knowledge and innovations. For example, the early development of Minanha's terrace system would have helped the community maintain productivity during times of declining precipitation, such as the droughts documented for C.E. 141, and the period between C.E. 490 and 580 (Webster et al. 2007). At the same time, the loose integration would have also hindered access to heartland innovations, and it apparently limited the ability to acquire certain key commodities, such as larger obsidian blades (Menzies 2003), leading to some potential vulnerabilities.

The nature of integration changed dramatically sometime around the beginning of the 8th century C.E., during an era of significant political change across the Maya Lowlands. At this time some elite migrants, likely from Caracol, established a petty royal court in what would rapidly emerge as the new Minanha epicenter (Iannone 2005; Figure 11.5).

The evidence does not support the notion that Minanha shifted from being a hinterland to a new, independent heartland, as in the African examples discussed by Kopytoff (1987, 1999). Rather, Minanha's rapid growth and adherence to certain cultural practices suggest the formation of a new client-kingdom under the auspices of the larger Caracol hegemonic polity, albeit one with comparative autonomy, given its distance from the Caracol metropole (Iannone 2009). This may fit the scenario described by Gil Stein (1999) wherein empires or hegemonic polities foster "internal migrations" to encourage state initiatives; although migrants from the heartlands may not necessarily control land in the hinterlands, they can focus on pacification and military development, support craft specialization and trade, and initiate engineering programs aimed at increasing agricultural production (see also Earle et al. 2011:213).

In light of these ideas, it is significant that the new political body that established itself at Minanha seems to have effectively inserted itself as a new "patron" by incorporating existing courtyards into new construction projects (Longstaffe and Iannone 2011), encasing extant ritual nodes within new shrine structures, and aligning new ritual offerings with those previously made by the local community (Schwake and Iannone 2010). The success of this assimilation project varied, with some of the largest, and longest-standing residential courtyard groups apparently benefiting from, and therefore supporting, the new patrons, whereas other sizable, and equally deep-rooted, courtyard groups seem to have entered into a period of decline, which implies that they contested the authority of the newcomers (Iannone 2010; Longstaffe and Iannone 2011; Macrae and Iannone 2011). That the resulting Minanha polity was syncretic in character is confirmed by a degree of adherence to certain Caracol-style caching and burial practices at the same time that more local traditions were continued, such as the extensive use of slate as capstones in buildings and grave chambers, and as burial and cache offerings (Iannone 2005, 2010).

Regardless of the apparent unevenness with which they were accepted by Minanha's traditional power-brokers, the migrant elites that arrived at the beginning of the 8th Century C.E. were able to marshal enough corvée labor to construct an impressive court complex, and to quickly expand the agricultural productivity of the micro-region by linking the previously separate terraced fields with longer, but poorer quality terrace sections (Macrae and Iannone 2011; McCane et al. 2010). They also commissioned the construction of a wall around a sizable bajo to create a larger and more reliable source of water (Primrose 2003). These innovations, likely borrowed from the more densely settled Caracol heartland settlement (e.g., A. Chase and D. Chase 1998), allowed for significant population growth, facilitated monumental construction, and for a brief moment transformed Minanha from a hinterland to a small heartland, as is one of the expectations of Kopytoff's cyclical model for hinterland development.

Nevertheless, it is important to consider that many of the initiatives of this time would have been aimed at providing taxes to support the new Minanha rulers, and tribute for their Caracol overlords, which would have drawn increasingly more resources away from the primary producers over time. These investments also locked the fledgling Minanha polity into reliance on an increasingly integrated, artificial environment. This new polity exhibited less biodiversity and

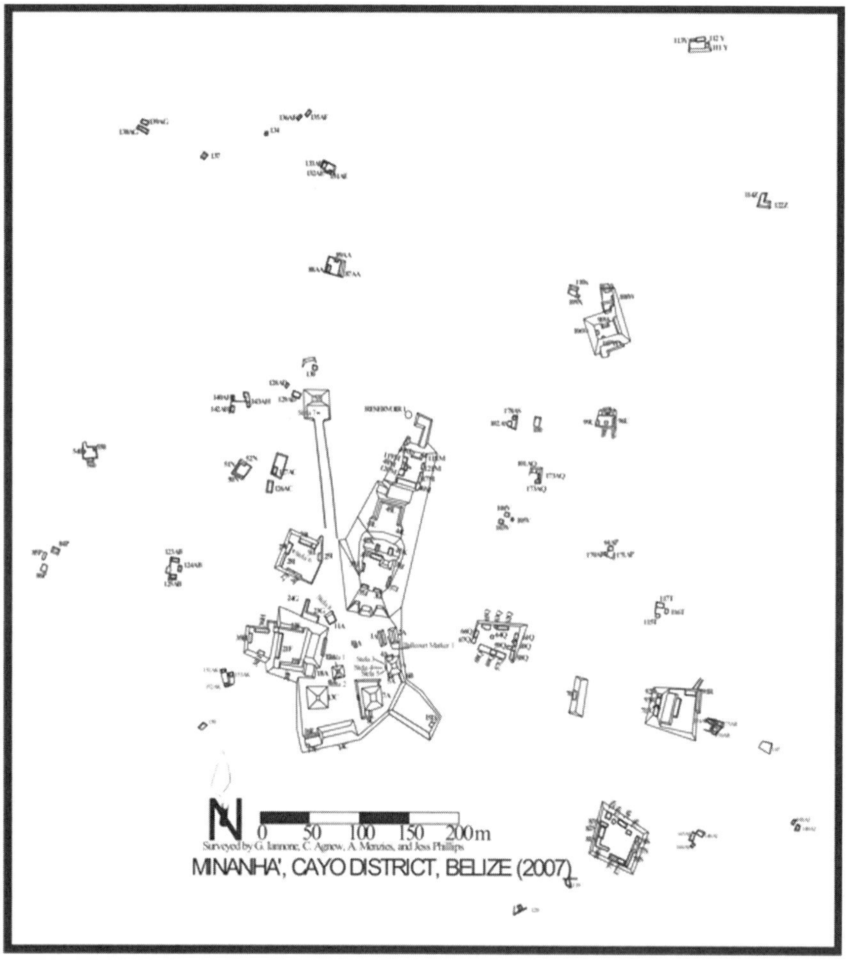

Figure 11.5. Rectified isometric plan of the Minanha epicenteral court complex.

did not benefit from some of the support services present at Caracol (A. Chase and D. Chase 2007), such as extensive road and market systems (there is only one intrasite causeway, and as yet, no well-defined market zone at Minanha), a significant level of craft specialization (with the exception of the production of granite tools; Longstaffe 2011), and a far-reaching, efficient trade network. Thus, even though it was expanding in size and complexity, the Minanha polity likely entered a risk spiral and began to exhibit the effects of path dependency, meaning it was increasingly "locked-in" to a specific developmental trajectory that left fewer options to respond to perturbations. This would have led to ever-increasing levels of vulnerability to unexpected environmental or cultural distresses.

Although the Minanha community was more firmly interconnected with the wider Maya world during the 8th century, this did not translate into significant enhancements to its economic resilience, above and beyond the innovations associated with its water management and agricultural systems. For example, an evaluation of the average width of a sample of obsidian blades concluded that Minanha was the "end of the line" for that particular commodity (Menzies 2003). In other ways, greater integration also led to a certain degree of vulnerability to broader political machinations. For example, a major destruction event occurred in the mid-to-late 8th century, resulting in: (1) the razing and burning of the royal residential courtyard and the emptying of a number of caches and burials, likely in conjunction with the rapid departure of the Minanha ruling family; (2) the sealing off of the epicenter's principal multiple entry tomb beneath a new shrine structure fronted by a slate stela and two uncarved limestone monuments; and (3) the construction of a new royal residential courtyard with a bi-level throne, possibly indicating a form of patron-client style, joint rule (Iannone 2010; Longstaffe and Iannone 2011; Schwake and Iannone 2010).

This new political regime would apparently not last long. Sometime in the early 9th century Minanha's royal residential courtyard was buried beneath 5 meters of rubble, many of its stucco friezes and important stelae were destroyed, and some elite building projects were left abandoned prior to completion (Iannone 2005, 2010; Schwake and Iannone 2010). The elites of the "new political regime" apparently deserted the community, or were forced out, along with a large segment of the support population, primarily the lowest status commoners who may not have had any direct control over key land and water resources (Macrae and Iannone 2011). From the perspective of resilience theory, this scenario fits well with that documented for the American Southwest, where emigration during periods of sociopolitical downturns has been envisioned as a form of adaptive transformation (Hegmon et al. 2008; Nelson et al. 2006). It is likely that a combination of unsustainable growth, overexploitation of resources, droughts, increasing political and economic competition, ideological disillusionment, and the progressively greater interconnectedness of the various elites across the Maya Lowlands, contributed to the downfall. However, this was not the end of the Minanha community. After the demise of the Minanha royal court, the traditional powerbrokers began building anew in their courtyards, once again taking advantage of their control over improved land, perennial water sources, and limited incorporation into the polities that were crumbling around them (Longstaffe and Iannone 2011; Macrae and Iannone 2011). These long-standing, highly resilient residential groups left a footprint not that dissimilar to their Preclassic and Early Classic ancestors (Longstaffe and Iannone 2011).

In summary, the Minanha case study documents the resilient and adaptive quality of some of the larger rural courtyard groups whose roots extend back to the earliest occupation of the micro-region. By improving some of their land through terrace construction and settling near perennial springs, these pioneers—and generations of their descendants—were able to live successfully for a millennium in an environment that is only sparsely populated today. In part, it was the lack of integration into the broader Maya world—and the short-lived Minanha polity—that may have contributed to their success. In contrast, the petty Minanha royal court that emerged in the 8th century was not only more firmly ensconced within the broader network of regional politics, but also reliant on an increasingly more tightly integrated, but also hypercoherent, economic and political system encompassing the micro-region over which it ruled. This is particularly evident in terms of the expansion and control of the surrounding agriculture and water management features. Ultimately, the elite segment of Minanha society proved to be far less resilient, with this experiment in political complexity only lasting for a century (Longstaffe and Iannone 2011). A significant portion of the support population, especially recent immigrants drawn into the micro-region because of the "full-service" nature of the Minanha royal court, ultimately demonstrated a comparable level of vulnerability to perturbations, primarily because they did not control vital resources, such as good agricultural land and reliable water sources (Macrae and Iannone 2011).

Santa Rita Corozal

Our third case study focuses on Santa Rita Corozal, located between the Rio Hondo and the New River in northern Belize, adjacent to Corozal Bay (Figure 11.6). Ancient occupation is present both on the shores of the bay (some low mounds are actually visible under the waters of the bay) and on an inland bluff. The site was well placed relative to both riverine and maritime trade. It was an ecologically advantaged hinterland that was well connected with both inland and maritime neighbors. This access was key throughout its development.

Santa Rita Corozal has been investigated for over a century, first by a local medical doctor (Gann 1900, 1918), subsequently by a series of regional archaeological projects (Green 1973; Pring 1976; Sidrys 1976, 1983), and most recently by the Corozal Postclassic Project (Chase 1981, 1982, 1990; D. Chase and A. Chase 1988, 2004a). While the site is best known for its Postclassic period (post-C.E. 1000) remains and was likely the capital of the Postclassic period province of Chetumal (D. Chase and A. Chase 1988), Santa Rita Corozal (Figure 11.7) was successfully and continuously occupied for the entire span of ancient Maya civilization—and is still occupied today. In contrast to many Maya sites, its population peak was during the Late Postclassic period. Located at a distance from the Classic period (C.E. 250–900) capitals of Tikal, Calakmul, and Caracol—as well as the Late Postclassic period (C.E. 1250–1450) capital of Mayapan—Santa Rita Corozal also maintained greater political and economic autonomy than most centers, in spite of its advantageous location. Thus, it served variously as an innovation receptor, creator, and modifier.

The first sound evidence of occupation of Santa Rita Corozal dates to the Early to Middle Preclassic period (ca. 1200 B.C.E.). Investigations indicate a well-established and precocious regional northern Belize Swasey Ceramic Sphere affiliation for a relatively small village of perhaps 150 inhabitants with population concentrated in the bluff area above the bay. By the Late Preclassic period (300 B.C.E. to C.E. 200), population and settlement had expanded to at least 1000 inhabitants. Sierra Red ceramics from funerary contexts suggest a broad, connected lowland Maya focus during this time. Toward the end of the Late Preclassic (C.E. 1 to

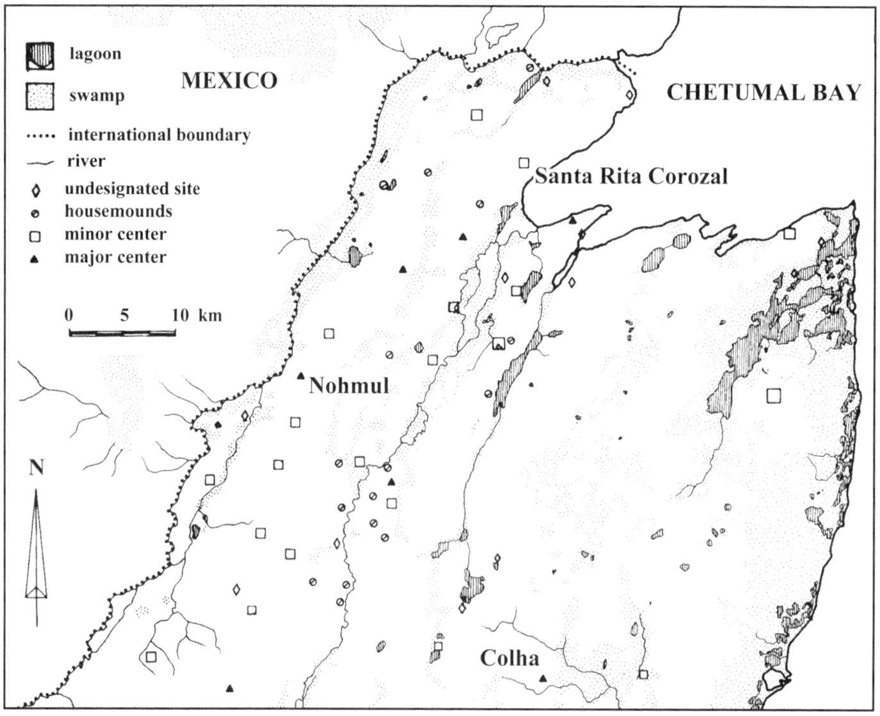

Figure 11.6. Map showing the location of Santa Rita Corozal and other centers in northern Belize (after Hammond 1975:figure 11.1).

250) and Early Classic periods (C.E. 250 to 550) population also grew in size. Evidence of prosperity and status differentiation in interments and constructions is evident, with ceramic and other artifactual ties extending to both the southern and northern Lowlands. The site was a receptor of innovations and trade items, but its connectedness was expressed within its own sociopolitical framework.

While the early population of the central portion of the site was never large, numbering no more than perhaps 1500 people, interments from Santa Rita Corozal Structure 7 suggest that the rulers of this site maintained a high standard of material well-being (D. Chase and A. Chase 2005). In fact, if taken out of context, grave goods within these interments might be taken to suggest that Santa Rita Corozal individuals were far more important politically within the overarching Maya realm than was likely the case (D. Chase and A. Chase 2004a). Late Classic period (C.E. 550–900) population likely increased to approximately 2500. Interestingly, material well-being, as indicated by the presence and similarity of burial offerings, was more widely distributed than in previous periods, and the extreme status distinctions of the Early Classic period were not in evidence, a situation similar to that found in the varied environmental and socio-political situation of the distant Belize Late Classic period capital city of Caracol (D. Chase and A. Chase 2004b). Terminal Classic period and Early Postclassic period (C.E. 900–1200, 1200–1300) remains are present at the site, suggesting continued access to external trade, but likely with flat population numbers.

However, the largest and most extensive occupation at Santa Rita Corozal dates to the Late Postclassic period (C.E. 1300–1550), well after the collapse of inland, mainstream, Classic period centers. The Postclassic period Maya of Santa Rita Corozal substantially reframed Classic period traditions. In particular, ritual caching practices appear to have served to unify the community through calendric ritual (D. Chase and A. Chase 2008). While Santa Rita Corozal prospered during its entire history, it was particularly advantaged following the Classic period collapse, perhaps being able to take even greater advantage of its location on a major trade corridor (see also Scarborough and Valdez, Ch. 9 this volume for a discussion of trade). Postclassic Santa Rita Corozal evinced particularly strong ties with the northern lowlands; both ritual practices and material remains (in some cases) are nearly identical to those delineated for Mayapan, some 300 kilometers to the north (D. Chase and A. Chase 2008). Site population more than tripled; a conservative estimate of the site center population in the Late Postclassic is over 7,000 people. The site prospered until the advent of Spanish conquistadors in C.E. 1532. Later Colonial occupation by the British indicated some limited population continuity with the modern town of Corozal.

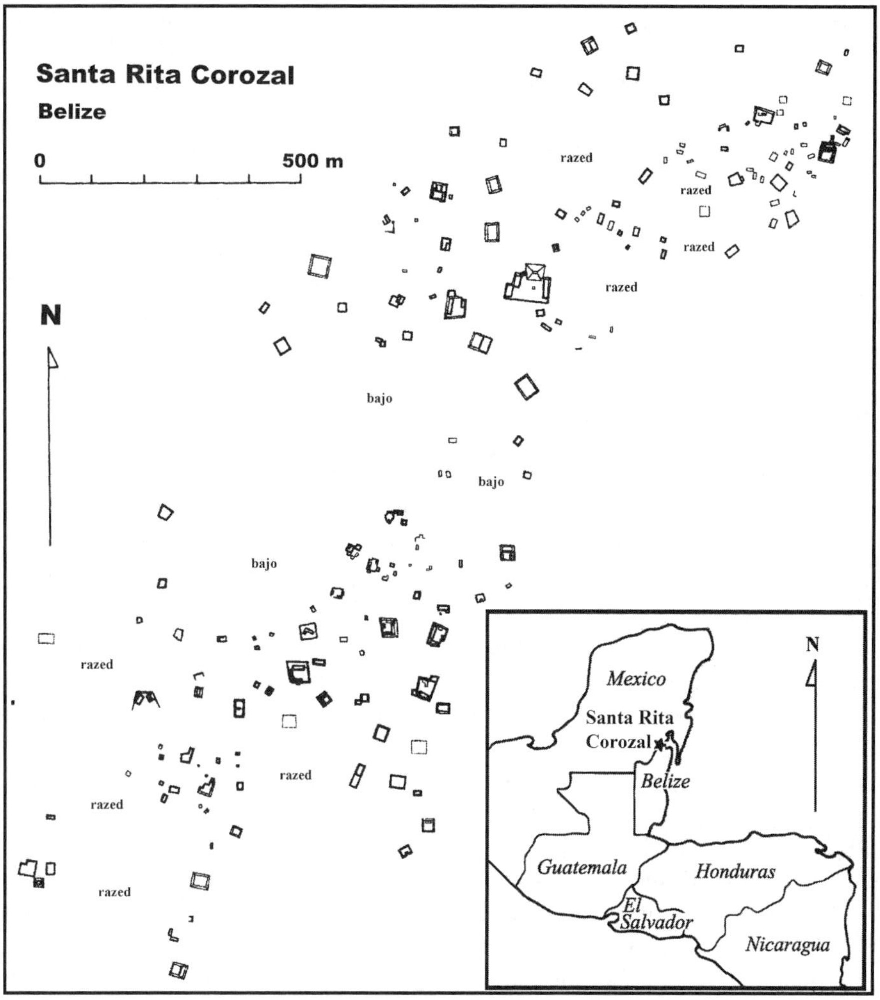

Figure 11.7. Rectified plan of Santa Rita Corozal, Belize showing its location in Belize.

Unlike many southern lowland sites, Santa Rita Corozal was continuously occupied for over three millennia. The site does not appear to have been under direct control of either southern or northern lowland polities, but rather maintained a connection to both. During much of its history, the site appears to have been peripheral to political machinations recorded in hieroglyphic texts. Preclassic and Classic period Santa Rita Corozal remained a small, seemingly independent hinterland polity. Economic ties were extensive, but political integration with neighboring areas was limited—so much so that its Early Classic leaders amassed a vast array of symbols to stress their importance at the "edge" of the Maya world. Ultimately, the site came to serve as the capital of the Postclassic province of Chetumal (D. Chase and A. Chase 1988). The peripheral, yet pivotal, location of Santa Rita Corozal at the juxtaposition of the northern and southern lowlands—with easy access to multiple trade routes—enabled this resilience, but other mechanisms supported its longevity. For example, while settlement was more densely concentrated than at many Classic period sites, Santa Rita Corozal's population remained manageable throughout its history—and was easily supported by surrounding agriculture land, a diversity of locally available marine resources, and the resources made available by its position as a transit point for regional trade. Postclassic period cultural adaptations, specifically ritual caching practices, evolved to focus on greater integration of the community as population numbers increased. Postclassic period Santa Rita Corozal—rather than being a site characterized by depopulation, decadence, or decline—was itself a successful dynamic and innovative adaptation. Thus, Santa Rita Corozal's exceptional location, in conjunction with its smaller size and politically peripheral positioning, led to a more nimble and resilient settlement.

Conclusions

While each of these sites was situated in a hinterland location, their physical placements and cultural adaptations varied substantially, being alternatively inland (Uxbenká and Minanha) or riverine and coastal (Santa Rita Corozal). Their "hinterland" position also differed. Uxbenká's placement in southern Belize partially isolated it from the southern lowland heartland, though it was well integrated in regional and pan-Mesoamerican economies for more than five centuries (Nazaroff et al. 2010). Uxbenká was located in an area of unusual agricultural fertility, lending to it a degree of resilience through reduced agricultural fallow periods and obviating the need for large-scale intensification, such as the terracing found a Minanha. Santa Rita Corozal was positioned at the juxtaposition of the northern and southern Maya Lowlands. Its access to fresh water and marine resources may have afforded it a degree of resilience to food shortages and agricultural uncertainties. Over time, Minanha became increasingly dependent on innovative agricultural and water management systems to sustain its population, which increased integration but reduced biodiversity and led to path dependency.

Both Uxbenká and Santa Rita Corozal have little or no evidence of being under the control of other, larger, polities for any extended period, though both were deeply integrated into regional geopolitical structures. Minanha started as an independent – albeit small and deeply rural community – but as it grew in size and complexity it eventually fell under the sway of its larger neighbor, Caracol. Located intermediate to the Belize Valley, Naranjo, and Caracaol, Minanha was marginalized to some degree by being set at the eastern edge of the southern Lowlands against the largely un-farmable and uninhabitable terrain in the Mountain Pine Ridge. Both Minanha and Uxbenká were always hinterland polities, while Santa Rita Corozal's hinterland status changed dramatically following the collapse of most southern Lowland polities when it became the capital of the province of Chetumal. Minanha was never really well connected economically (it was the end of the line for trade, and did not exhibit much craft specialization). Uxbenká and Santa Rita Corozal were both situated to take advantage of important trade routes. Uxbenká took full advantage of its location between the Caribbean Sea and the central Petén, and engaged in and mediated trade in obsidian blades and exotic ground stone from distant sources. Similarly, Santa Rita Corozal actively engaged in broad economic networks, though it uniquely allowed the fruits of these relationships to be spread broadly across its populace.

Besides differing in terms of strategic locations, the archaeological histories of these three sites also are varied. Uxbenká and Santa Rita Corozal were each home to Preclassic village occupations and were the largest sites in their zones for at least portions of their histories; Minanha never approached the size of the neighboring site of Caracol, but grew to be as least as large as the Belize Valley sites found to its north. Each site sustained a large and well-established Classic period population; however, only Santa Rita Corozal grew to prominence in the Late Postclassic period. Uxbenká and Minanha utilized stone monuments; Santa Rita did not.

The case studies presented here demonstrate the regional and temporal diversity that existed in ancient Maya adaptations in the southern lowlands—even amongst sites that may, in some way, be considered "hinterland." Despite each of these polities being part of the greater southern Maya Lowlands, each displays unique combinations of subsistence, economic, and political strategies. In each case, decision-making was geared to maximize adaption to local ecological conditions and to maintain resilience to demographic, environmental, and geopolitical stresses. In each case the consequences of these actions, intended or otherwise, resulted in periods of growth and periods of decline. None of these hinterlands was immune to events occurring in the broad social and economic networks in which they participated. Nor were they exempt from the impacts of changing ecological and climate systems. Uxbenká, Minanha, and Santa Rita Corozal were each nodes in overlapping and interacting economic and sociopolitical networks, and they both impacted, and were effected by, other nodes in the network. By the 9th century C.E. all three of these hinterland polities were deeply impacted by the political and economic disintegration sweeping across the Maya Lowlands (Kennett and Beach in press). At Uxbenká and Minanha this resulted in the abandonment of political institutions, collapse of agricultural systems, and population dispersal. Santa Rita Corozal was able to weather the collapse, albeit initially in a diminished capacity, rising again during the Late Postclassic as an important node in the then dominant economic and political landscape of the northern Lowlands.

Acknowledgments

The authors would like to thank the Institute of Archaeology in Belize, and in particular Jaime Awe and John Morris, for both facilitating and collaborating on our long-term research programs. We also extend our gratitude to the National Science Foundation (Chase, Prufer) and the Alphawood Foundation (Iannone, Prufer) for funding some of the key components of the Santa Rita Corozal, Uxbenká, and Minanha research. Iannone also wishes to thank the Social Sciences and Humanities research Council of Canada, and Trent University, for their ongoing support of the Minanha investigations.

References Cited

Anderies, John M.
2006 Robustness, Institutions, and Large-Scale Change in Socio-ecological Systems: The Hohokam of the Phoenix Basin. Journal of Institutional Economics 2(2):135–155.

Aquino, Valorie V., Keith M. Prufer, Clayton Meredith, Brendan J. Culleton, and Douglas J. Kennett
2013 Constraining the Age of Abandonment of Uxbenká Site Core Using Archaeological Stratigraphy and AMS 14C Dates. Research Reports in Belizean Archaeology 10: 269–279.

Bedford, Peter R.
2009 The Neo-Assyrian Empire. *In* The Dynamics of Ancient Empires. Ian Morris and Walter Scheidel, eds. Pp. 30–65. New York: Oxford University Press.

Browman, David L.
1997 Political Institutional Factors Contributing to the Interpretation of the Tiwanaku State. *In* Emergence and Change in Early Urban Societies. Linda Manzanilla, ed. Pp. 229–243. New York: Plenum Press.

Chase, Arlen F., and Diane Z. Chase
1998 Scale and Intensity in Classic Period Maya Agriculture: Terracing and Settlement at the "Garden City" of Caracol, Belize. Culture and Agriculture 29(2):60–77.
2007 Ancient Maya Urban Development: Insights from the Archaeology of Caracol, Belize. Journal of Belizean Studies 29(2):60–71.

Chase, Diane Z.
1981 The Maya Postclassic at Santa Rita Corozal. Archaeology 34(1): 25–33.
1982 Spatial and Temporal Variability in Postclassic Northern Belize. Ph.D. thesis, Department of Anthropology, University of Pennsylvania.
1990 The Invisible Maya: Population History and Archaeology at Santa Rita Corozal. *In* Prehistoric Population History in the Maya Lowlands. T. P. Culbert and D. S. Rice, eds. Pp. 199–213. Albuquerque: University of New Mexico Press.

Chase, Diane Z., and Arlen F. Chase
1988 A Postclassic Perspective: Excavations at the Maya Site of Santa Rita Corozal, Belize. Pre-Columbian Art Research Institute Monograph 4, San Francisco: Pre-Columbian Art Research Institute.
1998 The Architectural Context of Caches, Burials, and Other Ritual Activities for the Classic Period Maya (as Reflected at Caracol, Belize). *In* Function and Meaning in Classic Maya Architecture. Stephen D. Houston, ed. Pp. 299–332. Washington, DC: Dumbarton Oaks.
2004a Santa Rita Corozal: Twenty Years Later. Research Reports in Belizean Archaeology 1:243–255.
2004b Archaeological Perspectives on Classic Maya Social Organization from Caracol, Belize. Ancient Mesoamerica 15:111–119.
2005 The Early Classic Period at Santa Rita Corozal: Issues of Hierarchy, Heterarchy, and Stratification in Northern Belize. Research Reports in Belizean Archaeology 2:111–129.
2008 Late Postclassic Ritual at Santa Rita Corozal, Belize: Understanding the Archaeology of a Maya Capital City. Research Reports in Belizean Archaeology 5:79–92.

Culleton, Brendan
2012 Human Ecology, Agricultural Intensification and Landscape Transformation at the Ancient Maya Polity of Uxbenka, Southern Belize. Ph.D. dissertation, Department of Anthropology, University of Oregon.

Culleton, Brendan, Keith M. Prufer, and Douglas J. Kennett
2012 A Bayesian AMS 14C Chronology of the Classic Maya Urban Center of Uxbenká, Belize. Journal of Archaeological Science 39: 1572–1586.

Cumming, Graeme S.
2011 Spatial Resilience in Social-Ecological Systems. New York: Springer.

Earle, Timothy, Clive Gamble, and Hendrik Poinar
2011 Migration. *In* Deep History: The Architecture of Past and Present. Andrew Shryock and Daniel Lord Smail, eds. Pp. 191–218. Los Angeles: University of California Press.

Fauvelle, Mikael, Chelsea R. Fisher, and Geoffrey E. Braswell
2013 Return to the Kingdom of the Eagle: Archaeological Investigations at Nim Li Punit, Belize.

Research Reports in Belizean Archaeology 10:23–21.

Gann, Thomas
1900 Mounds in Northern Honduras. Nineteenth Annual Report, 1897–1898. Bureau of American Ethnology, Part 2. Pp. 661–692. Washington, DC: Smithsonian Institution.
1918 The Maya Indians of Southern Yucatan and Northern British Honduras. Bureau of American Ethnology Bulletin, 64. Washington, DC: Smithsonian Institution.

Green, Ernestine
1973 Location Analysis of Prehistoric Maya Sites in Northern British Honduras. American Antiquity 38(3):279–293.

Gunderson, Lance H., and C. S. Holling, eds.
2002 Panarchy: Understanding Transformations in Human and Natural Systems. Washington, DC: Island Press.

Hammond, Norman
1975 Introduction. *In* N. Hammond, Ed., Archaeology in Northern Belize: British Museum –Cambridge University Corozal Project: 1974–75 Interim Report. N. Hammond, ed. Pp. 6–14. University of Cambridge: Centre of Latin America Studies.

Hassig, Ross
1992 War and Society in Ancient Mesoamerica. Los Angeles: University of California Press.

Hegmon, Michelle, Matthew A. Peeples, Ann P. Kinzig, Stephanie Kulow, Cathryn M. Meegan, and Margaret C. Nelson
2008 Social Transformation and Its Human Costs in the Prehispanic U.S. Southwest. American Anthropologist 110(3):313–324.

Hartshorn, G. S., L. Nicolait, L.Hartshorn, G. Bevier, R. Brightman, J. Cal, A. Cawich, W. Davidson, R. Dubois, C. Dyer, J. Gibson, W. Hawley, J. Leonard, R. Nicolait, D. Weyer, H. White, and C. Wright
1984 Belize Country Environmental Profile: A Field Study. USAID Contract No. 505–0000-C-00-3001–00. San José, Costa Rica: Trejos Hermanos Sucesores, S.A.

Holling, Craford S.
2001 Understanding the Complexity of Economic, Ecological, and Social Systems. Ecosystems 4: 390–405.

Holling, Craford S., and Lance H. Gunderson
2002 Resilience and Adaptive Cycles. *In* Panarchy: Understanding Transformations in Human and Natural Systems. L. H. Gunderson and C. S. Holling, eds. Pp.25–62. Washington, DC: Island Press.

Iannone, Gyles
2005 The Rise and Fall of an Ancient Maya Petty Royal Court. Latin American Antiquity 16:26–44.
2009 The Jungle Kings of Minanha: Constellations of Authority and the Ancient Maya Socio-Political Landscape. Research Reports in Belizean Archaeology 6:33–41.
2010 Collective Memory in the Frontiers: A Case Study from the Ancient Maya Center of Minanha, Belize. Ancient Mesoamerica 21(2):353–371.

Kennett, Douglas J., and Tim Beach
In press Archaeological and Environmental Lessons for the Anthropocene from the Classic Maya Collapse. Anthropocene.

Kennett, Douglas J., Sebastian F. M. Breitenbach, Valorie V. Aquino, Yemane Asmerom, Jaime Awe, James U. L. Baldini, Patrick Bartlein, Brendan J. Culleton, Claire Ebert, Christopher Jazwa, Martha J. Macri, Norbert Marwan, Victor Polyak, Keith M. Prufer, Harriet E. Ridley, Harald Sodemann, Bruce Winterhalder, and Gerald H. Haug
2012 Development and Disintegration of Maya Political Systems in Response to Climate Change. Science 338:788–791.

Kopytoff, Igor
1987 The African Frontier: The Reproduction of Traditional African Societies. Bloomington: Indiana University Press.
1999 The Internal African Frontier: Cultural Conservatism and Ethnic Innovation. *In* Frontiers and Borderlands: Anthropological Perspectives. M. Rösler and T. Wendl, eds. Pp. 31–44. New York: Peter Lang.

LeCount, Lisa J., and Jason Yaeger
2010 Provincial Politics and Current Models of the Lowland Maya State. *In* Classic Maya Provincial Politics: Xunantunich and its Hinterlands. L. J. LeCount and J. Yaeger, eds. Pp. 20–45. Tucson: University of Arizona Press.

Lightfoot, Kent G., and Antionette Martinez
1995 Frontiers and Boundaries in Archaeological Perspective. Annual Reviews in Anthropology 24:471–492.

Lomitola, Lisa
2012 Ritual Use of the Human Form: A Contextual Analysis of "Charlie Chaplin" Figures in the Maya Lowlands. M.A. thesis, Department of Anthropology, University of Central Florida.

Longstaffe, Matthew Stephen
2011 Ancient Maya Site Core Settlement at Minanha, Belize: Development, Integration, and Community Dynamics. M.A. thesis, Department of Anthropology, Trent University.

Longstaffe, Matthew, and Gyles Iannone
2011 Households and Social Trajectories: The Site Core Community at Minanha, Belize. Research Reports in Belizean Archaeology 8:45–59.

Macrae, Scott, and Gyles Iannone
2011 Investigations of the Agricultural Terracing Surrounding the Ancient Maya Center of Minanha, Belize. Research Reports in Belizean Archaeology 8:183–197.

Malpass, Michael A., and Sonia Alconini
2010 Distant Provinces in the Inka Empire: Toward a Deeper Understanding of Inka Imperialism. Iowa City: University of Iowa Press.

McCane, Carmen A., Scott A. Macrae, and Gyles Iannone
2010 A Consideration of the Spatial Arrangement of Settlement Groups and Terraces in Contreras, Minanha, Belize. Research Reports in Belizean Archaeology 7:141–152.

Menzies, Adam C.
2003 A Technological Analysis of the Obsidian Assemblage from Minanha, Cayo District, Belize. M.A. thesis, Department of Anthropology, Trent University.

Moyes, Holley, Jaime J. Awe, George A. Brook, and James W. Webster
2009 The Ancient Maya Drought Cult: Late Classic Cave Use in Belize. Latin American Antiquity 20:175–206.

Moyes, Holley, and Keith M. Prufer
2013 The Geopolitics of Emerging Maya Rulers: A Case Study of Kayuko Naj Tunich, a Foundational Shrine at Uxbenká, Southern Belize. Journal of Anthropological Research 62(2):225–248.

Nazaroff, Adam J., Keith M. Prufer, and Brandon L. Drake
2010 Assessing the Applicability of Portable X-ray Fluorescence Spectrometry for Obsidian Provenance Research in the Maya Lowlands. Journal of Archaeological Science 37:885–895.

Nelson, Margaret C., Michelle Hegmon, Stephanie Kulow, and Karen Gust Schollmeyer
2006 Archaeological and Ecological Perspectives on Reorganization: A Case Study from the Mimbres Region of the U.S. Southwest. American Antiquity 71:403–432

Primrose, Ryan J.
2003 The Ancient Maya Water Management System at Minanha, West Central, Belize. M.A. thesis, Department of Anthropology, Trent University.

Pring, Duncan
1976 Outline of the Northern Belize Ceramic Sequence. Ceramica de Cultura Maya 9:11–42.

Prufer, Keith M., Holley Moyes, Brendan J. Culleton, Andrew Kindon, and Douglas Kennett
2011 Uxbenká: The Development of a Complex Polity in the Eastern Periphery of the Maya Lowlands, Latin American Antiquity 22(2): 199–223.

Schortman, Edward E.
1989 Interregional Interaction in Prehistory: The Need for a New Perspective. American Antiquity 54(1): 52–65.

Schortman, Edward E., and Patricia Urban
1994 Living on the Edge: Core/Periphery Relations in Ancient Southeastern Mesoamerica. Current Anthropology 35(4):401–430.

Schwake, Sonja, and Gyles Iannone
2010 Ritual Remains and Social Memory: Maya Examples from West Central Belize. Ancient Mesoamerica 21(2):331–339.

Sidrys, Raymond
1976 Mesoamerica: An Archaeological Analysis if a

Low-energy Civilization. Ph.D. dissertation, Department of Anthropology, University of California at Los Angeles.
1983 Archeological Investigations in Northern Belize, Central America. Institute of Archaeology Monograph 17. Los Angeles: University of California at Los Angeles.

Stein, Gil
1999 Rethinking World-Systems: Diasporas, Colonies, and Interaction in Uruk, Mesopotamia. Tucson: University of Arizona Press.

Thompson, Amy, and Keith M. Prufer
2013 Shifting Dynamics in the use of Space at Uxbenká. Research Reports in Belizean Archaeology 10: 255–270

Turner, Nancy J., Iain J. Davidson-Hunt, and Michael O'Flaherty
2003 Living on the Edge: Ecological and Cultural Edges as Sources of Diversity for Social–Ecological Resilience. Human Ecology 31(3): 439–461.

Van Andel, T. H., and N. C. Runnels
1995 The Earliest Farmers in Europe. Antiquity 69:481–500.

van der Leeuw, Sander
2005 Climate, Hydrology, Land Use, and Environmental Degradation in the Lower Rhone Valley during the Roman Period. C. R. Geoscience 337(1–2):9–27.
2007 Information Processing and Its Role in the Rise of the European World System. *In* Sustainability or Collapse? An Intergrated History and Future of People on Earth. R. Costanza, L. J. Graumlich, and W. Steffan, eds. Pp. 213–241. Cambridge: MIT Press.

Walker, Brian, and David Salt
2006 Resilience Thinking: Sustaining Ecosystems and People in a Changing World. Washington, DC: Island Press.
2012 Resilience Practice: Building Capacity to Absorb Disturbance and Maintain Function. London: Island Press.

Walsh, Megan, Keith M. Prufer, Brendan J. Culleton, and Douglas J. Kennett
In press A Late Holocene Paleoenvironmental Reconstruction from Agua Caliente, Southern Belize, Linked to Regional Climate Variability and Cultural Change at the Maya Polity of Uxbenká. Quaternary Research.

Webster, James William, George A. Brook, L. Bruce Railsback, Hai Cheng, R. Lawrence Edwards, Clark Alexander, and Philip P. Reeder
2007 Stalagmite Evidence from Belize Indicating Significant Droughts at the Time of the Preclassic Abandonment, the Maya Hiatus, and the Classic Maya Collapse. Paleogeography, Paleoclimatology, and Paleoecology 250:1–17.

Wells, E. Christian
2006 Recent Trends in Theorizing Prehispanic Mesoamerican Economies. Journal of Archaeological Research 14:265–312.

Wells, Peter
2013 Rome Beyond Frontiers: Imports, Attitudes and Practices, Journal of Roman Archaeology Supplementary Series, 94.

Wright, A. C. S., D. H. Romney, R. H. Arbuckle, and V. E. Vial
1959 Land Use in British Honduras. Colonial Research Publications, 24. London: Her Majesty's Stationary Office.

12

Transformative Relocation in the U.S. Southwest and Mesoamerica

Ben A. Nelson
Arizona State University
Adrian S. Z. Chase
Arizona State University
and
Michelle Hegmon
Arizona State University

ABSTRACT

A comparative perspective, drawing from cases in the U.S. Southwest and Northern Mexico, is used to illuminate the iconic Classic Maya "collapse," and to define the concept of *transformative relocation.* In some of the cases we discuss—including La Quemada and Classic Mimbres, as well as Maya—the end of a social configuration is not the end of a people. Rather, a broad temporal and regional perspective demonstrates that the dramatic change we see in the archaeological record is best characterized as a transformative relocation in which people relocated themselves and adopted new ways of life. The comparative perspective allows us to identify factors that contribute to this kind of transformation, including a compounding of vulnerabilities and situations of path dependence. [transformative relocation, Maya, U.S. Southwest, northern Mexico, archaeology]

The Classic Maya "collapse" ca. C.E. 900 is an iconic case of a society's failure to sustain key relationships internally and with its biophysical environment (D. Chase and A. Chase 2004; Demarest 2004; Dunning 1996; Hodell et al. 2001; Houston and Inomata 2009; Rice 2007; Stuart 1993; Webb 1973; Webster 2002). As such, the Maya case begs comparison with other similar ancient instances. Diamond (2005) has undertaken such a comparison on a global scale, predictably bringing criticism by archaeologists familiar with the details of the various cases (McAnany and Yoffee 2010). Others too have independently examined socio-ecological disruptions in such disparate regions as the circum-Mediterranean (van der Leeuw and de Vries 2002), the North Atlantic (Dugmore et al. 2012), Africa (McIntosh et al. 2000), Polynesia (Kirch 2005), and the U.S. Southwest (Kohler et al. 2010). The many ancient instances of collapse and reorganization from the past continue to intrigue the public and scholars alike. While the Maya case has much to say about these issues on its own, framing the collapse of the Classic Maya as one of many in the past may allow for a more general understanding of these issues.

The chapters in this volume examine the transformations of the Classic Maya with awareness of their complexity, but also with the intent of teasing out the most salient explanatory variables and their interactions. Ultimately we seek to portray these explanations in a manner understandable to a wide audience. Part of that process is identifying principles that operate across cultural contexts by comparing multiple cases. Currently under exploration is a set of approaches to identifying key interactions with the labels "resilience approach" (e.g., Redman 2005; Hegmon et al. 2008) or "social-natural approach" (van der Leeuw and Redman

ARCHEOLOGICAL PAPERS OF THE AMERICAN ANTHROPOLOGICAL ASSOCIATION, Vol. 24, pp. 171–182, ISSN 1551-823X, online ISSN 1551-8248. DOI: 10.1111/apaa.12036.

2002) to past social complexity. Out of these approaches, conceptual frameworks are emerging for analyzing and comparing commonalties in cases of collapse and other major transformations. On an archaeological time scale, such transformations are frequently recurring phenomena. Many archaeologists, including Mayanists, assume that such transformations have multiple but not infinite underlying causes (Demarest 2004).

In this chapter we highlight a particular process manifested in the Classic-to-Postclassic Maya transition and compare it to similar aspects of change in the U.S. Southwest and Northern Mexico (Figure 12.1). We call this process *transformative relocation*, in contrast to in-situ transformations wherein significant reorganization occurs while populations remain in place, and in contrast to total collapses, where the society (and people) disappears (e.g., the end of the Norse settlements of Greenland [Dugmore et al. 2012]). The instances that we consider are not all contemporaneous nor were the societies organized at the same scale, but we will examine the proposition that some of their changes were structurally and processually similar and may involve similar social agency. Of particular interest are instances where settled groups (villages, ceremonial centers, cities) disintegrated in the face of socionatural difficulties and other similar groups were constituted, albeit with different membership and leadership, some distance away from the originally settled area. We suggest that these transformations may have shared two properties: multiple vulnerabilities and path dependence.

This kind of explanation takes the focus away from collapse and abandonment and allows us to see that within a given context, transformation and reconstitution are a continuum of results that stem from human efforts to resolve common issues. This kind of inference also may be of relevance to the human future, because it suggests how societies can paint themselves into corners where there are no alternatives to radical change, and therefore be forced to reorganize profoundly.

After briefly considering the resilience approach, we describe the collapse of southern Lowland Maya cities and the rise of new forms of cities in the northern Lowlands. This process has long intrigued archaeologists and has become even more interesting as a result of recent research, because of new details about some of the actions of affected people (Inomata and Webb 2003 at Aguateca; Demarest et al. 1997 at Dos Pilas). We also describe three other cases of transformative relocation in central and northern Mexico and the U.S. Southwest, pointing out the ways that they are similar to and different from that of the Maya. The depiction of these cases in the idealized framework of transformative relocation allows us to identify some aspects of the socio-ecological status of these groups at the time of their transformation. Doing so demonstrates the need for research about specific vulnerabilities to which particular societies were subject. The northern Mexican case of La Quemada illustrates how such research into ancient vulnerabilities—using a combination of archaeology, paleobotany, geomorphology, and formal modeling—is currently being conducted and could be extended elsewhere.

The resilience approach seeks to comprehend how socio-ecological systems may change while retaining aspects of their structure and identity, or alternatively fail to do so and undergo significant transformations. The focus of the resilience approach is on the indivisible relationship between human societies and their environments. Its terminology is general in an attempt to characterize processes that underlie many kinds and scales and scales of socio-ecological change. The Classic Maya collapse is an instance of transformation that has great potential for shedding light on the principles that govern socio-ecological change.

Researchers in many fields, including scholars who use a resilience perspective, are concerned with identifying vulnerabilities, especially their cumulative and combined effects. Vulnerabilities are conditions, which can sometimes be described as particular states of variables such as rainfall quantities, that threaten the viability of a socio-ecological system (e.g., a city-state). A key finding is that socio-ecological transformations are often preceded by multiple vulnerabilities (Anderies et al. 2006). In the face of multiple vulnerabilities, change may become dynamic, non-linear, or even catastrophic (e.g., epidemics). Such changes are often constituted or preceded by previously uncharacteristic feedbacks between components of different orders (Peters et al. 2011). Thus, understanding the nature of individual vulnerabilities as well as conditions that lead to their joint occurrences becomes a critical focus of analysis. Collapses are perhaps best viewed as radical transformations that occur when multiple vulnerabilities materialize simultaneously.

One very important question is why systems sometimes fail to change even when people in the system perceive vulnerabilities. Path dependence connotes a sense of becoming increasingly stuck in a particular way of doing things, an inability to change even when change would be advantageous (Hegmon in press). Vulnerabilities may compound in path dependent social configurations, leading to situations known as rigidity traps (Hegmon et al. 2008). In such situations change is resisted (whether consciously or as a consequence of the overall social and technological configuration); thus when change does come, it is often abrupt and severe, because relatively profound adjustments are required. Recent examinations of prehispanic cases in the U.S. Southwest have shown that path dependence may have had a powerful

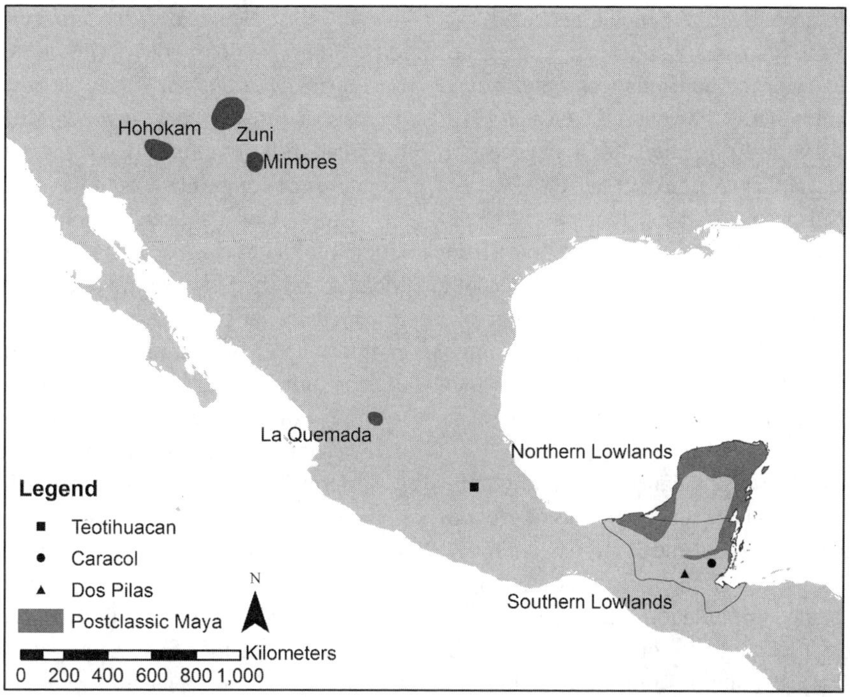

Figure 12.1. Sites and regions in the U.S. Southwest and Mesoamerica (with the Hohokam, Zuni, and Mimbres regions of the US Southwest, La Quemada in Northern Mexico, and the southern Maya Lowlands and Caracol and Dos Pilas within, and northern Maya Lowlands).

effect on the histories of some populations (Hegmon et al. 2008; Hegmon in press). This paper explores the potential of the Classic Maya collapse ca. C.E. 800–900 for adding data and perspectives to the understanding of collapse, especially instances of collapse that involve large-scale relocations of people.

Classic Maya

The ancient Maya occupied a semi-tropical environment stretching from contemporary Chiapas and the Yucatan Peninsula of Mexico, through Guatemala and Belize, into portions of Honduras and El Salvador. Access to fresh water, good agricultural soils, high quality flaked and ground stone raw materials, salt, hardwood, and marine resources varied through this region. From C.E. 250 with the widespread occurrence of polychrome ceramics to C.E. 900 with the political collapse in the southern Lowlands, Classic period site hierarchies existed in which polities combined smaller and larger centers. The largest centers maintained populations of over 100,000 people (Chase et al. 2011:389), integrating populations through market economies and internal road systems. However, the Maya context was not without its stresses and vulnerabilities. Agriculture was substantially dependent on seasonal rainfall and could be disrupted by excessively wet or dry conditions (Lucero et al., this volume).

Elite infrastructure, which included elaborate systems of personal glorification (inscriptions, murals, tombs, sculptural portraiture), as well as public spaces controlled by the elite (plazas, temples, palaces) was expensive to maintain, with sites and polities managing these stresses in different ways. Some, like Dos Pilas, Guatemala (Houston 1993; Demarest 2004), maintained smaller polities and population densities, with room for agricultural expansion. Others, like Caracol, Belize (A. Chase and D. Chase 1998), substantially modified their environments, probably both to intensify production and to buffer against climatic fluctuations by improving the retention of moisture and sediments.

The Classic period Maya ceased monumental construction and discontinued erection of dated stone monuments at some point during the 8th or 9th centuries. Significantly, the collapse and abandonment of the Lowland Maya cities took place over an extended period of time (A. Chase and D. Chase 2004) that was characterized by both unusual alliances and strife. For example, the Maya occupants of Dos Pilas left that site in the middle of the 8th century (Demarest 2004:108), but only after walling off parts of their city in an attempt to protect themselves from attack.

While 8th century Caracol also experienced increased warfare, it occurred at a time when major architecture was renovated, settlement expanded, and new alliances were formed with neighboring centers (A. Chase and D. Chase 1998; this volume; Chase et al. 1991). Elite diet and access to trade goods continued at Caracol throughout the 9th century, but cross-societal distribution mechanisms were not in place. Instead, the elite differentiated themselves from the rest of society (A. Chase and D. Chase 2007). Despite variation in timing, both Dos Pilas and Caracol succumbed to difficulties, which may have included climate change, warfare, and or political and economic failures—and which ultimately led to collapse, abandonment, and transformative relocation.

Postclassic period Maya populations generally relocated to sustainable locations near concentrations of groundwater (Chase and Rice 1985)—to some degree spawning the idea that the Maya collapse was drought inspired. Beginning in the 8th century, refugee populations may have further compounded problems, leading to sequent collapses elsewhere (Demarest 2004). Populations moved, but often not great distances; settlements do not appear to have relocated en masse. Disjunctions in ceramic transitions suggest intermingled populations and movements. There was no simple relocation from the south to the north, as was once thought (Cowgill 1964; Morley 1946); in some cases, it appears that northern populations moved further south (Chase and Chase 1982; Adams 1999).

The relocation was transformative not only because of population movement, but because institutions surrounding rulership were altered or discontinued, for example, as marked by cessation of several of the kinds of personal glorification of rulers mentioned above. Although more densely settled, Postclassic sites were not as spatially expansive as their Classic period counterparts and contained fewer people (Culbert and Rice 1990). Postclassic centers maintained some traditional aspects of Maya culture, but did not replicate others (D. Chase and A. Chase 2004). Ritual caches for both the Late Classic and Postclassic Maya were used for site integration, but the emphasis on eastern mortuary ritual found at many Classic period centers in the southern Maya Lowlands is not replicated in Postclassic sites. Many residential groups in the Classic period Maya area contained eastern ritual structures, something that is extremely pronounced at Caracol (A. Chase and D. Chase 2014). Monumental architecture also diminished between the two periods with the Late Classic practice of recording dynastic history on stone largely disappearing in the Postclassic period. Thus, the Classic period Maya provide an excellent example of both innovative adaptation and rigid path dependency. While changing environmental conditions may have set the stage, an accumulation of human choices led to the abandonment of Classic Maya cities and their transformative re-establishment in new locations. Although urban structures were re-invoked, it appears doubtful that the populations remained devoted to Classic period political structures or community identities.

The process of transformative relocation is not restricted to the Maya region. Prehispanic groups in northern Mexico and the U.S. Southwest, ca. C.E. 500–1400, manifested such changes at certain times and places. Co-authors of this chapter Nelson and Hegmon are part of a group of collaborators that has been examining the socio-ecological dynamics of five prehispanic cases in those regions. Some of these northern groups (with respect to the Maya) exhibit a pattern similar to the Classic-Postclassic Maya region, which makes them interesting to compare because they represent societies that were organized on much smaller scales than the Maya. While one might expect that different dynamics operate in societies of such different scale, we suggest to the contrary that many of the same issues, human responses, and systemic consequences were involved. In what follows we briefly describe three of these cases, La Quemada, Salt River Hohokam, and Mimbres, as comparative background for the explanations and methodological suggestions with which we conclude our observations about the Maya collapse.

Northern Mesoamerican Frontier

The northern frontier region of Mexico, which includes parts of Zacatecas, Durango, Jalisco, and Sinaloa, may have been at the distant end of a zone affected by population displacements from Central Mexico, in a pattern similar to that linking the different parts of the Maya region. As is noted above, Maya settlements began to develop in new locations well before C.E. 900, and the collapse was in part an attraction of population to those already established settlements. The northern frontier has a similar occupational history in relation to central Mexico. New centers began to form in the Bajío region north of the Rio Lerma-Santiago C.E. 350–600 (Cárdenas and Fernández 2004) and subsequently, as exemplified by La Quemada (Nelson 1997) in the northern frontier ca. C.E. 500/600–900. Throughout the latter period, central Mexico was experiencing the replacement of its major power center, Teotihuacan, by a series of smaller capitals such as Tula (Mastache et al. 2002), Teotenango (Piña Chan 1973), and Xochicalco (Hirth 1995), coupled with demographic shifts and stylistic changes implying connectivity with the northern frontier (Beekman and Christensen 2003; Crider 2011; Braniff and Hers 1998; Gaxiola 1999;

Jiménez Moreno 1959; Mastache and Cobean 1989; Nelson and Crider 2005; Rattray 1996).

La Quemada is the most intensively studied of several northern frontier ceremonial centers that were occupied from about C.E. 550–1000, corresponding to the Late Classic 1 through Late Terminal Classic as used in this volume. Abandoned ca. C.E. 900, the site was a spectacular mountaintop fortress and ceremonial center comprised of about 60 terraces (Nelson 1997). Architecture on the terraces includes a monumental core of masonry structures such as a 75 meter-long ball court, a roofed colonnaded hall about 20 × 25 meters in area. Smaller replicas of these features were placed around sunken patios on other, smaller terraces. Staircases, causeways, and walkways connected different parts of La Quemada, and causeways descended from the mountaintop to connect with more rural spaces occupied by over 200 villages.

The roughly synchronous abandonment of some of these northern frontier centers (Jiménez and Darling 2000; Kelley 1985; Nelson 1997; Trombold 1990) has been implicated in socio-ecological debates because ancient populations would have been vulnerable to crop failure. Pedro Armillas (1964) argued that appearance of these Late Classic–Early Postclassic centers suggested a climatically driven northward shift in the northern limit of Mesoamerica He proposed that Mesoamerican groups colonized the region when increased precipitation temporarily made maize agriculture viable, only to abandon their settlements when the old climatic conditions returned. Chronometric dates were not available at the time Armillas wrote, but his model implies that the climatic shift back to less favorable conditions should have happened ca. C.E. 900–1000. A key point is that, as legend suggests (Jimenez Moreno 1959), the centers in northern Mexico could have grown as a direct or indirect result of dispersive relocations in central Mexico. Armillas emphasized that the climatic element of his proposition required empirical testing. Sauer (1963) held that the semiarid conditions of northern Mexico meant that sedentism was contingent on agave cultivation. Parsons (2010) expands this hypothesis, arguing that the colonists would have needed to import algae and insects from the lake zones to the south. Why the northern frontier became Mesoamericanized (Foster 1986) remains an important question, as does the extent to which this transformation involved in situ lifeways changes as opposed to the arrival of immigrants. There are also questions about why some centers in the region were abandoned ca. C.E. 900. Other centers appear to have absorbed people from the ones that collapsed. Some of our recent work at La Quemada has focused on gauging the vulnerabilities of these seemingly oversized northern Mexican populations (see below).

U.S. Southwest

People in the Hohokam region seem to have experienced a transformation in place ca. C.E. 1150, followed by continued occupation till ca. C.E. 1350–1400, when they dispersed and reorganized in such a way as to be almost invisible archaeologically (Wells et al. 2004; Hill et al. 2004). The sequence is suggestive of resilience initially but later of path dependence leading to a difficult decline (Abbott 2003; Hegmon in press). Farmers in the Phoenix Basin became increasingly committed to a humanly modified landscape in which they built the largest prehispanic irrigation system in North America (Hunt et al. 2005), possibly supporting as many as 40,000 people. Hohokam territory as a whole expanded, and approximately 200 ball courts were constructed (Wilcox 1991). Analyses of ceramic production sources and exchange lead Abbott et al. (2007) to infer that by ca. C.E. 875 the ball courts became foci for markets at which pottery was exchanged for food and other products. The authors intentionally refer to "markets" because the scale and geography of distribution implies exchange among parties unknown to one another. The in-situ transformation came ca. C.E. 1150, possibly as a result of a change in the rainfall regime, reduction in river flow, and lessened ability to produce a crop surplus for exchange. Thus large scale specialist pottery production came to an end, and at the same time, the ball courts went into disuse. Marking the beginning of the misnamed Classic period, the population aggregated into the Phoenix Basin and territorial extent decreased, while platform mounds reminiscent of Mesoamerican structures became the focal points of social integration. The end of the Hohokam sequence came at ca. C.E. 1350 with dispersal so thorough that archaeologists are uncertain how to identify subsequent sites. Subsistence agriculturalists in this region would have been vulnerable to recurrent droughts, but that was not their only serious vulnerability. Large flood events in the late 1300s may also have damaged the canal systems. More deeply, this case can be considered one of path dependence in that the Phoenix Basin occupants had made a social commitment to a canal system that was robust to fluctuations of rainfall only within a certain range (Anderies et al. 2006; Hegmon in press).

The Mimbres region in the U.S. Southwest, long known for spectacular pottery, is now also known as a case of what resilience theorists call "reorganization." During the Classic Mimbres period (C.E. 1000–1130) people lived in large villages, and population grew, moving into marginal areas. Around C.E. 1130, a time of climatic downturn, many (but not all) people moved out of the villages and the pottery tradition ended. In contrast to earlier accounts, which argued that the Mimbres Valley and much of the region were abandoned at the end of the Classic period (e.g., Shafer and Taylor 1986), recent work (Hegmon et al. 1998; Nelson 1999; Nelson et al. 2006) finds that it is better understood as a regional reorganization, in which some people moved (tens of kilometers) from aggregated villages to dispersed hamlets, while others left the region. In other cases, people seem to have moved between river valleys (Nelson and Anyon 1996). The reorganization phase hamlets are different from the earlier villages. An inward focus and intra-regional interaction was replaced by a broad network of inter-regional ties, indicated by the import of numerous kinds of decorated pottery. Household organization changed and came to be focused on a single multi-functional room as household mobility increased. This increase in autonomy lasted only a generation or two—possibly because of threats of violence—and by the end of the 13th century most people had moved back into aggregated villages.

Characterizing Vulnerabilities and Explaining Transformations

How do we get inside the dynamics of past societies to identify vulnerabilities and evaluate their roles in social transformations, for example to understand why relocation sometimes needs to be part of change? The above examples demonstrate the need for in-depth examination of specific vulnerabilities. It does not suffice to say that a population is vulnerable to drought because it inhabits a semiarid environment, or to say that land degradation could be a problem for agriculturalists who were deforesting portions of a landscape. We need rigorous ways of characterizing variable changes and their impacts, including vulnerabilities, response mechanisms, and the tradeoffs among different strategies as conditions change (again, in part recursively as a result of attempts to reduce vulnerabilities). Our approach in northern Mexico (e.g. Anderies, et al. 2008) and the U.S. Southwest (e.g., Anderies and Hegmon 2011) has been to work iteratively between socio-ecological data and formal models. Real-world data about vegetative change (some of which can be parsed between climatic and anthropogenic causes), stream behavior, precipitation, and temperature provide realistic input for models that characterize interactions among key variables. In the La Quemada case an interdisciplinary team tested both empirically (Elliott et al. 2008) and with formal models (Anderies et al. 2008) for environmental causes of the prehispanic abandonments ca. C.E. 900–1000. This approach did not identify environmental causes per se, but did afford insight into the socio-ecological challenges faced by prehispanic farmers, as two examples from La Quemada will illustrate.

Socio-ecological data-gathering has been crucial to evaluating Armillas's (1964) model of settlement opportunism, i.e, intrusive farmers' colonization of lands during a period of favorable climate followed by failure to cope with increasing aridity, outlined above. Armillas basically argued that centers such as La Quemada in the northern Mesoamerican frontier were occupied and later abandoned because of climatic change. To address this possibility, Elliott et al. (2010) collected pollen, phytolith, sedimentary, paleomagnetic, and radiocarbon samples from an area of productive floodplain in the Malpaso Valley at the heart of the La Quemada agricultural system. They cut backhoe trenches to expose off-site soil and sediment deposits dating before, during, and after the main occupation of La Quemada (C.E. 500–900).

The hypothesis of settlement opportunism led Elliott et al. (2010) to expect indications of decreased temperature and aridity, floodplain stabilization, pedogenesis, and differing vegetative cover corresponding to the time when dense, sedentary human settlement began, ca. C.E. 500. The converse hypothesis of succumbing to drought vulnerability implied that those conditions reversed ca. C.E. 900, producing increased temperature and aridity, erosion, downcutting, and vegetative change. Elliott et al. tested the floodplain and tributary arroyos that must have provided the main agricultural support for several thousand people. These occupants constructed a cluster of over 200 villages surrounding a massive regional ceremonial center, a road system, and agricultural terraces, all of which they abandoned after several centuries of sustained development. Was their settlement system made possible, and then made to fail, by climatic change as Armillas (1964) interestingly proposed? Indices of aridity and vegetative changes were constructed from phytoliths, indices of stream behavior and soil formation from loss on ignition, magnetic susceptibility, anhysteretic and saturation remanence, and sediment characterization. The changes were dated by radiocarbon analysis and compared to human settlement history.

The results indicate no correlation between these measures of environmental change and the settlement history of the Malpaso Valley (Elliott et al. 2010). The onset of the current level of aridity occurred long before the main prehispanic occupation, ca. 525–230 B.C.E., yet this climate still permitted pedogenesis, streambed aggradation, and regular overbank flooding, implying favorable conditions for floodplain agriculture. These conditions persisted for centuries before, during, and after the episode of dense prehispanic occupation and were interrupted only by the deforestation and overgrazing of the Spanish colonization, beginning ca. C.E. 1550 (Elliott et al. 2010). We concluded that the prehispanic abandonment was not associated with strong environmental perturbation and that the environment experienced by the prehispanic population was markedly more productive than that of today. Either the perturbations were too short-lived to be detected by the measures used or the causes were in the social realm as opposed to the natural.

Because of the possibility that the types of socio-ecological data collected thus far may not be sensitive enough to capture short-term droughts, the archaeologists and other scientists dealing with the La Quemada case are experimenting with other approaches. One is to model subsistence security under different sets of crop mixes and climatic conditions. If farmers were vulnerable to droughts, it should be possible to simulate conditions under which farmers would be forced to migrate due to famine. Geographers and archaeologists have suspected that prehispanic people could not occupy the Northern Frontier without cultivating agave as a backup to maize, because maize is too sensitive to rainfall fluctuations. Agave, on the other hand, is a nutritionally productive perennial that stores its own supply of moisture (Parsons 2010; Parsons and Parsons 1990; Sauer 1963). Anderies et al. (2008) set out to determine how much difference agave cultivation made to the robustness of Northern Frontier farmers to drought. For example, in 100 years, how many famine events severe enough to cause migration would be avoided by a mixed maize and agave crop portfolio as opposed to one relying on maize alone? The model assumes that all farmers are employing the same crop mix and are subject to the same (stochastic) fluctuations in rainfall. Simulations were run with mean rainfall set at different percentages of the saturation point of maize (the point beyond which more precipitation makes no difference to yield).

Several key findings are suggested by the Anderies et al. (2008) model. First, mixing agave cultivation with that of maize can make a tremendous difference in a simulated context, eliminating as many as 95% of simulated famine events, but secondly, this difference is only achieved if the mean rainfall is within 70% of the saturation point of maize and variance of rainfall is relatively low, about 20% of the mean. Thirdly, these results suggest that increasing crop diversity does not automatically increase robustness. Thus one can conclude that under certain circumstances the vulnerability of northern frontier populations to drought can be significantly mitigated by the mixed annual-perennial strategy. Obviously, the populations had other ways of reducing vulnerability, such as using the most drought-resistant varieties of maize, terracing, building irrigation ditches, and hand-watering plants during dry years. Potentially, these practices could have made it possible to develop institutions that created short- or medium-term security but would not be adaptive in the long run because the practices or institutions were difficult to change.

As in the Mimbres, Hohokam, and Classic Maya cases, in the La Quemada example people stopped living in large settlements in what had been their main area of occupation, and many families must have relocated to form new social configurations. The environmental testing and formal modeling done this far have not pinpointed the causes of the relocation, but have identified some of the issues that the inhabitants were facing. Additional environmental testing and modeling are planned to sharpen the understanding of vulnerability to rainfall fluctuations, how plants and people responded to those fluctuations, and why some prehispanic groups ultimately dispersed to new environments and social settings.

Conclusion

One thing that should be clear from the above examples is that the processes that characterized the Classic Maya collapse may be echoed in many other cases, at a variety of scales, and in different institutional contexts. Path dependence, or the tendency of societies to follow established practices beyond the exhaustion of their utility, may contribute to many cases of collapse. Yet examples of greater resilience also exist in the prehispanic Americas (e.g., Zuni and its ancestral communities [Nelson et al. 2010]). We are quite far from understanding the mechanisms that permit societal transformations to occur with limited disruption, locational or otherwise, but significant advances are being made in data accumulation and conceptualization as we consider both empirical cases and broad concepts such as rigidity and path dependence. Mayanists of course are very active in these kinds of advances. The great questions raised by the Maya collapse can be asked of many other settings, and the comparative analysis of highly specific vulnerabilities may lead to further understanding of how security is promoted in complex human systems.

A benefit of the resilience approach is that it is amenable to formalization in mathematical models. By working between empirical cases and such models, researchers are able to explore possibilities and create better approximations of the key variable interactions in systemic transformations than they might with other, less formal analytical operations. Some of our work has been in these directions, and we believe that it has potential not only for improving the understanding of the Maya collapse but also for analyzing sets of collapses and understanding their common causes.

We suspect that southern Lowland Maya cities succumbed to ordinary issues that either assumed unusual proportions, "flared" simultaneously, or both. In the face of these vulnerabilities, the social groups were not flexible enough to respond by changing, and instead disintegrated because the enactment of solutions in place was precluded by established social practice. While individual ecological and social stresses may not have led to collapse on their own (McAnany and Negrón 2010), the combination of these societal stresses may have made the problems facing the Classic Maya intractable. In such circumstances relocation to the northern Lowlands, not by cities wholesale, but in smaller social aggregates that were recruited to new, growing centers, may have been a way of escaping entrenched political regimes and other regimes of value (Appadurai 1986) that bound groups to untenable patterns of behavior. Relocation may have permitted the substitution of new leadership and social principles that could not occur in place.

Transformative relocation would not force people to wholly abandon their social identities, nor would it permanently free them from path dependence. Turner and Sabloff (2012) suggest that the people who abandoned southern lowland centers did not return, because once established in the north, they became engaged in oceangoing trade to an extent that returning to the southern Lowlands would have been problematic. The La Quemada, Hohokam, and Mimbres cases described above provide strong parallels to the paradoxically permanent abandonment of fertile areas that (at least until the availability of carbon-fuel powered irrigation) would have had potential for economic reintensification after a human generation or two of ecological recovery.

In comparative perspective, the Classic Maya collapse appears large and spectacular, but not unique. Hopefully the above juxtaposition of U.S. Southwestern and northern Mexican cases identifies some of the basis on which the Maya collapse can inform more broadly about collapse in general.

Acknowledgments

We are grateful to Arlen Chase and Vernon Scarborough for the invitation to participate in the IHOPE-Maya conversation, and also to Sander van der Leeuw for his support and encouragement. We thank the editor of the AP3A series and anonymous reviewers for their corrections and improvements of our expressions about the tricky interactions among social and ecological variables. What remains of course is not their responsibility. Fieldwork at La Quemada was supported by grants from the National Science Foundation (BCS-0211109 and BECNH-0508001) as well as the National Endowment for the Humanities, the Wenner-Gren Foundation, the Foundation for the Advancement for Mesoamerican studies, and an anonymous donor. The Turner Foundation and the National Geographic Society supported fieldwork in the Eastern Mimbres area. Our ideas about resilience are the product of conversations with members of the Long Term Vulnerability and Transformations Project at Arizona State University, which has been funded by the Biocomplexity and Coupled Human and Natural Systems programs of the National Science Foundation (05008001 and BCS-1113991). The authors will be ever thankful to these sponsors.

References Cited

Abbott, David R., ed.
2003 Centuries of Decline during the Hohokam Classic Period at Pueblo Grande. Tucson: University of Arizona Press.

Abbott, David R., Alexa M. Smith, and Emiliano Gallaga
2007 Ballcourts and Ceramics: The Case for Hohokam Marketplaces in the Arizona Desert. American Antiquity 72:461–84.

Adams, Richard E. W.
1999 Rio Azul: An Ancient Maya City. Norman: University of Oklahoma Press.

Anderies, John M., and Michelle Hegmon
2011 Robustness and Resilience across Scales: Migration and Resource Degradation in the Prehistoric U.S. Southwest. Ecology and Society 16(2):22. http://www.ecologyandsociety.org/vol16/iss2/art22/, accessed June 2, 2014.

Anderies, John M., Ben A. Nelson, and Ann P. Kinzig
2008 Analyzing the Impact of Agave Cultivation on Famine Risk in Arid Prehispanic Northern Mexico. Human Ecology 36(3):409–422.

Anderies, John M., B. H. Walker, and Ann P. Kinzig
2006 Fifteen Weddings and a Funeral: Case Studies and Resilience-Based Management. Ecology and Society 11(1):21. http://www.ecologyandsociety.org/vol11/iss1/art21/, accessed June 2, 2014.

Appadurai, Arjun
1986 Introduction: Commodities and the Politics of Value. *In* The Social Life of Things: Commodities in Cultural Perspective. A. Appadurai, ed. Pp. 1–63. Cambridge, UK: Cambridge University Press.

Armillas, Pedro
1964 Condiciones Ambientales y Movimientos de Pueblos en la Frontera Septentrional de Mesoamérica. *In* Homenaje a Fernando Marquez-Miranda. Pp. 62–82. Madrid: University of Madrid.

Beekman, Christopher S., and Andrew F. Christensen
2003 Controlling for Doubt and Uncertainty Through Multiple Lines of Evidence: A New Look at Mesoamerican Nahua Migrations. Journal of Archaeological Method and Theory 10(2):111–164.

Braniff, Beatriz, and Marie-Areti Hers
1998 Herencias Chichimecas. Arqueología 19:55–80.

Cárdenas García, Efraín, and Eugenia Fernández-Villanueva
2004 Apuntes Para el Estudio de la Arqueología del Bajío. *In* Introducción a la Arqueología del Occidente. B. Braniff Cornejo, ed. Pp. 497–523. México, D.F.: Universidad de Colima y Conaculta-Instituto Nacional de Antropología e Historia.

Chase, Arlen F., and Diane Z. Chase
1998 Scale and Intensity in Classic Period Maya Agriculture: Terracing and Settlement at the "Garden City" of Caracol, Belize. Culture and Agriculture 20(2):60–77.
2004 Terminal classic Status-Linked Ceramics and the Maya "Collapse": De Facto Refuse at Caracol, Belize. *In* Terminal Classic in the Maya Lowlands: Collapse, Transition, and Transformation. P. M. Rice, A. A. Demarest, and D. S. Rice, eds. Pp. 342–366. Boulder: University Press of Colorado.
2007 "This is the End": Archaeological Transitions and the Terminal Classic Period at Caracol, Belize. Research Reports in Belizean Archaeology 4:13–27.
2014 Houses, Households, and Residential Groups at Caracol, Belize. Research Reports in Belizean Archaeology 11:3–17.

Chase, Diane Z., and Arlen F. Chase
1982 Yucatec Influence in Terminal Classic Northern Belize. American Antiquity 47:596–613.
2004 Hermeneutics, Transitions, and Transformations in Classic to Postclassic Maya Society. *In* The Terminal Classic in the Maya Lowlands: Collapse, Transition, and Transformation. P. M. Rice, A. A. Demarest, and D. S. Rice, eds. Pp. 12–27. Boulder: University Press of Colorado.

Chase, Arlen F., Diane Z. Chase, John F. Weishampel, Jason B. Drake, Ramesh L. Shrestha, Jaime J. Awe, K. Clint Slatton, and William E. Carter
2011 Airborne LiDAR, Archaeology, and the Ancient Maya Landscape at El Caracol, Belize. Journal of Archaeological Science 38:387–398.

Chase, Arlen F., Nikolai Grube, and Diane Z. Chase
1991 Three Terminal Classic Monuments from Caracol, Belize. Reports on Ancient Maya Writing, 36. Washington, DC: Center for Maya Research.

Chase, Arlen F., and Prudence M. Rice, eds.
1985 The Lowland Maya Postclassic. Austin: University of Texas Press.

Cowgill, George L.
1964 The End of Classic Maya Culture: A Review of Recent Evidence. Southwestern Journal of Anthropology 20 (145–159).

Crider, Destiny L.
2011 Epiclassic and Early Postclassic Interaction in Central Mexico As Evidenced by Decorated Pottery. Ph.D. dissertation, School of Human Evolution, Arizona State University.

Culbert, T. Patrick, and Don S. Rice, eds.
1990 Precolumbian Population History in the Maya Lowlands. Albuquerque: University of New Mexico Press.

Demarest, Arthur
2004 Ancient Maya: The Rise and Fall of a Rainforest Civilization. Cambridge, UK: Cambridge University Press.

Demarest, Arthur A., Matt O'Mansky, Claudia Wolley, Dirk Van Tuerenhout, Takeshi Inomata, Joel W. Palka, and Héctor L. Escobedo
1997 Classic Maya Defensive Systems and Warfare in the Petextabún Region. Ancient Mesoamerica 8(2):229–253.

Diamond, Jared M.
2005 Collapse: How Societies Choose to Fail or Succeed. New York: Viking.

Dugmore, Andrew J., Thomas H. McGovern, Orri Vésteinsson, Jette Arneborg, Christian Keller, and Richard Streeter
2012 Cultural Adaptation, Compounding Vulnerabilities and Conjunctures in Norse Greenland. PNAS 109(10):3658–3666.

Dunning, Nicholas
1996 An Examination of Regional Variability in the Prehispanic Maya Agricultural Landscape. *In* The Managed Mosaic: Ancient Maya Agriculture and Resource Use. S. L. Feddick, ed. Pp. 53–68. Salt Lake City: University of Utah Press.

Elliott, Michelle, Christopher T. Fisher, Ben A. Nelson, Roberto S. Molina Garza, Shawn K. Collins, and Deborah M. Pearsall
2010 Climate, Agriculture, and Cycles of Human Occupation over the Last 4,000 Years in Southern Zacatecas, Mexico. Quaternary Research 74:26–35.

Foster, Michael S.
1986 The Mesoamerican Connection: A View from the South. *In* Ripples in the Chichimec Sea: New Considerations of Mesoamerican-Southwestern Interactions. F. J. Mathien and R. H. McGuire, eds. Pp. 55–69. Carbondale: Southern Illinois University Press.

Gaxiola González, Margarita
1999 Huapalcalco y las Tradiciones Alfareras del Epiclásico. Arqueología 21:45–72.

Hegmon, Michelle
In press Path Dependence. *In* Oxford Handbook of Southwest Archaeology. B. J. Mills and S. Fowles, eds. Oxford University Press.

Hegmon, Michelle, Margaret C. Nelson, and Susan M. Ruth
1998 Abandonment and Reorganization in the Mimbres Region of the American Southwest. American Anthropologist 100(1):148–162.

Hegmon, Michelle, Matthew Peeples, Ann P. Kinzig, Stephanie Kulow, Cathryn Meegan, and Margaret C. Nelson
2008 Social Transformation and its Human Costs in the Prehispanic U.S. Southwest. American Anthropologist 110(3):313–324.

Hill, J. Brett, Jeffrey J. Clark, William H. Doelle, and Patrick D. Lyons
2004 Prehistoric Demography in the Southwest: Migration, Coalescence, and Hohokam Population Decline. American Antiquity 69(4):689–716.

Hirth, Kenneth G.
1995 Urbanism, Militarism, and Architectural Design: An Analysis of Epiclassic Sociopolitical Structure at Xochicalco. Ancient Mesoamerica 6(2):237–250.

Hodell, David A., Mark Brenner, Jason H. Curtis, and Thomas Guilderson
2001 Solar Forcing of Drought Frequency in the Maya Lowlands. Science 292:1367–1370.

Houston, Stephen D.
1993 Hieroglyphs and History at Dos Pilas: Dynastic Politics of the Classic Maya. Austin: University of Texas Press.

Houston, Stephen D., and Takeshi Inomata
2009 The Classic Maya. Cambridge, England: Cambridge University Press.

Hunt, Robert C., David Guillet, David R. Abbott, James Bayman, and Paul Fish
2005 Plausible Ethnographic Analogies for the Social Organization of Hohokam Canal Irrigation. American Antiquity 70:433–56.

Inomata, Takeshi, and Ron Webb
2003 War, Destruction, and Abandonment: The Fall of the Classic Maya Center of Aguateca, Guatemala. *In* Archaeology of Settlement Abandonment in Middle America. T. Inomata and R. Webb, eds. Pp. 43–60. Salt Lake City: University of Utah Press.

Jiménez Betts, Peter F., and J. Andrew Darling
2000 Archaeology of Southern Zacatecas: The Malpaso, Juchipila, and Valparaiso-Bolaños Valleys. *In* Greater Mesoamerica: The Archaeology of West and Northwest Mexico. M. S. Foster and S. Gorenstein, eds. Pp. 155–180. Salt Lake City: University of Utah Press.

Jiménez Moreno, Wigberto
1959 Síntesis de la Historia Pretolteca de Mesoamérica. *In* El Esplendor del México Antiguo, vol 2. Pp.

1109–1196. Mexico, D.F.: Centro de Investigaciones Antropológicos.

Kelley, J. Charles
1985 The Chronology of the Chalchihuites Culture. *In* The Archaeology of West and Northwest Mesoamerica. M. S. Foster and P. C. Weigand, eds. Pp. 269–288. Boulder: Westview Press.

Kirch, Patrick Vinton
2005 Archaeology and Global Change: The Holocene Record. Annual Review of Environmental Resources 30:409–440.

Kohler, Timothy A., Mark D. Varien, and Aaron M. Wright, eds.
2010 Leaving Mesa Verde: Peril and Change in the Thirteenth-Century Southwest. Tucson: University of Arizona Press.

Mastache, Alba Guadalupe, and Robert H. Cobean
1989 The Coyotlatelco Culture and the Origins of the Toltec State. *In* Mesoamerica After the Decline of Teotihuacan, A.D. 700–900. J. C. Berlo and R. A. Diehl, eds. Pp. 49–67. Washington, DC: Dumbarton Oaks Research Library and Collection.

Mastache, Alba Guadalupe, Robert H. Cobean, and Dan M. Healan
2002 Ancient Tollan: Tula and the Toltec Heartland. Boulder: University Press of Colorado.

McAnany, Patricia A., and Tomás Gallareta Negrón
2010 Bellicose Rulers and Climatological Peril? Retrofitting Twenty-First-Century Woes on Eighth Century Maya Society. *In* Questioning Collapse: Human Resilience, Ecological Vulnerability, and the Aftermath of Empire. P. A. McAnany and N. Yoffee, eds. Pp. 142–175. New York: Cambridge University Press.

McAnany, Patricia A., and Norman Yoffee, eds.
2010 Questioning Collapse: Human Resilience, Ecological Vulnerability, and the Aftermath of Empire. New York: Cambridge University Press.

McIntosh, Roderick J., Joseph A. Tainter, and Susan K. McIntosh, eds.
2000 The Way the Wind Blows: Climate, History, and Human Action. New York: Columbia University Press.

Morley, Sylvanus G.
1946 The Ancient Maya. Stanford: Stanford University Press.

Nelson, Ben A.
1997 Chronology and Stratigraphy at La Quemada, Zacatecas, Mexico. Journal of Field Archaeology 24(1):85–109.

Nelson, Ben A., and Roger Anyon
1996 Fallow Valleys: Asynchronous Occupations in Southwestern New Mexico. Kiva 61(3): 275–294.

Nelson, Ben A., and Destiny Crider
2005 Posibles Pasajes Migratorios en el Norte de México y el Suroeste de los Estados Unidos Durante el Epiclásico y el Postclásico. *In* Reacomodos Demográficos del Clásico al Posclásico en el Centro de México. L. Manzanilla, ed. Pp. 75–102. México, D.F.: Instituto de Investigaciones, Universidad Nacional de México.

Nelson, Margaret C.
1999 Mimbres During the Twelfth Century: Abandonment, Continuity, and Reorganization. Tucson: University of Arizona Press.

Nelson, Margaret C., Michelle Hegmon, Stephanie Kulow, and Karen Gust Schollmeyer
2006 Archaeological and Ecological Perspectives on Reorganization: A Case Study from the Mimbres Region of the U.S. Southwest. American Antiquity 71(3):403–432.

Nelson, M. C., K. Kintigh, D. R. Abbott, and J. M. Anderies
2010 The Cross-Scale Interplay between Social and Biophysical Context and the Vulnerability of Irrigation-Dependent Societies: Archaeology's Long Term Perspective. Ecology and Society 15:31. http://www.ecologyandsociety.org/vol15/iss3/, accessed June 2, 2014.

Parsons, Jeffrey R.
2010 The Pastoral Niche in Pre-Hispanic Mesoamerica. *In* Precolumbian Foodways: Interdisciplinary Approaches to Food, Culture, and Markets in Ancient Mesoamerica. J. E. Staller and M. D. Carrasco, eds. Pp. 109–136: Springer Science+Business Media.

Parsons, Jeffrey R., and Mary H. Parsons
1990 Maguey Utilization in Highland Central Mexico: An Archaeological Ethnography. Anthropological Papers, 82. Ann Arbor: Museum of Anthropology, University of Michigan.

Peters, Debra P. C., Roger A. Pielke Sr., Brandon T. Bestelmeyer, Craig D. Allen, Stuart Munson-McGee, and Kris M. Havstad
2011 Cross-Scale Interactions, Nonlinearities, and Forecasting Catastrophic Events. PNAS 101(42): 15130–15135.

Piña Chan, Román, ed.
1973 Teotenango, Segundo Informe de Exploraciones Arqueológicas. México, D.F.: Dirección de Turismo, Gobierno del Estado de México.

Rattray, Evelyn
1996 A Regional Perspective on the Epiclassic Period in Central Mexico. *In* Arqueología Mesoamericana: Homenaje a William T. Sanders. A. G. Mastache, J. R. Parsons, R. S. Santley, and M. C. Serra Puche, eds. Pp. 213–231. Mexico City: Instituto Nacional de Antropología e Historia.

Redman, Charles L.
2005 Resilience Theory in Archaeology. American Anthropologist 107(1):70–77.

Rice, Prudence M.
2007 The Classic Maya "Collapse" and Its Causes: The Role of Warfare? *In* Gordon R. Willey and American Archaeology: Contemporary Perspectives. J. A. Sabloff and W. L. Fash, eds. Pp. 141–186. Norman: University of Oklahoma Press.

Turner, B. L., II, and Jeremy A. Sabloff
2012 Classic Period Collapse of the Central Maya Lowlands: Insights about Human–Environment Relationships for Sustainability. PNAS 109(35):13908–13914.

Sauer, Carl O.
1963 Land and Life: A Selection from the Writing of C. O. Sauer. Berkeley: University of California Press.

Shafer, Harry J., and Anna J. Taylor
1986 Mimbres Mogollon Architectural Dynamics and Ceramic Style Change. Journal of Field Archaeology 13:43–68.

Stuart, David
1993 Historical inscriptions and the Maya collapse. *In* Lowland Maya Civilization in the Eighth Century A.D. J. A. Sabloff and J. S. Henderson, eds. Washington, DC: Dumbarton Oaks Library and Research Collection.

Trombold, Charles D.
1990 A Reconsideration of the Chronology for the La Quemada Portion of the Northern Mesoamerican Frontier. American Antiquity 55(2):308–323.

van der Leeuw, S. E., and B. de Vries
2002 Empire: the Romans in the Mediterranean. *In* Mappae Mundi: Humans and Their Habitats in a Long-Term Socio-Ecological Perspective. B. de Vries and J. Goudsblom, eds. Pp. 209–256. Amsterdam: Amsterdam University Press.

van der Leeuw, Sander E., and Charles L. Redman
2002 Placing Archaeology at the Center of Socio-natural Studies. American Antiquity 67(4): 597–605.

Webb, Malcom C.
1973 The Peten Maya Decline Viewed in the Perspective of State Formation. *In* The Classic Maya Collapse. T. P. Culbert, ed. Pp. 367–404. Albuquerque: University of New Mexico Press.

Webster, David L.
2002 The Fall of the Ancient Maya. London: Thames and Hudson.

Wells, E. Christian Wells, Glen E. Rice, and John C. Ravesloot
2004 Peopling Landscapes between Villages in the Middle Gila River Valley of Central Arizona. American Antiquity 69:627–652.

Wilcox, David R.
1991 Hohokam Social Complexity. *In* Chaco and Hohokam: Prehistoric Regional Systems in the American Southwest. P. L. Crown and W. J. Judge, eds. Pp. 253–275. Santa Fe: School of American Research Press.

13

Comparative Landscape Analysis: Contrasting the Middle East and Maya Regions

T. J. Wilkinson
University of Durham

ABSTRACT

The Maya Lowlands and the Middle East occupy two contrasting latitudinal zones of ancient settlement, the former comprising part of the semi-tropical belt of low-density urbanism whereas in the Middle East dense nucleated settlement has predominated. Building upon the foundation lain down by Robert McC. Adams and published in 1966, but primarily drawing upon new evidence from archaeological landscape surveys, this paper explores the commonalities and contrasts between these two landscapes. Emphasis is placed upon settlement and landscape dynamics, specifically those features that contribute to our understanding of settlement sustainability or fragility. In addition, the different responses of large and small sites to both internal and external stresses are examined with particular reference to models of collapse and resilience. This paper selectively draws upon evidence from case studies from each geographical zone. These include those previously presented from the Maya region together with case studies drawn from the large data base available from Durham University's Fragile Crescent Project. Key features of settlement landscape dynamics include: agricultural intensification, polity size, transport networks, and patterns of exchange. In addition, reference is made to settlement landscapes in the sub-humid and semi-arid Yemen highlands which occupy a latitudinal zone equivalent to the Yucatan Peninsula and which show some characteristics of low density urbanism. [Middle East, Maya, landscape archaeology, collapse, sustainability, resilience]

Introduction

After a period of quiescence, comparative archaeology has returned as a valid approach to the study of the ancient world. However, as a recent volume emphasizes, there is no single "best method" for comparative analysis and proponents of the comparative method tilt toward either the more theoretical or empirical ends of the spectrum (Smith 2012:325). With the increased attention paid to the archaeological landscape, this topic too can be subjected to comparative analysis. However, what may be described as a derivate of comparative settlement and landscape archaeology, namely the sustainability or resilience of the component communities, presents a number of challenges as discussed below.

Michael Smith and Peter Peregrine (2012:7) recognize two extremities of comparisons, namely *intensive comparative methods* in which a small number of case studies are compared using a large number of variables, versus *systematic comparative methods* in which a larger number of case studies employ a small number of variables. The present chapter adopts the latter approach, with emphasis being placed upon soil erosion, soil management, water use, and the scale of archaeological sites.

In addition, so-called "dimensions of comparison" contribute to a more systematic approach to comparative study, namely: sample size and selection, context (see below), scale, and the use of primary versus secondary data as well as archaeological versus historical data. It is also possible to pursue synchronic or diachronic comparisons, as well as to take account of the stage in the research itself and whether the comparison is undertaken at the regional or global level (Smith and Peregrine 2012:9–15). Among these dimensions of comparison, the various environmental, demographic, and

ARCHEOLOGICAL PAPERS OF THE AMERICAN ANTHROPOLOGICAL ASSOCIATION, Vol. 24, pp. 183–200, ISSN 1551-823X, online ISSN 1551-8248. DOI: 10.1111/apaa.12037.

historical contexts of the regions being compared must be taken into account. For example, in the Maya area ancient populations were usually larger than the modern populations currently living in the same area (Culbert and Rice 1990; Chase and Scarborough, this volume). This was also the case for much of the Middle East, where by the 17th–19th centuries C.E. the landscape was quite sparsely settled, only attaining its present high level of settlement density in the 20th century C.E. Marked differences are also evident in the climate and vegetation: thus the rainfall range of the Maya Lowlands (ca. 500 millimeters to 2500 millimeters per annum), albeit with a significant dry season, is significantly greater than that of most of the Middle East, and of course forest vegetation plays a lesser role in Middle Eastern settlement and archaeological prospection except in some mountainous areas.

This chapter is written from the perspective of a Middle Eastern archaeologist: I have tried to demonstrate areas of commonality between Old and New World examples, which may provide useful insights into how cities coped with problems of agricultural supply and increasing scale. Necessarily, this study focuses upon global comparisons of archaeological landscapes, with emphasis on a small number of dimensions of landscape analysis, primarily soil and water management, as well as aspects of low density urbanism and settlement dispersal. Relations between climate and human settlement, although important to both Old and New World cases, are not treated here for limitations of space.

A key question for this comparative landscape analysis is whether cycles of settlement growth and decline are evident and whether there is evidence for long-term sustainability. To stress some of the initial IHOPE objectives as laid out by Costanza et al. (2011:253): "Simple deterministic relationships between environmental stress (e.g., a climatic event) and social change are inadequate."

My aim in this paper is first to compare selected aspects of water supply and soil management in the Middle East and Maya Lowlands (Figure 13.1) and to suggest where there are points of comparison and contrast. Second, I compare certain key features of settlement patterns between the two regions. However, because the Maya Lowlands include the phenomenon of "low-density urbanism," it is necessary here to extend the comparison to parts of South Asia as well. Necessarily, the focus is upon long-term use of the landscape, especially archaeological evidence for positive and negative aspects of soil and water management (see below). The questions discussed can be viewed from the perspective of "socio-natural studies" as outlined by van der Leeuw and Redman (2002), but in addition, I touch upon questions of human–environment dynamics of global concern. Because definitions and perceptions of the term "sustainability" vary, and according to Fisher (2009:230) can be scale dependent and "can be in the eye of the beholder," the term must be used with care. Here the value of archaeological studies, which uniquely present long-term records of both human settlement and associated environmental changes, come into their own. Archaeological data are particularly well suited to estimating whether past landscapes of settlement endured or did not; however, explaining such endurance or change is much more of a challenge.

During the Holocene, human settlements will have had very different scales of economic support depending upon the prevailing political economies. In the Middle East these will have ranged from more local economies, in the earlier prehistoric phases, to those that formed part of the economies of the extensive and powerful empires of the first millennium B.C.E. and later. Consequently, the response of communities to any type of external event, whether environmental, social, or political, will have varied. Therefore the present paper does not proceed as a diachronic study; rather, I have mainly chosen to focus upon the last two-to-three millennia in both Old and New World cases, not simply to make certain that comparisons are chronologically equivalent (which on the face of it seems somewhat arbitrary), but also to enable the comparison to take into account what may be a similarly evolutionary stage in settlement (as justified below).

For much of the Middle East, Holocene settlements tend to be bounded and to some degree nucleated, and they also show evidence, not only of cycles of growth and decline, but also of nucleation and dispersal (Wilkinson 2003; Ur 2010b). Nevertheless, the more dispersed patterns of settlement that prevailed for the duration of the later empires (post-1000 B.C.E.) do enable some degree of comparison to be made with the New World, and although cases of low density urbanism are rare in the Middle East, the high densities of rural settlement that prevailed during both the first millennium B.C.E. and C.E. may be significant in terms of trends of long-term landscape degradation.

The complexities of human impact on ancient environments should not be under-emphasized. In this context the editors of a recent volume remind us that "the non-linear, recursive, and multi-scalar qualities of eco-dynamic processes clearly indicate that causal relationships exist in multiple dimensions and are inherently unsuitable to explanations relying on universal driving mechanisms" (Hill et al. 2009:250). Such complexities are relevant to both the Maya Lowlands and the Middle East. For example, in the Middle East evidence of long-term landscape degradation varies considerably through time, and although there was probably a significant increase in human impact on the environment during the early Holocene (Redman 1999:107–110;

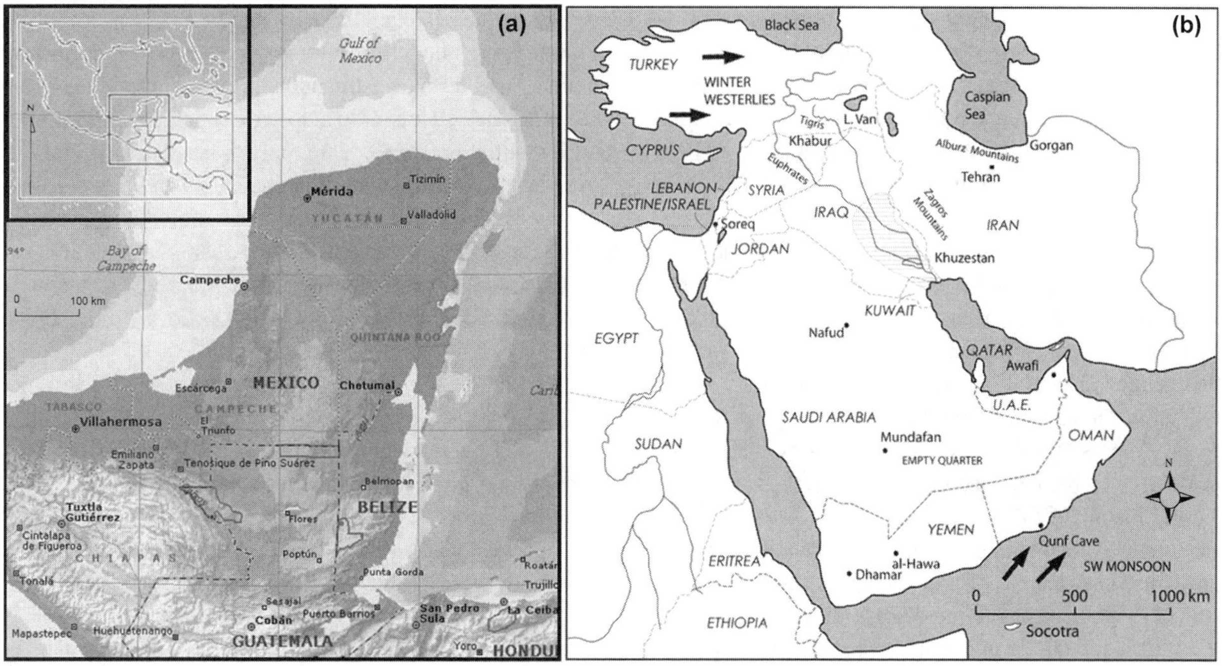

Figure 13.1. Maps showing (a) main places in Mesoamerica and (b) the Middle East discussed in text.

Rollefson and Köhler-Rollefson 1992), it is difficult to define any clear onset of major landscape degradation during the early Holocene. Nevertheless, studies in Jordan have recognized various "crises" or "hinge points" which have occurred as a result of a combination of demographic increases, landscape degradation, and climatic drying (Cordova 2007; Hill 2009). In the northern Fertile Crescent, although the Early Bronze Age (3200–2000 B.C.E.) represents a short-term peak in both settlement and landscape instability, it is during the later period of settlement and growth corresponding to the later territorial empires of the Neo-Assyrians, Seleucids, Roman-Parthian, Byzantine-Sasanian, and Early Islamic empires (1200 B.C.E. to C.E. 1000) that we see some increases in valley floor aggradation (Wilkinson 2010). Unfortunately, because valley floors receive episodic delivery of sediments from the neighboring terrain and sedimentation rates vary depending upon local geomorphology and river basin conditions, it is difficult to quantify rates of erosion and sedimentation. However, where large geoarchaeological data bases occur, patterns are emerging. For example, reviews of patterns of erosion and sedimentation by Dusar and colleagues (2011, 2012) demonstrate that although human impacts increased after the Bronze Age as landscape sensitivity increased, the increase is especially evident from the mid-first millennium B.C.E.

The Role of Climate

It is tempting to assume that in pre-modern times climatic fluctuations acted as a primary driver of socioeconomic change and particularly societal collapse (see de Menocal 2001; Staubwasser and Weiss 2006). However, not only were non-environmental factors important, human and naturally induced factors interacted in complex and often non-linear ways (Crumley 1994; Fisher 2009; Redman 2011:143). Therefore, despite the fact that climate change played an important role in societal change, even environmental scientists are starting to recognize that the role of climate change is more complex and nuanced than hitherto appreciated. For example, a recent global assessment of sustainability during the Holocene considered that "non-environmental factors" were at least as important as climatic fluctuations in driving social change (Roberts 2011). Moreover, when estimates of long-term settlement are put alongside climate proxy curves it becomes evident that human strategies were often capable of over-riding the limitations of climate change.

Despite these caveats, the role of climate has to be seen as a significant mechanism within the multi-component mix of factors that influenced both societal development and the assessment of soil management and erosion. In the Middle

East, interpretations of valley fills have bounced back and forth between the role of climate and human settlement as drivers. Whereas Butzer (1974) described a fine grained temporal record and inferred more complex inter-relations between humans and the environment, Vita-Finzi (1969) focused on region-wide climatic change as a causal factor (see also Brückner 1986; Cordova 2000; Goldberg 1998; Rosen 1986). Nevertheless, in recent years there has been an increasing tendency to focus upon the complexity of the relationship between humans and the environment and the role of humans in mediating some of the effects of climatic change (Casana 2008; Rosen 2007). Moreover, when both climate and human population are seen as together imposing a stress on the landscape, this combined impact presents greater explanatory power than each factor on its own (Wilkinson 2005).

In the Maya Lowlands, complex mechanisms are also regarded as fundamental to processes such as societal collapse. These include a combination of high population densities, loss of sustainability under hegemonic control, episodic droughts, and consumption of essential resources—all of which have been blamed for the Maya collapse (Redman 2011:137–38).

Whereas ancient communities were incapable of manipulating the weather, they were able to manage both soil and water resources, and it is these latter aspects of the environment which receives the bulk of the attention in this paper.

Managed Natural Resources

Here I discuss two aspects of resource management: first, soil management in the form of terraced agriculture together with soil erosion; and second, the management of water resources. Both of these types of management are widely evident in the Middle East and Maya regions.

Soil

In both the Middle East and the Maya regions, the complex intertwining of human–environment interactions can entail both "negative management" (such as soil erosion), as well as "positive management," the latter acting to stabilize the landscape and create new soils. Positive management can include the development of anthrosols, which result from the accumulation of organic residues, waste products from settlements, and sediments accumulated upon slopes or contained within irrigation waters. In addition, the creation of so-called landesque capital, namely "any investment in land with an anticipated life well beyond the present crop, or crop cycle" (Blaikie and Brookfield 1987:9), was important in both regions under discussion. Landesque capital, which entails longer term investment in built structures, such as terraces and check dams, also helps create deeper soils (Blaikie and Brookfield 1987:9). Here, only those classes of cultural landscape and associated geoarchaeology that are common to both the Middle East and the Mayan region are discussed. Summaries of other aspects of landscape degradation and erosion in the Maya region are provided by Dunning et al. (2009) and for the Middle East by Cordova (2007; Dusar et al. 2011).

Positive land management. In the Maya region, terraced field systems at (for example) Caracol and Taramarindito (Chase and Chase 1998; Dunning and Beach 2010; Whitmore and Turner 2001) can be compared at a general level with those in Palestine, parts of the Zagros Mountains, and particularly southern Arabia. For example, although field terraces in southern Arabia result mainly from the deliberate interception of hillslope deposits as a result of localized gravity accumulations and runoff, some are engineered, planned, and built up by soil introduced from elsewhere. However, most are a product of the efforts of thousands of households who have constructed vast numbers of walls to accumulate and thicken the soil to grow crops within a classic system of landesque (Blaikie and Brookfield 1987; Erickson 2006). Most examples of terraced fields in both the Middle East and the Maya Lowlands have been constructed in relatively moist regions where rainfall, sometimes supported by localized run-off, is sufficient to support crop growth. In contrast, their counterparts in South America concentrate in semi-arid mountains where irrigation is required to maintain crop growth (Denevan 2001:173).

Soil accumulations behind terrace walls provide a rich archive of sedimentary history and soil formation (Fish 1994:figure 3.1). Not only do terraced fields provide thicker soil horizons capable of holding more moisture and contribute greater rooting depth, in addition, the fertilization of fields on terraces results in the development of anthrosols. These over-deepened soil horizons result in more sustained levels of production and can buffer environmental impacts, as well as over-ride the limitations of the original soils. Ultimately this leads to a process of positive feed-back in which rather unproductive hillslopes eventually result in increased agricultural productivity and positive returns.

More generally, agricultural terraces can be regarded as belonging to the lower end of the runoff spectrum, ranging from large masonry dams at the largest end down to modest field terraces at the bottom (Wilkinson 2006).

In southern Arabia, the construction of terraced fields was not necessarily intended to conserve soil, but rather to deepen the soil profile on steep slopes where soils were

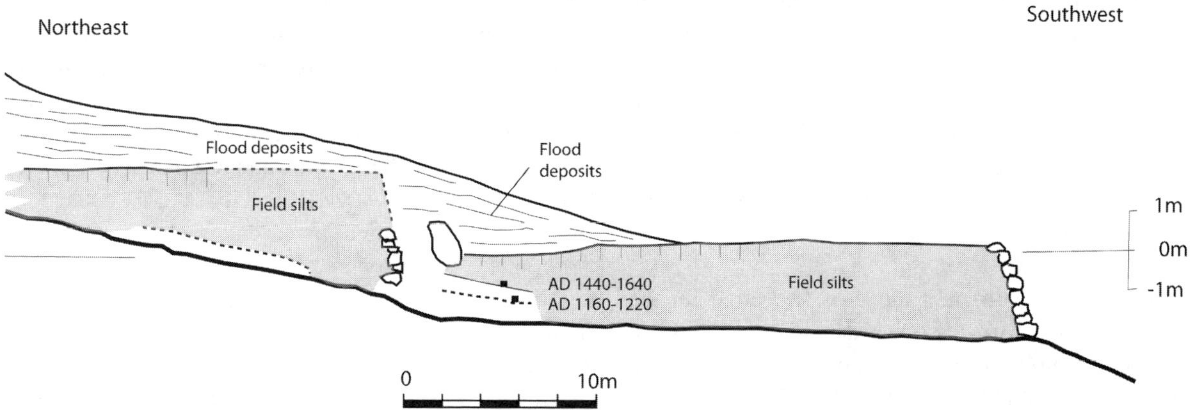

Figure 13.2. Section indicating post-terrace erosion of previously intact terrace walls (in grey, the pre-collapse terrace being defined by broken lines) in Yemen (amended from Wilkinson 2003:figure 9.4).

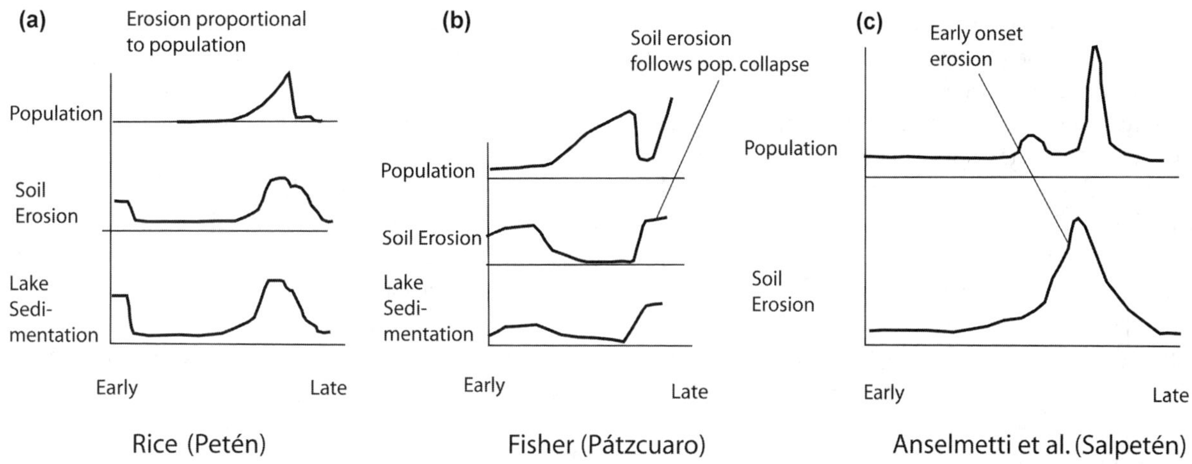

Figure 13.3. Graphs sketching the soil-erosion models discussed (re-drafted without scales to show comparative trends only): (a) Petén (Rice 1996); (b) Lake Pátzcuaro basin of Mexico (Fisher 2009); (c) Lake Salpetén, Petén, (Anselmetti et al. 2007). The Highland Yemen terrace model most closely resembles that of Fisher.

shallow. Consequently, in aggregate, systems of terraced fields had the effect of producing remarkably stable landscapes, ideal for rain-fed, irrigated, or runoff agriculture. This is caused by the tendency of terraces to be constructed in order to gradually infill all parts of the landscape, from valley bottom to hillcrest, with the result that not only are erosive slopes rendered stable, but also valley floors are infilled and constrained by walls and terraces so that their catchment areas become stabilized and runoff amplitudes diminish. Because terrace construction is contingent upon labor pools being available to maintain the terrace walls (Blaikie and Brookfield 1987), any decline in available labor, as has occurred episodically in Yemen, can result in the neglect and collapse of field terraces as well as a reduction in landscape stability (Figure 13.2). In addition, not only can the clearance of vegetation on exposed slopes above the terraces promote run-off, but the incidence of heavy rainfall or the neglect of terrace walls can then fuel a cascade of down-slope movement of soil and sediment (Pietsch and Mabut 2012; Varisco 1991; Wilkinson 2003:188–190). In other words, what starts as a policy of positive soil management can turn into a serious problem when either or both demography or environmental changes result in a change in the balance of soil accumulation.

Both soil erosion and landscape degradation are commonly perceived as significant factors of negative management (Blaikie and Brookfield 1987). This is the case in both the Middle East and the Maya Lowlands, and particularly pertinent to the present papers are relationships between population and soil erosion as they play out on valley slopes, river flood plains, and lake basins.

Several models of the relationship between population size and soil erosion are evident in the geoarchaeological literature for Mesoamerica. For example, Rice

(1996; Figure 13.3a) suggests that soil erosion had been roughly proportional to population increase. This is because soil erosion increased as a result of the removal of vegetation and the exposure of soils, which in turn were proportional to population size. Increased soil erosion then continued as population grew until there was a demographic collapse, after which soil erosion declined as the surrounding land surfaces became reforested and stabilized.

However, a very different model is suggested for the Lake Pátzcuaro basin of Mexico where sedimentation in nearby lakes is employed as a proxy measure for increased soil erosion (Fisher 2009; Figure 13.3b). At Pátzcuaro, sediment accumulation and associated landscape degradation remained at a reduced level as a result of increased land management which took the form of the construction of terraced fields. Sedimentation and soil erosion only followed demographic collapse as a result of a lack of maintenance of terraces and other measures.

A third model uses estimates of soil erosion rates (in Lake Salpetén, Petén) to suggest that human impacts, largely through deforestation and the exposure of soils, resulted in the deposition of a thick deposit of up to seven meters of Maya Clay (Anselmetti et al. 2007; Figure 13.3c). However, rather than relating increased erosion to the period of maximum population as implied by the Rice model (1996), maximum soil erosion was evident during the Middle to Late Pre-Classic (700 B.C.E.–C.E. 250), a period of relatively low population. In other words, erosion took place during the initial period of land clearance. Significantly in Salpetén, when population declined around C.E. 1000, soil erosion also declined. The data from Anselmetti and colleagues (2007) clearly demonstrate that population numbers are not the only driver of soil erosion, because the nature of human actions on the landscape are as important as numbers alone. Unlike the Fisher model, where population *decrease* may increase soil erosion because the protective terraces would not be maintained, it appears that absolute population decrease has resulted in some degree of stability. Furthermore, where much soil cover has already been removed, sediment delivery to the lakes will be reduced as a result of diminished soil supply. This "early onset" erosion is echoed in other parts of Yucatan where it is evident that relatively small populations can generate significant amounts of erosion if they reduce vegetation without taking appropriate steps to manage the exposed soils (Dunning et al. 2009). It is therefore evident that factors other than population size alone must be considered when explaining landscape degradation and soil erosion.

The above scenarios compare with geoarchaeological studies in the Middle East, where in addition to human activities, seasonal rainfall and aridity-induced vegetation loss are also considered to contribute to the formation of so-called valley fills. For example, in Yemen, a substantial pulse of erosion occasionally occurs during initial phases of vegetation clearance and terrace construction (Wilkinson 2005:179), as is found in the Maya region and Mexico. There was also frequently a *decrease* in soil erosion and associated sedimentation as population increased and landscapes became more stable (Wilkinson 2005). Subsequently, the collapse of terraces has been known to initiate a pulse of down-slope erosion as observed in the Lake Pátzcuaro basin of Mexico (Figure 13.3b; Fisher 2009). This is clearly evident on Figure 13.2 where post collapse sediments (flood deposits) overlie earlier phases of terraced fields (grey on Figure 13.2). Because variations in basin geomorphology as well as the timing of terrace construction or abandonment within any one river basin can result in very different histories of sediment delivery, it follows that sediment accumulation can also be complex. For example, in parts of the Middle East where demographic growth has occurred in under-managed uplands, soil erosion can increase, either because terrace fields (if constructed) were inadequately maintained, or they were too spatially discontinuous to stabilize the land surface. Moreover, where rural settlement has spread from lowlands on to erodible hillslopes, rates of soil erosion and downslope sedimentation can increase abruptly (Casana 2008).

From the foregoing, at least three temporal patterns of soil erosion are recognizable (Figure 13.3): (a) first, the original model of Rice (1996), which sees soil erosion resulting from a peak of maximum population as established in Petén (this is also when settlement moves on to vulnerable terrain and slopes); (b) when terraces collapse following a population decline (Fisher 2009); and (c) at the onset of vegetation and soil disturbance (Anselmetti et al. 2007). Although all three patterns are evident in the Middle East, the second case is comparable to that presented for Yemen (Figure 13.2).

These scenarios indicate that conditions of land management and settlement practice set the framework for soil erosion, and these depend upon local circumstances. Moreover, changing agricultural practices can result in new pathways for sediment transport (i.e., increased connectivity) as well as changes in contributing source areas (Lexartza-Artza and Wainwright 2011). In addition, estimates of soil erosion depend upon the temporal resolution of the sedimentary record. Consequently, although they may be locally applicable, none of the above models can necessarily translate across all areas, because each basin will exhibit a different geometry and geomorphology and will also consist of different proportions of terraced, wooded, or open terrain. Hence when aggregated, the resultant soil erosion will consist of the sum of contrasting conditions extending over different basin areas. Moreover, landscape stability depends upon local labor investment and management as well as "external" environmental factors.

Despite their seemingly different long-term trajectories of development, the terraced landscapes of the Maya Lowlands and the Middle East can also exhibit uncanny similarities, both at the macro and micro level. Contrast, for example, the mode of construction and pattern of terraced fields in Yucatan with those of highland Yemen (Figure 13.4). Except for enclaves of state-planned fields, both Old and New World terrace systems provide classic examples of "organic" landscapes that are closely sculptured to the natural topography. Such "bottom up" landscapes, as argued by Erickson (2006), appear to ultimately derive from the incremental additions of small-scale structures to formative stages which were essentially "natural" landscapes. This degree of similarity between Old and New World terrace systems may ultimately derive from the operation of equivalent processes that produced landscapes that evolved from similar initial conditions. Arguably, they therefore resulted from similar long term processes of human niche construction.

"Human niche construction," which originated as a branch of evolutionary biology, "emphasizes the capacity of organisms to modify their environment and thereby influence their own and other species' evolution" (Kendal et al. 2011:785; O'Brien and Laland 2012). Within mountainous valleys, terraced agriculture forms a classic example of niche construction because the thickened soil profiles not only provide an enhanced soil environment for food production, but also the terrace flats extend the area of cultivable land. As a result of such enhanced food production, agriculture produces positive returns so that the carrying capacity of the landscape increases significantly through time.

Moreover, by beginning at roughly the same formative stage, namely essentially similar "natural" initial conditions, and by building up the agricultural infrastructure incrementally, both Old and New World communities could end up with an essentially similar type of landscape, a process akin to convergent evolution. Such landscapes can be perceived from an evolutionary perspective using the following example: when investigating the evolution of multiple populations of *E. coli* bacteria, Lenski and colleagues "found that a population of a given generation is in many respects more similar to the other independent lineages than to its own ancestors" (German 2012:11). Other, perhaps even more relevant examples of convergent evolution can be found in the case of sharks and dolphins. In the case of terraced agriculture, if it is assumed that field terraces were constructed from a formative stage in (for example) the mid-Holocene and gradually expanded to fill any given valley system, then after a given number of years the evolved terrace systems on both sides of the Atlantic would be more similar to each other than they would be to their own ancestral landscape. As a result, the general appearance of terraced landscapes converges towards a mature and evolved state. Moreover, as long as the population is sufficient to maintain the terraces and areas of open terrain are limited, such systems attain a stable state—that is, until these conditions are disrupted.

Although at this stage the *E. coli* evolution can only be used as a metaphor, there is an inherent logic to the development of similar landscapes from similar initial conditions. This also implies that if similar formative (i.e., natural) landscapes are not found on opposites sides of the Atlantic, there is little chance of the resultant cultural landscapes being the same. Hence, some of the most characteristic landscapes of the Yucatan Peninsula, such as karstic landscapes with *aguadas* or *cenotes*, are unlikely to be replicated in the Old World unless the physical geography, human agency, and demography are appropriate. This difference in initial conditions reduces our ability to compare many landscapes between Old and New Worlds. Nevertheless, this is not to say that equivalent natural landscapes necessarily develop toward a similar end point, nor that such developments are environmentally determined. Not only is human agency (and ingenuity) a key factor in the development of similar cultural landscapes, but also (taking an analogy from chaos theory), slight differences in initial conditions might be expected to result in rather different outcomes.

Water Management

Water management is a key strategy in the mitigation of climatic or demographic limitations and enables agricultural production to be increased and or rendered more predictable. Although it is tempting to compare the irrigated landscapes of southern Mesopotamia with those of the lands of the Maya, not only are southern Mesopotamian hydraulic works significantly earlier in date than those of the Maya, they also have developed within very different hydrological environments. Therefore rather than using the earlier *southern* Mesopotamian evidence for hydraulic management, I have chosen to compare Maya hydraulic landscapes with the later systems of Upper Mesopotamia as well as those of Sri Lanka.

From the Neolithic through the Bronze Age (i.e., from roughly the sixth millennium to the second millennium B.C.E.), Upper Mesopotamian communities were predominantly dependent upon rain-fed cultivation, although limited amounts of irrigation occurred at Mari on the Euphrates and perhaps one or two other localities. This was followed around 1200–800 B.C.E. and later by the spread of canals

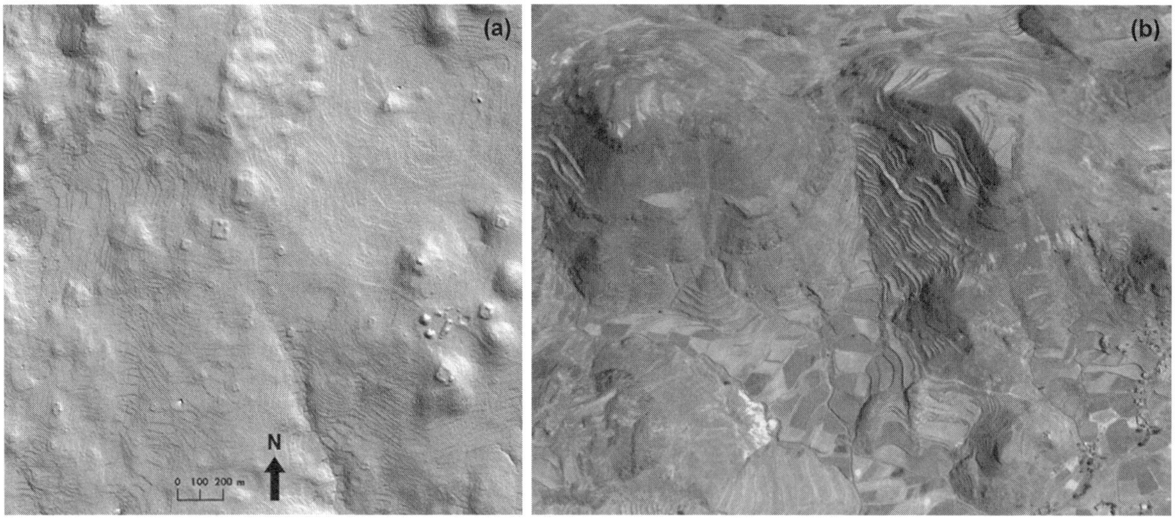

Figure 13.4. Images of terraced landscapes in both Mesoamerica and the Middle East (Yemen). (a) Caracol (LiDAR Image from Chase et al. 2011); (b) Google Earth Image from the Yemen highlands near Yarim.

throughout Upper Mesopotamia as communities aimed not simply to mitigate the effects of the semi-arid climate, but also to increase or stabilize yields. This process is now becoming clear especially through the records of the Middle and Neo-Assyrian empires, but also by the use of remote sensing, which together suggest that major irrigation schemes attained a high point of development during the Neo-Assyrian, Achaemenid, Hellenistic, Partho-Sasanian, Roman, Byzantine, and Islamic empires (i.e., roughly between about 1200 B.C.E. and C.E. 1000). Not only is this phase chronologically closer to the development of the Classic Maya cities and their water systems, but it also represents a fundamental shift toward large-scale water management in an agricultural economy that previously relied on rainfall. In Upper Mesopotamia, this shift enabled large areas of marginal land to be colonized as well as previously lightly settled areas to be settled more densely (Wilkinson and Rayne 2010).

An equivalent process of landscape transformation was also taking place in parts of the Maya lowlands, where swamp margin (i.e., *bajo* edge) locations in the Late Formative (400 B.C.E.–C.E. 150) were replaced in the Classic period by convex hydraulic systems located on more elevated land that enabled greater control to be exerted over the distribution of water (Scarborough 2003:111; Scarborough and Lucero 2010). Whereas in both regions a major change in the use of the landscape resulted in the adoption of novel systems of hydraulic management during the period 1000 B.C.E. to C.E. 1000, Upper Mesopotamia, with its more uniform physical landscape, probably lent itself more to large-scale hydraulic management than did the variegated landscape of the Maya. Hence in both the bajo edge locations and the subsequent convex micro watersheds, development was slow and accretionary. On the other hand, the larger scale hydraulic networks of Upper Mesopotamia often developed relatively rapidly and conversely could be disrupted, because the lengthy canals were vulnerable to being severed or damaged by eroding rivers and their floods, as was the case of the Nahrawan Canal in Iraq (Adams 1965). In addition, the nature of water provisioning to the settlements themselves was also very different: Upper Mesopotamia witnessed a boom in canal construction for urban water supply for cities such as Neo-Assyrian Nineveh and Roman Antioch, as well as for cereal cultivation, parks and gardens, and for the supply and taxation of a growth of dispersed rural settlements.

Maya projects were often very different. Thus the huge settlement complex of Early (or Late) Classic Dzibanché covering some 15–20 square kilometers or more included extensive fields and associated canals which contributed to "a grand experiment in a different kind of Maya garden city, wetter than others" (Dunning and Beach 2010:378). Nowhere in Upper Mesopotamia do we see such massive sprawls of low-density urbanism being supported by irrigation. Instead, Upper Mesopotamian towns, villages, and cities were circumscribed and bounded, extending for no more than 750 hectares (i.e., 7.5 square kilometers), usually much less.

A key contrast between the Maya Lowlands and Upper Mesopotamia is that the bajos-type system, which fluctuated between perennial and ephemeral (Dunning et al. 2002), arguably lacked the hydraulic connectivity between basins and sub-basins. In addition, the low relief, karstic nature of much of the terrain would preclude the construction of long canals.

In Upper Mesopotamia, after around 1000 B.C.E. when irrigation systems became common, the gentle and steady gradient of the terrain enabled small hydraulic systems to be "scaled up" to ever larger systems. Equally, the numerous interweaving canals obvious in valleys such as the Balikh in northern Syria produced a degree of redundancy in the channel network so that, in following times of crisis, the canals systems could be "scaled down" to more manageable lengths. On the other hand, in the Maya lowlands such scaling up and down may have been difficult because of the localized nature of hydraulic basins.

Although there is some equivalence of chronological progression in both the Maya lowlands and Upper Mesopotamia, the hydraulic landscapes show a very different relationship to the political economies in question. Whereas Upper Mesopotamia experienced a shift from relatively small-scale, rain-fed cultivation (Neolithic to Bronze Age) to a significant amount of large-scale, valley-side canals (Iron Age and later), frequently under imperial control, the Maya lowlands experienced a shift from lowland bajos-edge and concave watersheds to convex systems and more complex upland reservoirs that rarely manifested "absolute elite control" (Scarborough 2003:113; Scarborough et al. 2012).

For a more realistic comparison we should therefore turn to the areas of the Old World subject to low-density urbanism which also exhibit substantial developments of hydraulic landscapes during the past 2500 years. Particularly relevant are the tanks of Sri Lanka (Dharmasena 2010; Scarborough 2003:134–7, 63). This hydraulic system, which developed in a region of relatively high rainfall (1250–5000 millimeters per annum) and former tropical forest, was based around a series of tanks and reservoirs which received water as a cascading sequence along rivers and streams (Dharmasena 2010:348). Water diversion was effected via weirs, from rivers, as well as from micro-catchments (Gunawardana 1971). When initially developed, perhaps in the first millennium B.C.E., these did not form an integrated system, but any lack of connectivity was compensated for by the construction of a series of linking canals during the first millennium C.E. (Dharmasena 2010:351). Moreover, the system exhibits some evolution as increased water interception was enabled by raising dams, which ultimately supplied a more centralized economy (Scarborough 2003:136). Overall, the tank system is very well adapted to the Sri Lankan physical landscape and its "wet and dry" environment and is nested within a mosaic of shifting cultivation (called *chena* in Sri Lanka) to provide a resilient and sophisticated water management system. As pointed out by Scarborough (2003:135), the Sri Lankan hydraulic landscape closely resembles many in the Maya Lowlands. In part this similarity may derive from their development within semi-tropical wet and dry environments so that the initial conditions for both systems exhibit similar topographic relief (although Sri Lanka lacked the karstic element). In both cases the Maya and Sri Lankan populations were able to successfully enhance the natural environment to meet challenges such as the lack of hydraulic connectivity, demonstrating that human populations were active agents capable of sculpting the terrain to creative and productive ends and thereby supporting a high degree of sociopolitical complexity and agricultural productivity.

However, in the case of the Maya Lowlands, this was not without its costs and particularly relevant is the change in the karstic wetlands (bajos) as a result of forest removal by humans. As Dunning and colleagues (2002:279) noted, "our findings demonstrate the potentially devastating and long-term consequences of tropical deforestation. The transformation of bajos from perennial to seasonal wetlands occurred about 2,000 years ago. Even after the general abandonment of the region around 900 CE, most bajos remained seasonal wetlands, with only a few pockets of perennial moisture (*civales*) slowly being reestablished."

Settlement and Cities

Here, following a brief discussion of the dynamics of settlements in part of the Middle East, I discuss the relative scale of towns and cities in both the Middle East and the Maya region, with specific emphasis on the topic of low density urbanism.

In the Middle East, most cities before about 1000 B.C.E. were of relatively modest size, usually being much less than 400 hectares in total area. Temporal modeling of settlement trends demonstrates both the dynamics of urban growth and decline as well as the different dynamics of different classes of settlement. Thus, when the area of individual Early Bronze Age "towns" is plotted using a century-scale time sequence, it is evident that some, such as Titrish Höyük (Turkey), rise and fall extremely rapidly. In contrast, smaller sites (those less than five hectares) show a much more stable long term trajectory with relatively muted rises and falls, perhaps implying a more sustainable pattern of settlement (Figure 13.5a; Wilkinson et al. 2012). Not only do many towns fluctuate in size more than the settlements in the neighborhood, the amplitude of these fluctuations is often greater than those of environmental factors such as estimated rainfall for the period. Moreover in certain cases, such as Tell es-Sweyhat, Syria, settlement growth is out of sync with climate fluctuations as estimated from climate proxy data, in this case from Soreq Cave, Israel (Figure 13.5b).

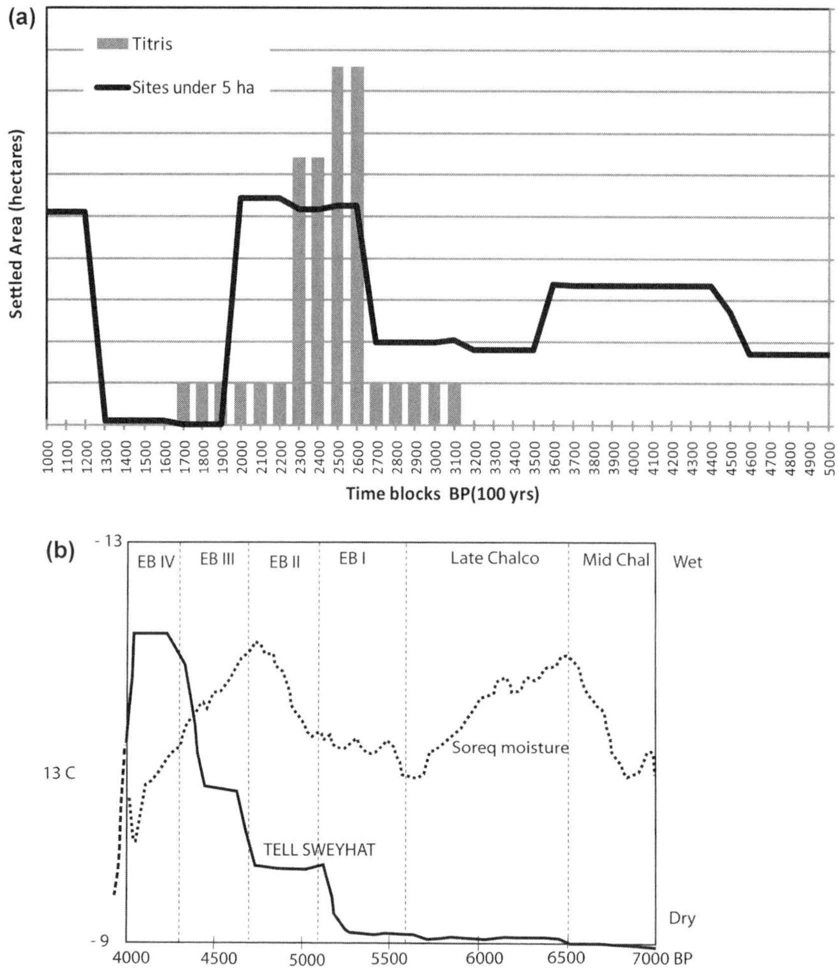

Figure 13.5. (a) Urban dynamics of large and small Early Bronze Age settlements in the Turkish Middle Euphrates (courtesy of Dan Lawrence: Fragile Crescent Project). (b) The approximate trajectory of growth and decline of the site of Tell es-Sweyhat (northern Syria) against the climate proxy curve for Soreq Cave (broken line). (Based upon data in Bar-Matthews and Ayalon [2011]; Wilkinson et al. [2012]; and Zettler [1997]).

However, just because the smaller settlements exhibit long-term stability does not mean that they were necessarily sustainable; they may simply exhibit path dependency as a result of cultural factors. For example, they may have functioned as "place holders" in the landscape for the resident communities in order to demonstrate tenure or long-term allegiance to the land. If climatic factors were significant to such settlement dynamics, it implies that settlements of different size reacted rather differently to similar climatic fluctuations. Moreover, detailed plots from individual expansive sites suggest a pattern of rise and fall that although similar in the sub-humid and semi-arid areas, are not contemporaneous (Wilkinson et al. 2012).

Low Density Urbanism

In contrast to the modest scale of these Bronze Age Middle Eastern "cities" or "towns," those of Mesoamerica and South Asia are manifestly vast. Particularly pertinent is the debate concerning the belt of low density agrarian-based urbanism in southeast Asia and the humid tropics of Mesoamerica (Coe 1957; Fletcher 2004, 2012). Such low density urbanism may constitute a global belt which extends throughout the sub-tropics, where specific ecological and transportation circumstances of bulk products apply as discussed by Fletcher (2012) and Scarborough and Lucero (2010). In contrast, in the Middle East, even where large cities are surrounded by dense patterns of rural settlement, the estimates of settlement patterns hardly seem to fit the description of low density urbanism as recognized in the Yucatan. Thus for Neo-Assyrian Upper Mesopotamia (a period of particularly dense rural settlement), estimates of rural population densities of 32–118 persons per square kilometer (Wilkinson et al. 2005:41–44; Ur 2010a:127) are much lower than those of the Maya heartland at a somewhat later date. For example, more recent estimates of 100–200 persons per square kilometer (Whitmore and Turner 2001:236) and 220–880 persons per square kilometer, or even higher, made for Puuc and the Copan valley (Dunning et al. 2009:91–92), indicate that rural settlement patterns of the Middle East were apparently significantly lower than those of the Maya Lowlands.

Unfortunately, because data sources on settlement patterns are rarely standardized, it is difficult to compare patterns of low density urbanism between regions (but see Peterson and Drennan 2012). Witness, for example, the pattern of sites around Anuradhapura, Sri Lanka, which are nearly all relatively small (less than 250 square meters, or 1/40 hectare), and which are difficult to compare with equivalent patterns around either Angkor Wat or Mesoamerican cities (see Fletcher 2012:figure 11.7). Although a case can be made that the signature landscape of the Anuradhapura region is one of low density urbanism (Coningham et al. 2007), when excavated these sites appear to be the remains of temporary dwellings of agriculturalists who were employed in slash and burn agriculture (i.e., swiddening). Consequently, the survey data might equally be interpreted as forming a dense scatter of primarily small rural settlements. In other words, some South Asian settlement patterns could be defined as either dense rural settlement or low density urbanism, depending upon the criteria applied. Clearly, such attempts at distinguishing between dense rural settlement versus low density urbanism are not easy, and may seem little more than a quibble. However, because such distinctions also contribute to how urban areas are delimited and defined, they are ultimately very important, as discussed below.

As stated above, low density urbanism appears less significant in most of the Middle East than in parts of South Asia. Nevertheless, not only were later cities, such as those of the early Islamic caliphates, extremely extensive in area, they were probably surrounded by a belt of high density rural settlement which may have formed a continuum with the city itself. This might, for example, have been the case around the Islamic cities of Zafar and Sohar in Oman, although unfortunately such areas are mainly obscured by the modern day spread of suburban settlement and gardens or expunged by recent developments and fields. Nevertheless, in the case of Sohar, surveyed in the 1970s, there existed a five- to six-kilometer radius scatter of intensive agriculture and conduit-irrigated gardens west of the city (Costa and Wilkinson 1987). These might, in addition, have accommodated a dense scatter of impermanent palm frond dwellings. Such penumbras of dense rural garden settlements might bring these Islamic cities more in line with those of low density urbanism.

Whether low density urbanism (or high density rural settlement) actually formed a belt around the globe is less clear. The dense pattern of rural settlement characteristic of the terraced landscapes of highland Yemen (> 2000 meters) during the late first millennium B.C.E. and early C.E. occurred within a similar landscape to sites such as Cerro Jazmin in the Mixteca Alta, Mexico or Caracol, Belize (Chase et al. 2011). But whereas the Mexican and Yemeni cases occupy the same latitudinal belt (ca. 15 degrees N +/-), examples from the Yucatan are located within lower terrain than both, and therefore experience significantly different ecological conditions.

More profound is the relationship between city size and longevity, which implies the existence of "an operational ceiling" for the development of cities (Fletcher 2004: figure 13.7). In other words, the larger the (ancient) city, the shorter its life-span when at its maximum size. Therefore although eighth–ninth century C.E. Baghdad may have housed a population of around 500,000, and perhaps as high as 1.6 million, this figure was sustained for less than two centuries (Fletcher 2004; but see Kennedy 2011:189 for more modest estimates). The overall relationship for larger pre-industrial compact cities globally is illustrated in Figure 13.6, which demonstrates how the largest cities lasted for little more than 60 years, whereas smaller cities in the region of 20–40 square kilometers endured for 660–730 years.[1] A similar generalization also holds for a sample of smaller and mainly older compact cities of the ancient Middle East (Figures 13.7a and 13.7b). In the case of Figure 13.7, the settlements are drawn from the rain-fed zone of northern Syria and Iraq as far south as early Islamic Samarra, located just beyond the limit of rain-fed cultivation. This sample includes sites ranging in date from Late Chalcolithic 3–4 Tell Brak (ca. 3900–3200 B.C.E.), through the Assyrian capital cities of Nineveh, Nimrud, and Khorsabad (ninth to seventh centuries B.C.E.), to early Islamic Samarra (ninth century C.E.). However, unlike the configuration of pre-industrial compact cities plotted by Fletcher, the distribution is concave up when plotted on normal axes (Figure 13.7a) but attains a more linear, roughly power-law relation when plotted on logarithmic axes (Figure 13.7b). Although it is not yet clear how this relationship holds for a larger sample, it illustrates the differences between early Middle Eastern cities versus the pre-industrial cities analyzed by Fletcher (2004).

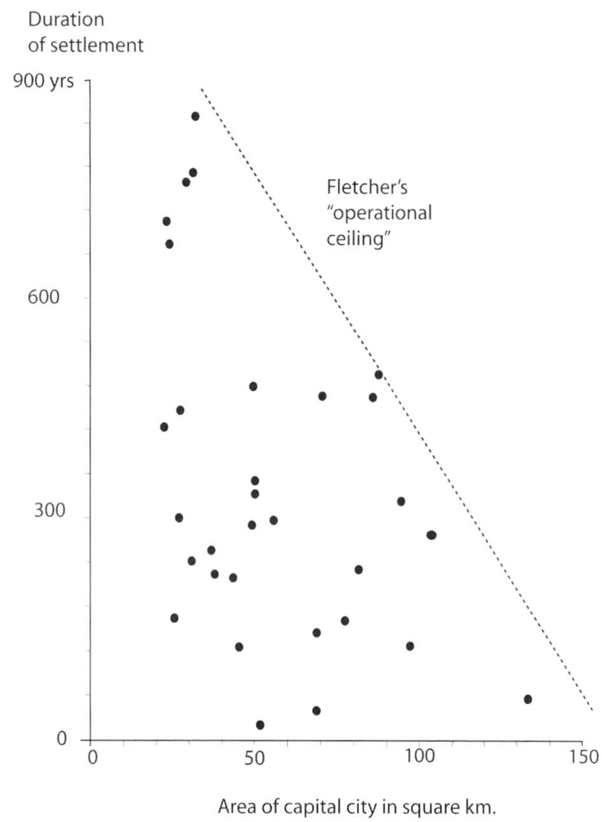

Figure 13.6. Urban dynamics of major pre-industrial cities represented by their duration (vertical axis) and maximum size in square kilometers (horizontal axis) (re-drawn from Fletcher 2004:figure 13.7).

What is evident from the analysis of Middle Eastern cities is that only during their very late stages, namely during the first millennium C.E., do cities start to attain the scale of those in Mesoamerica and South Asia. Comparisons between South Asia and Mesoamerica demonstrate that cities in the former area were significantly larger than those of Mesoamerica (Fletcher 2012:300): compare greater Angkor, which covered ca. 900–1,000 square kilometers with the 100–150 square kilometers of Tikal (Evans et al. 2007:14279). On the other hand, the LiDAR survey of Caracol defines an urban core of some 177 square kilometers and places that city within the scale of low density urbanism elsewhere in the ancient world (Chase et al. 2011). Such figures overwhelm the Early Islamic cities of Baghdad and Samarra (Iraq) which fell within the range of 5700 to 7000 hectares (57–70 square kilometers) in the eighth–ninth century and ninth century (C.E. 836–892), respectively, and were significantly smaller than their Maya counterparts. Clearly, such estimates show huge differences in scale between those cities defined as exhibiting low density urbanism. Therefore if the above relationship between city size and duration is to be tested, it is necessary to obtain some degree of consistency in the definitions of urban areas and estimates of their populations. This is not to say that the above estimates are wrong, only that they may be based upon rather different criteria.

Fletcher (2004:132) argues that there is no deterministic relationship between city size and duration; nevertheless, if such a ceiling existed it implies either that factors such as internal interactions or communications influenced the trajectories of these cities, or perhaps they were so vulnerable that any environmental or political event could have brought them down. In the Middle East and South Asia, although not all cities characterized by low density urbanism developed under the rule of kings of large, powerful states or empires, many did. Therefore, polity size does appear to provide one factor in the relationship between the growth of expansive polities and massive cities.

Particularly significant in terms of sustainability, was that it was necessary to supply the population with food. In the case of the mega cities of the Islamic Middle East, this not only presented a major problem for the administration of the caliphate, but the *rate* of rise and fall of such cities must have imposed an additional burden on supply systems. Thanks to both historical and archaeological sources, there is good evidence to indicate that the systems of water supply and irrigation were expanded significantly in order to provision these Abbasid cities (Kennedy 2011; Wilkinson and Rayne 2010). Moreover, it would have been necessary for such systems of supply to have been extremely flexible in order to re-direct the supply of bulk produce if cities were moved to new locations and demand in that sector collapsed, as was the case of Baghdad and Samarra. In the case of the Early Islamic Middle East, the supply of bulk foodstuffs was effected by integrated and efficient transportation networks, specifically by maritime and riverine boats (Kennedy 2011).[2] That this challenge of supply extended beyond the capital cities is illustrated by the case of trading cities such as Siraf (Iran), which had a very limited agricultural hinterland in contrast to Sohar (Oman) which possessed extensive areas of fields and gardens. Any supply deficits at Siraf could therefore have been met by maritime transport of bulk goods from other parts of the maritime network including Sohar (Wilkinson 2009).

Whereas the food supply of cities such as Angkor Wat and Caracol seem to have been met by the dense pattern of surrounding gardens and associated settlements (Chase et al. 2011:397; Evans et al. 2007:14280–14281), equivalent Islamic cities in the Middle East required a much larger hinterland which was integrated via efficient networks of maritime and riverine transport. Despite (or perhaps because of) their size, the mega cities of the Middle East did not endure

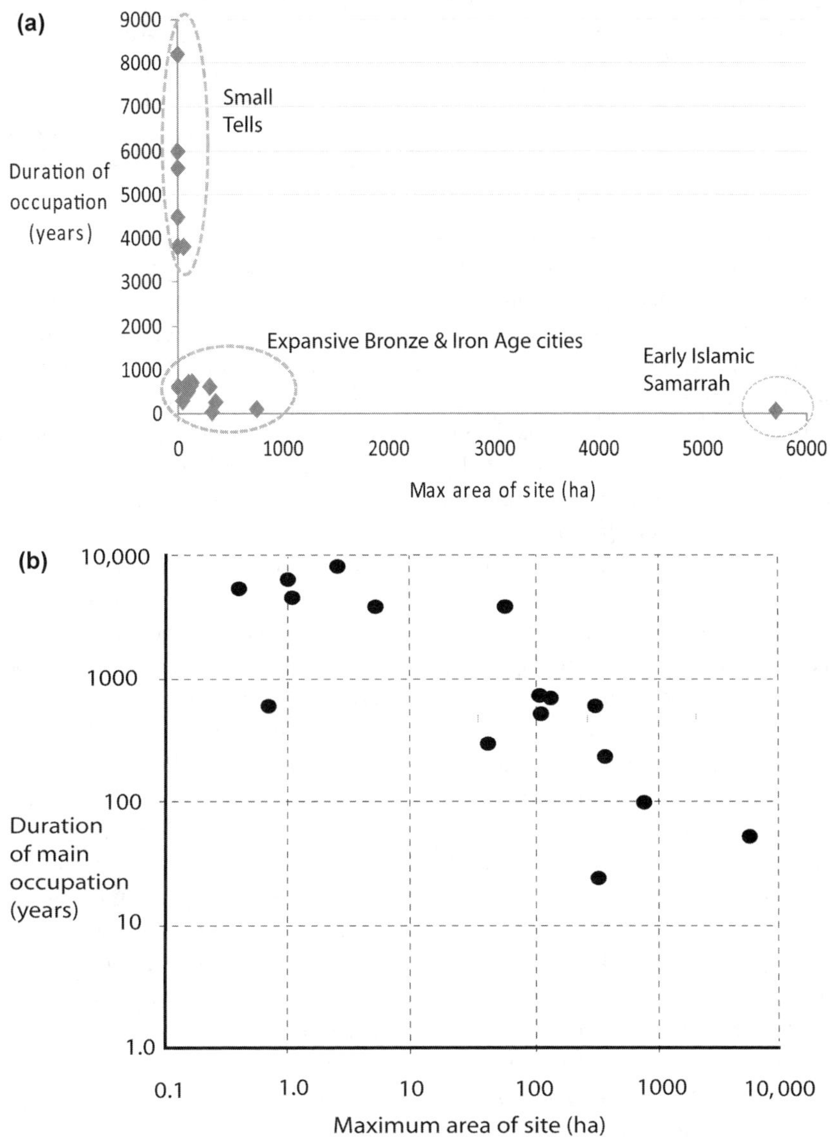

Figure 13.7. Urban dynamics of ancient Upper Mesopotamian towns and cities represented by their duration (vertical axis) and size, in hectares (horizontal axis): (a) Sample of sites according to normal scales; site classes are encircled in broken lines; (b) the same sites plotted according to log-log scales.

for long periods. This was in part because the rulers chose to re-locate their cities (Fletcher 2004:129; Kennedy 2011), but also because of internal socioeconomic factors or political and environmental crises. This raises the question: can settlement duration be equated with sustainability? Although this is difficult to explain in terms of process, the empirical evidence implies that when ancient cities become particularly large they were equally likely to decline rapidly. It is too early to say whether modern cities follow such trajectories: factors of governance, global economies, and social interactions all play critical and rather different roles today than in the past. Nevertheless, the archaeological evidence for both the Maya and the Old World mega cities raises interesting "grand challenge" questions, and the best way to tackle these is by comparative analysis and the provision of detailed, well defined empirical data.

Discussion and Conclusions

This broad and selective chapter suggests that questions of sustainability relate to both top-down and bottom-up situations. The bottom-up view is provided through the lens of landscapes managed at the household level, whereas the top-down perspective derives from a macroscopic view of cities and their trajectories of rise and fall. However, when crises did occur it was essential to have coping methods in place, otherwise it would have been necessary for communities to relocate in order to survive.

The co-occurrence, in both the Middle East and Yucatan, of increasing population *and* greater landscape stability echoes Michael Mortimore's (1998) argument for Africa, namely that population increase and land use intensification can occur together and without landscape degradation. Consequently if landscapes are well managed, such management initiates measures that stabilize the agricultural landscape. This of course requires a considerable depth of local knowledge of soils and agriculture, but with appropriate land management (such as investment in landesque capital or increased use of fertilizers), population density can actually increase in line with increased soil fertility (Mortimore 1998:156–58).

In other words, as long as practices of land management are appropriate, the landscapes in question are capable of supporting remarkably high population densities. Therefore archaeological evidence for investment in soil management is important for demonstrating how the carrying capacity of the land can be increased in line with population. Of course, how labor is deployed and landscapes managed vary depending upon the local environment and demography as well as the scale of investments.

At the macro-level, cities demonstrate disquieting tendencies to collapse as they become larger. However, because the evidence as compiled is rather preliminary, and importantly depends upon how the size of the city is defined, further empirical studies are necessary. Nevertheless, it appears from case studies from the Euphrates region of Turkey and Syria that the dynamics of cities can be very different from those of rural settlements. In addition, processes of landscape transformation matter, because any investments in large-scale terracing or irrigation systems may result in traces of earlier activities such as low density urbanism being erased. Before low density urbanism can be compared globally, it is essential to estimate the density of settlement per square kilometer in a wide range of localities and according to consistent criteria. It may also be necessary for archaeologists to sub-divide settlements into different land use or settlement zones that reflect different levels of sustainability. The most obvious contrast, therefore, between the later imperial cities of the Middle East and those of South Asia and the Yucatan is that the former commanded large supply hinterlands lubricated by hydraulic transport networks, whereas the latter were supplied to a significant degree by their surrounding agrarian garden settlements.

This chapter has argued that city dynamics and urban support systems were based upon a wide range of variables (Costanza et al. 2011); it is also evident that numerous vulnerabilities existed. If de-stabilizing factors occurred, the entire settlement system could unravel. In the case of landscape degradation and soil erosion, different scenarios prevailed under different circumstances as discussed above. Hence in the case of Yemen, the neglect of terraced fields as a result of demographic decline, conflict, or extreme climatic events could initiate the irreversible collapse of terraced agriculture, therefore bringing to an end some four to five millennia of incremental investment. However, are such systemic collapses of terraces evident where terraced landscapes occur within re-grown tropical forest? In the case of mega cities in both Old and New Worlds, these too were vulnerable to extreme events (climatic, social, or political) which could result in failure of the supply systems. In the Middle East, because most major Islamic cities were supplied by a well-integrated supply network, any shortfalls in provisioning could have been met, at least in part, by the transport of bulk foods by water. That this supply network was sufficient to sustain an entire city is, however, unlikely. If Maya cities were faced with stresses resulting from collapse or shortfalls in food supply, those located inland and away from efficient bulk transport routes could have been faced with a major crisis. From the perspective of Mayan urbanism, it is therefore not surprising that there was a relocation of Post classic settlement away from the interior toward more northern and coastal locations (McAnany and Negrón 2010:159–60). Nevertheless, it seems clear from the examples presented that the long-term sustainability of cities and their landscapes must be seen as a complex question entailing the operation of numerous variables, not simply one or two fundamental "drivers."

Notes

1. For a summary of criteria applied and estimates of the length of occupations for the pre-industrial cities, see Fletcher 2004:136n2.

2. Sometimes overlooked is the crucial role that canals and navigable rivers played in the transport of bulk products (Algaze 2008). Thanks to cuneiform records from the Ur III state, it is quite clear that the bulk transport of products such as cereals was extremely important, perhaps even more important than the role of irrigation in increasing crop yields, and it is crucial to appreciate that Mesopotamian channels acted as the superhighways of the time, overriding the limitations of overland transport. The incorporation of a hydraulic transport factor in the present models of the Maya region

is therefore important, that is if there is sufficient network connectivity (see Scarborough and Valdez, this volume).

References Cited

Adams, Robert, McC.
1965 Land behind Baghdad. Chicago: University of Chicago Press.
1966 The Evolution of Urban Society: Early Mesopotamia and Prehistoric Mexico. Chicago: Aldine.

Algaze, Guillermo
2008 Ancient Mesopotamia at the Dawn of Civilization. Chicago: University of Chicago Press.

Anselmetti, Flavio S., David A. Hodell, Daniel Ariztegui, Mark Brenner, and Michael F. Rosenmeier
2007 Quantification of Soil Erosion Rates Related to Ancient Maya Deforestation. Geology 35(10):915–918.

Bar-Matthews, M., and A. Ayalon
2011 Mid-Holocene Climate Variations Revealed by High-resolution Speleotherm Records from Soreq Cave, Israel and Their Correlation with Cultural Changes. Holocene 21(2):163–172.

Blaikie, Piers, and Harold Brookfield, eds.
1987 Land Degradation and Society. London: Methuen.

Brückner Helmut
1986 Man's Impact on the Evolution of the Physical Environment in the Mediterranean Region in Historical Times. GeoJournal 13:7–17.

Butzer, Karl W.
1974 Accelerated Soil Erosion: A Problem of Man–Land Relationships. *In* Perspectives on Environment. I. R. Manners and M. Mikesell, eds. Pp. 57–78. Washington, DC: Association of American Geographers.

Casana, Jesse J.
2008 Mediterranean Valleys Revisited: Linking Soil Erosion, Land Use and Climate Variability in the Northern Levant. Geomorphology 101:429–442.

Chase, Arlen F., and Diane Z. Chase
1998 Scale and Intensity in Classic Period Maya Agriculture: Terracing and Settlement at the "Garden City" of Caracol, Belize. Culture and Agriculture 20(2):60–77.

Chase, Arlen F., Diane Z. Chase, John F. Weishampel, Jason B. Drake, Ramesh L. Shrestha, K. Clint Slatton, Jaime J. Awe, and William E. Carter
2011 Airborne LiDAR, Archaeology, and the Ancient Maya Landscape at Caracol, Belize. Journal of Archaeological Science 38:387–398.

Coe, Michael
1957 The Khmer Settlement Pattern: A Possible Analogy with That of the Maya. American Antiquity 22:409–410.

Coningham, Robin, P. Gunawardhana, M. Manuel, G. Adikari, M. Katugampola, R. Young, A. Schmidt, K. Krishnan, I. A. Simpson, G. McDonnell, and C. Batt
2007 The State of Theocracy: Defining an Early Medieval Hinterland in Sri Lanka. Antiquity 81:699–719.

Cordova, Carlos
2000 Geomorphological Evidence of Intense Prehistoric Soil Erosion in the Highlands of Central Jordan. Physical Geography 21:538–567.
2007 Millennial Landscape Change in Jordan: Geoarchaeology and Cultural Ecology. Tucson: University of Arizona Press.

Costa, Paolo M., and Tony J. Wilkinson
1987 The Hinterland of Sohar. Archaeological Surveys and Excavations within the Region of an Omani Seafaring City. Journal of Oman Studies 9:1–238.

Costanza, Robert, Lisa J. Graumlich, and Will Steffen, eds.
2011 Sustainability or Collapse? An Integrated History of People on Earth. Cambridge, MA: MIT Press.

Crumley, Carole L., ed.
1994 Historical Ecology: Cultural Knowledge and Changing Landscapes. Santa Fe: School of America Research.

Culbert, T. Patrick, and Don S. Rice, eds.
1990 Prehistoric Population History in the Maya Lowlands. Albuquerque: University of New Mexico Press.

de Menocal, Peter B.
2001 Cultural Responses to Climatic Change during the Late Holocene. Science 292:667–673.

Denevan, William M.
2001 Cultivated Landscapes of Native Amazonia and the Andes. Oxford: Oxford University Press.

Dharmasena, P. B.
2010 Evolution of Hydraulic Societies in the Ancient Anuradhapura Kingdom of Sri Lanka. *In* Landscapes and Societies: Selected Cases. I. P. Martini and W. Chesworth, eds. Pp. 341–352. Dordrecht, Netherlands: Springer.

Dunning, Nicholas P., and Timothy Beach
2010 Farms and Forests: Spatial and Temporal Perspectives on Ancient Maya Landscapes. *In* Landscapes and Societies: Selected Cases. I. P. Martini and W. Chesworth, eds. Pp. 369–389. Dordrecht, Netherlands: Springer.

Dunning, Nicholas P., Timothy Beach, Sheryl Luzzadder-Beach, and John G. Jones
2009 Creating a Stable Landscape: Soil Conservation and Adaptation among the Ancient Maya. *In* The Archaeology of Environmental Change: Socionatural Legacies of Degradation and Resilience. C. T. Fisher, J. B. Hill, and G. M. Feinman, eds. Pp. 85–105. Tucson: University of Arizona Press.

Dunning, Nicholas P., Sheryl Luzzadder-Beach, Timothy Beach, John G. Jones, Vernon Scarborough, and T. Patrick Culbert
2002 Arising from the Bajos: The Evolution of a Neotropical Landscape and the Rise of Maya Civilization. Annals of the Association of American Geographers 92 (2):267–283.

Dusar, Bert, Gert Verstraeten, Koen D'haen, Johan Bakker, Eva Kaptijn, and Marc Waelkens
2012 Sensitivity of the Eastern Mediterranean Geomorphic System towards Environmental Change during the Late Holocene: A Chronological Perspective. Journal of Quaternary Science 27(4):371–382.

Dusar, Bert, Gert Verstraeten, B. Notebaert, and Johan Bakker
2011 Holocene Environmental Change and Its Impact on Sediment Dynamics in the Eastern Mediterranean. Earth Science Reviews 108:137–157.

Erickson, Clark L.
2006 Intensification, Political Economy and the Farming Community: In Defense of a Bottom-Up Perspective of the Past. *In* Agricultural Strategies. J. Marcus and C. Stanish, eds. Pp. 334–363. Los Angeles: Cotsen Institute of Archaeology.

Evans, Damien, C. Pottier, R. Fletcher, S. Hensley, I. Tapley, A. Milne, and M. Barbetti
2007 A Comprehensive Archaeological Map of the World's Largest Preindustrial Settlement Complex at Angkor, Cambodia. Proceedings of the National Academy of Sciences 104:14277–14288.

Fish, Suzanne K.
1994 Archaeological Palynology of Garden and Fields. *In* The Archaeology of Garden and Field. N. F. Miller and K. L. Gleason, eds. Pp. 44–69. Philadelphia: University of Pennsylvania Press.

Fisher, Christopher T.
2009 Landscape and the Tarascan State. Labor, Intensification and Land Degradation. *In* Polities and Power: Archaeological Perspectives on the Landscapes of Early States. S. E. Falconer and C. L. Redman, eds. Pp. 80–98. Tucson: University of Arizona Press.

Fletcher, Roland
2004 Materiality, Space, Time and Outcome. *In* A Companion to Archaeology. J. Bintliff, ed. Pp. 110–140. Oxford: Blackwell.
2012 Low-Density, Agrarian-based Urbanism. *In* The Comparative Archaeology of Complex Societies. M. E. Smith, ed. Pp. 285–320. Cambridge: University of Cambridge Press.

German, John
2012 Watching Evolution Unfold for 54,000 Generations and Counting. SFI Bulletin 26:10–12.

Goldberg, Paul
1998 The Changing Landscape. *In* The Archaeology of Society in the Holy Land. T. E. Levy, ed. Pp. 40–57. Leicester, UK: Leicester University Press.

Gunawardana, R. A. L. H.
1971 Irrigation and Hydraulic Society in Early Medieval Ceylon. Past and Present 53:3–27.

Hill, J. Brett
2009 What Difference Does Environmental Degradation Make? Change and Its Significance in Transjordan. *In* The Archaeology of Environmental Change: Socionatural Legacies of Degradation and Resilience. C. T. Fisher, J. B. Hill, and G. M. Feinman, eds. Pp. 160–173. Tucson: University of Arizona Press.

Hill, J. Brett, Christopher T. Fisher, and Gary M. Feinman
2009 The Socionatural Connection: Closing Comments. *In* The Archaeology of Environmental Change: Socionatural Legacies of Degradation and Resilience. C. T. Fisher, J. B. Hill, and G. M. Feinman, eds. Pp. 249–258. Tucson: University of Arizona Press.

Kendal, Jeremy, J. J. Tehrani, and Kevin N. Laland, eds.
2011 Human Niche Construction in Interdisciplinary Focus. Philosophical Transactions of The Royal Society (Series B) 366(1566):785–792.

Kennedy, Hugh
2011 The Feeding of the Five Hundred Thousand: Cities and Agriculture in Early Islamic Mesopotamia. Iraq 73:177–199.

Lexartza-Artza, Irantzu, and John Wainwright
2011 Making Connections: Changing Sediment Sources and Sinks in an Upland Catchment. Earth Surface Processes and Landforms 36:1090–1104.

McAnany, Patricia A., and Tomás Gallerata Negrón
2010 Bellicose Rulers and Climatological Peril? Retrofitting Twenty-First-Century Woes on Eighth-Century Maya Society. *In* Questioning Collapse: Human Resilience, Ecological Vulnerability, and the Aftermath of Empire. P. A. McAnany and N. Yoffee, eds. Pp. 142–175. Cambridge: Cambridge University Press.

Mortimore, Michael
1998 Roots in the African Dust: Sustaining the Drylands. Cambridge: Cambridge University Press.

O'Brien, Michael J., and Kevin N. Laland
2012 Genes, Culture, and Agriculture: An Example of Human Niche Construction. Current Anthropology 53(4):434–470.

Peterson, Christian E., and Robert Drennan
2012 Patterned Variation in Regional Trajectories of Community Growth. *In* The Comparative Archaeology of Complex Societies. M. E. Smith, ed. Pp. 88–137. Cambridge: University of Cambridge Press.

Pietsch, D., and L. Mabit
2012 Terrace Soils in the Yemen Highlands: Using Physical, Chemical and Radiometric Data to Assess Their Suitability for Agriculture and Their Vulnerability to Degradation. Geoderma 185–186:48–60.

Redman, Charles, L.
1999 Human Impact on Ancient Environments. Tucson: University of Arizona Press.
2011 Group Report: Millennial Perspectives on the Dynamic Interaction of Climate, People and Resources. *In* Sustainability or Collapse? An Integrated History of People on Earth. Robert Costanza, Lisa J. Graumlich, and Will Steffen, eds. Pp. 115–148. Cambridge, MA: MIT Press.

Rice, Don S.
1996 Palaeolimnological Analysis on the Central Peten, Guatamala. *In* The Managed Mosaic: Ancient Maya Agriculture and Resource Use. S. L. Fedick, ed. Pp. 193–206. Salt Lake City: University of Utah Press.

Rollefson, Gary O., and Ilse Köhler-Rollefson
1992 Early Neolithic Exploitation Patterns in the Levant: Cultural Impact on the Environment. Population and Environment: A Journal of Interdisciplinary Studies 13(4):243–254.

Roberts, Neil
2011 Living with a Moving Target: Long-Term Climatic Variability and Environmental Risk in Dryland Regions. *In* Sustainable Lifeways. N. Miller, ed. Pp. 13–38. Philadelphia: University of Pennsylvania Press.

Rosen, Arlene M.
1986 Cities of Clay: The Geoarchaeology of Tells. Chicago: University of Chicago Press.
2007 Civilizing Climate: Social Responses to Climate Change in the Ancient Near East. Lanham, New York: Alta Mira Press.

Scarborough, Vernon L.
2003 The Flow of Power: Ancient Water Systems and Landscapes. Santa Fe: School of American Research.

Scarborough, Vernon L., and Lisa J. Lucero
2010 The Non-Hierarchical Development of Complexity in the Semitropics: Water and Cooperation. Water History 2(2):185–205.

Scarborough, Vernon L., Nicholas P. Dunning, Kenneth B. Tankersley, Christopher Carr, Eric Weaver, Liwi Grazioso, Brian Lane, John G. Jones, Palma Buttles, Fred Valdez, and David D. Lenz
2012 Water and Sustainable Land Use at the Ancient Tropical City of Tikal, Guatemala. Proceedings of the National Academy of Sciences 109(31):12408–12413.

Smith, Michael E., ed.
2012 The Comparative Archaeology of Complex Societies. Cambridge: University of Cambridge Press.

Smith, Michael E., and Peter Peregrine
2012 Approaches to Comparative Analysis in Archaeology. *In* The Comparative Archaeology of Complex Societies. M. E. Smith, ed. Pp. 4–20. Cambridge: University of Cambridge Press.

Staubwasser, Michael, and Harvey Weiss
2006 Holocene Climate and Cultural Evolution in Late Prehistoric–Early Historic West Asia. Quaternary Research 66(3):372–387.

Ur, Jason A.
2010a Urbanism and Cultural: Landscapes in Northeastern Syria: The Tell Hamoukar Survey 1999–2001. Oriental Institute Publications, 137. Chicago: Oriental Institute.
2010b Cycles of Civilization in Northern Mesopotamia, 4400–2000 BC. Journal of Archaeological Research 18:387–431.

van der Leeuw, Sander E., and Charles L. Redman
2002 Placing Archaeology at the Center of Socio-Natural Studies. American Antiquity 67:597–605.

Varisco, Daniel
1991 The Future of Terrace Farming in the Yemen: A Development Dilemma. Agriculture and Human Values 8:166–172.

Vita-Finzi, Claudio
1969 The Mediterranean Valleys: Geological Changes in Historical Times. Cambridge: Cambridge University Press.

Whitmore, Thomas M., and B. L. Turner II
2001 Cultivated Landscapes of Middle America on the Eve of Conquest. Oxford: Oxford University Press.

Wilkinson, Tony J.
2003 Archaeological Landscapes of the Near East. Tucson: University of Arizona Press.
2005 Soil Erosion and Valley Fills in the Yemen Highlands and Southern Turkey: Integrating Settlement, Geoarchaeology and Climate Change. Geoarchaeology 20(2):169–192.
2006 From Highland to Desert: The Organization of Landscape and Irrigation in Southern Arabia. *In* Agriculture Strategies. J. Marcus and C. Stanish, eds. Pp. 38–68. Los Angeles: Cotsen Institute Publications.
2009 The Hinterland (of Siraf). *In* Siraf: History, Topography and Environment. D. Whitehouse, ed. Pp. 54–76. BIPS Archaeological Monographs Series, 1. Oxford: Oxbow.
2010 Empire and Environment in the Northern Fertile Crescent. *In* Landscapes and Societies—Selected Cases. I. P. Martini and W. Chesworth, eds. Pp. 135–151. Dordrecht: Springer.

Wilkinson, Tony J., and Louise Rayne
2010 Hydraulic Landscapes and Imperial Power in the Near East. Water History 2(2):115–144.

Wilkinson, Tony J., Nikolaos Galiatsatos, Dan Lawrence, Andrea Ricci, Rob Dunford, and Graham Philip
2012 Late Chalcolithic and Early Bronze Age Landscapes of Settlement and Mobility in the Middle Euphrates: A Reassessment. Levant 44(2):139–185.

Wilkinson, Tony J., E. Wilkinson, Jason Ur, and M. Altaweel
2005 Landscape of Empire: The Assyrian Countryside in Context. Bulletin of the American Schools of Oriental Research 340:23–56.

Zettler, R. L., ed.
1997 Subsistence and Settlement in a Marginal Environment: Tell es-Sweyhat, 1989–1995 Preliminary Report. MASCA Research Papers in Science and Archaeology, 14. Philadelphia: University of Pennsylvania, University Museum.

14

Collapse and Sustainability: Rome, the Maya, and the Modern World

Joseph A. Tainter
Utah State University

ABSTRACT

The factors that make a society sustainable, or vulnerable to collapse, can rarely be discerned within a human lifetime. Sustainability challenges develop over periods of decades, generations, or centuries. Sustainability must therefore be a historical science. A major challenge of the IHOPE program is how to draw valid comparisons among different kinds of societies, existing at different times, that can clarify our contemporary problems of sustainability. This paper develops and illustrates a theory for understanding sustainability and collapse that has cross-cultural applicability. Illustrating the theory by the collapse of the Western Roman Empire yields new insights into what it means to be a sustainable society. Comparison to the Maya reveals that, despite many differences, the Roman Empire and Maya polities underwent similar patterns of cultural evolution, and developed similar vulnerabilities. Comparison of both historical cases to the sustainability challenges of today demonstrates that contemporary industrial societies face evolutionary processes similar to those experienced by the Romans and the Maya. This analysis yields several points that are worthwhile for policy makers to understand. [collapse, complexity, energy, Maya, Roman Empire, sustainability]

The key question for societies of today and the future is whether we can sustain a way of life that is materially prosperous in the face of scarce supplies of oil and other resources, degraded environments, a changing climate, and numerous major problems that will converge in the near future. Those of us who are concerned about these issues and also study the past realize that sustainability is a long-term process. The factors that make a society sustainable or not evolve over periods of decades, generations, or centuries. Sustainability must therefore be a historical science.

One might wonder how a paper on the Roman Empire fits into a volume on how study of the ancient Maya contributes to understanding today's problems. The answer is that sustainability challenges have much in common, including the sustainability challenges faced by states. Understanding the sustainability problems faced by an individual state can, in the proper framework, clarify some of the challenges faced by all states, including both Maya polities and today's societies. This can be best accomplished if a generalizing framework is adopted at the outset, searching for regularities or common patterns in how institutions address problems, and how problem-solving changes in its effectiveness over time.

Sustainability is often defined by the definition of sustainable development offered in 1987 by Gro Harlem Brundtland, then Prime Minister of Norway: "Sustainable development is development that meets the needs of the present without compromising the ability of future generations to meet their own needs" (World Commission on Environment and Development 1987:43). While Brundtland's definition will continue to be widely cited, it is not genuinely useful. Fundamentally it borders on tautology: *of course* sustainable development concerns tending to the future. The definition is, moreover, too general to guide decisions. As befits a political leader, it is so vague "as to be consistent with almost any form of action (or inaction)" (Pearce et al. 1994:457).

ARCHEOLOGICAL PAPERS OF THE AMERICAN ANTHROPOLOGICAL ASSOCIATION, Vol. 24, pp. 201–214, ISSN 1551-823X, online ISSN 1551-8248. DOI: 10.1111/apaa.12038.

In understanding the meaning of sustainability, it is useful to resort to basics. The term "sustain" comes originally from the Latin *sustinere*, and into English through the Old French *soustenir*. Both terms mean literally "to hold underneath"—in other words, to uphold or support. The *Shorter Oxford English Dictionary*, sixth edition, lists nine definitions of "sustain." Two of these are particularly useful. Number three reads "cause to continue in a certain state; maintain at the proper level or standard." Number five, which is consistent with biophysical concepts of sustainability, reads "support life in; provide for the life or needs of" (Stevenson 2007:3126). Both definitions are consistent with the original Latin and French terms: to sustain something is to support its continuation. Sustainability is the science of continuity. Sustainability emerges therefore from success in addressing existential problems, that is, problems of continuity. As a historical endeavor, sustainability concerns the long-term success of problem-solving efforts.

If sustainability is the attempt to maintain continuity, unsustainability manifests itself in transformation or collapse. The difference between transformation and collapse involves simplification and the rate of changes in complexity. Cultural complexity consists of differentiation in structure (more parts, and especially, more kinds of parts), combined with increasing constraints on behavior, the latter termed "organization" (for organization, see Gatlin [1972]). Both transformation and collapse may mean that an existing way of life is not sustained. As defined elsewhere, a collapse is the rapid loss of an established level of complexity (Tainter 1988). Transformation is a term that is popular today, but rarely, if ever, defined. Transformation is cultural change that may be more gradual than a collapse, or not involve major changes in complexity. "Transformation" is simply another term for "cultural change." If cultural change is not what people want, then transformation is a sustainability issue. Both collapse and transformation are legitimate topics in the study of sustainability, but collapse is primarily of interest here.

Complexity and Sustainability

Complexity is central to issues of sustainability and collapse. One of the most certain generalizations of history and prehistory is that human societies over the past 12,000 years have increased greatly in complexity. Prehistorians once thought that this came about through the development of agriculture. Agriculture, it was thought, gave our ancestors surplus food and, concomitantly, free time to invent craft specialization, industry, trade, urbanism, hierarchy, and the other things that are commonly called "civilization" (e.g., Childe 1944). The implicit assumption of this line of reasoning is that complexity emerges because it can, and will do so given surplus energy. Complexity in this perspective is therefore voluntary, and presumably desirable.

One problem with this view is that complexity is not free. In any living system, increasing complexity carries a metabolic cost. This is a matter of basic thermodynamics: It takes energy to maintain any system—human or otherwise—in a state of complexity. Among non-human species the cost is a straightforward matter of additional calories that must be consumed. Among humans, the cost of complexity is usually counted in surrogate currencies such as time, labor, money, or annoyance. These are all transformations of energy, which is the ultimate basis of complexity, as Leslie White pointed out (1949, 1959). Before the development of fossil fuels, increasing the complexity of a society meant that people worked harder. In the human past, the cost of complexity must always have constrained its growth.

If complexity costs, why did human societies ever grow more complex, let alone as complex as they are today? At least part of the answer is that complexity is a basic problem-solving tool. Confronted with problems, humans often respond by developing more complex technologies, establishing new institutions, adding more specialists or bureaucratic levels to an institution, increasing organization or regulation, or gathering and processing more information. Increases in complexity work in part because they can be implemented rapidly, and typically build on what was developed before. While we usually prefer not to bear the cost of complexity, our problem-solving efforts are powerful complexity generators. All that is needed for growth of complexity is a problem that requires it. Since problems continually arise, there is persistent pressure for complexity to increase.

Two examples illustrate this point. In response to the problem of terrorism, especially the attacks of September 11, 2001, nation-states increased complexity. In the United States, for example, this has involved differentiation in structure (new agencies such as the Department of Homeland Security and the Transportation Security Administration) and increases in organization (e.g., constraints on the kinds of behavior thought to be threatening). This response involves costs that are both monetary and personal. The report of the government commission convened to investigate the attacks of 9/11/2001 (colloquially called the 9/11 commission) recommended steps to prevent future attacks. The recommended actions amount, in effect, to more complexity, imposing more costs in the form of resources, time, or annoyance (9/11 Commission 2004). The second example concerns how we are responding to the problems of pollution and fuel availability in transportation. One way that we have responded is by developing automobiles that have two means of propulsion, where previously one was enough. The structure is differentiated (an engine and an electric motor), with the organization to make them work together provided by electronics and software.

Not all complexity comes from problem solving. There have been occasions when humans adopted energy sources of such great potential that, with further development and positive feedback, there followed great expansions in the numbers of humans and the wealth and complexity of societies. These occasions have, however, been so rare that we designate them with terms signifying a new era: the Agricultural Revolution and the Industrial Revolution. It is worth noting that these unusual transitions have not resulted from unbridled human creativity. Rather, they emerged from solutions to problems of resource shortages (Cohen 1977; Wilkinson 1973), and were adopted reluctantly because initially they created diminishing returns on effort in peoples' daily lives. As discussed below, when we do have surplus or inexpensive energy, we do not have it for long. Humans (and organisms in other living systems) quickly find ways to use extra energy (Boulding 1959:vii).

The costliness of complexity is not a mere annoyance or inconvenience. It conditions the long-term success or failure of problem-solving efforts. Complexity is an economic function. Societies and institutions invest in problem solving, undertaking costs and expecting benefits in return. In any system of problem solving, early efforts tend to be simple and cost-effective. That is, they work and give high returns per unit of effort. This is a normal economic process: humans, if they have the knowledge and technology, tend first to pluck the lowest fruit, going to higher branches only when those lower no longer hold fruit. In more formal terms, this is known as the *best-first* principle (e.g., Cleveland 2008). In problem-solving systems, over the long term inexpensive solutions are adopted before more complex and expensive ones. In the history of human food-gathering and production, for example, labor-sparing hunting and gathering gave way first to horticulture, then to more labor-intensive agriculture (Boserup 1965; Clark and Haswell 1966; Cohen 1977), which in some places has been replaced by industrial agriculture that barely produces an energy surplus, and that sometimes consumes more energy than it produces (Hamilton et al. 2013). We produce minerals and energy whenever possible from the most economical sources (Cleveland 2008). Our societies have changed from egalitarian relations, economic reciprocity, ad hoc leadership, and generalized roles to social and economic differentiation, specialization, inequality, and full-time leadership. These characteristics are the essence of complexity, and they increase the costliness of any society.

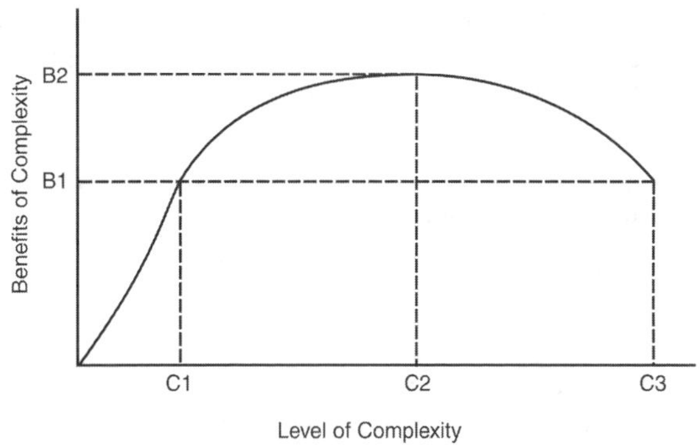

Figure 14.1. The marginal product of increasing complexity.

As high-return solutions are progressively implemented, only more costly solutions remain. As the highest-return ways to produce resources, process information, and organize society are applied, continuing problems must be addressed in ways that are more costly and less cost-effective. As the costs of solving problems grow, the point is reached where further investments in complexity do not give a proportionate return. Increments of investment in complexity begin to yield smaller and smaller increments of return. The *marginal* return (that is, the return per extra unit of investment) starts to decline (Figure 14.1). This is the long-term challenge faced by problem-solving institutions: diminishing returns to complexity. If allowed to proceed unchecked, eventually it brings ineffective problem solving and even economic stagnation. A prolonged period of diminishing returns to complexity is a major part of what makes problem solving ineffective and societies or institutions unsustainable (Tainter 1988).

Complexity that emerges through problem solving will often appear *before* there is energy allocated or even available to support it. Complexity compels at least reallocation of resources, and often compels increases in resource production. Rather than following the availability of energy, as Childe and others have thought, cultural complexity often precedes it. As discussed in a later section, this understanding of the temporal relationship between complexity and resources has implications for sustainability that diverge from what is commonly assumed. At this point, the preceding theory can be illustrated in the history of the Roman Empire.

Case Study: The Roman Empire

The energetic basis of the Roman Empire was, of course, the sun. Through agriculture, solar energy was transformed into food for the cities, manpower for the army, and the production of precious metals with which to pay the soldiers. Vaclav Smil (1994:66, 74) estimates that Roman and medieval wheat farmers in northern Europe could produce about 1/2 metric ton per hectare, and a yield of 3 to 4 times the seeding rate. Of this, in the late empire, the Roman state took up to 1/3 in taxes, while farmers needed about 1/3 to 1/2 for seed and subsistence. The tax amounted to 1/2 to 2/3 of surplus production, but all of the surplus in bad years (Wickham 1984:11; Smil 1994:37).

The economics of an empire such as the Romans assembled are seductive but illusory. The returns to any campaign of conquest are highest initially, when the accumulated surpluses of the conquered peoples are appropriated. When the Romans conquered a region, typically they would seize the accumulated surpluses of past solar energy, transformed into precious metals, works of art, and people. In 167 B.C.E., for example, the Romans captured the Macedonian treasury, and promptly eliminated taxation of themselves. When Pergamon was annexed in 130 B.C.E. the state budget was doubled, from 25 million to 50 million denarii. (The denarius, discussed below, was a coin initially of very pure silver.) After he conquered Syria in 63 B.C.E., Pompey raised it to 85 million denarii. Julius Caesar relieved the Gauls of so much gold that its value in Rome fell 36 percent (Cornell 1992; Lévy 1967:62–65).

After an initial series of victories over neighbors in Italy, Rome's conquests became, at least in part, economically self-perpetuating (Jones 1974:114–115). Some of the manpower of conquered peoples, and some of their wealth, went to fund new conquests (Cornell 1992). After subjugation, however, the conqueror assumes the cost of administering and defending a province. These responsibilities may last centuries, and are paid for from yearly agricultural surpluses.

An agrarian empire must therefore shift from consuming stores of past solar energy to a budget dictated by annual solar energy. This transition is inevitable, because imperial expansion cannot go on indefinitely. As an empire would expand, travel times to the frontiers would increase and the length of borders to defend would grow. Eventually an expanding empire encounters people and territory whose conquest is either impossible or not worth the cost. This was the situation experienced by the Roman Empire by the first century C.E. Territorial growth ended soon thereafter.

The Roman government was financed by agricultural taxes that barely sufficed for ordinary administration. Low-productivity subsistence agriculture paid 90% of taxes, and 80% of government revenues went to support the military (Duncan-Jones 1994:45; Jones 1964:464–465). When extraordinary expenses arose, typically during wars, the precious metals on hand frequently were insufficient. Facing the costs of war on the eastern frontier with Parthia and rebuilding Rome after the Great Fire, Nero began in 64 C.E. a policy that later emperors found irresistible. He debased the primary silver coin, the denarius, reducing the alloy from 98 to 93 percent silver. It was the first step down a slope that resulted two centuries later in a currency that was worthless and a government that was insolvent (Figure 14.2).

In the half-century from C.E. 235 to 284 the empire nearly came to an end. There were foreign and civil wars almost without interruption. The period witnessed 26 legitimate emperors and perhaps 50 usurpers. Cities were sacked and frontier provinces devastated. The empire shrank in the 260s to Italy, the Balkans, and North Africa (MacMullen 1976). The silver coinage, once 98% pure, reached a low of 1.9% precious metal. By prodigious effort the empire survived the crisis, but it emerged at the turn of the fourth century C.E. as a very different organization.

In response to the crises, the emperors Diocletian (284–305) and Constantine (306–337) designed a government that was larger, more complex, and more highly organized (Table 14.1).

These emperors subdivided provinces, creating many new ones, to prevent governors from rebelling. Each new province required a new administration, staffed with personnel. They expanded the size of the government, and the number of capital cities went from one to, at some times, four. The empire was increasingly ruled by separate governments in the east and the west. The empire doubled the size of its army and increased the proportion of cavalry, the latter being particularly expensive. There were also increasing controls on behavior. Workers were frozen into hereditary occupations that the government deemed essential, including the army. The government conscripted workers and guilds for such things as shipping and building new walls around cities. Farmers were tied to their land. The government assessed every plot of land across the entire empire—every field, every orchard, every pasture—for tax. This had to be done within a few years, and the recording alone must have been an enormous task.

To pay for this the government taxed its citizens more heavily, conscripted their labor, and dictated their occupations. Taxes on land doubled between C.E. 324 and 364. Villages were responsible for the taxes on their members, and one village could even be held liable for another. Despite several monetary reforms a stable currency could not be found (Figure 14.3).

As masses of worthless coins were produced, prices rose higher and higher (Figure 14.4). Money-changers in the east would not convert imperial currency, and the government refused to accept its own coins for taxes. People

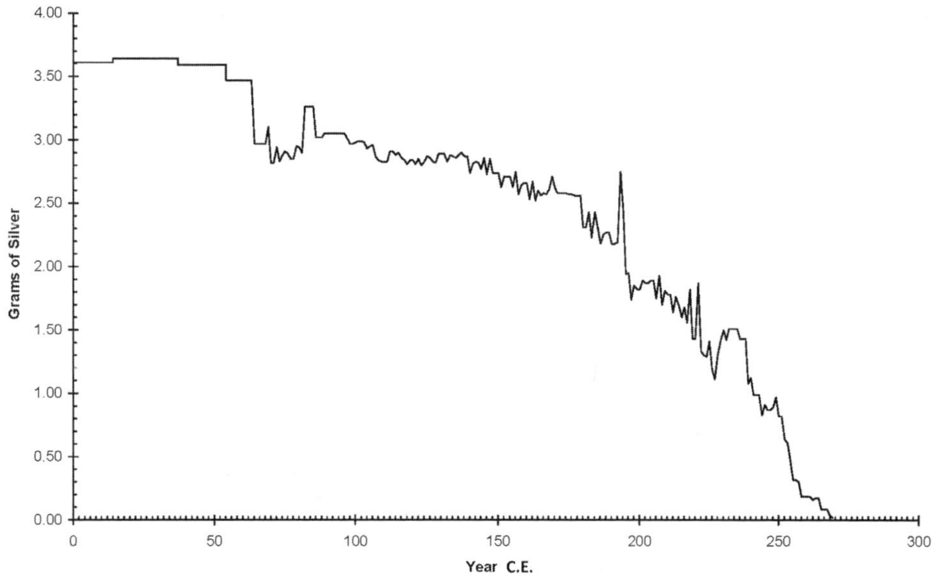

Figure 14.2. Debasement of the denarius to C.E. 269. Data from Cope (n.d., 1969a, 1969b, 1978); King (1982); Le Gentilhomme (1962); Tyler (1975); and Walker (1976, 1977, 1978).

Table 14.1. Increasing Complexity in the Late Roman Empire

Increases in structural differentiation	**Increases in organization**
Subdivided provinces	Attempted to freeze prices
Differentiated imperial leadership	Critical occupations made hereditary
Expanded size of government	Conscripted soldiers
Expanded seats of government	Requisitioned supplies
Expanded number of administrations	Conscripted guilds to provide services
Expanded numbers of administrative personnel	Other compulsory labor services
Separated civil and military functions of government	Farmers tied to land
Subdivided financial functions	Assessed all lands for tax

would make payments carrying sacks of coins. In response to empire-wide inflation, Diocletian issued in C.E. 301 an Edict on Maximum Prices. It was, however, ineffective.

With the rise in taxes, population could not recover from plagues in the second and third centuries. Subsistence farmers could not raise large families. Because of population decline, there were chronic shortages of labor. Faced with taxes, peasants would abandon their lands and flee to the protection of a wealthy landowner. Marginal lands went out of cultivation because often such lands would not yield enough for taxes plus a surplus for the farmer. As a result of these processes, by C.E. 400 most of Gaul and Italy were owned by about 20 senatorial families (Boak 1955; Duncan-Jones 1990; Harl 1996; Hodgett 1972; Jones 1964, 1974; MacMullen 1976; Russell 1958; Wickham 1984; Williams 1985; Williams and Friell 1994).

From the late fourth century the peoples of central Europe could no longer be kept out. They forced their way into Roman lands in western Europe and North Africa. The government came to rely almost exclusively on troops from Germanic tribes. When finally they could not be paid, they overthrew the last emperor in Italy in C.E. 476.

In response to the crises of the third century, the Roman Empire engaged in a sustainability effort that succeeded for a time, but that could succeed only for a time. The Romans attempted to sustain both their empire as a territorial entity, and the Graeco-Roman way of life. The strategy of the later Roman Empire was to respond to a near-fatal challenge in the third century by increasing the size, complexity, power, and costliness of the primary problem-solving system—the government and its army. The empire went metaphorically from living off interest (annual agricultural production) to consuming its capital resources: producing lands and

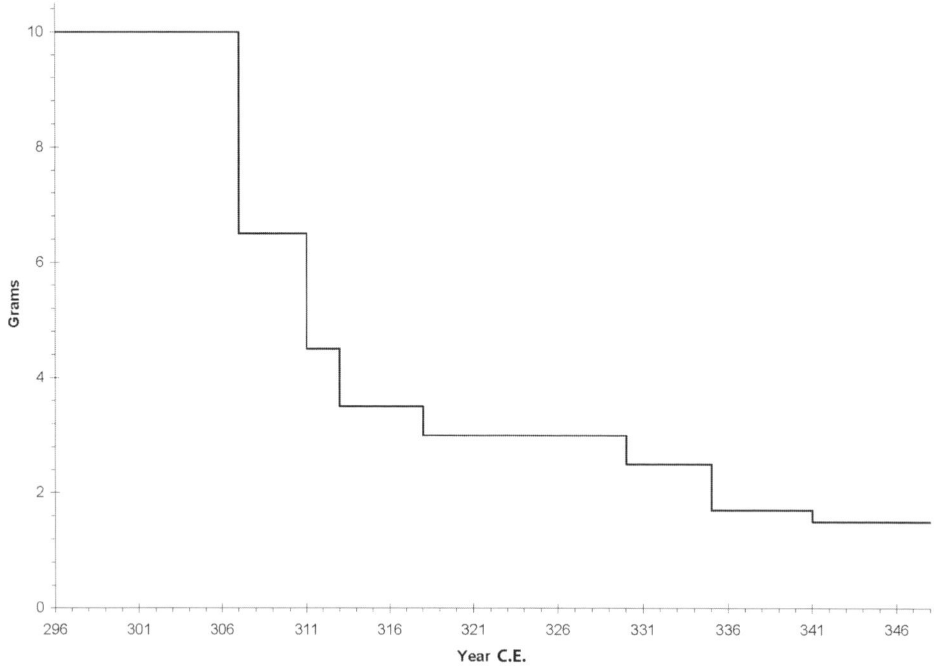

Figure 14.3. Reductions in the weight of the Roman follis, C.E. 296–348 Data from Van Meter (1991:47). A follis was a bronze coin with a silver coating, initially weighing about ten grams.

peasant population. The higher costs were undertaken not to expand the empire nor to acquire new wealth, but to maintain the status quo of imperial rule and the Graeco-Roman way of life. The benefit–cost ratio of imperial government declined. In the end the Western Roman Empire could no longer afford the problem of its own existence.

Sustainability and the Roman Collapse

Much that is written about sustainability is based on beliefs that go mostly unexamined. The most common belief is that sustainability emerges as a function of resource conservation, resource replacement, and/or technical innovation. That is, sustainability is thought to be a passive consequence of consuming less (e.g., Brown 2009; Rees 2002; Smith et al. 2010), resource substitution (Neumayer 2000), and/or developing new or more efficient technologies (Barnett and Morse 1963:139; Sato and Suzawa 1983:81; Smith et al. 2010). Thus the focus of most sustainability discussions has been on voluntary conservation (Murphy 2008), or on improvements in technical efficiency that reduce resource use per unit of consumption (Brown 2009; Smith et al. 2010). There are three reasons why conservation, substitution, and technical efficiency do not, by themselves, produce sustainability.

Firstly, there is the Jevons Paradox (Jevons 1866), often known today as the Rebound Effect (Greening et al. 2000; Polimeni et al. 2008). William Stanley Jevons, a noted 19th century economist, worried that Britain's industrial development and global leadership would outrun the supply of coal. Improvements in the technical efficiency of engines using coal, moreover, would only make the problem worse. Jevons observed that

> *It is wholly a confusion of ideas to suppose that the economical use of fuel is equivalent to a diminished consumption. The very contrary is the truth....* As a rule, new modes of economy will lead to an increase of consumption .... Now, if the quantity of coal used in a blast-furnace, for instance, be diminished in comparison with the yield, the profits of the trade will increase, new capital will be attracted, the price of pig-iron will fall, but the demand for it increase; and eventually the greater number of furnaces will more than make up for the diminished consumption of each. (Jevons 1866:123–125)

In short, as technological improvements increase the efficiency with which a resource is used, total consumption of that resource may increase rather than decrease. The Jevons Paradox has been observed in effect at the level of national economic statistics (Polimeni et al. 2008). It can also be seen in many facets of daily life (Tainter 2008), including fuel economy and miles driven in the United States.

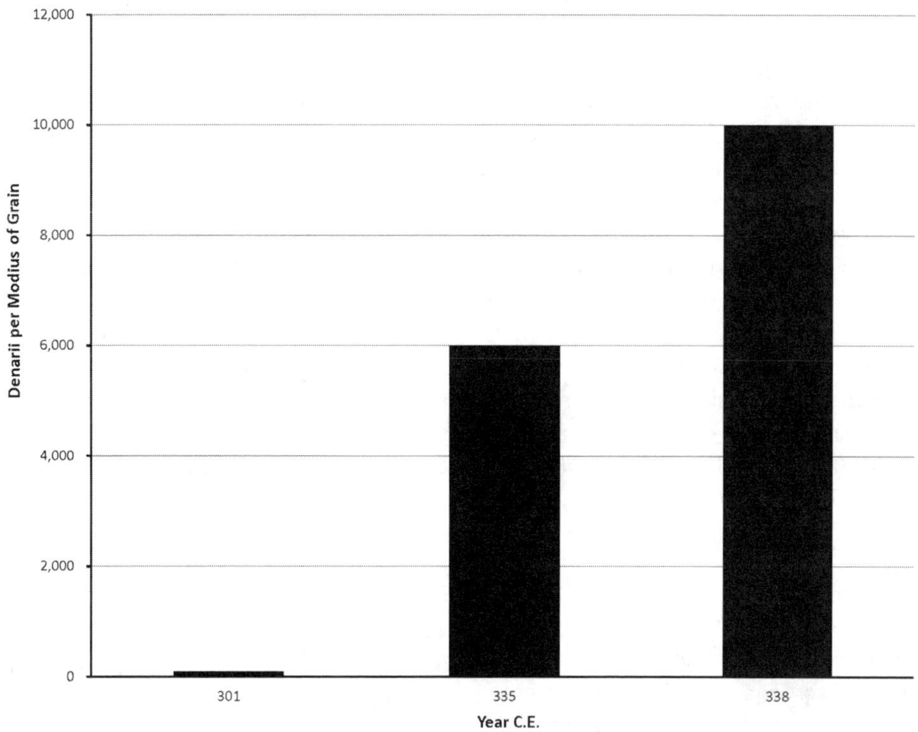

Figure 14.4. Inflation in the price of wheat in Egypt, C.E. 301–338 A modius was about nine liters. Data from Jones (1964:119).

As Americans responded to the fuel crises of the 1970s and began to buy more fuel-efficient vehicles in the 1970s and 1980s, for example, they responded to the savings, as Jevons would have predicted, by driving more (Tainter and Patzek 2012:93).

Following similar reasoning, Kenneth Boulding derived from Malthus's essay on population three theorems. The first is called the Dismal Theorem: "If the only ultimate check on the growth of population is misery, then the population will grow until it is miserable enough to stop its growth" (Boulding 1959:vii).

Theorem two is the Utterly Dismal Theorem, and it directly challenges the view that conservation or technical improvements produce sustainability:

> Any technical *improvement* can only relieve misery for a while, for as long as misery is the only check on population, the improvement will enable population to grow, and will soon enable *more* people to live in misery than before. The final result of improvements, therefore, is to increase the equilibrium population, which is to increase the sum total of human misery. (Boulding 1959:vii)

In other words, technical improvements produce only temporary savings, and ultimately make matters worse. Boulding's third theorem is called the moderately cheerful form of the Dismal Theorem:

> If something else, other than misery and starvation, can be found which will keep a prosperous population in check, the population does not have to grow until it is miserable and starves, and can be stably prosperous. (Boulding 1959:xi)

Boulding observed that how to implement the Cheerful Theorem "is a problem which has so far produced no wholly satisfactory solution" (1959:xi).

Secondly, the contemporary approach to sustainability assumes that complexity and resource consumption are mere choices. This reasoning can be traced back to the old suppositions of Childe and others that agriculture (i.e., surplus energy) *permitted* the evolution of complexity. If so, this implies that complexity is voluntary. We could, therefore, choose to live without it. The problems with this view should now be clear. To begin with, the implication of Boulding's Utterly Dismal Theorem is that humans have rarely had surplus energy. Surpluses are quickly depleted by increases in consumption. Furthermore, if complexity increases to solve problems, as argued here and elsewhere, then complexity is not usually voluntary. It is, rather, necessary (or necessary if one wants to solve problems), and causes resource consumption to increase. To suppose that contemporary societies can voluntarily simplify and reduce consumption for the long term is to assume that the future will hold no challenges.

Finally, there is the problem that knowledge production, like other problem-solving efforts, is subject to increasing complexity and costliness, and in time produces diminishing returns (Tainter 1988:99–107, 111–115). As a consequence of this dilemma, the productivity of technical innovation in the United States and elsewhere has declined by 22 percent in the last 30 years (Strumsky et al. 2010). This trend indicates that we cannot expect technical innovation to improve efficiency into the indefinite future, nor to produce a society that is sustainable for the long term.

The case study of the Roman Empire, and other case studies (Allen et al. 2003; Tainter 2006), lead to a different set of conclusions about what it means to be a sustainable society. These are:

1. Sustainability is a function of success at solving problems. Sustainability does not emerge, as is commonly thought, as a passive consequence of consuming less.
2. Complexity in human societies grows through the mundane process of solving problems, as just discussed, including problems of sustainability.
3. Complexity is an economic function, with benefits and costs, and can reach diminishing returns.
4. Since sustainability depends on solving problems, it promotes the growth of complexity and complexity's associated costs. Sustainability of a society or way of life may therefore require greater consumption of resources, not less.
5. A society or other institution can be destroyed by the cost of sustaining itself. Sustainability is always, therefore, a temporary state.

Implications for Study of the Maya

The Roman Empire was a very different kind of state from the Maya polities, and both were quite different from societies of today. Moreover, the history and sustainability challenges facing the Romans were seemingly different from those of the Maya, or those of today. How, then, can the lessons of one apply more broadly?

The answer lies in understanding three of the points just made. The first is that sustainability emerges from success at solving problems. The second is that problem solving causes complexity to grow, increasing costliness. The third is that complexity in problem solving can reach diminishing returns, rendering a society fiscally weakened and unable to respond to challenges. Therefore, one approach to understanding sustainability or collapse in a comparative framework is to analyze the evolution of complexity in problem solving over long periods of time.

The challenges for students of the Maya are to document changes over time in major sectors of societal investment, and to explain those changes. Maya polities undertook to engage in several sectors of public investment, a number of which would have been rather costly for a subsistence agricultural society. In such a society, 90% or more of the economy involves the production of energy, mainly from agriculture (Fouquet 2008:269). This leaves little energy for anything else. Yet the Maya produced public architecture and monuments, and hydraulic engineering of both sites and landscapes. They created and maintained agricultural ecosystems, and conducted wars. How did these evolve over the period of Maya history?

Public architecture and monuments included such features as pyramids, temples, ball courts, elite residences, stelae, and causeways. These were meant to impress, and they still do to this day. It is noteworthy that the construction of dated monuments at Classic Maya sites increased over time (Erickson 1973:51; Kennett et al. 2012:790), although individual sites varied in their construction programs (Demarest 2004:111). As the Classic period proceeded, the Maya overall invested more and more in building monuments. The costliness of this sector of public investment grew and grew, reaching a peak just prior to the collapses of the Maya polities.

To cope with a challenging environment, in which rainfall varied by season and year, the Maya developed major projects of hydraulic engineering. Late Preclassic communities (ca. 400 B.C.E.–C.E. 250) developed concave microwatersheds at the margins of natural sinks or large depressions that held water year round. Communities were situated to capture seasonal rainfall and channel it for future use. It was a passive system employing the natural resources of geology and gravity. By the Early Classic period (ca. C.E. 250–550), major centers relocated to high ground, which was then sculpted to catch and store water. Large, surfaced plazas caught and channeled water, which was stored for release during the dry season (Scarborough 1998, 2007). The hydraulic system thus changed from passive, employing natural forces, to active management, involving more human intervention. This is a certain way to increase costs (Allen et al. 2003). Moreover, water management did not involve engineering alone. It also required systems of community ritual, which seem to have become grander and more public over time (Lucero 2006:176).

The Maya invested heavily in creating and maintaining an agricultural support system. Across the Lowlands they built terraces, canals, raised fields, check dams, walled fields, and facilities for water channeling and storage (see Lucero et al., Chapter 3, this volume and Chase and Chase, Chapter 10, this volume). The distribution of these facilities varied with the features of individual locations, and with political economy ((e.g., Dunning 1996; Fedick 1996a, 1996b; Pyburn 1996). Webster (2002:328–337) emphasizes how, through time, agriculture required increasing investments of labor, producing both diminishing returns and soil erosion. Timber, moreover, was becoming exhausted toward the end of the Classic period (Lentz and Hockaday 2009). Students of the Maya have long thought that problems of agriculture contributed to, or even precipitated, the collapses of polities.

Warfare was a major cost for ancient societies, and a significant activity among the Maya. There were conflicts between polities at various levels of severity. At least 20 sites had fortifications (Webster 2000:73), many built in the Late Classic, and some shortly before a center collapsed (Ambrosino, Ardren, and Stanton 2003:110). Glyphs tell of victories and defeats (Martin and Grube 2008). Warfare increased in complexity over time, as the Late Classic saw an increase in the variety of arms and armor (Hassig 1992:95). Piedras Negras may have "... organized a conventional army more in the central Mexican mold," giving it a tactical advantage (Hassig 1992:95). Caracol also seems to have had a substantial army, allowing wars to be fought even during the planting season (D. Chase and A. Chase 2002:35). Such developments would have forced other polities to try to develop countering capabilities, or face defeat.

Spoils of war apparently fueled a building boom at Caracol, while defeat by Caracol curtailed Tikal's ability to build. Glyphic references to war increased late in the Classic period, suggesting that war itself became more frequent, severe, or consequential, and that it became more important publicly to display information about wars. By the Late Classic, wars were a facet of life of sufficient centrality to be classified into types of conflict (A. Chase and D. Chase 1989, 1998; D. Chase and A. Chase 2002, 2003; Golden 2003:33). Warfare would have shaped much else in Maya society (Webster 1977), including the production systems that supported it. War influenced political alliances and different levels of society, and was a part of daily life year-round (D. Chase and A. Chase 2003:179).

Given the importance of energy and other resources in sustainability, students of the Maya could begin to address IHOPE goals by asking the following two questions: (1) What did it cost to be Maya society? And (2), How did those costs change over time? Everything the Maya did came from solar energy via their biophysical environment, and from the geological endowment of that environment. Thus these questions concentrate attention on the environmental issues that are of interest to IHOPE, and on the related issue of complexity and its costs. We know that Maya society grew more complex over time, and that complexity requires resources. Those resources came primarily from the landscape of the Maya, especially from its agricultural systems. As in other ancient societies, such as those of the Mediterranean Basin, solar energy and geological resources were converted into precious items, in the Maya case fabricated from such materials as jade, obsidian, clay, pigments, common stone, and wood. Solar energy was also transformed into Maya craft production. Agriculture was the medium through which solar energy was transformed into crafts, specialists, and amenities. As Maya society grew more complex, agriculture intensified, apparently leading to environmental degradation (see Lucero et al, Chapter 3, this volume). Complexity, as manifested in monumental construction, hydraulic engineering, agricultural intensification, warfare, and other factors, is central to understanding how the Maya succeeded for so long in their landscape, and why so many of their polities ultimately proved unsustainable.

Viewed in the light of these processes, the Maya look more like the Roman Empire than is commonly thought. In each of the areas of Maya society examined here, complexity and costliness increased over time. Investments in monumental construction and stone carving grew and grew, reaching a peak shortly before the collapses of polities. Hydraulic engineering changed from employing natural subsidies in the Preclassic to greater human management in the Classic. In the use of natural resource systems, changing from natural subsidies to human management increases costs and can make a resource system less sustainable (Allen et al. 2003). Public water management rituals added to the costs. The Maya invested heavily in the agricultural landscape, apparently intensifying production over time even as the environment was degraded (Webster 2002; see also Chase and Chase, Chapter 10, this volume). Finally there was warfare, which would have grown more costly as conflict intensified, armies were supported, and new weapons adopted, and as warfare was publicized in stone in the Late Classic. In short, the Maya seem to have experienced an evolutionary course much like that of the Roman Empire. They experienced increasing complexity and costliness in an economy limited by proximate solar energy. To pay for increasing complexity they intensified production, degrading their resource base (that is, consuming their capital) in the process. As with the Roman Empire, the collapse of Maya polities is no mystery.

Problem Solving and Sustainability Today

A critical factor that undermined the Roman Empire is that, late in its history, it increased in complexity and costliness just to sustain itself, that is, *merely to maintain the status quo*. The goals were the survival of the empire in its established territory, and the continuation of Graeco-Roman civilization. No new lands were conquered and no major booty acquired. It is axiomatic that increasing in complexity and costliness to maintain the status quo yields diminishing returns. Diminishing returns to investment in complexity will, in time, lead to fiscal weakness and alienation of the support population. Such developments reduce resiliency and problem-solving capacity, and make a society increasingly vulnerable to collapse (Tainter 1988).

The general principles that clarify the Roman and Maya collapses contribute also to understanding sustainability challenges today. While superficially our societies appear very different from those of the past, in fact they are subject to many of the same constraints. Just as ancient societies did, we increase in complexity and costliness to solve problems. There are at least seven major challenges that contemporary, industrialized societies (especially the United States) face:

1. Funding retirements for the baby-boom generation;
2. Continuing increases in the cost of health care;
3. Replacing decaying infrastructure;
4. Adapting to climate change and repairing environmental damage;
5. Developing new sources of energy;
6. Continuing high military costs; and
7. Continuing need to innovate.

These problems will converge over the next generation. In a historical perspective, that is nearly simultaneously. Resolving these problems will require increasing complexity and expenditures. Addressing these problems individually would perhaps be feasible. The challenge is that we will have to respond to them more or less simultaneously (Tainter and Patzek 2012:200–205). Moreover, we will have to do so at a time when our two major engines of wealth—oil and innovation—are becoming less abundant and less productive. Reserves of oil are declining, and we are experiencing severely lower net returns from searching for and producing oil from new sources. It is, furthermore, unlikely that renewable sources of energy will be able fully to replace declining supplies of oil (Hall and Klitgaard 2012; MacKay 2009; Tainter and Patzek 2012). At the same time, we are seeing diminishing returns to our system of technical innovation (Huebner 2005; Peirce 1879; Strumsky et al. 2010), which reduces the potential for technology to continue to offset declining quantity and quality of natural resources. Moreover, recent innovations seem less able to boost economic growth and produce wealth than previous ones (Gordon 2012), which further reduces our problem-solving capacity.

These problems present a clear threat to well-being in and of themselves, exacerbated by the timing of their occurrence. There is a further problem, one of great consequence: these challenges must be resolved merely to maintain the status quo. Of course, for a time innovation (problem 7) may produce additional wealth, but its productivity is declining. Renewable sources of energy (problem 5) do not have the energy density of fossil fuels, and so cannot be expected to support the wealth creation and problem-solving abilities that fossil fuels have given us (Hall and Klitgaard 2012). Resolving the seven problems will not generate new net wealth over the long term. Rather, we must solve them merely to keep our lives as they are now. Like the Romans, and perhaps also the Maya, we must increase the complexity and costliness of our way of life just to maintain the status quo. This will produce diminishing returns and serious consequences, including a reduction in our problem-solving abilities, and political discontent as incomes stagnate and shrink.

This analysis offers several points that are worthwhile for policy makers to understand. Firstly, while the term *complexity* has negative connotations, complexity in problem solving is not inherently good or bad. It is either useful and affordable, or it is not. Secondly, complexity grows by small increments, as challenges arise and are addressed. Each increment seems reasonable and affordable at the time. It is the cumulative costs that do the damage. Thus the first step in coping with complexity is to be aware of the processes by which it grows. Thirdly, there are several strategies for coping with complexity, as detailed elsewhere (Tainter 2006:99–100). The most common are to (a) pay the cost of complexity by exploiting resources and taxing the support population (as the Romans did, and probably the Maya); (b) shift or defer costs (as the Romans did through debasement, and we do through borrowing); (c) find subsidies to pay the costs (as we do with fossil fuels); or (d) don't solve the problem. In any case, all solutions to complexity are temporary. In the arena of sustainability and collapse, success consists of staying in the game.

It is important to point out that we understand the consequences of the seven converging problems because we have the historical examples to guide us. Were it not for our understanding of the Romans, the Maya, and other past societies, we would not have our present understanding of the consequences of increasing complexity to maintain the status quo. If we accept the lesson, the misfortunes of the Romans and the Maya will be to our benefit. One point is clear: historical science is key to understanding sustainability.

Acknowledgements

I am pleased to express my appreciation to Arlen Chase and Vernon Scarborough for advice on recent literature on the Maya, and to two anonymous reviewers for their comments.

References Cited

9/11 Commission
2004 The 9/11 Commission Report: Final Report of the National Commission on Terrorist Attacks Upon the United States. New York: Norton.

Allen, T. F. H., Joseph A. Tainter, and T. W. Hoekstra
2003 Supply-Side Sustainability. New York: Columbia University Press.

Barnett, Harold J., and Chandler Morse
1963 Scarcity and Growth: The Economics of Natural Resource Availability. Baltimore: Johns Hopkins Press.

Boak, Arthur E. R.
1955 Manpower Shortage and the Fall of the Roman Empire in the West. Ann Arbor: University of Michigan Press.

Boserup, Ester
1965 The Conditions of Agricultural Growth: The Economics of Agrarian Change under Population Pressure. Chicago: Aldine.

Boulding, Kenneth E.
1959 Foreward. In Population: The First Essay. Thomas Robert Malthus, author. Pp. v–xii. Ann Arbor: University of Michigan Press.

Brown, Lester
2009 Plan B 4.0: Mobilizing to Save Civilization. New York: W. W. Norton.

Chase, Arlen F., and Diane Z. Chase
1989 The Investigation of Classic Period Maya Warfare at Caracol, Belice. Mayab 5:5–18.
1998 Late Classic Maya Political Structure, Polity Size, and Warfare Arenas. *In* Anatomia de una Civilizacion: Aproximaciones Interdisciplinarias a la Cultura Maya. Andrés Ciudad Ruiz, María Yolanda Fernández Marquínez, José Miguel García Campillo, María Josefa Iglesias Ponce de León, Alfonso Lacadena García-Gallo, and Luis Tomás Sanz Castro, coordinators. Pp. 11–29. Madrid: Sociedad Española de Estudios Mayas.

Chase, Diane Z., and Arlen F. Chase
2002 Classic Maya Warfare and Settlement Archaeology at Caracol, Belize. Estudios de Cultura Maya 22:33–51.
2003 Texts and Contexts in Maya Warfare: A Brief Consideration of Epigraphy and Archaeology at Caracol, Belize. *In* Ancient Mesoamerican Warfare. M. Kathryn Brown and Travis W. Stanton, eds. Pp. 171–188. Walnut Creek: AltaMira Press.

Childe, V. Gordon
1944 Progress and Archaeology. London: Watts and Company.

Clark, Colin, and Margaret Haswell
1966 The Economics of Subsistence Agriculture. London: MacMillan.

Cleveland, Cutler J.
2008 Natural Resource Quality. *In* The Encyclopedia of Earth. Cutler J. Cleveland, ed. http://www.eoearth.org/view/article/154798/, accessed May 21, 2014.

Cohen, Mark N.
1977 The Food Crisis in Prehistory: Overpopulation and the Origins of Agriculture. New Haven: Yale University Press.

Cope, Lawrence H.
n.d. Unpublished metallurgical analyses on file in the Department of Coins and Medals, British Museum, London.
1969a The Nadir of the Imperial Antoninianus in the Reign of Claudius II Gothicus, A.D. 268–270. The Numismatic Chronicle 7.
1969b The Nadir of the Imperial Antoninianus in the Reign of Claudius II Gothicus, A.D. 268–270. The Numismatic Chronicle 9.
1974 The Metallurgical Development of the Roman Imperial Coinage During the First Five Centuries A.D. Ph.D. dissertation, Liverpool Polytechnic University.

Cornell, T. J.
1992 The Effects of War on the Society of Ancient Rome. *In* Effects of War on Society. G. Ausenda, ed. Pp. 133–148. San Marino: Center for Interdisciplinary Research on Social Stress.

Demarest, Arthur
2004 Ancient Maya: The Rise and Fall of a Rainforest Civilization. Cambridge: Cambridge University Press.

Duncan-Jones, Richard
1990 Structure and Scale in the Roman Economy. Cambridge: Cambridge University Press.
1994 Money and Government in the Roman Empire. Cambridge: Cambridge University Press.

Dunning, Nicholas P.
1996 A Reexamination of Regional Variability in the Pre-Hispanic Agricultural Landscape. *In* The Managed Mosaic: Ancient Maya Agriculture and Resource Use. Scott L. Fedick, ed. Pp. 53–68. Salt Lake City: University of Utah Press.

Erickson, Edwin E.
1973 The Life Cycle of Life Styles: Projecting the Course of Local Evolutionary Sequences. Cross-Cultural Research 8:135–160.

Fedick, Scott L.
1996a Introduction: New Perspectives on Ancient Maya Agriculture and Resource Use. *In* The Managed Mosaic: Ancient Maya Agriculture and Resource Use. Scott L. Fedick, ed. Pp. 1–14. Salt Lake City: University of Utah Press.
1996b An Interpretive Kaleidoscope: Alternative Perspectives on Ancient Agricultural Landscapes of the Maya Lowlands. *In* The Managed Mosaic: Ancient Maya Agriculture and Resource Use. Scott L. Fedick, ed. Pp. 107–131. Salt Lake City: University of Utah Press.

Fouquet, Roger
2008 Heat, Power and Light: Revolutions in Energy Services. Cheltenham: Edward Elgar.

Gatlin, Lila
1972 Information Theory and the Living System. New York: Columbia University Press.

Golden, Charles W.
2003 The Politics of Warfare in the Usumacinta Basin: La Pasadita and the Realm of Bird Jaguar. *In* Ancient Mesoamerican Warfare. M. Kathrun Brown and Travis W. Stanton, eds. Pp. 31–48. Walnut Creek: Altamira Press.

Gordon, Robert J.
2012 Is U.S. Economic Growth Over? Faltering Innovation Confronts the Six Headwinds. National Bureau of Economic Research Working Paper 18315.

Greening, Lorna A., David L. Greene, and Carmen Difiglio
2000 Energy Efficiency and Consumption—the Rebound Effect—a Survey. Energy Policy 28:389–401.

Hall, Charles A. S., and Kent A. Klitgaard
2012 Energy and the Wealth of Nations: Understanding the Biophysical Economy. New York: Springer.

Hamilton, Abbe, Stephen B. Balogh, Adrienna Maxwell, and Charles A. S. Hall
2013 Efficiency of Edible Agriculture in Canada and the U.S. over the Past Three and Four Decades. Energies 6:1764–1793.

Harl, Kenneth W.
1996 Coinage in the Roman Economy, 300 B.C. to A.D. 700. Baltimore: Johns Hopkins University Press.

Hassig, Ross
1992 War and Society in Ancient Mesoamerica. Berkeley: University of California Press.

Huebner, Jonathan
2005 A Possible Declining Trend for Worldwide Innovation. Technological Forecasting & Social Change 72:980–986.

Hodgett, Gerald A. J.
1972 A Social and Economic History of Medieval Europe. London: Methuen.

Jevons, W. Stanley
1866 The Coal Question: An Inquiry Concerning the Progress of the Nation and the Probable Exhaustion of Our Coal-Mines. 2nd edition. London: Macmillan.

Jones, A. H. M.
1964 The Later Roman Empire, 284–602: A Social, Economic and Administrative Survey. Norman: University of Oklahoma Press.
1974 The Roman Economy: Studies in Ancient Economic and Administrative History. Oxford: Basil Blackwell.

Kennett, Douglas J., Sebastian F.M. Breitenbach, Valarie V. Aquino, Yemane Asmerom, Jaime Awe, James U.L. Baldini, Patrick Bartlein, Brendan J. Culleton, Claire Ebert, Christopher Jazwa, Martha J. Macri, Norbert Marwan, Victor Polyak, Keith M. Prufer, Harriet E. Ridley, Harald Sodemann, Bruce Winterhalder, and Gerald H. Haug

2012 Development and Disintegration of Maya Political Systems in Response to Climate Change. Science 338:788–791.

King, Cathy E.

1982 Issues from the Rome Mint During the Sole Reign of Gallienus. Actes du 9ème Congrès International de Numismatique, Berne, 1979. Pp. 467–485. Louvain-la-Neuve: Association Internationale des Numismates Professionels.

Le Gentilhomme, Pierre

1962 Variations du Titre de l'Antoninianus au IIIe Siècle. Revue Numismatique VI(IV):141–166.

Lentz, David L., and Brian Hockaday

2009 Tikal Timbers and Temples: Ancient Maya Agroforestry and the End of Time. Journal of Archaeological Science 36:1342–1353.

Lévy, Jean-Philippe

1967 The Economic Life of the Ancient World. John G. Biram, trans. Chicago: University of Chicago Press.

Lucero, Lisa J.

2006 Water and Ritual: The Rise and Fall of Classic Maya Rulers. Austin: University of Texas Press.

MacKay, David J. C.

2009 Sustainable Energy–Without the Hot Air. Cambridge: UIT Cambridge.

MacMullen, Ramsey

1976 Roman Government's Response to Crisis, A.D. 235–337. New Haven: Yale University Press.

Martin, Simon, and Nikolai Grube

2008 Chronicle of the Maya Kings and Queens: Deciphering the Dynasties of the Ancient Maya. 2nd edition. London: Thames and Hudson.

Murphy, Pat

2008 Plan C: Survival Strategies for Peak Oil and Climate Change. Gabriola Island, BC: New Society Publishers.

Neumayer, Eric

2000 Scarce or Abundant? The Economics of Natural Resource Availability. Journal of Economic Surveys 14:307–335.

Pearce, D. W., G. D. Atkinson, and W. R. Dubourg

1994 The Economics of Sustainable Development. Annual Review of Energy and Environment 19:457–474.

Peirce, Charles S.

1879 Notes on the Theory of the Economy of Research. *In* United States Coast Survey, Showing the Progress of the Work for the Fiscal Year Ending June, 1876. C. P. Patterson, compiler. Pp. 197–201. Washington, DC: U.S. Government Printing Office.

Polimeni, John M., Kozo Mayumi, Mario Giampietro, and Blake Alcott

2008 The Jevons Paradox and the Myth of Resource Efficiency Improvements. London: Earthscan.

Pyburn, K. Anne

1996 The Political Economy of Ancient Maya Land Use: The Road to Ruin. *In* The Managed Mosaic: Ancient Maya Agriculture and Resource Use. Scott L. Fedick, ed. Pp. 236–247. Salt Lake City: University of Utah Press.

Rees, William E.

2002 Carrying Capacity and Sustainability: Waking Malthus' Ghost. *In* Introduction to Sustainable Development in Encyclopedia of Life Support Systems. David V. J. Bell and Y. Annie Cheung, eds. Oxford: EOLSS Publishers. http://www.eolss.net, accessed July 13, 2014

Russell, J. C.

1958 Late Ancient and Medieval Population. Transactions of the American Philosophical Society 48(3):1–152.

Sato, Ryuzo, and Gilbert S. Suzawa

1983 Research and Productivity: Endogenous Technical Change. Boston: Auburn House.

Scarborough, Vernon L.

1998 Ecology and Ritual: Water Management

and the Maya. Latin American Antiquity 9: 135–159.

2007 The Rise and Fall of the Ancient Maya: A Case Study in Political Ecology. *In* Sustainability or Collapse? An Integrated History and Future of People on Earth. Robert Costanza, Lisa J. Graumlich, and Will Steffen, eds. Pp. 61–75. Dahlem Workshop Report, 96. Cambridge: The MIT Press.

Smil, Vaclav

1994 Energy in World History. Boulder: Westview.

Smith, Michael H., Karlson C. Hargroves, and Cheryl Desha

2010 Cents and Sustainability: Securing Our Common Future by Decoupling Economic Growth from Environmental Pressures. London: Earthscan.

Stevenson, Angus (ed.)

2007 Shorter Oxford English Dictionary on Historical Principles. 6th edition. Oxford: Oxford University Press.

Strumsky, Deborah, José Lobo, and Joseph A. Tainter

2010 Complexity and the Productivity of Innovation. Systems Research and Behavioral Science 27:496–509.

Tainter, Joseph A.

1988 The Collapse of Complex Societies. Cambridge: Cambridge University Press.

2006 Social Complexity and Sustainability. Ecological Complexity 3:91–103.

2008 Foreward. *In* The Jevons Paradox and the Myth of Resource Efficiency Improvements. John M. Polimeni, Kozo Mayumi, Mario Giampietro, and Blake Alcott, authors. Pp. ix–xvi. London: Earthscan.

Tainter, Joseph A., and Tadeusz W. Patzek

2012 Drilling Down: The Gulf Oil Debacle and Our Energy Dilemma. New York: Copernicus Books.

Tyler, Philip

1975 The Persian Wars of the 3rd century A.D. and Roman Imperial Monetary Policy, A.D. 253–68. Einzelschriften, 23. Stuttgart: Historia.

Van Meter, David

1991 The Handbook of Roman Imperial Coins. Nashua: Laurion Numismatics.

Walker, David R.

1976 The Metrology of the Roman Silver Coinage, Part I: From Augustus to Domitian. BAR Supplementary Series, 5. Oxford: British Archaeological Reports.

1977 The Metrology of the Roman Silver Coinage, Part II: From Nerva to Commodus. BAR Supplementary Series, 22. Oxford: British Archaeological Reports.

1978 The Metrology of the Roman Silver Coinage, Part III: From Pertinax to Uranius Antoninus. BAR Supplementary Series, 40. Oxford: British Archaeological Reports.

White, Leslie

1949 The Science of Culture. New York: Farrar, Straus and Giroux.

1959 The Evolution of Culture. New York: McGraw-Hill.

Webster, David

1977 Warfare and the Evolution of Maya Civilization. *In* The Origins of Maya Civilization. Richard E. W. Adams, ed. Pp. 335–372. Albuquerque: University of New Mexico Press.

2000 The Not So Peaceful Civilization: A Review of Maya War. Journal of World Prehistory 14:65–119.

2002 The Fall of the Ancient Maya: Solving the Mystery of the Maya Collapse. London: Thames and Hudson.

Wickham, Chris

1984 The Other Transition: From the Ancient World to Feudalism. Past and Present 103:3–36.

Wilkinson, Richard G.

1973 Poverty and Progress: an Ecological Model of Economic Development. London: Methuen.

Williams, Stephen

1985 Diocletian and the Roman Recovery. New York: Methuen.

Williams, Stephen, and Gerard Friell

1994 Theodosius: The Empire at Bay. New Haven: Yale University Press.

World Commission on Environment and Development

1987 Our Common Future. Oxford: Oxford University Press.

15

Transforming Lessons from the Past into Lessons for the Future

Sander E. van der Leeuw
Arizona State University and Santa Fe Institute

ABSTRACT

This paper argues that we would massively increase the value of our archaeological understanding of the past for the present if we cast it differently. Rather than use a reductionist, ex-post approach (which explains the present by invoking the past, looking for origins), we should be using an "ex ante" approach that looks at the emergence of change, linking past and present to the future. This would allow us to learn from the past for the future. The paper examines some of the difficulties encountered in implementing such a different approach, at the level of our cognition, our scientific practices, and our paradigms, and then illustrates some of the changes in perspective such a shift would bring about by referring to the different discussions of Maya archaeology presented in this volume. [emergence, complex systems, problem-solving, information processing]

Introduction

In most of the sustainability debate, the discussions refer to the past much more specifically than to the future. For example, we want to keep our current energy use level, but change the nature of energy generation; we want to keep our heavily consumerist and materially focused lifestyle, but rid ourselves of the pollution it causes and reduce the resource use that it entails. Collectively, we seem to select things from our current lifestyle that we'd like to keep, others which we think we might do without, or yet others for which we expect to find the substitute technologies that allow us to maintain our comforts while mitigating their impact. But the predominant tendency has been to focus on those things that we don't want for our future: resource scarcity, lower comfort levels, destruction of ecosystem services or increases in air pollution or waste. On the other hand, there is relatively little positive reflection or discussion on "What kind of future do we want?" which starts from first principles or is detached enough from the past or the present to draw a different "Gestalt" of that future (Lévèque and van der Leeuw 2003).

Why would this be so? Does our intellectual tradition, and in particular our scientific tradition, have anything to do with that? This paper argues that our scientific tradition, and the institutional framework that underpins it, have handicapped our scientific communities in thinking freely about the future. Increasingly, since the 14th century, science has emphasized thinking about *origins rather than emergence*, about *feedback rather than feed-forward*, about learning *from* the past rather than learning *for* the future. The empiricist scientific tradition of the western world, with its emphasis on proof, seems to have favored that because after all, proof can only relate the past to the present (and vice-versa), rather than to the future, because the future is unknown. With our society's emphasis on the role of science as a motor of progress since the industrial revolution, this seems to have affected many aspects of our societies.

If this is so, is it uniquely a result of our scientific tradition or is our bias in favor of an "a posteriori" or "ex-post" perspective as opposed to an "a priori" or "ex ante" point of view part of the way our human cognition works? Atlan (1992) seems to argue in favor of the latter thesis when he proposes that the theories by which we link observations

ARCHEOLOGICAL PAPERS OF THE AMERICAN ANTHROPOLOGICAL ASSOCIATION, Vol. 24, pp. 215–231, ISSN 1551-823X, online ISSN 1551-8248. DOI: 10.1111/apaa.12039.

to ideas are underdetermined by our observations. If that is so, then those theories are necessarily over-determined by prior experience. Over time, past experience would thus seem to have limited the range of our conceptions of possible futures and emphasized extrapolation from the present or past.

Can we change the way we are collectively thinking about the future? Many individuals, from Plato to Thomas More, have been able to design utopias. Others have been able to extrapolate from their experience into scenarios for the future, such as Jules Verne who introduced novelties (submarines, sending people to the moon) in his books that have become reality a century or more later. Inventors have also been able to anticipate, as in the case of Leonardo da Vinci, whose drawings of many inventions came to be realized independently, many centuries later. Finally, most of us call on our "intuition" when we need to anticipate. The question is thus raised whether it could possibly be the case that many individuals have the capacity to think about the future, but that collectively, that capability is much rarer. And that in turn poses the question whether there are, in our culture and other cultures, cultural or social constraints that limit thinking about the future.

The IHOPE Maya project attempts to scientifically "learn for the future" by linking past, present, and future through a combination of archaeological and historical studies of the dynamics of various civilizations in co-evolution with their environments (e.g., van der Leeuw et al. 2011). It compares the socio-environmental co-evolution of eight differently structured societies within the Maya cultural area, in different environments, and elicits how each of these societies has emerged in the context of similar changes in the global climate dynamics over the ca. 1500 years of Maya civilization.

The papers also show, however, that the global climate change processes affected the different sub-regions ("hotspots") in the Maya area differentially, and thus poses the question how to relate global scale changes to local and regional scale ones. This is a highly relevant point with respect to the current CO_2 negotiations, which have been handled by the UN and IPCC on a global scale, whereas the reality is that greenhouse gases have very different roles in different regional subsystems in different parts of the world.

The project explicitly chose a Complex Adaptive Systems approach to better focus from an "ex-ante" perspective on the emergence of Maya societies and their socio-environmental trajectories through time. Once these dynamics were identified and understood, the team built a dynamic model representing them over the whole of the Maya area, which allowed it to explore multiple alternative scenarios that could have happened, but did not. Each of those scenarios may now be assessed against the intended and unintended consequences of the choices made earlier in the system's trajectory.

In doing this, the project's participants attempted not only to understand Maya societal dynamics and their evolution, but also to prepare the material for comparison with other case studies that are currently being worked on in comparable ways (the mobile and egalitarian societies of the interior of Australia, the agricultural village societies of the Southwestern United States, and the Roman Empire). Interesting ideas may thus be derived from the Maya model that are relevant to the transition to urbanism in other places and that have implications for modern sustainability issues.

Why Aren't We Thinking Constructively about Our Future?

At first sight, this focus on learning from the past rather than learning for the future seems at least in part a consequence of our society's reluctance to call into question ideals and ideas underpinning our current social organization and lifestyle. We often ignore such issues as the exploding world population, inequity between rich and poor, the impact of democratic institutions on decision-making, etc. Indeed, cultural, social, institutional, economic, and educational norms preclude such discussions as a way of transforming society except in a widely acknowledged crisis.

But upon further consideration, there are other roadblocks to learning for the future. Through time, every society develops its own intellectual tradition. Such a tradition is in essence *path-dependent*; that is, the history of that tradition determines, at any time and to an important degree, its current state, and thereby the options the society has for dealing with its current challenges and shaping its future.

That path-dependency is fundamentally a reflection of the fact that our ideas (theories, etc.) are under-determined by our observations. This is illustrated by an example from Atlan (1992): five traffic lights can assume 3^5 (=243) combinations of colors (i.e., "system states"). But the possible configurations of the connections between these lights that could explain any combination of colors numbers 3^{25}, about a thousand billion. That is also the number of random observations we would need to decide scientifically which configuration is the one actually connecting the lights. Evidently we never have anywhere near that number of observations. Hence, our theories and ideas are indeed under-determined by our observations. It follows that they must be over-determined by pre-existing ideas—existing patterns of thinking that shape our interpretation of new data—thus causing intellectual traditions to be difficult to change.

Moreover, our reductionist scientific tradition, together with the institutional framework that underpins it, has handicapped us, preventing us from thinking freely about the future. Science, ever since the 14th century, has emphasized the need to solidify the relationship between observations and interpretations. These interpretations linked the phenomena investigated to the past (phenomena that were already in existence at the time of observation), rather than to what was still to come (and therefore could not be observed). This kind of (natural) history, which has been the predominant explanatory paradigm at least until the 18th century (cf. Girard 1990), emphasized the explanation of observed phenomena in terms of chains of cause-and-effect linking the present to the past. As we conceive of past phenomena by reducing the number of dimensions[1] that we observe in the present into a more or less coherent narrative, this has resulted in reductionism. An inevitable corollary is the fragmentation of our world-view, which is currently one of our main handicaps in any attempt to understand the full complexity of the processes going on around us. It has been institutionalized in the way academia is structured in disciplines.

This kind of reductionist "ex post" science has in the last twenty-five years come under increasing attack from the Complex Systems approach that emerged beginning in the 1980s (Bentley and Maschner 2003; Kohler 2011; Mitchell 2009; Morin 2008; Prigogine 1982; van der Leeuw and McGlade 1997). It assumes that in order to improve our understanding, we need to develop a generative ex ante perspective in which the amplification of the number of cognized dimensions is essential. Such a perspective would help us to study emergence and feed-forward rather than origins and feedback. At least in theory, it should thus be possible to transcend our relative incapacity to focus on the future.

Of course this would require us to develop fundamentally different ways of practicing science and thinking about the future (and changing the nature of our academic institutions). Instead of following the classic, reductionist, approach to Occam's razor and choosing the simplest explanation for a set of observed phenomena, we would need to increase the number of dimensions of the phenomena that we consider, and look for a range of more complex interpretations that take the wider context of these phenomena into account. Moreover, we would need to consider the fact that in complex systems highly similar causes can have widely different effects, but that highly different causes can also have very similar results. In thinking about the future, we would therefore need to think in terms of alternatives, and when choosing between them, we would need to consider the unintended consequences of each of these alternatives. Adopting this kind of approach would seem a necessary (but not necessarily sufficient) condition for developing a desirable perspective on the future and adopting a road map to attain it.

Why is Constructing a Different Perspective on the Future So Important?

The way our ideas are generated is only one side of the (asymmetric) interaction between people and their environment, the one in which the perception of the multidimensional external world is reduced to a very limited number of cognized dimensions. The other side of that interaction is human action on the environment, and the relationship between cognition and action is exactly what makes the gap between our needs and our capabilities so dramatic. Every human action upon the environment modifies the latter in many more ways than its human actors perceive, simply because the dimensionality of the environment is so much higher than can be captured by the human mind. Hence the well-known and oft-observed fact that, no matter how careful one is in designing human interventions in the environment, sooner or later, something is highly likely to go "wrong." In sustainability science we call these events "unanticipated consequences." Indeed, as one anonymous reviewer of this paper remarked, "everything has unintended consequences."

Imagine a group of people moving into a new environment, about which they possess little knowledge. After a relatively short time, they will observe challenges that this environment poses, and they will do something about them. Their actions will be based on a reduced perception of these challenges, in which the observed short-term dynamics involved dominate. Yet these same actions transform the environment in (unknown) ways that affect not only the short-term, but also the long-term. Little by little, over time, all the frequent challenges become known and are modified by the society's action upon the environment, while the unknown longer-term challenges that are introduced accumulate. Ultimately, this necessarily leads to "time-bombs" or "crises" in which so many unknowns emerge simultaneously that the society risks being overwhelmed (van der Leeuw 2009 et al.). The society will initially deal with this by innovating faster and faster, as our society has done for the last two centuries or so, but it ultimately is a battle that the society can only lose. Whether it wants to or not, there will come a time at which it drastically needs to change the way it interacts with the environment, so that the whole cycle begins anew (Redman and Kinzig 2005; Scarborough and Burnside 2010).

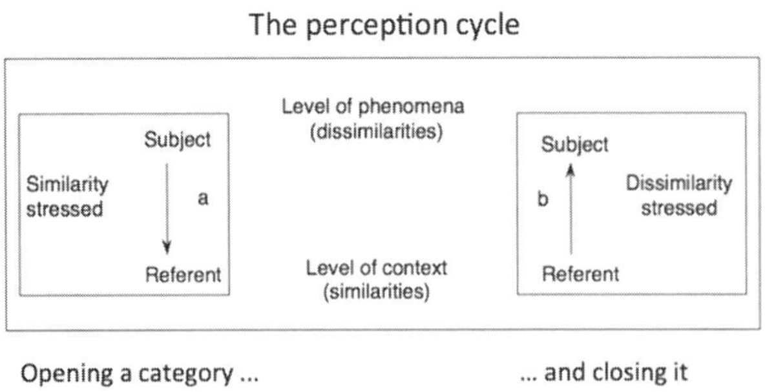

Figure 15.1. The categorization cycle.

All signs seem to point to the fact that we are currently getting rather close to such a "tipping point" (Rockström, Steffen, Noone, et al. 2009; Rockström, Steffen, Schellnhuber, et al. 2009), so that it becomes urgent to accord more importance to the unintended consequences of our actions, and to devise ways to include them in our decision-making. That requires better ways of anticipation.

Why Has the Need for a Different Perspective Remained Hidden for So Long?

If we accept the need of a different approach as essential to not only learn from the past, but also to learn for the future, the next question to ask is: why has such an approach only been emerging in the last thirty years or so, and relatively slowly at that? It seems to me that one possible explanation lies in the nature of human perception and categorization itself.

Categorization is of course based on the perception of similarities and differences. Following a range of experiments, the behavioral psychologists Kahnemann, Slovic, Tverski, and their associates (Kahnemann et al. 1982; Tverski 1977; Tverski and Gati 1978) concluded that the perception of similarity and dissimilarity is relative and contextual rather than absolute. On the basis of their conclusions, one can argue for the following model of categorization (Figure 15.1)

An initial comparison between unknown phenomena leads to the tentative conception of one or more categories by comparing their characteristics. These categories are then tested against other phenomena to establish which phenomena might be subsumed in them. In such testing, the category is the subject and the phenomena are the referents, and there is a bias in favor of *similarity*. But when the relevant categories are firmly established, the process is inverted: the categories become the referents and the phenomena the subjects, so that the comparisons are biased towards *dissimilarity*, and it is determined which phenomena, after all, did not belong in the categories established (e.g., Selby and El Guindi 1976). For example: assume that one is faced with a number of objects, among which there are some that resemble each other more or less and could fulfill the same function (e.g., "chairs"). The first comparison would pick these out, note their similarities, and put the objects together in a class ("chairs"). But next, once this class was established, further comparisons would note the dissimilarities between the definition of this class and the other objects (the "non-chairs").

Because of the fact that societies in effect define their environment, it is thus relevant to ask how the above dynamic of categorization applies to that process. The important point here is that we are dealing with the definition of a relationship between two phenomena—society and environment—which can be viewed from the perspective of either (Table 15.1).

Society can be seen as the referent and what surrounds it as the subject of the comparison, or the environment is the referent and society is the subject.

Table 15.1. Two perceptions of the relationship between society and its natural environment, depending on which of the two is taken as referent

Two ways to perceive a relationship . . .	
Milieu . . .	**Environment . . .**
• Humanity is compared to nature	• Nature is compared to humanity
• The cohesion of nature, its unknown aspects, its strangeness and force are amplified	• The cohesion and strength of nature is diminished, its known aspects emphasized
• The confusion and the handicaps of humanity are accentuated	• Cohesion and strength are accentuated in humanity
• Humanity is *passive* in a natural environment which is *active* and aggressive	• Humanity is *active* and aggressive in a natural environment that is *passive*
• Change is attributed to nature, and people have no other choice but to adapt to nature	• Humanity is the source of all change; people create their environment
• Natural changes tend to be viewed as dangerous, because they are beyond human control	• Natural changes seem more controllable and lose their dangerous appearance

Although in everyday usage we do not make a clear distinction between these two cases, looking at them very closely reveals an interesting paradox (Table 15.2). Notably, it emerges that in the interaction between these complementary perspectives, the dangerous aspects of the natural dynamics are systematically exaggerated, and the dangerous aspects of the societal dynamics undervalued. This encourages society to increasingly intervene in its natural environment by giving the impression that society's actions can reduce the risks it runs, whereas in reality, society reduces by its actions the predictability of natural phenomena.

If one now projects this process over the longer term, and takes into account that the dimensionality of the real world is much greater than that of our perception of it, I would argue that, over time, if our knowledge increases at a certain rate, it may well be that our impact on the environment changes that environment at a much faster rate than our understanding of that environment increases. We would therefore need to examine whether it is not true that the more a society learns about its environment, the less it understands it.

The cognitive feedback loop that we have just described induces society to intervene more and more in its environment—generating more and more long-term, hidden (or unanticipated) consequences. Because of this shift from known short-term challenges to unknown longer-term ones, we get the (in my opinion erroneous) impression that we can indeed control the natural environment as long as we keep intervening in it more and more drastically.

Table 15.2. Characteristics of the interaction between the two relational perceptions

. . . and their interaction
• The "milieu" and "environment" perspectives are complementary
• Their interaction exaggerates natural dangers and underestimates those of human intervention
– This encourages society to intervene in its natural environment
– It gives the impression that society's actions reduce risks
• In reality, society reduces by its actions the predictability of natural phenomena
– Society loses control: the more it transforms its surroundings, the less it understands them
• This seems to be irreversible tendency?
– It ties in to the risk spectrum shift argument

Societies as Innovating and Problem-Solving Organizations

Most chapters in this book have presented recent changes in Mayanists' general perspective on their domain of study and described in some detail what one may observe in the different socio-environmental "hot spots" in the region. These chapters show: (1) how, in the different areas, societies have forged different ways of interacting with the environment; and (2) how these different approaches have changed over time under the impact of both (a) climate change and (b) the unintended consequences of each of the different approaches to dealing with the environment. Three other chapters compare developments in the Maya area to socio-environmental interactions occurring in other areas of the world, and point to some long-term dynamics to which all four societies have been subject. This paper goes a step further and tries to explain some of the second-order changes that we can observe in the Maya case, asking *how the balance between the societal and the environmental dynamics changed over time.*

A quick scan of this volume shows immediately that most of its papers consider "managing" externalities such as the climate, water, cultivable land and crops, energy and other resources as essential challenges for Maya societies to address in order for the society to emerge and grow, and view a deficiency in the ability to do so as one of the reasons for their demise. The papers of Lucero et al. (this volume) and Isendahl et al. (this volume) show this most clearly, following the perspective developed by Tainter (1988, this volume; Tainter and Patzek 2011), but close reading will reveal the same perspective in some of the others as well. They all view the environment from the perspective of society, by asking how the environment enabled the rise of Maya society or how it was impacted by it. But to study the second order change, we must also look at the societal dynamics themselves, and ask the question "What drove the Maya towards organizing themselves in the kind of complex, urban societies that emerged in the area?" Hence, I will next outline a model of that process that applies to human societies in general (van der Leeuw 2007, 2010, 2012).

Humans differ from most other species in that they can learn and learn how to learn; that they can categorize, make abstractions and hierarchically organize them; and that they communicate between themselves by various kinds of symbolic means. That capacity to process information is genetically encoded, but the information they process, and the ways in which they do so, is not. It is socio-culturally and self-referentially developed and maintained in each different culture.

Human learning involves the recognition of patterns of all kinds, whether temporal, spatial, semantic, syntactic or yet other. By identifying such patterns, we organize the world around us, infuse it with structure and meaning, make it possible for us to understand where we live and or know things about it, intervene in it, etc. As part of that process, human beings have the capacity to transform their natural and material environment in many different ways, and at many spatial and temporal scales.

Our relations with our environment are part of that uninterrupted process of human learning, which may be seen as a positive (reinforcing) cycle that creates order out of our experiences of the world, by isolating patterns, defining them in terms of a limited number of dimensions, and storing the latter in the form of knowledge. The more cognitive dimensions have thus been acquired and stored, the more problems can be tackled, and the more quickly knowledge is accumulated, according to the following feedback loop:

> Knowledge is structured by problem-solving; more knowledge increases the information processing capacity; that [increase] in turn allows the cognition of new problems and creates new knowledge; [that] knowledge creation [also] involves more and more people in processing information, [thus] increasing the size of the group involved and its degree of aggregation; this [in turn] creates more problems and increases the need for problem-solving; [such] problem-solving structures more knowledge . . . etc. (van der Leeuw 2012:34)

The result of this process is the continued accumulation of information-processing capacity, which enables a concomitant increase in matter, energy and information flows through the society, and thus enables the society to grow. That information-processing capacity includes the sum total of the understanding, know-how and skills of the people involved, including both their technical and organizational means of solving problems and their means to maintain group cohesion.

Prigogine (1980), a Nobel-winning chemist and one of the fathers of the "Complex Systems" approach, proposed to change our usual perspective on the relationship between order and disorder. As an example, Prigogine argued that rather than see a flow in a liquid as a *disturbance* of the stable structure of the rest of the basin, the flow could be seen as a *dynamic structure* in an entropic environment (the rest of the basin). He called such dynamic structures that dissipate entropy "dissipative structures" or "flow structures."

I would argue that human societies can be seen in the same way as "flow structures." Their existence is dependent upon flows of information that allow the needs of the individual participants to be met by distributing resources throughout the society. Material and energetic resources (ores, plants, animals, wind, oil) are identified as such in the natural environment, transformed by human knowledge and energy in such a way that they are suitable for use in the society (actions, artifacts, foods), and again transformed during use into forms with higher entropy (heat, waste). These can then be recycled, or they are released by the society. The first kind of transformation increases the information content of the resources by relating them more closely to the information processed in society, and thus making them useful, whereas the second one reduces their information content.

But the flows of matter, energy, and information do not follow the same pattern. Matter and energy are subject to the laws of conservation, and *cannot in the strict sense be shared*. Thus, if A gives B an object, A no longer has it. The same is true of energy expenditure. But if A teaches B something, they both share the knowledge, and that shared knowledge then becomes the basis for the interactions between them, including shared exploitation of resources. Though they do indeed function as the substrate enabling the transmission of information, matter and energy could therefore never have created durable human social institutions, let alone societies. Human societies are shaped and held together by shared information, shared expectations, shared institutions, shared world-views, etc. The artifacts and other elements of the material culture of societies are essential aspects of the transmission of such information that enable the sharing of cultural information. But their culture is in the minds of the people participating in it—it is in itself intangible.

The channels through which information is processed in society emerge through a recursive communication process that aligns people's perceptions, ideas, language, technology, culture, and environmental resources. It draws more and more individuals into a network in which they can communicate (and obtain resources) with less effort and or less risk of error than they would experience individually, outside the network. Simultaneously, it transforms more and more of the known environment in ways that are compatible with, and support, the needs of the society. On the other hand, when the recursive communication falls or remains below a certain threshold, it keeps people out of a network because they cannot sufficiently maintain their alignment.

The shared information also creates the channels through which energy and matter flow, whether these channels are material (e.g., roads, cables, trade patterns [Sahlins 1974], etc.) or virtual (e.g., ideology or exchange networks such as the *kula* [Malinowski 2010(1922)]). Sometimes the channels for information, matter, and/or energy are the same, but that is not necessarily so: electricity, petroleum, and coal are transported, processed, and delivered in different ways, as are virtually all goods in everyday life that we do not collect or process ourselves. The fabric of society thus consists of flows through multiple networks, held together by different kinds of (information) relations (kin, business, friendship, exchange, client-patron, power, etc.), and transmitting different combinations of matter, energy, and information. Ultimately, as Luhmann (1992) reminds us, the information processing occurring in society is also determinant for the society's definition of its environment, its environmental challenges, and the solutions it might propose for them, as the society does not communicate *with* the environment, but communicates within itself, auto-referentially, *about* its environment.

As Leslie White argued (1949), maintaining a society's growth requires a continuous increase in the quantity of energy and matter flowing through the society, implying the identification, appropriation, and exploitation of more and more resources. But it seems to me that not enough attention has been paid to the fact that this dynamic is enabled and driven by the information-processing loop. If not enough information is processed, the members of the society will not be able to acquire sufficient matter and energy to satisfy all of them; that increases the chances that people will act in their own immediate interests and the society loses coherence.

Because that transition may take time, it is often not directly visible on the timescales studied by most cultural or social anthropologists. However, on archaeological timescales, such as the slow disintegration of the Roman Empire, one clearly observes that as central control begins to falter, the Empire breaks up into constituent parts. Initially, this concerns the breakup of the Empire into four parts, but a few centuries later, local *latifundia* (estates) and municipalities in the Western Empire gain their independence and become centers of attraction in their own right, strengthening their own information flows at a regional scale. A good example of this is the municipality of Trier in Germany, which transforms itself from an outpost of the Empire to a regional center in its own right. In the Eastern Empire, the same process leads to a complete, bottom-up restructuration of its sociopolitical organization that accords an increased degree of independence to most political units. Avoiding such disintegration, it would seem, requires a continual stream of innovations spreading from the center to the periphery.

Recent research on the relationship between city size and innovation seems to indicate that continued innovation is facilitated by higher interaction densities of individuals and more rapid information processing (Bettencourt et al. 2009; Florida 2002, 2005;). Hence, it would seem that the innovation density of a social system is, over the long term, usually higher in its centers.

Innovations create value for those people for whom the innovation represents something desirable but difficult to attain. The farther from the centers of a society, the more unattainable the innovations created in those centers are, because of the greater distance from the know-how that created them. The value gradient is therefore inversely proportional to the information-processing gradient. I would hypothesize that the perceived value of innovations prompts export of raw materials and resources from the periphery to the center. Hence these raw materials and resources, in turn, are transformed into (objects of) value wherever the (innovative) know-how to do so has spread. The objects are then exchanged with whomever considers them of value—i.e., whomever cannot make them (or not make them as well, or as efficiently)—thus closing the loop between the two flows.

The Emergence of Maya Polities as a Result of Local Problem-Solving

What strikes one when reading the case studies in this volume is the great diversity of ways in which the Maya have dealt with very diverse environments. This is particularly clear with regard to the primary resources of their existence—water and soil—but concomitantly also with respect to the diversity of crops and agricultural techniques, settlement location, and social organization.

From their traditional "ex post" perspective most archaeologists search for the origins (and later the demise) of "Maya civilization," emphasizing the similarities among the different regional Maya groups. Differences in subsistence techniques are interpreted as merely ways in which the Maya adjusted their approach in order to deal with local environments and to procure the resources they needed. From this ex post perspective, the unity of the Maya world is more important than the existence of many different modes of subsistence; culture is more important in the interpretation than the environment. In terms of Table 15.1, the *environment is viewed from the perspective of society*. The fundamental question to be answered from this perspective is: *How have the Maya adapted to different environments, and how have these adaptations impacted their institutions and material remains?*

But from an "ex ante" perspective we get a different picture, one which emphasizes that, while the various Maya entities ultimately became part of a social community (the "Maya world") that shares many cultural traits, these societal entities are in essence home-grown, and have created their own ecologies (in the wider sense, encompassing their environments, their ways of exploiting them, and the societal institutions and material infrastructure to go with them) through an ongoing interaction between the local population and its environment. Hence, diversity is emphasized over similarity in the emergence of the "Maya world" (Scarborough and Valdez 2009). The diversity of subsistence techniques is interpreted in terms of the different environmental contexts of the different Maya polities or societies (e.g., Liendo et al., this volume), rather than the different subsistence adaptations of a "Civilization." In the terms of Table 15.1, *society is viewed from the perspective of the environment*. The fundamental questions now are: *How have the different regional Maya groups interacted with their local environments? How has that interaction shaped the local societies? and How have the different regional societies converged to leave a relatively uniform material culture that we, as archaeologists, have interpreted as "Maya civilization"?*

The IHOPE-Maya group that is responsible for this volume has prepared the way for such an approach by working assiduously towards a comparative systemic framework for the study of the different Maya polities. Only in the context of such a framework is it possible to achieve the kind of modeling that allows us to view, analyze, and experiment with the various scenarios developed by the Maya for dealing with their regional and local environments (e.g., Heckbert 2012; Heckbert et al. in press) and to understand the path-dependent development of each region to the point where long-distance trade and crafts emerge as novel resources that have the side-effect of enhancing the information flows between the different polities to such an extent that one may begin to speak of a "Maya world," which must have resembled a shared set of values.

The "ex ante" perspective that we propose here thus enables us to study the regional development of each polity as an instance of socio-environmental problem solving in which the environment offers both opportunities and challenges. As each of these is encountered and dealt with, the polity transforms itself, grows, invests, creates new institutions, mobilizes new resources (or increasing quantities of the same resources), and ultimately reaches a plateau and declines.

The paper by Isendahl, Dunning, and Sabloff (this volume) presents a good case in point. The authors present the case of the Puuc Maya as a boom-and-crash economy enabled by fertile lands and constrained by a lack of water because there are few sources of (sub-) surface water, and little seasonal rainfall. Under the circumstances, effective water management was essential and was achieved at two societal levels, that of the family (the *chultun*, a small underground cistern) and that of the neighborhood or settlement (the *aguada*, an open still-water reservoir). The management level of the latter was decided based on location, degree of investment, and storage capacity. Clearly, therefore, water management itself was directly connected to the emergence of the administrative and political organization. As water was such a precious resource in this area, it may also have been the basis for some of the territorial organization of these early polities. Moreover, needing to combine water and land, the geography of Puuc settlement combined fertile lands with nearby karstic subsoils in which one could dig out the water reservoirs needed to irrigate during the dry season.

The Early Institutionalization of Maya Polities

The authors of Chapter 4 (Isendahl, Dunning, and Sabloff) discuss the emergence of Puuc social organization as the result of the ample availability of underexploited agricultural lands, which facilitated the amassing of ample resources to sustain larger and more stratified settlements characterized by monumental architecture and costly ceremonialism. I would put a question mark here: "Does the availability of ample resources directly lead to greater social complexity or not?"

Let us look at this in some detail as a case study in the interaction between problem solving and growth of societies. From that perspective, it seems that as long as there are ample resources, their availability will indeed drive an increase in the size of the interactive group, as well as stimulate a variety of resource exploitation methods. In that phase, most families should be able to manage more or less on their own, and a political hierarchy does not seem necessary.

But as the authors state, "while a key resource is ... abundant it is typically inefficiently managed and rapidly depleted" (Isendahl, Dunning and Sabloff, this volume: Chapter 4). Once the limits of the resource are becoming evident, one would expect (a) a drive towards more efficient use of the crucial resources, which often entails closer interaction and collaboration between individuals; and (b) a concomitant increase in conflict within the polity and therefore a need for arbitration and authority. This seems to be an interesting candidate for the drive towards monumental architecture and more complex institutional hierarchies that one observes (cf. Johnson, 1982).

In the case of the Puuc, the trend towards increasingly complex hierarchies is not limited to the individual settlements (which are rapidly growing out into large, low-density towns), but is also reflected in the spatial organization of the region.[2] Though necessary from an information-processing perspective (Johnson 1982), the creation of hierarchies has as a consequence that the people at the top become more and more distant from the decision-making going on at the level of the individual farmsteads, and this may easily lead to a degree of scalar mismatch between decisions made and their application in (somewhat) different conditions (cf. Flannery's classic 1972 paper). This is especially relevant as the size of the polities and their population grows, and decision-making becomes more and more centralized across settlements.

Overall, one could thus characterize the Puuc phase of regional evolution, therefore, as one in which population aggregation and density as well as social and societal challenges and costs grow in importance, while environmental challenges seem to be manageable due to increasingly efficient management and technology.

Arguably, one encounters among the Maya polities both the initial phase of emergence in an environment in which resources are ample, and this next phase of increasing efficiency in exploitation (in terms of return on investment in human, social, and environmental capital) accompanied by growing societal size and complexity. However, the specific resource challenges are different in each case. In the case of Caracol, for example (Chase and Chase, this volume), precipitation is ample but the availability of fertile lands in a very karstic landscape is a challenge that leads to the creation of terraces, which in turn poses other challenges.

In northern Yucatan, recent research (Fedick, this volume) has shown that the availability of both water and fertile soils is greater than expected, thus finally providing an explanation for the relatively dense settlement of that area in the Maya period. But the environment poses particular resource challenges all of its own. In the absence of a *cenote*, it requires people to dig about 10 meters below the surface to tap into a plentiful aquifer (which had not been noticed before). It also limits cultivation to an important extent to natural pockets in the karstic landscape (*rejolladas*) that are filled with good soils.

In each case the investment in both environmental and societal structuring—material infrastructure and societal institutions—is so substantial that it becomes increasingly difficult for the society concerned to change course. Indeed, the local and regional societies are from this point on seriously path-dependent. The diversity of potential solutions to experienced problems has been reduced in order to achieve the increased efficiency needed to cope with growth, and the cost of the investments made over time effectively precludes adopting an "out of the box" approach. Moreover, the size of the polity or society has grown to such a point that implementing a new solution would be very cumbersome, requiring a mobilization of collective action that would require substantive means of enforcement.

The Transition toward Partial Dependency on Long-Distance Interaction

Whereas the "emergence" phase of the local Maya societies involves the local population and occurs against the backdrop of solving challenges in the local environment, there inevitably comes a point at which the footprint of the local societies begins to exceed the local environment. This is in effect a response to the combination of resource exhaustion and path-dependency that each society or polity eventually is likely to reach. Let us see how this might have happened.

I argued above that all societies are necessarily held together by shared information processing, which results in a shared value system, which allows members of the society to draw upon one another and upon the collective knowledge to solve problems more easily than one would do single-handedly. That information-processing system grows as a function of the problems a society encounters on its path, and the ways in which they are solved. As the population in a polity grows, the total set of dimensions in which a society recognizes value (the society's "value space") thus expands together with the knowledge base and the information-processing capacity of the society's members. How it expands depends on the interactions the society's members have with their environments (in the widest sense, both natural and social).

In the initial phase of emergence of a polity, when environmental and subsistence challenges predominate in the preoccupations of its members but the relatively small group size limits social challenges, these values seem mainly related to the environment, subsistence, technology, and economy. But there comes a point where the growing size of the society keeps pushing for expansion of the total "value space" (the collection of all the values, whether material or symbolic), but the domain of environmental and subsistence values (and related ones) is shared by everyone and cannot grow any further through innovation. At that point new domains for value creation need to be opened.

As a polity's spatial expansion is what keeps confronting it with novel environmental challenges, and thus expanding its total value space, the point where new value domains need to be opened up more or less coincides with the moment in time when a polity is in the process of attaining its greatest spatial footprint.

Heckbert's (2012) dynamic model of Maya societies illustrates what then seems to have happened. He finds that he cannot derive from his model the conditions for further demographic expansion of individual polities without invoking a growing value space based on manufacturing of secondary agricultural and tertiary (artisanal) products, as well as long-distance trade that brings other novel objects and ideas into the polities concerned. This idea fits many antecedent archaeological theories and case studies that relate long-distance trade and (artisanal) manufacturing to the emergence of urbanism and, with it, the introduction of writing, counting, administration, laws, and adjudication (e.g., Algaze 2008; Wilkinson, this volume; Wright 1969).[3]

What does the lead-up to that state actually look like? As a result of the above process of expansion of their value space, the Maya polities have ultimately focused on externalized material values, creating monuments, material wealth, etc., in order to foster a bond between their members. A characteristic of such an externalized, artifact-based value system is that it can be cross-cultural because sharing objects (and valuing them) can be integrated into many different value systems. This results in relationships between many polities in which the exchange of both (rare) raw materials and craft products serves as a basis for more and more intense interactions between the polities and connects larger and larger parts of an encompassing information-processing system, as exemplified in Scarborough and Valdez's study (this volume). These relationships might also have served as "risk insurance" for shortages by establishing a network that links polities in highly diverse environmental circumstances, and thus with very different subsistence risks (cf. Cherry 1986 for prehistoric Crete, for example). The process may have resulted in either household-based or more centralized local storage facilities similar to the ones known from the Inca (D'Altroy et al. 1985), as well as elaborate road systems and shared scheduling of exchange events between polities (necessitating a refined calendar?). Increased social coherence and legitimation among the polities that are thus linked together could initially have achieved a potential degree of resilience with respect to the environment that none of the polities concerned could achieve on their own.

This process would have allowed more and more people to aggregate at each center, and spawned more urban centers. The most efficient urbanization would have been based on "buy-in" from the food producing communities rather than coercion, and that buy-in would best have been reinforced by a shared value or aspiration system. If the areas were connected by roads, they were probably also connected by values. To strengthen the latter, there would have needed to be a mechanism for the outlying communities to participate meaningfully.

Because this process involved an increase in value per capita, it would have accelerated information processing, increased innovation and specialization at the urban centers. This, in turn, would further have accelerated information processing, drawing in ideas from the whole of the area connected by a road system through long-distance (but not bulk) trade. Slowly but surely, this would have impacted on the local value systems, increasing the value of ideas and objects obtained from elsewhere, to the detriment of values attached to local products such as primary resources, crops, etc. As these "new" values took the form of manufactured items rather than resources extracted from the environment, they more directly reflected the different social value systems of the polities that produced them, for example by differences in shape, effectiveness, or decoration. Such objects thus may have served as "identity markers," whether at the individual, the group, or the society level (A. Chase and D. Chase 2009; D. Chase and A. Chase 2004), adding yet another dimension of value. But because they were ultimately widely exchanged, they became familiar to the members of the different polities, and thus came to represent the material expression of the *koinè*[4] that in our eyes was the Maya world.

The Role of Unintended Consequences

Because of increased population aggregation in the cities, the local environment of the centers probably at some point was no longer to be able to provide the necessary subsistence resources, while bulk transport of foodstuffs was too costly in energy to relieve this situation. At the same time the path dependency of the polities' trajectories hampered the capacity of the population to quickly adopt a different mode of life. As a result, local crises emerged, the expansion of the centers came to an end, and the disintegration of the individual polities began.

There are two main approaches to explain the net effect of this conundrum. The first looks at the energy flows that a society maintains to keep its members alive and to maintain its infrastructure. In its early phases, a society's expansion depends on using energy and material resources that are easily accessible in the environment or have been accumulating through either natural or human processes. As the society grows, it needs more and more energy in the form of food. Ultimately, the rate of food return on energy invested will decrease as the resources on which the society is based become locally scarcer or require access from further afield. In the extreme, this throws the society back on the net food productivity of the sun alone and only over an area that the society directly controls or impacts.

This—in my opinion entirely correct—energy perspective on the rise and fall of civilizations is the perspective that is currently dominant for our contemporary societies and is beginning to be considered for ancient societies. It is most clearly represented in this volume by the contributions of Tainter (this volume) and Isendahl et al. (this volume). But there is another, somewhat more general, way of explaining the disintegration dynamic that is inexorably pushing any society towards dissolution. It is related to the evolution of societies' information-processing dynamics (Scarborough and Valdez, this volume; van der Leeuw 2007, 2010).

In fact, there are some particularities of human information processing that create their own limitations to the growth of societies. Individually, we are limited in the number of dimensions we can observe or manipulate (Read and van der Leeuw 2008, in press). Collectively, by dividing tasks and communicating and coordinating activities, as well as developing more effective and efficient communication and information-processing technologies, such as writing, printing, telecommunication, and so forth, clearly a society can handle (many) more dimensions. But it is nevertheless limited to a selection from among the infinite number of dimensions that constitute the complex system in which any society is embedded. Whether individually or collectively, therefore, any action that we humans undertake is based on a reduced perception of the challenges with which that action attempts to deal. But these actions impact on the full set of complex system dimensions, inherently creating "unanticipated consequences" that result from any actions we as humans undertake.

If we suppose for a moment that our knowledge and understanding expands linearly or even geometrically (as in the case of our current phase of very rapid societal innovation) with time, the difference in dimensionality between the complex system itself and the representation we have of it clearly lead to unanticipated consequences, increasing in orders of magnitude faster. Hence, *though we think we know more every day, proportionately we in fact know less and less about the socio-environmental system that we are continuously modifying.*

Not only do we know less and less about our changing, highly dynamic environment as time proceeds, but what we know also changes. Clearly, through time, any society will initially tackle the challenges that it encounters most frequently—that is, the ones that involve rapid temporal rhythms (annual, decadal). But as society tackles them, human impact will transform the complex system that is the context in which the society functions in many different ways, involving many different temporal rhythms, including much slower ones (e.g., centennial, millennial). The cumulative effect of that process over the long term is *a shift in the risk spectrum the society deals with, taking out known short-term risks and introducing unknown longer-term ones.* Ultimately, that will lead to a "risk barrier," a moment in time when unexpectedly many such hidden longer term risks emerge more or less simultaneously or at least in quick succession. In fact, as the members of a society become ever more adept at solving short-term problems, they shift the risk to longer-term problems—such as climate change—which do not match the skills they have developed. They are inevitably headed into a trap of their own devising. Or to put it differently, *over time any society comes to a point when it is overwhelmed by the unintended consequences of its own actions.* That is the tipping point that we commonly call "a crisis."

Because of the explosion in the dimensionality of the system the society is entangled in, the last part of the trajectory leading to such a crisis is characterized by an increasing focus of the society on short-term, tactical interventions rather than the strategic ones that characterized the early stages of the societal growth process: "problems" (challenges due to unintended consequences) are indeed emerging everywhere simultaneously, and there is not enough time to deal with all of them in depth. Moreover, such tactical decisions generally require fewer resources, so that investment takes less away from the surplus that supports the standard of living and the organizational complexity of the society. This shorter-term focus enhances the risk that unintended consequences may at any time overwhelm the society.

The Decline of Maya Societies: Overcome by the Unanticipated Consequences of Their Own Actions

The perspective I have just outlined prompts me to argue that Mayanists must try and identify many more facets of Maya polities' demise than only the energy shortages or the environmental degradation that have been called upon to explain them. For one, we need to extend the energy shortage concept to resource shortages in general, including shortages in raw materials that do not immediately serve subsistence purposes. Among the latter are precious stones, ceramic trade wares, obsidian, and other materials from which tools are made, used, and discarded. In effect, we must include any material shortages that interrupt, change, or limit the cycle of value creation and the expansion of the value sphere in our accounts of the "rise and fall" of polities. But over and beyond immediate shortages, unintended consequences lead to all kinds of other stresses.

We see such stresses as part of the conundrum facing Maya polities towards the end of the Classic and in the Post-Classic periods. They may take many forms that seem at first sight imposed by the natural environment, such as the landscape constraints on expansion of further terracing for cultivation (e.g., Chase and Chase, this volume); limitations in the surfaces to be cultivated in non-terraced environments (e.g., Fedick, this volume); limitations in the availability of household water within a reasonable distance of a settlement (Lucero et al., this volume); and mis-harvests due to insufficient precipitation as a result of oscillations in climate (Cobos et al., this volume; Gunn et al., this volume). But many other stresses are socio-environmental. These include insufficient capacity to maintain water-cleaning biotopes in reservoirs (Lucero et al., this volume); deforestation (e.g., Liendo et al., this volume); migrations (e.g., Isendahl et al., this volume; and Chase and Chase, this volume); soil exhaustion due to overexploitation and or erosion (Gunn et al., this volume); and overreliance on an engineered landscape that is costly to maintain (Lucero et al., this volume; and Iannone et al., this volume). Yet other stresses occur entirely in the societal domain: growing economic distance between the top and the bottom of societal segments; warfare and conflict within or between polities; loss of shared identity (all three in Chase and Chase, this volume); miscommunication or deficiencies in the information-processing apparatus of societies (e.g., Scarborough and Valdez, this volume), interruptions in long-distance trade; and so forth.

Many of the stresses that directly involve the environment, resources, or material culture have the advantage that they can often be observed in archaeological data and, indeed, all of them have been observed in different instances in the Maya archaeological data and are mentioned in this volume. The others are more difficult to trace because they are only indirectly observable (such as fluctuations in the demography of the population) or because they need the help of epigraphers to decipher texts on stelae (e.g., Gunn et al., this volume)—social unrest, economic problems, organizational and or institutional barriers, dysfunctions, and the like (cf. Flannery in a classic paper [1972], based on work done by H. A. Simon [1996] and R. A. Rappaport [1977]).

Clearly, if we are to pursue this approach, archaeologists will need to start looking for other kinds of information in their excavations and interpretations. That process has hardly begun, and I cannot, in this paper, present a substantive case study drawing upon such novel data. But, in my opinion, the merit of this approach would be that it moves us away from single-cause explanations of the demise of ancient societies (van der Leeuw 1987).

Lessons from the Maya Past for the Study of the Future

One important message of this volume is that we have to move away from explanations in terms of chains of causes and consequences, whether single or multiple, and begin to think in terms of syndromes occurring in complex, multi–temporal and multi–scalar interactions in which the unintended consequences of decisions made earlier by individuals or collectivities, whether consciously or unconsciously, play an important role (van der Leeuw 2007). Indeed, we have to look at Maya polities and their interactions through time in terms of complex adaptive systems that completely integrate the dynamics of the geosphere, hydrosphere, atmosphere, biosphere, and anthroposphere (e.g., McGlade 1995; van der Leeuw and McGlade 1997). In doing so, we approach the Maya in a way that is much closer to the sustainability challenges that our modern world is actually facing, and thus enhance the chances that the detailed study of the archaeological data will enable us to draw lessons that actually apply to the present and the future. After all, we live in a period during which many so-called "crises" have been identified as occurring at the same time: demographic, economic, financial, social, environmental. It is only one step from there to realize that these are actually all manifestations of one and the same phenomenon: our society is close to being overwhelmed by the unintended and unanticipated consequences of our own (earlier) actions.

Another lesson from this study is that once one takes a truly long-term perspective, the second-order changes in environmental, socio-environmental, and societal dynamics can be observed and taken into account, whereas this is not possible from a shorter-term perspective such as is generally applied to the current sustainability debate (Brand 1999; Carpenter 2002). The long-term approach enables us to identify both the path-dependencies and the tipping points that one may observe in individual societal trajectories. Moreover, such a long-term perspective has two other advantages: (1) it takes into account the very slow dynamics involved, both environmental and social; and (2) it highlights many more "basins of attraction" that the society has explored in the course of its evolution than if one only focuses on the recent past. In the Maya case, it turns out that in the Yalahau lowlands, large populations could be sustained by harnessing underground water resources and small pockets of good agricultural soils in hollows in the karstic subsoil (Fedick, this volume). In the modern, large-scale perspective on agriculture, this opportunity has not been seen or exploited.

Thirdly, we need to remind ourselves that it is essential to study the long term from an "ex ante" perspective, looking at every point in time for the emergence of new phenomena, institutions, behaviors, and dynamics, rather than taking an "ex post" point of view and looking for the origins of phenomena that we currently observe in our own world. This applies both to archaeological case studies and to the study of sustainability issues in the modern period. That inherently implies (again) that we do not try and isolate individual cause-and-effect chains to which we accord explanatory value (knowledge), but that we approach our efforts to gain understanding by looking at multiple strands of connections in terms of possibilities and probabilities. In evaluating these, it is fundamental to look at as wide a range of the potential consequences of different scenarios as possible.

A fourth lesson concerns the need to view the emergence of polities simultaneously from the societal and the environmental perspective (e.g., Figure 15.1). After all, environmental constraints and opportunities impact on the subsistence of all populations, and as a society grows in size, these initial environmental conditions shape the society's path dependencies and opportunities. The latter cannot be realized unless they are both offered by the environment and perceived by society. In the absence of such a double window of opportunity (both environmental and social), they remain latent and do not contribute to the further development of the socio-environmental system. This is most evident when one reminds oneself that a potential resource (such as land) does not become useful for the society until that society has recognized that potential, has put the institutions and technologies in place to exploit it (by hunting, gathering, raising animals or cultivating one or more crops), and has identified the uses of that resource (in this case food). The same is the case for oil, coal, uranium, and other resources. Indeed, these did not become part of our human way of life until complex scientific knowledge and technology were available, thus opening the societal "window of opportunity" that enabled their exploitation (and set us up for our current sustainability dilemmas).

Another scalar issue is that of the urban landscape. Cities are the theater in which networks and communities of different sizes interact. The way in which this interaction is organized inevitably has an impact on urban dynamics and infrastructure. Were the low-density cities of the Maya with their urban cultivation systems more sustainable in their landscape than the dense cities of today? If so, what may have been the factors influencing this? Clearly, these cities had a very different relationship between their energy network and their information network than modern cities. Did that impact their innovativeness and, thereby, the sustainability of the polities of which they were part? Did it impact on their maximum size? An interesting study in that respect is the work of Fletcher (2007, 2012), but more detailed work is necessary before one can hope to come to any conclusion. For example, Sanders (1999) argues cogently that these variables need to be seen in the context of the distance between a city and its neighbors; however, while such a perspective may hold true for Western traditions, it may not have applicability to the Maya or other tropical civilizations (e.g., Chase et al. 1990; Fletcher 2007).

A lesson of great importance for our current sustainability debate is the need to look at a wider range of spatiotemporal scales and their interactions, both to better understand the past and to better assess the future. For our understanding of the past, for example, it is important that we look at the differences in spatiotemporal scale of various dynamics (e.g., demographic vs. environmental), but also at the very long-term consequences of our actions, far beyond the timeframes we usually take into account.

But this also has important implications for our vision of our own future. Throughout this volume one observes, for example, that the Maya managed to sustain very large populations in an area that is at present considered incapable of doing so—not because the environment has become more unfriendly, but because our perception on what is a friendly environment has changed from one that is small-scale and uses a very diverse set of subsistence techniques into one which is large-scale and only takes a much narrower set of techniques into account. In the process, we have shifted from a perspective that stresses the quality of life to one that emphasizes the quantity of production. This shift is clearly part of our economy-driven globalization, as it searches for the *economically* cheapest and most efficient kinds of resource exploitation to the detriment of the *socially* cheapest and most efficient ones.

There are many examples of issues that are important to us in the modern world to which archaeology can contribute by offering novel ideas and, in some cases, solutions (e.g., van der Leeuw and Redman 2002). The chapters within this book have consciously tried to develop a change in perspective that will facilitate the use of Maya archaeological data in seeking lessons for the future.

Notes

1. Dimension is here used in the mathematical sense and signifies any yardstick (or "dimension") against which one can measure phenomena: height, width, and length, but also color, pointedness, density, cleverness, etc.

2. Note that the (ethno-historic) data about the hierarchical organization of Puuc settlements date from the 16th century, even though Isendahl et al. notice their good fit with the four-tiered settlement structure of the region.

3. Work on the emergence of cities in France (Schmitt 2014) argues that there is another such threshold in the growth of urban systems, which occurs when full-time craft specialization needs to be introduced to allow further expansion of population sizes in Medieval cities. Spufford's work on the emergence of medieval trade routes in Europe points in the same direction (2002).

4. Geographical area in which different cultural and political entities interact—the term is used, for example, for the hellenistic period in the Eastern Mediterranean.

References Cited

Algaze, Guillermo
2008 Ancient Mesopotamia at the Dawn of Civilization: The Evolution of an Urban Landscape. Chicago: University of Chicago Press.

Atlan, Henry
1992 Self-Organizing Networks: Weak, Strong and Intentional: The Role of Their Underdetermination. La Nuova Critica N.S. 19–20:51–70.

Bentley, R. Alexander, and Herbert D. G. Maschner, eds.
2003 Complex Systems and Archaeology. Salt Lake City: University of Utah Press.

Bettencourt, Luis M. A., Jose Lobo, and Deborah Strumsky
2009 Invention in the City: Increasing Returns to Patenting as a Scaling Function of Metropolitan Size. Research Policy 36(1):107–120.

Brand, Stuart
1999 The Clock of the Long Now. New York: Basic Books.

Carpenter, Steven R.
2002 Ecological Futures: Building an Ecology of the Long Now. Ecology 83:2069–2083.

Chase, Arlen F., and Diane Z. Chase
2009 Symbolic Egalitarianism and Homogenized Distributions in the Archaeological Record at Caracol, Belize: Method, Theory, and Complexity. Research Reports in Belizean Archaeology 6:15–24.

Chase, Diane Z., and Arlen F. Chase
2004 Archaeological Perspectives on Classic Maya Social Organization from Caracol, Belize. Ancient Mesoamerica 15:111–119.

Chase, Diane Z., Arlen F. Chase, and William A. Haviland
1990 The Classic Maya City: Reconsidering The Mesoamerican Urban Tradition. American Anthropologist 92:499–506.

Cherry, John
1986 Polities and palaces: Some Problems in Minoan State Formation. *In* Peer Polity Interaction and Socio-political Change. Colin Renfrew and John Cherry, eds. Pp. 19–46. Cambridge: Cambridge University Press.

D'Altroy, Terence N., Timothy K. Earle, David L. Browman, Darrell La Lone, Michael E. Moseley, John V. Murra, Thomas P. Myers, Frank Salomon, Katharina J. Schreiber, and John R. Topic
1985 Staple Finance, Wealth Finance, and Storage in the Inka Political Economy. Current Anthropology 26(2):187–206

Flannery, Kent V.
1972 The Cultural Evolution of Civilizations. Annual Review of Ecology and Systematics 3:399–426.

Fletcher, Roland
2007 The Limits of Settlement Growth: A Theoretical Outline. Cambridge: Cambridge University Press.
2012 Low-Density, Agrarian-Based Urbanism: Scale, Power, and Ecology. *In* The Comparative Archaeology of Complex Societies. M. E. Smith, ed. Pp. 285–320. Cambridge: Cambridge University Press.

Florida, Richard
2002 The Rise of the Creative Class. New York: Basic Books.
2005 Cities and the Creative Class. London: Routledge.

Girard, René
1990 Innovation and repetition. SubStance 62/63:7–20.

Heckbert, Scott
2012 Maya Simulation. Model (beta version), posted August 8, 2012 at http://www.openabm.org/model/3063/version/3/view.

Heckbert, Scott, Christian Isendahl, Joel Gunn, Sarah Brewer, Vern Scarborough, Arlen F. Chase, Diane Z. Chase, Robert Costanza, Nicholas Dunning, Timothy Beach, Sheryl Luzzadder-Beach, David Lentz, and Paul Sinclair
In press Growing the Maya Social-Ecological System from the Bottom Up. In Handbook of Historical Ecology and Applied Archaeology (in press). C. Isendahl and D. Stump, eds. Oxford: Oxford University Press.

Johnson, Gregory A.
1982 Organizational Structure and Scalar Stress. *In*

Theory and Explanation in Archaeology. Colin Renfrew, Michael Rowlands, and Barbara A. Segraves-Whallon, eds. Pp. 431–457 New York: Academic Press.

Kahnemann, Daniel A., Paul Slovic, and Amos Tverski
1982 Judgment under Uncertainty: Heuristics and Biases. Cambridge: Cambridge University Press.

Kohler, Timothy A.
2011 Complex Systems and Archaeology. Working Paper 2011–06–023, Santa Fe Institute, Santa Fe NM

Lévèque, Christian, and Sander van derLeeuw
2003 Quelles natures voulons nous ? Pour une approche socio-écologique du champ de l'environnement. Paris: Elsevier.

Luhmann, Niklas
1992 Ecological Communication. London: Polity Press.

Malinowski, Bronislaw
2010 [1922] Argonauts of the Western Pacific: An Account of Native Enterprise and Adventure in the Archipelagoes of Melanesian New Guinea. New York: Benediction Classics.

McGlade, James
1995 Archaeology and the Ecodynamics of Human-Modified Landscapes. Antiquity 69:113–132.

Morin, Edgar
2008 La Méthode, Paris: Seuil, Collection Opus (2 vol.)

Mitchell, Melanie
2009 Complexity: A Guided Tour. Oxford: Oxford University Press

Prigogine, Ilya
1993 Time, Structure and Fluctuations. *In* Nobel Lectures, Chemistry 1971–1980. Tore Fräng-smyr and Sture Forsén, eds. Pp 263–285. Singapore: World Scientific Publishing Co.
1982 From Being to Becoming. San Francisco: Freeman.

Rappaport, Roy A.
1977 [1968] Maladaptation in Social Systems. Boletín Ciudades para un Futuro más Sostenible 37. Posted September 30, 2009. http://habitat.aq.upm.es/boletin/n37/arrap.en.html, accessed December 15, 2012.

Read, Dwight W., and Sander E. van der Leeuw
2008 Biology Is Only Part of the Story.... Philosophical Transactions of the Royal Society Series B 363:1959–1968.

Read, Dwight W. and Sander E. van der Leeuw
In press The Extension of Social Relations in Time and Space during the Palaeolithic. *In* Festschrift in Honor of Clive Gamble. F. Coward and F. Wenban-Smith, eds. In press.

Redman, Charles L., and Ann P. Kinzig
2005 Resilience of Past Landscapes: Resilience Theory, Society, and Longue Duree. Conservation Ecology 7(1):14–32.

Rockström, Johan, Will Steffen, Kevin Noone, Åsa Persson, F. Stuart Chapin III, Eric F. Lambin, Tim M. Lenton, Marten Scheffer, Carl Folke, Hans-Joachim Schellnhuber, Björn Nykvist, Cynthia A. de Wit, Terry Hughes, Sander E. van der Leeuw, Henning Rodhe, Sverker Sörlin, Peter K. Snyder, Robert Costanza, Uno Svedin, Malin Falkenmark, Louise Karlberg, Robert W. Corell, Victoria J. Fabry, James E. Hansen, Brian Walker, Diana Liverman, Katherine Richardson, Paul Crutzen, and Jonathan A. Foley
2009 A Safe Operating Space for Humanity. Nature 461:472–475

Rockström, Johan, Will Steffen, Hans-Joachim Schellnhuber, Sander E. van der Leeuw, Diana Liverman, James E. Hansen, Tim Lenton, Sverker Sörlin, Victoria J. Fabry, Kevin Noone, Eric Lambin, Robert W. Corell, Robert Costanza, Marten Scheffer, Carl Folke, Uno Svedin, Terry Hughes, Henning Rodthe, and Paul Crutzen
2009 Planetary Boundaries: Exploring the Safe Operating Space in the Anthropocene. Ecology and Society 14(2):32. http://www.ecologyandsociety.org/vol14/iss2/art32/, accessed December 13, 2013.

Sahlins, Marshall
1974 Stone Age Economics. London: Tavistock.

Sanders, Lena
1999 A Multiscalar Investigation into the Dynamics of Land Abandonment in Southern France. *In* Final

Report: ARCHAEOMEDES II: Policy-Relevant Models of the Natural and Anthropogenic Dynamics of Degradation and Desertification and Their Spatiotemporal Manifestations, Vol. 2 (part 1). Pp 71–74. Brussels: DG XII of the European Union.

Scarborough, Vernon L., and William R. Burnside
2010 Complexity and Sustainability: Perspectives from the Ancient Maya and the Modern Balinese. American Antiquity 75(2):327–363.

Scarborough, Vernon L., and Fred Valdez
2009 An Alternative Order: The Dualistic Economies of the Ancient Maya. Latin American Antiquity 20(1):207–227.

Schmitt, Clara
2014 *Modélisation de la dynamique des systèmes de peuplement: de SimpopLocal à SimpopNet*. Unpublished Ph.D. Thesis in Geography, Université de Paris I (Panthéon-Sorbonne)

Selby, Henry A., and Fadwa El Guindi
1976 Dialectics in Zapotec Thinking. *In* Meaning in Anthropology. Keith Basso and Henry A. Selby, eds. Pp. 181–196. New Mexico: University of New Mexico Press.

Simon, Herbert A.
1996 [1969] The Sciences of the Artificial. 3rd edition. Cambridge: MIT Press.

Spufford, Peter
2002 Power and Profit: The Merchant in Medieval Europe. London: Thames and Hudson.

Tainter, Joseph
1988 The Collapse of Ancient Societies. Cambridge: Cambridge University Press.

Tainter, Joseph, and Tadeusz W. Patzek
2011 Drilling Down: The Gulf Oil Debacle and Our Energy Dilemma. New York: Springer.

Tverski, Amos
1977 Features of Similarity. Psychological Review 84:327–352.

Tverski, Amos, and Itamar Gati
1978 Structures of Similarity. *In* Cognition and Categorization. E. Rosch and B. B. Lloyd, eds. Pp. 79–98. Hillsdale, NJ: Erlbaum.

van der Leeuw, Sander E.
1987 Revolutions Revisited. *In* Studies in the Neolithic and Urban Revolutions. L. Manzanilla, ed. Pp. 217–243. BAR International Series, 349. Oxford: British Archaeological Reports.
1998 La nature serait-elle d'origine culturelle? Histoire, archéologie, sciences naturelles et Environnement. *In* Nature et Culture. A. Ducros, J. Ducros, and F. Joulian, eds. Pp. 83–98. Paris: Errance.
2007 Information Processing and Its Role in the Rise of the European World System. *In* Sustainability or Collapse? R. Costanza, L. J. Graumlich, and W. Steffen, eds. Pp. 213–241. 96th Dahlem Workshop Report. Cambridge, MA: MIT Press.
2010 The Archaeology of Innovation: Lessons for Our Times. *In* Innovation: Perspectives for the 21st Century. Pp. 33–53. Madrid: BBVA.
2012 Global Systems Dynamics and Policy: Lessons from the Distant Past. Complexity Economics 1:33–60.

van der Leeuw, Sander E., and James McGlade
1997 Archaeology and Nonlinear Dynamics: New Approaches to Long-Term Change. *In* Archaeology: Time, Process and Structural Transformations. S. E. van der Leeuw and J. McGlade, eds. Pp. 1–31. London: Routledge.

van der Leeuw, Sander E., and Charles L. Redman
2002 Placing Anthropology at the Center of Environmental Studies. American Antiquity 67(4):597–605.

van der Leeuw, Sander E., David A. Lane, Dwight W. Read
2009 "The long-term evolution of social organization", Chapter 3 in: David A. Lane, Denise Pumain, Sander E. van der Leeuw and Geoffrey West (eds.) Complexity Perspectives on Innovation and Social Change, pp. 85–115, Berlin: Springer (Methodos series)

van der Leeuw, Sander E., Robert Costanza, Steven Aulenbach, Simon Brewer, Michael Burek, Sarah Cornell, Carole Crumley, John Dearing, Catherine Downy, Lisa Graumlich, Michelle Hegmon, Scott Heckbert, Katherine Hibbard, Steven T. Jackson,

Ida Kubiszewski, Paul Sinclair, Sverker Sörlin, and Will Steffen
2011 Toward an Integrated History to Guide the Future. Ecology and Society 16(4):2. http://www.ecologyandsociety.org/vol16/iss4/art2, accessed December 11, 2013.

White, Leslie
1949 The Science of Culture: A Study of Man and Civilization. New York NY: Farrar, Straus and Giroux.

Wright, Henry T.
1969 The Administration of Rural Production in an Early Mesopotamian Town. Anthropological Papers, 38. Ann Arbor: University of Michigan Museum of Anthropology.

List of Contributors

About the Editors

Arlen F. Chase (Ph.D. 1983, University of Pennsylvania) is a Pegasus professor of Anthropology and an Associate Dean in the College of Sciences at the University of Central Florida. His research interests focus on archaeological method and theory in the Maya area with particular emphasis on contextual, settlement, and ceramic analysis and secondary interests on urbanism, ethnicity, and epigraphic interpretation. For thirty years he has co-directed excavations at Caracol, Belize; before that he worked on a seven-year project at Santa Rita Corozal in the same country. He has also carried out fieldwork in Guatemala and Mexico as well as in Arizona and Pennsylvania in the United States. He has authored over 150 articles and book chapters as well as five previous books. PDFs of his writings may be found at www.caracol.org.

Vernon L. Scarborough (Ph.D. 1980, Southern Methodist University) is Distinguished University Research Professor and Charles P. Taft Professor in Anthropology at the University of Cincinnati in Cincinnati, Ohio. He has taught and conducted fieldwork at the University of Texas at El Paso; the University of Khartoum, Sudan; and the University of Peshawar, Pakistan. In addition to ongoing water management studies in Belize and Guatemala, he has worked in the Argolid, Greece, and in Bali, Indonesia. His topical interests are settlement, land use, and water management in the context of the archaic state. He has published eight books and over 90 scholarly journal articles and book chapters.

Cover image

The cover illustration is a 2.5 LiDAR rendition of a small portion of the anthropogenic landscape of Caracol, Belize (courtesy of the UCF Caracol Archaeological Project).

Adrian S.Z. Chase
adrian.chase@asu.edu
School of Human Evolution and Social Change
Arizona State University
Phoenix, AZ 85006

Arlen F. Chase
arlen.chase@ucf.edu
Department of Anthropology
University of Central Florida
Orlando, FL 32816

Diane Z. Chase
chase@ucf.edu
Academic Affairs and Department of Anthropology
University of Central Florida
Orlando, FL 32816

Rafael Cobos
rachcobos@aol.com
Facultad de Ciencias Antropologicas
Universidad Autónoma de Yucatán
Km 1 carretera Mérida-Tizimín, Cholul
Mérida, 97305, Yucatán, México

Guillermo de Anda Alaniz
cenote@prodigy.net.mx
Facultad de Ciencias Antropológicas
Universidad Autónoma de Yucatán
Km 1 carretera Mérida-Tizimín, Cholul
Mérida, 97305, Yucatán, México

María del Rosario Domínguez Carrasco
mrdoming@yahoo.com
Centro de Investigaciones Historicas y Sociales
Universidad Autonoma De Campeche
Av. Agustin Melgar S/N
Entre Juan De La Barrera Y Calle 20
Col. Buenavista, C.P. 24030
Campeche, Campeche, Mexico

Nicholas P. Dunning
nicholas.dunning@uc.edu
Department of Geography
University of Cincinnati
Cincinnati, OH 45221

Betty Faust (c/o Dr. Carnevali)
bettybfaust@gmail.com
Depto. Recursos Naturales, Herbario
Calle 43 No. 130, Col. Chuburná de Hidalgo
Merida, Yucatán, México CP 97200

Scott L. Fedick
scott.fedick@urc.edu
Department of Anthropology
University of California at Riverside
Riverside, CA 92521

Vilma Fialko
fialkovilma@yahoo.com
Instituto de Antropologia e Historia
Ex-Convento de Santo Domingo
12 avenida y 11 calle, Zona 1
Guatemala 01001

William J. Folan
wijfolan@gmail.com
Centro de Investigaciones Historicas y Sociales
Universidad Autonoma De Campeche
Av. Agustin Melgar S/N
Entre Juan De La Barrera Y Calle 20
Col. Buenavista, C.P. 24030
Campeche, Campeche, Mexico

Roberto García Moll
gmoll@prodigy.net.mx
División de Estudios Arqueológicos, INAH
Licenciado Primo de Verdad No. 3
Colonia Centro, México, D.F.

Joel D. Gunn
jdgunn@uncg.edu
Department of Anthropology
University of North Carolina at Greensboro
426 Graham Bldg, UNCG, P.O. Box 26170
Greensboro, NC 27402

Michelle Hegmon
hegmon@asu.edu
School of Human Evolution and Social Change
Arizona State University
Phoenix, AZ 85006

Gyles Iannone
giannone@trentu.ca
Department of Anthropology
Trent University
Peterborough, Ontario K9J 7B8
Canada

Christien Isendahl
christian.isendahl@gu.se
Department of Historical Studies
University of Gothenburg
P.O. Box 200
SE-405 30 Gothenburg
Sweden

David L. Lentz
david.lentz@uc.edu
Department of Biological Studies
University of Cincinnati
Cincinnati, OH 45221

Rodrigo Liendo Stuardo
rodrigo@liendo.net
Instituto de Investigaciones Antropológicas UNAM
Circuito Exterior s/n
Ciudad Universitaria, 04510, Mexico D.F.

Lisa J. Lucero
ljlucero@uiuc.edu
Department of Anthropology
University of Illinois at Champaign-Urbana
Urbana, IL 61801

Ben A. Nelson
bnelson@asu.edu
School of Human Evolution and Social Change
Arizona State University
Phoenix, AZ 85006

Mario Arturo Ortiz-Pérez
maop@igg.unam.mx
Instituto de Geografía, UNAM
Circuito de la Investigación Científica s/n
Ciudad Universitaria, 04510, México, D.F.

Keith Prufer
kmp@unm.edu
Department of Anthropology
University of New Mexico
Albuquerque, NM 87131

Jeremy A. Sabloff
jsabloff@santafe.edu
Santa Fe Institute
1399 Hyde Park Road
Santa Fe, NM 87501

Vernon L. Scarborough
Vernon.scarborough@uc.edu
Department of Anthropology
University of Cincinnati
Cincinnati, OH 454221-0380

Sergey Sedov
serg_sedov@yahoo.com
Instituto de Geología, UNAM
Circuito de la Investigación Científica s/n
Ciudad Universitaria, 04510, México, D.F.

Berenice Solís-Castillo
bsolisc.geologia@gmail.com
Ciencias de la Tierra, UNAM
Circuito de la Investigación Científica s/n
Ciudad Universitaria, 04510, México, D.F.

Elizabeth Solleiro-Rebolledo
solleiro@geologia.unam.mx
Instituto de Geología, UNAM
Circuito de la Investigación Científica s/n
Ciudad Universitaria, 04510, México, D.F.

Joseph A. Tainter
joseph.tainter@usu.edu
Department of Environment and Society
Utah State University
Logan, UT 84322

Fred Valdez, Jr.
fredv@mail.utexas.edu
Department of Anthropology
University of Texas
Austin, TX 78712-1086

Sander E. van der Leeuw
vanderle@asu.edu
School of Sustainability
Arizona State University
Phoenix, AZ 85006

Beniamino Volta
bvolta@ucsd.edu
Department of Anthropology
University of California – San Diego
La Jolla, California 92093

Tony J. Wilkinson
t.j.wilkinson@durham.ac.uk
Department of Archaeology
University of Durham
Durham, England DH1 3LE